Medicare at maturity

The Banff Centre
School of
Management

Medicare at maturity

Achievements, lessons & challenges

Edited by Robert G. Evans and Greg L. Stoddart

Publication of proceedings funded
by Extendicare Ltd.

Taken from the
Proceedings of the Health
Policy Conference on
Canada's National Health Care
System

Management Studies Programs

© 1986 The Banff Centre for Continuing Education

ISBN 0-919813-38-0

The University of Calgary Press
2500 University Drive N.W.
Calgary, Alberta, Canada T2N 1N4

Canadian Cataloguing in Publication Data

Main entry under title:
Medicare at Maturity

    Bibliography: p.
    ISBN 0-919813-35-6

    1. Medical care — Canada. I. Evans, Robert G., 1942-. II. Stoddart, Gregory Lloyd, 1948-
RA412.5.C3M43   1986   368.4'2'00971   C86-091351-1

No part of this book may be stored in a retrieval system, translated or reproduced in any form, by print, photoprint, microfilm, microfiche, or any other means, without written permission from the publisher.

Printed in Canada

CONTENTS

FOREWORD	vii
ACKNOWLEDGEMENTS	ix
PREFACE	x

I. HISTORICAL AND CURRENT PERSPECTIVE

The Canadian Health Care System 1974-1984 3
    Malcolm G. Taylor

Commentary 41
    Maureen M. Law

II. HEALTH COSTS AND EXPENDITURES

Riding North on a South-bound Horse?
Expenditures, Prices, Utilization and Incomes
in the Canadian Health Care System 53
    Morris L. Barer and Robert G. Evans

Commentary 165
    K.G. Moore and Y.M. Cheung

III. CHOICE OF TECHNIQUE

Choice of Technique: Patterns of Medical Practices 181
    Renaldo N. Battista, Robert A. Spasoff
    and Walter O. Spitzer

Commentary 215
    Fernand Turcotte

IV. MANPOWER POLICY

And Who Shall Represent the Public Interest?
The Legacy of Canadian Health Manpower Policy 221
    Jonathan Lomas and Morris L. Barer

Toward an Improved Work Organization in the
Health Services Sector: From Administrative
Rationalization to Professional Rationality 287
    André-Pierre Contandriopoulos, Claudine Laurier
    and Louise-Hélène Trottier

Commentary 325
    René Dussault

Commentary 329
    Pierre Bergeron

V. ORGANIZATION OF DELIVERY

Health Services Organization and Delivery:
    Promise and Reality 337
        John E.F. Hastings and Eugene Vayda

Commentary 385
    Jacques Brunet

VI. CONFLICT MANAGEMENT

Conflict and Accommodation in the
    Canadian Health Care System 393
        Carolyn Tuohy

Commentary 435
    K.J. Fyke

VII. REFLECTIONS AND SYNTHESIS

American Perspective:
    If the War of 1812 Had Turned Out Differently,
    Would There Now be PPOs in Manitoba or Global
    Budgeting in Vermont? Some Concluding Observations 443
        Bruce C. Vladeck

Canadian Perspective:
    Learning From Our Experience 451
        Richard Van Loon

List of Contributors 473

List of Participants 477

FOREWORD

This book is unusual — in its origins, contents and anticipated audiences. A broad survey of Canada's medical circumstances in the 1980s, the work, though comprised of chapters by different authors, is of high quality, intellectually coherent, capably edited and accessible to those readers interested in Canadian medicine and the preoccupations of North American health policy deliberations. Careful reading of it would improve the quality of medical discussion on both sides of the Canada/United States border.

The origins of *Medicare at Maturity* are special in at least two respects. While it grew out of a scholarly conference — held at The Banff Centre School of Management in the Summer of 1984 — it is not the typical "proceedings" of such scholarly meetings. The editorial mandate to the authors made sure that the topics discussed would constitute a broad contemporary survey of Canadian health policy. The book's chapters testify to the editors' success in producing a book of appropriate scope. Equally important, the editors have reduced the major problem of conference proceedings — sharp differences in tone, quality of discussion and format in the separate scribblings of busy authors. How this was accomplished is not clear to me, but the fact of its accomplishment is. Generated from a conference, the book is free of the major liabilities of the proceedings genre.

Medicare at Maturity is also unusual in that it is the successor volume — more than a decade later — to an earlier book that was similarly conceived. The earlier effort, *National Health Insurance: Can We Learn from Canada?* (Wiley, 1975), is among the most widely cited sources about how Canada came to its Medicare program in the period 1945 to 1971. The 1975 work had a North American focus as well, but its largely Canadian authors were explaining Canadian developments to their southern neighbours. The 1975 volume became a widely used text *in* Canada, while, ironically, its contents focussed on lessons *for* America. The twin efforts — a review of similar materials in a comparable volume — is a quite unusual example of follow-up materials in cross-national policy studies.

The contents of this book, however, do reflect a different focus, and an unusual one for Canadian scholars. The largest North American market for health policy studies is, of course, the United States, ten times larger in population. Nonetheless, *Medicare at Maturity* presumes the interest of attentive publics in Canada and trusts there will be some parallel attention in the United States. Volume two balances the "foreign aid" posture of the 1975 study and is, in that sense, a more Canadian centred work.

The balance sought is evident in the concluding chapters — which separately address what Canadian and American audiences might learn from recent developments in Canada. The focus of all the substantive chapters is on Canadian experience. Yet the book has a genuinely North American quality to it. How is that so? It is because the authors each discuss their subjects with an eye to policy concerns on both sides of the border. The chapter on the costs of Canadian Medicare proceeds from the knowledge that health care cost inflations — the rate of which is substantially less in Canada than in the United States — is firmly on the agenda of North American politics. The discussion of manpower issues reflects the North American fact of sharp expansion in physician supply and considerable controversy over its consequences. The subject of conflict management in Canadian medical politics recognizes that this substantial industry — vital, expensive, with large opportunity costs for other public and private spending — can never mirror the fantasy world of rational planning and frictionless adjustment.

The audiences for whom this book is relevant are quite diverse. Conceived as an analytical portrait of an industry, it is obviously directed at Canadians professionally interested in health policy. Government officials in Canada will, I believe, welcome this survey as an authoritative guide to what has taken place in their policy domain. So should journalists and policy analysts anxious to have a clear view of trends in progress and sources of present and prospective conflict. For the teacher interested in the place of health care in the modern welfare state it will be a usable guide and substantial help to the students who understandably seek order from the claims and counterclaims of advocates in scholarly and non-scholarly publications. Directed at Canadian audiences most clearly, *Medicare at Maturity* should be of great interest in the United States as well. Canada and the United States differ, of course. But the two nations are as close as any pair in medical arrangements, economic circumstances and range of political conflict. Canadian Medicare represents, in one sense, a road not taken for the United States. Conversely, the pluralism of American medicine reveals options Canadian policy-makers can consider as Canadian Medicare evolves over time. This book will make the task of cross-national interpretation considerably easier.

Theodore R. Marmor

ACKNOWLEDGEMENTS

The Banff Centre School of Management would like to thank those who generously supported the Health Policy Conference on Canada's National Health Care System.

Advanced Education, Alberta
Hospitals and Medical Care, Alberta
Health and Welfare Canada
Ontario Economic Council
Commonwealth Fund
Robert Wood Johnson Foundation
Kaiser Foundation
Milbank Fund

* * * * * *

The Banff Centre School of Management gratefully acknowledges the continuing interest and assistance received from Extendicare Ltd. Their support has made the publication of this book possible.

PREFACE

Health care in Canada is never long out of the headlines of the daily newspapers, or the attention of those concerned with public policy. As the largest, most comprehensive, probably most successful, and easily the most popular public programs in the country, the insurance systems for hospital and medical care receive the lion's share of that attention. And despite the great popularity and generally conceded success of Medicare in Canada, the reimbursement issues remain bitterly contentious, for readily apparent reasons. The famous "Doctors' Strike" in Saskatchewan, which greeted the introduction in 1962 of the provincial program that was to become the prototype of the nation-wide federal-provincial system, has recently been surpassed in both length and scale by the Ontario strike in the Summer of 1986.

Yet behind these inevitable and occasionally highly dramatized conflicts, the broad structure of the health care and health insurance system, as perceived by patients, providers and the general public, has remained relatively stable since the provinces each established their medical insurance programs in the late 1960s or early 1970s. The hospital programs go back another decade or more, to the late 1950s. By the mid-1980s, therefore, the Canadian Medicare system(s) is clearly a mature or "established" program which has generated a wealth of experience, good and bad, for those responsible for making it work.

Making that experience more generally available for interpretation and analysis, however, is an additional and separate process. The Canadian federal and provincial governments have generated a large number of reports on particular aspects of health care funding and delivery, and have commissioned periodic reviews and analysis by external individuals and groups, some of which have been excellent. The academic community has also continued to scribble away, again often with very useful results.

But it is remarkable that one of the most consistently and widely quoted sources, for both description and analysis of the Canadian health care system, has been the collection of papers prepared for a conference on the Canadian experience, held in the United States in the Summer of 1974. This volume, *National Health Insurance: Can We Learn from Canada?*, with contributions by Canadian and American authors, describes the evolution leading up to the universal and comprehensive (for hospital and medical care at least) public insurance system. But analyses in the early 1970s could provide only preliminary indications as to how the completed system would perform.

By the early 1980s, a number of us involved in teaching programs related to health care were increasingly uncomfortable that this volume was becoming rather "long in the tooth", and that no more recent, and similarly comprehensive, work was available. Conversations on this theme at The Banff Centre Senior Health Administration program in 1982 led to the obvious solution — why not hold another conference, ten years later, in Canada this time, to reflect on the lessons of the intervening decade?

Such a conference should pull together health care people from a variety of backgrounds, with a strong emphasis on "doers" as well as "talkers" — providers and administrators as well as academics — and provide enough time and an appropriate environment for an in-depth study. Building around a set of carefully related commissioned papers, it should address both the evaluation of past policy and the development of future policy — what has worked, what has not and where do we go from here?

Participants were also invited from the U.S., the U.K. and Australia. While the primary focus of discussion was quite clearly Canadian experience, with the intent of assisting the development of Canadian policy, it is obvious that the broader range of external experience gives one a clearer view of what also might have been done, and how it might have turned out. It also suggests a number of possibilities for the future.

The American comparisons and contrasts are particularly apt, because, as Professor Marmor points out in his foreword to this volume, the past two decades in North America display virtually a social policy experiment. Two very similar cultures, with very similar health care systems, adopted in the 1960s very different ways of paying for care. Cross-border comparisons now permit us to draw some quite clear conclusions as to the results; the "lessons" of the Canadian experience become a great deal clearer in the light of the U.S. alternatives. Thus the present conference, while focused on Canada, is inevitably about health care in a North American context — as was the earlier conference in 1974.

The structuring of the conference topics, over a period of five days, and the commissioning of papers and discussants, was a critical part of the process. This was carried out by a conference steering committee, some of whom had been involved in the 1974 conference, who accepted The Banff Centre's invitation to take responsibility for developing the program and running the meetings. The Committee consisted of:

Dr. Robert Evans (Chairman)
Professor
Department of Economics
University of British Columbia
Vancouver, British Columbia

Mr. David Rochefort
Manager
Management Studies Programs
The Banff Centre, School of
   Management
Banff, Alberta

Mr. Gary Chatfield
President
Extendicare Ltd.
Toronto, Ontario

Mr. Gary Frey
Vice-President
The Banff Centre
Banff, Alberta

Dr. Philip Lee
Professor
Institute of Social Policy Studies
University of California
San Francisco, California

Dr. Ted Marmor
Professor
Centre for Health Studies
Institute for Social Policy Study
New Haven, Connecticut

Dr. Jean Rochon
Dean
Faculté de médecine
Université Laval
Ste. Foy, Québec

Dr. Greg Stoddart
Associate Professor
Department of Clinical Epidemiology and Biostatistics
McMaster University
Hamilton, Ontario

Dr. Eugene Vayda
Associate Dean
Community Health
Faculty of Medicine
University of Toronto
Toronto, Ontario

Their efforts, in planning meetings and during the conference itself, were fundamental to the success of the conference.

But a first-class program is only necessary, not sufficient, for a successful conference. Equally important is the quality of the site and the organization of administration and support services. Here The Banff Centre was the key ingredient. The Centre itself provides a unique setting, and the staff of the School of Management, particularly David Rochefort and Carol Walker, brought to the conference operations "the art which conceals the art" — the machinery which runs so smoothly that it is rarely noticed.

Once the conference was over, the second phase of the work began. It seems a universal law of (academic) publishing that all books take longer. Not longer than anything in particular, just longer. The specific reasons may vary from book to book, but the outcome is always the same. This conference was not designed, however, nor the papers written, as a commentary on current events. The trends and issues which the authors were asked to address did not suddenly surface in the early 1980s, and have not vanished since. The particular topics which reach the daily headlines may change (although that is not always true either!) but the underlying structural forces are much more constant.

The editorial process was managed by David Rochefort, while we took responsibility for bringing the manuscripts into final, publishable form. Special thanks to Ellen Andersen who spent many hours wordprocessing and updating the papers for publication. She was assisted in this process by Kim Dobson and Wilma Neish. Also, Gary Frey should be singled out for special mention for his courage to commit The Banff Centre and its resources to undertake this project.

We are grateful to the authors and participants for their patience (well, most of them) in waiting for the final product, and hope that they will feel that it has justified their efforts. We think it does.

Robert G. Evans
Greg L. Stoddart

I

HISTORICAL AND CURRENT PERSPECTIVE

THE CANADIAN HEALTH CARE SYSTEM 1974-1984

Malcolm G. Taylor

Historical Perspective

Our purpose at this conference is to build on the analyses, expositions, insights and forecasts so cogently presented at the Sun Valley Conference on the Canadian Health Care System in 1974.[1] The background to the two major decisions on hospital insurance in 1957 and medical care insurance in 1966 was presented at that conference by Dr. Maurice LeClair, then Canadian Deputy Minister of National Health and Welfare. My assignment is to review briefly what has happened since then. Because some may be unfamiliar with the specific characteristics of Canada's national hospital and medical care insurance programs, it is desirable to describe briefly how the programs were achieved and to highlight the characteristics of their design.

The early decades of the 1900s had witnessed a variety of voluntary efforts to pre-pay part or all of the costs of unpredictable medical and hospital care. These efforts included friendly societies, mining company and railway employees' contracts, and the beginnings of commercial insurance. In Saskatchewan and Alberta municipal doctor and municipal hospital programs had been introduced. From 1935 to 1937 the government of British Columbia struggled to introduce a province-wide program, but in the face of opposition from the B.C. Medical Association and the Manufacturers' Association, the proposal was abandoned.

But it was the deprivations of the Depression of the 1930s and the growing demands and sacrifices of World War II that pushed the issue of public health insurance onto the national political agenda. With Canada's declaration of war in September 1939, the Honourable Ian Mackenzie had been transferred from his portfolio as Minister of Defence to the more tranquil post of Minister of Pensions and National Health. Disappointed with this demotion, he directed his attention to health insurance. An inter-departmental task force was established; five health professions and nine other associations were invited to set up advisory committees; proposals for federal subsidies to provincially administered programs were presented at public hearings of a House of Commons Select Committee on Social Security in 1943.

Few public proposals have ever achieved such support, for they were endorsed not only by labour, farmer and women's groups, but also by the Canadian Medical Association and spokesmen for the life insurance industry. In 1944 a Gallup Poll revealed that 80 percent of the Canadian adult population wanted, and were willing to pay for, a comprehensive national health program.

Responding to this build-up of public expectations, the government of Canada offered, at a special Dominion-Provincial Conference on Post War Reconstruction beginning in August 1945, federal subsidies to the provinces to support the introduction of health insurance providing medical, hospital, dental, nursing and diagnostic services, in addition to other social security and reconstruction measures. But the costs for the provinces were high: transfer of the fields of personal and corporation income taxes to the national government. The price tag was more than the wealthier provinces would accept; accordingly, failure to achieve agreement on the fiscal proposals aborted the health and social security proposals.

In the health field, the vacuum of unfulfilled expectations was immediately entered by commercial insurance companies and the creation and expansion of hospital and medical profession-sponsored and controlled Blue Cross and Blue Shield pre-payment plans. The era of voluntary pre-payment of unpredictable health care costs had begun. Although the "service type" contracts (first dollar coverage and no extra-billing) introduced by the Blue Cross and physician-sponsored programs were more expensive than commercial indemnity plans, the service contract was clearly the most acceptable to Canadians. By 1952, more than five million Canadians were insured for varying degrees of hospital insurance, and nearly four million had some degree of protection against medical and surgical costs.

The only major federal government action was to introduce in 1948 the National Health Grants program (which had been proposed and lost in 1945-1946), providing grants both for a variety of public health services including professional training and health surveys, and for hospital construction similar to those offered by the Hill-Burton Act in the United States.

The lack of Hospital Association-Blue Cross initiative in Saskatchewan had led the Co-operative Commonwealth Federation (CCF) government there to introduce a universal hospital insurance program in January 1947, based on the federal government proposals of 1945. This action was followed by British Columbia in 1949 and Alberta in 1950. Newfoundland entered Confederation in 1949 with about one-half of its population covered by the Cottage Hospital system. Four of the ten provinces thus had government hospital insurance programs in operation by 1950. But because of Prime Minister Louis St. Laurent's opposition to a government program, the 1953 Liberal election platform ingeniously placed the onus for further initiatives on the provinces. Federal action would take place only when "most (six? seven? eight?) of the provinces are ready to join in a nation wide scheme".

At the 1955 Conference on the Tax Agreements, and much to Mr. St. Laurent's dismay, Premier Leslie Frost of Ontario proposed a national program. Prime Minister St. Laurent resisted, but when Health Minister Paul Martin threatened to resign, he reluctantly agreed. In January 1956 the federal Hospital Insurance and Diagnostic Services (HIDS) offer was made. The federal proposal adopted the typical grant-in-aid formula: federal funds would be forthcoming to provinces that met federal conditions. In general, these conditions included universal coverage, comprehensive inpatient services at the standard ward level, portability of benefits and availability on equal terms and conditions to all provincial residents.

The financial formula was unique; it discriminated among the provinces according to provincial costs. The federal contribution to each province in respect of its shareable costs would be (a) 25 percent of the average *per capita* cost in Canada as a whole, plus (b) 25 percent of the average *per capita* cost in the province itself, multiplied by the number of insured persons in the province.

On the surface, the formula appeared benign; it contributed more than half the costs to low cost provinces and less than one half to high cost provinces. But in another sense it discriminated against the low cost, low income provinces by providing higher *per capita* subsidies to the richer provinces. By 1975-1976, the *per capita* federal payments in respect of residents of Prince Edward Island were $89.67. In Ontario, they were $106.96, or 18.6 percent more. Nevertheless, in 1958 a national, provincially-administered hospital insurance system was born.

With the undoubted success of the hospital insurance program, the pressures for government medical care insurance mounted, as did the activities of the commercial insurance industry and the profession-sponsored Trans-Canada Medical Plans (a national association of provincially-based, not-for-profit medical insurance organizations) to prevent such an outcome.

Three major events at the beginning of the 1960s were to be instrumental in triggering the introduction of Medicare. The first was the decision by the CCF government of Saskatchewan in 1959 to use the new federal hospital insurance funds to help finance the medical care insurance program to which it had been committed for fifteen years. The legislation was passed in November 1961. Despite a withdrawal of services by the profession in July 1962, the program began operation.

Simultaneously, the national Liberal Party, out of office since 1957, and with a new coterie of leaders under Lester Pearson, held a national policy convention in January 1961 that committed the party to a federally subsidized, provincially administered national Medicare program.

Aware of the threat to its control of the Trans-Canada Medical Plans system, the Canadian Medical Association requested Prime Minister John Diefenbaker in the Fall of 1960 to appoint a Royal Commission to investigate the field of health services. Its objective was clearly to prevent medical care insurance from becoming a "political football" as it had in Saskatchewan and to ensure that the issue would be resolved by the rational advice of an independent commission rather than through the unpredictable and uncontrollable "hauling and pulling" of politics.

Prime Minister John Diefenbaker and his government agreed. A Royal Commissioh, chaired by The Honourable Emmett Hall, Chief Justice of Saskatchewan, was appointed in June 1961.

In the June 1962 national elections, the Progressive Conservative party lost its overwhelming majority and was forced to form a minority government. This lasted until April 1963 when the Liberals under the leadership of Lester Pearson came to power, but also with a minority government. The Honourable Judy LaMarsh was appointed Minister of Health and Welfare, responsible for the two major social programs to which the Liberal platforms of the 1962 and 1963 elections had committed them: pension reform and Medicare. But the most significant appointment in the Cabinet, certain to affect Medicare, was that of the Honourable Walter Gordon, Chairman of the Liberal Party Policy Committee, to be Minister of Finance. He was the only strong supporter of health insurance to occupy that post in the fifty years that health insurance was a public issue. And it made the difference.

The Royal Commission on Health Services reported in June 1964. To the surprise and dismay of the medical associations and the insurance industry, as well as of several provincial governments, it endorsed a comprehensive range of benefits that would be federally subsidized and provincially administered. It was, indeed, an unusual political melange: a Royal Commission appointed by the Progressive Conservatives recommending a medical care program that, despite extraordinary medical opposition, a New Democratic government had introduced in Saskatchewan and to which the federal Liberal government was now committed on a national scale.

Despite opposition from the medical profession, the insurance industry, chambers of commerce and several provincial governments, in July 1965 the Pearson government offered a Medical Care Insurance program to be subsidized in the aggregate to the extent of 50 percent by the federal government, and to be administered by the provinces. The legislation was passed in 1966 and, following a one year's delay, went into effect on July 1, 1968, with only two provinces — British Columbia and Saskatchewan — immediately qualifying.

The conditions for the federal contribution were similar to those under the hospital insurance program: services were to be comprehensive, the program universal and benefits portable. Administration was to be by public authority, giving "reasonable access" to insured services.

The federal cost-sharing formula differed from that of the Hospital Insurance Act in that it was not adjusted to provincial *per capita* costs. All provinces received one half the national *per capita* cost multiplied by the number of insured persons. The effect of disregarding provincial *per capita* costs was to increase the proportion of the costs in low income provinces (and lower that in high income provinces) paid by the federal government relative to that provided under the hospital insurance formula.

By January 1, 1971, all provinces had joined the system and virtually the total population of Canada was thus provided with insurance against the costs of all necessary medical and hospital services.

The two decisions to launch such large-scale and complex programs were, indeed, great social, political and economic achievements — and so the people of Canada have recognized them to be. But it was also understood by their architects that the financing arrangements were means to further ends: providing the resources of qualified health care personnel and the institutional resources in which many or most of them would work. And these, too, were means, but to an ultimate end: enhancement of the health status of the members of Canadian society.

Since all three of these elements — institutional resources, health manpower, and costs and financing — will be considered in depth in succeeding chapters, this Introduction will provide only a brief overview before proceeding to discuss the major events in the decade under review.

Programs in Operation, 1968-1976

Hospital Facilities

In the late 1940s and early 1950s, Canada began a vigorous campaign to renew and expand its social capital, neglected during the Depression and the War. Spurred by the Hospital Construction Grant included in the 1948 Health Grants program, a total of 46,000 new beds were built in the short space of five years, 1948 to 1953. Construction continued, so that by the end of the decade when the national hospital insurance plan became fully operational, Canada had approximately 96,000 short-term beds and 19,000 long-term beds or, respectively, 5.4 and 1.1 beds per 1,000 population. In the 1960s an additional 22,000 short-term beds were built, but the beginning of a new trend was evident as 10,000 long-term beds, nearly half as many as the increase in short-term beds, were also added. In the decade of the 1970s this trend was even more pronounced; the number of short-term beds was reduced by almost 6,000 while 20,000 long-term beds were added. The respective ratios by (fiscal) 1979/80 were 4.8 and 2.2 beds per 1,000. Preliminary data indicate that the changing patterns set in the 1970s are continuing into the 1980s.

Hospital utilization statistics follow the same trends. Hospital admission rates increased from 143.4 per 1,000 in the mid-1950s to 154.7 per 1,000 in 1960, a rise of only 7.9 percent, remarkably low given that the proportion of the population insured had more than doubled. The rate rose to 165.9 per 1,000 in 1970 and then began to decline in the 1970s to a low of 155.5 in (fiscal) 1979/80. [*Editors' Note:* The bed and utilization data quoted here differ from those tabulated in the paper below by Barer and Evans. They refer to *all* hospitals, regardless of ownership or function. The Barer-Evans data refer only to Public General and Allied Special hospitals, for which more detailed operating statistics are available. Discrepancies are less than 5 percent, just enough to uphold the tradition of health statistics that no two numbers shall ever match. A listing and discussion of data sources is provided in the appendix to Barer and Evans.]

Several factors or forces (some of them offsetting) may have been at work here: a gradually aging population with its concomitant needs for long-term care; provision of facilities in under-serviced areas; new high technology that reduced length of stay; increases in home care services; fiscal restraints affecting all levels of government; and, not least, a growing perception in the 1970s that Canadians had placed too much emphasis on inpatient hospital care and that resources should now be re-directed to preventive measures, health promotion and non-institutional care, if not outside the health care system entirely. The restraints on growth in the hospital sector were associated with increasing restraints on growth in the whole health care system.

Health Personnel

Physicians

When the Royal Commission on Health Services was appointed in 1961, the physician to population ratio was 1:857, ranging from a high of 1:758 in British Columbia to a low of 1:1,990 in Newfoundland. Several factors guided the Commission in framing its recommendations with respect to medical manpower: the population projections submitted by its consultants, which, based on the high birth rates and immigration of the 1950s, turned out to be grossly exaggerated; the serious disparities in medical manpower among the provinces; the higher utilization of medical services by insured persons (and the fact that under universal Medicare the number of insured persons would be more than doubled); and the constant reiteration of medical association spokesmen that the introduction of health insurance (termed by them "socialized medicine") would lead to an exodus of doctors from the country. This latter prediction was reinforced during the Commission's deliberations by the fact that at least 10 percent of the doctors had left Saskatchewan on the introduction of its Medicare plan in July 1962, and that another 200 departed in the next eighteen months, although all had been replaced by the middle of 1964. Taking all these factors into account, the Commission recommended that five new medical schools be created and that several of the existing schools be expanded.

With the assistance of the Health Resources Fund introduced by the federal government in 1966 for the specific purpose of expanding educational resources for health sciences personnel, four new medical schools were launched and twelve others expanded and upgraded, increasing Canada's medical school capacity from 881 graduates in 1966 to 1,770 in 1983. Meanwhile, however, the threats of a mass emigration of doctors had proved wholly unfounded. From a low of 242 physicians moving abroad in 1975, the numbers increased gradually to a high of 663 in 1978 and gradually declined to a low of 372 in 1981 and a slight increase to 450 in 1982. In fact, at no time after the introduction of Medicare did the percentage of physicians emigrating from Canada exceed the percentage of physicians emigrating in the 1950s when the supply of physicians was much more restricted.

In contrast, however, the number of physicians immigrating to Canada reached unprecedented levels. In the five years prior to 1971, the annual number of immigrants averaged 470. Beginning in 1970, the numbers began to rise, reaching a maximum of 1,170 in 1973. At the request of a number of provinces, immigration regulations were changed in February 1975 to restrict the flow; during the past five years annual immigration has averaged 357.

The effects of expanding medical school capacity and the unexpected surge in physician immigration, together with modest rates of emigration, resulted in a steady increase in the physician to population ratio in every province. The total number of active civilian physicians (including interns and residents) increased in the decade 1971 to 1981 from 32,942 to 45,542, while the physician to population ratio in Canada as a whole increased from 1:659 to 1:538, and the annual percentage increase in physicians continues higher than the percentage increase in the population.

Nurses

The largest single group in the health services sector is, of course, the professional nurses, and the increase in their numbers (47 percent from 1971 to 1981) exceeded even the increase in physicians (38 percent). Again, as with physicians, the ratio of nurses to population varies from province to province but the gap between the low- and high-income provinces has been substantially reduced.

Perhaps no other professional group has been subject to so many changes: the transfer in most provinces of their basic education from hospital-based schools of nursing to the community colleges; assumption of responsibility for many procedures previously the domain of physicians; greater demands for specialization in skills in intensive care, dialysis units and other high-tech areas. One result of this up-grading has been rapid expansion in baccalaureate courses in universities (1,379 graduates in 1981, a 186 percent increase over 1971). Many nurses are also completing graduate Health Services Administration degrees, and others are completing doctoral programs for teaching and research.

Dentists

Except for a number of childrens' dental programs, the insuring or pre-payment of dental services remains almost solely a private-sector function, mainly through employer-employee negotiated contracts. The most recent survey conducted (in 1982) indicated that approximately 55.4 percent of the Canadian population was insured by third-party pre-payment plans, and, of these, three-fourths were insured through private plans. Nevertheless, without the stimulus of universal coverage, the increase in the number of dentists (54 percent from 1971 to 1981) is even more dramatic than that of either doctors or nurses.

But even with this increase, the distribution of dentists reveals shocking disparities among the provinces. The dentist to population ratio in Canada as a whole in 1982 was 1:2,087, but among the provinces the ratio ranges from a high of 1:1,585 in British Columbia to lows of 1:3,554 in New Brunswick and 1:4,457 in Newfoundland. We thus have the anomaly of cut-backs in dental school enrolment in major urban centres while a survey conducted in 1978-79 revealed that 49.7 percent of the population had had no consultation with a dentist in the preceding twelve months.[2] Dental health, as observed by the Royal Commission in 1964, remains one of our most serious health problems.

Other Professions and Para-professions

While physicians, nurses and dentists traditionally have been, and remain, the core of the health services delivery system, the explosion in medical technology and its increasingly widespread use have introduced new, specialized occupations and have expanded others. Health and Welfare Canada now reports on twenty-seven different occupations in its annual *Health Manpower Inventory* (from which all manpower data in these sections have been derived).[3] Not all these will be referred to, but in the 1971 to 1981 period, some increases have been spectacular. At the end of 1981, there were 258 audiologists (an increase of 2500 percent from 1971); 4,191 dietitians (200 percent); 4,453 respiratory technologists (318 percent); 4,124 dental hygienists (386 percent); 15,097 laboratory technologists (108 percent); 9,660 radiation technologists (108 percent); 1,852 occupational therapists (75 percent from 1973); and 4,453 physiotherapists (95 percent). The list goes on, but enough has been shown to indicate the variety of health occupations and their extraordinary expansion made possible, mainly, by a publicly financed educational system and the publicly financed health insurance system.

Cost of the Programs

As reported by Dr. Maurice LeClair (Footnote 1), the total costs of the hospital insurance program had reached slightly over $3 billion in 1973/74, of which the federal government contributed 50.1 percent. Expenditures on the Medicare program had reached $1.37 billion, of which the federal government contributed 50 percent.

By 1975/76, the combined costs of the two programs had reached $6.45 billion, of which the federal government contribution amounted to 50.8 percent. This $6.45 billion figure was to become the base-line for calculating federal contributions beginning in 1977 when the provisions of the Established Programs Financial Arrangements Act would come into effect. Further discussions of health expenditures will be reserved for the section dealing with that Act.

Financing

As noted above, the federal government was committed to paying one-half of the costs of the two programs in the ten provinces and two territories. Under hospital insurance, the federal government's contribution came from the Consolidated Revenue Fund. When Medicare was introduced, however, the federal government imposed a 2 percent surtax on the income tax (to a maximum of $120), which it designated the "Social Development Tax". Because of opposition from several of the provinces that intended to use an increase in the provincial income tax to finance their share of costs of the new program, the federal government dropped the separate identification of the surtax and simply incorporated it into the general income tax.

What was remarkable about provincial decisions on revenue sources was that the pre-payment plans and the insurance industry had "educated" Canadians to pre-pay their hospital and medical costs through the payment of premiums, a high proportion subsidized by employers. It was a ready-made tax source, and the first two provinces to introduce universal hospital insurance programs (Saskatchewan and British Columbia) made full use of it. In 1954, however, because of the difficulties of collecting from individuals not in large employee groups, B.C. abolished premiums and increased the retail sales tax from 3 percent to 5 percent. As the rest of the provinces came into the system in the late 1950s, most also began by imposing premiums but, with the exception of Ontario, all later abandoned that source for funding hospital insurance. With the introduction of Medicare, both British Columbia and Alberta re-imposed premiums for that coverage; but no other province save Ontario imposes them.

One other source of financing used by some of the provinces has been "user fees" or charges to patients at the time of receiving service. The only example of government-imposed user charges for physicians' services was that of Saskatchewan in 1968, an experiment abandoned, on a change of government, in l971. But hospital user fees have been imposed in British Columbia and Alberta since the inception of their programs, and, in a number of other provinces, *per diem* fees are charged for extended care when it is anticipated that the patient will not be maintaining a separate residence. User fees will be further discussed under the section on the Canada Health Act.

Established Programs Financing Arrangements, 1977

There are two basic problems in any federal system: (1) balancing the fiscal resources of the central and regional governments with the constitutional responsibilities assigned to each of them, and (2) removing, or at least reducing, the disparities in the fiscal capacities of the respective units forming the federation. In Canada, these issues were formally addressed by the Royal Commission on Dominion-Provincial Relations in 1937 to 1940 and have been a preoccupation of both levels of government ever since.

The first problem has been addressed by the transfer of personal income and corporation income tax points (as they are called, a point being 1 percent of the federal income tax) from the federal to the provincial governments. The second challenge has been approached in two ways: (1) by unconditional equalization payments to lower income provinces to enable them to provide reasonably comparable levels of service at reasonable levels of taxation, and (2) by conditional grant-in-aid programs in areas of provincial jurisdiction, in which there is held to be a clear national interest. Health insurance and higher education are the two major examples of the latter approach.

Despite the acknowledged success of the hospital and medical care insurance programs, as indicated by the degree of public approval and the perceived quality of the health services, experience has revealed two basic flaws in the conditional grant-in-aid systems.

From the provincial point of view, there were constant complaints about the inflexibility of the administrative details of the Agreements under the Hospital Insurance Act, the fact of federal auditing to determine "shareable" costs and, more importantly, claimed distortions in provincial priorities in health services created by the fact that federal funds were available to subsidize only two — and the most expensive — of an increasing range of health services programs.

Ottawa's concern was that it had lost control of its ever- and rapidly increasing health budget, since it was forced to match all expenditures incurred by provincial governments. There were several factors enhancing federal officials' rising sense of alarm. The first was the uneasy feeling that provincial governments were not as prudent in their decisions on cost-shared medical and hospital insurance programs as in other alternative programs for which they were wholly responsible to allocate "100¢ dollars".

Yet another factor was the growing conviction that, as a result of introducing hospital insurance first, Canada had grossly overbuilt its hospital system. On this base, believed to be thus inflated, there were extraordinary annual increases in costs in the mid-1970s (22 percent in 1974 and 26 percent in 1975). These, together with the unprecedented increase in the numbers of physicians, created a mentality of a health cost "crisis", which was exacerbated by the flood of literature on the efforts in the U.S. (most of them futile) to achieve some degree of control over rising health costs there.

The Economic Council had earlier sent up warning flares. In its 1970 Annual Review, *Patterns of Growth*, the Council projected that "if the rate of increase of the past five years (1964 to 1969) were to continue unabated, these two areas of activity (health and education) alone would absorb the entire national product before the year 2000".[4] All ministers of Finance and provincial treasurers got the message.

There was one new element, the conviction among growing numbers of health officials and health analysts that the outer limits of what a high-technology, treatment-oriented system could contribute to improved health status had been reached, if not, indeed, exceeded. As World Bank surveys had shown, a link exists between life expectancy and the availability of health services. Among seventy-five countries, roughly four-fifths of the variations in life expectancy are associated with access to physicians, nurses and hospitals. With diminishing returns from additional inputs, however, a point is reached at which further increases yield little or no gain, and indeed several analyses show that they generate losses. This critical point appears to be in the neighbourhood of 150 physicians per 100,000 people.[5] As a report by the Economic Council of Canada observes, "If [these figures are] realistic, it would put Canada, with over 170 physicians per 100,000 people, beyond this point".[6]

Taking all these factors together, it was clear that the stage was being set for a major restructuring of the financial underpinnings of the federal-provincial health insurance system.

The direction that new federal initiatives would likely take had been indicated as early as 1966, before Medicare had been introduced. At a meeting of the Federal-Provincial Tax Structure Committee, Finance Minister Mitchell Sharp had announced the federal government's intention to end conditional grants for "certain well established and continuing" programs and the provinces were offered a transfer of seventeen income tax points in lieu of the grants for hospital insurance and for the Canada Assistance Plan. Fearing that the increases in the income tax yield would not keep pace with the increasing costs of the two programs, all of the provinces, with the exception of Quebec, refused.[7]

At this point it is necessary to refer to one of the better working relationships of the federal system: the income tax collection agreements whereby (with the exception of Quebec) the provinces accept the federal definitions and exemptions respecting income, and the federal government collects without charge to the provinces the additional percentage income taxes levied by the provinces. With the reduced federal "base" resulting from the Income Tax Reforms of 1971 (a process quite separate from issues of health care finance), provincial governments would have had either to accept lower revenues or to bear the onus of raising the percentage to be levied on their behalf. Recognizing the provincial position, the federal government agreed that for the first three years of the 1972 to 1977 Tax Agreements (during which the provincial governments could make the necessary adjustments), the federal government would ensure that the provinces would receive no less under the reformed income tax than they would have received had the federal income tax base not been reduced. This became known as the Revenue Guarantee. Becoming entangled with health insurance funding, it has bedevilled federal-provincial relations ever since.

Following its preoccupation in the early 1970s with tax reform and the negotiation of the 1972 tax agreements, the federal government renewed its efforts to resolve the impasse over financing post-secondary education and the two health programs. In 1973, the government proposed a variant of the 1966 offer that would have linked increases in federal contributions to increases in the GNP. This was rejected by the provinces. Alarmed by the inordinate increases in health care costs in 1974 and 1975, the federal government then announced that increases in its contributions to medical care would be limited to 14.5 percent *per capita* in 1976/77, 12 percent in 1977/78 and 8.0 percent in 1978/79. It also gave the mandatory five-year notice to terminate the Hospital Insurance Agreements, effective in 1980. It was evident that more than equalization payments would be on the agenda of the upcoming negotiations for the 1977 Tax Agreements, and that fundamental restructuring of the system was in order.

Those negotiations began at the Federal-Provincial Conference in June 1976. Prime Minister Pierre Trudeau introduced his proposals with a statement of objectives:

1. To maintain across Canada the standards of service to the public under these major programs, and to facilitate their improvement.
2. To put the programs on a more stable footing, so that both levels of government are better able to plan their expenditures.
3. To give the provinces flexibility in the use of their own funds which they have been spending in these fields.
4. To bring about greater equality among the provinces with regard to the amount of federal funds they receive under the programs.
5. To provide for joint policy discussions relating to the health and post-secondary fields.[8]

The proposals directed to these objectives signalled the end of the open-ended 50-50 cost-sharing arrangements for post-secondary education and the two health programs. In their place, the federal government proposed to vacate 12.5 points of personal income and 1.0 percent of corporation income "tax room" which would thus become available for the provinces to occupy. This was calculated to approximate one-half of the federal contribution under the existing cost-sharing formula. In addition, the federal government would contribute a cash grant equal to one half of its 1975/76 payments for the three programs, escalated annually in accordance with a three-year moving average of increases in the GNP. Since a tax point yields less revenue in low income than in high income provinces, the tax points would be equalized to the national average. Moreover, in the event that revenue from the tax points fell below the amount payable in the escalated cash grant, a transitional payment equal to the difference would be added.

The negotiations that began in July 1976 were lengthy, often bitter, and always complex. The provincial finance ministers and their officials held an unprecedented number of meetings. During these, Saskatchewan and the four Atlantic provinces finally abandoned their insistence on retaining the 50-50 cost-sharing formula, permitting the finance ministers to present an unanimous counter-proposal in early December that included a demand for an additional transfer of four tax points as a continuation of the Revenue Guarantee. The federal Finance Minister rejected this proposal and the issues were left for the scheduled First Ministers Conference on December 13-14.

While the fundamental change from cost sharing to block funding was accepted, the provinces were adamant that the Revenue Guarantee must be maintained. Finally, to achieve agreement, the federal government offered an additional transfer of one tax point and its equivalent in cash (or one-half the amount the provinces had demanded).

Despite the fact that the origins of the Revenue Guarantee lay in the 1971 income tax reforms, and had absolutely nothing to do with Established Programs financing, the Revenue Guarantee amounts (the equivalent of two tax points) were included in the omnibus legislation and published as one part of the federal government's three "contributions". Although it had the short-term effect of magnifying the federal contribution, it was a political decision that would come to embarrass the government, and that would finally be withdrawn.

The essentials of the agreement were incorporated in the Federal-Provincial Fiscal Arrangements and Established Programs Financing Act and became operational for the period April 1, 1977 to March 31, 1982.

Extended Health Care Services Program

In addition to the provisions already outlined, the federal government introduced a new grant of $20 *per capita* (also to be escalated annually in accordance with increases in GNP) to assist provinces in providing less expensive support services, including nursing home intermediate care services, adult residential care services, converted mental hospitals, home care services and ambulatory health services. No conditions (other than information reporting) were attached to this grant.

For purposes of relating federal contributions to the respective health programs and post-secondary education, the allocations obtaining in 1975/76 were adopted. These were determined to be: higher education, 32.4 percent; hospital insurance, 49.9 percent; and Medicare, 17.7 percent.

The financial results in contributions to the provinces under EPF in comparison with the final years of the cost-sharing period (1975/76 and 1976/77) are presented in Table 1. Note that the federal "contribution" includes the 12.5 percent income tax and 1 percent corporation income tax transfer equalized to the national average yield, but excludes the one tax point and its equivalent cash payment constituting the extension of the Revenue Guarantee.

With the introduction of the EPF arrangements, the major objectives of the two levels of government were achieved. The federal government obtained a greater degree of predictability and control over its health expenditures, and the provincial governments achieved their goal of greater flexibility in determining their health care program priorities. The new block grant also provided a greater degree of equity in that by the third year, the *per capita* payments to provinces were equal, whereas under the Hospital Insurance Act formula, low cost provinces received lower *per capita* grants than did high cost provinces. At the same time, it should be noted that this new-found autonomy and equity were not achieved without commensurate responsibilities. The provinces are now solely responsible for program cost increases that exceed increases in the GNP. On the other hand, since all provincial expenditures on medical care and hospital insurance are now 100¢ rather than 50¢ dollars, the federal contribution no longer has any steering effect on provincial decision-making.

A primary objective of the federal government in shifting to block funding was to induce a greater degree of urgency and action in containing costs of the two increasingly expensive health programs. But it is not clear whether EPF had any major impact on provincial government cost containment policies. Almost all provinces had already taken a tougher bargaining stance in negotiating with their respective medical associations and in granting hospital rate increases below the level of inflation. These efforts had been enhanced by the anti-inflation program of the federal government from 1975 to 1978.

With the expiry of controls on incomes and prices in 1978, the latter part of that year and 1979 saw large increases in the number of doctors extra-billing, an increased militancy among nurses and other hospital unions, and the beginning of charges that, as a result of EPF, provinces were diverting federal "contributions" to non-health purposes. With the election of the Progressive Conservatives in 1979, the new Minister of Health, the Honourable David Crombie, became the focal point of charges that the federal government was not fulfilling its obligations to ensure that the "national standards" were maintained and the principles

TABLE 1

PROVINCIAL GOVERNMENT EXPENDITURES AND FEDERAL CONTRIBUTIONS FOR HOSPITAL AND MEDICAL CARE INSURANCE PROGRAMS, (in $ million) BY PROVINCE, FISCAL YEARS ENDING MARCH 31, 1975/76 to 1982/83

	1975/76	1976/77	1977/78	1978/79	1979/80	1980/81[b]	1981/82[b]	1982/83[b]
Provincial Expenditures[a]								
Nfld.	147.8	162.0	171.5	188.2	211.4	248.3	291.3	338.8
P.E.I.	24.1	27.2	29.8	33.8	37.7	43.6	51.0	62.6
N.S.	207.4	239.2	258.2	284.5	320.6	365.5	445.3	513.5
N.B.	154.5	176.2	190.1	208.2	233.2	287.5	351.8	380.8
Que.	1,870.7	2,154.5	2,243.8	2,599.3	2,807.8	3,185.9	3,590.6	4,110.4
Ont.	2,309.1	2,645.4	2,846.3	3,030.9	3,222.3	3,735.4	4,260.5	5,039.0
Man.	272.5	308.7	334.5	348.5	383.6	445.8	547.7	656.9
Sask.	223.6	257.6	300.3	325.2	361.8	418.0	467.3	577.6
Alta.	481.0	568.3	620.8	710.7	820.8	1,010.1	1,283.8	1,518.0
B.C.	742.3	805.7	887.7	979.9	1,113.3	1,425.1	1,853.9	2,061.0
Yuk.	3.9	7.0	7.4	8.6	9.0	9.8	10.9	12.3
N.W.T.	12.0	11.6	16.9	17.8	21.0	22.4	24.8	28.4
Canada	6,448.9	7,363.4	7,907.3	8,735.6	9,542.5	11,197.3	13,178.9	15,299.3
Federal Contributions[c]								
Nfld.	76.4	90.8	95.5	113.1	130.0	144.6	161.1	181.1
P.E.I.	14.8	16.7	19.5	23.8	28.1	31.4	34.8	39.1
N.S.	111.6	131.2	147.2	170.5	194.4	216.1	240.4	271.1
N.B.	92.8	107.2	116.8	138.4	159.8	177.8	197.6	222.5
Que.	914.5	1,055.4	1,180.7	1,310.0	1,465.0	1,632.9	1,826.6	2,062.6

TABLE 1 (cont'd)

PROVINCIAL GOVERNMENT EXPENDITURES AND FEDERAL CONTRIBUTIONS FOR HOSPITAL AND MEDICAL CARE INSURANCE PROGRAMS, (in $ million) BY PROVINCE, FISCAL YEARS ENDING MARCH 31, 1975/76 to 1982/83

Federal Contributions(c)	1975/76	1976/77	1977/78	19178/79	1979/80	1980/81(b)	1981/82(b)	1982/83(b)
Ont.	1,181.7	1,349.2	1,511.9	1,733.3	1,962.8	2,191.3	2,447.0	2,773.2
Man.	148.8	172.1	186.3	212.1	237.7	262.1	291.2	329.4
Sask.	127.6	149.8	163.3	191.1	219.8	245.3	274.8	311.6
Alta.	257.3	303.2	347.9	413.0	501.2	601.7	701.7	737.2
B.C.	341.4	390.3	426.4	505.4	597.7	691.3	784.9	887.8
Yuk.	2.7	4.1	4.3	5.5	6.7	7.1	8.6	8.8
N.W.T.	8.5	8.4	12.7	15.1	16.8	18.6	20.3	22.9
Canada	3,278.1	3,778.4	4,212.5	4,831.3	5,520.9	6,220.4	6,989.9	7,847.1

Percent Federal Contribution

	1975/76	1976/77	1977/78	19178/79	1979/80	1980/81(b)	1981/82(b)	1982/83(b)
Nfld.	51.7	56.0	55.7	60.1	61.5	58.2	55.3	53.5
P.E.I.	61.4	61.4	65.4	70.4	74.5	72.0	68.2	62.5
N.S.	53.8	54.8	57.0	59.9	60.6	59.1	54.0	52.8
N.B.	60.1	60.8	61.4	66.5	68.5	61.8	56.2	58.4
Que.	48.9	49.0	52.6	50.4	52.2	51.3	50.9	50.2
Ont.	51.2	51.0	53.1	57.2	60.9	58.7	57.4	55.0
Man.	54.6	55.7	55.7	60.9	62.0	58.8	53.2	50.1
Sask.	57.1	58.2	54.4	58.8	60.8	58.7	58.8	53.9
Alta.	53.5	53.4	56.0	58.1	61.1	59.6	54.7	48.6
B.C.	46.0	48.4	48.0	51.6	53.7	48.5	42.3	43.1
Yuk.	69.2	58.6	58.1	64.0	74.4	72.4	78.9	71.5
N.W.T.	70.8	72.4	75.1	84.8	80.0	83.0	81.9	80.6
Canada	50.8	51.3	53.3	55.3	57.8	55.6	53.0	51.3

(a) Including federal contributions (b) Provisional (c) Cash plus tax room.

SOURCE: Based on data from Health Economics and Data Analysis Division, Health and Welfare Canada.

of Medicare were not eroded. As an indication of public interest in the threats to Medicare, a number of provincial health coalitions held provincial conferences in 1979, leading up to a National Health Coalition "SOS Medicare Conference" in Ottawa in early November 1979.

Health Minister Crombie, however, had already begun to take action. In July 1979 he had convened a meeting of health ministers at which a general overview of the situation was discussed. He then proposed that a Special Commissioner be appointed to conduct a public inquiry. The provincial ministers (with the exception of Quebec which, in the event, co-operated fully) accepted the proposal and also agreed that the Honourable Mr. Emmett Hall, who had been the Chairman (1961-1964) of the Royal Commission on Health Services, should be the Special Commissioner.

The terms of reference for the new Commission (Health Services Review '79) were broad:

1. Consider the extent to which the goals of the Charter of Health for Canadians have been met.

2. Examine the extent to which the principles of portability, reasonable access, universal coverage, comprehensive coverage, reasonable compensation, and uniform terms and conditions are being achieved.

3. Consider whether there should be other basic principles underlying health insurance delivery.

4. Consider the nature and extent of necessary revisions to the Hospital Insurance and Diagnostic Services Act and the Medical Care Act and related legislation.

5. Consider other means by which public authorities may best comply with the principles referred to above.[9]

From the government's point of view there were really only two major questions: Were the provinces, as charged, diverting federal health funds to non-health programs? And were extra-billing by physicians and user charges by provinces violating the principle of reasonable access and thus eroding Medicare?

But the public took the appointment of a Commission seriously. After eleven years of Medicare, a comprehensive in-depth examination of the system was essential. Both provider and consumer groups responded with an overwhelming total of 450 briefs that, in the main, lauded the system, observed its shortcomings, demanded new services and pointed in new directions.

As Research Consultant to the Commissioner, I was primarily responsible for ascertaining whether provincial governments were indeed diverting federal health funds, for analyzing the briefs to prepare for questioning of witnesses in the public hearings, and for preparing drafts for parts of the rest of the Report.

Expert staff in Health and Welfare Canada analysed pre-EPF and post-EPF health expenditures. That group completed a monumental task of examining provincial public accounts and all their data were submitted to provincial Health and Treasury departments for verification. This was followed up by personal interviews with federal and provincial Finance and Health officials. The results were indisputable: provinces were not diverting federal health "contributions" to non-health purposes. The whole issue had arisen because the federal government had included the Revenue Guarantee (one tax point and its equivalent in cash) as a "contribution" under EPF. The proportions of provincial budgets allocated to health pre -and post-EPF were identical. Revenue Guarantee funds, quite rightly, had been spent on other programs. That answered federal question number one.

On question number two, whether extra-billing and user charges were endangering the principle of reasonable access, Commissioner Hall was adamant. He concluded that "if extra-billing is permitted as a right and practised by physicians in their sole discretion, it will, over the years, destroy the program, creating in that downward path a two-tier system incompatible with the societal level which Canadians have attained".[10] But what if extra-billing were denied? What if government-medical association negotiations over the fee schedule broke down? The remedy, said the Commissioner, was binding arbitration, a solution that almost every witness speaking to the issue in the public hearings had rejected.

His views on extra-billing were a noble restatement of a fundamental principle of the Canadian health system and reflect credit on the ideals and sense of equity of a distinguished jurist. But the total Report, because of underfunding, understaffing and limited time, did not address adequately many of the issues and recommendations in many of the briefs.

The election of 1980 had returned the Liberals to power with the Honourable Monique Bégin reinstated as Minister of Health and Welfare. The campaign itself had devastated the National Health Coalition's 1979-1980 crusade as many of its leaders and front-line workers were redirected to election duties.

One effect of the Clark government's period in office and its return to Opposition benches was that the Progressive Conservatives now demanded a greater role for Parliament in the upcoming negotiations for the 1982 Fiscal Arrangements and Established Programs Financing Act. Previous negotiations had taken place solely between federal and provincial ministers and their officials, with their agreements rubber-stamped by Parliament and provincial legislatures. Professor Donald Smiley has described the process as "executive federalism". There now appeared a determination among Opposition members and Liberal backbenchers alike that it was time for members of the House of Commons to reassert their role in the parliamentary system.

The Conservative Opposition demanded and finally obtained agreement by the government to the appointment of a new investigative body, an all-party House of Commons Task Force that was commissioned to examine the whole field of federal-provincial fiscal relations including the impact of EPF. It was the last thing the government wanted in a period of restraint — a parliamentary committee holding public hearings across the country, providing highly publicized opportunities for a variety of interest groups demanding increases in government spending. The terms of reference endeavoured to head off this likelihood by authorizing the seven-member, all-party committee to examine "fiscal equalization, the tax collection agreements, the Canada Assistance Plan and Established Programs Financing, and that this examination take place *within the context of the government's expenditure plan as set out in the October 28, 1980 budget*".

The Task Force held public hearings in Ottawa and all the provincial capitals received briefs from a host of interest groups concerned, in the main, with financing higher education and the health care system. Both, it was claimed, were underfunded. The Canadian Medical Association and several of its provincial divisions cited evidence of the underfinancing of the system and urged that spending be increased immediately to at least 8.2 percent of GNP from the 7 percent characteristic of the 1970s. (In fact, Canadian spending on health services reached 8.4 percent of GNP in 1982.) Aided by an excellent research staff, the Task Force produced a remarkable Report, *Fiscal Federalism in Canada*, in less than a year.[11]

Acknowledging that it was re-crossing terrain traversed by the 1979-1980 Health Services Review, the Task Force nevertheless conducted an intensive analysis of the relevant briefs and statistical and financial data available to it. While praising the health program as a "major accomplishment of Canadian society" and approving the extension of EPF block funding, the Task Force was concerned about the erosion of national standards and the role of the federal government in a field of provincial jurisdiction. It concluded that despite the constitutional division of powers,

> there is an overriding national interest in the operation of health insurance plans and in the effectiveness of health care delivery. The question that follows is what actions the federal government may take to serve the national interest without itself becoming directly involved in health care delivery.

It concluded "that the proper role for the federal government is the formulation, monitoring and enforcement of conditions on its financial support of provincial programs". To perform this role it urged that the Hospital Insurance and Medical Care Acts be consolidated in order to establish clear program conditions supported by explicit criteria against which satisfaction of those conditions can be monitored, and to provide for some withholding of federal financial support from provincial plans that do not fully meet those conditions. It also urged the Minister of Health to report annually to Parliament the results of the department's monitoring and any withholding actions taken, for reference to a parliamentary committee.

The Task Force divided its report on the health system into three sections: the delivery system, program conditions and the national commitment to health care including the question of underfunding. Only the highlights will be summarized here.

With respect to the delivery system the Task Force reported on five major areas of concern: (1) the further development of extended health care resources to meet more effectively the needs of an aging population; (2) the need to develop alternative health care services and to counteract the tendency of the present system to emphasize an "illness care" or "treatment oriented" approach; (3) the geographical imbalance in the distribution of medical manpower, facilities and services; (4) the under-utilization of non-physician health workers, associated with an alleged oversupply of physicians; and (5) more effective coordination among all those concerned with health care in Canada.

In addition to this concise but comprehensive overview of the health care system, the Task Force dealt at some length with three major issues.

The first was the imbalance in the system resulting from the over-emphasis on medical and hospital services, and the lack of resources allocated to extended care, prevention and health promotion. It endorsed the health field concept of the Lalonde Report [12] and the recommendations for the development of community health centres in the Hastings Report of 1972.[13] Moreover, it recommended that the federal and provincial governments work together to identify more specifically the program conditions or criteria that would lead to better implementation of the community-based health care philosophy.

The second major issue was the extent to which user fees and extra-billing by physicians violated the principle of reasonable access. Examining hospital user fees imposed in three provinces, the committee concluded that it had no evidence, given the exemptions prevailing in those provinces, that user fees constituted a barrier to accessibility. Nevertheless, it endorsed the view of the Health Services Review that appeal to the "user pay" concept is contrary to the principle and spirit of the national health program.

The committee found the issue of extra-billing more complex; indeed, it was unable to achieve consensus on its recommendations. It summarized the arguments presented by the medical associations as follows:

1) It (extra-billing) is said to promote the "economic and fiscal responsibility" of the user;

2) It increases the private financing of the system (thus reducing the burden on the general taxpayer); and

3) It enhances the patient-physician relationship.

And, finally, extra-billing was described as a barometer of physician discontent and a safety valve for physicians who feel alienated and under-compensated.

It then summarized some of the arguments advanced in opposition to extra-billing:

> All or almost all of the members of a specialty group may be opted out — as is frequently the case with such specialists as obstetricians or ophthalmologists, for example;
>
> All or almost all general practitioners in a given area may be extra-billing, so that choice is seriously limited for many people;
>
> In its actual application, extra-billing is not, as claimed, a means by which a mediocre income is raised to a moderately acceptable one. In fact, most of the revenues collected from extra-billing flow to high-income physicians; and
>
> Although physicians claim not to extra-bill low income patients, there are some documented cases of pensioners and those on unemployment insurance being billed, and indeed of those bills being placed in the hands of collection agencies.

The Task Force then repeated the conclusion of the Health Services Review:

> If extra billing is permitted as a right and practiced by physicians at their sole discretion, it will, over the years, destroy the system, creating in that downward path a two-tier system incompatible with the societal level which Canadians have attained.

Following further analysis of the medical association's position the committee concluded "that the legitimate interests of doctors must give way to the broad public perception that uncontrolled billing of patients beyond the levels of provincial medical insurance plan schedules will ultimately destroy medicare".

The majority of the committee recommended that "doctors who either bill a provincial medical plan directly, or whose patients are reimbursed by the plan, not be allowed to charge fees in excess of those permitted under the plan's approved fee schedule". It then added: "However, consistent with the need to ensure fair remuneration for doctors, the majority believes that this proposed ban on extra billing should be combined with a fair negotiation process, followed, if necessary, by binding arbitration to set the plan's schedule of fees". This was followed by a second recommendation of the majority that "following federal-provincial negotiations, any plan that does not meet fully all the accessibility criteria be ineligible for full federal financial support under Established Programs Financing".

The minority of the committee was not prepared to go that far, recommending only that if individual doctors choose to bill patients directly, they must opt out of the plan, and they must opt out entirely for all patients. This would end the practice of billing some patients directly and billing the plan on behalf of others, as well as the billing of both patients and the plan for the same services.

The third and final major issue was whether Canadians were committing a sufficient proportion of national resources to meet their essential health care needs. The committee carefully analyzed the claim, most forcefully enunciated by the Canadian Medical Association, that the health system was underfunded. With health expenditures of 7.1 percent of GNP in 1979, of eight western nations only the United Kingdom and New Zealand were lower. The alleged manifestations of underfunding included delays in treatment of acute care patients, waiting lists for elective surgery, reduction of personnel, closing of facilities, lack of extended care facilities, outdated equipment and overburdened facilities. Underfunding was also claimed to have resulted in an increase in the numbers of physicians opting out and extra-billing.

The counter-arguments were summarized as follows:

1. International comparisons of the percentage of GNP allocated to health services are misleading; they dwell on expenditures and say nothing about the mix of services or results. In the United States, overhead costs of insurance are four times higher than in Canada; hospital administrative overhead (because of billing for each service) is much higher; there is far greater duplication of facilities and high technology.

In essence, the Report concluded that comparisons of the percentage of GNP spent on health services by Canada and the U.S. were irrelevant. "The difference is in our philosophy: Canadians are endeavouring to develop a health care system directed to health needs — not a competitive system to serve an illness market".

2. The switch to block funding from cost-sharing had injected a major infusion of new funds into the system. In 1978-79 provinces received between 1.5 and 1.8 billion dollars more than they would have under the old formula. The federal share of provincial spending on health and post-secondary education had increased from 42 percent in 1976-77 to 47 percent in 1979/80. In constant dollars, *per capita* spending on health had increased by almost one-fifth in the decade of the seventies.

3. While physicians' incomes, like those of all other self-employed professional groups, had not kept pace with inflation during the 1970s, following the extraordinary increases resulting from the introduction of Medicare, nevertheless, physicians continued to remain in first place.

Taking all the evidence presented to it, and the findings of its research staff, the Task Force concluded:

> Provincial determination to contain cost growth in the health care system is strengthened by the argument that added investment in the acute care system will yield low marginal improvements in health . . . .
> It now seems that the next great advances must be made through better nutrition, more healthful lifestyles, cleaning up the environment,

greater safety in the workplace, and measures to reduce automobile accidents; . . . Having rejected the general argument that the health system is underfunded, the Task Force finds it impossible to recommend that increased expenditures be allocated at this time to the treatment system . . . in aggregate, and in present circumstances, federal government funding for health care services in Canada appears to be generally adequate. Despite this conclusion, there may remain specific areas of the health care system — for example, preventive care — that require expansion.

It was a unique episode in the Canadian governmental system — an all-party committee of Liberal back-benchers and Opposition members gathering evidence at the grass roots on one of Canada's most important social programs. It paved the way for the Canada Health Act of 1984.

The Canada Health Act, 1984

From the point of view of the federal and provincial Health ministries, the major concern in the decade we are examining (1974 to 1984) was making the system work: the proper allocation of acute and chronic care beds in hospitals and nursing homes; the scale of home care programs and the like; negotiations with medical associations; determining rates of payments to hospitals; increasing worries in several provinces about a perceived oversupply of physicians; the desire to expand preventive services and health promotion; constraints imposed by the continuing financial commitments to a high inventory of physicians and perceived oversupply of acute treatment beds in many areas; making rational decisions about the need for and efficacy of an ever-expanding range of available high technology; and managing relationships with increasingly militant hospital unions and nurses' and medical associations. It was daily a very full plate of decision-making for harassed health ministry officials.

The two major events in the decade were, however, the switch to block funding for hospital and medical care under the Established Programs Financial Arrangements legislation in 1977 and the Canada Health Act of 1984. The first of these, EPF, had represented the most massive transfer in our history of revenues (and therefore of the substance of power) from the federal to the provincial governments. The Canada Health Act, on the other hand, appeared to the provinces and the medical profession to be the reverse: an unwarranted and powerful federal intrusion into a field of provincial jurisdiction.

The issue appeared simple: whether physicians should be permitted, at will, to extra-bill insured patients and whether provincial governments could authorize "user fees" to be charged to patients admitted to hospital outpatient or inpatient facilities. The questions were simple, but they arose from the fundamental principle of the Medical Care Act that:

> The plan provide(s) for the furnishing of insured services upon uniform terms and conditions . . . by the payment of the cost of insured services in accordance with a tariff of authorized payment established pursuant to the provincial law . . . on a basis that provides for reasonable compensation for insured services rendered by medical practitioners and *that does not impede or preclude*, either directly or indirectly whether by charges made to insured persons or otherwise, *reasonable access* to insured services by insured persons.

The controversy leading to the Canada Health Act exceeded that over the National Energy Policy in that it involved all the provinces, and even that over reform of the Constitution in that while it, too, involved all the provinces, the proposed policy changes to be accomplished through a new Canada Health Act also brought into the fray the powerful medical associations.

Like so many aspects of our health care delivery system, the government-administered payment policies had their genesis in the methods of paying doctors before the advent of pre-payment and in the policies adoped by the physician-controlled pre-payment plans beginning in the late 1930s and continuing in their operation until the passage of the Medical Care Act in 1968. It is necessary, therefore, to introduce this discussion by tracing the evolution of the payment methods developed by the pre-payment plans.

In private practice, prior to any form of pre-payment, the medical practitioner billed his patients on a fee-for-service basis, taking into consideration the presumed "intrinsic" worth of the medical "act" and, in many cases, also the patient's ability to pay. Through this custom (known as "the sliding scale of fees"), the physician performed a "Robin Hood" function as he provided lower cost or free (sometimes not intentionally but because the bill remained unpaid) medical care to the poor who were obviously subsidized by his higher charges to the more affluent. The system could work effectively, of course, only if the physician's practice encompassed a reasonable spectrum of both low and higher income patients.

As the provincial medical associations became more involved with fee issues, their "tariff" committees developed standardized fee schedules as guidelines or "suggested minimum fees" for an ever-increasing range of procedures.

When commercial insurance companies introduced medical and/or surgical indemnity contracts, they used these fee schedules in setting their indemnity rates, usually providing reimbursement at less than the official minimum, thus requiring a degree of co-insurance by the patient as well as, usually, a fixed deductible before the insurance took effect.

The profession-sponsored pre-payment plans, on the other hand, introduced a wholly new concept — the so-called "service contract" (or "first-dollar coverage") providing, insofar as the patient was concerned, payment of the fee in full. There were three important elements in the new arrangements:

1. The participating physician was required to sign a contract with the pre-payment plan agreeing to accept the plan's payment as payment in full.

2. Because the plan was serving, in effect, as the physicians' collection agency, it was agreed that the plan would deduct 10 percent (in Saskatchewan, 15 percent) for overhead administration.

3. If the funds available from premium revenues were insufficient to meet the 90 percent obligation, the plan was empowered to "pro-rate" the payment downward so that expenditures and revenues were in balance. As the Ontario Physicians Services Incorporated (PSI) contract stated: "Unpaid balances of approved accounts shall constitute a charge against any surplus funds available for payment to participating physicians (i.e., those who had signed a contract with PSI) at the termination of the fiscal year". But the contract also provided that "the Board of Governors may, by resolution approved by two-thirds of the members of the Board, cancel such unpaid balances . . . and the Corporation shall thereafter cease to be liable in respect thereof".

It is unknown how often this provision was exercised by PSI, but a similar clause in the contract of Manitoba Medical Services was frequently used. The reason was that, in anticipation of the introduction of a government program, the Manitoba Medical Association had established a fee schedule that was, for most items, the highest in Canada. Pro-rating frequently was as low as 75 percent of the inflated (compared with most other provincial fee schedules) accounts. The unpaid "balances" were cited in the MMS Annual Reports as a "contribution" by the profession to the subscribers.

Four essential points emerge from this discussion of the profession-sponsored pre-payment experience:

1. In contrast to the medical associations in the U.S., Canadian provincial medical associations had established uniform province-wide minimum guideline Fee Schedules that became the uniform fee payment schedules for their pre-payment plans.

2. Ten percent was deducted from accounts for the plan's overhead administrative costs. Ninety percent was more than most physicians billing uninsured patients typically received. This precedent was adopted by provincial governments when Medicare was introduced.

3. In contrast to the strongly voiced contention of the medical associations that under Medicare the "contract" is only between the patient and the government, the creators of the pre-payment plans believed that the service contract could not work unless there was also a contractual relationship with the participating physicians.

4. Payments to physicians were made from a predetermined total fund. If volume of services, multiplied by the unit costs of the services rendered, exceeded revenues, accounts were pro-rated. Interestingly, this was foreseen in the comprehensive report on Medical Economics by the CMA Committee on Economics in 1934. Commenting on the various methods of paying physicians (salary, capitation, fee-for-service), the Committee said: "There does not appear to be any reason why a uniform system of payments should be advocated . . . . There is a sum for distribution; the method used will neither decrease nor increase it, otherwise the fund would not be solvent".[14]

The reason that the pre-payment plan funds in any fiscal year period were more or less predetermined was that, although there were periodic increases in premiums, the plan administrators warned association tariff committees that inordinate increases in fees would require commensurate increases in premiums that would result in their losing subscribers to the insurance companies. In other words, some forms of market forces were at work, in contrast to the present open-ended system we now have.

However, in every province having a profession-sponsored pre-payment plan, there were some physicians who did not sign contracts and were thus non-participating physicians, or what are now called (in two provinces) "opted out" physicians. These physicians set their own fees; those of their patients who were subscribers were reimbursed the amount provided in the operative fee schedule. The practice of "extra-billing" insured patients (though not "double-billing", of both plan and subscriber) was thus established.

The issue of extra-billing under a government-sponsored medical insurance program surfaced, naturally, in the first proposed Medicare program in Canada, that of Saskatchewan.[15] The major issue was whether there should be a government program at all, but the right of doctors to practise outside the plan and to extra-bill their patients was also of primary concern. Under the pressures generated by the withdrawal of all physicians' services (excepting emergency services in hospitals) for twenty-three days, the government accepted in the Saskatoon Agreement what is known as Mode Three billing:

> The doctor may practice partly, largely, or entirely outside any voluntary agency and not be enrolled for direct payment by the Commission. He will bill patients entirely at his own discretion . . . the patient must claim reimbursement from the Commission and pay any difference between the doctor's fee and eighty-five percent of the minimum fee schedule.

About 30 percent of physicians use Mode Three for some of their patients and the total amount extra-billed is approximately $2 million.

The issue of the right to extra-bill also triggered the withdrawal of services by the Federation of Medical Specialists of Quebec in October 1970. But with the doctors' strike becoming inextricably bound up with the FLQ crisis, the kidnapping of James Cross and the murder of Pierre Laporte, the National Assembly met in emergency session on October 15 and gave three readings to Bill 41, ordering the specialists back to work, and providing for three methods for physicians to practice with respect to the Medicare plan:

1. *Les engagés*: those who opt in and collect their fees in full from the Quebec Health Insurance Board.

2. *Les désengagés*: those who opt out but agree to charge no more than the authorized fees to their patients who would then be reimbursed in full.

3. *Les non-participants*: those who do not participate at all, charge their self-determined fees, and whose patients would *not* be reimbursed in any amount.

The effect was to preclude virtually all extra-billing. In only two provinces, Manitoba and Ontario, are physicians required to opt out of the system in order to charge more than the fees negotiated between the government and the medical association. This means that they bill all of their patients directly, and the patients must, in turn, seek reimbursement from the Medicare plan. In Ontario, however, there is an exception: opted-out doctors forming "billing groups" within a hospital (such as a group of anaesthetists) may bill OHIP for their (presumably non-affluent) hospitalized patients or outpatients.

In the other provinces (with the exception of British Columbia where there is no admitted extra-billing; but, if there were, extra-billers would be required to opt out) doctors are not required to opt out. They may bill their patients, the plan, or both. Unlike opted-out physicians in Ontario and Manitoba, they run no risk of unpaid bills.

In Ontario, the proportion of physicians opting out has fluctuated between 11 percent and 18 percent and now appears to have levelled off at about 15 percent, but it is reported by the Ministry that only about 5 percent of accounts are extra-billed. This means that fewer than 5 percent of patients (that is, of only those who chance to be ill or injured) contribute an additional estimated $50 million to physicians' incomes. In Nova Scotia approximately 53 percent of physicians extra-bill; and in Alberta about 47 percent (Edmonton 55 percent and Calgary 62 percent), adding about $14 million to physicians' incomes.

It is estimated by Health and Welfare Canada that the total of extra-billing charges approximated $100 million in 1983. The Canadian Medical Association emphasizes that this adds about 2 percent to the total cost of physicians' services. This aggregate figure is, of course, irrelevant. The central question is the impact of a specific extra charge on a specific patient or family.

While the practice of extra-billing had been criticized by consumer groups since the beginning of Medicare, the rapid increase in the number of opted out physicians in Ontario (from 10-12 percent from 1972 to 1977 to 18 percent in

1978) and of doctors extra-billing in other provinces when the Anti-Inflation Board restrictions were lifted in 1978 brought public discussion of the issue to a higher level in the election of 1979.

As we have seen, one of the first measures to be taken by the new Health Minister, the Honourable David Crombie, was to commission the Health Services Review to examine whether the increase in extra-billing was the result of provinces diverting federal contributions to non-health purposes, thereby reducing payments to physicians, who then augmented their incomes by extra-billing. Before Mr. Justice Hall could report, the Clark government was defeated and during the election campaign the former Health Minister, the Honourable Monique Bégin, spearheaded the attack on extra-billing and user fees and vowed to end both practices on the Liberals' return to power. Reinstated in the Health Ministry, and supported by the 1980 Health Services Review judgement that extra-billing, if allowed to continue, would create an unacceptable two-tier system, Madame Bégin continued her criticism of the practice and of the provinces that permitted it. She promised federal legislation that would penalize provinces that authorized hospital user fees and permitted extra-billing. There appears not to have been strong support in the Cabinet, especially during the period of negotiations on the Constitution, but the proposed policy was given substantial impetus, as we have seen, by the recommendations of the all-party parliamentary Task Force in August 1981.

The angry reactions of the provincial governments, and particularly of the ministers of Health in British Columbia, Alberta and Ontario, were matched only by the vehement outcries of spokesmen for the Canadian Medical Association and its provincial divisions. Massive publicity and lobbying campaigns were launched by all the medical associations, and Dr. Marc Baltzan of Saskatoon, during his term as President of the CMA from September 1982 to August 1983, became almost as prominent a media figure as Madame Bégin herself.

Senior officials of Health and Welfare Canada had begun preparation of a position paper, at the request of the Minister, shortly after her return to office. The initiation of official discussions began at a meeting of federal and provincial Health ministers in Ottawa on May 26, 1982, followed by a meeting of federal and provincial Deputy Ministers of Health in Vancouver on September 29, where a second draft of the White Paper was discussed. This was followed on the next day by a meeting of provincial ministers of Health. That meeting resulted in a press statement that the provinces would consider challenging the constitutional authority of the federal government to proceed with a Canada Health Act based on the proposals of the White Paper. The battle lines were now clearly drawn.

The confrontation escalated throughout 1983 as hyperbolic rhetoric flooded the news media. On the one side were the Liberal party and the government with their front-line spokesperson, the Minister of Health. They were championed by the federal NDP, provincial Liberal and NDP Opposition parties (where they existed), and by consumers' associations and the national and provincial health coalitions. On the other side were most of the provincial ministers of Health and the national and provincial medical associations. Not since the issue of Medicare itself in the mid-1960s had there been such a torrent of editorials and letters to the editor.

A flurry of actions and statements during 1983 fanned the flames of discord. In February the Ontario Cabinet passed a regulation under the Health Disciplines Act making it professional misconduct for a physician to charge a patient more than the OHIP fee schedule without warning the patient in advance. At its annual meeting in June, the Ontario Medical Association delegates voted overwhelmingly against the regulation, and various spokesmen said that "the law is incompatible with our status as private, independent businessmen". A *Toronto Star* editorial countered that "no businessman worth his salt fails to tell a customer how much something costs before the customer buys it". In March the Alberta budget raised premiums by 47 percent, and Health Minister David Russell announced that Alberta would authorize hospitals to collect a $20-a-day user fee beginning October 1, 1983 (so far no hospital has imposed that charge).

An analysis of Alberta Medical Care payment data by Professor Richard Plain showed that although the fee schedule negotiated with the Alberta Medical Association had increased 50 percent in three years, extra-billing had continued to increase, rising to a total of $14.5 million in 1983. Moreover, the data showed that physicians were extra-billing thousands of welfare recipients, low income earners and senior citizens.[16]

In July the provincial Treasurer of British Columbia announced in his budget a new Health Care Maintenance Tax that added 8 percent to the provincial income tax, and an increase in hospital daily user fees from $7.50 to $8.50.

Ontario provincial Treasurer and former Minister of Health, the Honourable Larry Grossman, defended extra-billing in an interview with reporters on December 13 by saying that only "the top three or four percent" of the income scale were charged, despite numerous cases that the NDP and Liberal Opposition members had reported of low income families and pensioners who had been extra-billed.

What is perhaps surprising is that it is not the affluent but the low income citizens who are speaking out against extra-billing, when, in fact, it is the affluent who have a very strong case. A study by the Economic Council of Canada revealed that the bottom 20 percent of income earners receive in dollar terms two and a half times more medical and hospital services than the top 20 percent. But the bottom 20 percent contribute 1 percent of the cost of the two plans while the top 20 percent contribute 48 percent of the cost; indeed, the top 40 percent of income earners contribute 73.7 percent of the cost of the two programs, and the lower 60 percent of income earners contribute 26.3 percent while receiving (in dollar terms) 72.4 percent of services.[17] Thus, when an affluent patient is extra-billed he is, in effect, being taxed *twice* (unlike the non-sick or injured who are taxed only once) to subsidize lower income patients who constitute the bulk of the practice of the average physician. Many of those patients would, in the absence of a government program, be able to pay only part or none of the physicians' fees.

On July 25, 1983, The Honourable Monique Bégin issued the long anticipated Position Paper entitled *Preserving Universal Medicare*.[18] Its main theme is that Medicare is threatened by "growing and spreading" direct charges to patients. In a surprisingly low-key discussion the paper examined, in turn, user charges, extra-billing, federal and provincial health spending, and premium financing in B.C., Alberta and Ontario, where uninsured persons may not be entitled to insured services.[19] It commented on the existing hospital insurance and medical insurance legislation, pointing out the inadequacy of their definition of "reasonable access", and stated that the penalty available to the federal government with respect to a province not meeting the federal conditions — withholding of the total federal cash contribution — was too blunt an instrument. It concluded by saying:

> We cannot preserve Medicare by charging the sick; we cannot preserve Medicare by judging who is poor and who is not; we can only preserve Medicare by ensuring its basic principles.

The reactions were not unexpected: unqualified condemnation by the provinces — "electioneering", "blackmail", "a poor example of federal-provincial cooperation", "will seriously damage the health care system". President Marc Baltzan of the CMA said that:

> the proposals do not begin to address the major problems of Medicare which (are) underfunding and worn out facilities . . . . It is an obvious backdoor intrusion into an area of provincial jurisdiction . . . . Ottawa cannot directly legislate how health care programs are financed and administered, so Madame Bégin plans to use Ottawa's fiscal leverage, some would call it financial blackmail, to force provincial governments to operate provincial health care programs according to the dictates of the federal government.

The national and provincial health coalitions praised the document.

On September 7 Madame Bégin met in Halifax with her provincial counterparts, but to no avail. The stalemate was complete.

On December 13 the Canada Health Act was introduced in the House of Commons and given first reading. The reactions of provincial governments, the medical associations and the health coalitions duplicated those of early summer. But the surprising new development, indicating the extent of popular support, was that the Bill was supported in principle by *both* federal Opposition parties, the NDP *and* the Progressive Conservatives. Following the Christmas recess, Bill C-3 was given second reading on January 16, and the debate continued on January 17 and 20. It was then referred with all-party support to committee, which held extensive public hearings and reported back to the Commons on March 21, 1984. It was passed by the House on April 9, by the Senate on April 17, and was proclaimed law on April 17, its requirements to become effective July 1, 1984.

The purpose of the Canada Health Act was to consolidate the Hospital Insurance and Diagnostic Services Act of 1957 and the Medical Care Act of 1966 and to define more precisely the conditions on which the federal payments would continue to be made. The overall policy was declared thus:

> It is hereby declared that the primary objective of Canadian health policy is to protect, promote and restore the physical and mental well-being of residents of Canada and to facilitate reasonable access to health services without financial or other barriers.

The five conditions were restated as: (1) public administration, (2) comprehensiveness, (3) universality, (4) portability and (5) accessibility.

Since all provinces were meeting the condition of public administration, that condition need not concern us here. The condition of universality was altered by requiring that 100 percent of residents (rather than the 95 percent required under the Medical Care Act) be entitled to insured services on uniform terms and conditions. This provision affects only those provinces requiring payment of premiums as a condition for entitlement to insured services.

The conditions with respect to comprehensiveness and portability were, in the main, restatements of the earlier legislation and existing practice.

The condition of accessibility was expanded by providing, for the first time, the procedures for negotiating payments to providers of insured services. The relevant section of the Act reads as follows:

> 12 (1) In order to satisfy the criterion respecting accessibility, the health care insurance plan of a province:
> (a) must provide for insured services on uniform terms and conditions and on a basis that does not impede or preclude, either directly or indirectly, whether by charges made to insured persons or otherwise, reasonable access to those services by insured persons;
> (b) must provide for payment for insured health services in accordance with a tariff or system of payment authorized by the law of the province;

> (c) must provide for reasonable compensation for *all* insured health services rendered by medical practitioners or dentists; and
>
> (d) must provide for the payment of amounts to hospitals, including hospitals owned or operated by Canada, in respect of the cost of health services.
>
> (2) In respect of any province in which extra-billing is not permitted, paragraph 12(1)(c) shall be deemed to be complied with if the province has chosen to enter into, and has entered into, an agreement with the medical practitioners and dentists of the province that provides:
>
> (a) for negotiations relating to compensation for insured health services between the province and provincial organizations that represent practising medical practitioners or dentists in the province;
>
> (b) for the settlement of disputes relating to compensation through, at the option of the appropriate provincial organizations referred to in paragraph (a), conciliation or binding arbitration by a panel that is equally representative of the organizations and the province and that has an independent chairman; and
>
> (c) that a decision of a panel referred to in paragraph (b) may not be altered except by an Act of the legislature of the province.

The most significant new requirements are two: (1) a province must provide reasonable compensation for *all* insured health services; and (2) the provinces are not required to adopt binding arbitration; but, if they do, the decision of the arbitration panel cannot be altered by the government but can only be reviewed by the Legislature, where, it may be assumed, the award would be intensely debated.

The Act also requires the province to provide the Minister of National Health and Welfare with such information as the Minister "may reasonably require" for the purposes of the Act, and to give recognition to the contributions and payments by Canada in any *public* documents (i.e., budget statements and health care plan annual reports) or in any advertising or promotional literature related to the health care plan.

The Act next provides a detailed procedure for action to be taken by the Minister in the event of a province's failing to meet any of the criteria and the requirements for information and visibility. When a default has been perceived, the federal Minister must first consult the responsible Minister in the province concerned, send by registered letter to the Minister a notice of concern with respect to the problem, seek additional information through bilateral discussions, make a report to the province within ninety days, and, if requested by the province, meet to discuss the report. If the province has not given an undertaking satisfactory to the Minister to remedy the default within a period that the Minister considers reasonable, the Minister shall then refer the matter to the Governor-in-Council. The Governor-in-Council may thereupon direct that any cash contribution for a fiscal year be reduced by an amount considered to be reasonable, or where appropriate, direct that the whole of the cash contribution payable to that province for a fiscal year be withheld.

Sections 18-20 provide for the withholding from the cash payment to a province of an amount equivalent to the total amount of extra-billing permitted, and/or the amount of user charges authorized, by the province.

The Act also provides for such deductions to be accounted for separately in the Public Accounts and, if the practice of extra-billing or user charges is eliminated within three fiscal years, the total amount deducted is to be repaid to the province.

Although the Liberal party's advocacy of the policy of banning extra-billing and user charges had been formally announced in the government's White Paper in July, and the New Democratic Party's criticism of the practice had been known for years, there were many commentators who believed that the Liberals, responding to government-sponsored public opinion polls, had introduced the bill as a potential election issue. It would seriously embarrass the federal Progressive Conservative Party and its new leader Brian Mulroney if they were trapped by the Opposition to the measure expressed by so many provincial governments controlled by Progressive Conservatives. But Mr. Mulroney eluded the trap by ignoring the provincial premiers and health ministers and announcing his party's support for the legislation in December. There is no doubt that his statement muffled the opposition of the medical associations. Quite clearly Medicare had been defused as an issue in the forthcoming national elections.

The responses of the eight provincial governments now facing up to the new requirements are as yet unknown, with the possible exception of Manitoba where Premier Pawley supported the legislation. [*Editor's Note*: Subsequent to this writing, the governments of Manitoba, Nova Scotia and Saskatchewan have taken steps to end the practice, and that of Ontario is pledged to do so.] Dire warnings have been issued by medical spokesmen that first-rate doctors will leave Canada and the quality of medical services will decline. Whether a major exodus will, indeed, occur is difficult to predict with certainty, but three pieces of evidence suggest that a wholesale departure is unlikely.

The first is that British Columbia, where there is no extra-billing, has the highest physician to population ratio in the country and is attempting to introduce measures to limit the number of physicians entitled to bill the Medicare plan.

The second is the experience of Quebec where extra-billing is, in effect, not permitted. Since 1970 when Medicare was introduced, the physician to population ratio has increased from 1:681 to 1:489 (the second highest ratio in Canada) in 1983. It is hard to believe that that number of physicians would have voluntarily accepted the "civil servant" status that spokesmen in other provinces say the new legislation will force upon them, if that perception were true.

The third is that the most likely destination for departing physicians would be the U.S., and most experts have concluded that there is already a surplus of physicians in that country, especially in urban areas where Canadian physicians would undoubtedly prefer to locate.

There is no doubt, however, that the right to set their own fees, that is, to extra-bill, is a key element in most physicians' belief structures. In a recent survey of more than 2,000 physicians in five provinces representing the five regions of Canada,[20] 53 percent of respondents agreed with the statement that "because benefit fee schedules are too low, doctors cannot provide adequate time to patients without extra billing", and 64 percent agreed that extra-billing is "primarily a means by which the profession can maintain its autonomy". On the question of not reimbursing patients of physicians who extra-bill (that is, the Quebec model), 72 percent were opposed, while 78 percent opposed any proposal for withholding federal funds from provinces that permitted the practice. The proportion of doctors believing in the principle of extra-billing is clearly much larger than the proportion engaging in its practice.

Although the President of the Canadian Medical Association condemned the measure as "constitutional rape" and provincial government spokesmen have protested this federal intrusion into a field of exclusive provincial jurisdiction and have threatened to take legal action against the federal government, there is no doubt about the constitutional right of the federal government to attach conditions to its contributions to the provinces. If the conditions are too onerous or politically repugnant, the only provincial recourse, it would appear, is to reject the grants.

There is also no doubt, on the other hand, that provincial governments authorizing hospital user fees and/or permitting extra-billing now face difficult choices. While EPF payments to the provinces in respect of their medical and hospital programs remain at 50.3 percent, the ending of the Revenue Guarantee payments (estimated to be approximately $5.7 billion overall in the 1982 to 1987 period) and declining rates of increase in revenues resulting from slow growth in the economy make the financial decisions extremely difficult, as well as politically unpalatable. If Ontario, for example, continues to permit extra-billing, it will lose $50 million annually in federal contributions. To meet that will require increases in annual premiums (now $354 for an individual and $714 for a family), or an increase in income taxes, or an increase in the deficit. To prohibit extra-billing is to abandon a policy to which it is committed. [*Editor's Note*: This was written in 1984. As of mid-1985, the commitment appears rather to be to prohibition.] It is also to confront an increasingly militant profession. This militancy will be enhanced by the increased pressures from the 15 percent of the profession who are opted out and who could previously live with a negotiated settlement because they could augment their incomes by extra-billing. The government will also face increased difficulties in collecting premiums from individual premium payers who apparently can no longer be denied entitlement to insured services when their premiums have not been paid. And if more funds are diverted to pay higher income to physicians (to buy them out of extra-billing), the problems of financing increasing hospital costs will be increased.

Because of the unanimous support of the Progressive Conservative members of Parliament for the legislation, it appears that the earlier hopes of provincial governments that a victory for Mr. Mulroney would reduce their burdens have been dashed (although one cannot be sure).

When the Saskatchewan government, committed to a policy of payment from the Medical Care Commission as payment in full, was forced in the Saskatoon Agreement in 1962 to compromise and accept that patients could be extra-billed, I wrote: "It [the costs added by extra-billing] appeared to be a price that would have to be paid for a principle about to be abandoned".[21] One could now say that the political and financial choices faced by provincial governments referred to above are a price to be paid for a principle about to be reinstated!

Notes

1. Those desiring a more complete background analysis should consult the papers by LeClair and others in S. Andreopoulos, ed., *National Health Insurance: Can We Learn From Canada?* New York: John Wiley, 1975, or Taylor, M.G., *Health Insurance and Canadian Public Policy*. Montreal: McGill-Queen's University Press, 1978. The latter in particular provides sources for the historical outline in this paper.

2. Statistics Canada, *Perspectives on Health*. Ottawa: Department of Supply and Services, 1983.

3. Health and Welfare Canada, *Canada Health Manpower Inventory 1983*. Ottawa: HWC, 1983.

4. Economic Council of Canada, *Patterns of Growth*. Seventh Annual Review. Ottawa: The Council, 1970.

5. World Bank, *Health*. Washington, D.C.: World Bank, 1975.

6. Economic Council of Canada, *Financing Confederation*. Ottawa: The Council, 1982.

7. Carter, G.E., *Canadian Conditional Grants Since World War II*. Toronto: Canadian Tax Foundation, 1971.

8. Prime Minister Pierre Trudeau, *Statement to the Federal-Provincial Conference*, June 14, 1976.

9. Hall, Emmett J., *Canada's National-Provincial Health Program for the 1980's: "A Commitment for Renewal"*. Report of Health Services Review '79. Saskatoon, Saskatchewan: 1980.

10. Hall, *op. cit.*, footnote 9, p. 27.

11. Parliamentary Task Force on Federal-Provincial Arrangements, *Fiscal Federalism in Canada*. Ottawa: Department of Supply and Services, 1981.

12. Lalonde, Marc, *A New Perspective on the Health of Canadians*. White Paper. Ottawa: Government of Canada, 1974.

13. Hastings, J.E.F., *The Community Health Centre in Canada*, 3 vols. Report of the Community Health Centre Project. Ottawa: Health and Welfare Canada, 1972.

14. Canadian Medical Association, Committee on Economics, *Report*, 1934.

15. For a thorough analysis of extra-billing, the following references should be consulted: Soderstrom, L., "Extra-billing and Cost-sharing", *Canadian Public Policy*, 7, 1981, 103-107; Stoddart, G.L. and C.A. Woodward, "The Effect of Physician Extra-billing on Patient Access to Care", May 1980, mimeo (a study commissioned for Health Services Review '79); Barer, M.L., R.G. Evans and G.L. Stoddart, *Controlling Health Care Costs by Direct Charges to Patients: Snare or Delusion?* Ontario Economic Council, Occasional Paper #10, 1979; Beck R.G. and J.M. Horne, "Medical Fee Determination", *Canadian Public Policy*, 7, 1981, 107-114; Wolfson, A.D. and C.J. Tuohy, *Opting Out of Medicare: Private Medical Markets in Ontario*. Toronto: University of Toronto Press, 1980; P. Manga, *The Political Economy of Extra Billing*. Ottawa: The Canadian Council on Social Development, 1983; Brown, M.G. and V.A. Hicks, "Billing Above Tariff by Physicians in the Absence of Opting-Out Penalties", 1983, mimeo.

16. Plain, R., "Charging the Sick: Observations on the Economic Aspects of Medical-Social Policy Reform". Paper presented at the Canadian Centre for Policy Alternatives Conference, Medicare: The Decisive Year. Montreal: McGill University, November 1982, published in Conference Proceedings.

17. Boulet, J.-A. and D.W. Henderson, *Distributional and Redistributional Aspects of Government Health Insurance Programs in Canada*. Discussion paper #146. Ottawa: Economic Council of Canada, 1979.

18. *Preserving Universal Medicare*. Government of Canada Position Paper. Ottawa: Minister of Supply and Services, 1983.

19. In Alberta, in October 1983, 135,000 registrations, involving approximately 270,000 people, were suspended for non-payment of premiums. Health Minister David Russell reported that unpaid premiums totalled approximately $4.5 million in the first six months of 1983, see *Toronto Star*, October 4, 1983.

20. Taylor, M.G., M.H. Stevenson and P. Williams, *Medical Perspectives on Canadian Medicare*. Toronto: York University Institute for Behavioural Research, 1984.

21. Taylor, *op. cit.*, footnote 20, p. 294.

COMMENTARY

Maureen M. Law

Introduction

Much has happened since the 1974 Sun Valley Conference to transform the health care delivery system in Canada. Legislative initiatives such as the Established Programs Financing (EPF) Arrangements (1977) and the Canada Health Act (1984) have helped to bring about some of these changes. Professor Taylor has touched on these and other events and initiatives over the past ten years.

With the recent passage of the Canada Health Act, the health policy debate in Canada entered a new, more challenging phase. Health insurance and health financing will undoubtedly remain on the national agenda. At the same time, however, there is an increasing awareness of the limitations of the conventional health care delivery system.

This Health Policy Conference comes at a most opportune time. The next phases in the development of our health systems will have to rely more on our intellect than on government largesse. The broad cross-section of participation in this conference provides an excellent opportunity to exchange information and ideas on the direction that health policy in Canada should take.

My comments will focus on three major topics. I will begin by commenting, from a federal perspective, on a few of the key public policy initiatives over the past ten years that Professor Taylor has covered in his paper. I will then shift to the most recent federal policy initiative, the Canada Health Act. Specifically, I want to outline some of the Act's key objectives and to draw attention to some of the more subtle but, I believe, significant changes embodied in it. Finally, I want to share with you our views on some of the challenges and choices that lie ahead. The next step is a critical one. And, as I see it, the federal government has a key role to play — indeed, it has an obligation to participate in determining both the direction and the pace of health care policy development.

Professor Taylor's Retrospective

Professor Taylor has indeed established himself as an authority on the evolution of Canadian health care policy. His book *Health Insurance and Canadian Public Policy: The Seven Decisions that Created the Canadian Health Insurance System* has become required reading for bureaucrats and academics alike. The "bridge paper" that Professor Taylor has prepared for this conference provides an insider's view on some of the key developments since 1974. This view draws on his involvement with the 1964 Royal Commission on Health Services, the original Hall Report, coupled with his more recent connection with the 1979 Health Services Review.

In an effort to provide a basis for discussion, I shall focus my attention on three specific aspects of Professor Taylor's paper. These are: (1) the shift to block-funding (under the Established Programs Financing (EPF) Arrangements), (2) the 1979 Health Services Review, and (3) The parliamentary Task Force Report on the Fiscal Arrangements.

Health Financing: The Shift to Block-Funding

While Professor Taylor identifies many of the pressures for introducing block-funding in 1977 and assesses some of the effects of EPF on the health care delivery system, there are other aspects of EPF that, in retrospect, and certainly from a federal perspective, take on special significance.

Cost-sharing for Hospital Services

Professor Taylor asserts that the cost-sharing arrangements under the Hospital Insurance and Diagnostic Services (HIDS) Act "discriminated against the low cost, low income provinces". While it is true that under the HIDS cost-sharing formula, provinces that spent less on hospital services received less *per capita* than those that spent more, it should be noted that HIDS was not the only fiscal arrangement in place with the provinces. Specifically, the Fiscal Equalization Program was designed to ensure that all provinces would be in a position to provide reasonably comparable levels of public services at comparable levels of taxation. The effectiveness of this program is reflected by the fact that the differences in overall revenue-raising capacity (on a *per capita* basis) between "have" provinces and "have not" provinces are significantly reduced.

Consequently, the fact that certain provinces chose not to allocate their equalized revenues to hospital services in the same proportion as other provinces, and thus not to receive commensurate federal contributions, is, I would argue, more a function of provincial priority-setting than of their ability to fund these services. Hence, to ascribe *per capita* discrepancies in provincial health spending to something inherent in the HIDS cost-sharing formula, as Professor Taylor appears to do, is, I believe, an incomplete representation of the fiscal and political context within which this formula operated.

The Shares Debate

Professor Taylor presents a table expressing federal contributions under EPF as a proportion of total provincial spending on health insurance programs. He also touches on the question of the allocation of EPF transfers among the three established programs: Hospital Insurance, Medical Insurance and Post Secondary Education. I would like to speak to both of these points in the context of the shift to block-funding and its impact on the health system.

First, I will address the question of federal-provincial shares. As Professor Taylor points out, one of the principal objectives of block-funding was to give the provinces more flexibility in the use of health care funds. The pursuit of this objective was, I believe, motivated by a key assumption that the health insurance programs were indeed established or mature programs. Federal cash contributions continued to be contingent on the provinces satisfying the five basic program criteria: accessibility, portability, comprehensiveness, universality, and public administration. But for all intents and purposes, the only real safeguard for these principles was the belief that any move on the part of the provinces to reduce their commitments to Medicare would meet with stiff public resistance. The federal government had the power to withhold *all* cash contributions in the event that any one of the five conditions was not met. However, this "all-or-nothing" instrument to enforce provincial compliance was not, in fact, a realistic option.

Accordingly, I believe that the question of shares is irrelevant with respect to assessing the shift to block-funding. While we know what the federal health contributions are, and therefore what the numerator is, settling on an appropriate denominator poses problems. On the one hand, the provinces argue that it is inappropriate to express federal contributions as a proportion of hospital and medical expenditures alone, since EPF was designed to encourage them to reallocate health resources. On the other hand, it would be inappropriate to use all provincial health expenditures as the denominator since the federal government has no influence over or responsibility for non-insured services.

The second facet of the shares debate, the allocation between health programs and Post Secondary Education (PSE), is also often misinterpreted. The allocation of EPF transfers was approximately as follows: HIDS, 1/2; Medical Care, 1/6; and PSE, 1/3. This allocation reflects national spending in the base year of EPF, and it has always been recognized that individual provinces, depending on their own priorities, had different distributions of spending at the time EPF was introduced. This national allocation was only necessary to enable the federal government to assign payment responsibility between the Department of National Health and Welfare and the Secretary of State, and to provide the Minister of Health and Welfare with designated amounts that could, if necessary, be withheld from a province.

It should be emphasized, therefore, that these percentages were never intended to be benchmarks or targets for the distribution of provincial spending across these three programs.

Hall Review 1979

The events leading up to the Hall Review are well covered by Professor Taylor. He indicates that two issues were dominant: (1) whether extra-billing and user charges were endangering the principles of Medicare, and (2) whether provinces were diverting federal funds from Medicare to other public programs. I will be addressing the issue of extra-billing and user charges in the context of my discussion of the Canada Health Act. I will restrict my remarks here to the diversion of funds and, in particular, to Professor Taylor's suggestion that "the whole issue had arisen because the federal government had included the Revenue Guarantee . . . as a 'contribution' under EPF''.

While the inclusion of the equivalent of two tax points in the EPF formula certainly confused the issue, it is possible that the question of diversion would have arisen even if the Revenue Guarantee had been excluded from the arrangements.

This diversion of funds allegation was largely based, I understand, on the fact that the federal share of health insurance costs increased fairly dramatically in the first few years following the introduction of EPF.

However, this increase was due not only to the inclusion of the Revenue Guarantee as a federal contribution, but also to the fact that provinces were constraining their expenditures while at the same time the GNP, and therefore federal contributions, was still growing strongly. This can be seen from Professor Taylor's table, which excludes the Revenue Guarantee element. It is interesting to note that substantial increases in provincial health spending, coupled with lower GNP growth, resulted in a reversal of the earlier trend after 1979/80.

The Parliamentary Task Force on Fiscal Arrangements

The "shares debate" gradually gave way to a debate over the adequacy of funding of the health care system. This question, *inter alia*, was addressed by the Breau Task Force. On the whole, I believe that the Canadian experience reflects the fact that universal coverage on a publicly-funded, pre-paid basis is not incompatible with containing health costs. However, recent efforts to contain costs have led to charges in some quarters that the system is underfunded. The allegation of "underfunding" presupposes some criterion of adequacy of funding. The typical benchmarks are (1) historical trends in terms of proportion of GNP spent on health, and (2) international comparisons of health spending in either *per capita* or proportion of GNP terms.

With respect to the percentage of GNP spent on health, it is worth noting that the President of the Canadian Medical Association, in his presentation to the

Breau Task Force, argued that the Canadian health care system was seriously underfunded. In May 1982, the CMA recommended that as a "minimum goal" health spending should be increased in an orderly way to reach a level of 8.2 percent of our GNP by 1985. Health spending in 1982, according to official statistics subsequently released, totalled $30.1 billion or 8.4 percent of GNP. While health spending in 1982 had increased by about 14.5 percent over the 1981 level, the increase in the proportion was in large measure due to a sharp decline in GNP. This, in my view, reveals the dubious value of this proportion as an appropriate indicator of the adequacy of funding.

With regard to international comparison, Professor Taylor touches on some of the problems involved, including accounting problems and variations in the mix of services from country-to-country. Caution must, therefore, be exercised to guard against inferring too much from such comparisons. With this in mind, I would like to draw attention to the results of a recent, as yet unpublished, study by the Organization for Economic Co-operation and Development. According to this study, which compares health spending in 1982 as a proportion of GDP (Gross Domestic, as opposed to National, Product), the average of all OECD member countries was 7.6 percent. This compares with 8.4 percent for Canada and 10.6 percent for the U.S.

The parliamentary Task Force, as is pointed out by Professor Taylor, concluded that the level of federal funding, in aggregate, appears adequate, although there may be specific areas that require expansion. I would also add that, in several presentations to the Commons Committee studying the Canada Health Act, it was also suggested that the health system is adequately funded. The President of the Canadian Hospital Association, for example, when asked whether the system was underfunded, responded that "based on information supplied by hospital and health associations across the country, the broad statement that hospitals are underfunded cannot be supported". He went on to say, however, that "there are some indications of a trend to capital underfunding mainly affecting the large, urban teaching institutions".

Before we sink more taxpayers' dollars into the replacement of existing capital, I believe that we have an obligation to consider whether or not more health care provided in an institutional or clinical setting would result in significant improvement in the health of Canadians.

Canada Health Act

Much was said and written about the Canada Health Act, before and after it received Royal Assent. During the committee stage it was alleged that it was merely "housekeeping" legislation, an affront to cooperative federalism, devoid of provisions to address "real issues" and backward looking rather than forward looking. I would like to deal with the question of what the Act does and does not do.

Basic Objectives: Preserve and Protect

The basic objectives of the Canada Health Act were outlined in the paper "Preserving Medicare" (July 25, 1983). These objectives include not only a consolidation of federal legislation of the last twenty-five years, but also a restoration of some federal influence over the direction of national health policy, including the safeguarding of the principles of Medicare.

The Act appears to be doing the job. A number of provinces have moved already to comply with it: Newfoundland has eliminated its user charges, Alberta has delinked premiums and entitlement to benefits (Bill 45), and Nova Scotia has banned extra-billing.

The Canada Health Act does not, however, guarantee that direct charges will be done away with. Many Canadians are probably quite surprised and perhaps irritated by the fact that some provinces have not subscribed to the federal view. This is, of course, a provincial prerogative and this discontent will be levelled at provincial governments.

Other Objectives: Clarify and Advance Federal Health Policy

Some of the less obvious changes embodied in the Canada Health Act have escaped detailed assessment except by those who have scrutinized it most intensely. The Act clarifies, as well as entrenches, these basic Medicare conditions:

1. *Portability.* I believe that, in general, the importance of moving to host-province rates (in Canada) and establishing national standards for out-of-country benefits is not yet fully appreciated.

2. *Comprehensiveness.* The Act defines insured hospital services in terms of level of care (acute, chronic, rehabilitative) rather than on the basis of a list of approved facilities. This, I believe, is an important conceptual change.

3. *Accessibility.* The entrenchment of medical necessity as the overriding determinant of reasonable accessibility is an important clarification.

4. *Public Administration.* Clearer guidelines regarding what provinces can and cannot contract out is also an important and often overlooked change.

Over and above these clarifications, the Act contains other provisions that, in a more subtle way, will guide and facilitate further health policy in Canada.

1. *A consultation process*, which should minimize the extent to which Medicare issues have to be resolved in the public, political arena.

2. *Consent provisions*, which will ensure that the provinces have the opportunity to participate in the development of federal regulations.

3. *An annual report*, which should encourage regular reassessment of where we are going. This discipline should help to avert haphazard, unintentional

developments, as well as to provide a means for detecting problems at an early stage, before they get out-of-hand.

Raised Expectations

The Canada Health Act raises certain expectations about where the health system is headed in terms of, for example, the valuable contribution of all health care practitioners to the system. However, certain false expectations may also have been created, to the degree that the Act did not, and could not, address issues unrelated to insurance. The Act does not deal, for example, with the overall funding issue. This issue will no doubt be reviewed in the process leading up to the renewal of the Fiscal Arrangements by April 1, 1987.

The Act, in short, addresses many of these preserving and clarifying objectives. While it does not directly address the difficult structural problems that we face, it has created a broader, firmer foundation upon which to build a better health system. It is to this range of broader, longer term issues that I would now like to turn.

Looking Ahead

The process leading to the Canada Health Act underlines what can happen when a coalition of health interests and public opinion gets behind an issue. Health care groups from across the country united forces to create pressures for change. Now, while the momentum of the Act is still alive, is the time for these same individuals and groups to press for further improvement and possibly a fundamental restructuring of the health system.

The debate surrounding the Hall Review, the parliamentary Task Force, and finally the Canada Health Act was marked by a call for structural reform and by a sincere desire to exchange and explore new ideas. This forum provides another, perhaps more appropriate, opportunity to debate these kinds of reforms.

There will be other opportunities. Indeed, the federal Minister of Health and Welfare has made a commitment to hold a National Health Policy conference to promote a full debate on these issues.

Challenges

I believe we now face at least five major challenges: the pressures of health care technology, a changing population profile, concerns about quality of life, the growing disparities in health status, and, of course, health financing. I will briefly address each of these in turn.

Health Care Technology

Technological advances will not only create difficulties in terms of health financing, but will also raise:

1. *Ethical dilemmas.* Not everyone can expect to have equal access to ever more expensive, elaborate, and exotic medical equipment or procedures.
2. *Role uncertainties.* The roles of all players in the health care system, from orderlies to medical practitioners, may have to change.
3. *False expectations.* As Canadians see these rapid advances taking place, they may develop false hope about what the health system can do for them. The concept of "spare parts" medicine already seems to be taking hold.

On the positive side, this technological revolution may create new market opportunities for Canadian industries. We must be in a position to encourage Canadian businessmen to take advantage of these opportunities.

Changing Demographic Profile

In general, the financial impact of the growing proportion and growing numbers of Canadians aged sixty-five and over is often overstated and misunderstood. Still, the capacity of the health care system to provide the appropriate mix and level of support services is increasingly being tested. This challenge will become more pressing, not only as service limitations are reached but also as the political voice of this cohort of Canadians increases and becomes more focused.

Quality of Life

Improved access to conventional health care services has not had the impact on the overall health of Canadians that many providers and consumers may have hoped. Flat-of-the-curve medicine (i.e., beyond the point at which there is no discernible improvement in health from increased consumption of health care) is a concern. While the evidence is more suggestive than conclusive, we would be remiss as a society just to stand back and do nothing.

Health Status Disparities

Universal access to medically required health care services is a reality in Canada. It stands out as one of the most important social accomplishments of Canadian society in the post-war period. Unfortunately, although perhaps not unexpectedly, eliminating inequalities of access to health care has not substantially affected inequalities in health status.

Financing

There seems to be little evidence to suggest that the system is currently underfunded in any global sense. The question of redistributing existing resources will, however, have to be addressed. The 1977 block-funding arrangements are conducive to resource reassignments. There are, however, impediments to reallocating health resources, including the income aspirations of established providers, continuing increases in provider supply relative to the population, consumer expectations, legal encumbrances and political realities. We must find ways to sidestep these impediments in a fair and effective way.

The Choices

Restructuring the health system in Canada will take time. It takes time to alter long-standing preconceptions, overcome system inertia, identify practical and effective alternatives, and garner sufficient public and political support.

We also know from experience that all the players must participate in identifying and making these choices. An ongoing debate among all interest groups must be fostered. Moreover, governments, I believe, have a critical role to play in this regard.

Canadians who banded together to participate in the Canada Health Act debate must not be discouraged. They must maintain their resolve and participate in this important dialogue. Canada, as a society comprised of progressive-minded citizens, will encounter some difficult moral and ethical problems. It would be unfair to expect health providers to bear all the burden of responsibility for making ethical decisions such as who will or will not benefit from medical advances. Protocols or guidelines must be developed at the national level. High-technology services must be rationalized, perhaps also at the national level (e.g., national referral centres may have to be identified.)

More than ever before, the challenges we face will cut across traditional health and welfare sectors and governmental boundaries. Because the challenges are multi-faceted, the choices will be wide-ranging. Accordingly, the need for multi-sectoral participation and planning is more acute now than ever. There has been a lot of rhetoric in the past about the need for integrated planning. This rhetoric must now gradually give way to breathing life into the concept by reforming the ways in which governments interact with one another and with the providers of health and social services.

The Public Sector's Role

The role for governments in the restructuring of the health system will have to be defined carefully. We have learned from past experiences that top-down policy changes have been of short-term value only. Future policy changes, if they are to be effective and to have long-term value, will require consensus building; that is, they will have to reflect bottom-up concerns and thinking.

Given the constitutional division of powers in Canada, responsibility for structural reform will largely rest with the provinces. More and more provinces have grown to appreciate that, wherever possible, they should encourage and facilitate change rather than impose it. Governments have never been able to impose their wills on either unconvinced consumers or unconverted providers. We must all be willing partners in developing a new vision of health care in Canada — one that goes well beyond the defence of Medicare.

II

HEALTH COSTS AND EXPENDITURES

RIDING NORTH ON A SOUTH-BOUND HORSE? EXPENDITURES, PRICES, UTILIZATION AND INCOMES IN THE CANADIAN HEALTH CARE SYSTEM

Morris L. Barer
Robert G. Evans

Introduction

Health expenditures capture a very large share of attention in discussions of health policy, perhaps more than they deserve. Catch-phrases such as "cost explosions", "cost-capping" and "underfunding" suggest that health policy is primarily about levels of expenditure. The same impression is created by intense negotiations and highly publicized political struggles between providers and provincial governments over fees and budgets. And the new Canada Health Act, while opening with a firm statement of national objectives for health care, is in fact entirely about patterns of expenditure.

Canadians share with the rest of the developed world this morbid fascination with money. In the United States, the words "health care" demand the word "costs" to complete the phrase. And in most European countries similar concerns are expressed, that an ever-larger share of national resources is being eaten up by health care. But the Canadian view of costs *is* somewhat different in being rather schizophrenic. In this country, "underfunding" is an important part of the rhetoric, along with intense concerns to hold costs down. In the U.S., Germany or Sweden, by contrast, "underfunding" (in a global sense) does not seem to enter the discussion as an issue or problem.

The schizophrenia arises, of course, from Canada's exceptional success, relative to most other countries, in limiting the growth of health expenditures over the past fifteen years. But the result has not been to remove expenditures from the arena of debate, or to lower their priority; quite the contrary. As perceptions of "cost explosion" become less acute, those of "underfunding" grow. If costs are not "too high", then they must be "too low"; in any case, they remain a central issue. The U.K., which like Canada has been relatively successful in limiting health care expenditures, is, we believe, the only other country in which the concerns of "too much" and "too little" manage to occupy the public stage simultaneously.

Yet the centrality of expenditures in health care policy may be deceiving, and can lead to misplaced attention and failure to address real issues. Expenditures and "costs" are not ends in themselves, but means to further ends. No particular level of expenditure or share of Gross National Product (GNP) devoted to health care is "right" in some absolute sense. The slogans that focus on costs — "cost explosions" or "underfunding", for example — are rhetorical summaries of more elaborate underlying intellectual frameworks: sets of beliefs, values, assumptions and objectives. These patterns of thought, partly shared and partly conflicting, extend across the health care system and beyond it to the wider economy and society. They underlie the conflicting views of participants in policy debates as to "what is to be done?" in the broadest sense.

Expenditure patterns, actual or desired, give concrete form to these patterns of thought and serve as the vehicle for translating them into action, in the same way that the budget for a single institution or a government (or even a household) summarizes and focuses its objectives and beliefs. But the comprehension, and perhaps to some degree the resolution, of conflicts over expenditure patterns requires us to move through them or beyond them to examine the activities and the objectives they represent. The debate may begin with expenditures, but it cannot end there, because expenditure information by itself is insufficient to answer the more fundamental questions involved.

Nevertheless, expenditure data *do* provide an essential starting point. They enable us to describe and clarify what has been happening in the Canadian health care system, in a broad aggregate sense, and so to save a good deal of time and effort that might otherwise be wasted debating misapprehensions. Descriptive data should serve to broaden the common ground of accepted fact, and to focus attention on the genuinely problematic issues.

Secondly, expenditure data can provide, in some cases, strong *prima facie* support for particular causal hypotheses. Analysis of non-experimental data, however sophisticated, can never "prove" causality. It can only isolate more or less subtle patterns of correlation, which is unfortunate, since all purposive action depends on hypotheses of causality. But aggregate data will sometimes display patterns so clear-cut that they are very strongly suggestive of causality, and may reasonably be interpreted as placing a heavy burden of argument, if not proof, on those who would deny.

Finally, patterns in the aggregate data may raise questions, presenting deviations or anomalies that invite explanation. The observation of peculiar behaviour, and attempts to explain it, can thus focus analysis in ways that may improve our understanding of how the health care system functions.

Outline of the Paper

The first section of this paper displays and discusses patterns of health expenditure in Canada as a whole, over the post-war period of about thirty-five years. Particular attention is given to the behaviour of different components of health expenditures, and to the contrasting experience of the U.S. over the same period. The significance of the Canadian form of reimbursement for hospital and medical services is indicated by the very different behaviour of these expenditure components in the two countries after 1971. The view often expressed in the U.S., that steady expansion in the share of national income devoted to health care is somehow natural or normal, or in any case inevitable, is clearly refuted.

The national data, however, can easily mislead one into inferring uniformity across provinces. Analysis of the data for individual provinces shows a substantial degree of variation in expenditure patterns both across provinces and over time. Provinces also differ in their emphasis on the various components of health expenditures. Such variations in historical experience underscore the extent of discretion in health policy — there is no "Iron Law" of health expenditures in either level or pattern.

From expenditures we turn to estimates of actual service volumes, focusing in the second section on the physician sector. Indices of physicians' fees by province and over time are developed from Health and Welfare and Statistics Canada sources, and divided into expenditure data, to derive estimates of actual *per capita* utilization of medical services, comparable across provinces. These are also combined with data on physician manpower, to yield estimates of relative output per physician that are related to productivity measures. The inadequacy of fee data prior to Medicare, and particularly during the years of introduction of Medicare, is apparent. Nevertheless, some important trends and variations in both *per capita* utilization and physician billing patterns show up in the cross-provincial data. In particular, there seems to be quite a marked slowing in rates of increase in billings per physician (adjusted for fee change) in recent years, together with a significant acceleration in fee increases.

We finish this section with a return to the national focus, and a comparison with U.S. data over the past decade, which brings out the remarkable parallelism of trends in the two countries in both physician stock and medical services use *per capita*, and in output per physician. The really sharp discrepancy is in fee growth relative to the general inflation rate in each country. In Canada, physicians' fees fell well behind inflation during the 1970s; in the U.S. they ran well ahead; and the discrepancy in real terms of 3.3 percent per year over ten years accounts for most of the difference in cost experience. Cost control in the medical care sector in Canada, relative to the U.S., has been achieved largely through fee and income control.

The third section continues our focus on service volumes, now within the hospital sector. After a brief look at trends in hospital capacity and utilization (patient days and separations), we develop hospital wage and then hospital input price indices for each province. While there has been little inter-provincial divergence in hospital wage trends since 1962, the hospital sector as a whole has fared well. Hospital workers have gained about 1.7 percent per year over the twenty years from 1962 to 1982, relative to a composite wage index for the general economy. But provinces have shown different patterns, with Newfoundland hospital workers gaining about 2.5 percent per year relative to general provincial wage levels, while B.C. hospital workers were forced to accept relative gains of only 1.3 percent per year.

The wage indices for each province form the largest component of the hospital input price indices developed by combining unpublished expenditure share data obtained from Statistics Canada with price indices for three categories of inputs: labour, pharmaceuticals, and all other resources (medical and surgical supplies plus other supplies and expenses). The resulting input price index for 1962 to 1982 for Canada as a whole is extended back to 1946 by bridging with a hospital rate series from the pre-universal insurance period. This linked hospital price index grew about 3 percent per year faster than the Gross National Expenditure (GNE) deflator over the whole thirty-six-year period, 1946 through 1982!

In keeping with our interest in service volumes and "productivity", the hospital input price indices are used to deflate cost per patient day data, effecting a disaggregation into real cost per day, and servicing intensity per day. Cost per patient day rose an average 11 percent per year over the thirty-six years from 1946 to (fiscal) 1982/83. This 11 percent may be partitioned into 5.4 percent per year general inflation, hospital sector-specific real input price growth of 3 percent per year, and growth in daily servicing intensity of 2.3 percent per year. Growth in servicing intensity appears to have slowed since about the mid-1970s, although this is far from uniform across provinces. At least part of the 2.3 percent servicing intensity growth appears to reflect declining sector productivity.

As with the physician services section, we close the third section with a brief comparison of Canadian and U.S. trends. Since 1971, U.S. real (adjusted for inflation) hospital costs *per capita* have risen nearly three times as fast as those in Canada. This marked difference in real cost experience can be attributed primarily to much higher U.S. growth in servicing intensity. Whereas the physician sector divergence was a price/income phenomenon, the story in the hospital sector is one of differences in resource use per patient day.

Finally, the fourth section provides a summary and discussion of the possible implications of the historical record for policy and performance during the rest of the 1980s and beyond.

Health Care Expenditures in Canada, by Component and Province

Tables 1-3 present Canadian National Health Expenditures and major components, in total, *per capita* and percentage of GNP form. The accompanying Figure 1 shows health expenditures as a percent of GNP for Canada and for the U.S. from 1950 to 1982. These data reflect the scale of the health care sector, as a major national industry, and indicate the dominant position in it of hospital and physician expenditures — the expenditures covered by universal public health insurance. Dentistry is financed through a mix of private pay and private insurance with some public subsidy and public delivery programs for special groups, much like pre-Medicare or U.S. physicians' services insurance. Several provinces have programs reimbursing some part of pharmaceutical costs, but they differ significantly from each other. Federal government policy has attempted to promote an environment in which competition would keep down drug prices, and has not assisted their reimbursement.

The Distribution of Expenditure Shares by Component

A number of patterns emerge from these data. First, it is important to note that while "doctors and hospitals" account for a dominant share of health spending, they are still only 56.1 percent of the total. Of every dollar of health expenditures, 44 cents goes to goods or services *not* covered by Medicare. The form of public health insurance that we think of as characteristic of "the Canadian system" covers only a bit more than half of total health expenditures.

The 56.1 percent going to "doctors and hospitals" in 1982 was essentially identical with the 1961 share, 56.2 percent, although in 1971 it had reached 61.9 percent. The pre-1960 data indicate a sharp increase in the hospital share in the immediate post-war years, followed by stability from 1951 to 1961.

But within this component the long-term trend, from 1946 on, is clearly one of a steadily increasing share for hospital expenditure, and of a decreasing share for physicians. From 1946 to 1976 (linking series in 1961) hospitals' share of health spending rose 38.6 percent. There were major jumps in the late 1940s and in the late 1950s and early 1960s, as first private insurance and then the public plans brought in more money. But these jumps are superimposed on a long-term uptrend that breaks only in the second half of the 1970s, when hospitals' share of the total begins to shrink for the first time in (at least) thirty years. And the decline is quite sharp, 10.8 percent in six years, or almost twice as fast as the previous uptrend.

The share of physicians, in contrast, shows a long-term downtrend. Their share fell 18.2 percent from 1946 to 1966, recovered rapidly from 1966 to 1971 with the gains from Medicare, then fell back even more rapidly in the early 1970s. From 1976 on, however, physicians have managed to maintain an almost stable share, dropping slightly at the beginning of the 1980s then rising somewhat into 1982 on sharply increased total expenditures.

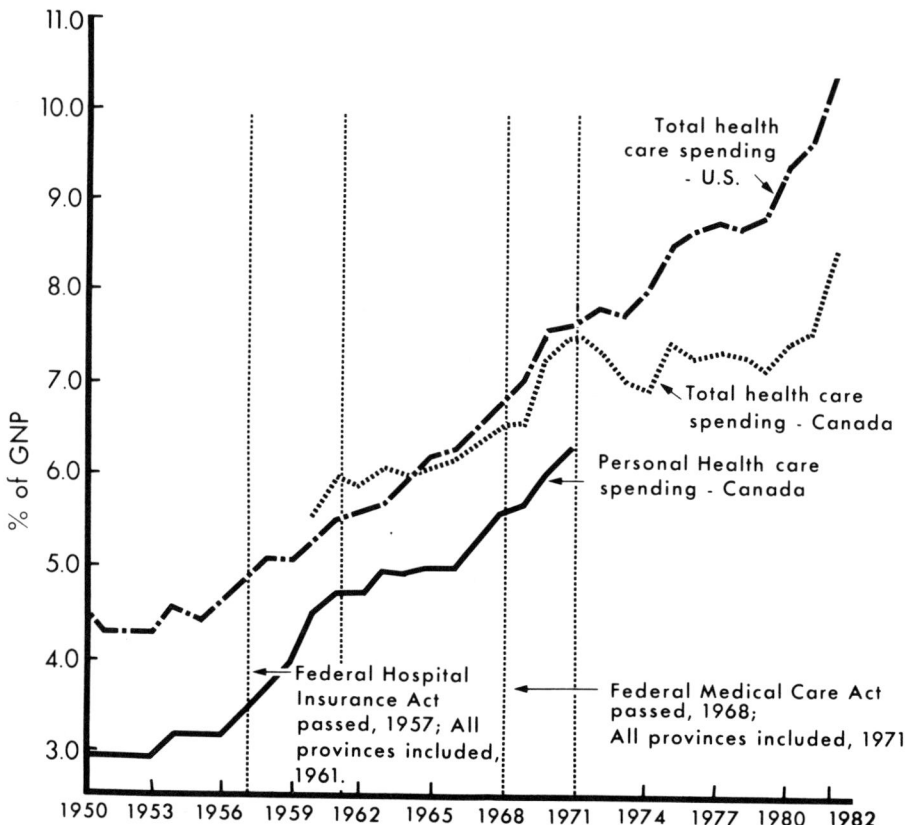

Figure 1

Health Care Expenditures as a Percentage of Gross National Product, Canada and U.S., 1950-1982

TABLE 1
EXPENDITURES ON HEALTH CARE IN CANADA (in $ millions), BY MAJOR COMPONENTS, 1946-1982
(Bracketed Figures are Percentages of Total)

YEAR	Hospitals	Physicians' Services	Dentists' Services	Prescription Drugs	Subtotal	National Health Expenditures
1946	150.7 (50.1)	86.7 (28.9)	36.3 (12.1)	26.8 (8.9)	300.5 (100.0)	n.a.
1951	326.4 (56.9)	153.0 (26.7)	51.0 (8.9)	42.9 (7.5)	573.3 (100.0)	n.a.
1956	541.5 (57.9)	240.1 (25.7)	81.5 (8.7)	71.8 (7.7)	934.9 (100.0)	n.a.
1961*	949.0 (59.7)	388.3 (24.4)	116.7 (7.3)	135.8 (8.5)	1,589.9 (100.0)	2,375.5 — (66.9)
1966	1,668.8 (43.5)	605.2 (15.8)	176.4 (4.6)	232.0 (6.0)	2,682.3 (69.9)	3,837.5 (100.0)
1971	3,152.8 (44.3)	1,250.4 (17.6)	311.5 (4.4)	402.5 (5.7)	5,117.2 (71.8)	7,122.3 (100.0)
1976	6,571.5 (46.4)	2,103.2 (14.9)	699.8 (4.9)	667.1 (4.7)	10,041.6 (70.9)	14,158.7 (100.0)
1977	6,928.3 (44.6)	2,309.0 (14.9)	827.6 (5.3)	746.0 (4.8)	10,810.9 (69.6)	15,532.6 (100.0)
1978	7,483.5 (43.8)	2,544.0 (14.9)	954.1 (5.6)	822.2 (4.8)	11,803.8 (69.1)	17,094.1 (100.0)
1979	8,239.5 (43.2)	2,843.5 (14.9)	1,106.0 (5.8)	918.2 (4.8)	13,107.2 (68.7)	19,067.2 (100.0)
1980	9,484.7 (42.8)	3,284.7 (14.8)	1,288.0 (5.8)	1,011.2 (4.6)	15,068.5 (67.9)	22,178.6 (100.0)
1981	10,724.4 (41.6)	3,741.0 (14.5)	1,482.9 (5.8)	1,205.0 (4.7)	17,153.3 (66.6)	25,769.3 (100.0)
1982	12,470.0 (41.4)	4,414.3 (14.7)	1,682.6 (5.6)	1,473.4 (4.9)	20,040.0 (66.6)	30,087.7 (100.0)

Average Annual Growth Rates (%)

	Hospitals	Physicians' Services	Dentists' Services	Prescription Drugs	Subtotal	National Health Expenditures
1951-61	11.3	9.8	8.6	12.2	10.7	n.a.
1961-71	12.8	12.4	10.3	11.5	12.4	11.6
1971-76	15.8	11.0	17.6	10.6	14.4	14.7
1976-81	10.3	12.2	16.2	12.6	11.3	12.7
1981-82	16.3	18.0	13.5	22.3	16.8	16.8
1946-82	13.1	11.5	11.2	11.8	12.4	n.a.
1961-82	13.0	12.3	15.1	12.2	12.4	13.7
1971-82	13.3	12.2	16.6	12.5	13.2	14.0

*Note: "National Health Expenditures" includes, in addition to the listed components, expenditures on homes for special care; services of other self-employed health professionals; non-prescription drugs, eyeglasses and other appliances; and public health, health research, expenses of prepayment, capital expenditures and miscellaneous. These additional components are not calculated prior to 1960. The 1961 components are shown as a percent both of the subtotal of the four major components, and of total National Health Expenditures.

This experience finds an interesting contrast in the U.S., where physicians' share of total health expenditures was 19.1 percent in 1970, 19.2 percent in 1982, and virtually unchanged in between (Gibson et al., 1983). In 1950 they were slightly higher, at 21.7 percent. American physicians thus began the period with a larger share of health spending, and have held on to most of it, while Canadian physicians started with a smaller share and saw it shrink more, at least down to 1976, with the Medicare gains being given up in subsequent years.

U.S. hospitals, however, increased their share of health spending by 38.2 percent from 1950 to 1982, an increase very similar to that in Canada. The major difference is that they did not reach a peak and fall back. Instead they continued to climb slowly in the late 1970s and early 1980s.

Of course, what one subsector gains in share, another loses. The drop in hospital share after 1976 was matched by a major surge in the components not itemized in Tables 1-3. These sectors increased from 28.2 percent in 1971 to 33.4 percent in 1981, most of the growth coming after 1976 and almost all of it in "homes for special care". There was apparently a significant redirection of resources away from hospitals and toward other forms of institutional care in the late 1970s, which preliminary 1982 data suggest may now have ceased.

The other itemized components, dentistry and prescription drugs, also show clear historical patterns. Their contrasting experience shows that neither is determined simply as a residual from the behaviour of "doctors and hospitals". Both sectors show a sharp drop in share in the immediate post-year years, which probably *is* simply a mirror of the rapid hospital expansion, particularly since these data exclude many of the other National Health Expenditure components. From 1961 to 1971, however, prescription drugs' share of health spending is relatively stable. The gain in the 1950s may be a result of the antibiotic boom. In the early 1970s this share drops sharply, then stabilizes in the late 1970s, and shows (in the preliminary data) a remarkable surge of growth in 1982. Dentistry, by contrast, loses ground (relatively) from 1951 to 1971, then begins a climb through the 1970s. The early 1980s suggest that this relative gain may have peaked, though it should be noted that spending on all the main competitors, hospitals, physicians and prescription drugs, increased significantly in 1982.

Health Care Expenditures as a Proportion of National Economic Activity

This brings us back to the fact that, as noted above, shares must add to unity. They tell us about the relative balance within the health care sector, but not about its growth or decline relative to the rest of the economy. For this information, we turn to Tables 2 and 3.

Table 3 shows the position of the components of health expenditure in the overall economy. It gives the ratio of health care spending to total national income, measured here by GNP, which implicitly adjusts health spending for

TABLE 2
EXPENDITURES ON HEALTH CARE IN CANADA, PER CAPITA ($) BY MAJOR COMPONENTS, 1946-1982

YEAR	Hospitals	Physicians' Services	Dentists' Services	Prescription Drugs	Subtotal	National Health Expenditures
1946	12.26	7.05	2.95	2.18	24.45	n.a.
1951	23.30	10.92	3.64	3.06	40.92	n.a.
1956	33.67	14.93	5.07	4.46	58.14	n.a.
1961	51.94	21.25	6.39	7.44	87.02	130.02
1966	83.24	30.19	8.80	11.57	133.79	191.42
1971	146.02	57.91	14.43	18.64	237.00	329.86
1976	285.49	91.37	30.40	28.98	436.24	615.12
1977	297.42	99.12	35.53	32.02	464.09	666.78
1978	317.98	108.10	40.54	34.94	501.56	726.34
1979	346.66	119.63	46.53	38.63	551.45	802.21
1980	394.05	136.46	53.51	42.01	489.98	921.42
1981	440.13	153.53	60.86	49.46	703.98	1,057.58
1982	505.71	179.02	68.24	59.75	812.72	1,220.18

Average Annual Growth Rates (%)

1951-61	8.4	6.9	5.8	9.3	7.9	n.a.
1961-71	10.9	10.5	8.5	9.6	10.5	9.8
1971-76	14.8	9.5	16.1	9.2	13.0	13.3
1976-81	9.0	10.9	14.9	11.3	10.0	11.4
1981-82	14.9	16.6	12.1	20.8	15.5	15.4
1946-82	10.9	9.4	9.1	9.6	10.2	n.a.
1961-82	11.9	11.8	13.7	10.8	11.9	12.3
1971-82	12.0	10.8	15.2	11.2	11.9	12.6

TABLE 3
EXPENDITURES ON HEALTH CARE IN CANADA AS PERCENTAGE OF GROSS NATIONAL PRODUCT BY MAJOR COMPONENTS, 1946-1982

YEAR	Hospitals	Physicians' Services	Dentists' Services	Prescription Drugs	Subtotal	National Health Expenditures
1946	1.27	0.73	0.31	0.23	2.53	n.a.
1951	1.51	0.71	0.24	0.20	2.65	n.a.
1956	1.69	0.75	0.25	0.22	2.92	n.a.
1961	2.39	0.98	0.29	0.34	4.01	5.99
1966	2.70	0.98	0.29	0.38	4.34	6.21
1971	3.33	1.32	0.33	0.43	5.41	7.49
1976	3.42	1.10	0.37	0.35	5.24	7.38
1977	3.30	1.11	0.40	0.35	5.15	7.39
1978	3.23	1.10	0.42	0.35	5.10	7.36
1979	3.12	1.08	0.42	0.35	4.96	7.21
1980	3.20	1.11	0.43	0.34	5.08	7.48
1981	3.16	1.10	0.44	0.36	5.06	7.60
1982	3.50	1.24	0.47	0.41	5.62	8.44

Average Annual Growth Rates (%)

1951-61	4.70	3.28	1.91	5.45	4.23	n.a.
1961-71	3.37	3.02	1.30	2.38	3.04	2.26
1971-76	0.53	-3.58	2.31	-4.03	-0.64	-0.30
1976-81	-1.57	0.00	3.53	0.57	-0.70	0.59
1981-82	10.76	12.73	6.82	13.89	11.07	11.05
1946-82	2.86	1.48	1.16	1.62	2.24	n.a.
1961-82	1.64	1.48	3.06	0.48	1.63	1.94
1971-82	0.45	-0.57	3.27	-0.43	0.35	1.09

inflation and population growth. Here the relatively well known, but still important story is the stabilization of that ratio from 1971 to 1981, a pattern that is unique in the developed world and, as shown in Figure 1, is in particularly sharp contrast to the U.S. experience.

It is also in sharp contrast to previous Canadian experience. And the coincidence of the timing — topping out of the ratio after completion of the public insurance plans — lends support to two important (and distinct) hypotheses. First, the specific form of funding system adopted by the Canadian provinces was essential to cost control. (Its features — universal comprehensive coverage in conjunction with sole-source funding by a level of government with major non-health responsibilities — can be contrasted with those of other countries, such as Germany or Sweden, where almost complete public coverage co-exists with cost escalation.) And second, in the absence of these plans, the parallel behaviour of health expenditures in Canada and in the U.S. would presumably have persisted. That behaviour suggests that, in the absence of external control, there is no *internal* self-limiting mechanism that constrains the share of national income going to health. It simply grows until an external constraint is reached.

The "stability" pattern, however, is broken in 1982. Is the Canadian funding system coming unstuck? The easy answer is no; 1982 is simply an aberration resulting from a large drop in GNP in that year. In particular, as Figure 1 shows, the 1982 jump is exactly paralleled in the U.S. So it cannot be attributed to a breakdown of control specific to Canada.

But this optimistic explanation is undermined somewhat by Tables 1 and 2, which show unusually high rates of increase in expenditures for both hospitals and physicians' services in 1982. General inflation (the Consumer Price Index) rose only 10.8 percent in 1982, so that hospital spending (*per capita*) was up 3.7 percent in real terms, total health spending up 4.2 percent, physicians 5.2 percent, and prescription drugs 9.0 percent. There appears to have been something of a health spending "breakout" in 1982, even as GNP was falling.

Looked at another way, prior to 1982 the Canadian GNP grew more rapidly than the inflation rate, by somewhat more that 2 percent per year. If one takes the average amount by which GNP growth exceeded inflation over the 1976 to 1981 period, and adds this to the actual inflation rate from 1981 to 1982, one can derive a hypothetical value for what the 1982 GNP might have been, had there not been a recession. Dividing this value into 1982 health expenditures yields a "recession-adjusted" value for the ratio of health expenditures to GNP for 1982. The result turns out to be virtually invariant as to whether one uses the Consumer Price Index or the GNE deflator as the measure of inflation, 7.8 percent in the former case and 7.86 percent in the latter.

While this adjustment clearly indicates the importance of the recession in driving up the ratio in 1982, it also shows that in the absence of recession the ratio would still have been higher than in any previous year. Indeed, from its

1979 value of 7.2 percent, the ratio has risen steadily for three years at about 0.2 percent per year, suggesting the possibility of a renewed uptrend. For the sake of comparison, a similar adjustment to the 1982 value of the U.S. ratio yields 10.12 percent with the CPI as an inflation measure, 9.98 percent with the GNE deflator. In the U.S. the ratio increases by 8 percent from 1981 to 1982, and between 54 percent and 72 percent of the increase appears to be the result of the recession (depending on which inflation measure one uses). In Canada, the increase in the ratio from 1981 to 1982 is 11 percent, and the recession accounts for about 70 percent on either measure.

One must not attach too much precision to these numbers, as the "recession-adjusted" GNP for 1982 could be computed on a number of different assumptions. But the general picture of the recession accounting for between two-thirds and three-quarters of the 1982 increase in Canada, and a somewhat more uncertain half to three-quarters in the U.S., would hold up on any estimate.

The 1982 "breakout", if that is what it is, shows up in each of the major components of health expenditure. Hospitals and dentists' services reached new highs in their share of national income, while prescription drugs and physicians' services shares moved most of the way back to their 1971 peaks. Apart from this single year, however, the components of health spending show rather different long-term patterns.

Hospitals took a steadily increasing share of national income from 1946 to 1976, with particularly rapid gains in the late 1950s and late 1960s. Their share continued to rise in the early 1970s even after the share of total health spending in GNP had peaked and begun to fall. In the latter half of the 1970s, hospitals' share declined somewhat, and from 1979 to 1981 it was virtually stable.

Physicians, on the other hand, seem to alternate between periods of stability (1946 to 1956, 1961 to 1966, 1976 to 1981) and rapid changes. Their share of national income went up in the late 1950s and late 1960s, and down in the early 1970s. It is interesting to note that when each form of public insurance was introduced — hospitals in the late 1950s and medical services in the late 1960s — both medical and hospital care increased their share of GNP. But, in each case, the form of care covered by the new public plan showed the larger increase. Dentists' services, outside the public programs, have increased their share of GNP at a steady, and indeed accelerating rate, without either the rapid rises or the flat spots or declines of the larger sectors. This steady growth is yet another indicator of what the experience of physicians' services expenditures might have been in the absence of public insurance plans: no dramatic surges, but no corrections either, just steady expansion.

Prescription drug expenditures, in contrast, show a decline in share of national income even more marked than that of physicians in the first half of the 1970s, followed by stability in the second. Except for the very peculiar spurt in the 1982 data, their growth period was the 1950s, and to a lesser extent, the 1960s.

The Growing Discrepancy between Canadian and U.S. Health Expenditures

The percent-of-GNP by component data in Table 3 afford an interesting comparison with U.S. experience in the post-1971 period (Gibson *et al.*, 1983). In 1971, Canada and the U.S. spent, respectively, 7.49 percent and 7.7 percent of GNP on health care; in 1981 they spent 7.60 percent and 9.8 percent. The discrepancy increased by 1.99 percentage points in this decade. (We disregard 1982 because of the perturbing effect of economic recession in both countries.) This gap is almost entirely a result of contrasting experiences with hospital and physician costs.

In 1971, Canada spent 3.33 percent of GNP on hospitals; the U.S. actually spent a markedly lower share — 2.86 percent. But, in the next ten years, the U.S. share rose to 4.02 percent while the Canadian fell to 3.16 percent. The U.S. share thus increased +1.16 percent - (-0.17 percent), or 1.33 percentage points relative to Canada. For physicians' services, Canada, in 1971, spent 1.32 percent of GNP compared with the U.S., 1.48 percent; but, ten years later, the Canadian share had fallen to 1.10 percent while the U.S. share rose to 1.87 percent for a net increase in U.S. share relative to Canada of +0.39 percent - (-0.22 percent), or 0.61 percent of GNP. Thus together the change in GNP shares of "doctors and hospitals" account for a U.S.-Canada spending gap of 1.94 percent, out of the total of 1.99 percent.

All other components of health spending in 1971 accounted for 2.84 percent of GNP in Canada, compared with 3.37 percent in the U.S. In both countries, the "all other" share grew at almost the same rate over the decade (17.6 percent in Canada, 16.3 percent in the U.S.) to reach 3.34 percent of GNP in Canada and 3.92 percent in the U.S. Health spending other than doctors and hospitals thus added only 0.05 percent to the total U.S.-Canada health spending difference of 1.99 percent.

Figure 2 provides the Canada-U.S. contrast for physician and hospital expenditures only, from 1948 to 1983. The impact of the public plans is even more apparent than in Figure 1. The 1982 surge carries total Canadian health spending to new (relative) heights; but "doctors and hospitals" merely reattain their 1971 and 1975 ratios.

The (Non-)Effects of Population Change — Thus Far

Behind all the discussion of rising and falling shares of national income, however, Table 2 serves to remind us that it is relative rates of increase that are in question. Health expenditures *per capita*, of course, keep growing, reaching an estimated $1,220.18, or about $5,000 for a family of four, in 1982. Apart from reducing the numbers to human scale, Table 2 shows, in conjunction with Table 1, the relatively small influence of population growth on overall costs. From 1946 to 1982, total Canadian expenditures on the itemized components of health

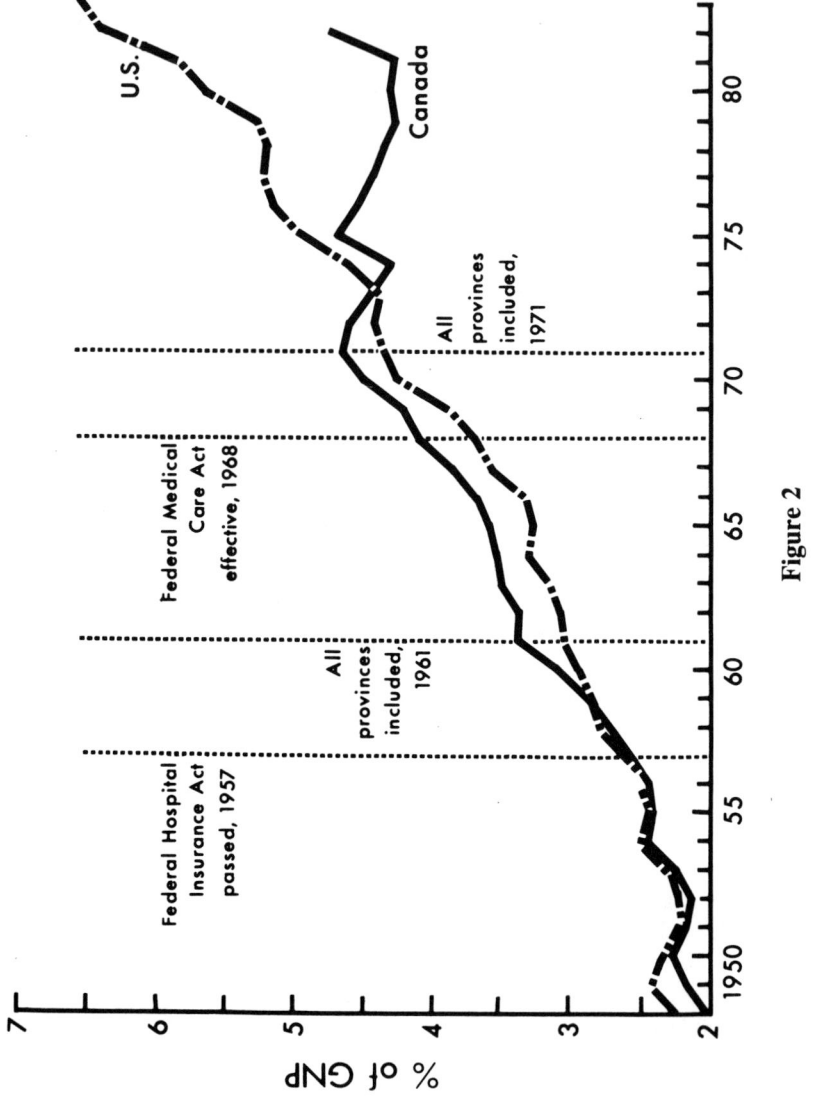

Figure 2

Hospital and Physician Expenditures as % of GNP, Canada and U.S., 1948 - 1983

care rose an average of 12.3 percent per year, *per capita* spending rose 10.2 percent, so population growth made up less than one sixth of the increase over this period. Since 1971, population has accounted for only one tenth of health care cost increases, as the rate of population growth continues to decline.

Of course, we are often reminded that the population (and not just we ourselves) are growing older. But the impact of such changes is very slow and does not affect the period under examination. A measure of Canadian hospital expenditure (public general and allied special) *per capita* standardized for age-specific hospital use patterns, which was generated by Irazuzta (1979), shows an average increase per year of 8.23 percent from 1950 to 1974, compared with the unadjusted rate of 8.38 percent. From 1960 to 1974 the figures are 7.76 percent and 8.05 percent. Comparable adjustments for the other components of health expenditures (except for homes for special care) would show even smaller effects. The aging of the population was simply not rapid enough to exert significant influence on short-term cost movements. It will become important in the future, but only over a time-span of decades (Denton and Spencer, 1983; Woods Gordon, 1984).

Inter-provincial Variation in Health Expenditure Patterns

Within the overall national picture, however, individual provinces often show very different trends. The "Canadian health care system" is in fact ten systems, each with its own history. Tables 4-7 show the pattern of changes across provinces in total health spending *per capita* and in three of its major components. The tables cover the period only from 1960 on, as published data by province are not available for earlier years. Each table shows the provincial values for a particular year as a percentage of the Canada average *per capita* value, so that the relative positions of the provinces are easily seen.

Table 4 shows a striking change in the relative positions of the provinces over time, and in particular very significant narrowing of differences in *per capita* spending. All but one of the provinces moved closer to the national average in the twenty-two-year period, with Quebec and the three most easterly provinces showing particularly spectacular gains. Only Alberta moved away from the national average — upwards from 5.5 percent above to 13.9 percent above.

There were, however, some very different patterns of change across the provinces. The far West, Alberta and B.C., shows a pronounced U-shape pattern, falling to the mean in the 1960s, staying quite close to it for over a decade, then moving up sharply in the late 1970s. It appears that, perhaps as a result of public hospital insurance, the rest of Canada caught up with the more affluent West in the 1960s, but that the constraints of the late 1970s have been less enthusiastic or less effective in these two provinces.

Saskatchewan shows the same U-pattern, falling to the mean (despite universal medical insurance) in the early 1960s, but going well below in the late 1960s,

TABLE 4
HEALTH CARE EXPENDITURES PER CAPITA, CANADA AND PROVINCES RELATIVE TO CANADA, 1960-1982

YEAR	Canada $	B.C. %	Alta. %	Sask. %	Man. %	Ont. %	Que. %	N.B. %	N.S. %	P.E.I. %	Nfld. %
1960	120.34	114.4	105.5	107.2	104.8	112.3	85.2	88.5	83.6	80.7	57.4
1965	170.85	99.5	106.4	97.2	100.7	110.1	93.9	82.2	89.4	74.9	63.6
1970	293.37	98.8	103.7	86.4	102.3	109.9	96.8	78.1	84.9	80.4	63.5
1971	329.86	96.9	100.4	86.6	100.0	109.0	99.4	79.2	85.0	79.6	64.1
1975	544.79	102.5	100.4	91.9	97.5	103.7	101.6	79.3	91.3	78.9	75.7
1976	615.12	102.3	99.3	93.8	100.1	103.3	101.4	77.4	93.3	78.3	78.9
1978	726.34	105.5	100.1	92.7	99.7	103.6	98.3	82.1	93.8	82.4	86.9
1980	921.42	109.0	110.5	91.6	100.0	98.6	99.5	84.2	94.2	97.1	85.1
1981	1,057.58	109.5	109.4	96.0	103.6	98.4	97.6	89.6	97.6	90.6	86.0
1982	1,220.18	107.4	113.9	95.7	101.9	98.5	95.6	92.8	103.8	89.2	87.7

Average Annual Growth Rates (%)

1960-65	7.26	4.33	7.44	5.18	6.40	6.82	9.37	5.70	8.71	5.68	9.49
1965-70	11.42	11.25	10.85	8.83	11.78	11.38	12.09	10.28	10.27	13.00	11.37
1970-75	13.18	14.01	12.45	14.58	12.10	11.87	14.28	13.52	14.84	12.75	17.23
1975-80	11.08	12.46	13.23	11.01	11.65	9.97	10.62	12.42	11.78	15.79	13.71
1980-82	15.08	14.23	16.83	17.62	16.16	15.02	12.80	20.81	20.80	10.29	16.82
1960-82	11.10	10.79	11.49	10.53	10.96	10.44	11.69	11.35	12.20	11.61	13.26
1971-82	12.63	13.69	13.93	13.66	12.82	11.60	12.23	14.26	14.69	13.80	15.88

TABLE 5
HOSPITAL EXPENDITURES PER CAPITA, CANADA AND PROVINCES RELATIVE TO CANADA, 1960-1982

YEAR	Canada	B.C.	Alta.	Sask.	Man.	Ont.	Que.	N.B.	N.S.	P.E.I.	Nfld
1960	46.62	114.3	108.8	126.1	103.0	107.4	83.0	103.3	92.4	78.1	68.7
1965	72.89	91.8	101.0	105.0	94.4	104.1	102.3	96.3	90.6	72.3	70.1
1970	132.00	87.5	103.8	88.6	92.6	104.2	107.5	82.6	92.0	52.1	68.9
1971	146.02	85.0	100.4	86.2	94.9	105.9	106.8	83.9	93.5	67.3	68.4
1975	245.41	97.3	106.4	85.6	102.5	106.4	111.8	86.2	96.8	71.6	81.7
1976	285.49	91.3	100.0	88.1	99.3	101.1	108.9	86.1	93.9	69.6	80.3
1978	317.98	92.5	94.3	85.7	95.9	96.9	114.3	89.0	99.6	73.8	89.0
1980	394.05	97.0	97.4	88.1	96.7	92.2	117.3	87.0	99.9	74.8	91.8
1981	440.13	98.1	97.1	90.3	100.4	91.6	116.2	85.7	106.7	66.9	91.1
1982	505.71	95.7	100.3	89.8	101.4	93.1	112.6	90.2	110.9	68.5	95.0

Average Annual Growth Rates (%)

	Canada	B.C.	Alta.	Sask.	Man.	Ont.	Que.	N.B.	N.S.	P.E.I.	Nfld
1960-65	9.35	4.67	7.72	5.41	7.46	8.65	14.02	7.81	8.90	7.66	9.78
1965-70	12.61	11.54	13.23	8.86	12.19	12.64	13.73	9.22	12.96	5.46	12.21
1970-75	13.20	15.62	13.77	12.41	15.52	13.67	14.10	14.17	14.38	20.64	17.13
1975-80	9.93	9.87	8.00	10.59	8.65	6.84	10.99	10.14	10.61	10.90	12.54
1980-82	13.29	12.50	14.96	14.35	16.04	13.82	11.00	15.33	19.37	8.41	15.24
1960-82	11.44	10.55	11.03	9.74	11.36	10.72	13.00	10.76	12.37	10.78	13.10
1971-82	11.96	13.17	11.94	12.38	12.63	10.65	12.49	12.69	13.70	12.13	15.35

TABLE 6
PHYSICIAN EXPENDITURES PER CAPITA, CANADA AND PROVINCES RELATIVE TO CANADA, 1960-1982

YEAR	Canada	B.C.	Alta.	Sask.	Man.	Ont.	Que.	N.B.	N.S.	P.E.I.	Nfld
1960	19.82	142.6	104.1	100.4	110.3	117.0	76.0	67.7	80.5	66.4	44.9
1965	27.70	122.8	96.2	100.6	103.5	119.7	82.7	64.5	74.1	61.2	43.4
1970	48.81	119.1	112.2	83.1	114.3	121.5	73.8	60.6	87.3	56.6	60.1
1971	57.91	107.7	107.1	77.8	98.6	114.3	92.5	63.1	78.7	70.5	53.6
1975	84.22	117.1	102.2	76.3	83.3	109.2	97.1	64.6	88.6	64.3	53.8
1976	91.37	125.4	102.0	78.7	88.3	107.4	95.2	60.5	86.9	69.2	58.4
1978	108.10	124.1	99.2	78.6	87.2	107.5	96.6	60.1	85.8	69.7	56.9
1980	136.46	123.0	100.7	80.9	87.2	110.2	92.2	59.5	84.2	69.2	59.9
1981	153.53	128.4	102.4	83.3	89.4	112.4	84.7	63.7	85.7	71.6	60.6
1982	179.02	134.0	107.1	88.3	87.9	112.1	80.4	65.4	84.5	71.9	59.8

Average Annual Growth Rates (%)

1960-65	6.92	3.78	5.24	6.96	5.58	7.43	8.75	5.89	5.18	5.19	6.22
1965-70	12.00	11.30	15.50	7.80	14.23	12.32	9.46	10.59	15.72	10.27	19.55
1970-75	11.53	11.15	9.48	9.65	4.70	9.17	17.83	12.99	11.86	14.39	9.08
1975-80	10.13	11.23	9.80	11.42	11.15	10.35	9.01	8.33	9.01	11.76	12.54
1980-82	14.54	19.54	18.08	19.67	14.97	15.47	6.97	20.10	14.74	16.75	14.37
1960-82	10.52	10.21	10.66	9.88	9.39	10.31	10.81	10.35	10.76	10.92	11.97
1971-82	10.80	13.03	10.80	12.09	9.65	10.61	9.41	11.17	11.52	11.00	11.90

TABLE 7
EXPENDITURES ON "HOMES FOR SPECIAL CARE", CANADA AND PROVINCES RELATIVE TO CANADA, 1960-1982

YEAR	Canada	B.C.	Alta.	Sask.	Man.	Ont.	Que.	N.B.	N.S.	P.E.I.	Nfld.
1960	6.22	107.6	68.8	109.3	146.3	128.5	78.0	92.6	33.8	96.6	37.1
1965	8.63	103.1	103.6	121.1	145.5	110.9	83.7	91.8	67.6	130.7	45.2
1970	21.03	70.8	74.8	91.4	89.3	102.1	128.8	67.6	75.7	160.0	37.2
1971	23.90	72.6	71.6	94.9	93.1	100.5	128.5	76.4	83.2	151.7	38.4
1975	49.97	79.6	66.0	111.4	127.0	93.4	130.5	81.7	75.5	127.6	48.3
1976	62.44	65.2	63.2	95.3	129.5	97.3	134.2	67.0	87.0	122.3	47.6
1978	85.20	87.8	93.1	115.2	134.3	112.1	84.8	100.1	99.8	108.1	85.1
1980	112.60	76.8	96.5	105.8	128.7	104.4	101.1	99.5	102.0	104.8	85.6
1981	144.90	75.5	91.0	105.3	134.3	108.5	96.9	118.8	93.1	116.4	82.0
1982	166.99	73.4	93.7	104.4	135.2	109.9	93.6	124.6	96.4	118.7	85.3

Average Annual Growth Rates (%)

1960-65	6.77	5.87	15.87	8.97	6.66	3.67	8.28	6.58	22.66	13.42	11.04
1965-70	19.50	10.84	11.98	12.96	8.39	17.54	30.26	12.42	22.27	24.43	14.93
1970-75	18.90	21.71	15.95	23.69	27.56	16.79	19.21	23.47	18.83	13.64	25.27
1975-80	17.64	16.82	26.92	16.43	17.96	20.31	11.79	22.38	24.92	13.09	31.92
1980-82	21.78	19.00	20.01	21.00	24.83	24.93	17.17	36.29	18.38	29.64	21.57
1960-82	16.13	14.13	17.77	15.89	15.72	15.31	17.10	17.71	21.80	17.22	20.60
1971-82	19.33	19.45	22.28	20.38	23.46	20.30	15.95	24.75	20.94	16.70	28.31

partially recovering by 1975, then holding its relative position, while Manitoba stays very close to the national average throughout.

The Ontario pattern, in contrast, is of alternating periods of loss of relative position (the early 1960s, the early 1970s, 1978 to 1980) interspersed with stability. The main downward adjustments come in the early 1970s, mirroring the large gain in relative position in Quebec, where a reverse U is seen. Quebec's position improved dramatically in the early 1960s (late entry to hospital insurance), rose again in the early 1970s (late entry to Medicare), but by 1982 was back close to its 1965 level.

Newfoundland and the Maritime provinces show the clearest pattern of relative gain. These gains seem to start at different times — from 1960 on in Newfoundland, 1965 on in P.E.I., and 1970 on in Nova Scotia — but the Medicare period is one of steady gain in relative status. In New Brunswick, however, the 1960s show a loss of relative position, the early 1970s a flat period, and not until 1981 does New Brunswick regain its 1960 position. P.E.I. lost ground sharply from 1980 to 1981, but otherwise the Maritimes appear to have been less affected by the expenditure restraints of the second half of the 1970s.

To summarize, the period as a whole shows the three top provinces in 1960, Ontario, B.C. and Saskatchewan, moving down sharply while Quebec, Nova Scotia, P.E.I. and Newfoundland all move up. Alberta begins above average and ends even higher. But much of the adjustment occurs in the early 1960s as Quebec moves into hospital insurance.

Focusing on the Medicare period, 1971-1982, indicates that central Canada, particularly Ontario, is the home of cost control. The three western and the four eastern provinces all showed *per capita* costs rising faster than the national average from 1971 to 1982; western expenditures outpace the average by from 10.5 percent (Saskatchewan) to 13.4 percent (Alberta), while in the east cost increases range from P.E.I.'s 12.1 percent above the average to Newfoundland's 36.8 percent. Only Manitoba stays solidly on the average.

What this indicates is that, had Canada as a whole followed the growth experience of the three western provinces, total health care costs in 1982 would have been 10.5 percent to 13.4 percent above their actual levels, or from 9.3 percent to 9.6 percent of GNP — almost halving the difference with the U.S. Had Canada followed the growth pattern of Nova Scotia or Newfoundland since 1971, we might now be spending as large a share as the U.S. or more.

Of course, this calculation is unfair with respect to the eastern provinces, since it neglects the fact that Quebec and particularly Ontario had *per capita* expenditure levels far above the Maritimes in 1971. Despite eleven years of relatively tighter cost control in Ontario, by 1982 its *per capita* expenditures still exceeded Saskatchewan and all the Maritime provinces but Nova Scotia. B.C. and Alberta, however, cannot as easily argue "catch-up": they begin the period at or near national average expenditure levels and end it well above, suggesting significantly weaker cost control especially in the past few years. If Canada's unique grip on health costs is slipping in the 1980s, these data suggest the slippage may have begun in the West.

Major Components of Health Expenditure — Contrasting Provincial Experiences

As always, aggregate data conceal as well as reveal, and there is more to the story. In Tables 5-7 we present provincial data for leading components of health expenditures, starting with hospitals in Table 5, physicians' services in Table 6, and "homes for special care" in Table 7. Taken together, these three tables throw into sharp relief important differences between the two high-spending western provinces over the past decade.

B.C. shows up as consistently below average on both forms of institutional spending. From well above average in 1960, B.C.'s *per capita* hospital spending dropped to 15 percent below average in 1971. It moved up toward the national average in the early 1970s, and since then has stayed about 5 percent to 10 percent below average. "Homes for special care" spending *per capita* in B.C. in 1970 was 30 percent below the national average, despite a more elderly population there than in Canada as a whole. Although the new provincial long-term care program in 1978 brought B.C. up to 87.8 percent of average, it has since dropped back down. The B.C. experience does not, then, support an argument of substitution of other institutional care for hospital care.

Nor does it seem explicable simply as rapid population growth with a lag in institutional building. The even more rapid growth in Alberta's population has been matched by hospital spending, as Alberta has stayed very close to the national pattern. Spending on homes for special care in Alberta was relatively very low in the early 1970s, but moved up after 1976 to run 5 percent to 10 percent below national averages, yet again this expansion did not seem to have much influence on inpatient costs.

The most striking feature of the western experience is physician costs. B.C. in 1960 was 42.6 percent above national levels. By 1971 this had fallen to 7.7 percent; the introduction of Medicare clearly enabled doctors in the rest of Canada to catch up. Since 1971, however, B.C. physicians appear to have escaped almost completely the pressures on physician incomes elsewhere in Canada and by 1982 were generating *per capita* costs fully a third higher than the national average. In Alberta, physician costs started the decade of the 1970s at 7.1 percent above average, dropped to average by 1978, and since 1980 have moved back up to 7.1 percent above. As we shall see later, however, the physician-to-population ratio in Alberta was virtually unchanged from 1975 to 1982, implying a drop in relative position to 20 percent below average in 1981. The fact that *per capita* physician costs were matching or outpacing national averages in the late 1970s and early 1980s, while physician numbers were falling well behind, indicates that in Alberta, as in B.C., physicians' average earnings were a major factor driving costs upward faster than in the rest of Canada. Yet, interestingly, the two provinces are at opposite ends of the national spectrum on both physician availability and extra-billing patterns.

There is one other point to the Alberta story. New construction expense *per capita* has been accelerating above national levels since 1977. By 1982 it was more than three times national levels — $199.97 compared with $64.29 — a difference large enough to explain the whole discrepancy between Canada and Alberta in total health spending. While some degree of above-average capital spending might be quite appropriate in a province with very fast population growth, it would appear that Alberta may have overestimated the longevity of the oil boom, in this field as in others. A relatively relaxed attitude toward the usual political pressures for physician income increases and new hospital construction, and toward cost escalation generally, was an affordable luxury in the late 1970s. But as the revenue and population boom has ended, the Alberta government must now confront the consequences. "Blaming the patients", though perhaps understandable, is unlikely to be helpful.

The Saskatchewan and Manitoba patterns of hospital expenditure show no striking changes over the 1971 to 1982 period. The rapid increases in Canadian hospital costs in the 1960s seem to have caught up with, and surpassed, Saskatchewan, which in 1960 was 26.1 percent above average and by 1970 was 11.4 percent below. But since then, Saskatchewan hospital costs *per capita* have been consistently 10 percent to 15 percent below national averages, while Manitoba costs have fluctuated in the range of average to 5 percent below.

This Manitoba pattern *is* interesting, however, when matched with the dramatic expansion in Manitoba's homes for special care expense. Since 1975, this has fluctuated between 25 percent and 35 percent above the (rapidly growing) national average, having moved up relatively very fast in the early 1970s. Yet there is no indication of a corresponding drop in hospital costs — indeed, these grew faster in Manitoba from 1971 to 1975 than in Canada generally. As noted below, the interprovincial comparability of data reporting in this sector may be questionable. The significant feature of this comparison, however, is not Manitoba's relative position at a point in time but its relative *expansion* in the early 1970s.

In both provinces, physician costs *per capita* have run behind the national *per capita* levels throughout most of the period. In Saskatchewan, however, the early (1962) introduction of public insurance enabled them to avoid the "medical boom" of the late 1960s. As a result, Saskatchewan costs fell well behind the national averages in the 1960s, and then grew in parallel in the 1970s. The data suggest, however, that since 1978 Saskatchewan has been catching the "western disease", and physician costs are rising much more rapidly. In Manitoba, in contrast, relative costs fell steadily from 1960 to 1975 and have been fairly stable since.

Ontario and Quebec show contrasting physician cost experience; one consistently well above average, the other below. The dramatic fluctuations surrounding Quebec's entry to Medicare, from 1970 to 1971, are large enough to influence relative patterns all across Canada; in particular, Ontario's drop in one year from 21.5 percent above average to 14.3 percent above mirrors the Quebec increase. But from 1971 to 1980, both provinces move more or less in line with the national averages — given their size, they *are* most of the averages. The interesting development since 1980 is the drop in Quebec's relative position, suggesting either that the pressures pushing up physician costs in every other province have, as yet, no counterpart there, or that public policies in response have been exceptionally successful.

In the institutional sector, in contrast, Quebec shows substantially higher costs *per capita* (which are not affected by the 1971 break) than does Ontario. While Ontario between 1975 and 1980 squeezed its hospital costs from about 5 percent above average to 7 percent to 8 percent below, Quebec has moved up to more than 10 percent to 15 percent above. In the homes for special care sector, Quebec data appear to be inconsistent between 1976 and 1977; the Ontario picture is of steady growth at or somewhat above the national average, with a dramatic spurt between 1975 and 1978. There may be an indication of some substitution away from acute care here, as the 1975 to 1978 period also shows a sharp drop in Ontario's relative position in hospital costs *per capita*. But no such substitution emerges from the Quebec data.

In the East, hospital cost experience in Nova Scotia and Newfoundland contrasts with that in New Brunswick and P.E.I., perhaps reflecting the significance of the location of medical schools and tertiary care referral centres. Costs generated on behalf of New Brunswick and P.E.I. residents may be being attributed to Nova Scotia in particular. All four provinces outpaced the national averages from 1971 to 1982, but the difference was much more marked in Nova Scotia and especially in Newfoundland. Over the period as a whole, 1960 to 1982, New Brunswick and P.E.I. actually ran behind the average because of very slow growth in the 1960s. The rise in Newfoundland's relative position is particularly dramatic; Nova Scotia has always been relatively high-cost. But by 1982, Nova Scotia was second only to Quebec in *per capita* hospital spending, and its growth since 1980 is suggestive of relatively weaker, or at least less successful, cost containment in that sector.

The "homes for special care" sector shows a pattern that raises questions about the classifications underlying the data. Newfoundland, Nova Scotia and New Brunswick all show spectacular increases in this class of spending during a relatively short period in the mid-1970s. Newfoundland comes up from well below half to 85 percent to 90 percent of average, while the other two move to the average. Nowhere is there any sign of a hospital cost offset. It appears that either a reclassification or a major increase in spending in this area took place very rapidly throughout the Maritimes, although the extraordinary drop in Quebec spending between 1976 and 1978 distorts all other provincial relatives.

In contrast with the fluctuations in institutional spending, *per capita* spending on physicians' services in the eastern provinces has maintained a remarkably stable relation to the national level. Newfoundland's spending increased from under half to 60 percent of the national average between 1960 and 1970, and has stayed there since. All have shared the acceleration of costs in the 1980s. Indeed, New Brunswick has had the most rapid increase in the country in physicians' costs *per capita*, from 1980 to 1982, though this still leaves the province at only two-thirds of the national average.

The diverse provincial experiences widen the range of observed relationships between policies and outcomes. They demonstrate clearly that the Canadian health care funding system is by no means monolithic. Different provincial policies, pressures and philosophies lead to very different performances, and the overall "Canadian" performance is an average or central tendency heavily weighted by Ontario and Quebec.

But all such data record only expenditures. They do not tell us how the changes over time are partitioned into prices and quantities, or into incomes, manpower and capacity. More or less spending may indicate more or less servicing, or simply richer or poorer providers. Accordingly, we turn our attention in the following two sections to the physician and hospital sectors, to try to identify the real service flows behind the expenditure statistics.

Fees, Utilization, Incomes and Numbers in the Physicians' Services Sector: 1960-1982

The evolution of patterns of expenditure for physicians' services, in Canada and in the individual provinces, reflects the development both of provision and utilization, and of average price levels. The latter, in turn, depend on changes in quoted fees — fee or reimbursement schedules — and (in the pre-Medicare period) changes in collections ratios. In the Medicare period, extra-billing also contributes an additional price increase factor that may be significant in some provinces.

The price/quantity distinction is of central importance if one is to draw inferences from expenditure data about differences in the availability and utilization of physicians' services, across provinces or over time. The implications for health policy of a particular expenditure differential are very different, depending on whether it reflects variations in actual service use, or merely different prices.

Trends in Average Levels of Physicians' Fees, Over Time and Across Provinces

Table 8 presents a compilation of fee schedule indices, based on unpublished material provided by Health and Welfare Canada. The Health Information Division compiles estimates of the percentage increase in fees represented by each revision of a provincial fee schedule, going back to December 1963. Cross-provincial relative fee levels are also compiled for certain years, subject to the difficulty of comparing different provincial schedules. In Table 8 the relative fee levels of the provinces in 1971 are expressed on a base of the Canada average equal to 100.0, and then carried forward and backward by the percentage changes in each province (see this paper's Data Appendix for details).

The major weakness of the Table 8 data in the pre-Medicare period, and particularly in the period of introduction of Medicare in each of the provinces, is that they make no allowance for changes in billing patterns and collections ratios. These exerted a very significant upward influence on prices, yet apparently there are no data indicating the magnitude of that effect. Barer and Evans (1983) calculated that over the period 1935 to 1979 the average Canada-wide fee for physicians' services (as reported in the Consumer Price Index Component in earlier years, and fee schedule changes in later years) rose at a rate of 3.2 percent per year. But increases in actual prices received were estimated, by an indirect procedure, at between 4.2 percent and 5.0 percent per year, most probably in the range of 4.7 percent to 4.9 percent. The overall Consumer Price Index rose at an average rate of 4.0 percent.

In the period 1960 to 1971, from the beginning of our provincial indices to the Canada-wide introduction of Medicare, the average annual increase in physician fee schedules was 3.3 percent, compared with a Consumer Price Index increase of 2.7 percent. But the estimated increase in fees actually received (Barer and Evans, 1983) is between 4.9 percent and 5.7 percent per year in this period. The big surge is, of course, in the late 1960s, when most provinces entered Medicare; from 1965 to 1971 the Barer/Evans estimates outrun list fees by from 3.3 percent to 4.0 percent per year (for six years!) even as list fees were outrunning the CPI by about 0.4 percent per year.

Table 9 makes the same point with different data, showing the increase in *per capita* expenditure on physicians' services in each province during the two-year period spanning its entry to Medicare, and then the increase in *per capita* utilization implied by deflating that increase by the change in list fees over the same two-year period. Four provinces show an increase in apparent *per capita* use of 40 percent to 50 percent; Newfoundland's increase is 67 percent! Yet there is no evidence of growth in physician numbers or workload anywhere close to large enough to generate these increases. Indeed, the well-known Enterline *et al.* (1973) study in Montreal showed *no* increase in physician workload in the twelve-month period spanning the introduction of Medicare. We may reasonably

TABLE 8
PHYSICIANS' FEE INDEXES, CANADA AND PROVINCES, 1960-1983 (Canada, 1971 = 100.0)

YEAR	Canada	B.C.	Alta.	Sask.	Man.	Ont.	Que.	N.B.	N.S.	P.E.I.	Nfld.	CPI
1960	69.9	84.3	78.1	64.5	65.2	69.3	71.3	62.7	66.7	?	64.4	74.3
1963	74.5	82.9	78.0	65.5	76.9	74.1	78.8	67.9	69.8	65.8	70.9	77.2
1964	76.1	86.0	79.4	65.5	76.9	74.1	82.1	67.9	69.8	73.8	70.9	78.6
1965	78.7	86.0	81.3	65.5	76.9	78.5	82.6	67.9	69.8	73.8	70.9	80.5
1966	80.1	86.0	85.0	65.5	76.9	79.9	83.2	76.5	69.8	74.1	70.9	83.5
1967	86.6	94.5	91.0	66.1	85.4	86.5	93.2	85.2	73.8	74.2	74.8	86.5
1968	90.6	94.5	97.0	74.1	102.4	88.7	92.8	85.2	85.7	85.0	82.7	90.0
1969	96.1	100.9	99.3	81.3	102.4	95.4	95.8	94.1	87.1	85.0	82.7	94.1
1970	97.8	100.9	102.7	84.0	102.4	97.6	100.3	94.1	87.5	97.8	82.7	97.2
1971	100.0	100.9	106.2	87.8	102.4	100.5	100.3	94.1	87.5	97.8	82.7	100.0
1972	101.4	105.2	106.3	90.3	102.4	102.0	100.3	94.1	93.5	100.3	83.4	104.8
1973	102.3	112.9	107.9	93.8	102.4	102.0	100.3	94.1	99.6	101.2	89.4	112.7
1974	107.4	123.1	112.3	96.9	108.5	107.2	100.3	95.4	107.3	107.5	91.6	125.0
1975	114.2	141.7	122.6	108.5	114.0	112.8	100.3	106.2	122.7	113.9	99.8	138.5
1976	121.8	157.4	135.1	118.1	124.4	120.4	101.3	109.7	133.7	122.5	108.4	148.9
1977	132.0	164.1	144.5	126.1	133.1	128.8	118.0	117.5	140.4	131.0	110.3	160.8
1978	140.2	175.2	153.9	134.2	140.2	137.0	121.8	124.8	148.4	138.9	116.9	175.2
1979	150.6	189.0	164.6	145.5	151.2	149.0	127.0	138.9	159.1	150.7	124.0	191.2
1980	164.8	206.6	190.1	165.2	168.3	166.1	128.7	151.9	175.0	170.2	140.5	210.6
1981	184.2	241.7	214.5	186.8	193.2	184.5	137.7	174.6	195.6	187.4	157.3	236.9
1982	208.3	279.9	261.7	224.8	215.6	206.4	147.4	204.6	220.5	208.7	178.1	262.5
1983	227.5	300.0	281.3	241.0	226.5	232.2	158.9	220.7	241.4	224.3	189.8	277.6

Annual Average Growth Rates (%)

	Canada	B.C.	Alta.	Sask.	Man.	Ont.	Que.	N.B.	N.S.	P.E.I.	Nfld.	CPI
1960-65	2.40	0.40	0.81	0.31	3.36	2.52	2.99	1.61	0.91	?	1.94	1.62
1965-70	4.44	3.25	4.78	5.10	5.89	4.45	3.96	6.74	4.62	5.79	3.13	3.84
1960-70	3.42	1.81	2.78	2.68	4.62	3.48	3.47	4.14	2.75	5.82	2.53	2.72
1970-75	3.15	7.03	3.61	5.25	2.17	2.94	0.00	2.45	7.00	3.09	3.83	7.34
1975-80	7.61	7.83	9.17	8.77	8.10	8.05	5.11	7.42	7.36	8.36	7.08	8.74
1980-83	11.35	13.24	13.95	13.41	10.41	11.81	7.28	13.26	11.32	9.64	10.55	9.64
1970-83	6.71	8.74	8.06	8.45	6.30	6.89	3.60	6.78	8.12	6.59	6.60	8.41
1960-83	5.26	5.67	5.57	5.90	5.56	5.40	3.55	5.62	5.75	6.32	4.81	5.90

TABLE 9
IMPACT OF ENTRY TO UNIVERSAL PUBLIC MEDICAL INSURANCE PROGRAMS ON PER CAPITA EXPENDITURES, BY PROVINCE

	Year of Introduction	Changes Measured Over	Change in Expenditure Per Capita	Change in List Fees	Change in Apparent "Utilization"
Nfld.	1969	68-70	67.26	0.00	67.26
P.E.I.	1970	69-71	48.45	15.07	29.00
N.S.	1969	68-70	46.65	2.09	43.64
N.B.	1971	70-72	42.80	0.00	42.80
Que.	1970	69-71	55.38	4.69	48.40
Ont.	1969	68-70	29.55	10.04	17.72
Man.	1969	68-70	48.82	0.00	48.82
Sask.	1962	61-63	32.18	0.96	30.92
Alta	1969	68-70	22.15	5.88	15.37
B.C.	1968	67-69	29.16	6.77	20.98

assume, then, that most of the apparent "utilization" increases in Table 9 are in fact increased prices through improved collections ratios or changes in billing patterns — but we do not know exactly how much. The Barer/Evans methodology for estimating these effects has not been applied at the provincial level, and in any case represents a fairly early stage of technique.

Subject to these *caveats*, however, the data in Table 8 do indicate what was happening to official fee levels through the 1960s, and provide a minimum estimate of price changes. Moreover, the post-1971 data do not suffer from the same collections ratio biases. The impact of extra-billing is primarily localized in Alberta and to a much lesser extent in Ontario. In any case, its effects are not of the same order of magnitude as the Medicare entry biases. The Table 8 data are on a common base; the Canada 1971 average is set equal to 100.0 and all other province and year index values are relative to that level. In 1971 the Maritime provinces and Saskatchewan had fee levels markedly below national averages, while Alberta and, to a lesser extent, Manitoba were above. By 1983, however, B.C. and Alberta had pushed their fees far above national averages, 31.9 percent above for B.C. and 23.6 percent above for Alberta. Only in B.C. did physician fees outrun the general inflation level from 1971 to 1983; in Alberta, as in Saskatchewan and Nova Scotia, fee increases almost matched inflation rates. As recently as 1980, however, even B.C.'s fees were slightly behind the general inflation level. (Since then, B.C. appears to have given away money with both hands.)

Thus the U-shaped pattern of relative costs in B.C. and Alberta is primarily a result of fee changes. In the 1960 data, both provinces had fee levels well above the national average. From 1960 to 1970, physicians in both provinces lost ground relative to the rest of Canada. But B.C. physicians' fees far outpaced national fee levels in the early 1970s, and Alberta sped up in the latter half. In the early 1980s, these two provinces were joined by Saskatchewan to form a western bloc in which fee increases substantially exceeded the national average even as that average was outrunning inflation for the first time since the late 1960s.

These provinces are thus an exception to the general Canadian story of fee gains in the 1960s, sharp losses in the early 1970s, slower losses in the late 1970s, and gains in the 1980s. Over the period 1970 to 1983, the three western provinces outran the national average by 1.3 percent (Alberta) to 1.9 percent (B.C.) *per year*, again suggesting that cost restraint is less restraining in the West.

Trends in Per Capita Utilization of Physicians' Services — Expenditures Adjusted for Fee Change

Table 10 uses these indices to deflate *per capita* expenditures on physicians' services, enabling us to look at the western provinces in a different way. Here we find that in the 1971 to 1982 period (avoiding the 1970-1971 bounce in Quebec) utilization *per capita* rose 3.65 percent per year in Canada as a whole, but the three western provinces ran behind by, from half a percent to 1.5 percent per year. In fact, from 1975 on *per capita* utilization in Alberta was virtually static in marked contrast to almost every other province and time period. By 1982, physicians' services utilization in Alberta was nearly 15 percent below the national average; in 1971 it was about 1 percent above. Saskatchewan dropped from about 12 percent below to 18 percent below, and B.C. fell from about 7 percent above to just about equal.

It should be emphasized that in each province, utilization *per capita* has indeed increased significantly since 1971, at a Canada-wide average rate of 3.65 percent per year; and even in Alberta the 1971 to 1982 increase averages 2 percent per year (though almost all of that increase came before 1975). But the relative growth in physicians' services costs in the three western provinces since 1971, compared with the rest of Canada, has been a result of relative fee, not utilization, differences.

The fee pattern in Manitoba and Ontario, in contrast, stays relatively close to the national average. Both provinces showed list fees increasing faster than the general inflation rate in the 1960s; Manitoba in 1971 had fees slightly above the national average while Ontario was almost dead on. From 1971 to 1983, Manitoba fluctuates between average and a few percentage points above, Ontario between average and a few points below. Both run behind the CPI by 4 percent to 5 percent per year in the early 1970s, and by about 3/4 percent in the late 1970s. They outrun the CPI again in the early 1980s.

While Manitoba and Ontario physician fees track the national average quite closely, their implied utilization rates differ. Both show a surge in apparent utilization in the late 1960s, a bit above national rates. During the period, both entered Medicare. But Manitoba's utilization growth lagged behind national rates in the early 1960s, while Ontario's was slightly ahead. The Manitoba growth rate of *per capita* use was the slowest in Canada in the early 1970s, ran above average in the late 1970s, and has slowed again in the 1980s. Ontario raced ahead in the early 1970s (highest annual rates west of the Ottawa river), slowed in the late 1970s, and speeded up again in the 1980s. From 1971 to 1982, Ontario's utilization rate grows over 1 percent per year faster than Manitoba's, finishing the decade *one third higher*, though fee levels are about the same. In 1971 Ontario utilization was 17.7 percent higher; in 1960 the two provinces were about equal. The post-Medicare pattern is thus a continuation of a pre-Medicare trend.

Physicians' fees in Quebec appear to have moved far out of line since 1971. In the 1960s Quebec fee data follow the national average quite closely. But from 1971 to 1975 fees in Quebec were absolutely flat, and from the mid-1970s on they have run well behind both national averages and general price levels. Quebec is the only province in which physician fees continue to run behind

TABLE 10
PER CAPITA APPARENT UTILIZATION OF PHYSICIANS' SERVICES, ADJUSTED FOR LIST FEE DIFFERENTIALS, CANADA AND PROVINCES, 1960-1982
(1971 $)

YEAR	Canada	B.C.	Alta.	Sask.	Man.	Ont.	Que.	N.B.	N.S.	P.E.I.	Nfld.
1960	28.35	33.52	26.43	30.85	33.53	33.45	21.12	21.40	23.91	n.a.	13.80
1965	35.20	39.56	32.77	42.53	37.30	42.25	27.74	26.32	29.41	22.97	16.95
1970	49.91	58.11	53.32	48.29	54.46	60.75	35.89	31.41	48.70	28.26	35.49
1971	57.91	61.79	58.39	51.30	55.94	65.85	53.39	38.84	52.06	41.75	37.55
1975	73.75	69.57	70.24	59.24	61.55	81.50	81.52	51.25	60.81	47.53	45.41
1976	75.02	72.82	69.00	60.88	64.83	81.50	86.12	50.36	59.39	51.61	49.22
1978	77.10	76.59	69.66	63.35	67.25	84.85	85.74	52.06	62.49	54.24	52.63
1980	82.80	81.24	72.30	66.82	70.72	90.57	97.77	53.47	65.63	55.46	58.22
1981	83.35	81.56	73.26	68.49	71.07	93.57	94.43	55.99	67.27	58.66	59.15
1982	85.94	85.69	73.23	70.33	72.97	97.19	97.69	57.26	68.58	61.65	60.08
Annual Average Growth Rates (%)											
1960-65	4.42	3.37	4.39	6.63	2.15	4.78	5.60	4.23	4.23	?	4.20
1965-70	7.23	7.99	10.23	2.57	7.86	7.53	5.29	3.60	10.61	4.23	15.93
1970-75	8.12	3.67	5.67	4.17	2.48	6.05	17.83	10.29	4.54	10.96	5.05
1975-80	2.34	3.15	0.58	2.44	2.82	2.13	3.70	0.85	1.54	3.13	5.10
1980-82	1.88	2.70	0.64	2.59	1.58	3.59	-0.04	3.48	2.22	5.43	1.58
1960-82	5.17	4.36	4.74	3.82	3.60	4.97	7.21	4.58	4.91	?	6.92
1971-82	3.65	3.02	2.08	2.91	2.45	3.60	5.65	3.59	2.54	3.61	4.37

inflation in the early 1980s; though P.E.I. just holds level, the other eight provinces run well ahead from 1980 on.

But Quebec also shows apparent "utilization" increases, 17.8 per cent *per capita* from 1970 to 1975, suggestive of very large increases in effective prices received during the introduction of Medicare. Thus the very low rates of increase in official fees are compensated by very high increases in either or both of collections ratios or effective fees per procedure. Even after 1975, utilization increases in Quebec are higher than in any other province but Newfoundland. This makes all the more striking the apparent dead stop of utilization increases in the 1980s, when list fees are still running well behind inflation.

The three Maritime provinces and Newfoundland all show the post-1971 pattern of fee increases running behind inflation rates by large amounts in the early 1970s, smaller in the late, and then outrunning inflation in the early 1980s. Nova Scotia, however, kept almost level with inflation in the early 1970s, matching B.C.; and P.E.I. has just matched inflation in the early 1980s. Except for Newfoundland, all made gains in the late 1960s. But the main story is in Table 10, the utilization increases.

All four provinces saw spectacular gains in "utilization", more than 10 percent *per year* (in Newfoundland's case, nearly 16 percent) for a five-year period in either the late 1960s or the early 1970s. Like Quebec, the eastern provinces appear to have achieved very high *de facto* rates of increase in prices received, which do not show up in list fees. These appear to be primarily associated with the introduction of Medicare. They were able to keep this process going over the decade from 1965 to 1975; but in the late 1970s, only P.E.I. and Newfoundland maintained above average rates of increase in utilization. In the 1980s, though, the other two provinces have accelerated growth in utilization rates.

For the post-1971 period as a whole, Nova Scotia has achieved above average fee increases while the other three have been about average. But correspondingly, Nova Scotia has below average rates of utilization increase, Newfoundland has above average, and the other two follow the averages.

One way of summarizing these adjustments is shown in Table 11, which reports *per capita* utilization rates, relative to the national average, by province, for selected years between 1960 and 1982. Also calculated are measures of dispersion — the ranges from highest to lowest and from second highest to second lowest, and the sum of the absolute values of provincial departures from 100.0, divided by the number of provinces. This table thus summarizes cross-provincial inequalities in medical services use. (They are not adjusted for provincial differences in age and sex structure, which, while important, are unlikely to change much over time. And in any case, such adjustments would make a difference of only two or three percentage points, except for Newfoundland, where the difference might be between five and ten.)

Table 11 shows that between 1960 and 1965 the dispersion of use rates changed little, becoming, if anything, more unequal. Six years later, Medicare *did* appear to have decreased inequality substantially, though the provinces with the highest rates of *apparent* increase in use are also those that have the most biased price data. Thus Table 11 overstates the degree of equalization. But since 1971, there has apparently been no reduction in inequalities of use. Newfoundland and B.C. have both moved toward the average, but Alberta and Nova Scotia have dropped down sharply, and Quebec has moved through and farther out the other side.

Where fees have risen fastest since 1971 — in B.C., Alberta, Saskatchewan and Nova Scotia — relative use rates have dropped, while where they have risen most slowly — in Quebec — use rates have risen fastest. (This observation is consistent with a "target income" view of physician behaviour, since, except for Alberta, out-of-pocket payments by users are trivial or non-existent in these provinces.) But the apparent, and to some degree overstated, equalization of service use that appears to have been a result of Medicare, has not persisted. If anything, Table 11 suggests a slight increase in dispersion after 1971.

The Growing Availability of Physicians' Services — Manpower and "Productivity"

Utilization rates *per capita*, of course, depend on both the availability of providers and on their levels of activity. Increased utilization could result either from increases in physician-to-population ratios, or from increased levels of output per physician (either increased hours of work or increased output per hour). In Table 12 we present data by province on the population per average civilian physician, for Canada 1960 to 1983, and on the value for each province as a percentage of the Canadian figure. (The provincial relatives are reversed, showing above-average physician-to-population ratios as 100+ percent.) Table 13 then calculates an index of physician "workload", estimated by multiplying each province/year value underlying Table 12 by the corresponding value in Table 10 [(services/population) x (population/doctor)], then dividing by the Canada 1971 index value, and multiplying by 100.0.

The index is synthetic, since Active Civilian Physicians (ACP) used in Table 12 is a broader concept than fee-practice physicians. It includes interns, residents and other physicians in salaried practice, as well as some not in clinical practice at all. The ACP series is thus a more comprehensive indicator of physician service capacity, but also overstates that capacity somewhat. The fee indexes in Table 8 and on which Table 10 is based, however, apply only to fee-for-service practitioners. Moreover, total expense for physicians' services is broader than simply fee payments; it includes sessional fees and other income from professional practice. As long as implicit prices of physicians' services supplied other

TABLE 11

RELATIVE (APPARENT) UTILIZATION OF PHYSICIANS' SERVICES, PER CAPITA, CANADA AND PROVINCES RELATIVE TO CANADA (in $ 1971)

Canada	1960 $ 28.35	1965 $ 35.20	1971 $ 57.91	1976 $ 75.02	1982 $ 85.94
B.C.	118.2	112.4	106.7	97.1	99.7
Alta.	93.2	93.1	100.8	92.0	85.2
Sask.	108.8	120.8	88.6	81.2	81.8
Man.	118.3	106.0	96.6	86.4	84.9
Ont.	118.0	120.0	113.7	108.6	113.1
Que.	74.5	78.8	92.2	114.8	113.7
N.B.	75.5	74.8	67.1	67.1	66.6
N.S.	84.3	83.6	89.9	79.2	79.8
P.E.I.	?	65.3	72.1	68.8	71.7
Nfld	48.7	48.2	64.8	65.6	69.9
Range	69.6	72.6	48.9	49.2	47.1
2nd Range	43.7	54.7	39.6	41.5	43.2
Avg.of Discrepancies	20.8	21.5	15.0	18.6	18.7

TABLE 12
POPULATION PER ACTIVE CIVILIAN PHYSICIAN,*
CANADA AND PROVINCIAL PHYSICIAN TO POPULATION RATIOS RELATIVE TO CANADA**
1960-1983

YEAR	Canada	B.C.	Alta.	Sask.	Man.	Ont.	Que.	N.B.	N.S.	P.E.I.	Nfld.
1960	879	113.1	87.3	88.1	104.1	110.4	100.5	65.2	82.1	74.6	43.0
1965	779	117.8	88.4	87.3	102.8	109.3	97.8	66.7	87.6	70.4	57.4
1970	689	110.3	96.2	85.6	98.1	106.6	101.2	62.1	90.6	60.2	61.8
1971	659	107.3	95.5	81.0	102.1	106.2	103.1	62.9	89.9	57.6	59.8
1975	585	103.0	88.3	83.3	99.5	107.5	102.1	64.4	98.3	59.5	77.2
1976	577	103.7	89.2	81.6	99.7	105.8	103.6	65.4	97.3	67.7	80.3
1978	560	105.3	87.3	83.0	100.2	105.8	102.8	63.7	102.6	67.7	80.3
1980	547	106.0	84.4	81.8	100.4	106.0	103.6	61.7	102.5	67.9	83.5
1981	538	104.7	84.0	81.3	99.8	105.7	105.3	62.8	101.1	67.8	84.0
1982	523	104.8	85.2	81.2	102.8	104.8	105.3	65.3	99.8	65.3	86.0
1983	512	104.9	85.8	80.3	102.4	104.9	104.7	66.9	102.1	61.6	86.2

Average Annual Growth Rates in Physicians Per Capita (%)

	Canada	B.C.	Alta.	Sask.	Man.	Ont.	Que.	N.B.	N.S.	P.E.I.	Nfld.
1960-65	2.44	3.29	2.71	2.27	2.17	2.23	1.88	2.91	3.80	1.25	8.54
1965-70	2.49	1.13	4.23	2.07	1.55	1.99	3.17	1.04	3.18	-0.67	4.03
1970-75	3.33	1.93	1.55	2.78	3.61	3.50	3.51	4.06	5.04	3.08	8.00
1975-80	1.35	1.94	0.46	0.97	1.53	1.06	1.65	0.51	2.19	4.05	2.96
1980-83	2.23	1.88	2.77	1.59	2.91	1.88	2.59	5.02	2.15	-1.01	3.31
1960-71	2.65	2.16	3.50	1.87	2.47	2.29	2.90	2.32	3.51	0.27	5.78
1971-83	2.13	1.93	1.21	2.04	2.14	2.03	2.25	2.66	3.22	2.71	5.28
1960-83	2.38	2.04	2.30	1.97	2.30	2.15	2.56	2.49	3.35	1.53	5.52

*Includes interns and residents.
**Provincial relative values are inverse; values above 100.0 are above average physician to population ratios.

than by fee-for-service (in each province) move more or less in line with fee levels, however, the index values will not be biased.

Table 12 indicates the substantial growth in available physician supply *per capita*, by nearly three-quarters since 1960, and nearly 30 percent since 1971. But as indicated in Table 10, growth in utilization *per capita* has consistently outstripped that of physicians *per capita*. Apparent output per physician grows by about 1.5 percent per year in the Medicare period. Over the whole period since 1960, output per physician appears to grow much faster — about 2.7 percent per year — but as emphasized, the late 1960s "utilization" growth rates are severely upward-biased.

Table 12 makes several general points (each with its exception!). First, physician supply appears to have become more equal across the provinces. Taking the average of the absolute percentage differences from the national value in 1983 yields 13.8, compared with 17.2 in 1971, and 18.8 in 1960. It appears, therefore, that equalization of physicians *per capita* has progressed substantially since 1971, though equalization of apparent service use has not. But this national result is virtually all accounted for by changes in Nova Scotia and Newfoundland. If we exclude the four eastern provinces, distribution appears to have equalized somewhat between 1960 and 1971 and then diverged between 1971 and 1983.

Once again, the provinces show very different histories. B.C. has always had above-average physician availability, but its relative status dropped steadily from 1960 to 1975, when it was only 3 percent above average. By 1983 it was back up to 4.9 percent above. Table 13 further indicates that in the Medicare period B.C. physicians increased their output at only a bit over two-thirds the national average rate. From 1960 to 1971, their output was about average; by 1982 it was 4.9 percent below, but their extraordinarily high fees have kept up *per capita* costs. British Columbians in 1960 had to pay more for physicians' services because they had many more physicians whose average output was about equal to the Canadian average, though they received about 20 percent higher fees per service than in Canada generally. By 1971 their fees were near the Canadian average, as were workloads, but extra numbers held up costs. By 1983, workloads in B.C. are below average, numbers of physicians are only a bit above average, but fees are now more than 30 percent higher. The fees are the interesting phenomenon in B.C. — do high fees lead to lower workloads, or vice versa?

Alberta is quite different. Here the growth in physician supply *per capita* virtually stopped from 1975 to 1981. Physicians continued to flow in, at above average rates, but not fast enough to keep up with population growth. As a result, the relative availability of physicians fell to 16 percent below the national average. Utilization *per capita* is below average by roughly the same proportion — nearly 15 percent (Table 10), while Table 13 shows that physicians' output has grown at almost exactly the same rate as the national average. Their output has remained in the neighbourhood of 5 percent above that average throughout the period, until

TABLE 13
INDEXES OF ACTIVITY PER PHYSICIAN, CANADA AND PROVINCES,
1960-1982 (Canada, 1971 = 100.0)

YEAR	Canada	B.C.	Alta.	Sask.	Man.	Ont.	Que.	N.B.	N.S.	P.E.I.	Nfld.
1960	65.3	68.2	69.7	80.7	74.2	69.8	48.4	75.6	67.1	n.a.	73.9
1965	71.9	68.5	75.7	99.4	74.1	78.9	57.9	80.6	68.6	66.6	60.3
1970	90.1	95.2	100.0	101.9	100.2	102.8	64.0	91.3	97.1	84.7	103.6
1971	100.0	99.4	105.6	109.3	94.5	107.2	89.4	106.7	100.0	125.3	108.3
1975	113.1	103.5	122.0	109.0	94.8	116.2	122.1	122.1	94.8	122.4	90.2
1976	113.4	106.1	117.0	112.8	98.4	116.4	125.7	116.5	92.3	115.4	92.7
1978	113.1	106.8	117.0	112.0	98.5	117.6	122.4	120.0	89.4	117.5	96.1
1980	118.7	109.8	122.8	117.1	101.0	122.5	135.3	124.1	91.8	117.1	99.9
1981	117.5	109.9	123.1	118.8	100.4	124.8	126.4	125.7	93.8	122.0	99.2
1982	117.8	112.0	117.8	118.7	97.3	127.1	127.2	120.2	94.2	129.4	95.7

Average Annual Growth Rates (%)

1960-65	1.94	0.09	1.67	4.26	-0.03	2.48	3.65	1.29	0.44	n.a.	-3.99
1965-70	4.62	6.80	5.73	0.50	6.22	5.43	2.02	2.52	7.20	4.93	11.43
1970-75	4.65	1.69	4.06	1.36	-1.10	2.48	13.85	5.99	-0.48	7.64	-2.73
1975-80	0.97	1.19	0.13	1.44	1.28	1.06	2.02	0.33	-0.64	-0.88	2.06
1980-82	-0.38	1.00	-2.06	0.68	-1.85	1.86	-3.04	-1.58	1.30	5.12	-2.12
1960-82	2.72	2.28	2.41	1.77	1.24	2.76	4.49	2.13	1.55	n.a.	1.18
1971-80	1.50	1.09	1.00	0.75	0.27	1.56	3.26	1.09	-0.54	0.29	-1.12

the sharp drop in 1982. Fees in Alberta have also been consistently above average, by 5 percent to 10 percent, but from 1980 on Albertan physicians have managed to extend this advantage to 20 percent to 25 percent. This recent "up-side break-out" in Alberta fees, like the long-term development in B.C., seems to be the main factor driving costs up, though it is masked in the Alberta expenditure data by the absolutely unprecedented stability in physician supply and utilization during the 1975 to 1981 period.

It might be tempting to construct a "market-type" argument here, that relative physician scarcity in Alberta has both encouraged extra-billing and enabled physicians to push up list fees. But the temptation should be resisted. If there is a large "excess demand" (patient-initiated) in Alberta, why would it not simply draw in more physicians? And why is extra-billing most prevalent in the doctor-dense urban areas? And finally, why are fees rising even faster in B.C.?

Saskatchewan has consistently been well below the national average in physicians *per capita*, by nearly 20 percent in both 1971 and 1982. But output per physician, which was nearly a quarter above average in 1960, had fallen to 10 percent above in 1971, and about equal in 1982. (Alternatively, the rest of Canada has caught up with Saskatchewan.) Accordingly, in 1982 utilization *per capita* in Saskatchewan is nearly 20 percent below the national average. Fees, though historically 10 percent to 20 percent below average, closed the gap to 5 percent in 1975, and caught up in 1980. Relative fees and output per physician thus moved in opposite directions in the 1970s, suggestive of "target income" behaviour by Saskatchewan physicians.

Manitoba, Ontario, Quebec and New Brunswick all follow the Canadian average physician-to-population ratio quite closely in the post-1971 period, though at different levels. Ontario and Quebec both run about 5 percent above the average (plus or minus a couple of percent), though that represents a decline in relative position since 1960 for Ontario (from 10 percent above to 5 percent, while Quebec was climbing from average to 5 percent above. Manitoba is consistently at or just above average, though its position slipped a bit in the 1960s. New Brunswick holds steady throughout the period at about two-thirds the Canada level.

But the activity per physician indices, fee-adjusted expenditures per active civilian physician, are dramatically different. In Manitoba, this index actually fell sharply between 1970 and 1971, then recovered, but in 1982 was still below its 1970 value. While differences in fee schedule structures make it deceptive to refer to this index as a measure of productivity, it does show that expenditure per physician in Manitoba has moved with the fee schedule, rather that outrunning it as in most other parts of Canada. Prior to 1971, the index was above average in Manitoba.

Quebec and Ontario, in contrast, both show index values about 8 percent above the national level in 1982. This pattern holds for Ontario throughout the period, but in Quebec it reflects very rapid increases in the early 1970s. By 1983, both provinces have almost identical levels of physicians *per capita* and fee-adjusted expenditures per physician. Their populations thus have (Table 10) almost identical service utilization rates, and their differences in *per capita* costs are entirely traceable to the large fee differential that has been growing throughout the 1970s. The increase in Quebec real expenditure per physician has not been rapid enough to compensate for this difference.

In New Brunswick, activity per physician runs a bit above average but the differential fluctuates, and is not nearly as large as the physician-to-population ratio differential. It more or less offsets the slightly below average New Brunswick fees, so that on balance, physician costs *per capita* are also about two-thirds of national levels, corresponding to the lower physician supply.

Prince Edward Island shows substantial shifts in its physician-to-population ratio, which in the 1980s has actually fallen. But as a small community whose population presumably uses the referral services of Nova Scotia, P.E.I. does not bear much independent interpretation. It is interesting that since the advent of Medicare, P.E.I.'s physicians, like New Brunswick's, have maintained above average activity levels; but *per capita* physician costs are well below average, though fees are not, simply because they are fewer.

Nova Scotia and Newfoundland, however, show the dramatic increases in physician supply. The big increases in Nova Scotia, relative to the rest of the country, came in the 1960s and early 1970s; in Newfoundland above average growth continues at least until 1982. The index of activity per physician, however, fell in both provinces in the early 1970s and has fluctuated but increased little since. In both, it lies well below the national average, suggesting the possibility of capacity absorption problems. Fees in Newfoundland are also below average; lower physician costs *per capita* are a result of fewer physicians *per capita*, much less activity per physician, and lower fees. In Nova Scotia, in contrast, fees since 1975 have been above average, and physician numbers have been at or above average. But by 1982, the Nova Scotia activity index was about 20 percent below average. Thus physician costs *per capita* in Nova Scotia appear to be below average because physicians there generate fewer billings. But they are well above costs in Newfoundland, where activity levels per physician are similar, because there are more physicians in Nova Scotia and their fees are higher.

Where the Expenditures Come Out — Average Incomes per Physician

Activity levels per physician, however, are a roundabout way of addressing physician incomes, which are presented directly in Tables 14-17. Table 14 is simply the ratio of physician expenditures *per capita* (Table 6) divided by active civilian physicians *per capita* (Table 12) with provincial values expressed as percentages of the national level. The Canada values are also indexed, to 1971 = 100.0. Table 15 presents average net physician incomes per (taxable) income tax

TABLE 14
INDEXES OF PHYSICIAN EXPENDITURES PER ACTIVE CIVILIAN PHYSICIAN, CANADA AND PROVINCES RELATIVE TO CANADA, 1960-1982 (Canada, 1971=100.0)

YEAR	Canada	B.C.	Alta.	Sask.	Man.	Ont.	Que.	N.B.	N.S.	P.E.I.	Nfld.
1960	45.7	125.9	119.1	113.9	105.8	105.8	75.6	103.7	98.0	88.9	104.3
1965	56.5	104.2	108.8	115.2	100.8	109.6	84.5	96.7	84.7	86.9	75.6
1970	88.1	108.0	116.6	97.1	116.4	113.9	72.9	97.5	96.4	94.0	97.2
1971	100.0	100.3	112.1	95.9	96.5	107.7	89.7	100.4	87.5	122.5	89.6
1975	129.1	113.6	115.9	91.6	83.7	101.5	95.1	100.4	90.1	108.0	69.7
1976	138.2	120.9	114.4	96.4	88.6	101.4	91.9	92.5	89.3	102.3	72.8
1978	158.6	117.9	113.5	94.8	87.1	101.6	94.0	94.4	83.6	102.9	70.8
1980	195.6	116.0	119.3	98.9	86.9	104.0	89.0	96.4	82.2	101.9	71.8
1981	216.4	122.7	122.0	102.5	89.6	106.4	80.4	101.4	84.7	105.7	72.1
1982	245.3	127.8	125.7	108.8	85.5	106.9	76.4	100.2	84.6	110.1	69.5
Average Annual Growth Rates (%)											
1960-65	4.37	0.46	2.46	4.58	3.33	5.06	6.69	2.88	1.34	3.86	-2.17
1965-70	9.28	10.06	10.81	5.61	12.48	10.12	6.09	9.45	12.16	11.02	14.92
1970-75	7.94	9.04	7.80	6.68	1.06	5.48	13.83	8.58	6.49	10.97	0.99
1975-80	8.66	9.11	9.30	10.36	9.47	9.19	7.24	7.78	6.68	7.41	9.30
1980-82	11.99	17.55	14.93	17.42	11.10	13.56	3.77	14.20	13.65	16.38	10.20
1960-82	7.94	8.01	8.20	7.71	6.90	7.99	7.99	7.77	7.22	8.99	5.96
1971-82	8.50	10.92	9.63	9.74	7.31	8.43	6.94	8.49	8.17	7.45	6.03

return, after expenses of practice but before tax, for self-employed practitioners. It thus refers to a smaller group than active civilian physicians, and excludes expenditures on services of physicians other than fee-for-service practitioners. These data, however, are believed by officials at Health and Welfare Canada to have become increasingly biased since 1973, because of changes in patterns of net income reporting for tax purposes. Thus Tables 16 and 17 present alternative estimates of average gross and net incomes, by province, constructed by Health and Welfare Canada (and unfortunately excluding Quebec).

These tables tell quite different stories about the rate of increase of physician incomes in Canada in the Medicare period. Table 15, based on taxation data, indicates an increase in average net incomes of 92.5 percent from 1971 to 1982 or 6.1 percent per year. But the alternative net income estimates prepared by Health and Welfare Canada for the same period indicate an increase of 147.4 percent, or 8.6 percent per year. The estimated gross incomes that correspond to these rise 171.0 percent from 1971 to 1982, rather more rapid than the 145.3 percent increase in expenditures per average civilian physician in Table 14. But the Canada averages in Tables 14 and 15 include Quebec, where expenditures per physician have increased much more slowly since the mid-1970s. If Quebec is excluded, about half the discrepancy between Tables 14 and 16 over the 1971 to 1982 period disappears. The Table 15 net income data from taxation statistics, however, indicate an increase in average net income per physician, 92.5 percent, which is less than the fee increase of 108.3 percent over the 1971 to 1982 period. If accepted at face value, this (in combination with increasing aggregate expenditures per physician) would imply either an extraordinarily rapid increase in expenses of practice, or a rapid increase in the proportion of physician expenditures generated outside the fee-for-service sector.

On any measure, of course, physician incomes in the 1970s ran behind the general level of incomes. The average weekly wage (industrial composite) rose 183.6 percent from 1971 to 1982. But the loss of relative status implied by the taxation data, of over 30 percent from 1971 to 1982, seems clearly too large. The loss suggested by the HWC estimates in Table 17 is probably more accurate, 20 percent from 1971 to 1980 with a recovery thereafter. By 1982 the drop in physician relative incomes indicated by Table 17, relative to 1971, is only 13 percent; and increases in real fees in 1984 and 1985 will bring physicians' incomes up further.

It must also be recalled that from 1946 to 1971 physician net incomes rose 429.1 percent, compared with 323.8 percent for the average weekly wage, for a relative gain of 24.9 percent. In the immediate post-war period, general wages rose rapidly; the physician relative gain from 1951 to 1971 was 44.3 percent. The year 1971 thus represents an historical peak in relative income status for Canadian physicians, from which they fell sharply in the early Medicare years. But it is notable that by 1983 they may be within 10 percent of that status again — and by 1985 they may have reached it.

TABLE 15

INDEXES OF NET INCOME, ALL SOURCES, OF SELF-EMPLOYED TAXABLE CANADIAN PHYSICIANS, CANADA AND PROVINCES RELATIVE TO CANADA, 1946-1982 (Canada, 1971 = $39,555)

YEAR	Canada	B.C.	Alta.	Sask.	Man.	Ont.	Que.	N.B.	N.S.	P.E.I.	Nfld.
1946	18.9	116.4	129.6	113.8	128.6	101.6	77.8	112.2	91.0	64.0	0.0
1951	25.2	112.3	120.2	105.2	136.5	108.3	72.2	71.0	97.2	54.4	76.2
1956	33.0	115.8	92.7	110.3	97.3	107.3	85.2	94.8	88.8	75.2	110.3
1961	43.0	107.0	108.8	107.7	90.0	107.0	88.1	92.8	94.7	80.5	128.2
1966	63.2	90.0	99.7	107.3	96.4	110.0	92.9	94.0	96.4	86.4	92.4
1971	100.0	74.6	101.9	89.5	99.6	106.2	106.4	99.6	91.8	94.0	109.2
1976	124.7	94.3	101.6	96.1	88.6	99.8	105.6	97.3	100.6	87.8	114.5
1977	130.7	92.0	93.0	93.6	89.6	101.4	106.8	97.1	103.5	84.9	99.6
1978	138.2	95.9	92.5	90.4	82.3	102.2	105.2	97.5	98.6	79.6	97.3
1979	147.6	93.0	99.5	91.8	93.8	103.5	102.1	100.2	99.0	80.0	98.0
1980	160.3	90.4	112.0	94.0	89.8	105.4	98.9	98.4	102.8	71.3	97.5
1981	172.9	95.8	104.4	105.7	92.9	104.4	97.1	106.8	105.0	85.6	80.9
1982	192.5	101.2	115.0	82.1	95.1	109.6	87.2	109.4	105.4	87.6	109.2

TABLE 16

INDEXES OF ESTIMATED AVERAGE GROSS PROFESSIONAL INCOMES,
CANADA AND PROVINCES RELATIVE TO CANADA,
1973-1982 (Canada, 1971 = $56,824)

YEAR	Canada	B.C.	Alta.	Sask.	Man.	Ont.	Que.	N.B.	N.S.	P.E.I.	Nfld.
1973	107.3	93.3	104.7	98.0	101.5	102.3	n.a.	94.1	93.2	89.4	98.6
1974	118.8	96.3	102.9	95.5	96.7	102.8	n.a.	90.5	91.1	91.4	92.6
1975	131.6	107.8	105.1	95.4	93.5	98.6	n.a.	89.6	98.9	86.6	92.0
1976	141.8	109.2	108.1	96.7	92.7	97.7	n.a.	88.0	96.5	84.6	94.3
1977	150.8	101.5	108.6	96.4	92.9	100.6	n.a.	90.6	93.8	86.5	84.4
1978	164.0	101.6	108.4	91.5	89.7	101.5	n.a.	88.1	92.5	85.2	87.4
1979	181.4	101.9	107.1	94.9	94.0	101.1	n.a.	89.0	90.4	83.5	88.0
1980	201.3	101.0	111.1	96.3	89.9	100.4	n.a.	88.2	90.2	86.9	93.6
1981	235.8	102.2	111.2	96.3	90.3	100.0	n.a.	91.1	86.6	84.4	88.8
1982	271.0	103.2	118.2	99.4	88.3	98.7	n.a.	92.9	85.7	83.1	85.7

TABLE 17
INDEXES OF ESTIMATED AVERAGE NET PROFESSIONAL INCOMES,
CANADA AND PROVINCES RELATIVE TO CANADA,
1973-1982 (Canada, 1971 = $39,203)

YEAR	Canada	B.C.	Alta.	Sask.	Man.	Ont.	Que.	N.B.	N.S.	P.E.I.	Nfld.
1973	101.3	88.4	102.0	96.0	97.7	103.5	n.a.	105.0	101.0	92.2	104.8
1974	110.5	92.6	99.7	93.8	94.4	103.4	n.a.	100.0	100.0	95.3	100.0
1975	121.7	105.8	99.3	92.4	97.7	99.6	n.a.	97.7	107.3	90.6	99.4
1976	132.1	108.9	105.6	92.3	87.5	97.9	n.a.	93.5	103.7	84.8	103.1
1977	138.5	100.0	105.6	93.4	90.6	101.1	n.a.	97.8	99.9	87.3	90.6
1978	150.0	97.5	104.7	86.5	87.6	102.9	n.a.	93.3	102.0	86.2	93.9
1979	165.5	97.7	103.0	92.0	91.2	102.7	n.a.	94.2	98.8	87.1	96.3
1980	183.9	97.0	108.6	95.3	87.2	101.7	n.a.	92.8	98.7	87.9	100.8
1981	214.3	98.8	109.5	95.2	88.1	101.2	n.a.	96.4	95.2	85.7	96.4
1982	247.4	99.0	115.5	97.9	85.6	100.0	n.a.	97.9	93.8	84.6	92.8

All four tables, however, show a relatively low level of dispersion in incomes across provinces. The HWC estimates of net income per physician (not including Quebec) show in 1982 a range of from 84.6 percent of the national average to 115.5 percent, but this represents a substantial increase over the previous year or indeed over the years back to 1973. (The 1982 data in Table 15 also show a marked increase in dispersion since 1981.) Furthermore, the average net incomes are less dispersed than the gross incomes. The contrast with the dispersion across provinces in physicians *per capita* or services *per capita* is very marked. Fee levels, as shown in Table 8, are by 1983 quite similar except for the B.C. and Alberta outliers on the high side and Quebec and Newfoundland on the low. Yet even these differentials get evened out; B.C.'s fees in 1982 were 34.4 percent above average but estimated gross incomes were only 3.2 percent up, and nets were one percent below. Average output per B.C. self-employed physician appears to be only about three-quarters of the national average. On the other hand, expenditures per active civilian physician in B.C. in 1982 were 27.8 percent above average, suggesting either that a substantial proportion of activity does not flow through the self-employed physician sector, or that the tax data may be downward-biased by the inclusion of larger numbers of semi-retired part-timers. In Alberta, by contrast, a 25.6 percent fee advantage in 1982 translated into a 22.0 difference in expenditures per active civilian physician, an 18.2 percent gross income differential, and a 15.5 percent net income differential. In Alberta, higher fees translate into higher incomes, not lower activity levels. B.C. physicians rank even lower in net incomes based on tax data (even though these include Quebec), suggesting that biases in these data may be quite severe in B.C. Only P.E.I. shows a discrepancy of similar magnitude.

Taxation data, however, are more reliable for the earlier years (and insurance data, of course, do not exist). Table 15 suggests that the inter-provincial dispersion in physician incomes was not always low. But the equalization of incomes predates Medicare, and seems to have taken place primarily in the 1950s. Medicare preserved this relative equality, but did not create it. The fee increases of the 1980s appear to have recreated a substantial degree of dispersion, but this may be a temporary phenomenon. The high degree of visibility given the provincial fee bargaining in the Medicare system, and the much lower degree of attention given to actual service use, may explain why the data above indicate that Medicare has served to maintain far more inter-regional equality in physician incomes than in population utilization of physicians' services. Convergence of expenditure data cannot be assumed to imply equalization of medical care use.

Comparisons of Canada and U.S. Physicians' Costs, Fees and Utilization

Before we began the detailed analysis of expenditures on physicians' services by province, we compared Canadian and U.S. health expenditures, total and by components, before and after 1971. It was apparent that the significant divergence in costs in the two countries has emerged and grown only since 1971, and is a result only of differing trends in hospital and medical care costs. We now return to the Canada-U.S. comparison during the post-Medicare decade, focusing on physicians' services only and attempting to isolate the critical factor or factors explaining the growing difference between the two countries.

Table 18 displays selected information on physicians' costs, fees, and expenditures in Canada and the U.S. over the 1972 to 1982 decade. It demonstrates some remarkable similarities, and enables us to isolate the key factor explaining the different performances in the two countries.

First, it is notable that physician costs *per capita* rose 1.5. percent per year faster in the U.S. for an entire decade, to gain 16.2 percent over the whole period. But physician numbers rose in parallel, implying that the difference was almost all in expenditures per physician. This, in turn, is a result of differences in fee trends: in Canada the index of physicians' fees ran behind the CPI by an average of 2.0 percent per year, while in the U.S. it ran 1.4 percent ahead. U.S. physicians' fees (adjusted for general inflation rates) outran Canadian by 3.3 percent *per year* for *ten years*! Inflation was more rapid in Canada than in the U.S. over this period, but the critical difference is the relative performance of physicians' fees.

Differences in real output per physician, however, are surprisingly small (and in any case somewhat suspect because of the possible effects of changes in fee schedule structures and billing behaviour). Canadian physicians may have reacted to tighter fee controls by increasing output more rapidly but not by enough to compensate for the decline in (real valued) fees. U.S. physicians' outputs, adjusted for the increase in fees, changed very little over the period. Also remarkable is the fact that annual average increases in service utilization *per capita* — costs adjusted for increases in physicians' fees — were so similar in both countries, despite the differences in funding systems. (The levels of utilization, however, cannot be compared in the absence of an inter-country index of relative fees.)

Data on physicians' net and gross incomes, and practice expenses, refer only to self-employed physicians in fee-for-service practice and thus represent a subset of the costs and practitioners covered by the aggregate data. In the U.S. they are based on self-reported questionnaires, and in Canada on tax records or Health and Welfare Canada estimates. These data show a substantial difference in practice overheads, but no difference at all in the growth of overheads over the decade, after adjusting for general inflation. The much-discussed effects of U.S. malpractice insurance may explain some of the difference in levels, but not the trends.

In fact, the net and gross income per physician data also show little difference between Canada and the U.S., because of a very large implicit difference in patterns of output per physician. The U.S. data show a significant *drop* in output per physician, of nearly one percentage point per year over the decade, while the Canadian data show a very large annual increase. But these sharply divergent trends, while consistent with an interpretation of physician behaviour that would have real output levels moving in opposite directions from real (inflation-adjusted) fee trends, are not reflected in the aggregate data based on total expenditures and all physicians. Nor is there supporting evidence from data on physician hours of work or other practice inputs. The discrepancies suggest either some problems in the compilation of the gross income estimates, or a shift in the extent to which self-employed and reporting physicians are representative of the profession as a whole.

Capacity, "Prices", and Utilization in the Hospital Sector: 1946-1983

The statistical and definitional bases for this section are primarily historical series reported or provided by Statistics Canada, for all Public General and Allied Special (PGAS) hospitals. This series is longer than the Health and Welfare Canada "general and allied special" hospitals series, and excludes federal hospitals. It is also more complete, at least in published sources, than Statistics Canada's "Public General" hospitals series, although the latter should at least theoretically represent a more intertemporally homogeneous set of hospitals. We have compiled data for Canada back to 1946 or 1947, and for the provinces variably back to 1947, 1953 or 1962 (some series being more complete than others).

In addition to the advantage of length, the PGAS series represents the lion's share of the hospital sector — 85.6 percent of all operating hospitals, and 96.1 percent of total bed capacity of operating hospitals in the most recent year for which data are available (Canada, Statistics Canada, 1984).

The data published by Statistics Canada on PGAS hospitals are based (and depend) on hospitals' submission of "Annual Returns". These bear some of the warts of any survey or questionnaire — less than 100 percent response rates for particular items — although the data base is remarkably complete, particularly since 1961. Nevertheless, some series are available only for *reporting* hospitals, others for all *operating* hospitals. Wherever possible, we use data for *operating* PGAS hospitals. Where data sources differ for any item and year, the latest source is used. A detailed account of data sources, and adjustments to published data, is provided in the Data Appendix below. More detailed data referenced there are available from the authors.

Capacity

The number of rated/approved beds in PGAS hospitals in Canada almost tripled in the thirty-five years from 1947 to 1982/83, from 58,414 to 152,584

(Table 19). (The figures for the years from 1976 to 1982 are net of mental institution beds in Quebec, which were re-classified in 1976 and after as extended care beds — see Data Appendix.) The number of hospitals increased by just over one-half during the same period, implying almost 70 percent growth in average hospital size (Table 21). About 45 percent of the growth in hospital complement came in the period 1947 to 1951, which saw an *annual average 4.6 percent* increase in the number of PGAS hospitals, plus the addition of Newfoundland to the 1951 figures. The rest of the growth, in the periods before and immediately after introduction of universal hospital insurance, was virtually over by 1966. Since then, however, bed capacity and average hospital size have increased by about one-quarter. The rapid growth in the number of hospitals from 1947 to 1951 was accompanied by a less rapid but still substantial run-up in bed capacity. The following fifteen years to 1966 saw much slower growth in numbers of hospitals (about 1.3 percent per year), but sustained increases in bed capacity (about 4 percent growth per year). Even after net addition of new hospitals virtually ceased (1966 onward), eleven further years of significant capacity increase followed, although the first five of these (1966 to 1971) saw more rapid growth than the last six. It is not until 1978/79, in fact, that we see a stabilization of bed capacity.

As usual, this national picture glosses over considerable provincial variation. Growth in the number of PGAS hospitals in Quebec was far more rapid than in any other province from 1951 to 1982/83. In fact, Quebec accounts for almost 35 percent of the growth in PGAS hospital complement over the period. Alberta, and to a lesser extent B.C. and P.E.I., also significantly exceeded the national growth in hospitals. At the other end of the spectrum, the number of PGAS hospitals in the Northwest Territories and Yukon and in Saskatchewan fell over this period, and there was no net growth in either Nova Scotia or New Brunswick.

The provinces differ not only in their long-term growth rates, but in the shorter period patterns as well. B.C. followed the national pattern, albeit with higher growth rates in each period, from 1951 through 1971. During the 1970s, however, B.C. kept growing while national growth was flat. The Alberta story is all 1961 to 1966, a period during which new hospitals appeared at an annual rate of 2.8 times faster than the national average of 1.47 percent! The Saskatchewan hospital stock declined relatively steadily over the entire period, while 1970s and 1980s drops in New Brunswick and P.E.I. approximately counterbalanced their 1950s growth. The only other figures of note are those for Quebec, which show well above national average growth right up until 1981/82, but particularly over the period 1961 to 1971 (perhaps again reflecting late entry into the national hospital program).

The bed expansion sweepstakes (Table 20) goes hands down to Alberta, where bed capacity tripled in the period 1951 to 1982/83. Average hospital size doubled over the same period (Table 21). Alberta's growth rates exceeded the national

TABLE 18

PHYSICIAN SUPPLY, FEES, AVERAGE INCOMES, AND OUTPUTS,
AND PER CAPITA EXPENDITURES ON AND UTILIZATION OF PHYSICIANS' SERVICES,
CURRENT AND CONSTANT DOLLARS,
CANADA AND U.S., 1972 and 1982

	U.S. 1972	U.S. 1982	Avg. Annual % Change	Canada 1972	Canada 1982	Avg. Annual % Change	Can./U.S. % diff.
Per Capita Expenditures for Physicians' Services (Current Dollars):	80	262	12.6	63.52	179.02	10.9	-1.5
Population per Physician:	637	506	-2.3	636	523	-1.9	0.3
Expenditures per Physician:	50,960	132,572	10.0	40,399	93,627	8.8	-1.1
Index of Physicians' Fees:	103.0	251.8	9.4	101.4	208.3	7.5	-1.7
Per Capita Utilization of Physicians' Services (Adjusted for Fee Change):	77.67	104.05	3.0	62.64	85.94	3.2	0.2
Real Service Output per Physician (A):	49,476	52,650	0.6	39,841	44,948	1.2	0.6
Consumer Price Index:	103.3	220.2	7.9	104.8	262.5	9.6	1.6
Real Value Index of Physicians' Fees:	99.7	114.3	1.4	96.8	79.4	-2.0	-3.3
Expenses of Practice per Physician (Current Dollars):	31,318	78,400	9.6	19,347	57,000	11.4	1.6
Expenses of Practice per Physician (Constant Dollars):	30,318	35,598	1.6	18,461	21,714	1.6	.0
Net Income/Physician (Current Dollars):	47,240	99,500	7.7	39,977	97,000	9.3	1.4
Net Income/Physician (Constant Dollars):	45,731	45,179	-0.1	38,146	36,952	-0.3	-0.2
Gross Income/Physician (Current Dollars):	78,558	177,900	8.5	59,324	154,000	10.0	1.4
Gross Income/Physician (Constant Dollars):	76,048	80,777	0.6	56,607	58,667	0.4	-0.2
Real Service Output per Physician (B):	76,270	70,651	-0.8	58,505	73,932	2.4	3.2

notes: Real Service Output (A) is calculated by multiplying together rows one and two. Population per Physician and Per Capita Expenditures on Physicians' Services to yield current dollar expenditures per physician (row 3), and then dividing by the index of physicians' fees (row 4). It thus includes all expenditures and all physicians, regardless of form of practice organization or physician employment. Real Service Output (B) is based on estimates of average gross receipts from professional practice deflated for fee change, and thus refers only to physicians in self-employed practice. Constant dollar measures of Real Service Output and of Utilization Per Capita are derived by deflating the corresponding current dollar measures by the Index of Physicians' Fees; constant dollar measures of gross and net incomes and practice expenses are derived using the price index for consumer expenditures. All values are in currency of the country reported, unadjusted for exchange rate differences. Such adjustments would lower Canadian cost increases, relative to the U.S. over this period.

TABLE 19

NUMBER OF HOSPITALS[1] AND BED CAPACITY,[2]
CANADA AND PROVINCES,
1947-1982/83

	47	51	56	61	66	71	76	77/78	78/79	79/80	80/81	81/82	82/83
Hospitals													
Canada	666	830	909	938	1,009	1,028	1,028	1,035	1,038	1,036	1,034	1,030	1,028
N.W.T. & Yukon	10	10	12	6	10	7	3	3	3	3	3	3	4
Nfld.	n.a.	34	44	41	47	47	47	47	47	47	47	45	44
P.E.I.	6	6	8	9	9	9	10	10	10	10	10	9	8
N.S.	39	47	46	47	47	47	46	47	48	48	48	48	47
N.B.	31	34	34	39	39	39	35	35	35	33	33	34	34
Que.	95	112	127	138	152	171	175	178	180	182	181	181	181
Ont.	166	178	201	211	221	227	234	233	232	230	229	229	226
Man.	41	66	80	78	82	85	80	80	80	80	80	80	84
Sask.	94	155	152	154	151	140	136	136	138	138	138	135	133
Alta.	102	101	106	116	142	145	146	146	146	145	147	147	148
B.C.	82	87	99	99	109	111	116	120	119	120	118	119	119

	47	51	56	61	66	71	76	77/78	78/79	79/80	80/81	81/82	82/83
Beds													
Canada	58,414	69,333	86,433	100,506	122,315	138,280	145,208	148,240	149,988	149,343	151,424	152,393	152,584
N.W.T. & Yukon	374	420	664	139	270	197	162	162	162	147	147	147	182
Nfld.	n.a.	1,719	1,868	1,730	3,089	2,997	3,183	3,195	3,251	3,304	3,311	3,255	3,242
P.E.I.	366	619	658	715	720	751	769	763	753	741	757	727	725
N.S.	2,838	3,317	3,542	3,641	4,366	4,814	4,978	5,114	5,512	5,420	5,395	5,418	5,348
N.B.	2,193	2,089	2,374	3,107	3,645	4,303	4,200	4,250	4,293	4,307	4,249	4,328	4,289
Que.	15,936	18,945	22,119	26,417	31,913	36,588	37,717	38,375	40,088	39,725	40,060	40,427	41,268
Ont.	17,077	19,461	28,679	34,505	42,857	48,108	48,405	49,216	48,798	48,244	47,846	48,545	48,757
Man.	3,828	4,884	5,020	5,497	5,947	6,322	6,414	6,336	6,282	6,261	6,606	6,429	6,489
Sask.	4,454	5,749	5,852	6,855	7,222	7,244	7,946	7,952	7,858	7,870	7,901	7,470	7,032
Alta.	5,355	5,627	7,575	8,776	11,784	14,048	14,269	14,674	14,677	15,006	16,150	16,491	16,747
B.C.	5,993	6,503	8,082	9,124	10,502	12,908	17,165	18,203	18,314	18,318	19,002	19,156	18,505

[1] Operating Public General & Allied Special Hospitals
[2] Rated Bed Capacity until 1975; Approved Bed Complement from 1976-1982/83.

TABLE 20
AVERAGE ANNUAL GROWTH RATES,
NUMBER OF HOSPITALS[1] AND BED CAPACITY,[2]
CANADA AND PROVINCES,
1947-1982/83

	Canada	N.W.T. & Yukon	Nfld.	P.E.I.	N.S.	N.B.	Que.	Ont.	Man.	Sask.	Alta.	B.C.
Number of Hospitals												
1947-51	4.56[3]	0	n.a.	0	4.77	2.34	4.20	1.76	12.64	13.32	-0.25	1.49
1951-61	1.32	-4.98	1.89	4.14	0	1.38	2.69	1.72	1.68	-0.06	1.39	1.30
1961-66	1.66	10.76	2.77	0	0	0	3.09	0.93	1.01	-0.39	4.13	1.94
1966-71	0.31	-6.89	0	0	0	0	1.82	0.54	0.72	-1.50	0.42	0.36
1971-76	0	-15.59	0	2.13	-0.43	-2.14	0.43	0.61	-1.21	-0.58	0.14	0.89
1976-81/82	0.04	0	-0.87	-2.09	0.85	-0.58	0.62	-0.43	0	-0.15	0.14	0.51
1981/82-82/83	-0.19	33.33	-2.22	-11.11	-2.08	0	0	-1.31	5.00	-1.48	0.68	0
1951-82/83	0.74	-2.91	0.84	0.93	0	0	1.82	0.77	0.78	-0.49	1.24	1.02
Bed Capacity												
1947-51	3.72[3]	2.94	n.a.	14.04	3.98	-1.21	4.42	3.32	6.28	6.59	1.25	2.06
1951-61	3.78	-10.47	0.06	1.45	0.94	4.05	3.38	5.89	1.19	1.78	4.54	3.44
1961-66	4.01	14.20	12.29	0.14	3.70	3.25	3.85	4.43	1.59	1.05	6.07	2.85
1966-71	2.48	-6.11	-0.60	0.85	1.97	3.37	2.77	2.34	1.23	0.06	3.58	4.21
1971-76	0.98	-3.84	1.21	0.47	0.67	-0.48	0.61	0.12	0.29	1.87	0.31	5.87
1976-81/82	0.97	-1.92	0.45	-1.12	1.71	0.60	1.40	0.06	0.05	-1.23	2.94	2.22
1981/82-82/83	0.13	23.81	-0.40	-0.28	-1.29	-0.90	2.08	0.44	0.93	-5.86	1.55	-3.40
1951-82/83	2.58	-2.66	2.07	0.51	1.55	2.35	2.54	3.01	0.92	0.65	3.58	3.43

[1] Operating Public General & Allied Special Hospitals
[2] Rated Bed Capacity until 1975; Approved Bed Complement from 1976-1982/83.
[3] Rate of growth excluding Newfoundland.

TABLE 21
AVERAGE HOSPITAL SIZE, AND BEDS PER 1,000 POPULATION, CANADA AND PROVINCES RELATIVE TO CANADA, 1947-1982/83

Beds/Hospital	1947	1951	1956	1961	1966	1971	1976	1977/78	1978/79	1979/80	1980/81	1981/82	1982/83
Canada	87.7	83.5	95.1	106.2	119.1	132.6	139.2	141.2	142.4	142.1	144.4	145.8	146.3
N.W.T. & Yukon	42.6	50.3	58.1	21.8	22.7	21.2	38.8	38.2	37.9	34.5	33.9	33.6	31.1
Nfld.	n.a.	60.6	44.7	39.7	55.2	48.1	48.6	48.2	48.6	49.5	48.8	49.6	50.4
P.E.I.	69.6	123.6	86.4	74.8	67.2	62.9	55.2	54.0	52.9	52.1	52.4	55.4	61.9
N.S.	83.0	84.6	81.0	73.0	78.0	77.2	77.7	77.1	80.6	79.5	77.8	77.4	77.8
N.B.	80.6	73.5	73.4	75.0	78.5	83.2	86.2	86.0	86.2	91.8	89.2	87.3	86.2
Que.	191.2	202.6	183.2	170.3	157.6	148.3	142.6	140.8	144.4	141.9	141.6	141.5	144.0
Ont.	117.3	130.9	150.1	154.0	162.8	159.8	148.6	149.6	147.7	147.6	144.7	145.4	147.4
Man.	106.5	88.6	65.9	66.4	60.9	56.1	57.6	56.1	55.1	55.1	57.2	55.1	52.8
Sask.	54.0	44.4	40.5	41.9	40.1	39.0	42.0	41.4	40.0	40.1	39.7	37.9	36.2
Alta.	59.9	66.7	75.2	71.3	69.7	73.1	70.2	71.2	70.6	72.8	76.1	77.0	77.4
B.C.	83.4	89.5	85.8	86.8	80.9	87.7	106.3	107.4	108.1	107.4	111.5	110.4	106.3
Beds/1,000 Population													
Canada	4.65	4.95	5.37	5.51	6.11	6.40	6.31	6.35	6.36	6.26	6.27	6.23	6.17
N.W.T. & Yukon	335.1	339.4	398.9	66.4	102.8	58.1	39.8	38.9	38.4	35.0	34.6	33.7	41.2
Nfld.	n.a.	96.2	83.8	68.6	102.6	89.5	90.3	89.8	90.9	93.3	93.1	92.0	91.7
P.E.I.	83.7	127.7	123.8	123.6	108.2	104.8	103.0	100.0	97.5	96.8	98.6	95.0	95.3
N.S.	99.1	104.2	95.0	89.7	94.6	95.2	95.1	96.5	103.3	102.7	101.6	102.4	101.3
N.B.	96.6	81.8	79.7	94.4	96.7	105.9	98.3	97.6	98.0	99.4	97.3	99.8	99.0
Que.	92.5	94.3	89.0	91.1	90.3	94.8	95.7	96.1	100.0	100.0	99.8	100.6	102.9
Ont.	88.0	85.5	98.9	100.4	100.8	97.3	92.7	92.4	90.7	90.4	88.8	90.2	90.3
Man.	111.4	127.1	110.1	108.2	101.1	99.8	99.5	97.0	95.9	97.6	102.9	100.5	101.3
Sask.	114.6	139.6	123.6	134.5	123.7	122.0	136.5	133.4	130.7	131.8	130.9	123.4	115.9
Alta.	139.6	121.0	125.7	119.6	131.8	134.7	122.7	119.2	114.9	115.2	118.2	116.4	116.4
B.C.	123.4	112.7	107.6	101.6	91.7	92.2	110.1	114.0	112.6	112.0	112.4	111.2	107.1

average by 50 percent during the period of fastest national growth (1961 to 1966). Also doubling average hospital size from 1951 to 1982/83 was British Columbia and, combined with above national average growth in hospital complement, these two western provinces exhibit the most dramatic expansion in bed stock over the period as a whole. New Brunswick and Ontario also approximately doubled their average hospital size. In the former, this represented the only source of sector growth, whereas about average concurrent growth in number of hospitals pushed Ontario well above the national average growth in bed supply. Quebec's rapid development of new institutions was accompanied by much slower increases in average hospital size (about 35 percent over the period 1951 to 1982/83), leaving it virtually at the national average in terms of growth in bed stock. Prince Edward Island was the only province in which average hospital size actually fell, but the numbers are small. Most of its bed capacity increase came in the 1947 to 1951 period. Saskatchewan compensated for a relatively continuous reduction in hospital complement with an expansion in average size, at least up to 1977/78. But the sharp drop in bed capacity in the last two years has served to return Saskatchewan's bed stock to early 1960s levels. Early growth in Manitoba gave way to much slower than national growth rates through the 1950s, 1960s and 1970s. Even with a 60 percent increase in average hospital size, Nova Scotia has also lagged well behind the national average in bed capacity growth. Finally, growth in Newfoundland's bed stock was confined almost exclusively to the period 1961 to 1966.

In the second part of Table 21, and in Table 22, bed stock is examined relative to population growth. For Canada overall, bed growth exceeded that of the population until the early 1970s, the excess being particularly pronounced during the "bed boom" from 1961 to 1966. While the population growth rate fell steadily over the entire period, bed stock growth has declined since the mid-1960s. This has created a pattern of first increasing and then sharply falling beds *per capita*. Downsizing of the hospital sector (at least relative to population growth) began in in earnest in the early 1970s; and this has been a fairly uniform trend, with the notable exceptions of B.C. and Saskatchewan, where beds *per capita* declined in the second half of the decade. In Alberta, continued rapid bed expansion has simply not kept up with the influx of population. In contrast, beds *per capita* in Quebec fell over the 1971 to 1976 period but have resisted the national trend since then with dramatic growth in bed supply for a slow-growing population. B.C. displays a particularly interesting growth trend, with bed expansion just keeping pace with population growth during the high growth (virtually everywhere else) period of 1951 to 1966. Then more recently it has been one of the slower provinces to join the downsizing movement. While Alberta, Ontario, New Brunswick and P.E.I. were leading the way during the first half of the 1970s, B.C. was building beds at an *annual* rate of 3.3 percent over and above population growth! B.C. continued to lag behind the lead of Ontario, Alberta, P.E.I. and now Saskatchewan in the 1976 to 1982 restricted growth period. It is

TABLE 22
AVERAGE ANNUAL GROWTH RATES, POPULATION[1] AND BEDS PER 1,000 POPULATION CANADA AND PROVINCES, 1947-1982/83

Population	Canada	N.W.T. & Yukon	Nfld.	P.E.I.	N.S.	N.B.	Que.	Ont.	Man.	Sask.	Alta.	B.C.
1947-51	2.79	1.03	1.73	1.05	1.12	1.40	2.25	2.44	1.23	-0.12	3.29	2.78
1951-61	2.67	4.28	2.41	0.69	1.37	1.49	2.63	3.09	1.74	1.07	3.56	3.41
1961-66	1.88	2.50	1.48	0.75	0.51	0.63	1.91	2.22	0.87	0.64	1.89	2.84
1966-71	1.53	4.27	1.19	0.54	0.88	0.58	0.85	2.08	0.53	-0.59	2.17	3.15
1971-76	1.28	4.04	1.31	1.10	0.97	1.32	0.68	1.40	0.65	-0.10	2.51	2.45
1976-81/82	1.21	1.62	0.36	0.75	0.48	0.54	0.67	0.88	0.12	1.05	4.30	2.28
1981/82-82/83	1.16	2.43	0.83	0.33	0.71	0.78	0.66	1.22	0.97	1.17	2.51	1.37
1951-82/83	1.85	3.46	1.50	0.74	0.92	1.00	1.53	2.10	0.94	0.54	2.98	2.87
Beds/1,000 Population												
1947-51	1.57[2]	1.90	n.a.	12.90	2.86	-2.55	2.09	0.84	4.97	6.71	-1.98	-0.70
1951-61	1.08	-14.13	-2.28	0.75	-0.43	2.53	0.73	2.72	-0.54	0.70	0.96	0.04
1961-66	2.09	11.40	10.65	-0.59	3.19	2.59	1.92	2.18	0.73	0.40	4.08	0
1966-71	0.93	-9.94	-1.79	0.30	1.05	2.78	1.92	0.23	0.67	0.65	1.38	1.05
1971-76	-0.28	-7.57	-0.10	-0.63	-0.30	-1.77	-0.10	-1.25	-0.35	1.97	-2.13	3.33
1976-81/82	-0.25	-3.50	0.11	-1.85	1.24	0.06	0.75	-0.80	-0.06	-2.23	-1.30	-0.06
1981/82-82/83	-0.96	20.95	-1.22	-0.68	-2.04	-1.77	1.28	-0.89	-0.16	-7.02	-0.97	-4.62
1951-82/83	0.71	-5.91	0.56	-0.23	0.62	1.34	1.00	0.89	-0.02	0.11	0.59	0.55

[1] As of June 1 from 1947 to 1969, July 1 from 1970.
[2] Rate of growth excluding Newfoundland.

only in the final year of the entire period (1982/83) that the province seems to have decided to get serious about bed stock reductions.

The bottom half of Table 21 contains beds *per capita* data for Canada, and then provincial "relatives" for each year. These data suggest considerable convergence toward the national average over the period. The four western provinces, and particularly Alberta, were "bed-rich" in 1947 and by 1951 had been joined by Prince Edward Island, which went from lowest to second highest (an increase of over 50 percent!) in the space of four years. B.C. and Manitoba fell off toward average through to 1966, by which time only Saskatchewan and Alberta stood out more than 10 percent on either side of the average. So both the pre- and post-universal hospital insurance periods saw narrowing inter-provincial bed availability differences. But the convergence did not stop there. Over the next five years, Newfoundland's relative position eroded somewhat. During the 1971 to 1976 period, B.C. and Saskatchewan were the only provinces in which bed capacity *per capita* was growing, and in B.C. in particular the growth was significant — more that 3 percent *per annum*. The major "losers" were Alberta and New Brunswick. Since 1976 the dominant patterns have been a marked decline toward average for Saskatchewan and a somewhat less marked but similar trend for Alberta; some upward movement in Nova Scotia (this being a result of relatively flat population and a relatively ambitious bed expansion from 1976 to 1981/82) and Quebec; and an erosion of position for P.E.I. The net effect was considerable further narrowing of dispersion from 1976 to 1982/83.

Over the entire period, the striking stories are clearly Alberta (40 percent above to 16 percent above), B.C. (23 percent above to 7 percent above) and, in the other direction, P.E.I. (16 percent below to 5 percent below). Of course, again one must not lose sight of the fact that the entire bed/population distribution was moving up over the period to 1971 and then gradually falling, even while becoming more concentrated. But the period since 1976 has been one of significant convergence largely through reductions in bed stock *per capita*.

In Table 23 bed capacity is viewed not from the perspective of *per capita* treatment capacity, but rather as available input to physicians' practices. The much shorter physician stock (by province) series curtails the historical period; nevertheless, some interesting trends emerge.

Most obvious (and reflected in the data for all provinces), is the rapid expansion in physician supply relative to bed capacity: physician stock in Canada grew an average 1.95 percent per year faster than PGAS bed stock over the twenty-two years from 1960 to 1982/83, and 2.31 percent per year faster over the shorter period from 1965 to 1982/83. Equally remarkable is the monotonicity in this trend, although that does not carry over to all the provinces.

While the overall trend has been expansion in physician supply relative to bed supply, there has also been considerable convergence among the provinces toward the national average ratio of PGAS beds per active civilian physician. The

TABLE 23
HOSPITAL BED/PHYSICIAN RATIOS,
CANADA AND PROVINCES RELATIVE TO CANADA,
1960-1982/83

Beds/Physicians	1960	1965	1971	1976	1978/79	1980/81	1981/82	1982/83
Canada	4.94	4.76	4.22	3.64	3.56	3.43	3.35	3.23
Nfld.	176.9	178.6	149.5	112.6	113.2	111.7	109.6	106.5
P.E.I.	158.1	153.6	182.0	152.2	144.1	145.2	140.3	145.8
N.S.	100.2	108.0	105.9	97.8	100.8	99.1	101.2	101.5
N.B.	142.3	145.0	168.2	150.3	153.9	157.7	159.1	151.7
Que.	105.1	92.2	91.9	92.6	97.2	96.2	95.5	97.8
Ont.	84.4	92.2	91.7	87.6	85.7	84.0	85.4	86.1
Man.	96.4	98.3	97.6	100.0	95.8	102.3	100.6	98.5
Sask.	150.8	141.8	150.5	167.3	157.6	160.1	151.9	142.7
Alta.	130.4	149.2	141.0	137.6	131.7	139.9	138.8	136.5
B.C.	83.4	77.7	85.8	106.3	107.0	106.1	106.3	102.2

Annual Average Rates of Growth in Bed/Physician Ratios

	Canada	Nfld.	P.E.I.	N.S.	N.B.	Que.	Ont.	Man.	Sask.	Alta.	B.C.
1960-65	-0.74	-0.56	-1.31	0.76	-0.37	-3.29	1.03	-0.34	-1.95	1.97	-2.13
1965-71	-1.99	-4.84	0.83	-2.30	0.48	-2.04	-2.08	-2.10	-1.01	-2.90	-0.36
1971-76	-2.91	-8.26	-6.32	-4.45	-5.08	-2.78	-3.79	-2.45	-0.83	-3.38	1.34
1976-81/82	-1.65	-2.19	-3.24	-0.97	-0.52	-1.03	-2.16	-1.53	-3.52	-1.48	-1.66
1981/82-82/83	-3.58	-6.27	0.21	-3.54	-8.44	-1.25	-3.15	-5.93	-10.02	-5.59	-7.87
1960-82/83	-1.91	-4.15	-2.27	-1.87	-1.65	-2.23	-1.84	-1.83	-2.19	-1.73	-1.03

"provincial relatives" for this ratio in Table 23 show Newfoundland, in 1960, 77 percent higher than average, and Ontario and B.C. with the lowest relative bed to physician ratios. Prince Edward Island, New Brunswick, Saskatchewan and Alberta were all at least 30 percent above average. From 1965 on, Newfoundland experienced continuous and substantial shrinkage in the ratio of bed stock to physician supply, far in excess of national trends for each sub-period (bottom of Table 23), so that by 1982/83 it is within 7 percent of average. In contrast, three of the other initial high-side provinces, P.E.I., New Brunswick and Saskatchewan, show almost no movement toward centre over the period, and remain the three provinces with the greatest abundance of beds per physician as of 1982/83. B.C., with the fastest expansion in bed stock since 1966, passed the national average bed to physician ratio during its remarkable bed growth from 1971 to 1976. Far below average growth in that ratio saw it slip back to just above average in 1982/83. The rapid expansion in bed stock and a recent slowing in the growth of physician numbers has kept Alberta well above average. Saskatchewan also remained above average, but for a different reason. Hospital bed supply has actually fallen since 1966, but growth in physician supply has been far below the national average. Manitoba has remained relatively stable. Ontario began the period with a below national average bed to physician ratio. Below average growth in bed capacity since 1966 (both in absolute terms — Table 20 — and relative to population — Table 22) has led to its spot as the province with the lowest such ratio in 1982/83. In contrast, Quebec was slightly above the national average in 1960, but rapid growth in physician supply dropped its bed to physician ratio to about 8 percent below average by 1965. That approximate position held until 1976; since then, Quebec has moved back to very near average. Finally, Nova Scotia shows some fluctuation but in 1982/83 was in virtually the same relative position as in 1960. These various trends are reflected as well in the bottom half of Table 23, where we show annual rates of change in the bed to physician ratio.

No province shows growth in bed stock relative to physician supply for more than one sub-period, and Manitoba, Saskatchewan, Quebec and Newfoundland join Canada overall with monotonically declining bed to physician ratios (at least based on five- and six-year periods). The rate of decline clearly picked up in the last year, as the western provinces in particular became more serious about restraint. Having little control over physician supply (which partially reflects politically irreversible decisions on medical schools from years past), provinces have tended in the short run to focus on the institutional sector.

Utilization

While we were able to rely on capacity data for all operating PGAS hospitals, utilization data in certain years have appeared for reporting hospitals only. For consistency, we applied the province-specific (or Canadian for Canada) operating/reporting bed capacity ratios to scale up patient days or separations (see Data Appendix below). This adjustment carries with it an implicit assumption that occupancy rates in non-reporting hospitals were the same as those in reporting hospitals. The figures in Tables 24 and 25 are based on complete data on operating hospitals for 1954 to 1975, and on estimated data for operating hospitals for 1947 to 1952 and 1976 to 1982/83. Particularly in the later years, the adjustments are minor as most operating hospitals reported utilization data. While utilization data were available for reporting hospitals in 1946, we were unable to find data on bed capacity of *operating* hospitals for that year. Thus, the estimation adjustment could not be implemented for 1946 and these tables begin in 1947. In addition, the bed re-classification in Quebec between 1975 and 1976 necessitated an adjustment similar to that for bed stock. (Details may be found in the Data Appendix.)

From Table 21 we saw that beds *per capita* increased about 33 percent over the thirty-five-year period, or at an annual rate of 0.8 percent. Patient days *per capita* increased substantially faster — 47 percent, or 1.1 percent *per annum*. That is, patient days increased an average 1.1 percent *per annum* faster than population, for thirty-five years!

The period 1947 to 1951 was one of extremely rapid growth, 3.6 percent *per capita* annual increase in patient days. In 1947 Prince Edward Island was about 16 percent below the national average rate of 1,241 days per 1,000 population, as the least hospitalized provincial population (Table 24). At the other end were the three western provinces, B.C., Alberta and Saskatchewan, the latter being 42 percent above average. In the following four years, P.E.I.'s growth in beds *per capita* of 12.9 percent *per annum* was associated with a 7.5 percent *per annum* increase in days *per capita* (Table 25)! This was more that 75 percent faster than the national growth rate. Little wonder then that by 1951 P.E.I. was only 5 percent below the national average of days *per capita*. Among the above average provinces in 1947, patient days *per capita* in Alberta and B.C. actually fell by 0.7 percent and 0.4 percent per year respectively leaving them only 11 percent above average in 1951 (down from 33 percent to 35 percent in 1947). Saskatchewan experienced utilization growth second only to P.E.I. in moving from 42 percent above average to 54 percent above in 1951. Ontario experienced the largest drop in utilization, and fell to 14 percent below average.

The period 1951 to 1961 was one of continued but smaller increases in utilization. Over the period, patient days *per capita* increased at an annual rate of about 1.1 percent. Utilization in Nova Scotia and New Brunswick fell somewhat, and then recovered at rates of 3.1 percent and 5.3 percent *per annum* respectively from 1956 to 1961. Alberta inched upward, Ontario led the country in growth to recover to average, and Quebec hit its lowest relative position in 1961. Saskatchewan's utilization growth slowed to a crawl, but its population continued to receive significantly more hospital care than those of other provinces, and B.C.'s growth continued well below average, leaving its utilization rate very

TABLE 24

HOSPITAL UTILIZATION PER 1,000 POPULATION,[1] CANADA AND PROVINCES RELATIVE TO CANADA, 1947-1982/83

Patient Days	1947	1951	1956	1961	1966	1971	1976	1977/78	1978/79	1979/80	1980/81	1981/82	1982/83
Canada	1,240.7	1,464.6	1,578.1	1,639.5	1,793.9	1,894.3	1,807.5	1,838.3	1,857.3	1,848.7	1,848.8	1,841.7	1,826.5
N.W.T. & Yukon	242.3	306.8	312.4	26.4	52.3	41.4	28.9	29.2	27.7	24.5	30.3	27.2	31.8
Nfld.	n.a.	n.a.	79.8	77.0	82.5	83.5	82.1	76.4	77.0	79.0	78.9	75.1	78.6
P.E.I.	83.7	94.6	95.2	97.5	94.0	95.5	100.5	94.4	92.6	90.6	90.2	89.4	91.1
N.S.	88.7	89.1	77.8	87.1	89.8	92.7	88.2	88.1	92.8	93.6	92.3	91.3	90.0
N.B.	92.9	91.5	81.7	101.9	99.9	102.4	96.7	99.0	98.7	96.6	96.6	99.6	100.2
Que.	88.9	89.1	91.1	85.7	88.1	91.5	93.9	98.3	101.2	100.4	103.7	103.1	104.6
Ont.	105.4	86.4	99.4	104.5	105.2	101.0	96.4	94.8	93.4	93.4	91.1	94.0	94.7
Man.	113.0	113.1	100.6	108.7	103.2	100.1	97.6	96.2	91.0	91.6	92.8	94.2	90.8
Sask.	141.6	153.6	134.4	137.4	126.8	121.3	125.6	123.0	120.5	122.0	123.1	113.4	106.7
Alta.	134.8	110.9	121.5	117.1	120.6	129.9	117.8	109.8	107.2	108.2	106.2	104.3	108.9
B.C.	133.0	111.1	112.4	102.3	96.4	96.0	116.3	118.5	119.2	119.1	119.1	115.4	109.0
Separations													
Canada	110.3	124.2[2]	141.3	145.7	152.0	164.7	158.7	155.5	153.4	149.6	148.2	146.2	145.8
N.W.T. & Yukon	82.5	65.1	112.1	41.6	70.3	56.0	45.0	35.0	34.5	39.2	50.4	44.6	32.1
Nfld.	n.a.	n.a.	64.2	74.5	87.0	95.8	102.6	102.4	107.1	109.8	110.4	107.9	113.0
P.E.I.	93.0	101.9	106.4	105.9	109.6	120.0	135.3	136.8	140.2	142.7	141.6	143.7	136.8
N.S.	98.4	95.5	93.1	98.2	99.2	101.8	101.5	107.0	111.8	114.1	113.4	114.9	113.6
N.B.	100.8	110.9	102.8	115.1	111.5	110.4	107.5	115.8	114.5	112.0	112.5	114.5	115.2
Que.	69.4	70.0	76.6	80.0	84.1	78.6	74.7	80.5	80.0	77.9	81.4	79.6	77.9
Ont.	98.7	86.9	98.8	98.7	96.6	101.2	107.1	101.1	100.6	101.2	98.5	100.9	100.6
Man.	108.2	128.3	103.5	114.1	112.8	111.9	103.6	104.3	103.1	103.0	107.7	110.3	108.7
Sask.	140.9	164.9	145.2	145.5	144.2	141.9	135.9	139.1	141.2	144.7	146.5	142.7	145.3
Alta.	154.2	144.8	159.9	130.0	128.3	131.1	122.3	120.0	119.2	118.6	113.5	111.1	120.3
B.C.	129.8	123.6	115.4	114.5	110.6	105.8	105.2	105.2	106.0	107.5	106.9	106.7	102.6

[1] In Public General & Allied Special Hospitals; Operating 1953-1975; Estimated for Operating for 1976-1982/83 and 1947-1952; Utilization does not include newborns.

[2] Excluding Newfoundland.

TABLE 25
AVERAGE ANNUAL GROWTH RATES, PATIENT DAYS AND SEPARATIONS PER 1,000 POPULATION, CANADA AND PROVINCES, 1947-1982/83

Patient Days	Canada	N.W.T. & Yukon	Nfld.	P.E.I.	N.S.	N.B.	Que.	Ont.	Man.	Sask.	Alta.	B.C.
1947-51	4.23	10.56	n.a.	7.47	4.36	3.83	4.31	-0.81	4.26	6.39	-0.73	-0.36
1951-61	1.13	-20.86	n.a.	1.45	0.90	2.24	0.74	3.07	0.74	0.01	1.68	0.31
1961-66	1.82	16.73	3.23	1.08	2.43	1.41	2.37	1.96	0.76	0.20	2.42	0.63
1966-71	1.10	-3.55	1.35	1.40	1.74	1.60	1.87	0.28	0.49	0.21	2.61	1.01
1971-76	-0.93	-7.79	-1.27	0.09	-1.90	-2.06	-0.42	-1.86	-1.43	-0.24	-2.86	2.93
1976-77/78	1.70	2.89	-5.37	-4.45	1.51	4.12	6.46	0.02	0.22	-0.41	-5.16	3.66
1977/78-78/79	1.03	-4.13	1.91	0.51	6.50	0.66	3.97	-0.45	-4.45	-1.04	-1.40	1.63
1978/79-79/80	-0.46	-12.11	2.15	-2.60	0.39	-2.29	-1.23	-0.47	0.21	0.80	0.46	-0.54
1979/80-80/81	0.01	-23.55	-0.21	-0.47	-1.43	-0.23	-3.31	-2.50	1.32	0.92	-1.87	-0.03
1980/81-81/82	-0.38	-10.55	-5.19	-1.21	-1.46	2.67	-0.99	2.86	1.14	-8.22	-2.11	-3.46
1976-81/82	0.38	-0.85	-1.40	-1.94	1.06	0.96	2.26	-0.12	-0.34	-1.65	-2.03	0.22
1981/82-82/83	-0.83	16.05	3.83	1.02	-2.20	-0.22	0.64	-0.17	-4.39	-6.73	3.51	-6.32
1947-82/83	1.11	-4.59	n.a.	1.36	1.15	1.33	1.58	0.80	0.48	0.30	0.50	0.54

Separations	Canada	N.W.T. & Yukon	Nfld.	P.E.I.	N.S.	N.B.	Que.	Ont.	Man.	Sask.	Alta.	B.C.
1947-51	3.01	-2.89	n.a.	5.41	2.24	5.48	3.23	-0.21	7.50	7.15	1.42	1.78
1951-61	1.61	-2.84	n.a.	1.99	1.89	1.99	2.96	2.91	0.42	0.34	0.51	0.82
1961-66	0.84	11.98	4.02	1.54	1.05	0.20	1.87	0.40	0.60	0.65	0.56	0.15
1966-71	1.62	-2.90	3.58	3.49	2.15	1.41	0.26	2.57	1.46	1.30	2.07	0.73
1971-76	-0.74	-4.97	0.63	1.66	-0.80	-1.27	-1.75	0.40	-2.24	-1.60	-2.12	-0.87
1976-77/78	-2.03	-23.81	-2.20	-0.97	3.23	5.56	5.59	-7.48	-1.42	0.31	-3.82	-1.97
1977/78-78/79	-1.34	-2.82	3.18	1.14	3.14	-2.43	-1.97	-1.84	-2.47	0.12	-2.04	-0.56
1978/79-79/80	-2.48	10.94	-0.04	-0.73	-0.53	-4.62	-5.09	-1.97	-2.54	-0.05	-2.95	-1.12
1979/80-80/81	-0.91	27.21	-0.36	-1.69	-1.49	-0.48	3.52	-3.46	-3.54	-0.33	-5.16	-1.46
1980/81-81/82	-1.36	-12.65	-3.56	0.11	-0.02	0.39	-3.52	0.99	1.08	-3.89	-3.43	-1.55
1976-81/82	-1.63	-1.81	-0.62	-0.43	0.85	-0.37	-0.38	-2.79	-0.39	-0.65	-3.49	-1.33
1981/82-82/83	-0.27	-28.35	4.38	-5.07	-1.43	0.34	-2.33	-0.54	-1.75	1.53	7.94	-4.09
1947-82/83	0.80	-1.89	n.a.	1.92	1.21	1.18	1.13	0.85	0.81	0.89	0.09	0.13

nearly on average in 1961. In 1961, Newfoundland was solidly entrenched as the low utilization province.

During the following five years, *per capita* utilization growth picked up again, particularly in Nova Scotia, Quebec and Newfoundland. Growth continued to be stagnant in Saskatchewan, in contrast to national rates which increased 1.8 percent per year faster than population. From 1966 to 1971, Alberta led the country in *per capita* growth, capping twenty years of steady, well above average growth that left it as the high utilization province. The national trend by this time was continued but slowing growth.

From 1971 to 1976 patient days *per capita* overall for Canada fell almost one percentage point per year. (It is worth noting that if one fails to adjust for the Quebec bed reclassification, patient days *per capita* in that province increase at an astronomical 5.3 percent *per annum*, a rate that leaves Canada with positive growth over the period.)

Leading the way in falling *per capita* utilization was Alberta, which in five years went from the highest rate at 30 percent above average, to the second highest at 18 percent above. In New Brunswick, Nova Scotia, Ontario and Manitoba utilization was also falling at least 50 percent faster than in Canada as a whole. Thus, in retrospect, the early 1970s represented the beginnings of bed capacity restraint being reflected as a slowdown in utilization. After a short pause from 1976 to 1978/79, utilization *per capita* resumed its capacity-driven downward trend. Only in B.C. was the bull not reined in during the 1971 to 1976 period. B.C. experienced 3 percent yearly *per capita growth* while the rest of the country was *falling* at a rate in excess of 1 percent *per annum*. This moved it from 4 percent below average to 16 percent above. In fact, B.C. continued to show well above average growth until 1978/79, by which time it was 19 percent above average, a position it held until 1980/81.

Per capita utilization resumed its upward ways in 1976/77 and 1977/78. Since 1978/79 there has been a more or less sustained decline in patient days *per capita*. The major relative moves of note since 1976 are to be found in P.E.I., Saskatchewan, Alberta and Quebec. The tightening of bed supply since 1980 in Saskatchewan dropped patient days with it, by 8.2 percent and 6.7 percent *per capita* in teh two most recent years. From 23 percent above average in 1980/81, it was only 7 percent above average in 1982/83. In Quebec the story appears to have been alternating years of strong growth and pauses for digestion. The net effect has been a move from 6 percent below average in 1976, to 5 percent above in 1982/83. However, the sharp changes in direction may be nothing more than a message that we attempted to smooth something that was not smooth in our adjustment for the transfer of mental institution days to extended care days. We are fairly confident of our figures for 1975, and 1979/80 on, less so for the intervening years (see Data Appendix below). P.E.I. experienced five consecutive years of *per capita* reductions, the largest coming in 1977/78, and only in 1982/83 did utilization show a return to the upside. The decline that began in the previous half-decade continued in Alberta, and for the second consecutive five-year period it led all provinces in the reduction of utilization *per capita.*

Separations (discharges plus deaths) *per capita* increased more rapidly (or fell more slowly) than patient days during the periods 1951 to 1961 and 1966 to 1976. Since 1976, there has been a steady decline in separations *per capita*, while patient days have fluctuated. This is not reflected precisely in the pattern for average length of stay in Table 26, because one cannot infer ALS directly from Table 24. "Patient days" does not represent the days stay incurred by "separated" patients. However, the steady increase in ALS since 1976 seems a reasonable reflection of the relative decline in separations.

Once again, provinces have followed remarkably different paths. In 1947, P.E.I. had the lowest *per capita* separation rate, some 7 percent below average and above only Quebec. By the end of the period it ranked second at the other end of the scale, behind only Saskatchewan, and 37 percent above average. In light of P.E.I.'s patient day experiences, it is not surprising to find in Table 26 a continuous and relatively rapid drop in ALS since 1961. Newfoundland experienced a similar move; its *per capita* separation rate increased 2.2 percent *per annum* over the period 1956 to 1982/83. Showing somewhat less marked but still noteworthy shifts in relative position were New Brunswick (from even to 15 percent above), Nova Scotia (2 percent below to 14 percent above), Alberta (54 percent above to 20 percent above), B.C. (30 percent above to 3 percent above), and Quebec (30 percent below to 22 percent below). Saskatchewan, which started the period about 40 percent above the national average in patient days and separations *per capita*, has clearly effected its relative utilization reductions through shortened lengths of stay (from about 10.4 days in 1956, to about 9.2 days in 1982/83, while the Canadian average was moving in the other direction). Saskatchewan in 1982/83 had the highest separation rate in the country, 45 percent above average.

P.E.I.'s relative surge occurred in two stages, during 1947 to 1951, and then from 1966 through to about 1979/80. It fell back dramatically in the most recent year, when separations *per capita* fell 5 percent in a year of little national change (these figures, however, being preliminary, may yet change). In contrast, Newfoundland's relative increase has been fairly uniform over the entire period. Nova Scotia's gains have largely been recent (since 1976), while New Brunswick has followed a roller coaster route, with high relative growth for 1947 to 1951, 1956 to 1961, and 1976 to 1977/78 and far below average growth during 1951 to 1956 and 1971 to 1976. Quebec's separation rate ran up dramatically from 1947 through to the post-hospital insurance period, at an annual *per capita* rate averaging 2.7 percent through to 1966. From 1966 to 1976, separations *per capita* fell while the national rate rose slightly. Since 1976, yearly growth has been erratic (far above Canada from 1976 to 1977/78 and from 1979/80 to

TABLE 26
AVERAGE LENGTH OF HOSPITAL STAYS,
CANADA AND PROVINCES RELATIVE TO CANADA,
1946-1982/83

	1946	1951	1956	1961	1966	1971	1976	1977/78	1978/79	1979/80	1980/81	1981/82	1982/83
Canada	11.1	10.5	11.0	11.1	11.7	11.3	11.0	11.4	11.4	11.4	11.9	12.2	12.3
N.W.T. & Yukon	n.a.	n.a.	449.1	62.2	73.5	76.1	n.a.	65.8	57.1	56.0	68.2	59.8	85.4
Nfld.	n.a.	n.a.	132.7	134.2	94.9	88.5	79.7	76.4	72.9	57.8	73.2	72.1	74.0
P.E.I.	n.a.	n.a.	86.4	93.7	87.2	81.4	78.8	69.4	66.8	63.9	58.9	65.6	65.1
N.S.	n.a.	n.a.	84.5	88.3	90.6	92.9	84.2	74.6	77.3	81.4	85.0	81.1	80.6
N.B.	n.a.	n.a.	79.1	89.2	90.6	94.7	91.5	86.9	87.0	89.3	88.4	85.2	87.9
Que.	n.a.	n.a.	114.5	104.5	106.0	114.2	129.1	137.1	122.2	122.3	123.9	129.1	136.3
Ont.	n.a.	n.a.	102.7	106.3	107.7	101.8	92.4	94.8	94.0	96.3	96.0	93.4	92.8
Man.	n.a.	n.a.	93.6	100.0	93.2	92.0	96.0	93.1	94.9	93.7	94.3	87.7	83.8
Sask.	n.a.	n.a.	94.5	93.7	87.2	85.8	91.5	84.3	96.7	83.2	85.0	83.6	74.9
Alta.	n.a.	n.a.	80.0	89.2	93.2	98.2	89.7	85.2	94.0	93.7	91.8	93.4	92.8
B.C.	n.a.	n.a.	97.3	91.0	82.9	88.5	103.3	89.6	108.1	109.5	102.7	107.4	103.3

Average Annual Rates of Change in Average Length of Stay

YEAR	Canada	N.W.T. & Yukon	Nfld.	P.E.I.	N.S.	N.B.	Que.	Ont.	Man.	Sask.	Alta.	B.C.
1946-51	-1.11	n.a.	n.a.	n.a.	n.a.	n.a.	n.a.	n.a.	n.a.	n.a.	n.a.	n.a.
1951-61	0.56	n.a.	n.a.	n.a.	n.a.	n.a.	n.a.	n.a.	n.a.	n.a.	n.a.	n.a.
1961-66	1.06	4.50	-5.72	-0.39	1.58	1.38	1.34	1.32	-0.36	-0.39	1.94	-0.80
1966-71	-0.69	0	-2.07	-2.04	-0.19	0.19	0.79	-1.81	-0.93	-1.00	0.36	0.61
1971-76	-0.46	n.a.	-2.52	-1.11	-2.40	-1.15	2.01	-2.37	0.38	0.81	-2.26	2.66
1976-81/82	2.02	n.a.	0	-1.66	1.26	0.59	2.02	2.25	0.19	0.20	2.86	2.82
1981/82-82/83	0.74	43.84	3.41	0	0	3.85	6.35	0	-3.74	-9.80	0	-3.05
1961-82/83	0.49	1.22	-3.11	-2.04	-0.76	-0.39	1.76	-0.99	-1.18	-1.39	-0.16	0.26

1980/81, and far below from 1978/79 to 1979/80 and from 1980/81 to 1982/83. Ontario fell during 1947 to 1951 and recovered by 1956, and has been relatively flat since then. Manitoba and Saskatchewan led the country during the fast growth period 1947 to 1951, then flattened out while most of the other provinces continued to grow rapidly in the following half decade. Manitoba then lost during 1971 to 1976 what relative position it gained in 1956 to 1961, while Saskatchewan's relative position has remained fairly stable since 1956. The erosion in the relative ranking of Alberta came during the two periods 1956 to 1961 and, to a lesser extent, 1971 to 1976. What it lost from 1976 to 1981/82 it picked back up with the highest provincial growth rate *per capita* during the most recent year. B.C.'s major "losses" came slightly earlier (1947 to 1956), and then flat separation rates *per capita* throughout the 1960s found it about 6 percent above average by 1971. That has changed little since.

The bottom half of Table 25 shows two distinct general periods of separation patterns. The period 1947 to 1971, covering the eras of medical and hospital insurance development, was almost exclusively one of growth in separations *per capita*. During 1971 to 1976 only Newfoundland, P.E.I., and Ontario showed growth. Then, with the notable exception of Nova Scotia, all the five-year growth rates (1976 to 1981/82) turned negative. Whether Alberta's experience from 1981/82 to 1982/83 portends things to come is still an open question. More likely it represents an Alberta-specific rebound from sustained larger than average reductions since 1971.

While there has been marked convergence of inter-provincial patient days *per capita*, with Newfoundland the sole "outlier" by 1982/83, separations *per capita* have yet to show any central tendency.

Table 26 has been touched on at various points in the discussion of patient days and separations. Lengths of stay crept up relatively steadily from 1951 to 1966, fell back to 1956 levels by 1976, and then have shown relatively steady increase since then. (The figures for Quebec were adjusted from published data as described below in the Data Appendix.) It is interesting that ALS was virtually flat over the thirty years 1946 to 1976. Since 1976, as provinces have begun to clamp down on bed capacity, ALS has increased 1.9 percent per year, possibly a reflection of a changing mix of case severity as bed supply becomes taut. But even this may be too simple or general an explanation. First, the major increase in ALS has been in Quebec, where some uncertainty remains as to the accuracy, or rather the strict comparability, of ALS figures. Second, two of the most vigorous bed reduction campaigns since 1976 have been staged in Saskatchewan and P.E.I. Yet ALS has fallen in both.

In summary, patient days *per capita* increased for Canada as a whole continuously from 1947 until 1971. But the period since then has been one of almost continuous yearly reductions. *Per capita* utilization fell relatively sharply form 1971 to 1976, returned briefly to pre-1971 growth rates in 1977/78 and 1978/79, and then turned down once again. By 1982/83 we had recorded four successive years of falling or flat *per capita* rates, with B.C. and Saskatchewan leading the way down. Separates *per capita* peaked at the same time (1971), and have been in a continuous national decline since then. The run up was led by the Maritimes and Quebec, while, despite a (preliminary) reverse blip in the most recent year, Alberta has been the fastest declining among the provinces since 1971.

Prices, Quantity Indexes and Implied Resource Use

Continuing our focus on the price/quantity split of expenditures, we begin this section by developing hospital input price indexes for Canada and for each province. These are then combined with *per diem* expenditure data to calculate daily service volume indexes.

Data limitations prevented the compilation of input price indexes prior to 1962. Accordingly, we have generated indexes by province for the period 1962 to 1982/83, and have extended this back to the beginning of the period, using a mix of other data, for Canada only.

Table 27 is taken, *mutatis mutandis*, from Barer and Evans (1983), Table 7. Over the fourteen years 1946 to 1960, the hospital rate index grew at an annualized 8.2 percent, or 4.4 percent *per annum* faster than the CPI. But the *per diem* grew even faster, at 9.8 percent *per annum*, pointing out the danger in adopting *per diems* as a hospital "price" series. The cost per day series has a significant servicing or utilization component built in and, as we will see below, if the servicing trends are other than inter-temporally invariant, there is no reason for a *per diem* series to proxy "prices" particularly well.

During 1946 to 1951 the hospital rate index increased 2.3 percent *per annum* in real terms, fuelled primarily by increases of 4.3 percent from 1947 to 1948 and 4.2 percent in the following year. The major jump in real terms, however, came from 1951 to 1952, when the rate index increased 15.8 percent, or 13 percent faster than the CPI. From 1954 to 1960, during the development and implementation of the provincial hospital insurance plans, hospital rates ran on average about 3.9 percent per year ahead of the CPI. Meanwhile the *per diem* increased 66 percent over the six years, or 7 percent faster than the CPI on an annualized basis.

As noted earlier, the major component of hospital operating costs is staff salaries and wages. Commencing in 1962, and then continuously since 1966 (with the exceptions of 1972 and 1978), Health and Welfare Canada has published information on monthly wages for subsets of forty-seven standard employment classifications of personnel. These data, which have appeared in the published series *Salaries and Wages in Canadian Hospitals* form the backbone of the data used to compute the labour component of our hospital input price index for the period 1962 to 1982/83. The data in these publications are derived from Depart-

TABLE 27

HOSPITAL RATES AND OTHER "PRICE" SERIES,
CANADIAN PUBLIC GENERAL AND ALLIED SPECIAL HOSPITALS,
1946-1960 (1949 = 100.00)

YEAR	Hospital Rate Index	CPI	Real Hospital Rate Index	$ Per Day
1946	70.80	77.52	91.33	5.73
1947	78.00	84.75	92.03	6.82
1948	93.10	97.03	95.95	7.81
1949	100.00	100.00	100.00	8.71
1950	102.10	102.84	99.28	9.11
1951	116.20	113.70	102.20	10.28
1952	134.60	116.54	115.50	10.94
1953	141.70	115.50	122.68	11.96
1954	154.20	116.15	132.76	12.85
1955	160.50	116.41	137.88	14.05
1956	169.50	118.09	143.54	14.91
1957	184.00	121.83	151.02	16.11
1958	197.10	125.06	157.60	17.84
1959	204.70	126.49	161.84	18.88
1960	213.50	128.04	166.75	21.32
Average Annual Rate of Change				
1946-1960	8.20	3.65	4.39	9.84

ment of Labour surveys. In 1962, wage level data were provided for only thirteen of forty-seven categories for Canada; even fewer were available for some provinces. By the early 1970s, data were available for about thirty categories, and in some of the years since 1977 all forty-seven categories have been reported, at least for Canada. Unpublished data for 1981, 1982 and 1983 were kindly provided by Health Information Division, Health and Welfare Canada.

The corresponding data on the number of employees in each category, year, and province, proved to be more elusive. While Health and Welfare Canada publications contain province-specific average wage levels, and numbers of full-time employees in Canada for each year since 1971, the provincial equivalents of the latter have not been published. Again, the Health Information Division was kind enough, at considerable effort, to produce these provincial data back to 1974.

Wage patterns have displayed far more inter-provincial similarity than capacity or utilization. And like capacity and utilization, the trend over the (much shorter) period has again been convergence toward the national average. In order to compare wage levels across provinces, we computed a series of indexes using a common (the Canadian) mix of full-time personnel, but province-specific wage levels. Formally, let

P_{ijt} = wage level, personnel category i (i = 1, ..., 47), province j (j = 1, ..., 10), year t (t = 62, 66-71, 73-77, 79-82)
Q_{ijt} = number of full-time employees, category i, province j, year t
P_{ict} = wage level, category i, Canada, year t
Q_{ict} = number of full-time employees, category i, Canada, year t

Then we can compute a modified Laspeyres index for each province, as:

$$PREL_{jt} = \sum_{i=1}^{47} \overline{P}_{ijt} Q_{ict} / \sum_{i=1}^{47} \overline{P}_{ict_0} Q_{ict_0} \quad (t_o = 1977)$$

where $\overline{P}_{ijt}$ = 0 for every t if P_{ijt} = 0 for any t
= P_{ijt} otherwise
$\overline{P}_{ict}$ = 0 if P_{ijt} = 0 for any t
= P_{ict_0} otherwise

Thus, the index for each province may be based on different numbers of personnel categories, depending on province-specific availability of wage data.

Six such indexes were computed for each province, in two sets. The first set of three covered the entire period from 1962, for three different base year Canadian personnel mixes (1971, 1977 and 1982). Since price data were available for a maximum of thirteen categories in 1962, these three indexes were constructed on, at most, those thirteen categories. As a validation of those indexes, and following the procedure employed in Barer and Evans (1983), we then reconstructed these three indexes for the shorter period 1971 to 1982-1983. With fewer

P_{ijt} values $= 0$, this meant an index based on close to thirty categories for most provinces. By comparing the values of the second set of indexes with the values for 1971 to 1982-1983 from the first set, we were able to satisfy ourselves that, indeed, the smaller set of categories suitably captured wage movements of the larger set, for all provinces. In addition, the choice of base year made little difference to the behaviour of the index.

The results in Table 28 are based on the 1977 Canadian personnel mix, with Canada, 1971 = 100. Rates of wage increase were both relatively high (10.1 percent *per annum* in contrast to the average weekly wages and salaries (standard industrial composite) increase of 8.2 percent *per annum* over the same period) and remarkably uniform across provinces: seven of the ten provinces averaged growth of between 10 percent and 11 percent per year, and the other three were not far off. Despite the uniformity, however, there is convergence. The provinces paying the lowest wages in 1962 (Newfoundland and Prince Edward Island) show the highest overall rate of growth. While they were both still below average as recently as October 1983, the gap closed considerably from 1962 (26 percent and 23 percent below average) to 1982 (10 percent and 12 percent below). Ontario wages grew least rapidly, moving Ontario from 2.3 percent above to 3.2 percent below average (although the latter deficit was made up in 1983). Alberta's combination of close to average wages in 1962 and the third fastest growth left it the wage leader in 1982. Far above average growth from 1982 to 1983 has since moved Saskatchewan very close to Alberta, and both are well clear of the rest of the country. In 1962, B.C. hospital wage rates were about 8 percent higher than average and the highest in the country. With below average growth since then, it had slipped to second by 1982, and to third by 1983.

The shorter periods are also interesting. The early 1960s growth was led by P.E.I. and Quebec, with the latter displacing B.C. as the wage leader by 1966. Wage increases began in earnest in the latter part of the 1960s, and carried on throughout the 1970s and early 1980s, apparently peaking with the phenomenal increases in 1982 (everywhere but in B.C. where the federal "6 and 5" wage and price restraint program, B.C. style, was getting an early start). By 1968, B.C. was almost 11 percent above average and had regained top spot from Quebec. That lead was stretched to 17 percent above average at the "peak" in 1974. Twenty and 24 percent national average increases occurred in 1974 and 1975 respectively. As recently as 1981, B.C. still led the nation, with wages almost 13 percent above average. But that province clearly foreshadowed things to come with a wage increase less than half the national average in 1982, and followed up in 1983 with a smaller increase than any province but Quebec, where wages actually fell.

For the purposes of generating hospital input price indexes, we computed province-specific Laspeyres wage indexes, which combined each province's wage levels with its own base year personnel mix. Because provincial data on

TABLE 28
RELATIVE HOSPITAL WAGE LEVELS, CANADA AND PROVINCES, 1962-1983 (BASE YEAR = 1977)
(Canada, 1971 = 100)

YEAR*	Canada	Nfld.	P.E.I.	N.S.	N.B.	Que.	Ont.	Man.	Sask.	Alta.	B.C.
1962	51.57	38.08	39.78	44.32	46.10	50.51	52.78	50.69	52.05	50.79	55.80
1966	65.21	47.45	54.62	54.57	55.47	68.55	65.82	61.70	62.84	62.75	67.64
1967	71.58	56.18	57.61	62.98	64.61	75.48	72.29	65.52	67.77	67.46	73.86
1968	77.66	64.69	59.52	69.75	69.04	76.28	80.35	73.30	73.43	73.47	86.03
1969	82.72	66.89	72.86	74.62	73.02	76.96	86.61	79.55	79.07	82.95	94.33
1970	92.56	74.20	83.18	80.97	76.61	93.88	93.93	87.07	86.93	89.64	104.12
1971	100.00	83.44	87.66	89.73	91.10	104.38	102.34	94.52	91.54	96.12	113.62
1973	119.31	91.91	102.73	102.85	104.40	126.63	119.34	108.29	108.83	110.65	130.04
1974	143.04	113.80	116.32	119.56	115.89	146.49	150.08	123.43	131.51	126.07	167.36
1975	177.04	131.93	137.76	142.01	136.40	176.91	184.92	165.04	150.12	172.00	201.92
1976	190.83	156.91	153.65	161.47	151.60	191.27	198.71	178.05	170.94	189.76	213.38
1977	207.54	162.49	176.26	172.38	178.14	206.79	212.46	192.14	194.28	201.81	230.90
1979	234.81	184.92	210.03	193.90	209.79	233.46	241.56	219.45	233.36	235.34	255.59
1980	269.79	222.02	221.88	221.84	221.38	282.30	264.38	244.42	243.84	285.14	312.36
1981	307.14	225.61	268.25	257.79	271.09	325.76	296.04	297.83	306.63	315.42	346.06
1982	351.27	309.03	316.73	308.65	315.34	368.01	340.03	342.05	360.77	378.89	368.26
1983	369.64	337.49	334.08	339.79	335.54	362.46	369.46	368.86	409.14	412.39	382.13
Average Annual Rates of Change											
1962-66	6.04	5.65	8.25	5.34	4.73	7.93	5.67	5.04	4.82	5.43	4.93
1966-71	8.93	11.95	9.92	10.46	10.43	8.77	9.23	8.90	7.81	8.90	10.93
1971-76	13.80	13.46	11.88	12.47	10.72	12.88	14.19	13.50	13.30	14.57	13.43
1976-81	9.99	7.53	11.79	9.81	12.33	11.24	8.30	10.84	12.40	10.70	10.15
1981-82	14.37	36.98	18.07	19.73	16.32	12.97	14.86	14.85	17.66	20.12	6.42
1982-83	5.23	9.21	5.48	10.09	6.41	-1.51	8.66	7.84	13.41	8.84	3.77
1962-82	10.07	11.04	10.93	10.19	10.09	10.44	9.76	10.02	10.16	10.57	9.89

*All rates are as of October 1.

numbers of personnel were available only since 1974, indexes were produced using 1977 and 1982 as base years. Again, and not surprisingly, the differences were minimal. The indexes were computed as:

$$PI_{jt} = \sum_{i=1}^{47} \overline{P}_{ijt} Q_{ijt_o} / \sum_{i=1}^{47} \overline{P}_{ijt_o} Q_{ijt_o}$$

Table 29 contains these province-specific indexes (1971 = 100 for each province) using 1977 as the base year for mix of personnel. Of course, the values for Canada are identical to those in Table 28, and, by and large, the patterns of growth are extremely close to those based on the Canadian mix of personnel. It is the wage indexes in this table that are carried forward as the labour price components in the construction of the hospital input price indexes.

Before turning to that task, we show in Table 30 each province's hospital wage experience, relative to its average weekly wages and salaries. This table standardizes the previous table for inter-provincial differences in general wage levels, and reveals disparate inter-provincial experiences. Overall, the Canadian story has been continuous and, at times, substantial relative gains for hospital sector employees. The twenty years since 1962 (almost the entire period of universal hospital insurance) have produced wage increases of 1.7 percent per year (for twenty years!) higher than a representative sampling of other sectors of the economy. During the half-decade 1971-1976, hospital wages ran ahead of the composite index at a rate of almost 3 percent per year, and in the "boom" year of 1982, when hospital wages increased an average 14 percent, hospital workers picked up 4 percent relative in one year!

We find in this table perhaps the most interesting inter-provincial differences. Newfoundland hospital workers made their largest relative gains from 1966 to 1971 and, more remarkably, in 1982. In that year average gains of about 27 percent were 24 percent higher than those being received by non-hospital workers! This looks like overkill in response to a half-decade of minor slippage. Not only did Newfoundland have the highest provincial hospital wage gains over the twenty years (Tables 28 and 29), but it led all provinces in hospital workers' relative gains. P.E.I. was a close second on both counts. In fact, with the exception of a loss in relative position from 1971 to 1976, P.E.I. hospital sector employees made relative gains during the other fifteen years of the period of about 3.7 percent per year. Nova Scotia's relative gains have been steady (gains in each period) although less spectacular and erratic. Among the Maritime provinces, New Brunswick's hospital sector fared least well, losing ground from 1962 to 1966, again in the early 1970s, and during 1982 (despite a 16.5 percent nominal wage increase). The province was the second lowest (to B.C.) in relative hospital worker gains over the entire period. Quebec workers picked up close to 2 percent per year on workers in other sectors, with the gains spread evenly over the period. Of particular interest was 1982, when hospital employees gained almost

TABLE 29

PROVINCE-SPECIFIC HOSPITAL WAGE LEVELS,
1962-1983 (BASE YEAR = 1977)
(1971 = 100 in Each Province)

YEAR	Canada	Nfld.	P.E.I.	N.S.	N.B.	Que.	Ont.	Man.	Sask.	Alta.	B.C.
1962	51.57	45.36	45.13	49.62	50.69	48.68	51.62	53.44	57.02	52.75	49.10
1966	65.21	57.28	62.14	60.74	60.84	65.78	64.38	65.00	68.70	65.17	59.41
1967	71.58	67.78	65.84	70.19	70.92	72.39	70.65	69.11	74.01	70.17	64.84
1968	77.66	78.12	68.12	77.75	75.86	73.15	78.55	77.38	80.24	76.40	75.56
1969	82.72	80.18	82.83	83.27	80.16	73.85	84.64	84.02	86.40	86.29	82.62
1970	92.56	89.32	94.60	90.26	84.18	89.93	91.83	91.88	95.08	93.22	91.46
1971	100.00	100.00	100.00	100.00	100.00	100.00	100.00	100.00	100.00	100.00	100.00
1973	119.31	109.69	117.74	114.79	114.71	121.24	116.60	115.18	119.22	115.32	114.52
1974	143.04	135.89	132.69	133.47	127.54	140.05	146.89	131.94	143.91	131.38	147.99
1975	177.04	157.91	158.83	159.21	150.81	169.09	180.75	175.69	164.15	179.72	178.04
1976	190.83	187.45	177.43	180.95	168.34	182.80	194.43	189.40	187.53	198.28	188.01
1977	207.54	193.80	200.74	192.95	196.48	197.62	207.48	204.69	212.98	211.08	203.44
1979	234.81	220.62	241.47	216.14	232.10	223.23	236.14	234.17	256.14	246.14	225.40
1980	269.79	264.40	256.41	247.44	245.56	270.11	258.41	263.19	267.87	297.10	276.17
1981	307.14	268.63	307.75	288.38	298.68	311.45	289.10	318.79	336.47	328.92	305.54
1982	351.27	367.90	360.22	344.41	348.52	351.91	332.16	364.81	397.24	394.97	325.73
1983	369.64	401.45	382.56	380.00	369.97	346.36	362.14	392.81	448.55	429.42	336.99

Average Annual Rates of Change

1962-66	6.04	6.01	8.33	5.18	4.67	7.81	5.68	5.02	4.77	5.43	4.88
1966-71	8.93	11.79	9.98	10.49	10.45	8.74	9.21	9.00	7.80	8.94	10.98
1971-76	13.80	13.39	12.15	12.59	10.98	12.82	14.22	13.63	13.40	14.67	13.46
1976-81	9.99	7.46	11.64	9.77	12.15	11.25	8.26	10.98	12.40	10.65	10.20
1981-82	14.37	36.96	17.05	19.43	16.69	12.99	14.89	14.44	18.06	20.08	6.61
1982-83	5.23	9.12	6.20	10.33	6.16	-1.57	9.02	7.68	12.92	8.72	3.46
1962-82	10.07	11.03	10.94	10.17	10.12	10.40	9.76	10.08	10.19	10.59	9.92

TABLE 30

HOSPITAL WAGE LEVELS RELATIVE TO INDUSTRIAL COMPOSITE
AVERAGE WEEKLY WAGES AND SALARIES, CANADA AND PROVINCES,
1962-1983

(1971 = 100 in Each Province)

YEAR	Canada	Nfld.	P.E.I.	N.S.	N.B.	Que.	Ont.	Man.	Sask.	Alta.	B.C.
1962	88.14	77.47	72.55	85.56	87.60	82.17	88.26	87.51	90.03	90.39	85.98
1966	93.16	83.74	87.10	88.94	87.07	91.59	92.63	95.32	93.84	95.33	84.35
1967	95.82	92.28	83.92	95.82	94.31	94.49	95.46	93.08	94.06	96.55	86.35
1968	97.28	97.53	84.64	99.46	96.04	89.50	98.96	95.38	95.64	98.15	95.42
1969	96.79	93.63	92.14	99.40	93.87	85.35	99.59	96.64	97.45	101.53	97.41
1970	100.45	93.94	101.52	97.72	91.74	97.02	99.86	98.20	100.74	100.95	101.10
1971	100.00	100.00	100.00	100.00	100.00	100.00	100.00	100.00	100.00	100.00	100.00
1973	102.34	91.07	95.27	96.34	97.07	103.74	100.65	98.54	101.97	99.33	97.95
1974	110.55	99.85	94.06	100.40	93.53	106.96	115.79	100.42	108.80	102.02	112.56
1975	119.84	99.51	95.36	104.19	93.73	112.07	126.19	116.91	106.10	120.27	118.06
1976	115.18	104.70	93.41	105.66	94.21	108.53	121.58	112.47	106.22	116.16	110.48
1977	114.29	98.96	96.19	102.64	99.73	106.60	118.95	112.02	110.04	111.82	109.19
1979	112.12	100.54	103.55	99.44	102.58	103.66	118.26	111.97	113.04	111.34	105.07
1980	117.00	113.29	100.28	104.97	98.07	113.10	118.66	115.09	107.35	120.58	115.86
1981	118.99	101.36	110.68	109.79	119.07	116.97	118.84	125.62	121.60	116.92	114.48
1982	123.73	125.87	116.34	118.06	115.47	120.34	124.40	130.39	129.34	125.87	111.52
1983	121.30	129.19	116.48	122.97	113.70	111.26	128.41	129.34	136.08	127.71	107.77

Average Annual Rates of Change

	Canada	Nfld.	P.E.I.	N.S.	N.B.	Que.	Ont.	Man.	Sask.	Alta.	B.C.
1962-66	1.40	1.97	4.67	0.97	-0.15	2.75	1.21	2.16	1.04	1.34	-0.48
1966-71	1.43	3.61	2.80	2.37	2.81	1.77	1.54	0.96	1.28	0.96	3.46
1971-76	2.87	0.92	-1.35	1.11	-1.19	1.65	3.98	2.38	1.22	3.04	2.01
1976-81	0.65	-0.65	3.45	0.77	4.79	1.51	-0.45	2.24	2.74	0.13	0.71
1981-82	3.99	24.18	5.11	7.54	-3.02	2.88	4.68	3.79	6.37	7.65	-2.58
1962-82	1.71	2.46	2.39	1.62	1.39	1.93	1.73	2.01	1.83	1.67	1.31

3 percent relative to other sector workers, despite a *fall* in wages of about 1.5 percent. Hospital employees fared almost as well in Ontario, but by making large gains in the early 1970s, giving back only a fraction of them in the later 1970s and early 1980s, and then in 1982 recouping what was lost. Prairie province workers all capped off steady relative gains with remarkable 1982s. Of the three, Alberta fared least well, "only" picking up 1.7 percent relative *per annum* because of almost no gain from 1976 to 1981 (despite average annual wage increases of more than 10 percent). The whole of Alberta was enjoying the euphoric late 1970s.

While B.C.'s wage increases were quite similar to those for the country as a whole from 1971 to 1981 (Table 29), 1982 saw hospital workers fare poorly relative to those in other provinces (except Quebec) and, it turns out, relative to the labour force more generally (Table 30). In relative terms, B.C.'s hospital sector lost ground from 1962 to 1966 while that sector in the rest of the country (except New Brunswick) was making substantial gains: B.C. did substantially better (in relative terms) than all but Newfoundland from 1966 to 1971, slipped back again with small increases to 1973, then moved to a relative peak in 1975. With the exception of significant recouping in 1980 (a result of a 23 percent increase in average wages), it has been all relative erosion since then. While B.C. appears to have moved slowly into the process of capacity and utilization control, it has evidently chosen to approach hospital sector cost containment through wage restraint. Since 1975, hospital workers in that province have lost 5 percent in relative wages, while in every other province except Ontario there have been further gains of as much as 26 percent in Newfoundland, 23 percent in New Brunswick and more than 20 percent in two other provinces. To be fair, of course, one needs to note that 1971 to 1975 had been a good period for B.C. hospital workers but an uneventful period for those in Newfoundland and even worse for those in New Brunswick. What is harder to argue with is the fact that B.C.'s average relative gain over the entire period has been the slowest of all the provinces, despite relative gains second only to Ontario from 1962 to 1975.

As noted above, the province-specific wage indexes of Table 29 were used as the labour price series in constructing the hospital input price indexes. Development of the latter indexes for the period 1962 to 1982 required two further steps: choosing price series for the other input components, and developing weights to apply to those prices. Since the composite input price index is intended as a means of estimating volume indexes by deflating expenditure data, a Paasche index is desirable. As developed elsewhere (Barer and Evans, 1983), the index

$$P_{jt} = 1/[\sum_i (PI_{ijt_0}/PI_{ijt}) \cdot ES_{ijt}]$$

(where ES_{ijt} is the share of total hospital operating costs attributable to input category i in province j and year t)

is appropriate for this purpose.

We chose to limit our expenditure disaggregation to three components: labour, drugs, and everything else. The Health Division, Institutional Statistics Section, Statistics Canada devoted considerable time and effort on our behalf to disaggregate expenditure data back to 1946 by province, into seven categories: medical salaries, intern and resident salaries, other salaries and wages, employee benefits, medical and surgical supplies, drugs, and supplies and other non-departmental expenses. Unfortunately, two factors limit the extent to which we can utilize this detail at present.

First, and most obvious, is the lack of available price series to apply to most of these components, particularly on a provincial basis. Second, the expenditure disaggregations on which the ES_{ijt} would be based are plagued by numerous inconsistencies and changes over the period, both across provinces and within series for any given province.

Examples of the former are the treatment of intern and resident salaries, apparently included in the catch-all "supplies and other expenses" until 1968, and then not split out from total salaries and wages in 1981/82 or 1982/83; and of medical staff salaries, excluded entirely in Quebec but not in other provinces since 1979. The intern/resident salary problem is particularly bothersome, because it causes an artificial jump in the salaries and wages share from 1968 to 1969, from 67 percent to more than 70 percent of total expenditures, with a corresponding discontinuity in the opposite direction for supplies and other expenses.

Quebec is the most acute example of the province-specific problems, having failed to break out either medical and surgical supplies or drugs since 1979/80, having for the most part excluded depreciation expenses during 1967 and 1968, and having employee benefits paid on non-departmental contracts falling into the employee benefits category from 1976 to 1980/81. It appears that even a monumental effort to produce inter-provincially and inter-temporally consistent expenditure share data would fail. On the other hand, we doubt that such an effort would substantially alter the expense proportions. The only adjustment we have made is to split out estimated drug expenditures for Quebec for the years 1979/80 through 1982/83 from supplies and other expenses totals for Quebec and Canada. Over the period 1971 to 1978, Quebec's drug expenditures ran about 2 percent of total operating costs, and ranged from a high of 2.9 percent in 1971 to 1.9 percent in 1978. Accordingly, we estimated drug expenses for Quebec at 2 percent of operating expenses for each of the four most recent years, subsequently deducting those amounts from supplies and other expenses for Quebec and Canada, and adding them to drug expenses for Canada. Our expenditure shares (ES_{ijt}), then, are based on unpublished data provided by Statistics Canada. The three categories carried forward to the construction of the input price indexes are employee labour costs (all salaries and wages plus employee benefits), drugs, and everything else (supplies and other non-departmental expenses, plus medical and surgical supplies). This treatment is slightly different from that in our earlier Canada-only analysis (Barer and Evans, 1983) but, with the benefit of two additional years of reflection, seems at least equally appropriate.

While the inconsistencies make analysis of trends somewhat hazardous, there are nevertheless some fairly obvious and incontrovertible patterns of note for Canada as a whole. In 1946, salaries and wages in Canadian hospitals (or at least those that reported) constituted about 47 percent of total expenses (keeping in mind that some share of supplies and other expenses was medical, intern, and resident salaries). This proportion increased steadily, to 51 percent by 1951, and then throughout the 1950s, apparently reaching a plateau of sorts in the early 1960s, at about 66 percent to 67 percent (including employee benefits). Further small increases occurred through to 1973, by which time the share reached about 74 percent, now including intern and resident salaries (the discontinuity appears to be in the order of 2.5 percent between 1968 and 1969). A large increase in labour cost share shows up between 1975 and 1976; from 75.8 percent in 1975 to 79.3 percent in 1976! Reference back to Table 28 shows no major wage increase in 1976 but, recalling that the wage data are as of October 1 each year, the major increase showing for 1975 (averaging 24 percent!) may have fallen largely into calendar 1976 hospital expenditures. This would have the effect of biasing hospital input prices upward in 1975, producing a corresponding downward bias in our daily service volume index. Without more detailed intra-year wage change data, we cannot confirm or refute this possible bias. Looking ahead a bit at the input price and implied service volume index series (see Tables 32 and 34 below) provides little help. Although the Canadian "price" index pattern over the period 1974 to 1976 is at least consistent with a pattern of over-stated average wages in 1975 relative to 1976, there is insufficient evidence on which to base any firm assertion. The service volume index in Table 34 is, at first glance, similarly suggestive of this sort of phenomenon. However, the 1975 dip in the Canadian index is, it turns out, largely attributable to much slower than average growth in the cost per patient day data for Quebec (Table 33), despite close to average growth in prices. But we are getting ahead of ourselves. The year 1976 is at least a local maximum for the wages and salaries component. Its share has slid steadily since then, to about 75 percent in 1982-1983.

The generally rising share of expenses absorbed by labour is also reflected in reductions for all other categories of expenditure. Medical and surgical supplies constituted about 6 percent of costs in 1946, and more recently have been in the neighbourhood of 2.5 percent to 2.8 percent. A similar decline shows for drugs. The residual "supplies and other expenses" component fell from about 40 percent (including intern/resident salaries) in 1946, to 24 percent in 1968, falling further to about 20 percent (now excluding intern/resident salaries) in the early 1970s. It reached a low in the labour cost peak year, at 15.6 percent, and since has climbed back close to 20 percent. In the last year for which medical and intern/resident salaries are split out (1980-1981), salaries excluding these two items accounted for 66.7 percent of total operating costs, down from the 1976 peak of 67.9 percent. Employee benefits took 6.4 percent in 1976, and an identical share in 1982/83. Thus, most of the fall in labour costs from 1976 to the present is attributable to medical salaries (down from 3.2 percent in 1976 to 2.2 percent in 1980/81) and interns' and residents' salaries (down from 1.8 percent in 1976 to 1.3 percent in 1980/81). But at this level of disaggregation the numbers begin to "soften". Quebec's medical salaries were transferred out of hospital budgets to the provincial medical insurance plan beginning in 1979, and a clear discontinuity shows in the Canadian total between 1978/79 and 1979/80.

Our decision to aggregate to three input categories for the purpose of constructing the hospital price indexes was dictated not only by the problems of inter-provincial and inter-temporal inconsistencies in expenditure share data, but also by the (un)availability of appropriate input price series. The national Pharmaceuticals and Medicines Industry Selling Price Index (from CSR — *Canadian Statistical Review*) was coupled with the drug expenditure share data for each province, and the Gross National Expenditure (GNE) deflator (also from the *CSR*) was combined with the residual (medical and surgical supplies plus other supplies and non-departmental expenses) category.

Table 31 represents the culmination of the work on wage indexes and expenditure shares. There the hospital input price indexes (based in 1971 for each province) are reported. To a large extent these series mirror the general trends in Table 29 because of the overwhelming influence of labour costs in hospital operating budgets. The fact that wage increases have outrun other price increases means that virtually all rates of wage growth exceed the corresponding period growth rates for the composite input price indexes. The only exceptions in the periods shown are B.C. in 1982, where general price increases had not yet been reined in and hospital workers received an increase averaging only 6.6 percent, and Newfoundland for the period 1976 to 1981. Reference to the individual year data for Newfoundland during that period indicates that other hospital input prices exceeded wage increases in each year except 1980. There are a few other shorter period exceptions to the general trend (e.g., Nova Scotia from 1977 to 1979; Ontario from 1979 to 1980), but the Canadian hospital wage index grew 0.9 percent per year faster over the twenty years 1962 to 1982 than the hospital input price index. Wages outran the composite index by the greatest extent in Newfoundland (1.58 percent per year) and were closest to the other price components in B.C. (0.77 percent per year ahead).

Hospital input prices increased most rapidly over this period in Prince Edward Island, although Alberta, Quebec and Newfoundland were right on its heels. At the "slow" end was Ontario, but in general there is not much aggregate variation across provinces. This is partly a contrived convergence, a function of our use of single national price series for two of the three input categories, but there was also little inter-provincial range in the aggregate wage increases.

TABLE 31
HOSPITAL INPUT PRICE INDEXES,
CANADA AND PROVINCES,
1946-1982/83
(1971 = 100 in Each Province)

YEAR	Canada	Nfld.	P.E.I.	N.S.	N.B.	Que.	Ont.	Man.	Sask.	Alta.	B.C.
1946	17.32										
1951	28.42										
1956	41.46										
1960	52.22										
1961	54.96										
1962	57.53	55.92	54.70	57.23	58.28	55.43	57.07	59.04	61.89	58.99	54.54
1966	70.15	67.16	69.05	68.19	68.31	70.26	69.30	70.07	73.09	70.74	65.07
1967	75.67	75.05	72.36	75.88	76.09	75.81	74.94	74.08	77.95	75.09	70.02
1968	80.89	82.38	74.93	81.73	80.20	77.04	81.52	80.80	83.14	80.28	78.94
1969	85.30	84.75	86.13	86.47	83.85	77.64	86.77	86.53	88.41	88.24	85.01
1970	93.68	91.98	95.34	92.51	87.86	91.46	93.14	93.32	95.67	94.28	92.71
1971	100.00	100.00	100.00	100.00	100.00	100.00	100.00	100.00	100.00	100.00	100.00
1973	117.50	110.65	116.08	114.12	114.12	119.09	115.53	114.41	117.16	114.57	114.06
1974	137.62	131.59	129.65	130.08	126.33	135.90	140.34	129.31	137.45	129.10	142.09
1975	167.63	153.30	153.82	154.44	148.69	162.27	170.34	165.82	157.84	169.28	170.00
1976	182.43	177.92	171.12	173.97	164.90	177.11	185.04	180.30	178.58	186.95	181.46
1977/78	197.03	185.77	189.99	185.08	187.13	190.52	197.04	193.75	198.89	198.56	195.36
1979/80	224.01	212.98	226.53	209.81	220.08	216.39	224.86	222.91	237.23	230.68	218.07
1980/81	255.04	248.97	243.61	238.01	237.12	256.55	246.61	249.25	253.28	271.35	261.43
1981/82	287.82	260.20	284.41	273.01	280.51	291.93	275.02	293.54	305.74	301.60	289.29
1982/83	325.54	331.05	328.81	318.56	322.44	326.37	312.56	331.48	353.89	353.78	310.49

Average Annual Rates of Change

1962-66	5.08	4.68	5.99	4.48	4.05	6.11	4.97	4.37	4.25	4.64	4.51
1966-71	7.35	8.29	7.69	7.96	7.92	7.31	7.61	7.37	6.47	7.17	8.97
1971-76	12.78	12.21	11.34	11.71	10.52	12.11	13.10	12.51	12.30	13.33	12.66
1976-81/82	9.55	7.90	10.69	9.43	11.21	10.51	8.25	10.24	11.35	10.04	9.78
1981/82-82/83	13.11	27.23	15.61	16.68	14.95	11.80	13.65	12.92	15.75	17.30	7.33
1962-82/83	9.05	9.30	9.38	8.96	8.93	9.27	8.87	9.01	9.11	9.37	9.08
1946-82/83	8.49										

In Table 31 the "price" index for Canada has been extended back to 1946, by combining the 1962 to 1982 values as described above with the 1946 to 1960 values for the hospital rate index from Table 27, and bridging the two using other data sources. We took the "average hourly wage" figures for Canada (computed in Barer and Evans, 1983, Table 9) for 1960 to 1962 and, using 1962 as a bridge, extrapolated the hospital wage levels for Canada in Table 29 back to 1960. This produced a value for 1961 of 48.47 and for 1960 of 44.98. These were combined with expenditure share and price data for the other two input components, for 1960 and 1961, to produce the hospital input price index values shown in Table 31 for those two years. The complete Canada series in Table 31 is then a result of combining the 1960 to 1982 input price index series with the 1946 to 1960 hospital rate series (Table 27), using 1960 as a bridge. The average rate of growth over the entire period 1946 to 1982 was 8.5 percent per year.

In Table 32 the input price index for each province is displayed relative to the GNE deflator. Since the latter is the price index used in combination with 15 percent to 30 percent of hospital expenditures in computing the former, we eliminate by construction some of the potential divergence in the two series. In fact, the differences between Tables 31 and 32 largely reflect the different behaviours of the provincial wage indexes relative to the GNE deflator.

Over the thirty-six years from 1946 to 1982, the composite hospital input price index for Canada grew on average 3 percent faster than the GNE deflator, *per annum*! The most rapid relative growth came during the insurance program development of the 1950s, with the index outrunning the GNE deflator by 5 percent per year from 1951 to 1961. But in all periods "prices" have moved up faster than the deflator, and 1966 to 1971, during the medical plan development, was another rapid growth period (3.3 percent above the deflator). During 1946 to 1971 the index outpaced the GNE deflator by 3.6 percent per year; since 1971 the relative yearly rate has been a considerably slower 1.6 percent.

Since all provincial series have been deflated by the same index in Table 32, the inter-provincial patterns match those in Table 31 and require no further comment. The instances of hospital prices lagging behind general price levels are few and far between.

With the price series of Table 31, we are equipped to disaggregate hospital operating costs per day into their price and input quantity or servicing components. Table 33 reports costs per day for adults and children, as pieced together from various Statistics Canada publications dating from the late 1950s. While these are reproduced here largely without modification, precise sources and adjustments may be found below in the Data Appendix.

Cost per adult and child patient day in Canadian PGAS hospitals increased from about $5.75 in 1946 to close to $250.00 in 1982/83, or about *11 percent per year, for thirty-six years*! During the hospital insurance years 1962 to 1982/83, growth has been an even more remarkable 12.2 percent per year. The provincial

TABLE 32

HOSPITAL INPUT PRICE INDEXES
RELATIVE TO THE GNE DEFLATOR,
CANADA AND PROVINCES, 1946-1982
(1971 = 100 in Each Province)

YEAR	Canada	Nfld.	P.E.I.	N.S.	N.B.	Que.	Ont.	Man.	Sask.	Alta.	B.C.
1946	41.23										
1951	46.51										
1956	61.51										
1960	72.42										
1961	75.80										
1962	78.37	76.19	74.53	77.96	79.40	75.51	77.75	80.44	84.31	80.37	74.31
1966	84.92	81.31	83.59	82.56	82.70	85.07	83.90	84.83	88.49	85.64	78.78
1967	88.09	87.37	84.24	88.34	88.58	88.25	87.24	86.24	90.75	87.41	81.51
1968	91.19	92.87	84.47	92.14	90.41	86.86	91.91	91.09	93.74	90.51	89.00
1969	92.01	91.42	92.91	93.28	90.45	83.75	93.60	93.35	95.37	95.18	91.71
1970	96.78	95.02	98.49	95.57	90.76	94.48	96.22	96.41	98.84	97.39	95.78
1971	100.00	100.00	100.00	100.00	100.00	100.00	100.00	100.00	100.00	100.00	100.00
1973	103.34	97.32	102.09	100.36	100.37	104.74	101.61	100.62	103.04	100.76	100.32
1974	110.10	105.27	103.72	104.07	101.06	108.72	112.27	103.45	109.96	103.28	113.67
1975	114.42	104.64	104.99	105.42	101.50	110.77	116.28	113.19	107.74	115.55	116.04
1976	113.73	110.92	106.68	108.46	102.81	110.42	115.36	112.41	111.34	116.55	113.13
1977	114.75	108.19	110.65	107.79	108.99	110.96	114.76	112.84	115.84	115.65	113.78
1979	111.28	105.80	112.54	104.23	109.33	107.50	111.70	110.73	117.85	114.60	108.33
1980	114.01	111.30	108.90	106.39	106.00	114.68	110.24	111.42	113.22	121.30	116.87
1981	115.54	104.46	114.18	109.60	112.61	117.19	110.40	117.84	122.74	121.08	116.13
1982	118.73	120.73	119.92	116.18	117.59	119.03	113.99	120.89	129.06	129.02	113.24

Average Annual Rates of Change

	Canada	Nfld.	P.E.I.	N.S.	N.B.	Que.	Ont.	Man.	Sask.	Alta.	B.C.
1946-51	2.44										
1951-56	5.75										
1956-61	4.27										
1962-66	2.03	1.64	2.91	1.44	1.02	3.03	1.92	1.34	1.22	1.60	1.47
1966-71	3.32	4.22	3.65	3.91	3.87	3.29	3.57	3.35	2.48	3.15	4.89
1971-76	2.61	2.09	1.30	1.64	0.56	2.00	2.90	2.37	2.17	3.11	2.50
1976-81	0.32	-1.19	1.37	0.21	1.84	1.20	-0.88	0.95	1.97	0.77	0.52
1981-82	2.76	15.58	5.03	6.00	4.42	1.57	3.25	2.59	5.15	6.56	-2.49
1962-82	2.10	2.33	2.41	2.01	1.98	2.30	1.93	2.06	2.15	2.39	2.13
1946-82	2.98										

TABLE 33
COST PER PATIENT DAY, ADULTS AND CHILDREN, PGAS HOSPITALS, CANADA AND PROVINCES RELATIVE TO CANADA, 1946-1982/83

YEAR	Canada	N.W.T. & Yukon	Nfld.	P.E.I.	N.S.	N.B.	Que.	Ont.	Man.	Sask.	Alta.	B.C.
1946	5.73		80.4	74.2	89.4	96.2	85.8	107.1	83.2	88.4	102.0	130.9
1947	6.82		82.6	73.9	88.2	96.9	88.9	107.8	87.1	89.3	103.3	118.3
1948	7.81		92.2	82.9	98.4	101.1	90.4	105.3	86.7	94.6	103.6	116.2
1949	8.71		94.9	75.7	95.2	100.6	90.8	105.8	93.1	97.6	99.0	112.1
1950	9.11		109.9	75.1	93.6	101.5	89.5	105.6	94.5	98.8	103.6	112.2
1951	10.28		93.0	72.1	96.4	102.1	93.4	103.8	97.1	99.4	102.0	108.0
1952	10.94		93.0	73.6	98.1	105.3	86.8	107.5	102.3	101.4	91.8	114.3
1953	11.96		92.6	78.5	100.3	100.1	96.9	105.0	98.4	95.6	86.7	105.3
1954	12.85		86.2	82.5	102.3	102.4	100.3	105.0	95.0	91.6	86.1	101.6
1955	14.05		85.2	75.8	102.2	102.9	101.4	105.6	91.9	91.9	85.9	100.3
1956	14.91		85.6	76.1	101.6	102.2	105.9	104.2	90.2	87.1	85.9	97.0
1957	16.11		90.0	77.8	100.6	98.3	111.0	102.3	87.8	87.8	83.2	94.1
1958	17.84		88.8	76.5	100.4	94.1	115.4	100.7	87.4	86.6	81.1	92.0
1959	18.88		89.4	73.8	94.3	89.4	121.9	99.0	86.9	84.6	80.6	87.5
1960	21.32		95.5	72.9	99.7	89.2	117.9	100.1	88.0	84.1	83.9	87.9
1961	23.10	135.3	99.7	70.3	99.9	87.1	110.7	104.3	88.6	85.8	81.9	91.0
1962	24.82	105.6	96.0	69.7	99.4	85.2	114.3	103.6	87.1	83.3	81.6	90.0
1963	26.87	89.1	93.1	69.6	98.5	79.5	117.4	103.5	88.2	78.7	79.2	89.4
1964	29.18	92.7	94.0	71.7	99.4	89.2	113.0	105.5	92.4	76.6	78.1	89.3
1965	31.92	91.9	95.1	70.0	98.6	89.2	116.8	105.3	94.8	74.7	76.9	85.1
1966	36.06	86.7	103.0	71.4	100.0	89.2	114.0	105.7	94.2	75.0	78.2	85.0
1967	40.38	87.9	102.8	69.9	98.6	88.8	114.4	104.4	95.5	76.3	76.5	87.9
1968	45.01	88.2	106.5	71.0	104.7	93.5	101.8	108.4	103.5	74.6	88.5	89.5
1969	50.69	91.6	110.1	69.0	107.0	96.6	102.1	108.8	101.7	78.1	87.9	84.5
1970	56.24	87.2	116.6									
1971	61.58	85.1										
1972	68.52	87.4										
1973	77.09	92.7										
1974	93.23	106.5										
1975	110.30	101.6										
1976	125.79	107.2										

TABLE 33 (cont'd)
COST PER PATIENT DAY,
ADULTS AND CHILDREN, PGAS HOSPITALS,
CANADA AND PROVINCES RELATIVE TO CANADA,
1946-1982/83

YEAR	Canada	N.W.T. & Yukon	Nfld.	P.E.I.	N.S.	N.B.	Que.	Ont.	Man.	Sask.	Alta.	B.C.
1977/78	135.65	97.0	130.5	75.8	111.1	97.6	98.9	110.0	102.8	77.4	91.2	84.6
1978/79	147.92	100.7	131.8	78.7	111.5	96.5	97.9	109.5	103.2	80.6	94.3	85.1
1979/80	162.25	173.1	133.3	81.5	112.7	96.4	99.1	107.0	103.8	79.4	96.6	86.6
1980/81	188.01	151.9	133.2	79.4	110.8	96.3	96.9	104.4	109.2	82.2	102.7	93.0
1981/82	217.14	173.6	143.1	77.0	120.0	97.1	93.9	104.8	111.6	85.5	103.4	93.8
1982/83	246.50	122.4	136.7	85.4	120.7	103.7	89.0	106.0	116.1	90.6	108.4	95.0

Average Annual Rates of Change in Cost-Per-Patient Day

1946-51	12.40											
1951-56	7.72											
1956-61	9.15		7.08	11.04	10.73	9.54	11.35	8.98	9.59	7.78	6.16	7.04
1961-66	9.32	0.01	10.09	6.90	7.54	6.39	13.66	8.03	7.39	7.60	7.87	6.08
1966-71	11.30	10.87	12.44	10.65	12.47	11.23	9.63	12.74	12.67	9.09	10.60	11.75
1971-76	15.36	20.80	20.43	14.47	17.08	17.21	13.03	16.07	17.59	15.81	18.12	14.09
1976-81/82	11.54	22.83	16.20	14.04	14.12	11.67	9.69	10.69	13.62	13.57	15.21	13.91
1981/82-82/83	13.52	-19.95	8.38	25.88	14.25	21.16	7.63	14.85	18.17	20.33	18.98	14.91
1953-82/83	11.00		13.05	11.54	12.15	11.29	11.14	10.96	12.28	11.09	11.23	9.78
1962-82/83	12.16	13.00	14.84	12.84	13.10	12.20	11.44	12.18	13.48	12.08	13.48	11.86
1946-82/83	11.01											

data from 1953 on reveal some striking relative trends and shifts in position. Immediately apparent is the extent to which B.C.'s *per diems* exceeded those of the rest of the country in 1953 (31 percent above average), and the almost continuous decline in B.C.'s relative position over the following thirteen years. After a brief surge in the late 1960s, B.C.'s relative *per diems* headed down again, reaching a relative bottom in 1976. Since 1976, B.C.'s growth in *per diems* has outrun the Canadian average by 2 percent per year, with most of that relative gain coming between 1979/80 and 1980/81.

While B.C.'s relative "costliness" was diminishing during the 1950s and early to mid-1960s, Quebec was following a reverse course (from 14 percent below average in 1953 to a peak 22 percent above average in 1966). But by 1982 it had returned very close to its original relative position. In fact, in 1982/83 Quebec's *per diem* exceeded that of only Prince Edward Island which, while edging toward centre over the period (or more precisely since 1976), managed to maintain the lowest *per diem* in Canada.

Three provinces made relatively steady and continuous "gains" over the sixteen years since 1966: Newfoundland, Nova Scotia and Manitoba. Newfoundland's *per diem* costs took off in the last half of the 1960s, increased even more rapidly from 1971 to 1976 (outrunning the Canadian growth of 15.4 percent per year, by about 5 percent per year!), then experienced a further one-year increase of 20.7 percent while the national increase was a much more modest 7.8 percent from 1976 to 1977/78. By 1982/83, Newfoundland's *per diem* stood 37 percent above the national average. Nova Scotia and Manitoba have followed roughly similar roads to the second and third highest 1982/83 *per diems*. In Manitoba, relatively rapid increases in the 1950s gave way to slippage throughout the mid-1960s. Growth in both provinces ran ahead of the national average throughout the 1970s and has been particularly brisk in the early 1980s. While the remaining provinces have had their relative movements, their positions in 1953 and 1982 were roughly similar. Ontario shows the least relative movement of all the provinces, while Saskatchewan and New Brunswick have taken the roller coaster route. Alberta began the period just above average, then had *per diems* actually fall from 1958 to 1959 and increase far less than average the following year. Continued slow growth from 1961 to 1966 (1.3 percent per year slower than average) left it 20 percent below average in 1966. That "deficit" increased to almost 25 percent below average in 1974, but since then Alberta has led all provinces in *per diem* growth.

Reference back to Table 29 confirms that one must be cautious in interpreting the wage and price series. Newfoundland's wages increased 37 percent from October 1981 to October 1982. Yet the increase in cost per patient day from 1981/82 to 1982/83 was a much lower 8.4 percent. This is likely the result of two effects, one real, the other resulting from our inability to compute accurate average yearly wage levels. First, there was a drop of just over 10 percent in

TABLE 34
DAILY SERVICE INTENSITY (PER DAY SERVICE VOLUME) INDEXES, CANADA AND PROVINCES,
1946-1982/83
(1971 = 100 in Each Province)

YEAR	Canada	Nfld.	P.E.I.	N.S.	N.B.	Que.	Ont.	Man.	Sask.	Alta.	B.C.
1946	53.74										
1947	58.05										
1948	55.70										
1949	57.83										
1950	59.24										
1951	58.74										
1952	53.97										
1953	56.04										
1954	55.33										
1955	58.12										
1956	58.40										
1957	58.13										
1958	60.10										
1959	61.24										
1960	66.30										
1961	68.26										
1962	70.06	65.31	77.90	72.46	79.82	65.21	70.69	67.94	78.21	75.13	83.01
1966	83.48	82.84	87.31	81.50	85.96	89.88	79.24	78.60	88.56	85.44	88.18
1967	86.65	88.73	92.14	86.70	86.20	90.24	82.97	84.33	92.34	93.78	92.24
1968	90.36	94.06	95.61	89.93	89.00	92.89	88.61	86.78	98.52	95.43	94.44
1969	96.51	99.15	92.88	95.25	93.77	107.17	93.10	89.64	101.24	97.40	97.62
1970	97.48	98.28	92.96	97.83	92.64	103.70	96.19	93.39	98.14	98.22	98.70
1971	100.00	100.00	100.00	100.00	100.00	100.00	100.00	100.00	100.00	100.00	100.00
1973	106.54	123.90	107.48	110.43	109.71	106.01	108.53	111.59	104.71	109.37	104.47
1974	110.01	125.78	113.91	115.56	119.36	112.74	106.75	121.05	109.70	114.79	104.93
1975	106.86	136.74	115.28	122.18	126.26	99.38	107.96	120.99	110.59	119.86	105.65
1976	111.97	142.38	114.84	126.44	134.13	104.15	113.83	124.72	116.64	123.02	106.53
1977/78	111.80	164.58	122.56	133.12	128.82	101.15	116.56	126.48	111.96	129.47	106.91

TABLE 34 (cont'd)
DAILY SERVICE INTENSITY (PER DAY SERVICE VOLUME) INDEXES,
CANADA AND PROVINCES,
1946-1982/83
(1971 = 100 in Each Province)

YEAR	Canada	Nfld.	P.E.I.	N.S.	N.B.	Que.	Ont.	Man.	Sask.	Alta.	B.C.
1979/80	117.62	175.34	132.18	142.49	129.40	106.69	118.79	132.76	115.21	141.28	117.20
1980/81	119.71	173.75	138.84	143.08	139.07	102.01	122.42	144.81	129.41	147.96	121.71
1981/82	122.51	206.26	133.26	155.97	136.92	100.34	127.26	145.07	128.72	154.81	128.13
1982/83	122.96	175.71	145.10	152.72	144.32	96.60	128.61	151.82	133.82	157.02	137.18

Average Annual Rates of Change

1946-51	1.80										
1951-56	-0.11										
1956-61	3.08										
1961-66*	4.48	6.13	2.89	2.98	1.87	8.35	2.90	3.71	3.16	3.26	1.52
1966-71	3.68	3.84	2.75	4.18	3.07	2.16	4.76	4.93	2.46	3.20	2.55
1971-76	2.29	7.32	2.81	4.80	6.05	0.82	2.63	4.52	3.13	4.23	1.27
1976-81/82	1.82	7.69	3.02	4.29	0.41	-0.74	2.26	3.07	1.99	4.70	3.76
1981/82-82/83	0.36	-14.81	8.89	-2.09	5.40	-3.73	1.06	4.65	3.96	1.43	7.06
1962-82/83	2.85	5.07	3.16	3.80	3.01	1.98	3.04	4.10	2.72	3.75	2.54
1946-82/83	2.33										

*1962-66 for the provinces.

average paid hours per patient day from 1981/82 (April 1, 1981 to March 31, 1982) to 1982/83. Second, the timing of the large wage increase may have been close enough to (although clearly after) October 1981 to cause at least some of the per day cost impact to fall within 1981/82. This is supported by the observation that cost per patient day increased 24 percent from 1980/81 to 1981/82.

On the other hand, B.C., with the smallest wage increase in 1982 (6.6 percent), nevertheless reported a substantial (and above average) *per diem* increase of 14.9 percent. But overall, the general Canadian trend in *per diem* growth appears to be closely correlated with wage increases.

Table 34 presents the results of the "deflation" of cost per patient day. Having examined the price experience in some detail, we are now able to analyze the implied per day service provision (or servicing intensity) experience of Canada since 1946 and the provinces since 1962. In our earlier work (Barer and Evans, 1983), we found that daily servicing intensity increased 1.8 percent per year over the period 1935 to 1946 (although the *per diems* were for adults, children, and newborns, and are less reliable at the beginning of that period). That is, of the 4.8 percent annual increase in *per diem* cost, 1.8 percent was not explainable by increases in factor prices. Therefore, it represented some combination of increased inputs per inpatient day and changing activity mix (inpatient vs. other). We consider these in more depth below.

Table 34 indicates that the period 1946 to 1951 was one in which servicing intensity continued to increase about 1.8 percent per year. But the apparent impact of universal hospital insurance in the late 1950s is marked. From 1951 to 1957, while *per diems* were increasing by almost 57 percent, servicing intensity was dead flat; the 57 percent increase was entirely a price-related phenomenon. Once the provincial insurance plans were in place, however, that all seemed to change. In the following five years (1957-1962), *per diems* increased another 54 percent; but this time only half could be attributed to price rises. Daily servicing intensity increased 3.8 percent per year for five years! In fact, this trend of rapidly increasing factor inputs continued unabated throughout the rest of the 1960s and the early 1970s. Over the ten years 1961 to 1971, the *per diem* increase of 167 percent (10.3 percent per year) is made up of an 82 percent price increase (6.2 percent per year) and a 47 percent increase in implied inputs per inpatient day of care (3.9 percent per year).

The run-up in daily resource use peaked temporarily in 1974, or at least dropped back so dramatically in Quebec in 1975 that the Canadian average settled back as well. This Quebec experience, noted earlier, results from far below average *per diem* growth (5 percent in Quebec vs. 18 percent nationwide) in conjunction with about average price increases. Whether this represents an artifact caused by institutional reclassifications, or differences in data bases for wage as opposed to *per diem* data, is not clear. It does seem to warrant further scrutiny.

While the rate of growth in servicing intensity since 1975 has been far slower than rates in the earlier periods (2 percent per year), still growth has continued. Only since 1979 has the rapid growth in *per diems* (15 percent per year) once again become price dominated (13.3 percent per year).

Provincial variation is by now no surprise. While the period analyzed is only 1962 to 1982, there are nevertheless numerous interesting similarities as well as differences. The first and most obvious similarity is that servicing intensity has increased substantially in every province (from 2 percent per year in Quebec to 5 percent per year in Newfoundland). A second similarity is the almost universal growth within shorter periods. Only in Quebec from 1976 to 1981/82 do we find servicing intensity falling over a five-year period. Finally, in general we find that price increases have accounted for a larger proportion of increases in *per diems* than has growth in servicing intensity.

During the period of overall fastest growth in servicing intensity (1962-1966), that in Newfoundland and Quebec was actually outstripping price growth in those provinces. Newfoundland's rate of servicing growth also far exceeded that for Canada throughout the 1970s, explaining most of its above-average growth in *per diems*. P.E.I. has experienced remarkably stable service volume growth over the period, running behind the Canadian average in the early period, and ahead more recently. Nova Scotia, with below average price increases, nevertheless had *per diems* rising 0.8 percent per year faster than average (for twenty years). Servicing intensity growth third behind only Newfoundland and Manitoba provides the explanation. New Brunswick and British Columbia both experienced slow growth in servicing intensity in the earlier years, but there the similarity ends. B.C. hospitals showed very little intensification in servicing from 1970 to 1977, while New Brunswick's data show extremely rapid increases through to 1976. From 1976 to 1981-1982, B.C.'s rate of increase was double the national average while New Brunswick's was flat. Both provinces had substantial increases in the most recent year. In Quebec, servicing intensity growth has declined continuously, turning to a reduction during 1976 to 1982/83. That province's index level in 1982 was lower than its value throughout the period 1969 to 1981/82. Thus, Quebec's servicing experience stands out as unique among the provinces. But this may well be yet another result of the mental institution reclassification. While we attempted to adjust for this in our utilization and capacity series, we were unable to do so in our cost per patient day and price series. We observed no sharp discontinuities in the price data for Quebec, but that series is largely dependent on wage rate surveys. If new institutions were introduced into PGAS stock, but not into the labour survey samples, both wage rate and labour mix changes in Quebec could have been overlooked in our series. In the cost per day series, there is a discontinuity of sorts, but it is between 1974 and 1975 rather than between 1975 and 1976 when most of the effect of the reclassification appears in the utilization data. Furthermore, it is not unique to Quebec. Cost per patient day in Alberta and Nova Scotia, for example, moved just as sharply relative to the national average, but in the opposite direction (Table 33). Our general unease with the Quebec data, however, does extend to the story apparently told by the service intensity index.

Ontario and Alberta show roughly comparable growth until 1973, from which point Alberta became one of the servicing growth leaders through to 1981/82. Servicing growth slowed for both provinces in the most recent year. Manitoba and, to a lesser extent, Saskatchewan have experienced above average increases since 1971.

While the overall figures for Canada suggest a slowing growth trend in daily servicing intensity, that trend is by no means reflected in all the provinces. In fact the Canadian figures result to a large extent from the dramatic and somewhat questionable decline in Quebec. Since 1976, all four western provinces and P.E.I. have experienced substantial growth in their service volume indexes. In particular, B.C. and P.E.I. have been showing more rapid growth than in any previous period. It would be difficult to call the direction of servicing trends for the remainder of the 1980s.

Of course there is more than one possible explanation for increases of this magnitude in a deflated expenditure per day index. While the most obvious is increased resource use per inpatient day, the construction of the *per diem* permits other explanations. Since the *per diem* is a combination of *total* operating cost (in the numerator), and *inpatient* days of care (in the denominator), and since hospitals may be involved in a number of non-inpatient-care activities, a significant shift in activity mix away from inpatient care could produce spurious inpatient servicing growth. A full-fledged historical activity cost allocation was beyond the scope of this paper. However, an earlier confrontation with this same issue (Barer and Evans, 1983) convinced us that no more than a small part of the growth could reasonably be attributed to such a shift in the mix of hospital activities. The index for B.C. increased 18 percent from 1966 to 1973. Yet, an extensive cost allocation exercise based on B.C. hospitals (Barer, 1977) showed a relatively constant 85 percent expenditure share for inpatient activity over this same period, indicating that activity shifts account for very little of the "servicing intensity" growth.

A second possibility is to be found in the construction of our price indexes. If for any reason they mis-state the "true" extent of price growth, the intensity growth rates will be biased in the opposite direction. A more costly mix of personnel over the period, for example, might be interpreted either as higher labour costs or as more intensive (more highly skilled) servicing. In earlier work (Barer and Evans, 1983), however, we found a Paasche index for Canada to move in almost perfect step with the Laspeyres index. There has been remarkably little shift in the mix of personnel among the forty-seven categories used in our index construction.

Still another concern is that the GNE deflator may do an inadequate job of proxying price movement for medical and surgical supplies and the myriad other supplies and expenses in the residual category. While this remains a possibility, there are two immediate reasons for believing that any impact would be small. First, we applied some alternative indexes and couplings for Canada (Barer and Evans, 1983, n. 10), and found such calculations to have almost no impact. Second, and related, is the overwhelming share of expenses attributable to labour. One would need substantial departures from the GNE deflator for alternative price series to affect significantly the implied servicing indexes. For example, even if costs per day for Canada were deflated by the wage index alone (which increased 10 percent per year for the twenty years 1962 to 1982), the servicing intensity index would still show a twenty-year average annual growth rate of 1.9 percent (down from 2.85 percent). There seems little doubt that a substantial portion of the growth in these intensity indexes is in fact growth in daily servicing.

While one may be tempted to dismiss the servicing growth as minimal relative to the price growth (2.85 percent per year vs. 9.05 percent per year, 1962 to 1982), one must bear in mind that only 2 percent of that annual price growth was hospital sector-specific. The GNE deflator was increasing at an average of 6.8 percent per year over those twenty years. So the increase in *per diems* was 6.8 percent general inflation, 2.1 percent relative increase in hospital sector input prices, and 2.85 percent servicing intensity growth. A growth rate of 2.85 percent compounded over the twenty years would, in itself, have raised the Canadian 1962 *per diem* of $24.82 to $43.50 by 1982 even in an environment of constant nominal prices. Or, put another way, in the absence of servicing intensity growth since 1962, the 1982 *per diem* would stand at about $140, or $106 lower than the actual. On fifty million days of care in 1982/83, that figure represents more than $5 billion for that year alone.

Accepting the existence of greatly increased daily resource use leaves another set of questions: What is behind that resource use growth? What is that sum buying us? Here again there are a number of possibilities. Quality of care may have been improving continuously, so that the absorption of additional resources was resulting in improved outcomes for comparable diagnostic/severity situations. Or the patient day may not be inter-temporally homogeneous in the sense of comparable diagnosis/severity mixes. Or patterns of care may have changed. Or productivity may have declined.

By and large we are content to leave this collection of possible explanations to the curious reader. Each is a research project in itself. But we cannot resist closing this section with a few germane observations that may guide any such investigations. In certain quarters there would be no question as to causality. The sophisticated quality fallacy builds a direct relationship *by assumption* between daily inputs of personnel and supplies (that is, servicing intensity) and quality of care (see, e.g., M. Feldstein, 1974, 1977); the view is also widely held among providers. While we would like to believe that at least a share of the 2.85 percent growth in resource use per day is being reflected in better outcomes *ceteris paribus*, the available evidence does not support any automatic linkage from inputs to outcomes. More is not necessarily better.

There may be more promise in the case mix explanation. An increasingly complex case mix would bring with it increases in resource requirements per patient day. After all, there are obvious reasons why chronic care *per diems* tend to be far lower than those for acute care. Some preliminary investigation over a shorter period, and focusing again only on B.C., found some shift toward a more complex case mix, but not nearly enough to explain (even one-third of) the growth in servicing intensity (Barer and Evans, 1980, 1983).

A third possibility, probably largely eliminated by the historical pattern of average lengths of stay, is changes in patterns of care. If lengths of stay had been falling and daily servicing intensity increasing, one might argue that changed care patterns, toward more intensive, shorter stays of comparable outcome, were being reflected in the servicing index. The argument is less convincing (although not wholly refuted) in light of a rising average length of stay over the period. It could still be argued, for example, that the ALS pattern would have shown even more rapid growth with flat servicing intensity.

The fourth explanation, and the last we offer by way of future research directions, is declining productivity. If the three explanations noted above (plus any others we may have overlooked) fail to account fully for the growth in servicing intensity, the residual is by default and definition, declining productivity (in terms of outcomes achieved, not necessarily in activities performed). This is not to point fingers exclusively at hospital personnel. As Table 35 shows, paid hours per patient day have increased far less rapidly than our service volume indexes. It is evidently other supplies and purchased services that have accounted for the larger share of the increase in resource use per day, at least since 1966.

The American Experience in Contrast

At the end of the discussion of province-specific physician data, we returned to a more aggregated comparison of Canadian and U.S. experience over the decade 1972 to 1982 to try to identify the sources of the growing divergence. Table 36 provides a similar comparison for hospital data. There, however, the data are presented for 1966 and 1982, and (annual average) rates of increase or decrease are calculated over the five-year period 1966 to 1971 and the eleven-year period 1971 to 1982. All indices are set to 1971 = 100.

The year 1971, however, has somewhat different significance for Canadian hospital data. The public hospital insurance plans had become universal and nation-wide ten years earlier, in 1961, so the year is not an institutional turning

TABLE 35
PAID HOURS PER PATIENT DAY, CANADA AND PROVINCES RELATIVE TO CANADA, 1961-1982/83

YEAR	Canada	N.W.T. & Yukon	Nfld	P.E.I.	N.S.	N.B.	Que.	Ont.	Man.	Sask.	Alta.	B.C.
1961	11.8	91.5	109.3	106.8	116.9	109.3	102.5	102.5	103.4	89.0	89.8	92.4
1962	12.1	103.3	101.7	97.5	114.0	110.7	104.1	103.3	100.0	89.3	86.8	90.9
1963	12.4	83.1	100.8	97.6	114.5	109.7	105.6	101.6	99.2	85.5	87.9	88.7
1964	12.7	81.1	105.5	97.6	110.2	108.7	109.4	100.8	99.2	86.6	85.8	89.8
1965	13.0	84.6	103.8	94.6	109.2	106.2	112.3	99.2	100.8	86.9	83.8	89.2
1966	13.4	77.6	108.2	92.5	106.0	104.5	114.2	99.3	101.5	85.1	84.3	85.1
1967	13.9	76.3	110.1	91.4	111.5	102.9	113.7	97.8	100.0	84.9	84.9	84.2
1968	14.0	72.1	114.3	91.4	111.4	102.1	110.0	100.0	102.1	86.4	85.7	85.0
1969	13.3		106.0	90.2	109.8	102.3	111.3	100.0	98.5	87.2	88.0	85.7
1970	13.3		106.0	85.7	105.3	102.3	112.0	100.0	102.3	84.2	86.5	83.5
1971	13.3		109.8	90.2	106.0	103.0	109.8	102.3	103.8	82.7	85.0	81.5
1972	13.5		108.9	88.9	104.4	101.5	111.9	103.0	105.2	81.5	85.2	81.0
1973	13.7	69.3	110.9	93.4	109.5	100.7	108.8	104.4	105.8	80.3	87.6	82.0
1974	13.9	98.6	111.5	95.0	112.2	102.9	109.4	101.4	112.2	82.0	87.8	80.9
1975	14.1	97.2	117.7	97.2	117.7	105.0	107.8	101.4	114.2	83.7	89.4	81.2
1976	13.8	108.0	129.7	97.8	123.9	105.1	110.1	102.2	115.2	84.8	89.9	83.1
1977/78	13.6	112.5	145.6	97.1	125.0	108.1	99.3	103.7	114.7	83.1	92.6	83.2
1978/79	13.7	120.4	147.4	98.5	125.5	105.8	97.8	104.4	115.3	85.4	94.2	82.1
1979/80	14.0	111.4	143.6	97.1	115.7	103.6	102.1	102.1	112.1	84.3	93.6	87.8
1980/81	13.9	140.3	148.2	94.2	125.9	107.2	97.1	102.9	118.7	86.3	97.8	87.8
1981/82	14.1	134.0	156.7	93.6	126.2	109.9	94.3	102.1	119.1	90.1	100.7	89.4
1982/83	14.0	102.9	141.4	104.3	132.1	114.3	91.4	103.6	122.1	92.9	102.9	91.4

Average Annual Rates of Change in Paid Hours-Per-Patient Day

	Canada	N.W.T. & Yukon	Nfld	P.E.I.	N.S.	N.B.	Que.	Ont.	Man.	Sask.	Alta.	B.C.
1962-66	2.58	-4.49	4.20	1.25	0.72	1.10	4.97	1.56	2.96	1.36	1.85	0.90
1966-71	-0.15		0.14	-0.65	-0.14	-0.43	-0.93	0.45	0.29	-0.71	0.00	-0.53
1971-76	0.74		4.16	-2.38	3.93	1.14	-0.28	0.72	2.87	1.24	1.88	0.18
1976-81/82	0.43	4.87	4.31	-0.45	0.81	1.34	-1.58	0.42	1.11	1.65	2.75	2.38
1981-82/83	-0.71	-23.81	-10.41	10.61	3.93	3.23	-3.76	0.69	1.79	2.36	1.41	1.59
1962-82/83	0.73	0.71	2.41	1.07	1.48	0.89	0.08	0.74	1.74	0.93	1.59	0.76

TABLE 36

HOSPITAL CAPACITY, UTILIZATION AND EXPENDITURES PER CAPITA, PER DIEM COSTS, AND INDEXES OF INPUT PRICES AND SERVICE INTENSITIES PER PATIENT DAY,
Canada and U.S. 1966-1971 and 1971-1982

	Canada				U.S.			
	1966	1982	Avg. Annual % Chg. 1966/71	% Chg. 1971/82	1966	1982	Avg. Annual % Chg. 1966/71	% Chg. 1971/82
Hospital Expenditures Per Capita ($)	83.24	505.71	11.9	12.0	78.46	573.67	13.2	13.3
Hospital Input Price Index	70.2	325.5	7.3	11.3	71.9	264.5	6.8	9.2
Hospital Input Price Index Relative to GNE Deflator	84.9	118.7	3.3	1.6	90.0	122.8	2.1	1.9
Hospital Expenditures Per Capita (Constant 1971 $)	100.67	184.41	7.7	2.1	98.21	266.18	8.2	5.6
Hospital Expenditures Per Capita (Real Output in 1971 $)	118.58	155.36	4.3	0.6	109.12	216.89	6.0	3.7
Hospital Per Diem Costs ($)	36	247	11.3	13.4	46	348	13.9	13.3
Index of Service Intensity per Patient-Day	83.5	123.0	3.7	1.9	72.7	149.5	6.6	3.7

Notes: Index Values are all based on 1971=100. Constant dollar values are deflated by the GNE deflator, while Real Values are deflated by the Hospital Input Price Index.

point. Rather it represents a change in emphasis and concern, from expanding coverage to cost control. The shift is one of policy and priorities, not of programs.

Table 36 shows first that the pattern of increase of hospital expenditures *per capita* in the two countries has been strikingly parallel, before and after 1971. But the increases are about 1 percent per year faster in the U.S., and this difference is the same on either side of 1971. Over sixteen years, it cumulates to a 20 percent increase in U.S. costs relative to Canada.

What is *very* different, however, is the pattern of *inflation-adjusted* costs *per capita*. (In this case we adjust by the GNE deflator, to reflect the fact that hospital expenditures are broader than simply wages and salaries.) It is striking that, although in both countries and both periods hospital costs *per capita* rose in real terms, the slowdown in growth after 1971 is much more pronounced in Canada where the rate of general inflation was more rapid than in the U.S. In both countries the latter half of the 1960s was a period of very rapid increases in inflation-adjusted hospital costs *per capita*, though even then the U.S. was rising faster, at 8.2 percent per year compared with 7.7 percent. After 1971, though, the Canadian rate of increase dropped by nearly three-quarters; that in the U.S. by about one-third. In real terms, since 1971, U.S. costs have risen two and a half times as fast as those in Canada.

One possible source of the difference is different rates of increase in input prices, in particular (but not exclusively), wages and salaries. We saw in Table 18 that differential rates of fee increases appeared to be the principal source of the difference in Canadian and U.S. physician costs. But Table 36 suggests that such differences in sector-specific inflation rates have been a much less important feature of the comparative hospital experience. Again, both countries in both periods have seen hospital input prices outrun general inflation. But in the 1971 to 1982 period the difference between Canada and the U.S. is only 0.3 percent per year, or about 3.5 percent over the whole period. In the late 1960s, such increases were much more rapid in Canada, but they were cut in half after 1971 (presumably because the general inflation level caught up). In the U.S., there is only a small difference before and after 1971.

What Table 36 shows clearly is that hospital expenditures adjusted for hospital-specific input price changes, i.e., hospital utilization and servicing intensity, have been dramatically different. In both countries, the late 1960s were a period of very rapid increases in real hospital inputs *per capita*; the U.S. figure of 6.0 percent per year cumulates to 34 percent in five years. But after 1971 the Canadian increases drop almost to zero. The U.S. rates also fall, but by a much smaller proportion. Over eleven years, the Canadian rate cumulates to 6.4 percent, the U.S. to 49 percent. This difference is then the major source of the divergence between Canadian and U.S. hospital cost trends after 1971.

Changes in deflated expenditures *per capita* can result from changes in utilization as usually measured — patient days per thousand population — or from changes in servicing intensity — inputs of personnel time and skills, drugs and supplies, services of capital equipment — per inpatient day. The latter in turn is influenced by shifting patterns of use within the hospital sector — more outpatient care, for example, raises *per diems* as commonly measured; a shift to more extended care and less acute care lowers them — or changes in the patterns of treatment within particular forms of care. Early discharge programs, for example, tend to raise the intensity of servicing per patient day, as may increasing diagnostic activity. The *per capita* data in Table 36 include the effects of all such shifts.

It would be interesting, but beyond the scope of this project, to assemble comparable Canada and U.S. data over time on utilization of different types of hospital care: patient days per thousand population by level of care and ambulatory use. This would enable us to identify and compare utilization *changes*, utilization *shifts*, and pure intensity changes.

Table 36 instead presents a rather cruder comparison, of Canadian *per diems* in general and allied special hospitals with those reported for U.S. community hospitals. (U.S. data are adjusted to exclude outpatient care, Canadian are not.) The denominators are not fully comparable, so not much should be made of the differences in levels. Nevertheless, these *per diem* data do show a substantial inter-country difference in service intensity per patient-day; i.e., *per diem* costs divided by input prices. In both countries these increases are cut by about half after 1971, but in both periods the U.S. increases are at about double the Canadian rate. And insofar as there may have been a shift toward more emphasis on outpatient care, the Canadian data are upward-biased relative to the U.S.

What seems clear in the case of hospital costs, then, is that the key difference between the Canadian and the U.S. experiences after 1971 has been in volumes of servicing, not in input prices. Furthermore, though these data do not permit too precise an allocation, that difference has been almost entirely a result of divergent trends, not in inpatient utilization, but in resources used — labour and supplies — per patient day.

Our data thus tend to reinforce the more detailed analysis by Detsky *et al.* (1983) for Ontario; the principal impact of cost-containment on Canadian hospitals, compared with their U.S. counterparts, has been to limit the growth of servicing intensity. Its relative effects on input prices and utilization have been much less.

Can We Escape From History?

Having surveyed the historical experience of the different provinces in some detail, we will in this section draw out some generalizations or common themes. From these, we attempt to forecast what the future of the physician and hospital sectors in Canada is likely to be through to the end of the 1980s and beyond. These forecasts are inevitably tentative, but they are consistent with the record

Expenditures, Prices, Utilization and Incomes in the Canadian Health Care System   145

thus far. On the other hand, the optimistic view of projections of this sort is that by drawing attention to the implications of present policies, they may encourage change and so become self-falsifying.

The first major point that emerges strongly from all the data above is the importance of the distinction between real and nominal expenditure. In both sectors, movements in relative prices and in associated provider incomes appear to be primarily responsible for expenditure shifts. There are underlying trends in utilization of both hospital and medical care, which are very significant over the long run — measured in decades. But the control of costs in the first decade of Medicare, like the dramatic increases in share of GNP going to health care in the pre-Medicare period, and the apparent resurgence of cost growth in the early 1980s, is primarily price/income driven.

This in turn implies that debates about under- or over-funding, which purport to focus on the appropriate balance between population need and health care resources, are seriously misleading if based solely on expenditure data. Of course, such debates are often simply struggles over relative income status, carried on in the emotive language of needs for care. But for those seriously interested in observing what has happened to the availability and use of services over time, or differences across provinces, it is essential that expenditure data be disaggregated to isolate shifts in relative prices from the underlying changes in quantities of services provided and used.

For Canada as a whole, the pre-Medicare and Medicare periods are quite distinct. The contrast between the rapid escalation in share of GNP devoted to health care during the twenty-five years prior to 1971, and the more-or-less stability since, commands immediate attention. And the expenditure component data show clearly that this resulted from a change in the forces determining hospital and physician costs; there is no trend break in the other cost components. In the pre-Medicare period, expansion occurred in capacity, utilization and relative prices; for the whole period all movements were relentlessly up often at quite remarkable rates. Since 1971, however, the patterns are no longer monotonic. Both relative prices, and capacity and utilization, show downward as well as upward movements in some cost components and time periods.

But the second significant point to emerge from the detailed data is that the Canadian experience is not monolithic. Performances differ among provinces. Ontario and Quebec seem to have been most successful in controlling overall costs; the far West and some of the Maritime provinces have had rates of cost escalation since 1971 that are closer to American patterns. Moreover, the balance between hospital and medical costs differs markedly across provinces. B.C. has by far the highest cost for physicians' services, and the most rapid escalation since 1971. But its hospital costs are consistently below the national average. Clearly there is room for considerable variety in policy emphasis, and for greater or lesser determination and success in managing overall costs. The form of the funding system does not guarantee the outcome in any lock-step fashion.

Taking the long view, however, it is clear that the real availability of facilities and services has become less unequal across provinces. The variety of provincial experiences has been superimposed on this underlying change. What is less clear is whether this represents a trend, or simply a one-time shift associated with the introduction of the public insurance programs. Particularly in the case of utilization of physicians' services, the data suggest that there has been no change in the degree of inter-provincial dispersion since 1971. There have, however, been considerable changes in *per capita* physician costs, reflecting changes in the dispersion of relative fees and incomes. Hospital wages also converged in the period leading up to the introduction of Medicare, but seem to have maintained about the same degree of inter-provincial dispersion since then.

Insofar as the various provincial experiences with cost control amount to more or less successful efforts to limit the growth of provider incomes, the third point that should be emphasized is the marked difference in income patterns between physicians and hospital workers. The rapid escalation of hospital workers' incomes in the pre-Medicare period has continued since 1971. Periods of stability in relative wages have been interspersed with dramatic forward movements, but in very few provinces and years have relative wages fallen. There is little indication in the data to 1982 that provincial payment agencies have found any way of stabilizing hospital relative wages. The one exception to this generalization is the period from 1975 to 1979, during most of which time the federal wage and price controls were in effect. But in all provinces but B.C., the lost ground was made up between 1979 and 1982.

Physician incomes, however, dropped sharply in the early 1970s. Fee schedules failed to keep up with the rate of inflation, falling in real terms by nearly 20 percent between 1971 and 1975. Increases in fee-adjusted billings per physician were not rapid enough to prevent significant relative income erosion. In the latter half of the 1970s, however, fee increases accelerated almost to the inflation rate, and since 1980 have significantly exceeded it. In combination with increases in fee-adjusted billing rates, this has enabled physician relative incomes to be at least maintained during the late 1970s and to move rapidly ahead again in the early 1980s.

The changing patterns of relative incomes suggest a shift in the focus of cost control policy at the provincial government level, according to perceptions of political feasibility and cost. In the early 1970s, physicians had just emerged from an extended period of extraordinary income gains. Moreover, they had yet to gear up politically and organizationally for the process of fee bargaining with provincial governments. Stringent fee controls were likely to meet relatively little professional resistance, nor would the income position of physicians generate much public sympathy. In the mid-1970s, the federal wage and price control program provided further support for provincial negotiators. But the steady acceleration of fees during the later 1970s and the jumps in the early 1980s suggest that the political cost of fee control has gone up sharply. In future it may be enough of a challenge to keep physician fees and incomes in line with general inflation rates, without again attempting to push relative incomes down.

Limitations on the supply of physicians, in contrast, seem to have been considered politically much more dangerous. With the exception of the change in federal immigration policy in 1975, which sharply cut back the in-migration of foreign physicians, there have been no significant policies to slow down the steady increase in physicians *per capita*. In the early 1970s when physician relative incomes were falling, the failure to address the manpower issue could be reconciled with overall cost control. But if it becomes more difficult to limit physician incomes, the control of numbers may begin to be taken more seriously.

In the hospital sector, the choice between controlling incomes and controlling capacity has been made differently. There does not appear to have been any independent effort by provincial governments to cap the growth in hospital workers' relative incomes. The only period of restriction was a result of federal policy, directed at the whole economy. Instead, provinces appear to have decided to limit the growth of hospital capacity. This shows up as stabilization of *per capita* bed capacity in the early 1970s, though the intensity of servicing continued to grow. *Per diem* costs, adjusted for input prices, were still climbing. But in the late 1970s, bed capacity began to be cut back, and service intensity was growing much less rapidly. After an increase in occupancy rates, utilization also began to fall, with the adjustments starting at different times in different provinces. It appears that in this case the politically most attractive, or least unattractive, approach has been to control expenditure through the budgetary negotiation process, rather than attempting to confront the hospital unions over relative wages. Looked at another way, in the hospital sector the hospital boards serve as a buffer between governments and workers, and in this buffering role appear to have chosen to let relative incomes rise. Budgetary pressures imposed on overall costs have then been translated into capacity reductions. But it seems most unlikely that this process could go on without provincial approval.

Implicit in these contrasting policies toward the physician and hospital sectors, however, is an enforced shift in patterns of medical practice. The steady increase in physicians *per capita*, in combination with the reduction in bed capacity, leaves fewer beds for each physician. The result must be that, on average, services to inpatients will become a decreasing share of medical practice. While some hospital-based physicians may continue to practice wholly or primarily on inpatients, primary care physicians are finding and will continue to find hospital access more and more difficult. From the point of view of effective health care, this may be a desirable trend. But no deliberate decision has ever been made to restructure practice patterns; it is simply the outcome of the different strategies of cost control that have been applied in the two sectors.

The steadily falling bed-to-physician ratio, which has every appearance of persisting into the indefinite future, places further pressure on physician incomes. The ability to generate billings depends to some extent on access to complementary hospital facilities and personnel. Thus, limitations on hospital capacity represent indirect limitations on physician earning power. Furthermore, since access to the increasingly scarce facilities is primarily controlled by physicians themselves, the internal political struggles over hospital access can only intensify. In these circumstances, it is not surprising that physicians perceive hospital facilities to be underfunded.

The data assembled above, however, emphasize that hospital beds are an incomplete measure of hospital capacity. The per day service volume index measures the increase in hospital costs per day adjusted for changes in wages and other input prices. This index has increased steadily throughout the period, indicating that the volume of services received by patients during each day in hospital has been increasing. This partially offsets reductions in utilization as measured by patient days *per capita*, since it allows for increases in hospital-based ambulatory care, or in more intensive servicing associated with increasingly complex interventions. Since 1975, however, this index too has been slowing its growth. Between 1971 and 1976, the index was increasing by much more than the reduction in beds *per capita*; but, since then, the drop in beds has accelerated and the growth in servicing intensity has slowed. This suggests further pressure on hospital facilities available to each physician.

These observations suggest that the relative cost performance during the first decade and a half of Medicare may deteriorate in future. The successful performance of the first decade was based on the use of "blunt instrument" policies, controls on the escalation of fee schedules, and global hospital budgets. Politically sensitive areas — physician supply and hospital workers' incomes — were avoided. In the early 1980s, provincial governments seem to be gearing up to tackle the physician manpower problem. So far, however, the most widely discussed approach has been B.C.'s effort to export the problem, by restricting the issuance of provincial billing numbers. In principle, a physician without a billing number may be licensed to practice in B.C., but neither he nor his patients can be reimbursed by the provincial plan.

It would probably be politically impossible to generalize this policy Canada-wide while still training increasing numbers of physicians. The obvious policy of reducing the production of new physicians would, if implemented immediately, have no significant impact before 1990. The medium term outlook, therefore, is for more cost pressure from the physician side, both on fee levels and on hospital capacity. Over the longer term, it has been suggested that changing physician lifestyles and personal priorities may lead to voluntary acceptance of reduced workloads and billing rates per physician. But so far this is pure speculation.

In principle, the hospital sector should be much more flexible because it is not constrained by the long lags that characterize the physician supply process. But, as emphasized above, the historical record does not show much success in the limitation of hospital workers' incomes; such increases seem as inevitable as those in physician supply. The key question for the future is whether the political costs of further constraining hospital capacity will escalate to the point where it is preferable to attempt to constrain hospital sector incomes. This would presumably imply increased labour unrest and more frequent strikes. Alternatively, or perhaps in addition, the process of supply constraint may continue. This will run into increasing resistance from physicians (assuming continued fee-for-service reimbursement and unrestrained medical school production) and possibly from the public. In principle, it should be possible to achieve further significant reductions in inpatient use by encouraging changes in patterns of medical practice along lines documented in the medical literature (see Hastings and Vayda, this volume). This would require, however, that provincial governments move beyond "blunt instrument" control mechanisms, and attempt to exert direct influence on those patterns. While the payoff to such initiatives could conceivably be very high, the political costs may be equally high. On balance, the path of least resistance is likely to be seen as more aggressive negotiation of incomes in the hospital sector. But even stability of hospital sector relative incomes may be insufficient to avoid escalation of hospital costs, particularly under pressure from the increasing physician supply.

Data Appendix

The data in Table 1 for 1971 and subsequent years are drawn from Canada, Health and Welfare Canada (1984a) Table 2, and for 1956 and prior years from Leacy, ed. (1983), Series B504-513. The 1961 and 1966 data are updated from Leacy on the basis of unpublished revisions to the institutions series by Health and Welfare Canada, Health Information Division. The new total expenditure figures for 1961 and 1966 are taken from Canada, *op. cit.*, Table 1, and the discrepancies between these and the totals in Leacy are assumed to be entirely in the institutions series since the physician, dentist, and prescribed drug series do not appear to have been revised. The allocation of these discrepancies between hospitals and homes for special care (included in National Health Expenditures but not in the pre-1961 sub-total) is on the basis of unpublished data supplied by Health and Welfare Canada, Health Information Division.

The data from 1970 on in Tables 2 to 7 are also drawn from Canada, Health and Welfare Canada (1984a), Tables 4, 6 and 31 to 40. Data prior to 1970 in Tables 2 and 3 are calculated from Table 1, using mid-year population data from Canada, Health and Welfare Canada (1979), Table 19.1 for 1966 and 1961, and 1 June data from Leacy, *op. cit.*, Series A1, for earlier years. Gross National Product data used to derive Table 3 are from *ibid.*, Series F13. Tables 4 to 7, data for 1960 and 1965, are calculated from Canada, Health and Welfare Canada (1979), Tables 18.1, 18.2, 18.11 and 18.12, using population data from Table 19.1.

Figure 1 is drawn using Canadian data from Table 1 of Canada, Health and Welfare Canada (1984a), for 1960 onward, and Leacy, ed. (1983), series B513 and F13 for earlier years. Figure 2 data are from the same sources, except that the break is at 1970. 1970 to 1982 data are from Table 6, earlier data from Series B504 and B505. U.S. data in both figures are from Gibson, Waldo and Levit (1983) for 1965 to 1982, and for earlier years from Cooper et al. (1973).

Table 8, the indices of physicians' fees by province from 1960 to 1983, is assembled from several sources. The Canada series was originally developed and described in Barer and Evans (1983). For 1971 and subsequent years, the Health Information Division of Health and Welfare Canada has prepared (unpublished) indices of the fee schedules in each province governing reimbursement of physicians by the provincial insurance plan, on a basis of 1971 = 100.0. The national index is a weighted average of these provincial indices, with provincial weights that are adjusted through time to reflect changes in the relative billings in the different provinces. Fee schedules change at a particular point in time, usually within a year. The Health and Welfare index represents the average over the year of fee schedules in force in a province during that year, weighted according to the proportion of time they were in force. The source for Table 8 is Canada, Health and Welfare Canada (1982a), with updated information provided by officials of Health and Welfare Canada. The most recent release ATP is Canada, Health and Welfare Canada (1984c).

This index forms the core of Table 8, with the modification that the base value in 1971 for each province has been adjusted to reflect the level of that province's fees relative to the national average. Health and Welfare Canada currently does not release the data in this form. But in the late 1960s and early 1970s, the Health Research Division of the Department of National Health and Welfare prepared (unpublished) comparisons of provincial fee schedules on a more or less annual basis, showing each province's schedule relative to that of Ontario. A tabulation by what was then the Health Economics and Statistics Division, in January 1975, gives these relatives for December 31 of 1970 and 1971, as well as the amounts and (in other sources) dates of schedule revisions during 1971. These, and provincial weights for 1972-1973 used by Health and Welfare Canada in constructing the post-1971 index (1984c), were used to calculate a national average index for 1971 against which each province's overall fee level could be compared in that year. These relatives were then used to re-base the post-1971 indices so that each province's fee level could be shown relative to that national average for 1971 (set equal to 100.0).

For provinces that entered Medicare prior to 1971, the periodic percentage changes in fee/benefit reimbursement schedules reported by Health and Welfare

Expenditures, Prices, Utilization and Incomes in the Canadian Health Care System 151

Canada could be used to compute appropriate changes in the index of fees in effect in each province, back to the date of entry to Medicare. Prior to that time, Health and Welfare Canada compiled estimates of the overall percentage change in fees represented by the periodic revisions in fee schedules issued by the provincial medical associations, and these are reported in unpublished tabulations (see also 1982a, 1984c). They can be used to carry each province's fee index back to December of 1963, and are so used here, although it must be kept clearly in mind that these were only guides to practitioners prior to Medicare. They were used as a basis for reimbursement by service benefit private insurance programs, but were not binding, and physicians may have made concessions from them either deliberately (differential billing) or unintentionally (uncollectible accounts) (Barer and Evans, 1983; Wolfson, Evans and Lomas, 1980).

For 1960, however, no such index exists. But at that time, data on physicians' fees were collected as a component of the Consumer Price Index. Unpublished data were provided by Statistics Canada for the major cities in each province, for April and October of each year, showing the value of this physicians' fees index as reported by practitioners surveyed by the Dominion Bureau of Statistics. A (population) weighted average of the index for the cities available in each province, for 1964 and 1960, was used to carry the fee schedule based index back to 1960. The 1963 value was not used, because this refers only to December of that year, and it was not known whether there were revisions to the fee guides in some provinces during that year. Since no city from Prince Edward Island was included in the CPI survey in those days, a 1960 index for that province could not be computed.

Quebec also represented a special case, as no fee guide was issued for all Quebec physicians prior to Medicare. The Quebec index in Table 8 from 1960 to 1968 is therefore the Consumer Price Index, physicians' fees component, for the city of Montreal. This specific index was not available after 1968, but for 1969 and 1970 the provinces that had already entered Medicare had been dropped from the CPI so that the national CPI physicians' fees component was almost entirely a reflection of Quebec fees. Accordingly, this component (as reported in Canada, Statistics Canada, *Prices and Price Indices*, Vol. 47, no. 12, p. 50, and Vol. 48, no. 12, p. 51) was used to form the bridge from 1968 to 1970, and fees in Quebec are assumed not to have changed during 1970. (Of course fees *collected* may well have risen sharply, as they appear to have done in several other provinces on the introduction of Medicare.)

Annual values of the Canadian Consumer Price Index are reported in Leacy, *op. cit.*, Series K8, down to 1975. Subsequent values are drawn from various issues of the *Canadian Statistical Review* (Canada, Statistics Canada, monthly).

Parenthetically, it should be noted that despite the potential inadequacies of the fee indices based on provincial fee guides prior to Medicare, they appear to parallel the CPI physicians' services component quite closely. From 1964 to

1968, both rose by 19.4 percent, although the latter includes Quebec and the former (since Quebec did not have a province-wide schedule) does not. There was, of course, some variation in individual years. From 1964 to 1970, the CPI component rises 29.1 percent and the fee schedule index 27.9 percent, but after 1968, as noted above, the CPI component was almost entirely Quebec, and the fee index was based on the other nine provinces, so there would be no reason for their values to coincide.

Tables 9 to 11 are calculated from prior tables or their sources. Table 9 combines data on *per capita* expenditures on physicians' services from Tables 31 to 40 of Canada, Health and Welfare Canada (1984a), and the relevant tables from Tables 18.1 to 18.32 and Table 19.1 from Canada, Health and Welfare Canada (1979), with fee data from Table 8 above, to compute the change in apparent *per capita* utilization during the period of introduction of Medicare in each province as the ratio of change in expenditure *per capita* over change in reported fees. Table 10 combines the data underlying Table 6 (which can be recovered from that table by computation) with those in Table 8, to yield estimates of expenditures *per capita* measured in constant, 1971, Canada-average fees, over time and across provinces. Table 11 presents this same information in the form of provincial relatives based on the national averages for selected years.

Table 12 introduces data on physician manpower, which are drawn from Canada, Health and Welfare Canada (1984b), Table 21.2, for 1972 to 1982. Data for 1983 are as yet unpublished, but were supplied by Health and Welfare Canada. Data for 1970 and 1971 are from Canada, Health and Welfare Canada (1980a), Table 21.2. For 1965, the number of active civilian physicians in Canada and population per physician were taken from Table 42 of Canada, Health and Welfare Canada (1972), p.132. This source does not give provincial breakdowns prior to 1970, but an earlier Research and Statistics Memo (Canada, Department of National Health and Welfare, 1967) gives a less complete count allocated by provinces. Table 12 uses the national data from the later source and allocates this total across provinces using the proportions in the earlier source. For 1960, the national total of active civilian physicians was taken from Judek (1964), Table 2-2, and then allocated across provinces using the proportions implicit in Judek's Table 2-3. That table reports province-specific data only for census years, but the provincial relatives for June 1, 1961, were used with the national data for December 31, 1960, in confidence that five months were unlikely to change the provincial relative standings significantly.

Table 13 is based on Tables 12 and 10. Utilization *per capita*, derived from Table 10, by province and year, is multiplied by population per physician, to yield utilization per physician, as a measure of physician activity levels or billings per physician in constant (Canada, 1971) fees. In Table 13 it has been indexed relative to the average value for Canada in 1971, and shows both the growth of output over time and relative outputs across provinces. Table 14 multiplies the underlying data of Table 12 with those of Table 6, expenditures *per capita* on physicians' services times population per physician, to yield expenditure per active civilian physician, and then indexes this too to Canada, 1971 = 100.0.

The data in Table 14 are not the same as average gross receipts per physician, for reasons spelled out in the text. Nevertheless, they should bear some relationship to average physician incomes, which are reported in Tables 15, 16 and 17, and are drawn from an unpublished document, "Earnings of Physicians in Canada", released by the Health Information Division of Health and Welfare Canada in February 1983 (Canada, Health and Welfare Canada, 1983). Table 15 is based on the data in Tables A.1.1 to A.1.10 and A.1.12 in that document, while Tables 16 and 17 are drawn from Tables 1 and 2 of Appendix A, which presents methodology and results of a calculation of average physician incomes from provincial insurance plan data by staff of the Health Information Division. An updated version of this document (Canada, Health and Welfare Canada 1985) is the source for the 1981 and 1982 data in Table 15, again using Tables A.1.1 to A.1.10 and A.1.12. These income data, while the best available, are subject to a number of biases and other problems. Full documentation that should guide their interpretation is provided in the HWC sources, while a more general discussion of the problems inherent in defining and measuring physicians' incomes is provided in Wolfson, Evans and Lomas, 1980.

U.S. data in Table 18 are assembled from Freeland and Schendler (1984); price and expenditure data from their Table 13 are combined with population and physician data from their Tables 2 and 4 respectively. The Canadian data are drawn from Tables 1 to 17 above, except for expenses of practice data. For 1982, these were the Health and Welfare Canada estimates from "Earnings of Physicians in Canada", *op. cit.*; for 1972 they were drawn from an earlier release, "Earnings of Physicians in Canada, 1962-1972" (Canada, Health and Welfare Canada, n.d. 1975?), Table A4.

The data in Table 19 are for all operating public general and allied special (PGAS) hospitals, as classified by Statistics Canada, modified for Quebec and Canada as noted below. These series include public general hospitals (some with long-term units), plus public paediatric, rehabilitation, extended care and nursing station/outpost hospitals. They exclude federal, psychiatric and tuberculosis institutions.

The number of operating PGAS hospitals from 1946 to 1952 was taken from Canada, Dominion Bureau of Statistics (1961); for 1953 to 1970 from Table 14 of Canada, Statistics Canada (1973a); for 1971 and 1972 from the respective annual editions of the same publication; for 1973 to 1975 from Canada, Statistics Canada (1976b, 1976c, 1978); for 1976 to 1980/81 from Canada, Statistics Canada (1981a, 1981b, 1981c, 1983a, 1983b), and for 1981/82 and 1982/83 from Canada, Statistics Canada (1982a, 1984).

From 1971 on, minor adjustments have been made to published data for Quebec, as noted below.

Beds data are reported as rated bed capacity until 1975, approved bed complement thereafter. This does not appear to have been a change affecting inclusions or classifications. There was, however, at least one change in classification, which made the generation of consistent series for Quebec and Canada from published data virtually impossible. This was symptomatic of Statistics Canada's more general failure to provide bridging information when series definitions, inclusions or exclusions changed. Specifically, the number of beds reported for operating PGAS hospitals in Quebec in 1975 was 41,835, up relatively sharply from the 1974 total of 38,629. This increase accounted for just over two-thirds of the entire Canadian increase. In 1976, the Quebec figure jumped to 47,917, an increase in bed stock of almost 15 percent during a year in which stock for the rest of Canada *fell* by more than 2 percent. Closer examination of the *Hospital Statistics* series (cat. no. 83-227 and 83-232) revealed that most of the PGAS increase from 1974 to 1975 was growth in extended care beds (2,400 out of the total increase of 3,200), and extended care bed growth from 1975 to 1976 was an additional 9,000 beds(!), in excess of the entire net PGAS increase of about 6,000 beds. By 1976 Quebec reported more than 60 percent of all operating extended care beds in Canada, and a much higher ratio of extended care beds to population than was found in any other province.

Our quest for information on the source of the sudden addition to extended care bed stock led to Canada, Health and Welfare Canada (1984a) and from there to Canada, Statistics Canada (1977, 1978c, 1979b, 1980b, 1981d, 1982b, 1983d). It turns out that from 1975 to 1976, concurrent with the second "leg" of the extended care bed expansion, mental institution bed capacity in Quebec fell by just over 11,000 beds. Canada, Health and Welfare Canada (1984a) notes that "starting early in the 1970's the province of Quebec transferred its mental-hospital beds to other uses. Some were converted to provide chronic care and are since then included with general and allied special hospitals" (p.96). But the 2,400-bed growth in extended care from 1974 to 1975 is unaccompanied by any particular running down of mental hospital bed capacity and, in fact, the number of operating mental institutions jumps from 64 to 76 (and then returns to 64 in 1976). To confuse the situation further, the number of separations from mental institutions between 1975 and 1976 (which one would expect might fall even if only long-term psychiatric beds and patients were being reclassified), remained relatively flat from 1974 through to at least 1978/79!

All this suggested the need for an inter-provincial comparability adjustment, but did little to suggest what that adjustment ought to be. The data reported in Table 19 for Quebec and Canada are based on the sources noted above, plus additional information obtained through the kind assistance and effort of Dr. Pierre Bergeron, Directeur, Evaluation des Programmes, Ministère des Affairs Sociales, Québec. He provided the following estimates of mental institution beds and patient days that would have been (pre-1976) or were (post-1976) reclassified as extended care and thus became part of Statistics Canada's PGAS hospital series from 1976 on:

	1974	1975	1979-80	1980-81	1981-82	1982-83
Beds	11,547	10,857	9,610	9,698	9,486	9,519
Patient Days	3,550,028	3,412,617	3,366,108	3,326,605	3,302,947	3,292,660

Unfortunately, data for the critical year, 1976, were not available. However, from the other sources noted above we knew that between 1975 and 1976 extended care beds increased by 9,000, and that mental institution bed capacity fell by just over 11,000 beds. The above data suggest that between 9,600 and 10,800 mental institution beds were reclassified in 1976.

Since 10,200 is the average of the 1975 and 1979-1980 numbers, close to the average of the 9,000 and 11,000+ figures on the two sides of the phenomenon in published sources, and not inconsistent with the 1974 and 1975 pattern in the above figures, we estimated that 10,200 beds reported as PGAS in 1976 were in fact reclassified mental institution beds. For 1977 and 1978 we reduced this to 10,000 and 9,800 respectively, and from 1979-1980 on we applied Bergeron's figures above. These beds were eliminated from the published PGAS figures for Quebec and Canada, to derive the data on which Table 19 and subsequent tables dependent on bed supply are based.

It turns out that Statistics Canada's published figures on number of hospitals included mental institutions in Quebec (but not their beds or utilization) as early as *1961!* In 1961, eight of the reported 146 PGAS hospitals were mental institutions, and from 1971 on, fifteen of the institutions were mental institutions. Our data in the top half of Table 19 have removed these institutions from the published figures for Quebec and for Canada.

The *published* figures (before the adjustments to Quebec and Canada) on rated/approved bed capacity for PGAS operating hospitals were taken from Canada, Dominion Bureau of Statistics (1961, Table 12) for 1947 to 1952; Canada, Statistics Canada (1973a, Table 14) for 1953 through 1970; Canada, Statistics Canada (1973b, 1974; Table 6) for 1971 and 1972 respectively; and Canada, Statistics Canada (1976b,c, 1978b; Tables 2 and 4) for 1973 through 1975. The data for 1976 through 1980-1981 are from Canada, Statistics Canada (1981a,b,c, 1983a,b; Table 1), and the two most recent years' figures come from the respective *Preliminary Annual Reports* (Canada, Statistics Canada 1982a, 1984). Table 20 rates of change are based on the figures in Table 19. The top half of Table 21 results from straightforward manipulation of Table 19. The bottom halves of Tables 21 and 22 (beds *per capita*) use Table 19 and population data taken from Canada, Statistics Canada (1972a, Table 1) for 1947 to 1969 (June 1); selected monthly editions of the *Canadian Statistical Review* for 1970 to 1976 (July 1);

and Canada, Statistics Canada (1984, Appendix B) for 1977 to 1982 (October 1, as mid-point of fiscal years). The physician data on which bed/physician ratios are computed in Table 23 are as described for Table 12.

Utilization data are reported in Tables 24 to 26, and once again adjustments were required to Quebec and Canada series because of the reclassification of mental institution beds. In this case, we compiled the following data for Quebec:

	1975	1976	1979/80	1980/81	1981/82	1982/83
A&C Patient Days in Reporting Extended Care Facilities	2,098,166	5,620,236				
Patient Days in Reporting Mental Institutions (Excluding Federal)	5,054,335	1,707,745				
Patient Days in Mental Institutions that would have been (pre-1976) or were (post-1976) reclassified as extended care from 1976 on	3,412,617		3,366,108	3,326,605	3,302,947	3,292,660

Line 1 was taken from Canada, Statistics Canada (1976a, 1978a), line 2 from Canada, Statistics Canada (1978e, 1979b), and line 3 is unpublished data from Pierre Bergeron. These suggest rather consistently that about 3.4 million patient days were reclassified in 1976. We smoothed the missing data for the subsequent years by assuming reclassification of 3.385 and 3.37 million days, respectively, in 1977/78 and 1978/79. For the later years, the Bergeron estimates were used. Again, these were deleted from the published data on PGAS hospital days in Quebec and in the Canadian totals.

Published PGAS hospitals' patient days data were not available in all years for all *operating* hospitals. As noted in the text, for the years in which we found patient days data only for *reporting* hospitals, those data were scaled up by the ratio of operating to reporting bed capacity in each province. For 1947 to 1952, patient days in *reporting* hospitals for Canada are taken from Leacy (1983), series B192, and for the provinces are based on average daily number of A&C patients (multiplied by 365 or 366 as appropriate) in *reporting* hospitals, from Canada, Dominion Bureau of Statistics (1961, Table 13). From 1953 to 1965, average daily number of patients in *operating* hospitals was taken from Canada, Statistics Canada (1973a). Statistics Canada Cat. no. 83-210 (Canada, Statistics Canada [1969, 1970, 1972b, 1973a,b, 1974], Table 11) provided annual data on patient days in operating hospitals for the years 1966 through 1972, and Cat. no. 83-227 (Canada, Statistics Canada [1976b,c, 1978b], Table 9) took over for

1973 to 1975. For reasons unclear to us, the only data we could find for years since 1975 were for *reporting* hospitals, although the numbers of PGAS hospitals not reporting are small. Table 5 of the later and published version of the 1981/82 *Preliminary Annual Report* (Canada, Statistics Canada [1983c]) provides patient days for 1976 through 1981/82, and the 1982/83 version (Canada, Statistics Canada [1984], Table 4) does the same for that year. Thus, for 1947 to 1952 and 1976 to 1982-1983, we scaled up patient days in reporting hospitals using the ratio of bed capacity in operating to reporting hospitals. This has the effect of assuming equivalent occupancy rates in those hospitals reporting and not reporting. Data on rated bed capacity in reporting hospitals were from the same sources as the patient day information (Canada, Dominion Bureau of Statistics [1961], Table 13) for 1947 to 1952, and Canada, Statistics Canada (1983a, 1984) for the years 1976 through 1982-1983).

Given the marked 1975 to 1976 break in the Quebec bed and patient day figures, the data on separations are an enigma. Separations of adults and children from extended care facilities in Quebec increased only marginally from 15,288 to 16,123 between 1975 and 1976 (Canada, Statistics Canada, 1976a, 1978a), while separations from non-federal mental and psychiatric institutions were 28,575 in 1975, 27,819 in 1976, and back up to 28,957 in 1977 (Canada, Statistics Canada, 1978d, 1979a, 1980a). In fact, total separations from PGAS hospitals in Quebec *fell* (according to the published data) by about 4 percent from 1975 to 1976. While we are left with some nagging unease about what happened to the separations represented by the 3.5 million reclassified patient days, we have no information that would allow us to make adjustments to the separations data. Thus the bottom half of Table 24 is taken from published sources. For 1947 to 1952, data for *reporting* hospitals were taken from Canada, Statistics Canada (1965), Table 13, as discharges plus deaths. These were scaled up as described above for reporting hospital patient days, to estimate separations in *operating* hospitals. Data for 1953 to 1970 are from Canada, Statistics Canada (1973a), Table 14, and for 1971 to 1975 from Canada, Statistics Canada (1973b, 1974, 1976b,c, 1978b). From 1976 forward we were again able to find data only for *reporting* hospitals, from the same sources as for patient days, and the bed capacity adjustment was applied. Table 25 reports the rates of change for the data in Table 24.

Because average length of stay is not simply total patient days in the year divided by separations (but rather patient days of separated cases divided by separations), Table 26 does not follow directly from Table 24. Rather, we took the ALS data from Leacy (1983), Series B285 for Canada, 1946 to 1952; Canada, Statistics Canada (1973a, 1974), Table 14 (Tables 13 and 14 for N.W.T. and Yukon) for Canada and provinces over the periods 1953 to 1960 and 1961 to 1971 respectively; *Hospital Annual Statistics* (Cat. no. 83-227, Table 17; Cat. no. 83-232, Table 4) as patient days of separated cases (SDS = separations' days stay) divided by separations for the years up to and including 1980/81; and from *Preliminary Annual Reports* (Canada, Statistics Canada, 1983c, 1984) for the most recent years. From 1973 forward the data were for *reporting* hospitals.

Of course, our earlier discussion of the problems with patient days data for Quebec suggests that adjustments were required to the Quebec ALS data. Indeed, the ALS in Quebec PGAS hospitals ostensibly jumped from 13.3 days in 1975 to 18.8 days in 1976, causing a full one day increase (10.97 to 11.97) in Canada's PGAS hospital length of stay. Since the ALS figures for 1976 through 1980/81 were computed from published series on days stay of separated cases (SDS) and on separations, and since we chose not to adjust separations, we simply reduced SDS as follows:

$$SDS_{adj} = SDS(1 - MH/DAYS);$$
$$ALS = SDS_{adj}/SEPNS$$

where MH are the patient days estimated to have been reclassified from mental health (MH) to extended care from 1976 forward. Rather than a straight subtraction of MH days, this first adjusts those days for the general PGAS relationship between total patient days (DAYS) and SDS. For Canada, SDS_{CAN} was reduced by $(SDS-SDS_{adj})_{QUE}$. This had the effect of lowering Quebec's 1976 ALS from the published figure for PGAS hospitals of 18.83 to 14.2, and Canada's from 11.97 to 11.0 (Table 26 suggests that even this may have been an incomplete adjustment.) In 1981/82 and 1982/83, when data on SDS were not published, we simply applied the published ALS figures for Quebec PGAS hospitals to the separations data (Table 24) to compute SDS, and then carried out the same adjustment as above.

Table 27 begins the development of the hospital input price series and is, as noted in the text, taken with minor modifications from Barer and Evans (1983), Table 7. The hospital rate index was a sub-component of the health and personal care component of the CPI prior to 1961, and is published in *Prices and Price Indexes* from 1955 only. Earlier unpublished data were provided by Statistics Canada. *Per diems* are from Canada, Statistics Canada (1964), Table 2. *Per diems* for adults and children (A&C) are reported for 1953 to 1960 only. We used a 1946 to 1960 *per diem* series based on adults, children, and newborns (AC&N) to extend the (A&C) series back to 1946. The ratio of A&C/AC&N was 1.11 in 1953 and 1954, 1.10 from 1955 to 1960. The AC&N figures for 1946 to 1952 were therefore scaled up by 11 percent in each year. This adjustment was not made in the earlier work, so lack of comparability between Table 27 and Barer and Evans (1983), Table 7, is partially attributable to this.

The indexes in Table 28 are based on the Canadian mix of personnel in 1977, and on province-specific wage levels, for those personnel categories for which data were reported in each province in 1962. Wage level data are from Canada, Health and Welfare Canada (1977, 1980b), Tables 1a to 11a, for the years 1962 to 1969 and 1970 to 1977 respectively; Canada, Health and Welfare Canada

Expenditures, Prices, Utilization and Incomes in the Canadian Health Care System   159

(1982b), Tables 1 to 11 for 1979 and 1980; and unpublished data supplied by Health and Welfare Canada for 1981 to 1983. The Canadian 1977 personnel mix is from Canada, Health and Welfare Canada (1980b), Table 1c. Table 29 is based on the same wage data as Table 28, but uses province-specific employee mix data for 1977, from unpublished data kindly provided by the Health Information Division, Health and Welfare Canada.

The series in Table 29 are related in Table 30 to provincial average wages and salaries, taken from the *Canadian Statistical Review* (*Historical Summary 1970*, p. 58, for 1962 to 1970; various monthly editions since then) and converted to indexes based on 1971 = 100.0. Thus, each column represents a province's hospital wage index from Table 29, divided by an industrial composite wage index for that province.

Expenditure share data for Table 31 were obtained from the Health Division, Institutional Statistics Section, Statistics Canada, and adjusted as described in the text. Price series in addition to the wage indexes in Table 29 were for pharmaceuticals, and all other supplies and expenses. For the former, we employed the pharmaceuticals and medicines industry selling price index, and for the latter the Gross National Expenditure implicit price deflator. Both were taken from the *Canadian Statistical Review* sources noted above in the context of average weekly wages and salaries. Table 32 is simply the division of the series in Table 31 by the same Canadian GNE deflator.

For 1946 to 1960, the first column of Table 33 is brought forward from Table 27. For 1953 and 1954, figures for Canada and provinces are from Canada, Statistics Canada (1967a), Table 2, for *reporting* hospitals. The same publication for 1970 (Canada, Statistics Canada [1973c]), Table 2) provides the data for 1955 to 1958, but for *operating* hospitals. Then Canada, Statistics Canada (1976d), Table 2 provides *operating* hospital average cost per day for 1959 to 1974. This source reports the Yukon and N.W.T. separately for the years 1961 to 1969. We computed a composite N.W.T. and Yukon cost per day series using average daily number of patients from Canada, Statistics Canada (1973a), Table 14 as weights for the region-specific costs per day. Canada, Statistics Canada (1978c), Table 2 provided data for 1975, and Canada, Statistics Canada (1984), p. 14 was the source for the period 1976 to 1982/83.

Table 34 is then calculated from Tables 31 and 33. The missing years are those for which no wage data were available. Table 34 figures are the cost per patient day from Table 33, re-based for Canada and each province at 1971 = 100.0, and divided by the respective input price indexes of Table 31.

The data in Table 35 are from *Preliminary Annual Reports* of hospital statistics from Statistics Canada. Canada, Statistics Canada (1967b), Table 1 provided the figures for 1961 to 1964, with the N.W.T. and Yukon composite computed by weighting each region's own paid hours per patient day by its share of the composite total patient days (from the same source). The years 1965 and 1966 were picked up from Canada, Statistics Canada (1975), Table 1b; and Canada, Statistics Canada (1978a), Table 1b provided 1967 to 1976 data. The N.W.T. and Yukon amalgamation for 1965 to 1968 was effected using data from Table 1A of the former publication. For the years from 1977 forward, annual editions of the *Preliminary Annual Reports* (Cat. nos. 83-217 and 83-X-202) were employed.

Finally, the U.S. data in Table 36 are from Freeland and Schendler (1984), Tables 12 and Q, and Gibson *et al.* (1983), Tables 1 and 2, and Canadian data are from the tables above.

Acknowledgements

This paper would have been impossible (or else much shorter) without the timely and heroic efforts of John Menic and Louis Fournier of the Institutional Statistics Section, Statistics Canada, and Gilles Fortin of Health and Welfare Canada. Revisions to the conference version were facilitated immeasurably by the generous assistance of Pierre Bergeron, Régie de l'Assurance-Maladie du Québec. Closer to home, Cheryl Jackson assisted with the data compilation and reconciliation, and Susan Chan converted the resulting mounds of data into the thirty-six tables that form the foundation of the paper. Susan Moloney, Mary Brunold and Jeanette Paisley had the unenviable task of getting two different word processors to convert what we wrote into what we meant. This research was funded in part by Health and Welfare Canada, under award 6610-1231-48.

References

Barer, M.L. *A Methodology for Derivation of Marginal Costs of Hospital Cases, and Application to Estimation of Cost Savings From Community Health Centres.* Unpublished doctoral dissertation. Department of Economics, University of B.C., 1977.

Barer M.L. and R.G. Evans. "Hospital Costs Over Time: Approaches to Price Deflation and Output Standardization". University of B.C., 1980, unpublished mimeo.

Barer, M.L. and R.G. Evans. "Prices, Proxies, and Productivity: An Historical Analysis of Hospital and Medical Care in Canada". In E. Diewert and C. Montmarquette, eds. *Price Level Measurement*, Ottawa: Statistics Canada, 1983, pp. 705-777.

Canada. Department of National Health and Welfare. "The Economics and Costs of Health Care". Research and Statistics Memo. Research and Statistics Directorate, Ottawa: DNHW, 1967.

Canada. Dominion Bureau of Statistics. *Hospital Statistics, Volume I — Hospital Beds*. Cat. no. 83-210. Ottawa: DBS, 1961.

Canada. Health and Welfare Canada. *Canada Health Manpower Inventory 1979*. Policy, Planning and Information Branch, Health Information Division, Ottawa: HWC, 1980a.

Canada. Health and Welfare Canada. *Canada Health Manpower Inventory 1983*. Policy, Planning and Information Branch, Health Information Division, Ottawa: HWC, 1984b.

Canada. Health and Welfare Canada. "Earnings of Physicians in Canada". Policy, Planning and Information Branch, Health Information Division, Ottawa: HWC, 1983, unpublished.

Canada. Health and Welfare Canada. *Earnings of Physicians in Canada, 1962-1972*. Health Programs Branch, Health Economics and Statistics Division, Ottawa: HWC, 1975.

Canada. Health and Welfare Canada. *Health and Welfare Services in Canada 1971*. Research and Statistics Directorate, Ottawa: HWC, 1972.

Canada. Health and Welfare Canada. "Increases in the Physicians' Benefit Schedules for Canada, the Provinces and Territories 1971 to 1984". Policy, Planning and Information Branch, Health Information Division, Ottawa: HWC, 1984c, unpublished.

Canada. Health and Welfare Canada. "Increases in the Schedules of Benefits for Physicians' Services under the Federal/Provincial Medical Care Insurance Plan". Policy, Planning, and Information Branch, Health Information Division, Ottawa: HWC, 1982a, unpublished.

Canada. Health and Welfare Canada. *National Health Expenditures in Canada 1960-1975*. Information Systems Branch, Ottawa: HWC, 1979.

Canada. Health and Welfare Canada. *National Health Expenditures in Canada 1970-1982*. Policy, Planning and Information Branch, Information Dissemination Unit, Ottawa: HWC, 1984a.

Canada. Health and Welfare Canada. *Salaries and Wages in Canadian Hospitals 1962 to 1975*. Health Programs Branch, Health Economics and Statistics Division, Ottawa: HWC. 1977.

Canada. Health and Welfare Canada. *Salaries and Wages in Canadian Hospitals 1970 to 1977*. Policy, Planning and Information Branch, Health Information Division, Ottawa: HWC, 1980b.

Canada. Health and Welfare Canada. *Salaries and Wages in Canadian Hospitals 1979 and 1980*. Policy, Planning, and Information Branch, Health Information Division, Ottawa: HWC, 1982b.

Canada. Health and Welfare Canada. "Earnings of Physicians in Canada". Policy, Planning and Information Branch, Health Information Division, Ottawa: HWC, 1985, unpublished.

Canada. Statistics Canada. *Canadian Statistical Review*. Cat. no. 11-003. Current Economic Analysis Division, Ottawa: SC, monthly.

Canada. Statistics Canada. *Canadian Statistical Review — Historical Summary 1970*. Cat. no. 11-505. Ottawa: SC, 1972a.

Canada. Statistics Canada. *Hospital Annual Statistics, 1976; 1977-78 — 1980-81*. Cat. no. 83-232, annual. Ottawa: SC, 1981a, 1981b, 1981c, 1983a, 1983b.

Canada. Statistics Canada. *Hospital Statistics Preliminary Annual Report, 1966, 1974 — 1976, 1981-82*. Cat. no. 83-217, annual. Ottawa: SC, 1967b, 1975, 1976a, 1978a, 1983c.

Canada. Statistics Canada. *Hospital Statistics Preliminary Annual Report 1981-82*. Ottawa: SC, 1982a, mimeo.

Canada. Statistics Canada. *Hospital Statistics Preliminary Annual Report 1982-83*. Cat. no. 83-X-202. Ottawa: SC, 1984.

Canada. Statistics Canada. *Hospital Statistics, Volume I — Beds, Services, Personnel, 1973 — 1975*. Cat. no. 83-227, annual. Ottawa: SC, 1976b, 1976c, 1978b.

Canada. Statistics Canada. *Hospital Statistics, Volume II — Expenditures, Revenues, Balance Sheets, 1974; 1975*. Cat. no. 83-228, annual. Ottawa: SC, 1976d, 1978c.

Canada. Statistics Canada. *Hospital Statistics, Volume I — Hospital Beds, 1963; 1966 — 1972*. Cat. no. 83-210, annual. Ottawa: SC, 1965, 1968, 1969, 1970, 1972b, 1973a, 1973b, 1974.

Canada. Statistics Canada. *Hospital Statistics, Volume VI — Hospital Expenditures, 1961; 1965; 1970*. Cat. no. 83-215, annual. Ottawa: SC, 1964, 1967a, 1973c.

Canada. Statistics Canada. *Mental Health Statistics, Volume I — Institutional Admissions and Separations, 1975 — 1977*. Cat. no. 83-204, annual. Ottawa: SC, 1978d, 1979a, 1980a.

Canada. Statistics Canada. *Mental Health Statistics, Volume III — Institutional Facilities, Services and Finances, 1974 — 1977; 1978-79 — 1980-81*. Cat. no. 83-205, annual. Ottawa: SC, 1977, 1978e, 1979b, 1980b, 1981d, 1982b, 1983d.

Canada. Statistics Canada. *Prices and Price Indexes*. Cat. no. 62-002. Ottawa: SC, various years.

Cooper, B.S., N.L. Worthington and M.F. McGee. *Compendium of National Health Expenditure Data.* DHEW Pub. No. (SSA)73-11903. Office of Research and Statistics, Social Security Administration, Washington, D.C.: U.S. Department of Health, Education and Welfare, 1973.

Denton, F. and B. Spencer. "Population Aging and Future Health Costs in Canada", *Canadian Public Policy*, 9, 2, 1983, 155-163.

Detsky, A.S., S.R. Stacey and C. Bombardier. "The Effectiveness of a Regulatory Strategy in Containing Hospital Costs — The Ontario Experience, 1967-1981", *New England Journal of Medicine*, 309, 3, 1983, 151-159.

Enterline, P.E. et al. "The Distribution of Medical Services Before and After 'Free' Medical Care — The Quebec Experience", *New England Journal of Medicine*, 289, 22, 1973, 1174-1178.

Feldstein, M. "Quality Change and Demand for Hospital Care", *Econometrica*, 45, 7, 1977, 1681-1702.

Feldstein, M. "The Quality of Hospital Services: An Analysis of Geographic Variation and Intertemporal Change". In M. Perlman, ed., *The Economics of Health and Medical Care*, pp. 402-419. London: MacMillan, 1974.

Freeland, M.S. and C.E. Schendler. "Health Spending in the 1980's: Integration of Clinical Practice Patterns with Management", *Health Care Financing Review*, 5, 3, 1984, pp. 1-68.

Gibson, R.M., D.R. Waldo and K.R. Levit. "National Health Expenditures 1982", *Health Care Financing Review*, 5, 1, 1983, 1-32.

Irazuzta, J.O. *A Trend Analysis of Hospital Utilization in Canada.* M.Sc. thesis. Department of Health Administration, University of Toronto, Toronto, 1979, unpublished.

Judek, S. *Medical Manpower in Canada.* Study prepared for the Royal Commission on Health Services. Ottawa: The Queen's Printer, 1964.

Leacy, F.H., ed. *Historical Statistics of Canada*, 2nd. ed. Ottawa: Statistics Canada and the Social Science Federation of Canada, 1983.

Wolfson, A.D., R.G. Evans and J. Lomas. "Physician Incomes in Canada". Background paper presented for *Health Services Review '79*, The Hon. Emmett M. Hall, Special Commissioner, Ottawa: Health and Welfare Canada, 1980.

Woods Gordon. *Investigation of the Impact of Demographic Change on the Health Care System in Canada.* Final Report submitted to the Task Force on the Allocation of Health Care Resources (Joan Watson, chairperson). Toronto: Woods Gordon, 1984.

COMMENTARY

K.G. Moore
Y.M. Cheung

Introduction

Barer and Evans have undertaken a difficult and time-consuming task — to assemble in one place historical data pertaining to expenditures for physician services and hospital care in Canada by province. Their objectives were three: (1) to broaden the common ground of accepted facts, (2) to identify clear-cut or emerging patterns in expenditure data, either to suggest causality among different variables or to place a heavy burden of argument on those who deny, and (3) to help improve our understanding of how the health care system functions in Canada. Although a sense of some frustration can be detected in the title of their paper, Barer and Evans have successfully accomplished what they set out to do. This makes our role as discussants of their paper, we hope, much easier. We have no basic disagreement with their descriptive, and little with their interpretive, analysis. But we would like to focus on some of the interpretations of their findings, particularly pertaining to Alberta because we are more familiar with Alberta than with other provinces.

Health Care Expenditures in Canada by Component and Province

Barer and Evans note that Canada allocated a more or less constant proportion of GNP for health care in the 1970s, while in the United States the share of national resources spent on health care was steadily increasing. They attribute the remarkable stability of the Canadian proportion to the specific forms of funding systems adopted by the provinces; i.e., global funding through a budget review process for institutional care and negotiations to determine not only the overall increase to the Schedule of Medical Benefits for physicians but also the structure of medical benefits. It is further conjectured that had Canada not adopted this specific form of funding system, the behaviour of health care expenditure in Canada would have been parallel to that in the U.S. In fact, we are actually looking at two hypotheses:

1. The first hypothesis concerns the relationship between the specific form of funding system adopted by the provinces and the proportion of GNP used for health care in Canada.
2. The second hypothesis pertains to how the proportion of GNP used would have changed in the absence of the specific form of funding system actually adopted.

When comparing Canada with the U.S., one can easily note the difference in funding as the source of difference in the proportion of GNP allocated to health care. It is more difficult, however, to accept the suggestion that if Canada had not adopted its specific form of funding system, the proportion of GNP used for health care in Canada would have resembled that in the U.S. in the 1970s. Since we are talking about a hypothetical case, there is no way to prove or disprove the conjecture, and it must remain hypothetical.

To shed some light on the second hypothesis, we examine the changes that the Alberta Dental Association (ADA) has introduced into its Fee Guide since 1970, and compare the ADA Fee Guide with the Schedule of Medical Benefits for Alberta physicians in terms of their respective changes. In making this comparison, we would like to note the following:

1. The physician and the dentist are required to spend almost the same number of years of schooling for their respective academic degrees. Also, the number of years for apprenticeship after schooling is quite similar for these two groups of health practitioners.
2. According to the ADA's recent survey, less than 10 percent of expenditures for dental care comes from public sources, such as the EHB program or welfare.
3. The ADA has autonomously established its Fee Guide to reflect changes in market conditions affecting dental practices in Alberta. In determining the structure of its Fee Guide for each year, the ADA normally considers the demand for and the supply of dental care, an acceptable level of average net income for dentists, changes in practice overhead, and other related factors.

To enhance comparability in this exercise, the medical benefit index is calculated for two different series, one for all medical practitioners and the other for general practitioners (GPs). Shown below are three different indices for selected years.

	Medical		
Years Ended December 31	**All Practitioners**	**General Practitioners**	**Dental Practitioners**
1970	100.00	100.00	100.00
1975	119.34	122.70	131.68
1979	160.37	168.71	178.53
1980	185.23	197.64	192.65
1981	208.95	224.70	215.38*
			206.62+
1982	248.36	276.65	255.66*
			225.22+
Annual Average % Increase (1970-82)	7.88%	8.85%	8.14%* 7.00%+

* General Practitioners   + Specialists

In the early part of the twelve-year period under review, changes to the ADA Fee Guide were larger than those to the Schedule of Medical Benefits. Toward the end of the period, however, the gap in annual increases began to be narrowed. As far as GP physicians are concerned, the increase in their benefit rate since 1970 exceeded that of dentists by 2.6 percent in 1980. This differential continued to increase, to 4.3 percent in 1981 and 8.2 percent in 1982. It is remarkable to note that over the entire period, the increase in the price of dental services was very similar to the rise in the price of physician services, although dentists as a group in Alberta had autonomous power to determine their price increases to reflect changes in market conditions affecting their practice. Is it then too speculative to suggest that absence of a specific form of funding system for physician services in Alberta would not have led to the rate of increase in the price of physician services that the U.S. experienced?

As we all know, about 70 percent to 75 percent of operating expense for hospitals is for labour costs. Therefore, what happens to wage negotiations between provincial hospital associations and their labour unions would influence a substantial part of the increase in operating expense. At times the federal and provincial governments have managed to influence the outcome of negotiations. However, their success in the 1970s is not that evident. In any event, the collective bargaining process that Alberta had during the 1970s would not have been any different even if Alberta had not adopted a global budget approach for hospital care. We think it is reasonable to suggest that the collective bargaining process was independent of a specific form of funding system, at least in Alberta.

We are afraid that the second hypothesis implicit in Barer and Evans's paper, while attractive, is too simple. Why has the U.S. not stampeded into adopting our global budget approach to control its hospital cost inflation, and paying fee-for-service physicians according to a fee schedule?

Fees, Utilization, Incomes and Numbers in the Physician Services Sector: 1960-1982

The "Western Disease"

In discussing the so-called "western disease", Barer and Evans observe (with, we think, some surprise) that British Columbia and Alberta are at opposite ends of the national spectrum in physician availability and extra-billing. Yet changes in physician availability, as measured by changes in the physician-to-population ratio, reflect changes in the supply of physicians in relation to changes in the demand for physician services. For example, if the physician-to-population ratio increases, the rate of increase in the supply of physicians can be regarded as exceeding the demand for physician services under suitable assumptions. In other words, the physician services market probably experiences excess supply. If physician prices are influenced by the relation between supply and demand, this would result in a deceleration of the increase in the price of physician services. If, on the other hand, the physician-to-population ratio decreases, the rate of increase in the demand for physician services exceeds (*ceteris paribus*) the supply of physicians. Under this condition, the physician services market experiences excess demand. Again, if physician fee setting responds to such shifts, the increase in the price of physician services tends to accelerate.

As shown in their paper, the increase in the physician-to-population ratio was faster in B.C. than in Alberta from 1971 to 1983. Thus one can speculate that, relatively speaking, Alberta experienced an excess demand situation that enabled extra-billing to persist as a form of additional increase in medical benefits over and above what the plan was prepared to pay for physician services. We must hasten to add, however, that excess demand was only one of many conditions conducive to extra-billing because we agree that it would not explain the difference in extra-billing between urban and rural areas within Alberta. But for the inter-provincial comparison that Barer and Evans were engaged in, an explanation based on excess demand is obviously convenient and easy to accept.

What about the effect of excess supply on the price of physician services in B.C.? What we can observe is inconsistent with the proposition that excess supply tends to depress the market price or to decelerate the increase of the market price. A common explanation is that the physician services market is different from a "normal" market where the mechanism outlined above is applicable. An explanation we would like to put forward is somewhat similar to a hypothesis Evans has suggested elsewhere; i.e., the target income hypothesis. It is well known that physicians, particularly when starting their medical careers, talk about building their practices. Building a medical practice in a locale is nothing more than market penetration to change the existing market shares. When a new physician opens his practice, the demand curve for each physician already in practice would tend not only to shift to the left but also to rotate, unless this particular locale suffers from a physician shortage. In other words, as the number of physicians increases in relation to the population at risk, the market share of each physician tends to shrink. This would have two different consequences, because physician earnings are a function of two variables; i.e., price and quantity. Since quantity is directly related to market share, which begins to shrink, it is natural for physicians to use the price variable to counter their shrinking market shares. Under our system, physicians as a group would have to negotiate with provincial health plans. Depending on the speed at which physician market shares shrink, the negotiating stance of a provincial medical association would be militant or conciliatory. In our view, the B.C. Medical Association has always taken a more militant stance with its negotiations than its counterpart in Alberta. And the former has managed to obtain higher increases than the latter.

Before moving to the next topic, we would like to comment briefly on an important reason for Saskatchewan to begin catching the "western disease". In the second half of the 1970s, we often heard that Saskatchewan physicians wanted to have their benefit rates raised to establish parity with Manitoba and Alberta. This, they insisted, was necessary to improve physician availability in the province. Essentially, what we observe is a leap-frogging effect.

Physician Workload

Barer and Evans attempt to determine physician workload using physician-to-population ratios and *per capita* utilization of physician services, after expenditure for physician services is adjusted for the price component. The formula used is as follows:

(POP/MD) × (Services/POP) = (Services/MD)

where POP denotes population, MD the number of physicians and Services the number of physician services provided. It is noted that their expenditure for physician services covers not only fee-for-service payments but also other payments and that their number of physicians encompasses fee-for-service physicians and other physicians either in salaried practice or not in medical practice, including interns and residents.

Since their calculations of physician workload are dictated by data availability, it would be interesting to see whether or not their results are consistent with the results derived from better data pertaining to fee-for-service physicians alone. Based on their Tables 10, 12 and 13, calculations are made to identify Alberta physician workload from 1971 to 1982, which is shown under B-E along with Alberta fee-for-service physician workload (FFS). In calculating FFS, Alberta fee-for-service payments compiled on a date-of-payment basis are used in conjunction with the number of physicians billing the plan and the increase to the Schedule of Medical Benefits. Summarized below are the two different results for Alberta physician workloads:

Years	B-E	FFS
1971	100.00	100.00
1975	115.59	103.92
1976	110.81	106.12
1978	110.83	112.12
1980	116.28	115.32
1981	116.37	116.68
1982	111.60	119.66
Average Annual Increase (1971-1982)	1.01%	1.65%

As can be seen in the above table, the growth rate of physician workload varies depending on which data are used. By any standard, the magnitude of the difference is rather significant. This leads us to wonder whether the difference can be attributed to data pollution from which the B-E series suffers.

[*Editors' Note*: One possible source of such "pollution" is variation in the point in time, during a year, at which changes are carried into a given data series. Moore and Cheung base their series on date of *payment* of physician claims, which may lag weeks (in some cases months) behind date of *service*. Barer and Evans use averages of fee schedules *in force* during a year, so carry in price changes more rapidly. Further, Barer and Evans use end-of-year (December 31) data on physician supply, which may not exactly reflect average numbers of physicians *active* during a year. Note that in Moore and Cheung's table, the discrepancy between B-E and FFS is in the 1982 data. Over the period 1971 to 1981, their series are almost identical. But the B-E data seem to go badly "off-line" in 1982, and also in 1975. If the problem is primarily timing of data changes, they should converge again in 1983. Note also that Moore and Cheung's previous table shows fee changes for medical practitioners, which match Barer and Evans's data almost exactly from 1970 to 1981, but which rise less rapidly from 1981 to 1982. This difference in estimated fee increases in itself "explains" about a third of the difference between B-E and FFS in output per physician. The federal data used by Barer and Evans indicate a higher Alberta fee level in 1982, and thus a lower output per physician, than do Moore and Cheung's data. (Some of the remainder might be due to differences in types of physicians counted and date of count.) In any case, Moore and Cheung's data look more plausible, lacking the sharp fluctuations in the Barer and Evans series. The problem in the latter may arise in part from combining federal expenditure series based on dates of payment with fee schedules measured at date of coming into force; moreover, the 1982 expenditure data used by Barer and Evans are (still) preliminary.]

Commentary 171

Physician Income

In Canada, there are essentially three different sources of physician income data. They are income tax returns, plan payments and income surveys that most of the provincial medical associations regularly conduct to prepare for their fee negotiations. On the surface, it looks very easy to obtain reliable data. But those who have ventured into this area would all agree that it is almost impossible to get reasonably accurate gross and net income data.

Since the medical associations never share the findings of their surveys with the provincial plans, four western provincial plans made a proposal in 1979 to Health and Welfare Canada to see whether tax return data could be used more effectively. We still hope that something will be done to improve the quality of physician income data. As an attempt to provide some interim measures, Health and Welfare Canada undertook a study to estimate average incomes for physicians. Since Barer and Evans use the results of this study in discussing the behaviour of physician incomes, it would be useful to highlight below some aspects of the methodology that Health and Welfare Canada used in its estimation process.

1. Based on an extensive review of physician earnings data from income tax returns, Health and Welfare Canada concluded that a progressive understatement of physician earnings reported in taxation data had begun about 1973.

2. Covered were only those physicians who had been considered as self-employed in the eyes of the tax laws using 1973 as a bench mark.

3. Changes in the average gross incomes of physicians were assumed to be proportionate to changes in plan payments per fee-for-service physician.

4. In determining plan payment per physician, radiologists and pathologists (including laboratories), and associated dollar amounts, were excluded.

5. For 1983, overhead expenses were adjusted for clinic distortions. (Fee-for-service clinics may hire salaried physicians, reporting their earnings as overhead expenses, not physician incomes.)

6. To be consistent with (5) above, excluded were those physicians whose overhead expenses in 1979 and 1980 had been less than 5 percent or more that 300 percent of their net income. For the years 1981 and 1982, it was assumed that expenses as a percentage of gross income had remained the same as in 1980.

7. A method of interpolation was used to calculate average overhead expenses between 1973 and 1979.

8. By definition, average net income is the difference between average gross income and average overhead.

Shown below are data for Alberta physician incomes from two different sources, one provincial and the other federal.

	1973	1982	% Increase
Average Plan Payment*	$39,674	$111,985	182.3%
Average Gross Income	$63,800	$182,000	185.3%

* Excludes laboratories — radiology and pathology

Since the average Plan payment of $39,674 in 1973 covers all physicians receiving at least one payment from the plan, it is necessary to exclude physicians with low payments to bring the average plan payment for 1973 to a level close to $63,800. The average plan payment for physicians receiving at least $40,000 in 1973 was $62,291 excluding laboratories (radiology and pathology). Therefore, it is reasonable to suggest that the average gross income as reported in income-tax returns for 1973 — i.e., $63,800 — covered a group of "full-time" physicians. In 1982, the average plan payment for physicians receiving at least $126,000 was $181,854 excluding laboratories (radiology and pathology).

We do have some concern about the way average net incomes were calculated, especially for 1979 and 1980. Health and Welfare Canada calculated the average overhead expenses for those physicians whose expenses were more than 5 percent or less than 300 percent of their net incomes. Then, average overhead was subtracted from average gross incomes to arrive at average net incomes. Since there is no guarantee that these averages were calculated for the same group of physicians, it is entirely possible that potential distortions embodied in the way of calculating average net incomes were rather significant. However, the magnitude of such distortions is unknown.

Capital, "Prices" and Utilization in the Hospital Services Sector: 1946-1983

The analysis of the detailed economic calculations is summarized as follows:

1. The increasing *per diem* experience is not just a wage rate story.

2. The servicing growth is a significant area of increase although less than the price growth.

3. The shift in the mix of personnel has been small and unlikely to distort the servicing index.

4. It is likely that the GNE deflator does an adequate job of adjusting for changes in the price of hospital supplies.

5. No more than a small part of the growth in hospital costs per patient day can be attributed to changes in the mix of hospital activities; e.g., shifts away from inpatient care to outpatient care.

Commentary 173

6. There may be more promise in the case mix explanation — i.e., that the patients treated have, on average, become "sicker" — but not nearly enough to explain the growth in servicing intensity.

7. Increasing lengths of stay do not lend support to the hypothesis that more intensive, shorter stays of comparable outcomes are reflected in the servicing index.

8. The final possible explanation for the growth in servicing intensity is declining productivity. However, paid hours per patient day have increased far less than service volume indexes and purchased services or other services may account for a larger share of the increases.

Further analysis would be necessary to confirm each of the above points as they apply to Alberta. Moreover, as mentioned in the paper, Alberta is uniquely high compared with other provinces in the area of capital construction costs. However, some observations on what has occurred over the past few years, at least in Alberta, would lend a significant amount of support to the above analysis. Only a few of the many variables will be highlighted. Some of the following factors will be relatively insignificant and some will be extremely difficult, if not impossible, to measure, but taken together they may account for a major portion of the servicing increases that Barer and Evans were unable to explain, at least for Alberta.

First of all, one of the areas that has been difficult to measure has to do with certain items in the employee benefit package. Recent negotiations in Alberta, through arbitration, provide that in addition to paying increased shift premiums, the employer has lost flexibility in the drawing up of shift schedules. When temporary wage staff are readily available, these restrictions may have little economic impact; but for some facilities, additional paid hours have been necessary to provide adequate coverage. The requirement for two staff to be on every unit was also part of the arbitration decision, and had some economic impact, particularly for hospitals with small nursing units.

Hospitals recently opened as part of the major construction program in Alberta have more single rooms, in some cases smaller nursing wards, enhanced diagnostic support, and expanded ambulatory care facilities. Significant cost increases have taken place to support the staff for these new programs, and housekeeping, utilities and other associated supplies costs have also multiplied in relation to the facility replaced. Due to the burgeoning growth in the province, provision had been made for expansion that is now also showing up in increased costs per patient day until the optimum capacity of the facility is utilized.

Relatively recent new programs such as neonatal intensive care beds, cardiac care/heart surgery, organ transplant programs and other high-technology procedures, are of course centres of increasing cost for the larger hospitals. In Alberta, hospitals are responsible for the costs of diagnostic procedures and face the

TABLE 1
ALBERTA HOSPITAL UTILIZATION BY SELECTED INDICATORS
FISCAL YEARS 1979/80 TO 1983/84

INDICATORS	79/80[1]	80/81[1]	81/82[1]	82/83[2]	83/84[3]
Population (October 1)	2,037,400	2,179,600	2,272,500	2,336,000	2,364,300[4]
Separations					
- General	379,102	370,523	368,264	406,628	N/A
- Auxiliary	2,870	2,922	2,920	3,869	N/A
- Total	381,972	373,445	371,184	410,497	408,335
Seps/1000					
- General	186.1	170.0	162.1	174.1	N/A
- Auxiliary	1.4	1.3	1.3	1.7	N/A
- Total	187.5	171.3	163.4	175.8	172.7
Days Stay					
- General	3,205,756	3,100,515	2,973,748	3,214,308	N/A
- Auxiliary	956,296	1,040,670	1,133,214	1,232,315	N/A
- Total	4,162,052	4,141,185	4,106,962	4,446,623	N/A
DS/1000					
- General	1,573.4	1,422.5	1,308.6	1,376.0	N/A
- Auxiliary	469.4	477.5	498.7	527.5	N/A
- Total	2,042.8	1,900.0	1,807.3	1,930.5	N/A
Patient Days					
- General	3,160,729	3,060,694	3,021,622	3,251,058	N/A
- Auxiliary	1,145,399	1,201,029	1,234,588	1,329,715	N/A
- Total	4,306,128	4,261,723	4,256,210	4,580,773	4,640,919

August 23, 1984
Health Economics & Statistics
Alberta Hospitals & Medical Care

TABLE 1 (cont'd)
ALBERTA HOSPITAL UTILIZATION BY SELECTED INDICATORS
FISCAL YEARS 1979/80 TO 1983/84

INDICATORS	79/80[1]	80/81[1]	81/82[1]	82/83[2]	83/84[3]
PD/1000					
- General	1,551.4	1,404.2	1,329.6	1,391.7	N/A
- Auxiliary	562.2	551.0	543.3	569.2	N/A
- Total	2,113.6	1,955.2	1,872.9	1,960.9	1,962.9
ALOS					
- General	8.5	8.4	8.1	7.9	N/A
- Auxiliary	332.2	356.1	388.1	318.5	N/A
- Total (using DS)	10.9	11.1	11.1	10.8	N/A
- Total (using PD)	11.3	11.4	11.5	11.2	11.4
Paid Hours					
- General	50,073,332	52,042,378	54,457,028	58,337,132	N/A
- Auxiliary	6,618,532	7,109,738	7,648,532	8,638,217	N/A
- Total	56,691,864	59,152,116	62,105,560	66,975,349	66,403,851
Paid/Hrs/PD					
- General	15.84	17.00	18.02	17.94	N/A
- Auxiliary	5.78	5.92	6.20	6.50	N/A
- Total	13.17	13.88	14.59	14.62	14.31

Source:
(1) AHMC, Annual Report "Hospital Utilization Selected Indicators" based on (HS1/2) Annual Returns.
(2) Preliminary data based on 82/83 (HS1/2) Annual Returns.
(3) 1983-84 Monthly Information Report form 160/161.
(4) Alberta Treasury, Bureau of Statistics Quarterly Population Growth 4th Quarter, 1983.

Notes:
- 1983-84 data includes Bonnyville Duclos and patient days and separations for nursing and auxiliary beds at Dickinsfield Extended Care Centre.
- All figures for 1983/84 are total and include both general and auxiliary hospitals.

TABLE 2

DISTRIBUTION OF NURSING PAID HOURS

	1973*	1981*
Graduate Nurses	51.58%	60.32%
Qualified Nursing Assistants	25.26	20.12
Orderlies	5.93	2.42
Other Nursing Staff	17.23	17.14
Overall	100.00	100.00

Source: Monthly Reports (106 and 161).

* Refers to the year ended December 31.
* Refers to the year ended March 31.

compound effect of technical support for new technologies such as ultrasound as well as increases in professional fees paid for professional interpretation.

A recent funding study in Alberta involving independent consultants working with three selected hospitals and the government to determine reasonable staffing levels has served to increase staffing levels significantly in two of the three hospitals involved. Similar studies in other provinces have often resulted in staff enhancements without measurable activity increases, particularly when the hospitals were well below the funding levels of their "peers".

Hospitals using patient classification systems have claimed that service needs have increased over the past few years. In Alberta, the average length of stay has remained relatively constant as shown in Table 1 and further study would be necessary to understand why this is occurring.

Paid hours increased from 1979/80 to 1983/84 as new facilities and new programs were introduced. A hospital strike in 1981/82 caused a decline in patient days and this possibly caused a backlog resulting in peak activity in 1982/83. A significant number of beds were also closed in Alberta during 1981 and 1982, due to renovation projects and a shortage of nursing staff. Table 2 indicates that in Alberta there has been a shift in the mix of nursing personnel, which may not show up as significant in the Canadian data.

We have outlined some of the reasons for the service intensity increase in Alberta. Further study is required to document the magnitude of each and to determine how much remains unexplained. We have, of course, been unable to determine how much quality of care has improved over time in the absence of an overall easily quantified measurement tool, but through many hospital visitations across Canada we have gained the impression that given a minimum level of staff for a particular case mix, quality of care outcomes is more accurately correlated with quality of care organization, as well as management and employee competence, than with staffing levels *per se*. The difficulty government faces is that of determining what this minimum is, and applying the "standard" to all hospitals.

Can We Escape From History?

Evidence is now available to show that provincial governments are sufficiently alarmed about health cost increases to attempt at least a partial escape from history. Recent legislation in Alberta makes it illegal to strike in the hospital and public service sectors. Settlements for nurses this year (1984) have been 0 percent, with a 3 percent increase next year. A similar firm stance has been taken in the medical sector regarding fee increases. The control of physician numbers is possible but limiting fee increases and an increasing number of women physicians graduating who may not remain in full-time practice throughout their careers could temper the perceived need for such controls. The changing male/female ratios of physicians may also limit the pressure on hospital beds. If the imposition of fee and salary limits does not work, then government must pay greater attention to the negotiation process and limit the domino effect of possible future fee changes on the rest of the health care income structure. Certain members of the nursing profession have pushed for the bachelor degree to become the minimum standard of education. Physicians in their negotiations relate increasing costs of nursing personnel to their increased practice costs and argue for increased fees. Every negotiation process is vital in the control of labour and fee-for-service costs. The threat or act of strike in these health sectors has perhaps limited the involvement or firmness of governments in the past, but change is taking place — the question is whether or not the firm position can be maintained.

Barer and Evans suggest that Ontario and Quebec have been the most successful in controlling costs. Although Table 4 in their paper would tend to support this conclusion, it does not mean that Ontario and Quebec have the best *performance* with respect to costs. We know that hospitalization of the elderly is significantly higher than for other age groups, and although age standardization receives brief mention in their paper, it would be useful to examine utilization patterns of both physician and hospital services adjusted for the wide variation in the sixty-five and over population shown in our Table 3. Adjusted for age, Barer and Evans's Table 4 might show that in spite of the pressure placed on them by the large fee and salary increases granted in B.C. and Alberta, these provinces have shown the best performance.

Finally, limiting beds, staff and salaries, physician numbers and fees are necessary for cost control, but the growing number of elderly will continue to

TABLE 3

POPULATION BY PROVINCE (1981)

	Total Population (000)	Total 65+ Population (000)	Percent Population 65+
Newfoundland & Labrador	567.7	43.8	7.7
Prince Edward Island	122.5	14.9	12.2
Nova Scotia	847.4	92.5	10.9
New Brunswick	696.4	70.6	10.1
Quebec	6,438.2	569.3	8.8
Ontario	8,624.7	868.0	10.1
Manitoba	1,026.2	121.8	11.9
Saskatchewan	968.3	116.2	12.0
Alberta	2,237.7	163.4	7.3
British Columbia	2,744.5	298.1	10.9
N.W.T. and Yukon	68.9	2.0	2.9
Alberta June 1, 1983 ABS Estimate	2,362.3	173.9	7.6

Source: Intercensal Estimate of the Population by Sex and Age, Canada and Provinces, Alberta Bureau of Statistics, April 1983.

increase the need for hospital beds and staff. As well, public emotions surrounding costly interventions such as heart surgery, dialysis, transplants and cancer treatment will no doubt make cost control increasingly difficult. Will our provincial government be able to implement and enforce such increasing controls involving life or death decisions?

III

CHOICE OF TECHNIQUE

CHOICE OF TECHNIQUE: PATTERNS OF MEDICAL PRACTICES

Renaldo N. Battista
Robert A. Spasoff
Walter O. Spitzer

Introduction

The choice of preventive, diagnostic, therapeutic or rehabilitative techniques by the providers of health care services profoundly affects the health care system as a whole; conversely, changes in the health care system have a critical effect on the manner in which individual clinicians choose the techniques they will use. Throughout the remainder of this paper, the word "technique" will encompass preventive, diagnostic, therapeutic or rehabilitative procedures as clinical manoeuvres. Our purpose is to examine the process of choice of technique in the Canadian health care system. Canadian/American comparisons will be presented to elicit the elements in the Canadian health care situation that singularly affect this process.

The Canadian Health Care System and the Health Status of Canadians

Eliminating financial barriers to access to health care has been the guiding principle of Canada's successive moves toward a national health insurance program over the past three decades. An equilibrium was sought between equity and respect for individual liberties.[1] The first step in that direction was taken in 1947 by Saskatchewan and showed that hospitalization and diagnostic services could be provided through a universal coverage plan at reasonable cost. Through the federal Hospital Insurance and Diagnostic Services Act of 1957 and the Medical Care Act of 1966, the government of Canada introduced a powerful incentive for provinces to develop a comprehensive health insurance plan. Approximately 50 percent of the costs of the program were paid from federal tax revenues and the provinces agreed to comply with the principles of universality, comprehensiveness, accessibility, portability and public administration. In 1977, the previous 50-50 cost-matching formula was replaced by block funding through tax transfer and cash payments for hospital and medical insurance.

How successful have we been in improving the health status of Canadians through these major changes? The evolution of major health indicators over the past decade is informative. Whether any change can be attributed to the modifications in our health care system is a matter for scholarly debate. Comparisons with data from the United States, however, provide one perspective.

Life expectancy at birth increased at an accelerated rate during the 1970s, after slowing its increase during the 1960s. The 1980-1982 life tables report life expectancies of 71.9 years for males, and 78.9 for females, compared with 69.3 and 76.4 in 1971. At age 40, male and female life expectancies were 34.7 and 40.7, compared with 33.2 and 39.0 in 1971. The increase for males was particularly interesting, since prior to 1971 almost all life expectancy gains were experienced by females and children. In the forty years from 1931 to 1971, life expectancy for 40-year-old males increased only from 32.0 to 33.2 years, while for females it rose from 33.0 to 39.0, and for males at birth, from 60.0 to 69.3.[2,3]

Similar developments, however, appear to have been under way in the U.S.; between 1970 and 1980, life expectancies at birth increased from 67 to 70 years for males, and from 74 to 77 years for females. The increases at age 40 were from 31 to 33 years for men, and 37 to 39 years for women.[4,5]

In addition to the accelerated improvements in life expectancies, other health indicators have improved quite impressively. Infant mortality in Canada, which was 17.5 deaths per 1,000 live births in 1971, decreased to 9.6 deaths per 1,000 in 1981. The neonatal death rate, which was 12.4 deaths per 1,000 live births in 1971, declined to 6.4 deaths per 1,000 live births.[6,7] For the same decade in the U.S., the infant mortality rate decreased from 20 to 12.6 per 1,000 live births and the neonatal mortality rate dropped from 15.1 to 8.5 per 1,000 live births.[8,9]

Turning to age-standardized mortality rates (ages twenty-five to seventy-four) in Canada from 1970 to 1979,[10] we notice an overall age-standardized mortality decline of about 12 percent (1022.9 to 920.0 per 100,000 population for men and 534.4 to 458.9 per 100,000 population for women). A 25 percent decline in both ischemic heart disease and cerebrovascular disease has also occurred during this period. Ischemic heart disease rates have decreased from 379.0 to 299.6 per 100,000 population for men and 131.4 to 97.1 per 100,000 population for women. Cerebrovascular disease rates have decreased from 65.9 to 49.7 per 100,000 population for men and 49.9 to 36.6 per 100,000 population for women. Similar trends have been observed in the U.S.[11,12]

The overall cancer rate has increased by 5 percent for males (from 230.3 to 241.8 per 100,000 population), while decreasing by 1.8 percent for females (from 173.4 to 170.2 per 100,000 population). However, the most striking trend for any specific site has been the continuing rise of lung cancer in Canada, particularly in women. The rate for men has risen 21.3 percent, from 71.3 to 86.5 per 100,000 population, whereas for women the rate has jumped 99.1 percent from 11.5 to 22.9 per 100,000 population.[13] Again, similar trends have been observed in the U.S.[14]

Deaths in Canada due to accidents have decreased from 71.2 per 100,000 population in 1971 to 57.5 per 100,000 in 1982. An important portion of that variation can be ascribed to the decrease in mortality due to motor vehicle accidents, from 26.9 to 17.1 deaths per 100,000 population. Mortality rates for suicide have increased moderately in Canada, from 11.9 to 14.3 per 100,000 population from 1971 to 1982. For homicide, the rates have remained constant around 2.3 deaths per 100,000 population.[15,16]

We also note that the number of cases of venereal diseases reported in the nation rose from 34,000 in 1970 to 54,000 in 1976. By 1980, the number of cases approached 60,000.[17] Part of the increase can undoubtedly be explained by better reporting; but we believe that the difference over the decade 1970 to 1980 is a true indicator of rising incidence. In contrast, German measles declined steadily from 1970 to 1980 (12,000 cases vs. 3,000).[18] An attainable benefit *not* attained is exemplified by red measles, which is preventable by primary means. There were 25,000 cases in 1970, and only 9,000 in 1976. In 1980, however, we had 13,000 cases. The U.S., with ten times the population and without universal health insurance, had only 1,714 cases in 1982,[19] thanks to mandatory immunizations for school entrants (introduced only very recently in some Canadian provinces).

Smoking behaviour can be taken as one indicator of lifestyle changes. Smoking cessation has occurred mainly among the more highly educated segments of the population; the decrease has been 41 percent (from 26.3 percent to 15.5 percent) among individuals holding university degrees but much less among others.[20] Young women, however, constitute a group in which smoking has increased. The situation is similar in the U.S.

This small array of indicators depicts the health status of Canadians as having improved in some aspects, as witnessed by the decrease in overall mortality rates, infant and neonatal mortality rates, and mortality rates due to ischemic heart and cerebrovascular disease. However, death rates from cancer and from accidents are still high, if not rising. Comparisons with U.S. figures do not show marked differences in mortality trends. Consequently, it is difficult to attribute the trends observed in the health status of Canadians over the past decade to the specific features of the Canadian system of National Health Insurance, to its success either in equalizing access *or* in controlling cost escalation.

Determinants of Choice of Technique

The process by which providers choose the particular techniques they will employ when dealing with individual patients is the result of a complex interplay among the many factors that shape the health care system. The cumulative effect of such choices of technique determines, in turn, the orientation and content of the health care system. As a consequence, a multi-directional interaction between choices of technique and other factors affecting the system is established.

Few have suggested explanatory models of adoption of patterns of practice.[21,22] We propose a conceptual framework that encompasses the several determinants of choice of technique. As suggested in Figure 1, clinical decisions immediately result from the interaction between physicians and patients. Internal determinants of physician and patient behaviours will ultimately shape clinical decisions. The practice setting, however, will set the stage for such decisions and will markedly influence patterns of practice. The shaping of these settings and their functioning will be greatly determined, in turn, by the broad policy environment. Research and technological development will constitute an important phase in the adoption of innovative technology. Finally, the overall process of adoption of patterns of practice will be constantly modulated by prevailing societal trends. Although seemingly static, the model we propose should be viewed rather as a tentative elucidation and simplification of a complex dynamic process. Let us now review the various factors that may influence the choice of technique.

Technology

For more than thirty years, technology has undergone rapid growth. Development of new technologies, and more specifically medical technology, has been triggered to a large extent by private industry.[23] Governments have also participated in this development, directly or indirectly, through research grants given to scientists working in university settings.

The diffusion of new techniques has often occurred, however, before any formal evaluation of their effect on health outcomes. Consequently, it has become apparent that the payoff to investments in new technology has been less than it might have been if development and diffusion were better channelled.[24]

The need for formal evaluation of medical procedures has been emphasized by many.[25-27] Although pharmaceutical products have been subjected to evaluation for some time, the same rigour has not been applied to medical procedures and very few have been formally assessed in terms of efficacy, effectiveness and efficiency before their widespread diffusion. The timing of evaluation has considerable importance; rigorous assessment using randomized clinical trials can be done prior to diffusion but it becomes more difficult after diffusion is initiated, for both methodological and ethical reasons.

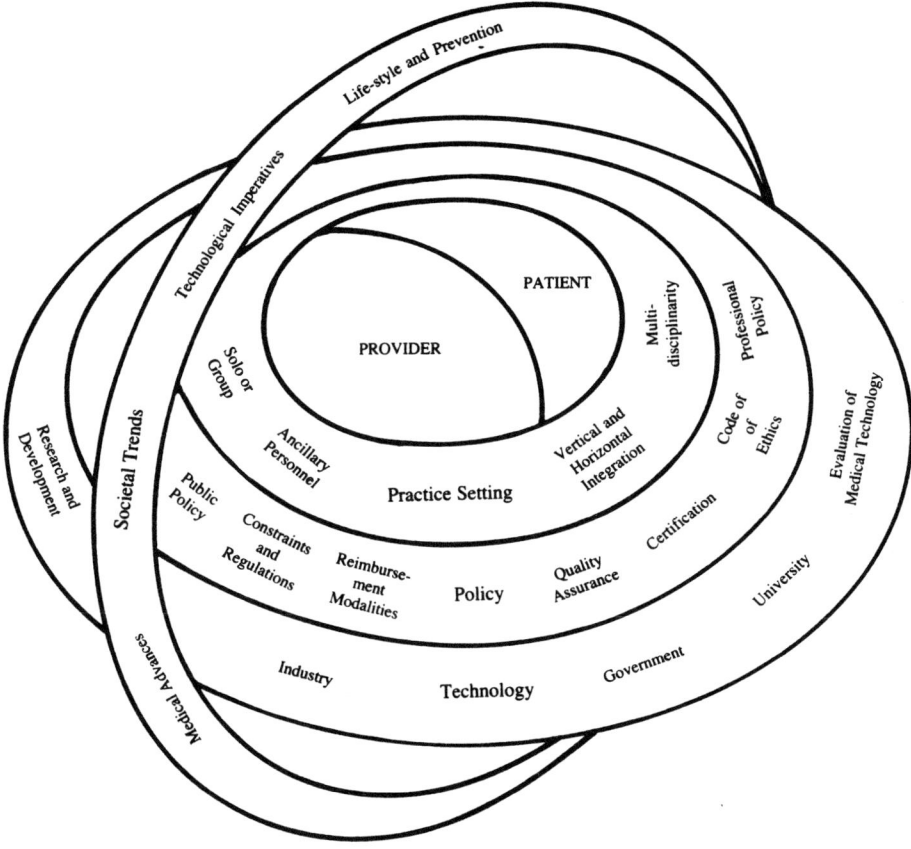

Figure 1

Choice of Technique: Conceptual Framework

Policy Environment

Patterns of practice develop and evolve in a policy context. Two levels of policy making can be distinguished: public policy and professional policy.

Policy statements can constitute an important element in the choice of technique. Decisions emanating from governing bodies, or specially created task forces, can establish practice guidelines for clinicians. Decision makers may have to go beyond merely making recommendations to the extent of providing operational incentives, invoked either before or after the initial diffusion of procedures. The ultimate expression of policy is the allocation of resources, e.g., in the form of global budgets for hospitals that constrain the choice of technique made by administrators and health care providers.

Reimbursement modalities exert an important influence on patterns of practice.[28-31] Where a National Health Insurance plan prevails, they are selected by governments through a negotiation process with the medical associations. Reimbursement alternatives and, more specifically, fee schedules, create a complex network of incentives within which medical practice will flourish.

Professional policies are established through several channels. By setting codes of ethics and controlling medical licensure, Colleges of Physicians, whose major role is the protection of the population, have a direct impact on manpower supply. Medical associations usually defend the interests of their members and are the official organizations of physicians for negotiating with governments. They are, nevertheless, also actively involved in continuing education programs and activities and are in a good position to suggest, influence and reinforce patterns of practice.

Quality assessment and assurance activities can also modulate the choice of techniques or patterns of practice. These activities provide the feedback required by providers to bring their practice behaviours into accord with the criteria of optimal practice.[32] Certifying and accreditation bodies have pursued quality assessment activities mainly in institutional settings. Similar activities have been undertaken by Colleges of Physicians in some provinces.[33] Such activities have been targeted not only to in-hospital but also to ambulatory practices.

Practice Setting

The organizational environment in which physicians practise appears to exert a significant influence on patterns of practice.[34,35] The structuring of practices (e.g., solo or group), the multi-disciplinary nature of health care teams, the presence of ancillary personnel, the horizontal integration of practice settings with other ambulatory care settings, and the vertical integration of such primary care settings with other levels of health care are some of the many factors shaping the practice environment of physicians and ultimately determining their practice behaviours.

The development of types of practice setting is very much dependent on the various policy forces that shape the health care system. Likewise the evolution, the success or failure, of some forms of practice organizations influences the formulation of policy aimed at improving the overall functioning of the system.

Provider

Ideally, the adoption of new patterns of practice by health care providers should follow the preceding steps since they, in effect, give physicians a body of knowledge, a policy environment and an organizational setting that will enable them to embrace new practice behaviours. In this context, providers shape their beliefs, crystallize their attitudes and, at times, adopt new behaviours.

An array of factors has been found, by different investigators, to be related to physicians' behaviours, e.g., socio-demographic characteristics and continuing education activities.[36-38] But the findings are not all consistent, and disentangling the separate effects of these factors is difficult. Statistical tools, as applied to observational data sets, are helpful but have well-known limitations. Common trends are suggested, however, by the literature. These elements can be viewed as facilitators of the process of diffusion of techniques at the provider/patient level. The practice environment, however, remains a key determinant of patterns of practice.

This approach does not demean the importance for physicians of pursuing greater rationalization with respect to their practice behaviours. Clinicians, as a result of the impetus provided by health care researchers and clinical epidemiologists, are becoming more aware of the necessity of critically assessing their choices of technique.[39,40] The application of decision analysis, for example, to clinical decision-making is one of the steps leading in that direction.[41,42] The utilization of clinical algorithms and protocols in clinical management has also received some attention.[43,44] Computerization of such aids to clinical decision-making is being explored and its limitations are yet to be completely ascertained.[45,46]

In short, external forces create a context in which physicians will develop styles of practice. Policy makers can exert control in the careful creation of this practice context. Beyond this, the onus is on providers to improve their clinical decisions and, as a result, to retain the professional autonomy required to reconcile the science and the art of medicine.

Patient

Patients' participation in the health care system can occur at several levels — in the functioning of organizations, in clinical decision-making and in self-initiated health behaviours. Given the limitation on the scope of this paper, we will focus attention on the last two.

Patient compliance with therapeutic strategies is a crucial element in any process of adoption of new techniques or patterns of practice.[47] In relation to prevention, compliance takes on an even greater meaning since it may require profound behavioural and lifestyle changes.

Consumers' involvement in the choice of technique usually occurs as a response to suggestions made by a health care provider. Occasionally, however, an approach will be formulated and initiated by consumers themselves, e.g., the self-help movements.[48]

Again, we realize that patients' involvement in the process of choice of technique will depend very much on the practice environment in which encounters with providers occur. The objective of policy makers should be the creation of contexts that facilitate patients' participation. As patients become more eager to take an active part in decisions concerning their health, providers may progressively integrate their views into the decision-making process. Conversely, as providers invite and encourage patients' participation, they may become more interested in participating in the process and a new equilibrium between patients and providers may be achieved.

Societal Trends

The complex process of choice of technique occurs in a broader societal environment that comprises an array of beliefs and social trends arising from the interaction of consumers, providers and socio-cultural and economic imperatives. Such beliefs and trends culminate in societal tensions that may initiate a series of technological developments and policy formulations. Conversely, societal trends may themselves be ultimately determined by technological developments.

Societal trends are constantly changing. The technological imperative and great enthusiasm for medical advances in recent decades have modulated the evolution of the health care system. The new concept of health conveyed by the "avant garde" Lalonde report is just starting to be translated into operational behaviour.[49] A greater preoccupation with health promotion may influence the evolution of the health care system significantly in the next few decades.

We have presented a conceptual framework that facilitates understanding of the complex interactions among the several determinants of patterns of practice. We turn now to consideration of several examples of choice of technique in Canada in order to assess their importance and to determine whether the process can be ascribed to the particularities of our health care system.

Patterns of Choice of Technique

The examples are drawn from the three broad domains of prevention, diagnosis and treatment. On the topic of prevention, we shall explore the integration of preventive activities into clinical practice through the periodic health examination and the development of patients' responsibility for health maintenance. With respect to diagnosis, CT scanners will be discussed as being representative of high technology diagnostic tools while laboratory tests will represent low technology tools. To illustrate choice of technique in treatment, three therapeutic manoeuvres will be presented: one medical (hypertension control) and two surgical (hysterectomy and day-care surgery).

Prevention

The Periodic Health Examination

Use of the periodic health examination as a strategy for prevention is not a new idea. As early as 1850, Shattuck suggested the importance of integrating preventive activities into clinical practice.[50] The concept, as traced by Yankauer, went through cycles of popularity but always fell short of breaking through because of lack of plans for implementation.[51] During the technological boom of the 1950s and 1960s, the idea of prevention fell somewhat into disfavour, as a consequence of being overshadowed by the glamorous achievements of curative medicine. In the 1970s, however, the rising costs of medical care, the reality of impending economic recession, and an increasing awareness of the limits on the ability of the curative health care system to improve the health status of the population, set the stage for a rebirth of the concept of prevention. In Canada, these ideas found their most eloquent expression in the now legendary Lalonde report.[52] The most explicit expression presenting prevention as a stated objective of the health care system was in the Castonguay-Nepveu report, which preceded the health care reform in the province of Quebec.[53]

All of these developments combined to create a favourable societal trend for prevention in Canada and, among other preventive strategies, a renewed interest in the Periodic Health Examination. It was against this background that the federal Conference of Deputy Ministers established the Canadian Task Force on the Periodic Health Examination in 1976. Its primary task was to formulate, from an exhaustive review of the relevant worldwide literature, clear practice recommendations regarding preventive activities that ought to be integrated into clinical practice. Responsibility for carrying out implementation of the strategy was not part of the Task Force's mandate.

The Task Force Report was published in 1979 in English and French and has been widely distributed to physicians.[54,55] Eighteen months after publication of the report, a study of primary care physicians in Quebec showed only limited integration of selected preventive activities into clinical practice.[56,57] The investigators estimated that not more than 28 percent of the population was being effectively reached by this physician-mediated strategy for prevention. The study was replicated in New Brunswick and it corroborated the findings in Quebec.[58]

There is general agreement that preventive and curative services are fundamental, interdependent ingredients of good health care. Their joint integration into medical practice, however, seems problematic; several barriers related to providers, consumers and the organizational features of practice settings have been identified.[59] Although the message about prevention and more specifically about Periodic Health Monitoring has been spreading in Canada, it has not been supported by incentives designed to increase the integration of preventive activities into clinical practice. This deficiency has recently been identified by the reconvened Task Force as a major priority and challenge for the coming years.[60]

Nevertheless, interest and concern about the quality of preventive care have prompted professional organizations to issue practice guidelines directed toward their constituencies, as witnessed by the Health Maintenance Guide recently published by the College of Family Physicians of Canada[61] and the College's even more recent report documenting the quality of medical practice (including preventive activities) among a sample of primary care physicians.[62]

In Canada, the adoption by providers of the Periodic Health Examination as a strategy for prevention is following a societally initiated model. Indeed, it was societal receptivity regarding prevention that prompted the Canadian government to create the Task Force. Failure to attain maximum benefit from this strategy could be imputed, in part, to the absence of implementation plans that would give operational support to the existing rhetoric and knowledge.

The secondary task assigned to the Task Force was to identify research requirements and approaches. As a result, research into the efficacy, effectiveness and efficiency of preventive manoeuvres has been stimulated and encouraged, as witnessed by an ongoing clinical trial on breast cancer screening.[63]

In the U.S., societal preparedness for prevention has been encouraged by sweeping statements such as the one emanating from the Office of the Surgeon General that emphasizes the importance of prevention in the pursuit of health objectives.[64] Periodic Health Monitoring as a means of achieving this objective has also been suggested and supported by the well-known work of Frame and Carlson,[65] Breslow and Somers,[66] and the Institute of Medicine.[67] As is often the case for our neighbours, the message appears to have diffused directly to providers and consumers without the intermediary activities of governmentally mandated bodies such as those in Canada. The net effect, however, as indicated by American studies, is probably not very different from that observed in Canada.[68-70] The implementation of preventive practices and incentives is being addressed in the U.S. in the context of private insurance payments through a demonstration project initiated by the Metropolitan Life Insurance Company. The project's major purpose is to ascertain whether monetary incentives for preventive practices will increase the number of such services offered by providers to patients.[71] Related experiments are being developed in the Health Maintenance Organizations network; evaluation research on the efficacy, effectiveness and efficiency of preventive services has also been generated.

Also in the U.S., several recent authoritative statements indicate a need for further direction.[72,73] The recent formation of an American Task Force on Preventive Services similar to its Canadian counterpart underscores the importance of policy guidelines and implementation plans. Thus the American scenario also follows a societally initiated model, but one in which policy formulation tends to reflect a pattern of practice that is already beginning to be adopted.

Canadian and American approaches to prevention and, more specifically, the Periodic Health Examination, differ somewhat but the diffusion of the related practice patterns is similar. We may, in fact, travel some of the road together, as witnessed by recent exchanges and promises of coordinated efforts by both Task Forces.

Patient's Responsibility for Health Maintenance

The Health Charter for Canadians in the Hall Report refers to "the responsibility of the individual to observe good health practices and to use available health services prudently".[74] The Lalonde Report includes patient participation in its Health Promotion Strategy.[75] As members of the public, patients exert considerable influence on the health care *system* through their membership on regional planning councils, boards of health, and hospital boards, but this involvement does not directly affect the choice of preventive, diagnostic or therapeutic techniques in individual patient/health-care provider contacts.

Little has been done by way of systematic evaluation of the impact of greater patient responsibility on health outcome; those who believe there has been a significant effect base their arguments largely on theory, if not ideology. Canadian government policy regarding patient responsibility has been limited to public education regarding healthy lifestyles, while governments have passively discouraged patient input into medical care by supporting the *status quo*, e.g., by entrenching the medical profession in its monopoly on first contact care, and by retaining the traditional focus on institutional care. There has been some rhetoric (e.g., in Ontario) about individual responsibility, aimed mainly at saving money, but there has been little action. The medical profession has been generally negative to a larger role for patients, as illustrated by its opposition to community health centres and nurse practitioners, both of which favour a larger role for patients. The nursing profession has been more favourable to a larger role for patients, but this may simply reflect a desire to reduce medical domination of the health care system.

Given the medical profession's monopoly on primary care, patients must exert whatever influence they may have on the choice of preventive, diagnostic and therapeutic technique during their visits to medical practitioners. One measure of the strength of this influence would be the growth of Community Health Centres (CHCs), which are favourably disposed to promoting an active role for the patient. CHCs have certainly not been overwhelmed by patients: the number of CHCs remains very small (except in Quebec), and some of them suffer from a lack of patients.[76] We estimate that not more than 3 percent of the Canadian population receives its primary care from such centres.

Under universal health insurance in Canada the only reason for a patient to choose a CHC is ideological, and the ideological motivation has apparently not been strong enough to overcome both tradition and professional opposition. A more positive example is the steady (albeit slow) growth of birthing centres and other "humane" approaches to obstetrical care, growth that seems to be motivated largely by patient demand.

Part of this situation may be explained by the fact that patients, both in Canada and in the U.S., are reluctant to embrace a philosophy that transfers undue responsibility to themselves for the choice of therapy, especially in difficult situations. A vivid example of a patient's reluctance to retain control of the choice of therapeutic technique has been described in an article by F.J. Ingelfinger about a personal episode in which he strongly advocated leaving control of treatment of his oesophageal cancer to the attending physician. Here was one of the world's best known gastroenterologists, a man who had devoted a lifetime to the study of the oesophagus, the editor of a most prestigious journal, advocating that decisions about his own care be taken out of his hands. His own words express this most eloquently:

> Finally, when the pangs of indecision had become nearly intolerable, one wise physician friend said, "What you need is a doctor." He was telling me to forget the information I already had and the information I was receiving from many quarters, and to seek instead a person who would dominate, who would tell me what to do, who would in a paternalistic manner assume responsibility for my care.[77]

In summary, we have found no evidence that patients have had a significant influence on the choice of technique in the Canadian health care system. Indeed, there is little reason to expect that the "security blanket" provided by comprehensive health insurance would lead patients to develop such a role. We conclude that the Canadian health care system has not encouraged the development of a more active role for patients in the choice of the approach to health care.

Diagnosis

Imaging Technology (High Technology)

Computerized tomography (CT scanning) is now seen as one of the unquestioned quantum jumps in technology during the 1970s and as the prototype of a new generation of diagnostic techniques. The diffusion of this new technology has, in the main, preceded any rigorous evaluation of its effectiveness or proper role. This is especially the case in the U.S. where there have been few barriers to its spread; any medical group or institution that sees an advantage to itself or its patients in having a CT scanner can purchase one and pass the costs along to its patients. The Canadian system of universal health insurance has virtually eliminated private health care institutions and insurance, and almost no one would be prepared to pay the extra charges required to purchase services from privately owned major equipment installations.

As a consequence, governments have an unusual degree of control over the proliferation of expensive new technologies: If the relevant government does not agree to pay for the operation (let alone the purchase) of a new machine, any professional individual, group or institution must analyse the advantages and financial consequences of such a purchase very carefully before acting. It is our perception that governments in Canada have effectively limited the spread of CT scanning. The evolution of CT scanning in Ontario will serve as an example.

The first Canadian CT scanner was installed at the Montreal Neurological Institute in 1973. The first machines in Ontario were installed in March 1974 in Toronto and Hamilton. By early 1980, there were twenty-two machines in Ontario, all in hospitals and nearly all in teaching hospitals; some were funded by the Ontario government, just over half were approved but not funded, and four were neither approved nor funded. The untidiness of this situation and the pressure to fund all the installed and additional machines prompted the Ontario Ministry of Health to refer the matter to its senior advisory body, the Ontario Council of Health. A Task Force carried out surveys of institutions having any of the new technologies, approached the District Health Councils (regional planning councils), consulted experts, commissioned a set of guidelines for the assessment of new technologies, and held a Consensus Development Conference. The Task Force submitted its reports to the Ontario Minister of Health in December 1980 and October 1982.[78] The reports contained a total of twenty-six recommendations on all aspects of imaging technology, including the recommendation that one CT scanner be made available for every 200,000 population (with special consideration to children's hospitals, cancer centres and northern Ontario), that their location be determined by District Health Councils and that the province promote the development of integrated diagnostic imaging services or units to which physicians would refer patients for investigation.

A rapid succession of Ministers of Health in Ontario may have been the cause of an absence of any official response to either report. The Ministry of Health has, however, developed a set of guidelines for the distribution of CT scanners, sent them to District Health Councils, and requested the councils not only to select the institutions that should receive the equipment but also to assign them appropriate placement in their list of priorities for funding. On the basis of District Health Council recommendations, the Ministry produced an implementation scheme and placed several scanners on a "probable approval" list for future years. The number of CT scanners in Ontario has now risen to thirty-two; all have been approved by the Ministry and funded up to a maximum of $150,000 per year. Since $150,000 is less than the actual annual operating cost for one shift per day, institutions are required to make a financial commitment from other resources and are automatically discouraged from increasing the number of operating hours per day. The result has been a ratio of one scanner per 250,000 people, which contrasts with one per 150,000 in the U.S. in 1980.[79]

The situation in Quebec is somewhat less orderly. For a population of six million, there are now thirteen scanners — eleven in Montreal and one each in Quebec City and Sherbrooke. The Quebec Ministry of Social Affairs has only recently agreed to pay part of the operating expenses of two of these installations. Consequently, acquisition of this technology has been based solely on the ability to attract private funds. There has been no systematic public examination of needs and no specific government policy is apparent.

The distribution of the CT scanning equipment in other provinces is variable, ranging from a high of one per 120,000 population in Prince Edward Island (a special case because of its small population) to roughly one per 200,000 in Alberta and British Columbia and one per 500,000 in most other provinces. The national average is of the order of one per 350,000.[80] All Canadian scanners are located in hospitals, and, in Ontario at least, this has been made a legal requirement.

It is obvious that uncontrolled proliferation of CT scanning technology has not occurred in Canada. Although Canadian physicians are as enthusiastic about CT scanning as their American colleagues, provincial governments have successfully rationed its use by limiting the supply of machines and the hours of operation. Physicians often refer a patient to a specialist as a means of getting a scan more rapidly; but the effect is still to restrict both the range of indications for CT scanning and its unjustified use. Although the long queues for use of the machines tend to restrict use of the technology to cases where it is really needed, is the approach to the population's benefit? Although generally available in urban areas, the inaccessibility of the machines to important portions of the Canadian population living in such areas as the Gaspé, the Kenora area or northern Manitoba has undoubtedly been a barrier to their justified and appropriately *urgent* use. The Canadian Neurological Society has argued that the lack of machines is causing unwarranted reversion to invasive investigations, with the attendant unnecessary hospital admissions, long hospital stays, and increased risks for patients.[81]

Laboratory Investigation (Low Technology)

Conventional laboratory investigations can be classified as low technology. Even though they are not individually very expensive, the aggregate of such activities accounts for a significant proportion of the ultimate cost of providing health services to the population. In Canada, the estimated direct costs for laboratory tests totalled $450 million in 1971 and $828 million in 1975, an 84 percent increase in four years.[82] An estimated 8 percent of all health care expenditures went for clinical laboratory tests in 1975. In the U.S., Fineberg estimated that, in 1980, $17 billion, or 7 percent of the $245 billion spent on health care, went for clinical laboratory tests.[83]

Knowledge about and experience with this low technology diffuses to physicians in a variety of ways, albeit less spectacularly than the high technology discussed in the preceding section. The methods range from the interpretation of the value of new techniques by laboratory directors and subsequent provision of only those considered effective, to the marketing of such procedures to physicians by manufacturers of the reagents or equipment. The fact that the introduction of the individual components of low technology developments is characterized by a gradual evolution and by the absence of dramatic cost impacts may account for the relative lack of constraints on the use of laboratory technology both in Canada and in the U.S. There is also very little regulatory interference with decisions to employ new techniques or to implement decisions regarding which conventional technique should be used.

The choice of technique in the low technology area is almost invariably left to the exclusive clinical judgement of physicians. Patients rarely interfere with such investigations except in the rare instances when they are excessively invasive. In neither country do physicians have any incentive to limit their ordering of laboratory tests. While in Canada the costs are passed on to the provincial billing agencies, in the U.S. private insurance, Medicare and Medicaid cover at least 80 percent of in-hospital laboratory costs and 50 percent of ambulatory laboratory costs.[84] Moreover, there is convergent evidence that cost awareness might not be an important factor for physicians in their test ordering decisions. Spitzer reported that among the physicians and students of McGill University teaching hospitals, about half of all decisions to order laboratory investigations were made on the basis of clinical factors without consideration of the costs involved.[85] Campbell and Marker reported a similar observation in an American federal institution,[86] while Cohen et al. suggested that simple cost feedback mechanisms are not sufficient to assure adequate reductions in test utilization.[87] Further testing this hypothesis, Hoey et al. conducted a comparative study of physicians in the teaching hospitals of McGill University and the University of Pennsylvania.[88] The evidence indicated that while some tests were ordered on the basis of price, a large proportion of tests were considered to be absolutely necessary or unnecessary regardless of their cost. Thus, educating physicians on the cost of tests may only have a limited impact on their pattern of test utilization. Canadian and American physicians did not demonstrate striking differences in their ordering profiles.

A number of factors seem to influence physicians' ordering behaviour.[89-91] The overriding philosophy of medical care dominated by the science-based "technologic imperative" is a powerful trigger.[92] It is reinforced by the medical education system that values procedures more highly than clinical examination. Fear of malpractice has also contributed to increasing laboratory utilization, thus stimulating the practice of defensive medicine.

Meagre efforts have been made by the Canadian federal government and the provincial governments to curtail utilization of diagnostic services. A Task Force was formed in Canada in 1969 to assess the cost of health services in Canada. Its report, which contained several recommendations regarding diagnostic services, was submitted to the provincial governments, the Canadian Medical Association, and the medical profession in general.[93] Most recommendations fell short of implementation. A similar endeavour was undertaken in 1974 by the Federal-Provincial Advisory Committee on Health Services. Its mandate was to formulate guidelines for the appropriate use of medical laboratory services in Canada. The final report was published in 1979 but had minimal impact on utilization of laboratory services.[94]

Thus, in Canada, it is clear that provider-related factors have initiated and modulated the patterns of diffusion of low technology procedures. In this area the Canadian and American experiences exhibit more similarities than major differences.

Therapy

Hypertension Control

Antihypertensive therapy has assumed great importance in the past decade or so. Despite the technological development of antihypertensives as a necessary prerequisite and their vigorous marketing, we do not view the emphasis on antihypertensive therapy as being primarily technologically driven. Rigorous evaluation largely preceded the encouragement of diffusion of the therapy by the medical profession and governments. Adequate clinical management of the disease became important from a policy perspective when it was discovered that control of mild and moderate hypertension reduces the incidence of such complications as heart attacks, strokes and premature death.[95]

Accordingly, governments have encouraged the use of recommended protocols for the management of hypertension, e.g., through the Task Force on Hypertension.[96] In Canada, we attribute this policy emphasis largely to the efforts of one individual, D.L. Sackett, who has made a personal mission of extending our epidemiologic knowledge of hypertension and of applying existing therapeutic knowledge. Although the presence of universal health insurance might be expected to have brought a higher proportion of patients under treatment in Canada than in the U.S., the effect may have been counterbalanced by programs specifically directed at the treatment of hypertension in the U.S. where the government thrust has been considerably stronger and where the emphasis was placed, in the 1960s, on the health of disadvantaged populations.

There is some evidence that physician compliance with recommended protocols has improved in Canada.[97] The much greater use in the U.S. of medical audits and other quality assurance techniques may have led to greater compliance with protocols than in Canada.

In conclusion, this is an area in which scientific evaluation has played a relatively large role. We find no evidence that the Canadian health care system has appreciably affected Canadian physicians' choice of technique in the management of this condition, relative to physicians in the U.S.

Hysterectomy

Wide variations in surgical rates have been reported across the Canadian provinces.[98,99] Similar findings have been documented in the U.S. and England and Wales.[100-102] Hysterectomy is one of the most commonly performed major surgical procedures in these countries and also exhibits a wide variation in rates.

The explanation of the variation is complex and requires discussion of data from several sources.

An examination of international variations in hysterectomy rates provides some insight into "macro level" determinants of surgical patterns of practice. Vayda et al. compared the surgical experience of Canada, England and Wales, and the U.S. for the period 1966 to 1976.[103] During that decade, the age-standardized hysterectomy rate in Canada declined from 541 per 100,000 women to 484, an 11 percent decrease. The rate for England and Wales fell very slightly from 230 to 224 per 100,000 women. In the U.S., the hysterectomy rate climbed from 484 per 100,000 women to 575 during the same decade, i.e., an 18 percent increase.

The factors most likely to explain these variations were explored. Despite a constant increase in the surgeon to population ratios in all three countries during the ten-year period under study, only the U.S. experienced a dramatic increase in overall surgical rates and, more specifically, in hysterectomy rates. England and Wales had the lowest number of hospital beds *per capita*, while Canada had 30 percent more than the U.S. in 1974 and 1976. The difference in surgical rates could hardly be explained by the availability of beds *per capita* even when the latter was corrected for the 20 percent greater length of stay in Canada than in the U.S. Mortality due to malignant gynecologic diseases in women sixty-five and over did not differ in the three countries.

The most likely explanation offered by the investigators for the observed differences in rates was that it was simply a reflection of the difference in overall health care expenditures in the three countries. Indeed, as reported for the decade studied, England and Wales spent 4.3 percent to 5.8 percent of their GNP on health care, Canada 6.1 percent to 7.2 percent, and the U.S. 5.8 percent to 8.6 percent.[104] The authors suggest that these cross-national differences in hysterectomy rates reflect differences in control of technology, as reflected in a slower increase in health expenditures in the United Kingdom and Canada. Hysterectomy being an in-hospital procedure, the comparison was not confounded by the increase in day-care surgery that will be discussed in the next section.

Variation in hysterectomy rates could also be examined at the "micro level" of regional differences. Roos studied hysterectomy rates in Manitoba for the years 1974 to 1976, focusing on areas of high and low hysterectomy rates.[105] The overall rate in Manitoba of 440 per 100,000 women during that period was comparable with the national rate. The rates reported across the thirty-three areas into which Manitoba was divided varied, however, from 300 to 1,500 per 100,000 women. No relation was found between hysterectomy rates and the supply of either physicians or beds. The investigators suggested, however, that a combination of patient characteristics, such as ethnicity and physician decision-making behaviour, could explain much of the variation in hysterectomy rates across small areas. The hypothesis of inter-physician variation is supported by other similar evidence.[106,107]

The effectiveness of a quality assurance system with respect to appropriate indications for hysterectomy was shown in Saskatchewan in the mid-1970s by Dyck et al.[108] In the early 1970s, the Department of Health in Saskatchewan had observed that the number of hysterectomies carried out in the province had increased by 72.1 percent during the period 1964 to 1974, while the number of women over age fifteen had increased by only 7.6 percent. When the three largest cities of Saskatchewan were compared, hysterectomy rates varied from 499 to 1,258 per 100,000 women. The College of Physicians and Surgeons of Saskatchewan developed a surveillance program, provided a list of specific indications for hysterectomy, and reviewed five hospitals. Two years later, the proportion of unjustified hysterectomies had dropped from 23.7 percent to 7.8 percent in the hospitals reviewed. Also, a 32.8 percent drop in the number of hysterectomies being done was registered in the province as a whole during the same period.

In summary, it can be argued that health care policies in Canada have indirectly contributed to a stabilization, if not a decrease, in hysterectomy rates over the past decade. A greater awareness and effort in containing health care expenditures could be the triggering incentive for this practice behaviour as suggested by Vayda et al.[109] and more recently by Wennberg et al.[110] This would concur with a model proposed by Rutkow, in which the importance of the policy environment in determining surgical rates is underscored.[111] Once the overall framework is set, surgical rates are modulated by provider-related factors, patient characteristics and quality assurance activities.

Day-care Surgery

The history of day-care surgery in Canada is a good example of the complexities of the choice of technique in health care and of the possible interactions between cost imperatives, policy formulation, generation of scientific evidence, clinical decisions by providers and patient involvement in such decisions.

As reported by Shah, day-care surgery was widely used at the turn of the century for many minor procedures.[112] The paucity of hospitals and the prevailing standards for anaesthesia and asepsis were important factors supporting this surgical approach. For example, day-care surgery was first reported at the Hospital for Sick Children in Toronto in 1910. Over the period 1910 to 1914, 83.1 percent of all operations were done in the day-care setting; of these, 78 percent were for tonsillectomy.[113] A similar situation prevailed in England.[114]

Changes in antiseptic and anaesthetic techniques and the ensuing ability to undertake more elaborate surgical procedures were major incentives for shifting outpatient practices into hospital facilities. This trend accelerated in the 1930s and 1940s with private health insurance providing some coverage for hospital care in all provinces. It became even more prevalent after the introduction of universal hospitalization plans in Saskatchewan in 1947, and shortly afterward in British Columbia and Alberta. Construction of hospitals was stimulated by the federal government's national health grant-in-aid program in 1948. The in-hospital trend was further accelerated by the introduction of the Hospital Insurance and Diagnostic Services Act in 1957, through which the federal government reimbursed provinces for half of their hospitalization costs for specified services.[115] Since the cost of most outpatient services continued to be borne in full by provincial governments or by patients, a major disincentive for day-care surgery was established. The number of hospital beds in Canada increased rapidly from 5.9 per 1,000 population in 1948, to 7.0 in 1974.[116] The Canadian health care system had already become very hospital-centred when the Medical Care Act providing for cost-shared universal medical care insurance was passed in the Parliament of Canada in 1966.[117]

Cost issues and acute awareness of the limitations on resources became recurring themes in the mid-1970s. Budgetary cuts and the decrease in available beds have prompted health institutions and providers to look for solutions; one solution is day-care surgery. Day-care surgery and recent developments in anaesthesiology can make the whole surgical experience less cumbersome and traumatic. Day-care units have been initiated in pediatric centres in Vancouver and Toronto and are now spreading throughout the country. Shah's article on day-care surgery in Canada presents 1977 statistical data on the number of day surgery procedures as a percentage of total surgical procedures;[118] the total percentage for Canada at that time was 29.1 percent. Of the 916 acute-care hospitals surveyed, 436 (47.6 percent) had day-care surgery services. (Private centres outside the mainstream hospital system have developed rather slowly.)

Although this changing pattern of surgical practice was triggered by the need to reduce costs and bed shortages, it is unclear whether these objectives have been successfully met where the new approach has been implemented. Indeed, as discussed by Freiberg, a new technique will have an impact on cost insofar as it becomes a well-accepted substitute for an existing and more costly procedure;[119] otherwise, it may well add to overall health care costs. The issue has also been explored by Evans and Robinson with respect to British Columbia.[120] They observed an expansion of the total volume of surgical activity in the early 1970s and a partial substitution of day-care surgery for inpatient surgery in the mid 1970s. They concluded that while savings were possible, potential savings were not achieved in the absence of incentives to reduce the use of inpatient care. Societal forces and imperatives in Canada have apparently initiated the diffusion of day-care surgery into the practice of providers, although it is mainly a hospital-based phenomenon for lack of incentives to create private centres. The interest in day-care surgery has also resulted in research efforts aimed at evaluating this new technique. Shah et al.[121] and, more recently, Pineault et al.,[122] conducted randomized trials of day-care surgery and documented results comparable with inpatient care in terms of efficacy, rate of complications and patients' satisfaction.

The diffusion of day-care surgery has followed somewhat similar channels in the U.S. The combined effect of cost concerns, advances in anaesthesiology and better educational preparation has spurred the rapid development of the required facilities.[123] The American Hospital Association conducted a survey of hospital involvement with ambulatory surgery in 1980 and found that offering ambulatory surgery were 70.5 percent (1,506) of all U.S. non-federal hospitals, 79.7 percent (1,107) of not-for-profit hospitals, 55.4 percent (180) of for-profit hospitals and 51.8 percent (219) of state or local government-owned hospitals.[124]

Freestanding surgical centres (i.e., physically separated from other health care facilities) were first established in the U.S. in the early 1970s.[125] By 1981, 100 such centres had been started and were handling 200,000 patient visits per year.[126] An estimated 900,000 visits per year to a total of 270 freestanding, privately-owned surgical centres are predicted by 1986.[127] Ambulatory surgery is obviously a growing area of the American health care delivery system that has been favoured by important revisions in reimbursement modalities by Blue Cross-Blue Shield and other third party payers.[128] Growing competition between freestanding and hospital-based units will accelerate this practice trend.[129]

In the case of ambulatory surgery, diffusion of the technique appears to be more rapid in the U.S. than in Canada, the difference being mainly attributable to the ability of the American system to adjust reimbursement schemes quickly to promote it.

Discussion

We now return to our classification of the factors affecting choice of technique, assessing the impact of each and suggesting opportunities for influencing the system in desired directions.

Although *societal trends* are presumably to be accepted (or endured) as givens, there may be opportunities for using them to influence the choice of technique. We have argued that such trends have already been reflected in major changes in the *system*, most notably the introduction of universal health insurance. Similarly, the expectation of greater resource deployment for prevention is beginning to show some effect at the level of commissioning policy formulation and of evaluating important preventive strategies; e.g., the national breast cancer screening trial. However, health care professionals — especially physicians — have been slow to respond to these trends, continuing their focus on curative and technological interventions. The result is that societal trends have not yet affected choice of technique in a material way in Canada. The similarity in patterns of practice between Canada and the U.S. supports this conclusion. But society would respond favourably to a re-orientation of the health care system toward a greater role for prevention; e.g., greater emphasis on health education and on nutrition. Some elements of society are calling for a greater role for consumers, and this trend could be used to support initiatives directed at self-care. Even the public's enthusiasm for technology might be harnessed, by using it to support such activities as health promotion through electronic media and sophisticated approaches to screening. Thus, although the impact of societal trends on choice of technique has so far been limited, there is considerable scope for harnessing these trends to achieve greater influence.

Research and technological development have influenced choice of technique largely by making new techniques available; for example, nuclear magnetic resonance did not exist ten years ago and hence could not have been chosen. New techniques have tended to serve as supplements (add-ons) to those already in use, although CT scanners have replaced invasive procedures and thus reduced risk to patients. In general, technological developments have had a smaller influence on choice of technique in Canada than in the U.S. because of the smaller amounts of money within the system, the remoteness from the founts of high technology, the small market, which discourages vigorous marketing, and the stronger policy control that governments have been able to exert. Indeed, in some respects we may be suffering from too little technology. We should continue to maintain our control over the use of new technologies, while ensuring that their spread is encouraged to the extent that they have been proven cost-effective. It is crucial that we ensure that health professionals are well-informed regarding the strengths and weaknesses of new technologies and that appropriate control mechanisms are in place.

Technology assessment is a relatively recent development. There has been modest encouragement of evaluative research in Canada, through the Health Care Evaluation Seminars, the development of the National Health Research and Development Programme and the growth of training programs in epidemiology and health services research. The hypertension example illustrates the growing contribution of clinical epidemiology. Evaluative research is perhaps even more needed for commoner, individually cheaper and often older procedures, such as laboratory tests, than for new technologies. But the emphasis in the research community is still overwhelmingly on biomedical research. Much more could be done to foster evaluative research, e.g., through contract research and the formation of targeted research groups.

Although progress has been made in doing evaluations, much less has been accomplished in implementation of the results. Communication of results is necessary, but is not sufficient: policy initiatives are needed. Much existing knowledge is not acted upon; e.g., the value of day-care surgery. On the other hand, physicians have been quick to change their behaviour in some instances, especially when good evidence has become available that a procedure is useless or even harmful; e.g., the rapid disappearance of internal mammary artery ligation.

The *policy environment* within which health care is provided is determined by both the government and professional organizations. We see it as the responsibility of government and the professions to provide an environment that will encourage desirable or appropriate behaviour. Government policy formation has had a minimal effect on choice of technique to date. Despite the potential of a national health insurance system to give governments a stronger hand in influencing provision of medical care, Canadian governments have generally been hesitant to become involved directly, apparently not wishing to antagonize the medical profession unnecessarily. Indeed, the way in which universal health insurance was introduced appears to have entrenched existing modes of organization and practice, and stifled experimentation. This was a lost opportunity to introduce innovation and encourage diversity in the system. Governments have begun to develop policy guidelines in some areas. The Canadian Task Force on the Periodic Health Examination has produced a set of recommendations and rules of evidence for development of policy. The report has been well received in many countries, but the effect on choice of technique has been minimal to date. It may be that insufficient time has elapsed for physicians to change their behaviour. Canadian government policy on controlling access to CT scanners has, however, definitely affected the availability of this technique: a dramatic difference in population to equipment ratio is evident between Canada and the U.S. We believe this difference extends to other areas of high technology as well.

Policy formulation is the key mechanism for governments to influence choice of technique; it is more appropriate than direct intervention in the provider-patient interaction. As in any motivational situation, these efforts will have a much greater chance of success if they are positive (in the form of incentives) than negative (as constraints). A striking example is the alacrity with which British general practitioners organized themselves into groups when the National Health Service began to subsidize the office expenses of group practices. Governments can do more by way of encouraging providers to work in appropriate groupings with appropriate facilities. The policy environment should be such that a physician does not lose income if he adopts desirable behaviour. There is also room for governments to direct incentives at consumers, e.g., regarding their health behaviour or their choice of providers.

Professional organizations also contribute to the policy environment in which providers work. They can contribute to a desirable environment by developing appropriate standards and guidelines for medical practice, introducing algorithms and clinical decision-making models to assist physicians in making the most effective and efficient decisions in difficult clinical situations, and establishing quality assurance programs. In all these areas, professional organizations have an advantage over governments. Physicians are much more responsive to initiatives arising from other physicians than to those from government. Even as simple a procedure as providing physicians with feedback on their individual practice patterns may lead to desirable change, as in the hysterectomy review in

Saskatchewan. Quality assurance activities have not been as widespread in Canada as in the U.S., where they have been linked to the continuing efforts at cost control. The Canadian Council on Hospital Accreditation is hospital oriented, as its name implies, and functions as a quasi-regulatory control mechanism rather than as an agency designed to promote quality in a given institution. Development of quality assurance mechanisms for ambulatory care is very much in its infancy, although strong positive efforts are being made by the College of Family Physicians of Canada and certain provincial licensing authorities. Again, the existence of universal health insurance in Canada appears to have had little effect on the development of quality assurance programs.

The *practice setting* is determined jointly by the policy environment and the provider. We believe that where it has been demonstrated that a particular practice setting leads to desirable patterns of practice, e.g., some types of groups, it is appropriate for governments to encourage physicians to choose this setting. This will have an indirect effect on the choice of technique, and in our view is as close as governments should come to intervening in the provider-patient interaction. We need more research into the effect of practice patterns on physician behaviour, to serve as the basis for such policy initiatives. Similarly, if it has been determined that certain types of personnel improve the care provided, and at acceptable cost, then mechanisms must be developed to pay them. The failure of the nurse practitioner to be adopted in Canada is largely due to the lack of such mechanisms. Similar arguments might be made for health educators and social workers, although there is less evidence of their cost-effectiveness.

Provider-related factors are important determinants of choice of technique. Indeed, providers have the last word in ordering medical procedures. Demographic variables such as age, sex and the nature and location of training affect their choice of technique. Their training, orientation, and pursuit of scientifically-based medicine are all factors conducive to high utilization of medical procedures, quite apart from such environmental factors as fee-for-service payment and fear of malpractice litigation. As noted above, the free enterprise system in the U.S. provides them with even more latitude than in Canada. Although we believe that governments should not become involved in the physician-patient interaction, there are some indirect approaches to provider factors that could do much to influence choice of technique. Governments could apply pressure to medical schools to broaden their admission criteria (e.g., by accepting more students with backgrounds in the humanities and social sciences), and to modify the curriculum to place more emphasis on effectiveness of services and on rational decision-making.

Patient-related factors have had a negligible effect to date on the choice of technique. There is some scope for making patients more efficient consumers of health services, e.g., through encouraging self-care, reducing their fascination with technology and encouraging or allowing them to use alternate providers.

TABLE 1

FACTORS INFLUENCING CHOICE OF TECHNIQUE IN THE CANADIAN HEALTH CARE SYSTEM

Factor	Current Importance	Potential Importance
Technology development	+	+
Technology assessment	+	+++
Health policy	+	+++
Practice setting	++	+++
Provider	+++	+++
Patient	+	++
Societal trends	+	++

Public education may have some value, but incentives such as premium reductions or expanded coverage would no doubt be more effective.

Conclusions

Table 1 summarizes our conclusions regarding the choice of technique in the Canadian health care system. The evidence suggests that control of the choice of technique remains almost exclusively in the hands of the physician, and that the consequences are not all bad. Many of the critical indicators have demonstrated an improvement in the health status of the population, although the outcomes and the rate of improvement are not appreciably better in Canada than in the U.S. Choice of technique in both Canada and the U.S. occurs primarily at the bedside and in the consulting room. Strong initiatives created by research, expectations of accountability and evaluation, new policies, and the expectations and needs of the physician converge at the point of patient-physician interaction when a patient seeks help. The choice of technique has not been strongly influenced by the development of universal health insurance. This conclusion should not be surprising, since the system was designed to have a minimal restraining effect on medical practice. The results, noted above, have been at least satisfactory. But if the system is to improve in terms of effectiveness and efficiency, it will be necessary for governments to seek greater influence on choice of technique. We believe that the most promising and most appropriate avenue for this approach will be through the development of policy that would help shape practice organizations more conducive to desirable physician behaviours. Enlightened management of the practice environment might be as far as policy makers should go without unduly infringing on professional autonomy. Efforts to increase rationalization of clinical decisions should be pursued. The role of evaluative research and technology assessment should be emphasized as a means of providing health care professionals with the necessary knowledge that will guide their choices of technique.

Acknowledgements

The authors are grateful to Dr. N.J.B. Wiggin, Dr. J.I. Williams, Ms. Cynthia Palmer and Ms. Diane Telmosse for their professional assistance.

Notes

1. LeClair, M., "The Canadian Health Care System", in S. Andreopoulos, ed., *National Health Insurance: Can We Learn From Canada?* Toronto: John Wiley & Sons, 1975, Ch. 1.

2. Statistics Canada, *Life Tables, Canada and Provinces, 1980-1982*, Cat. no. 84-532. Ottawa: Ministry of Supply and Services, 1984.

3. Leacy, F.H., ed., *Historical Statistics of Canada*, 2nd ed. Series B65-B74. Ottawa: Statistics Canada and the Social Science Federation of Canada, 1983.

4. National Center for Health Statistics, *United States Life Tables, 1969-1971*. Maryland: DHEW, 1974.

5. National Center for Health Statistics, "Advance Report of Final Mortality Statistics, 1980", *DHEW Monthly Vital Statistics Report.* Maryland: DHEW, 1983, 32 (suppl.).

6. Statistics Canada, "Mortality: Summary List of Causes", *Vital Statistics*, Vol. III, 1982, Cat no. 84-206. Ottawa: Ministry of Supply and Services, 1984.

7. Statistics Canada, "Deaths, 1971", *Vital Statistics*, Vol. III, Cat no. 84-206. Ottawa: Ministry of Industry, Trade and Commerce, 1974.

8. United States Department of Health, Education and Welfare, "Mortality, Part A", *Vital Statistics for the United States 1970*, Vol. II. Maryland: DHEW, 1974.

9. United States Department of Health, Education and Welfare. Maryland: DHEW, unpublished data.

10. Health and Welfare Canada, *Chronic Diseases in Canada*, 3, 2, 1982, 19-22.

11. United States Department of Health, Education and Welfare, *op. cit.*, footnote 8.

12. United States Department of Health, Education and Welfare, *op. cit.*, footnote 9.

13. Health and Welfare Canada, *op. cit.*, footnote 10.

14. Terris, M., "Newer Perspectives on the Health of Canadians: Beyond the Lalonde Report", *The Journal*, May 1, 1984, pp. 9-10.
15. Statistics Canada, *op. cit.*, footnote 6.
16. Statistics Canada, *op. cit.*, footnote 7.
17. Laboratory Centre for Disease Control, "Notifiable Diseases Summary", *Can Dis Weekly Report*, 7, 2, 1981, pp. 8-9.
18. Laboratory Centre for Disease Control, "Notifiable Diseases Summary", *Can Dis Weekly Report*, 9, 6, 1983, pp. 22-23.
19. MMWR, *Annual Summary, 1982*. U.S. Department of Health and Human Services, Center for Disease Control, December 1983.
20. Terris, *op. cit.*, footnote 14.
21. Contandriopoulos, A.-P., "La logique de production et l'utilisation des services médicaux", *Administration Hospitalière et Sociale*, mai-juin, 1983, pp. 5-10.
22. Donabedian, A., *Aspects of Medical Care Administration*. Cambridge, Mass: Harvard University Press, 1973.
23. McKinlay, J.B., "Epidemiological and Political Determinants of Social Policies Regarding the Public Health", *Soc Sci Med*, 13A, 1979, pp. 541-558.
24. Hiatt, H.H., "Protecting the Medical Commons: Who is Responsible?", *N Engl J Med*, 293, 1975, pp. 235-241.
25. Cochrane, A.L., *Effectiveness and Efficiency*. London: Nuffield Provincial Hospitals Trust, 1972.
26. Frazier, H.S. and H.H. Hiatt, "Evaluation of Medical Practices", *Science*, 200, 1978, pp. 815-878.
27. Fineberg, H.V. and H.H. Hiatt, "Evaluation of Medical Practices, the Case for Technology Assessment", *N Engl J Med*, 301, 1979, pp. 1086-1091.
28. Contandriopoulos, A.-P., "Stimulants économiques et utilisateur des services médicaux", *L'Actualité économique*, avril-juin 1980, pp. 264-296.
29. Rice, T., "The Impact of Changing Medicare Reimbursement Rates on Physician-Induced Demand", *Med Care*, 21, 8, 1983, pp. 803-815.
30. Manning, W.G. *et al.*, "A Controlled Trial of the Effect of a Prepaid Group Practice on Use of Services", *N Engl J Med*, 310, 23, 1984, pp. 1505-1510.
31. Battista, R.N., J.I. Williams and M.A. MacFarlane, "Determinants of Practice in Adult Cancer Prevention". Submitted for publication.

32. Palmer, R.H., "Quality assessment", in Greene, R., ed., *Assuring Quality in Medical Care*. Cambridge, Mass.: Ballinger, 1976, pp. 11-134.
33. Roy, A., "Professional Inspection". Paper presented at the Canadian Medical Association Conference, 1979.
34. Ross, C.E. and R.S. Duff, "Quality of Outpatient Pediatric Care: The Influence of Physicians' Background, Socialization and Work/Information Environment on Performance", *J Health Soc Behav*, 19, 1978, p. 348.
35. Riedel, R.L. and D.C. Riedel, *Practice and Performance: An Assessment of Ambulatory Care*. Ann Arbor: Health Administration Press, 1979.
36. Peterson, O.L., L.P. Andrews et al., "An Analytic Study of North Carolina General Practice", *J Med Educ*, 31, 1956, p. 1.
37. Clute, K.F., *The General Practitioner: A Study of Medical Education and Practice in Ontario and Nova Scotia*. Toronto: University of Toronto Press, 1963.
38. Brook, R.H. and K.N. Williams, "Effect of Medical Care Review on the Use of Injection", *Ann Intern Med*, 85, 1976, p. 509.
39. Fineberg and Hiatt, *op. cit.*, footnote 27.
40. Sackett, D.L., "Clinical Diagnosis and the Clinical Laboratory", *Clin Invest Med*, 1, 1978, p. 27.
41. Lusted, L.B., *Introduction to Medical Decision-making*. Springfield, Ill.: Charles C. Thomas, 1968.
42. Weinstein, M.C. and H.V. Fineberg, *Clinical Decision Analysis*. Toronto: W.B. Saunders Company, 1980.
43. Pauker, S.G. and J.P. Kassirer, "Clinical Applications of Decision Analysis: A Detailed Illustration", *Semin Nucl Med*, 8, 1978, pp. 324-325.
44. Hopkins, J.A., W.C. Shoemaker and S. Greenfield, "Comparison of the Treatment of Surgical Emergency With and Without an Algorithm", *Arch Surg*, 115, 1980, pp. 745-750.
45. Pauker, S.G., G.A. Gorry, J.P. Kassirer et al., "Towards the Simulation of Clinical Cognition: Taking a Present Illness by Computer", *Am J Med*, 60, 7, 1976, pp. 981-996.
46. Cohen, D.L., B. Littenberg, C. Wetzel and D. Neuhauser, "Improving Physician Compliance with Preventive Medicine Guidelines", *Med Care*, 20, 1982, pp. 1040-1045.
47. Sackett, D.L. and R.B. Haynes, *Compliance with Therapeutic Regimens*. Baltimore, MA: Johns Hopkins University Press, 1976.

48. Farquharson, A., "Self-help Groups: A Health Resource", in Coburn, D., C. D'Arcy, P. New and G. Torrance, eds., *Health and Canadian Society: Sociological Perspectives*. Markham, Ont.: Fitzhenry and Whiteside, 1981, Ch. 20.

49. Lalonde, M., *A New Perspective on the Health of Canadians*. Ottawa: Ministry of National Health and Welfare, 1974.

50. Shattuck, L., *Report of the Sanitary Commission of Massachusetts, 1850*. Cambridge, Mass.: Harvard University Press, 1948, reprint.

51. Yankauer, A., "The Ups and Downs of Prevention (E)", *Am J Public Health*, 71, 1981, pp. 6-9.

52. Lalonde, *op. cit.*, footnote 49.

53. Castonguay, C., *Health Insurance: Report of the Commission of Inquiry on Health and Social Welfare*. Government of Quebec, 1, 1968.

54. Canadian Task Force on the Periodic Health Examination, "The Periodic Health Examination", *Can Med Assoc J*, 121, 1979, pp. 1193-1254.

55. L'examen médical périodique, *L'Union Médicale du Canada*, 108, 1979, suppl., pp. 1-48.

56. Battista, R.N., "Adult Cancer Prevention in Primary Care: Patterns of Practice in Quebec", *Am J Public Health*, 73, 9, 1983, pp. 1036-1039.

57. Battista, R.N. and W.O. Spitzer, "Adult Cancer Prevention in Primary Care: Contrasts Among Primary Care Practice Settings in Quebec", *Am J Public Health*, 73, 9, 1983, pp. 1040-1041.

58. Battista, R.N., *Adult Cancer Prevention in Primary Care: The New Brunswick Study*. McGill University, Scientific Monograph, unpublished department document, 1983.

59. Battista, R.N., M.D. Beaulieu, J.W. Feightner *et al.*, "The Periodic Health Examination: An Evolving Concept", *Can Med Assoc J*, 130, 1984, pp. 1288-1292.

60. Spitzer, W.O., "The Periodic Health Examination: 1. Introduction", *Can Med Assoc J*, 130, 1984, pp. 1276-1278.

61. College of Family Physicians of Canada, *The Patterns of Practice and Health Care Delivery Committee: Health Maintenance Guide*. Toronto: College of Family Physicians of Canada, 1983.

62. Borgiel, A.E.M., J.I. Williams, G.M. Anderson *et al.*, *Assessing the Quality of Care in the Practices of Family Physicians*. College of Family Physicians of Canada, November 1983.

63. Miller, A.B., G.R. Howe and C. Wall, "The National Study of Breast Cancer Screening: Protocol for a Canadian Randomized Controlled Trial of Screening for Breast Cancer in Women", *Clin Invest Med*, 4, 3/4, 1981, pp. 227-258.

64. U.S. Public Health Service, *Healthy People: The Surgeon General's Report on Health Promotion and Disease Prevention*. Washington, DC: U.S. Government Printing Office, 1979.

65. Frame, P.S. and S.J. Carlson, "A Critical Review of Periodic Health Screening Using Specific Screening Criteria. Part I: Selected Diseases of Respiratory, Cardiovascular and Central Nervous Systems", *J Fam Pract*, 2, 1975, pp. 29-36.

66. Breslow, L. and A.R. Somers, "The Lifetime Health-Monitoring Program: A Practical Approach to Preventive Medicine", *N Engl J Med*, 296, 1977, pp. 601-608.

67. Preventive services for the well population, *Report of the Institute of Medicine, National Academy of Sciences, Healthy People* (Appendices). Washington, DC: DHEW, 1978, pp. 1-22.

68. Sackett and Haynes, *op. cit.*, footnote 47.

69. Romm, F.J., S.W. Fletcher and B.S. Hulka, "The Periodic Health Examination: Comparison of Recommendations and Internists' Performance", *South Med J*, 74, 1981, pp. 265-271.

70. Dietrich, A.J. and H. Goldberg, "Preventive Content of Adult Primary Care: Do Generalists and Subspecialists Differ?", *Am J Public Health*, 74, 3, 1984, pp. 223-227.

71. Logsdon, D.N., M.A. Rosen and M.M. Demak, "The INSURE Project on Lifecycle Preventive Health Services: Cost Containment Issues", *Inquiry*, 20, 1983, pp. 121-126.

72. Bridgers, W.F., "A Brief Chapter in the Politics of Prevention Research", *J Public Health Policy*, 5, 1, 1984, pp. 5-9.

73. Roemer, M.I., "The Value of Medical Care for Health Promotion", *Am J Public Health*, 74, 3, 1984, pp. 243-248.

74. Canada, *Royal Commission on Health Services*, Vol. I. Ottawa: The Queen's Printer, 1964.

75. Lalonde, *op. cit.*, footnote 49.

76. Kagis, M., "Here's Looking Back at Us!", *Healthlink*, 2, Fall 1982, p. 4. (Newsletter of the Association of Ontario Health Centres)

77. Ingelfinger, F.J., "Arrogance", *N Engl J Med*, 303, 1980, pp. 1507-1511.

78. Ontario Council of Health, *Task Force on Diagnostic Imaging*. Final Report, Part I, November 1980. Part II, September 1982.

79. U.S. Congress, Office of Technology Assessment, *Policy Implications of the Computed Tomography (CT) Scanner: An Update*. Washington, DC: U.S. Government Printing Office, January 1981.

80. Fournier, L., Statistics Canada. Personal communication, 1984.

81. The Canadian Neurological Society, "Statement on Diagnostic Imaging Techniques", *Can J Neurol Sci* (in press).

82. MacIntosh, O.C., *Use and Abuse of Diagnostic Services, the Canadian Experience*. Montreal: Eden Press, 1982.

83. Fineberg, H.V., "Clinical Chemistries: The High Costs of Low-Cost Diagnostic Tests", in Altman, S.H. and R. Blendon, eds., *Medical Technology: The Culprit Behind Health Care Costs?* DHEW publication no. (PHS)79-3216. Washington, DC: 1979.

84. Fineberg, H.V. and L.A. Pearlman, "Low-Cost Medical Practices", *Annual Review of Public Health*, 3, 1982, pp. 225-248.

85. Spitzer, W.O., "Educational Determinants of Paraclinical Investigation by Physicians in Teaching Hospitals". Paper presented to the annual meeting of the Association of Canadian Teaching Hospitals and the Association of Canadian Medical Colleges, Vancouver, B.C., October 1976.

86. Campbell, J.A. and M.T. Marker, "Doctor Billing in a Federal Institution", in Benson, S., M. Desmond, M.D. Burke and D. Connelly, eds., *Clinical Decision Making and Laboratory Use*. Minneapolis: University of Minnesota Press, 1982, pp. 294-299.

87. Cohen, D.I., P. Jones, B. Littenberg and D. Neuhauser, "Does Cost Information Availability Reduce Physician Test Usage? A Randomized Clinical Trial with Unexpected Findings", *Med Care*, 20, 3, 1982, p. 286.

88. Hoey, J., J.M. Eisenberg, W.O. Spitzer and D. Thomas, "Physician Sensitivity to the Price of Diagnostic Tests: A U.S.-Canadian Analysis", *Med Care*, 20, 3, 1982, p. 286.

89. Moloney, T.W. and D.E. Rogers, "Medical Technology — A Different View of the Contentious Debate Over Costs", *N Engl J Med*, 301, 26, 1979, pp. 1413-1419.

90. Connelly, D. and B. Steele, "Laboratory Utilization, Problems and Solutions", *Arch Pathol Lab Med*, 104, 1980, pp. 59-62.

91. Grossman, R.M., "A Review of Physician Cost-Containment Strategies for Laboratory Testing", *Med Care*, 21, 8, 1983, pp. 783-802.

92. Fuchs, V.R., "The Growing Demand for Medical Care", *N Engl J Med*, 279, 1968, pp. 190-195.

93. Canada, Department of National Health and Welfare, *Task Force Reports on the Cost of Health Services in Canada*, Vol II. Ottawa: The Queen's Printer, 1969.

94. Health Services Directorate, Health Services and Promotion Branch, Department of National Health and Welfare, *Guidelines for the Appropriate Use of Medical Laboratory Services in Canada*. Ottawa: The Queen's Printer, 1979.

95. Hypertension Detection and Follow-up Program Cooperation Group, "Five-year Findings of the Hypertension Detection and Follow-up Program I. Reduction in Mortality of Persons with High Blood Pressure, Including Mild Hypertension", *JAMA*, 242, 1979, pp. 2562-2571.

96. Canadian Hypertension Task Force, D.L. Sackett (chairman), "Report from the Canadian Hypertension Task Force", *Can J Public Health*, 70, 1979, pp. 298-299; 71, 1980, pp. 12-15.

97. Logan, A., personal communication, 1984.

98. Vayda, E. and G.D. Anderson, "Comparison of Provincial Surgical Rates in 1968", *Can J Surg*, 18, 1975, pp. 18-26.

99. Vayda, E., M. Morison and G.D. Anderson, "Surgical Rates in the Canadian Provinces, 1968-1972: A Five Year Analysis", *Can J Surg*, 19, 1976, pp. 235-242.

100. Bunker, J.P., "Surgical Manpower: A Comparison of Operations and Surgeons in the United States and in England and Wales", *N Engl J Med*, 282, 1970, pp. 135-144.

101. Wennberg, J.E. and A.M. Gittelsohn, "Small Area Variations in Health Care Delivery", *Science*, 182, 1973, pp. 1102-1108.

102. McPherson, K., P.M. Strong, A. Epstein and L. Jones, "Regional Variations in the Use of Common Surgical Procedures; Within and Between England and Wales, Canada and the United States of America", *Soc Sci Med*, 15a, 1981, pp. 273-288.

103. Vayda, E., W. Mindell and I.M. Rutkow, "A Decade of Surgery in Canada, England and Wales, and the United States", *Arch Surg*, 117, 1982, pp. 846-853.

104. *Ibid.*

105. Roos, N.P., "Hysterectomy: Variations in Rates Across Small Areas and Across Physicians' Practices", *Am J Public Health*, 74, 1984, pp. 327-335.

106. Kassirer, J.P. and J.S. Pauker, "The Toss-up", *N Engl J Med*, 305, 1981, pp. 1467-1469.

107. Wennberg, J.E., "Factors Governing Utilization of Hospital Services", *Hosp Pract*, 14, 1979, pp. 115-127.

108. Dyck, F.J., F.A. Murphy, J.K. Murphy *et al.*, "Effect of Surveillance on the Number of Hysterectomies in the Province of Saskatchewan", *N Engl J Med*, 296, 1977, pp. 1326-1328.

109. Vayda *et al.*, *op. cit.*, footnote 99.

110. Wennberg, J.E., K. McPherson and P. Caper, "Will Payment Based on Diagnosis-Related Groups Control Hospital Costs?", *N Engl J Med*, 311, 5, 1984, pp. 295-300.

111. Rutkow, I.M., "The Surgical Decision-Making Process: Determinants of Surgical Rates", *Health Serv Res*, 17, 1982, pp. 379-385.

112. Shah, C.P., "Anaesthesia for Day-Care Surgery: A Symposium (I), Day-care Surgery in Canada: Evolution, Policy and Experience of Provinces", *Can Anaesth Soc J*, 27, 1980, pp. 399-405.

113. The Hospital for Sick Children, Toronto, Ontario, *Annual reports*, 1910-14.

114. Nicoll, J.H., "The Surgery of Infancy", *Br Med J*, 2, 1909, p. 753.

115. Hospital Insurance and Diagnostic Services Act 5-6 Elizabeth II, in *Regulations*. Ottawa: The Queen's Printer, 1957.

116. Soderstrom, L., *The Canadian Health System*. London: Croom Helm, 1978, p. 26.

117. Medical Care Act 14-15 Elizabeth II. Ottawa: The Queen's Printer, 1966.

118. Shah, *op. cit.*, footnote 112.

119. Freiberg, L., Jr., "Substitution of Outpatient Care for Inpatient Care: Problems and Experience", *J Health Polit Policy Law*, 3, 1979, pp. 479-496.

120. Evans, R.G. and G.C. Robinson, "Surgical Day Care: Measurements of the Economic Payoff", *Can Med Assoc J*, 123, 1980, pp. 873-880.

121. Shah, C.P., G.C. Robinson, C. Kinnis *et al.*, "Day-care Surgery for Children: A Controlled Study of Medical Complications and Parental Attitudes", *Med Care*, 10, 5, 1972, pp. 437-450.

122. Pineault, R., A.-P. Contandriopoulos, M. Valois *et al.*, "Randomized Clinical Trial of One-Day Surgery: Patient Satisfaction, Clinical Outcomes and Costs". Submitted for publication.

123. Detmer, D.E. and D.J. Buchanan-Davidson, "Ambulatory Surgery", *Surg Clin North Am*, 62, 1982, pp. 685-704.

124. Burns, L.A. and M.S. Ferber, "Ambulatory Surgery in the United States: Development and Prospects", *J Ambul Care Management*, 4, 1981, p. 1.

125. Reed, W.A. and J.L. Ford, "Outpatient Clinic for Surgery", *Med World News*, 12, 1971, p. 58.

126. Burns and Ferber, *op. cit.*, footnote 124.

127. "Tremendous Growth Predicted in Ambulatory Surgery Market", *Same-Day Surgery*, 5, 1981, p. 137.

128. Fontaine, S., "Marketing Concepts", *Same-Day Surgery*, 4, 1980, p. 109.

129. O'Donovan, T.R., "Ambulatory Surgery Up-Date", *Same-Day Surgery*, 5, 1981, p. 91.

COMMENTARY

Fernand Turcotte

In their discussion of factors affecting the diffusion of technology into medical practice, Battista, Spasoff and Spitzer shed revealing light on a range of aspects of health care as dispensed in Canada, aspects that might well explain why the Canadian health care system has fared so well in protecting all Canadians against indigence brought about by sickness, within what seems, in relation to the U.S., a relatively moderate share of our collective resources. Looking back on the experience gained over the past decade, this paper addresses two questions:

1. Do Canadian health care systems foster technological changes that enhance productivity?
2. Do Canadian health care systems encourage selectively the diffusion of services and techniques proven to be efficacious while selecting out others?

Some of the answers provided by the authors are quite straightforward, but others are ambiguous.

While supporting the view of health economists that centralized control over financing mechanisms is the single most powerful explanation for Canada's success in curbing the growth rate of its national health expenditures, the Battista, Spasoff and Spitzer review introduces evidence more readily found in the daily chores of medical practice than in the national accounts. Some of this evidence challenges the perennial assumption of medical educators that physicians' behaviour is primarily determined by their knowledge and by the health problems with which they are confronted. Most of the data used by the authors has been gathered recently in Canada, and it shows that the organizational environment in which medical practice takes place is a more powerful determinant of physician behaviour than are sickness patterns.

In order to respond adequately to the increases in demand induced by the elimination of financial barriers to access health care, Canada augmented the size of the health care sector as a whole, as described in the paper by Taylor and documented by Barer and Evans above. But in view of the current similarity of structure of the health care sector on both sides of the border, and of the commonality of professional values and quality standards, it appears that very little else was ever changed.

Of the few health indices that are sensitive to health care, most have continued to improve after insurance mechanisms were organized and made functional across the nation. While chronological association does not prove causation, it does suggest that the quality of services was kept constant, as long as one assumes that quality of care may improve health. Increasing the output of services while maintaining constant quality and aggregate inputs is a remarkable achievement in health care that deserves careful scrutiny. By reviewing one process, that of diffusion of technology into medical practice, Battista and his colleagues provide a credible and meticulous account of one important aspect of how this country's health system has performed so far.

They have chosen seven determining factors as the basis for their analysis. The interactions of these factors with each other are illustrated in seven examples drawn from the domains of prevention, diagnosis and treatment — fields predominantly, if not exclusively, controlled by physicians. Their time span of observation varies, but with the exception of the Task Force on Periodic Health Examination (eighteen months being too short a period to allow for much change), it is sufficient to observe variations and the direction of these variations.

That the periodic health examination was deemed a service item worth the attention of a multi-specialty consensus conference, controlled by epidemiologists, illustrates the Canadian way of dealing with sensitive issues. The value of medical check-ups was and is still well entrenched in lay and professional beliefs. And to entrust to a group of peers the responsibility for formulating policy guidelines on this subject was a clever initiative, even if the structural proximity of the experts to their sponsors was, at times, used to contest the intrinsic validity of their report. That the report has not permeated actual practice more, after eighteen months, is not as surprising as it may seem at first glance, since the report was not supported by immediate action on medical fees. It is only after fee schedules are modified along some of the directions suggested in the Task Force Report, that the potential impact of this policy formulation is likely to be realized.

Patient participation has been considered, over and above what Battista and colleagues report in relation to health maintenance, as an organizational means to increase the responsiveness of the health care sector to the evolving needs of the population. In Quebec, for instance, the proportion of board members who are elected by users of services increases progressively as one moves from regional health services councils to local community services centres, where users-trustees hold the majority of seats on boards of direction. Whether this structural device has been successful is still to be verified, but anecdotal evidence suggests that it may be influential. This mechanism is, for instance, responsible for the introduction of abortion services and birthing suites into previously reluctant institutions.

In their study of the dissemination of CT scanners, the authors describe the degree of control that has been attained over the introduction of this expensive new technology and over its consequent use. Isolation and separation of capital-acquisition from operating funds in our hospital sector remains the best technical explanation for this phenomenon, after centralized control over spending.

The authors present a convincing argument, based on empirical evidence, to explain the increase in the intensity of use of low-technology interventions. They attribute most of this increase to the absence of cost-sensitivity among physicians, a phenomenon that seems impervious to experience, training or insurance coverage. This lack of cost-sensitivity compounds the overrating by physicians of the predictive value of most laboratory tests. Widespread medical overconfidence in tests derives from clinical experience gained in populations of patients, in which prevalence of related clinical problems tends to be high. It is a well-known phenomenon that the predictive validity of a given test is directly proportional to the prevalence of a clinical problem in a population. Relying more on his experience than on evidence, the physician is easily coaxed into ordering an additional test, not necessarily related to the diagnostic options he is attempting to rule out, but just in case he might come across some unexpected finding. At other times, he will want to reduce his risk of "sinning by omission", a side effect of increased awareness, if not fear, of possible malpractice questions. At that level, the choice of technique might be more readily understood through the developing field of clinical decision analysis rather than through organizational theory.

The delicate and complicated interplay of provider-related factors, patient-related factors and quality assessment/assurance activities is best described in the section on therapeutics. Control of hypertension is, to put it mildly, incompletely achieved, despite considerable evidence supporting both its feasibility and its effectiveness. The sensitivity of unjustified hysterectomies to quality assessment activities does explain part of the variation in rates of this surgical procedure that are reported in the literature. The remainder might be attributable to the (geographic) density of surgeons, as well as to physicians' practice variations, which are themselves determined, as may be inferred from specific mortality studies, *inter alia* by training, beliefs, experience and methods of payment, rather than by diseases of the uterus itself.

The use of day-care surgery diffusion patterns in the present century to illustrate the effects of societal forces on the health care system is convincing, particularly when a long enough time interval is considered.

Battista and his colleagues make a convincing argument against firmly held opinions in medical circles that consider the health care systems of this country to be frozen in an obsolete technology and, consequently, isolated from the "mainstream" of contemporary medicine, which is implicitly understood to be represented by U.S. standards of medical practice. New technologies are introduced and diffused with varying patterns across the land, but they remain influenced by the same factors one may find in the literature. And as observed elsewhere, innovations proven to be efficacious do not necessarily nor rapidly supersede methods that have become obsolete. Innovations embodied in hardware find acceptance more readily than those calling for changes in patterns of practice or organization of labour. Finally, diffusion of proven therapies or preventive services is more often impaired by structural deficiencies than by scarcity of necessary resources.

IV

MANPOWER POLICY

AND WHO SHALL REPRESENT THE PUBLIC INTEREST? THE LEGACY OF CANADIAN HEALTH MANPOWER POLICY

*This paper was not part of the conference proceedings but commissioned after by the steering committee

Jonathan Lomas
Morris L. Barer

Introduction

There is no more succinct a description of the potential offered by national health insurance for the appropriate organization of health manpower roles than that provided by George Bernard Shaw more than seventy years ago:

> [An] advantage of public medical work is that it admits of organization and consequently of the distribution of the work in such a manner as to avoid wasting the time of highly qualified experts on trivial jobs. The individualism of private practice leads to an appalling waste of time on trifles . . . in the pursuit of private fees . . . . To put it in terms of the cases, there are cases that present no difficulties, and can be dealt with by a nurse or student at one end of the scale, and cases that require watching and handling by the very highest existing skill at the other. (Shaw, 1911, pp. 73-74)

How far Canada has strayed from realizing this potential of national health insurance, the policies that have affected health manpower both before and after health insurance, and some changes that might improve Canada's performance, are the subject of this paper.

In the first section we present such data as we could locate on the growth and changes in mix of health manpower since the late 1960s. In the second section we trace the development of policies that influenced these changes, by focusing specifically on the three critical areas of regulation of the professions (what we have chosen to call professional governance), manpower planning and the financial and organizational structure of the health care system. In the final section we look to the future and, by extrapolating from what we see as the current shortcomings, suggest some changes in health manpower policy to capitalize on the potential "advantage of *public* medical work"

The Data on Health Manpower:
Primaries, Complements and Substitutes

Reliable and comprehensive time series data on health manpower in Canada are not readily available. Of all the categories, physician data are the most comprehensive indicating where the focus of health manpower attention lies. The primary sources for data are the licensing authorities of the various health professionals, but these data, of course, are of little value for those occupations that either have no mandatory licensing requirements (e.g., dental assistants) or are not even considered to be a legal occupation (e.g., midwives). We therefore had to use a variety of sources for our data.

Our principal source was the consolidation of data in the *Canada Health Manpower Inventory* (CHMI) published first in 1969 and annually since 1972 by the Department of National Health and Welfare. Where possible we have supplemented this with information from the original sources of the CHMI and elsewhere. These original sources are of four main types: licensing authorities, educational institutions, employment settings and occupational associations. Each of these sources has its own particular problems. Licensing data provide no information on the practice status of licensed individuals, e.g., part-time or full-time, administrative or non-administrative, licensed in more than one province but practising only in one, and so on. Educational data give only the number of graduates; they tell us nothing about the number who actually go into practice or employment. More important, they are not necessarily proportionate to the stock of personnel currently available. Data from employment settings, usually hospitals by way of their reports to Statistics Canada, do provide actual employment figures but reveal nothing of the individuals who are in other employment settings or who are qualified but no longer working in the occupation. This latter consideration is of particular importance in nursing where the pool of qualified nurses seems to be far larger than the number who are in nursing employment. Finally, data from membership in provincial or national associations are quite variable in quality and are subject to year-to-year fluctuations that are unrelated to real changes in practice or employment; e.g., periodic removals or reinstatements of mandatory association membership. Wherever possible we have tried to select what we considered to be the most reliable data available and to note any potential biases. We have provided a consolidation of the sources for all our tables in a Data Appendix at the end of this paper.

A particular difficulty we encountered was data discontinuity from year to year. This was of two types: changes in the reporting process of a reasonably reliable data source, and discontinuities in inherently unreliable data sets. An example of the former were the licensing data for dentists in which the reporting period changed from a June to a December year end in 1974 giving rise to an apparent leap in numbers for that year. An example of the latter was the dental assistants' association membership, which twice became mandatory and was then returned to voluntary. These discontinuities highlight the problem for government of relying on the occupations themselves to collect relevant manpower data, and the consequent difficulty for planning when no attention is paid to year-to-year consistency. Without an active government role in collecting and analyzing manpower data, planning will continue to be severely hampered by the absence of comprehensive and reliable numbers reported in a consistent fashion from year to year.

Given these problems, we decided to focus on Canada-wide data. While these hide what might be important inter-provincial variations, they provide an overview that is less susceptible to error. We have also focused largely on the 1968 to 1982 period, both because this captures the Medicare years and because little data is available prior to this time. There was also little point in trying to be comprehensive by reporting all health occupations — we just did not have the data. Hence, we used selected manpower categories to illustrate general trends in the growth of absolute numbers and in the relative mix of manpower categories. Average annual growth rates over set time periods (1968 to 1970, 1970 to 1975, 1975 to 1980 and 1980 to 1982) were used for specific occupations; relative growth indices (explained later) were used for comparisons between the primary professions and other selected occupations.

We chose to report the data in three categories. First are the primary professions, those categories of health manpower that have been largely self-determining in their activities and employment: physicians, dentists, pharmacists and optometrists. These professionals, by virtue of significant self-regulatory power, have not depended very much on the activities of other professions or occupations for the definition of their own roles. Second are the complements, whose activities tend to be supportive of the primaries: nurses, laboratory technicians, dental assistants and so on. The complements have therefore not been self-determining but, while they are largely dependent on the primaries for their roles, their development is clearly in the interests of the primary professions. Third are the substitutes, who could directly replace some of the functions of the primaries and who might therefore be considered supportive of the health system's needs, but who are in competition with the primaries: nurse practitioners and dental therapists, for example. Unfortunately, the substitutes are not usually self-regulating and have largely been dependent for their roles on their competitor primaries, with predictable results for their relative growth. It is also interesting to note that it is in this category that we had most difficulty locating *any* data. Midwifery, for instance, is not a legal occupation in Canada, making collection of data on their supply an exercise in contacting subversives!

TABLE 1

NUMBER AND POPULATION PER PRACTITIONER, PRIMARY PROFESSIONS, CANADA, 1968-1983[a]

YEAR	PHYSICIANS (active) (inc. Int. & Res.)		DENTISTS (licensed)	
	Number	Population to Practitioner Ratio	Number	Population to Practitioner Ratio
1968	28209	740	6738	3100
69	29659	714	6933	3055
70	31166	689	7115	3017
71	32942	659	7453	2913
72	34508	636	7611	2883
73	35923	619	7825	2842
74	37297	605	8487[b]	2659[b]
75	39104	585	8738	2619
76	40130	577	9401	2463
77	41398	566	10058	2328
78	42238	560	10451	2262
79	43192	554	10763	2222
80	44275	547	11095	2183
81	45542	538	11484	2135
82	47384	523	11880	2087
83	48860	512	-	-

Average Annual Growth Rates (%)

1968-70	5.11	3.64	2.76	1.34
1970-75	4.64	3.33	4.21	2.89
1975-80	2.52	1.35	4.91	3.73
1980-82[e]	3.34	2.23	3.48	2.28
1971-82[e]	3.34	2.13	4.35	3.10
1968-82[e]	3.74	2.49	4.15	2.88

a. See data appendix for sources.
b. Data reporting changed from June (1968-73) to December (1974-82).
c. Data reporting changed from national (1968-73) to province of registration (1974-82).
d. Some of the growth in these years due to more accurate reporting, not to a real increase in numbers.
e. Period goes to 1983 for physicians.

Note: In this and subsequent tables, average annual growth rates refer to growth of the practitioner-to-population ratio, the inverse of the reported ratio.

TABLE 1 (cont'd)

NUMBER AND POPULATION PER PRACTITIONER, PRIMARY PROFESSIONS, CANADA, 1968-1983[a]

YEAR	PHARMACISTS (licensed)		OPTOMETRISTS (active)	
	Number	Population to Practitioner Ratio	Number	Population to Practitioner Ratio
1968	10390	2010	1442	14485
69	10587	2001	1440	14710
70	11084	1937	1497	14339
71	11330	1916	1511	14368
72	11629	1887	1527	14370
73	11779	1888	1547	14373
74	13267[c]	1701[c]	1604[d]	14070[d]
75	13872	1650	1685[d]	13581[d]
76	14687	1577	1764[d]	13128[d]
77	15328	1528	1841	12720
78	15709	1505	1869	12651
79	16052	1490	1919	12461
80	16588	1460	1916	12642
81	17039	1439	2070	11842
82	17569	1411	2180	11371
83	-	-	-	-
Average Annual Growth Rates (%)				
1968-70	3.30	1.88	1.91	0.53
1970-75	4.66	3.35	2.41	1.10
1975-80	3.65	2.49	2.62	1.46
1980-82[e]	2.92	1.72	6.68	5.45
1971-82[e]	4.11	2.86	3.41	2.18
1968-82[e]	3.86	2.60	3.02	1.77

a. See data appendix for sources.
b. Data reporting changed from June (1968-73) to December (1974-82).
c. Data reporting changed from national (1968-73) to province of registration (1974-82).
d. Some of the growth in these years due to more accurate reporting, not to a real increase in numbers.
e. Period goes to 1983 for physicians

Note: In this and subsequent tables, average annual growth rates refer to growth of the practitioner-to-population ratio, the inverse of the reported period.

Before reporting on the data in these categories we should point out, however, that the placement of particular occupations in these categories reflects what actually is rather than what could be. Dental hygienists, for example, have been classified as complements because they work in dentists' practices, under the supervision of dentists, providing periodontal services that extend the "product line" of the practice. The dentist owns the practice, collects the fees and reimburses the hygienist. But there is no technical reason why, in a different regulatory environment, freestanding hygienists' practices, run by self-employed hygienists, might not offer a range of periodontal and preventive dental services ("prophylaxis and fluoride") in direct economic competition with dentists. Similarly, substitutes can also become complements when it is in the interest of the primary profession (and when their activities are strictly circumscribed by geography or setting); e.g., nurse practitioners in the far north or paramedics tending to roadside victims. Our categorization is intended to be a description, not an endorsement, of how health manpower is currently deployed.

Primary Professions

Table 1 presents the numbers and practitioner to population ratios of the primary professions from 1968 to 1982. All of the primary professions have increased both in absolute numbers and relative to population growth for the entire period under study; increased availability has therefore occurred whether the health profession was part of public health insurance (physicians and partially pharmacists) or private health insurance (dentists and optometrists). The total stock of primary professionals has increased by about two-thirds. In the entire period (1968 to 1982) and in the Medicare period (1971 to 1982) dentists have shown the most significant increases, averaging an annual growth in practitioner to population ratios of 2.88 percent and 3.10 percent respectively in the two periods. In the 1968 to 1982 period, average annual growth of optometrist to population ratios was slowest (1.77 percent), but in the Medicare period of 1971 to 1982 it was physician to population ratios that grew slowest, averaging 2.13 percent per year. This latter observation may be more an indication of how fast the supply of other professionals has grown than of how slowly the physician supply has grown. Furthermore, physician supply *per capita* increased by more than 2 percent *per annum* despite the fact that this was the only professional group for which specific immigration controls existed from 1975 onward.

The effect of these specific immigration controls, however, shows up clearly in Table 1. The annual increase in the number of physicians averaged 5.11 percent in 1968 to 1970, 4.04 percent in 1970 to 1975, but only 2.52 percent from 1975 to 1980. The timing of these increases is in contrast to those for dentists, which were greatest in 1975 to 1980 (4.91 percent) and less in 1970 to 1975 (4.21 percent) and 1968 to 1970 (2.76 percent). Pharmacists, like physicians, showed larger average annual increases in the 1970 to 1975 period (4.66 percent) than in 1975 to 1980 (2.65 percent). Optometrists' annual increases have been

TABLE 2

NUMBER AND POPULATION PER PHYSICIAN OF INTERNS AND RESIDENTS, GENERAL PRACTITIONERS AND SPECIALISTS, CANADA, 1968-1983[a]

YEAR	INTERNS & RESIDENTS		GENERAL PRACTITIONERS	
	Numbers	Population to Practitioner Ratio	Numbers	Population to Practitioner Ratio
1968	5240	3986	11778	1773
69	5229	4052	12592	1682
70	5510	3896	13023	1648
71	5503	3946	13704	1584
72	5902	3718	14302	1534
73	5979	3719	14919	1490
74	6189	3646	15545	1452
75	6543	3497	16379	1397
76	6376	3632	17036	1359
77	6538	3582	17654	1326
78	6805	3474	17913	1320
79	6748	3544	18469	1295
80	6988	3466	18853	1285
81	7232	3389	19232	1275
82	7303	3394	20355	1218
83	7420	3372	-	-

Average Annual Growth Rates (%)

1968-70	1.55	0.30	5.16	3.74
1970-75	3.59	2.74	4.69	3.36
1975-80	1.36	0.21	2.86	1.69
1980-82	2.22	1.22	3.92	2.73
1971-82	2.64	1.41	3.67	2.43
1968-82	2.28	1.01	4.00	2.73

a. See data appendix for sources.

TABLE 2 (cont'd)
NUMBER AND POPULATION PER PHYSICIAN OF INTERNS AND RESIDENTS, GENERAL PRACTITIONERS AND SPECIALISTS, CANADA, 1968-1983[a]

YEAR	SPECIALISTS		GENERAL PRACTITIONER TO SPECIALIST RATIO
	Numbers	Population to Practitioner Ratio	
1968	11191	1866	51.3:48.7
69	11838	1789	51.5:48.5
70	12633	1699	50.8:49.2
71	13735	1581	49.9:50.1
72	14304	1534	50.0:50.0
73	15025	1480	49.8:50.2
74	15563	1450	50.0:50.0
75	16182	1414	50.3:49.7
76	16718	1385	50.5:49.5
77	17206	1361	50.6:49.4
78	17519	1350	50.6:49.4
79	17975	1330	50.7:49.3
80	18434	1314	50.6:49.4
81	19078	1285	50.2:49.8
82	19726	1257	50.8:49.2
83	-	-	-

Average Annual Growth Rates (%)

1968-70	6.25	4.80
1970-75	5.09	3.76
1975-80	2.64	1.48
1980-82	3.44	2.24
1971-82	3.35	2.11
1968-82	4.15	2.88

a. See data appendix for sources.

steadily rising throughout the period, with a major recent increase in average annual growth in 1980 to 1982 (6.68 percent).

In Table 2 the physician supply is broken down into the components of interns and residents, general practitioners and specialists. Although specialist supply increased slightly faster than general practitioners in the periods during and after the introduction of Medicare (1968 to 1970 and 1970 to 1975), this has been counter-balanced by a slightly greater increase for general practitioners in the latter half of the 1970s and in the early 1980s. The last column of Table 2 shows that Canada has maintained roughly equal numbers of generalists and specialists, in contrast to the U.S., where "primary care specialists" (internists, paediatricians, specialists in obstetrics and gynecology) have almost entirely replaced GPs (McNutt, 1981). If current plans to reduce the availability of specialty residency posts in medical schools are carried out (Canada, 1984; Ontario Council of Health, 1983), this balance may be tilted toward the generalists.

Although the number of interns and residents has increased steadily throughout the period, major growth occurred in 1970 to 1975 with an annual average increase in numbers of 3.59 percent. This presumably reflects the decisions in the mid-1960s to open new medical schools and increase undergraduate medical school enrolment, resulting in larger numbers of interns and residents in the early 1970s.

Thus, the picture for all the primary professions has been one of steady growth throughout the 1968 to 1982 period, indicating that the presence of public (rather than private) health insurance confers no special growth potential on a particular professional group. In fact, insofar as immigration controls on physicians can be attributed to governments' concern over expenditures on physicians' services, public health insurance has slightly moderated the growth in the yearly increases in supply. However, physician supply *per capita* is still increasing year by year, as is that of all the other primary professions.

Complementary Occupations

Beyond the primary professions, data on other health occupations become more difficult to find, and what is available is of poorer quality. No data on occupations related to pharmacy or optometry (e.g., pharmacy assistants or opticians) could be located. Therefore, the remaining data reflect physician- or dentist-related occupations. We deal first with physician complements, which we have divided into two tables. In Table 3, complements to all (or most) physician activities are represented by nurses, nursing assistants and physiotherapists. In Table 4, complements to hospital-based specialists (either all specialists or specific specialties) are represented by laboratory technologists, respiratory technologists and radiation technicians.

Data for nurses are for nurses employed full-time or part-time in all forms of nursing whether or not in the hospital or in direct patient care. For nursing

TABLE 3

NUMBER AND POPULATION PER PRACTITIONER; NURSES, NURSING ASSISTANTS AND PHYSIOTHERAPISTS, CANADA, 1968-1982[a]

YEAR	NURSES[b]		NURSING ASSISTANTS[c]		PHYSIOTHERAPISTS[d]	
	Number	Population to Practitioner Ratio	Number	Population to Practitioner Ratio	Number	Population to Practitioner Ratio
1968	92618	226	28764	726	2027	10298
69	100003	212	32230	657	2024	10463
70	104258	206	34098	630	2210	9717
71	108630	200	36151	601	2287[h]	9492[h]
72	110769	198	36293	604	2541	8637
73	115929	192	37045	600	2698	8242
74	125475	180	38180	591	2991	7544
75	140388	163	39478	580	3260	7017
76	137858	168	40909[f]	566[f]	3591	6448
77	139989	167	42141	556	3662	6398
78	161125[e]	147[e]	42663	544	3673	6440
79	148954	160	43060	555	3945	6066
80	155309	156	44445	545	4187	5784
81	161269	152	45559[g]	538[g]	4453	5502
82	164231	151	—	—	4536	5463

Average Annual Growth Rates (%)

1968-70	6.11	4.76	9.00	7.47	4.52	3.05
1970-75	6.19[k]	4.84[k]	2.99	1.68	8.11	6.76
1975-80	2.06	0.90	2.40	1.26	5.20	4.00
1980-82[j]	2.84	1.65	2.51	1.30	4.11	2.92

TABLE 3 (cont'd)

NUMBER AND POPULATION PER PRACTITIONER; NURSES, NURSING ASSISTANTS AND PHYSIOTHERAPISTS, CANADA, 1968-1982[a]

YEAR	NURSES[b]		NURSING ASSISTANTS[c]		PHYSIOTHERAPISTS[d]	
	Number	Population to Practitioner Ratio	Number	Population to Practitioner Ratio	Number	Population to Practitioner Ratio
1971-82[j]	3.89[k]	2.64[k]	2.34	1.10	6.52	5.21
1968-82[j]	4.23[k]	2.97[k]	4.58	2.38	6.02	4.69

a. See data appendix for sources.
b. Full-time and part-time employed in nursing.
c. Full-time and part-time employed in public hospitals; adjusted series (see Appendix).
d. Active members of the Canadian Physiotherapy Association.
e. Non-comparable year. Refers to only those nurses who registered in Canada during the first four months of the registration renewal period. This fact and less rigorous editing with a simplified method for eliminating inter-provincial duplicates hinders comparison with other years.
f. Reporting changed from calendar year (1968-76) to fiscal year ending March 31 (1977/78 to 1981/82).
g. Figures include psychiatric hospitals for the first time.
h. Reporting changed from calendar year (1968-71) to fiscal year ending March 31 (1972/73 to 1982/83).
j. Period in fact ends in 1981/82 for nursing assistants and 1982/83 for physiotherapists.
k. These figures use an imputed value for the non-comparable year of 1978. This imputed value was half way between the figures for 1977 and 1979 i.e. 144,472 for the number of nurses and 164 for the practitioner to population ratio.

TABLE 4

NUMBER AND POPULATION PER PRACTITIONER; LABORATORY TECHNOLOGISTS, RESPIRATORY TECHNOLOGISTS AND RADIATION TECHNICIANS, CANADA, 1968-1982[a]

YEAR	LABORATORY TECHNOLOGISTS[b]		RESPIRATORY TECHNOLOGISTS[c]		RADIATION TECHNICIANS[c]	
	Number	Population to Practitioner Ratio	Number	Population to Practitioner Ratio	Number	Population to Practitioner Ratio
1968	5345	3908	186	112301	3706	5636
69	6156	3441	234	90521	3920	5404
70	6502	3301	346	62038	4184	5130
71	7241	2998	466	46588	4627	4692
72	7969	2753	604	36328	4626	4743
73	9258	2402	894	24872	5258	4229
74	10210	2210	1106	20406	6957	3244
75	11274	2030	1054	21711	7652	2990
76	12066	1919	1309	17692	8012	2890
77	12813	1828	1494	15674	8544	2741
78	13012	1817	1543	15324	8751	2702
79	13655	1751	1736	13774	9064	2638
80	14252	1700	1834	13207	9464	2559
81	15097	1624	1929	12708	9660	2537
82	15721	1576	2161	11471	9357	2648

TABLE 4 (cont'd)

NUMBER AND POPULATION PER PRACTITIONER; LABORATORY TECHNOLOGISTS, RESPIRATORY TECHNOLOGISTS AND RADIATION TECHNICIANS, CANADA, 1968-1982[a]

YEAR	LABORATORY TECHNOLOGISTS[b]		RESPIRATORY TECHNOLOGISTS[c]		RADIATION TECHNICIANS[c]	
	Number	Population to Practitioner Ratio	Number	Population to Practitioner Ratio	Number	Population to Practitioner Ratio
Average Annual Growth Rates (%)						
1968-70	10.40	8.92	36.85	22.95	6.25	4.82
1970-75	12.78	10.23	26.26	24.66	13.31	11.86
1975-80	4.82	3.63	11.94	10.67	4.35	3.17
1980-82	5.00	3.86	8.60	7.36	-0.54	-1.66
1971-82	7.36	6.08	15.77	14.38	6.97	5.68
1968-82	8.09	6.78	20.14	18.67	7.12	5.82

a. See data appendix for sources.
b. Active and certified.
c. Registered.

assistants the data are restricted to those employed in public hospitals; nursing homes and other extended care facilities where nursing assistants are widely used are not included. For physiotherapy the data are for members of the Canadian Physiotherapy Association. From Table 3 it is clear that all these occupations have experienced growth in the entire 1968 to 1982 period, not only in absolute numbers but also in relation to population increases. This has been especially and consistently true for physiotherapists, although it is unclear how much improved reporting of association membership may have influenced apparent growth in the earlier years.

The moderation in growth rates from the late 1960s and early 1970s to the late 1970s and early 1980s, already noted for physicians and pharmacists, is also observed for nurses and physiotherapists. On a *per capita* basis, employed nurses dropped from an annual average increase of 4.84 percent in 1970 to 1975 to 0.90 percent in 1975 to 1980. The same figures for physiotherapists' membership are 6.76 percent and 4.00 percent. Nursing assistants have, with the exception of the 1968 to 1970 period, shown only moderate growth on a *per capita* basis, but still with a slowing of that growth in the 1975 to 1980 period (a 1.26 percent annual average increase compared with 1.68 percent in 1970 to 1975).

In Table 4 we find a similar picture for hospital technologists and technicians: all show significant growth across the 1968 to 1982 period, but with a moderation of that growth from the mid-1970s onward. Radiation technicians actually slipped back in the 1980 to 1982 period with an annual average decrease on a *per capita* basis (-1.66 percent). Respiratory technologists — an occupational area that has seen significant technological advances in the past fifteen years — exhibited phenomenal growth, averaging annual *per capita* increases of 18.67 percent from 1968 to 1982! For laboratory technologists the same figure is 6.78 percent, and for radiation technicians 5.82 percent. However, the growth in certified laboratory technologists has to be explained, in later years, in terms of the decline in the number of uncertified laboratory technologists. Our data relate to certified laboratory technologists only, who comprised about 85 percent of hospital laboratory technologists until 1975. By 1982, however, more than 98 percent of the laboratory technologists in hospitals were certified. Thus their moderate growth in the late 1970s does not represent new job opportunities for laboratory technologists but rather an upgrading of the qualifications of those in existing hospital jobs. This bias in the data means that our figures for laboratory technologists understate the fall in growth rates from the mid-1970s onward.

In Table 5 we present data to relate the growth of these complements to the growth in the physician supply. We constructed Relative Growth Indices (RGIs) for each occupation against all physicians (nurses, nursing assistants and physiotherapists), all specialists (laboratory technologists), the specialty of internal medicine (respiratory technologists) and the specialty of radiology (radiation technicians). The RGI compares the ratio of the supply of a complement with the supply of physicians across two separate years. It standardizes the ratio of the

TABLE 5
RELATIVE GROWTH INDICES[a] OF PHYSICIAN COMPLEMENTS, CANADA, 1968-1982[b]

YEAR	NURSES AND ALL PHYSICIANS	NURSING ASSISTANTS AND ALL PHYSICIANS	PHYSIOTHERAPISTS AND ALL PHYSICIANS	LABORATORY TECHNOLOGISTS AND SPECIALISTS	RESPIRATORY TECHNOLOGISTS AND INTERNISTS[c]	RADIATION TECHNICIANS AND RADIOLOGISTS[d]
1968 vs. 1970	1.02	1.07	0.99	1.08	1.68	0.97
1971 vs. 1975	1.09	0.92	1.20	1.32	2.19	1.30
1976 vs. 1980	1.02	0.98	1.06	1.18	1.20	1.10
1981 vs. 1982	0.98	—	0.98	1.01	1.08	0.93
1971 vs. 1982	1.05	0.91[e]	1.38[f]	1.51	2.76	1.35
1968 vs. 1982	1.02	0.98[e]	1.33[f]	1.67	10.17	1.34

a. A value greater than 1.0 indicates that the supply of complements has grown more than the physician supply across the two comparison years; a value less than 1.0 indicates more growth in physician supply than in the supply of the complement.
b. See previous Tables 3 and 4 and data appendix for sources and footnotes.
c. This includes all subspecialties of internal medicine.
d. This includes both diagnostic and therapeutic radiologists.
e. Comparisons are to 1981/82, not 1982.
f. Comparisons are to 1982/83, not 1982.

later year to the earlier year with the result that an RGI greater than 1.0 means more growth in the complement occupation, and an RGI less than 1.0 means more growth in the physician supply. Thus:

$$RGI = \frac{R_2}{R_1}$$

where,

R_1 is the ratio of the complement occupation to physicians in the earlier comparison year

R_2 is the ratio of the complement occupation to physicians in the later comparison year

It is important to recall that the growth in the complement occupations is therefore being compared with growth in a professional group that has itself exhibited significant increases in supply over the period under study.

A comparison between the first year that all provinces were in Medicare (1971) and the latest year for which data are available (1982) shows that, with the exception of nursing assistants, all the occupations increased their supply relative to physicians. The absence of relative growth in nursing assistants may indicate that they are better considered a complement to nurses rather than to physicians; it should also be recalled, however, that the nursing assistant data exclude extended care settings where they may have increased significantly in numbers.

Table 5 shows that the moderation in the growth of each occupation after the mid-1970s is also reflected in their growth relative to physicians, despite the fact that increases in physician supply were also slowed from the mid-1970s onward. In the comparison between 1981 and 1982, three of the five occupations for which we had data (nurses, physiotherapists and radiation technicians) were growing more slowly than physicians, with RGIs respectively of 0.98, 0.98 and 0.93.

In locating data on complementary dental occupations we were forced to consider numbers of graduates because data on total supply were unreliable. For example, dental assistants have, on more than one occasion, removed and then reinstated mandatory association membership. Therefore, Table 6 presents the number of dentist, dental assistant and dental hygiene graduates from 1968 to 1982. Both of the last two occupations perform preparatory work for dentists or procedures under the direction or personal supervision of the dentist. In the late 1960s and early 1970s there was tremendous growth in the numbers of both these complementary occupations. In 1970 to 1975 the annual average growth rate in the number of dental assistant graduates was more than 46 percent, and in the number of dental hygienists nearly 26 percent. However, in what is by now a familiar pattern for the health occupations discussed here, these growth rates drop sharply in the late 1970s and early 1980s, especially for dental assistants. Nevertheless, the number of dental hygienists graduating, although growing

TABLE 6

NUMBER AND POPULATION PER GRADUATE; DENTISTS, DENTAL ASSISTANTS AND DENTAL HYGIENISTS, CANADA, 1968-1982[a]

YEAR	DENTIST GRADUATES		DENTAL ASSISTANT GRADUATES		DENTAL HYGIENIST GRADUATES	
	Number	Population to Graduate Ratio	Number	Population to Graduate Ratio	Number	Population to Graduate Ratio
1968	306	68261	72	290111	86	242884
69	339	62484	100	211820	87	243471
70	344	62398	125	171720	110	195136
71	363	59806	199	109093	125	173677
72	398	55132	311	70554	144	152378
73	401	55450	516	43092	133	167183
74	448	50376	711	31742	164	137614
75	436	52486	815	28078	304	75276
76	465	49803	962	24073	355	65235
77	459	51018	1002	23371	476	49196
78	469	50415	1009	23434	530	44612
79	473	50554	1059	22580	454	52669
80	491	49330	1078	22469	402	60252
81	479	51173	1073	22844	370	66248
82	480	52130	1113	22268	495	50069

Average Annual Growth Rates (%)

1968-70	6.12	4.69	31.95	30.16	13.80	12.28
1970-75	4.99	3.66	46.76	44.91	25.98	24.38
1975-80	2.44	1.28	5.94	4.73	7.30	6.08
1980-82	-1.32	-2.72	1.62	0.48	12.90	11.63
1971-82	2.63	1.36	18.87	17.43	16.24	14.83
1968-82	3.34	2.05	23.62	22.11	15.70	14.29

a. See data appendix for sources.

more slowly, still increased by 7.3 percent per year in 1975 to 1980 and 12.9 in 1980 to 1982.

The number of dentist graduates has dropped steadily throughout the 1968 to 1982 period, such that between 1980 and 1982 they were actually decreasing in number by an average of 1.32 percent per year. This finding is not surprising if we recall from Table 1 that the supply of dentists showed the highest average annual growth rates of all the primary professions, presaging what appears to be a reduction in the output from dental schools. Presumably the sharp drop in the output of dental assistants in the 1975 to 1982 period is in direct response to this reduced output of dentists, although this does not explain why dental hygienists continue to be produced in increasing numbers.

In Table 7 we present the RGIs for these two dental complements in relation to dentists. RGIs calculated for numbers of graduates are clearly not as satisfactory as RGIs for actual supply numbers, because RGIs compare just two specific years and therefore the degree of fluctuation that can be found from year to year in the number of graduates will not be "cushioned" by the existence of the previous years' stock, as is the case for yearly supply figures. However, since there were no major unexplained fluctuations in yearly graduate numbers, we felt justified in reporting the RGIs for dental complements.

TABLE 7

RELATIVE GROWTH INDICES[a] OF DENTIST COMPLEMENTS, CANADA, 1968-1982[b]

YEAR	DENTAL ASSISTANT AND DENTIST GRADUATES	DENTAL HYGIENIST AND DENTIST GRADUATES
1968 vs. 1970	1.54	1.14
1971 vs. 1975	3.41	2.02
1976 vs. 1980	1.06	1.07
1981 vs. 1982	1.04	1.34
1971 vs. 1982	4.23	2.99
1968 vs. 1982	9.85	3.67

a. A value greater than 1.0 indicates that the supply of dental complement graduates has grown more than the supply of dentist graduates across the two comparision years; a value less than 1.0 indicates more growth in the supply of dentist graduates than in the supply of dental complement graduates.
b. See previous Table 6 and data appendix for sources.

Once more the data confirm the moderation of complement growth relative to the primary profession from the mid-1970s onward, although, in contrast to physician complements, we observe no periods in which dental complements grew more slowly than the primary profession. We cannot say whether this is attributable to our use of graduate numbers instead of numbers in practice for dentists. What is clear is that the RGIs for dental complements are far larger than for physician complements, suggesting perhaps that public health and hospital insurance slowed the growth of physician complements more than private insurance affected the growth of dental complements.

The complement occupations have therefore grown as fast as, or faster than, their primary professions in the 1968 to 1982 period. A marked time-trend exists, however, with much slower growth of complements from the mid-1970s onward and, for physician complements, a trend toward slower growth in their supply than in the growth of the physician supply. Public health and hospital insurance might, therefore, have moderated increases in the supply of physician complements. Finally, a weaker overall economy during the 1980s and the earlier large increases in supply in the 1970s (for physiotherapy and dental assistants especially) suggest that there will be continued moderation in the *increases* in supply of complements, although not necessarily any reduction in the current size of the available *per capita* supply.

Substitute Occupations

While locating data on complement occupations was difficult, locating any sort of numbers on potential substitute occupations approached the impossible. We tried to focus on two physician substitute occupations — midwives and nurse practitioners — and one dentist substitute occupation — dental therapists or dental nurses. We were unable to find any data on midwives (it is not even a legally recognized occupation), despite our personal knowledge that some midwives are indeed practising in Canada. The data we located for nurse practitioners and dental therapists were far from adequate and were restricted to a specific province or group of provinces and territories.

It is interesting to note that the Canada Health Manpower Inventory (CHMI), which is the comprehensive listing of classes of health manpower prepared by the federal government, carefully *excludes* consideration of these substitute occupations. It also excludes denture therapists/denturists/dental mechanics (labels vary) who are also direct substitutes for, and economic competitors of, dentists. Selective tabulation by official data sources thus supports the perceptions and interests of the primary professions.

Indeed, in the case of substitute dental occupations, the very imprecision and ambiguity of names reflects the conflict with the primary professions, a struggle carried out through the political process as well as the marketplace. The label "dental mechanic", for example, which is in the B.C. regulatory legislation, conveys a very different public image from "denturist", and is probably inferior for marketing purposes. But representatives of the dental society have opposed attempts by their competitors to relabel themselves officially.

It may clarify the confusion of labels somewhat to point out that dental mechanics, denturists and denture therapists are all alternative names for self-employed fabricators of full dentures, who serve (and bill) their own customer/patients, legally in some jurisdictions, though under varying restrictions, and illegally in others. They are not permitted to fabricate and place *partial* dentures (plates and removable bridges), though allegedly some do in some provinces. Dental *technicians* are complementary to the dentist, fabricating full or partial, removable or fixed, prostheses on a dentists's prescription and on contract *to the dentist*. They are not allowed to deal directly with the public; the dentist bills for their work as well as his own. Representatives of dental societies have consistently attempted to suppress competitive "denturism" through the regulatory system by forcing its practitioners to serve as dental technicians, "to get on the dental team" (and work for its captain). This would maintain the dentist's exclusive right of *economic* access to patients (Hazelkorn and Christoffel, 1984).

Dental therapists, in contrast, who in some jurisdictions are known as dental nurses, are trained for two years post high school to perform intra-oral diagnostic, preventive and restorative procedures. In particular, they can take and interpret radiographs, and can prepare cavities for restoration as well as place, carve and polish amalgam fillings ("drill and fill"). In combination with tooth cleaning and topical fluoride application, this makes up the bulk of general dentistry. While most such personnel are in public employ, where they exist at all, there is again no technical or clinical, as opposed to regulatory, reason why they could not be in freestanding competitive practice ("drill, fill and bill"). Indeed, the public programs for school children in Saskatchewan and Manitoba *have* represented very cost-effective competition, which is why they are under severe political pressure. The dental hygienist poses a much less severe threat, being "unable" to "drill and fill" (although it has been repeatedly demonstrated in a number of jurisdictions that these skills, "expanded function", can be acquired in a relatively short up-grading program.

Before discussing these data on substitutes, which are presented in Table 8, a more general discussion of the difficulties in locating substitute occupation data is required. The potential to substitute for some or all of the activities of members of the primary professions will often not reside in all members of a single occupation. Rather, members of an occupation who currently perform as complements might, by virtue of some additional training, become qualified to operate as substitutes. The very title of nurse midwives or nurse practitioners reflects this fact, and the example of dental hygienists "in expanded function" has already been noted. From a data perspective this presents the problem of separating out: (1) those in the occupation who may have the additional training and be employed to use it; (2) those who may have it but are not employed to use it; and (3)

TABLE 8

NUMBER AND POPULATION PER PRACTITIONER, NURSE PRACTITIONERS (ONTARIO) AND LICENSED DENTAL THERAPISTS (CANADA)[a]

YEAR	NURSE PRACTITIONERS[b]		DENTAL THERAPISTS[c]	
	Number	Population to Practitioner Ratio	Number	Population to Practitioner Ratio[g]
1973	-	-	11	2021391
1974	-	-	78	289342
1975	79[d]	104162	156	146692
1976	-	-	209	110806
1977	127[f]	66204	252	92926
1978	142[e]	59868	292	80974
1979	112[f]	76248	342	69918
1980	104[e]	82689	368	65819
1981	129[e]	67160	368	66608
1982	126[f]	69655	339	73109
1983	131[f]	67840	335	74693
1984	-	-	335	-[h]

a. See data appendix for sources.
b. Active Members of the Nurse Practitioners' Association of Ontario.
c. Licensed dental therapists, does not include dental therapists practicing in private offices.
d. This figure as of June 1975.
e. These figures for end of fiscal year April to March.
f. These figures for end of calendar year.
g. These are calculated in relation to Canadian population figures, although practitioners are located only in Yukon, North West Territories, Manitoba and Saskatchewan.
h. No population figures available.

those who do not have it at all. The proportions in these three categories will obviously be related to many factors, but one significant influence is the degree to which the primary professions will *allow* the use of the advanced training, a matter discussed in more detail in later sections of this paper. For our purposes here, however, it is important to note that there *are* circumstances in which the primary professions are agreeable to such substitution. The most obvious case is that of providing service in unattractive locations such as those encountered in the North. We were able to locate most of our data on dental therapists/dental nurses for precisely this reason, because they are used extensively as government employees in the Northwest Territories, Yukon and northern Saskatchewan and Manitoba to "provide selected dental services to the]Native Indian[reserves in the province and under the Territories" (Uti, 1985).

We were not successful in separating out nursing occupation data into substitutes and complements. Even when we tried to construct a data series on graduates of nurse practitioner programs by contacting the training centres directly, most centres had data only on nursing graduates and did not separate out nurse practitioners from these aggregate numbers. It would appear, therefore, that even the occupations' educational authorities see little value in collecting data on substitute or potential substitute occupations. We were finally forced to resort to data on membership of the Nurse Practitioners' Association of Ontario — a less than satisfactory resource.

The unavailability of data on substitute occupations reflects the success of the primary professions in suppressing development of substitutes for their functions. It also suggests complicity, as noted above, on the part of educational and government institutions, which have failed to keep track of even such substitute personnel as are available. Yet there is demonstrated consumer demand for at least some of the substitute roles. For instance, following the rejection by Alberta's and Ontario's Colleges of Physicians and Surgeons of home births as an option (College of Physicians and Surgeons of Ontario, 1983), midwives have been in increasing demand as substitutes for physicians who now almost unanimously refuse to attend home births.

Turning to Table 8, and keeping in mind the problems with the data, we find that we are dealing with very small numbers of both nurse practitioners and dental therapists. The nurse practitioner data are not very reliable from year to year because of frequent changes in the reporting period. It is still clear, however, that there are few practising nurse practitioners in Ontario and there has been little or no growth in their numbers since full membership reporting was started in 1977. This absence of growth is hardly surprising given the closing, by 1982, of all three of the educational centres in Ontario (University of Western Ontario, University of Toronto and McMaster University) that had previously been training nurse practitioners.

The dental therapist data, obtained from three different sources in Manitoba and Saskatchewan (see Data Appendix at end of paper), present a similar picture, with supply actually decreasing since 1981. While these data exclude dental therapists in private practices (rather than in government employ), the number in this category has never exceeded ten (1982) and by 1984 had dropped to five (Malazdrewich, 1985). These findings are predictable given the threatening (to dentists) substitute role of dental therapists in providing a broad array of services from exposure and interpretation of x-rays to anaesthesia and preparation of cavities/insertion of fillings, and performance of uncomplicated tooth extractions.

The restricted picture that we were able to construct for substitute occupations is therefore the opposite of that for the complementary occupations. Limited utilization of their services, slow and more recently no growth or reduction in their supply, and continuing training only to supplement primary professions in unattractive locations — such is the present fate of competitors to the primary professions. In the next section we review the policies that have resulted in these contrasting growth pictures for, on the one hand, the primary professions or their complements, and, on the other, for the substitute occupations.

The Field of Manpower Policy: The Three-Legged Beast

The objective of manpower policy in the health care field is presumably to contribute to the success of the broader set of resource allocation policies designed to improve community health status in the face of resource constraints. In the jargon of the economist, the intent of such policy is to ensure that health care services are delivered with the technically most efficient mix of personnel, equipment, space and materials.[1] Evidence that we will touch on briefly below, and that is elaborated in more detail elsewhere in this volume (see, for example, Contandriopoulos et al. below), suggests that we have some distance to go to reach a technically efficient use of health care resources. The data presented in the previous section of this paper imply that the distance is growing: manpower policy appears to have led to significant growth and ongoing dominance of the primary professions, controlled and equally significant growth of their complements, and a clear retardation, if not suppression, of the development of substitutes for these primary professions.

In this section we attempt to analyze the reasons for this failure to meet health manpower policy objectives. It is important in doing so to outline the separate but highly interdependent areas of policy that can and should play a role in determining and encouraging the optimal number and mix of health care personnel. There seem to us to be three such areas: professional governance and regulation, manpower planning and supply policy, and system financing and structure. While there have been independent policy and procedural failures in each of these areas, of at least equal import has been the failure to recognize their interrelationship. Elsewhere in this volume Dussault describes the failure of professional governance reform in Quebec to bring about improved delegation to substitute health care personnel. Contandriopoulos *et al.* expand this analysis by pointing out some of the difficulties caused by failure to match changes in professional governance policy with supportive system financing and structure initiatives.

In the following sections we take each of these three areas in turn, describing the development of current policies and the (lack of) influence of these policies on the achievement of the overall health manpower objective described above. Where possible we point out that unless the three legs of a three-legged beast move in a coordinated fashion toward a common goal, the beast (health manpower policy) will, barring extraordinary good luck, spend a great deal of time with its face in the mud.[2]

Professional Governance and Regulation Policy: Has Anybody Seen the Collective Public Interest?

The structure of modern professional governance emerged in the first part of this century (Macnab, 1970; Dussault, 1978; Hogan, 1983). It was designed to deal with a health care environment very different from the one we encounter today. Prior to World War II the Canadian health care system

> was characterized by the primacy of the physician in a structure that provided care largely in terms of services to individuals in a doctor-patient relationship. This model and the delivery system associated with it were consistent with the individualistic ethic of the times. (Weller and Manga, 1983)

Health care professionals were seen as largely autonomous, practising as self-employed individuals in geographically scattered settings, with no third parties (not even government) intruding on the direct relationship between practitioner and patient. However, the potentially dire consequences for patients who were not protected from incompetent practitioners were reflected in the only objective of government policy of that time: protection of the "individual public interest". The governance structures that were established to achieve this objective developed in this pre-1945 health care environment.

What were the characteristics of this practice environment? There was a small choice of mostly complementary professions. Most of their members practised as generalists in largely independent fields of slowly developing, broad but not deep, knowledge with little reliance on technology. If there was any overlap in scope of practice, dominant and subordinate professions were well defined; and such relationships were reinforced by the prescription convention by which access to the subordinates was achieved only by way of prescription from the primary profession — physician to nurse, dentist to dental technician, optometrist to optician.[3]

Protection of the "individual public interest" was therefore sought by defining mutually exclusive practice domains (monopolies) and controlling the qualifications of those who were entitled to enter a profession's defined area of practice. The slow speed of knowledge development in these monopolistic domains made it reasonable to assume that by ensuring appropriate qualifications at entry (i.e., at registration) one ensured competence for the entire working life of the professional.[4] Significant emphasis was therefore placed on control of the educational process and licensure requirements.

The fields of practice thus established were quite broad and their breadth was significantly related to the order in which professional categories achieved statutory power. Thus physicians, by virtue of obtaining statutory power in the late 1700s and early 1800s, claimed rights to a vast area of practice, so vast that many of the subsequent statutes governing other professional groups had to exempt physicians from the exclusive practice rights of those latterly established. In addition to physicians, the primary health professions that emerged (all of which were to some extent still secondary to the dominant influence of physicians) were: dentistry, pharmacy and optometry. There was some competition from other manpower categories for a claim on these defined practice domains, but the limited number of categories of personnel enabled a solution to be found in one of three ways: "partnership" established by physicians and homeopaths,[5] "subordination" through prescription as described earlier,[6] or "exclusion" as happened to osteopaths and chiropractors.[7]

Each of the primary professions had wide fields of specialized knowledge and practised in scattered settings. Ensuring the competence of individuals within the profession therefore presented a problem to government. Both patients and government had inadequate knowledge to judge the competence of the provider and the quality of care provided. Thus, the professions themselves were given the power to define the standards of practice expected within their service monopoly and the power to enforce those standards. Governments did not have the capability of maintaining standards. They had neither the funds nor the knowledge to monitor the scattered practice settings and, in any case, enforcement by peers would be considered more acceptable. Thus emerged self-regulation with the informational asymmetry between government and practitioners resulting in the profession acting as agent of the state in protecting the individual public interest. In addition, of course, each member of the profession acted as agent of his or her individual patients in both advising on and procuring appropriate care (Tuohy and Wolfson, 1978). In the absence of any third party interests in the financial or social aspects of the professional-patient encounter, and in the face of fairly uniform and accepted forms of service delivery, this seemed to be a reasonable policy solution.

From the perspective of today's health care system, however, it is possible to see in retrospect a number of difficulties attributable to this form of professional governance.

First, by granting self-regulatory power, governments had effectively disenfranchised themselves from what, at the time, was the only policy avenue available to influence the roles of and relationships between health manpower personnel. Should they later wish to alter the scope of practice or subordination rights of the primary professions, they could do so only through explicit legislative change, with all the political costs of exercising such power. Had governments been aware that their first attempt at a professional governance structure would, in effect, also be their last, there might have been somewhat more time and analysis put into its development. The effect was to entrench the monopoly of the primary professions in difficult to penetrate fortresses of exclusive practice rights.

Second, the relative uniformity and acceptability of the financial and organizational structure within which professionals worked — fee-for-service private practice — resulted in governments granting the self-regulatory right to set practice standards not only for the content of care but also for the conditions within which that care would be delivered. At the time, organizational and financial issues were neither contentious nor very variable. They were therefore largely overlooked and came to be controlled by the profession by default as part of the package called "practice standards", despite the fact that no significant informational asymmetry existed in this area.

Third, the largely independent practice domains of the complementary primary professions (despite the broad scope of each) meant that there was no particular reason to establish effective mechanisms for inter-professional communication and control: each operated independently under an individualistic ethic and with its own view of the public interest.

Finally, the governance structure of the professions failed to establish any mechanisms for the protection of the "collective public interest". By "collective public interest" we refer to the fact that, in addition to the public interest in ensuring adequate quality of care provided to each individual, there is a more global public interest in ensuring that resources are used in a technically efficient manner. Squandering resources in health care means either deficits from attainable community health status (technical inefficiency), or fewer resources available for other competing non-health care uses of greater social value (allocative inefficiency) (Lomas et al., 1985b).

This is not to imply that the primary professions can or should undertake the social responsibility to ensure efficiently delivered health services by an array of health professionals — the cost-conscious physician as agent of society as well as of individual patients. On the contrary, here the information asymmetry is likely to go the other way: governments or other third parties are more likely to possess efficiency information that is neither available to, nor sought by, nor consistent with the goals of the professions. That responsibility logically should rest with those third parties.

What is important to note is that the concept of a collective public interest had little meaning when professional governance was established in the 19th (or even 18th) century. The importance of the collective public interest only emerged as third parties came to have a stake in the resources consumed by the aggregation of these individual encounters, and as closer scrutiny of the distribution, roles and incentive structures of the health care system revealed that traditional and accepted work allocations and delivery institutions were far from optimal. Nevertheless, a governance system based on the individual public interest (quality assurance without resource constraints) became a powerful determinant of manpower policies because government had, where self-regulation had been granted, no obvious or painless method of forcing consideration of this new collective public interest. The primary professions themselves have become remarkably adept at *excluding* consideration of this interest by expressing their own countervailing economic and social desires as imperatives for the protection of the *individual* public interest: we must do everything possible for our patients whatever the cost (to third parties/benefit to ourselves)!

The activities of the Office of the Professions in Quebec (described later in this volume) are clearly an attempt to inject such a collective public interest role into the process of professional governance. However, not only were such activities unsupported by parallel policies in manpower planning and system finance and structure, but our discussion here would suggest that those activities were misguided. Professional governance in the form of self-regulation is fundamentally ill-suited to maintain or promote the collective public interest.

The emergence of the collective public interest has not been the only change in the health care environment that highlights the anachronistic nature of professional governance. Increased reliance on technology has led to concentrations of health manpower where the technology is housed (e.g., in hospitals), a proliferation of new categories of health manpower and increased specialization or fragmentation of existing professions. Concentration of personnel in hospitals and other health care facilities raises the question of whether the regulation of practice activity must continue to be performed by the profession, or whether the "corporate" liability of (say) the hospital (Somers, 1969; Carlson, 1972; Dubin, 1983; Smith 1984) or community health centre (Hastings, 1972; Krever, 1975; Lomas, 1985) could be a more appropriate substitute. These institutions would not have the problem of informational asymmetry (or could at least find economic ways around the problem) and may have incentives to consider at least part of the collective public interest.

The proliferation of new categories of health manpower has been both in the area of complements to the primary professions (with significant growth in each category, as demonstrated in the previous section of this paper) and in potential substitutes (with little significant growth in any category). Both complements and substitutes have sought the same form of professional governance as that granted to the primary professions, usually because they see it as legitimating their roles and, more importantly, facilitating access to public funds. However, the granting of self-regulatory powers and exclusive practice rights to these groups would be both inappropriate, given the changed practice circumstances and the limited basis for their being self-regulatory professions, and unthinkable for government given its experience with the professions to whom such privileges were previously granted. Unfortunately, no acceptable alternative governance mechanisms have been forthcoming. The result has been a concentration of new manpower categories within the hospital setting, where liability and accountability are more easily dealt with. The substitute categories have also placed pressure on the existing professions, as well as on the inadequacies of their governance structures to incorporate the collective public interest, for, as Friedman (1965) has noted, "The success of licensing laws depends upon the absence of organized economic adversaries" (p. 524). Thus, a series of disruptive "turf wars" has broken out, with (up to the present) consistent victories for the primary professions which control vast tracts of practice rights as well as heavier economic and political artillery.

Specialization within the primary professions, most notably medicine, has given rise to concerns that the informational asymmetry underlying the assignment of self-regulatory powers is no longer overcome in disciplinary matters by allowing judgement by one's peers: no single peer has a broad enough knowledge of the appropriateness of his specialized colleagues' activities. Ironically, this fragmentation has also led to intra-professional "turf" disputes where substitution *within* a profession is possible.[8] The magnitude of this phenomenon was hinted at by the GMENAC (Graduate Medical Education National Advisory Committee) proceedings on physician requirements in the U.S., where some individual specialty panels overlapped by as much as 45 percent in what they claimed as their own practice domains (McNutt, 1981).

Seen in this light, the difficulty of finding a mechanism for consideration and protection of the collective public interest dates back to the early establishment of professional governance structures and their failure to take account of modern changes in the environment in which professionals practise. The imposition of first hospital insurance and then medical insurance has merely accelerated or accentuated pre-existing strains on relationships between and roles of health manpower; national health insurance has not been the cause of the problems. The emergence of the collective public interest would have occurred anyway, given the increasing role for third party private insurers prior to the introduction of national health insurance (a role that would inevitably have continued in the absence of government intervention, as witness the U.S. experience). In fact, the increasingly aggressive policies of private insurance companies and business coalitions in the U.S. on practice modes and content (Egdahl, 1983), motivated by conventional for-profit and market share considerations, happen to coincide at least partially with changes in the collective public interest. However, they too have encountered the difficulty of pressing home this consideration in the face of professional governance that is based only on the individual public interest, and professional lobbying based only on the individual professional interest (Checkoway, 1982).

With the exception of Quebec, there have been no major policy changes in Canada regarding governance of the professions since the onset of health insurance. Rather, we have witnessed a series of what Tuohy (1982a) has called "symbolic" acts, signalling to the primary actors and the public alike the various positions of the entrenched powers. While the introduction of health insurance did generate some manpower policies designed to alleviate concerns about inadequate supply in the face of increased demand (discussed in the next section), these policies merely reinforced the existing power structures by training more of the primary professions and of their complements. The initial government conceptualization of national health insurance as a bill-paying mechanism to facilitate improved access to a "private" health system (Vayda and Deber, 1984; Stoddart, 1985; Lomas, 1985) left little room for interference in a structure of professional governance from which government at least had already disenfranchised itself. In fact, in Ontario, when the government did attempt to monitor billing practices of physicians and enforce this monitoring by way of a Ministry-based mechanism, without a corresponding modification of the statute regulating physicians, they were successfully challenged in the courts and the resulting Medical Review Committee was placed within the professional governance authority, the College of Physicians and Surgeons (Tuohy, 1982b). Even more difficult to explain or rationalize, however, is the placement of responsibility for monitoring patterns of practice that has been adopted in British Columbia. There this activity is carried out by a committee of the B.C. Medical Association, which is a voluntary organization established to represent and serve the interests of physicians, not the general public. It does not have even the formal statutory responsibility of a College, which in principle, at least, is an institution established and empowered by the state to protect the general public interest.[9]

The professions in and out of health care have quite successfully guarded their extensive rights to control not only the content of their practice, but also the context within which they practice. The most publicized example of this occurred in law (but with clear application to medicine) when the Supreme Court upheld the right of the B.C. Law Society (in the "Jabour" case) to restrict advertising by members of the profession, thereby giving paramountcy to the delegated statutory power of the profession over the Anti-Combines (or other) federal legislation (Hunter, 1982). The advertising issue is of particular importance because of the clear implications of the ban for the economic well-being of the profession rather than for the general well-being of the public (i.e., the allowance of advertising would clearly be in the collective public interest, even if the professions have been able to argue ingeniously and creatively that it would not be in the individual public interest). Hunter (1982) has commented that "it is perhaps in its effect on innovation that advertising may be most important. It is significant to note that the two public inquiries under the *Combines Investigation Act* concerning advertising prohibitions involved new and low-cost delivery systems" (pp. 12-13). Hunter's comments can be generalized well beyond the advertising issue and also beyond law (Taylor, 1960; Alford, 1975; Muzondo and Pazderka, 1979; Begun, 1981).

These examples serve to underline a failure to recognize that standards for the content of practice and standards for the context within which practice occurs are two separate issues. The result has been professional control over both forms of governance. This, coupled with governments' initial view that their insurance programs were merely bill-paying agencies, has ensured little encroachment on the forms of professional governance.

The changes that have occurred have been more symbolic than substantive. Some consumer representation on the disciplinary boards of the professions has occurred (Ontario, 1975), but the role has been minor and restricted to the "reactive" function of policing protection of the individual public interest. Ministers of Health have entered the process only in Quebec and Ontario where Ministers are now, in theory, able to refuse to pass a specific regulation recommended by a college or even to impose a regulation.[10] But these powers are little used and are still politically if not legally constrained by the very structure and actual functions of current professional governance and by the resulting confrontation with the profession that follows exercise of the power (see, for instance, College of Physicians and Surgeons of Ontario, 1982).

National health insurance may therefore best be viewed as a missed opportunity to impose organizational change and reformed health manpower roles. Instead, it has been merely a mechanism that solidified the pre-existing dominance of professional governance by the primary professions. Government responsibility for a large segment of health care expenditures did emphasize the need for consideration of the collective public interest, but the historical forms of governance, which provided no mechanisms for this to occur, were left unchanged. Some idea of what might have been achieved can be obtained from two examples where government provision of health services did *not* merely build on the pre-existing power structures. In Saskatchewan, a dental care program for school children was introduced in 1974 using dental nurses or dental therapists, not dentists, with the appropriate changes in regulatory statutes to enable this form of delivery to occur. In Ontario, the growing need for basic foot care for the elderly has been met by opening a new training program for chiropodists, not by producing more highly trained podiatrists. There are, however, few other examples of professional governance imperatives being subordinated to economic efficiency imperatives and to the collective public interest. All too often the existing regulatory structure and the number and mix of existing health manpower have been the primary determinants of by whom and how a particular health care service will be delivered. It is to these health manpower supply policies that we turn next.

Health Manpower Planning and Supply Policy: Is a Physician in the Hand Really Worth Two Substitutes in the Bush?

There are three clear historical phases to health manpower planning and supply policies in Canada, all of which focus primarily on physicians. In the 1950s and 1960s the onset of national health insurance was anticipated and every effort was made to alleviate a perceived shortage of physicians that would be exacerbated by an expected increase in utilization under universal hospital and medical insurance. Increasing the physician supply was the major policy. By the early 1970s the overwhelming success of this anticipatory policy, coupled with the assumption by governments of the role of sole third party payor for most hospital and physician care, led to a second policy phase characterized by two conflicting aims. Physician numbers had to be controlled because they had a strong influence on total health care expenditures; however, no direct confrontation could occur with physicians who had, after all, been dragged unwillingly into national health insurance in the first place. Indirect control of physician supply was the resulting policy, with attacks on the physicians' "tools" for expenditure generation, but not on physician numbers directly. Finally, the most recent phase in the 1980s has been a consequence of the failure of the "softly, softly" approach in the 1970s and represents some harsher direct policy responses to physician oversupply. The pendulum has swung a full arc in less than twenty years. It is fair to say that all other health manpower planning and supply policy has been a sideshow to this consuming concern with physician numbers. One consequence of this fixation has been, of course, the virtual ignoring of the relative and appropriate roles of *all* health manpower as a policy area.

The initial policy phase, increasing the physician supply, relied heavily first on immigration and later on domestic production supplemented by immigration. Prior to the Hall Royal Commission in 1964 — the foundation for introduction of national medical insurance — the onset of hospital insurance and the growth in private medical plans had been provided for with relatively unfettered immigration policies. The Hall Commission, however, performed the first major physician manpower planning exercise in this country (Judek, 1964). The Commission, as a consequence, alerted government to the need for increased domestic production as well. Unfortunately, while the *policy* of increasing domestic production can be introduced quickly, the *outputs* from that policy — Canadian-trained physicians — lag some four or more years behind. Thus, as Table 9 shows, immigration continued as a major source of supply increase for most of the 1960s, and the effects of four new medical schools and overall increased domestic production were not realized until the late 1960s and early 1970s.[11] Average annual growth in the physician supply between 1957 and 1967 thus exceeded average annual population growth by 0.82 percent (Evans, 1975), but between 1968 and 1975 the average annual excess was 3.4 percent (See Table 1),[12] reflecting the joint effects of immigration and domestic production. Table 9 shows that the annual number graduating from Canadian medical schools did, in

TABLE 9

SOURCES OF POTENTIAL ANNUAL ADDITIONS TO
PHYSICIAN STOCK, CANADA, 1961-1982[a]

YEAR	IMMIGRATION[b] (1)	GRADUATES OF CANADIAN MEDICAL SCHOOLS (2)	TOTAL (1)+(2)	IMMIGRATION AS PERCENT OF TOTAL	GRADUATES AS PERCENT OF TOTAL
1961	445	839	1284	34.7%	65.3%
62	530	854	1384	38.3	61.7
63	687	817	1504	45.7	54.3
64	668	786	1454	45.9	54.1
65	792	1032	1824	43.4	56.6
66	995	887	1882	52.9	47.1
67	1213	921	2134	56.8	43.2
68	1277	1017	2294	55.7	44.3
69	1347	1019	2366	56.9	43.1
70	1113	1108	2221	50.1	49.9
71	987	1133	2120	46.6	53.4
72	988	1278	2266	43.6	56.4
73	1170	1328	2498	46.8	53.2
74	1090	1567	2657	41.0	59.0
75	806	1546	2352	34.3	65.7
76	401	1710	2111	19.0	81.0
77	312	1688	2000	15.6	84.4
78	263	1766	2029	13.0	87.0
79	298	1755	2053	14.5	85.5
80	380	1747	2127	17.9	82.1
81	382	1770	2152	17.8	82.2
82	463	1753	2216	20.9	79.1

TABLE 9 (cont'd)

SOURCES OF POTENTIAL ANNUAL ADDITIONS TO PHYSICIAN STOCK, CANADA, 1961-1982[a]

YEAR	IMMIGRATION[b] (1)	GRADUATES OF CANADIAN MEDICAL SCHOOLS (2)	TOTAL (1)+(2)	IMMIGRATION AS PERCENT OF TOTAL	GRADUATES AS PERCENT OF TOTAL
AVERAGE ANNUAL % INCREASES/DECREASES					
1961-65	16.1	6.3	11.3		
1965-70	8.2	1.8	4.2		
1970-75	-5.1	7.1	1.5		
1975-80	-9.5	2.6	-1.9		
1980-82	10.9	0.2	2.1		
1961-71	9.4	3.6	6.2		
1971-82	-3.6	4.2	0.6		
1961-82	2.6	3.9	3.3		

a. See data appendix for sources.
b. See also footnote 11.

fact, increase by more than 50 percent between 1968 and 1975, and that the bulk of this increase occurred in 1970 to 1975 when the average annual increase in graduates was 7.1 percent.

This delayed effect of the domestic supply policy might have been of less concern had it not been for two important factors. First, as Evans (1975) has shown, the expected increase in demand for physicians' services as a consequence of the introduction of Medicare in the late 1960s and early 1970s did not materialize. The demand curve had already been significantly altered by the presence of private insurance for physicians' services, and government hospital insurance and the introduction of Medicare had a negligible additional influence. Thus the physician supply was increased in anticipation of an increased demand that never occurred.

The second, and related, factor was the effect of this burgeoning physician supply on health care expenditures. While demand from patients for services may not have increased, utilization of physician services certainly did, presumably as a consequence of the incomplete agency relationships fostered by that increased physician supply (Evans, 1984). As Evans (1975) pointed out, "Physicians reorganized their practice patterns and generated more income from a given number of initial patient contacts" and therefore produced "a linkage from supply of physicians through the quantity of services they choose to perform to total expense" (p. 162).[13] This observation of a link between total physician supply and total health care expenditures formed the basis of the second phase of manpower policy from the early 1970s to 1980.

Before we discuss this phase in more detail, two points about the first phase of the 1950s and 1960s are worthy of note. First, a portion of the increase in health care expenditures generated by the larger physician stock was the increased cost of salaries for the other health manpower categories that complemented physicians' activities. As complements, they initially rode the rising tide of numbers alongside the physicians. Although expenditures on these manpower categories (nurses, therapists, technicians, administrators and unskilled employees) were driven by significant relative wage gains, they were also driven by their increased numbers in the hospital budget. On a per patient-day basis, labour inputs to the hospital (hours worked) increased by 44.6 percent between 1953 and 1971, an average annual increase of 2.1 percent (Evans, 1975). There were few overt policies governing the supply of these non-physician manpower categories; their production was left largely to respond to the derived demand within the health care system for their services. By default, therefore, physicians, whose decisions were a primary determinant of manpower needs, had a significant influence on the numbers and types produced. As shown in the data of the first section in this paper, physician complements flourished, substitutes did not.

Second, the "overshoot" in physician supply that started to become evident in the early 1970s highlights the difficulty of planning when the consequences of the policies will not be felt until some years down the road. In the policy making arena, four or more years is long-run, and, historically, long-run plans in policy making have never received the same degree of attention as short-run (crisis) plans.

Thus, by the beginning of the 1970s it was clear that an already physician-dominated health care system had become over-burdened with them, with significant effects on total health care expenditures. An appropriate policy response to this situation was not, however, as obvious. While there was a need to constrain supply, approaches to the profession had to be cautious because of the implicit "Medicare pact"; i.e., if physicians would become part of Medicare, government would not interfere with either the profession or the "practice of medicine" (Taylor, 1978). Therefore, with one exception, the policies focused not on the supply of physicians but on the indirect policy levers that could affect the expenditures generated by physicians. The one exception was the introduction of controls on physician immigration in 1975 (see Table 9) which was the least threatening of the direct supply control policies available to government (Evans, 1976). Interestingly, it was also the only direct policy lever available to the federal government in light of the fact that health care is under provincial jurisdiction. By 1975, however, the full effects of the policy of increased domestic production were being felt, and reduced immigration was unable to stem the yearly increase in physician supply: between 1975 and 1980, average annual growth in the physician stock exceeded population growth by 1.35 percent (see Table 1). Domestic production had become sufficient to ensure growth in physician supply in excess of population growth for many years to come.

The other policy measures during the 1970s were directed at resources complementary to physician activity. Thus, in most provinces hospital bed supply and hospital budgets were restricted (see Barer and Evans, this volume), while medical school capacity was left unchanged or was allowed to increase slightly. The justifications for allowing increases were based on supposed distributional imbalances across specialty and region. The medical schools argued against production cut-backs on the grounds of indiscriminate effects on the supply of various specialties. The justifications for increases in output were the poor geographic distribution of physicians or, as in B.C., the argument of unequal inter-provincial opportunities for medical education.

By squeezing budgets in the hospital sector, governments achieved not only a new relationship between physicians and bed capacity (Barer and Evans, this volume), but also an increased imbalance between physicians and other health manpower categories. A significant proportion of hospital budgets (around 75 percent) goes to pay the salaries of personnel (already corralled in significant numbers into the hospital because of the distortions of the professional governance structure and remunerative and organizational policies), and therefore pressure on hospital budgets produced pressure on the funds available to pay non-physicians. Not only did absolute numbers of personnel employed by the hospital sector fall with bed supply, but the growth of the previous decade in paid hours per patient-day also virtually ceased. Thus in Ontario, for example, total annual paid hours per 1,000 population fell between 1971 and 1981 from about 26,000 to 24,900, and paid hours per patient-day crept up only 0.6 percent per year in contrast to the 1960s growth of almost 1 percent per year (Barer and Evans, this volume). While physician supply was allowed to increase, opportunities for employment of non-physicians were actually declining, ironically because of policies designed to restrict physician activity. This is reflected in our complement occupation data above, showing consistent moderation in growth rates for the 1975 to 1982 period.

The indirect policies chosen by government also took the form of "symbolic" actions to signal their concern to the medical profession. A series of commissions and studies had recommended the use of some "substitute" personnel in the health system, most notably nurse practitioners (NPs) (Hastings, 1972; Robertson, 1973; Ontario, 1974). Some provinces responded by training and producing nurse practitioners (see Table 8) who, by this time, had also been shown to be safe, effective, of good quality, acceptable to patients and efficient from the perspective of the health care system (Spitzer, 1978). This initiative, however, could only be viewed as a symbolic gesture — hinting to physicians at the potential for their replacement — because the training of nurse practitioners was never accompanied by appropriate policies to encourage their incorporation into the health care system. Despite the demonstrated value of NPs in replacing general practitioners (GPs), there was no planned reduction in the output of the latter to match the growing output of the former. Governments either failed to see the required and obvious link between manpower categories in planning for new divisions of function or, more likely, found the required GP reductions politically too distasteful. Even if phased GP reductions had been achieved, the failure to alter the professional governance structures that allowed physicians to control the activities of other professions (especially nursing), would have doomed the initiative from the start. Finally, the absence of any appropriate remuneration mechanisms for NPs was not addressed, leaving the clearly untenable result that physicians who hired NPs reduced their own incomes as a consequence (Spitzer et al., 1973). This situation illustrates the need for a three-track policy in health manpower: professional governance, manpower planning, and system financing and structure.

It was hardly surprising, therefore, that the NP initiative was short-lived; gradually the training programs were closed as NPs emerged into a market in which their value and efficiency were proven but policies for their integration were non-existent (Spitzer, 1984). A recent study has estimated the cost of this "missed opportunity" as 10 percent to 15 percent of total expenditures on physician services (Denton et al., 1983). This amounted to $300 million to $450 million in the year of the study (1980); by 1985 the estimate will be between one-half and three-quarters of a billion dollars. In real terms this represents a potential replacement of (very conservatively) between 20 percent and 32 percent of current general practitioners (Lomas and Stoddart, 1985).

Dentistry provides a similar example. Denture therapists or denturists have been prevented in some provinces from substituting as independent practitioners fabricating and inserting dentures (Hazelkorn and Christoffel, 1984). In Ontario, this initiative was actually blocked by an independent advisory council to the Ministry of Health, which in arriving at its conclusion recognized the merit of the proposal while bowing to the dominance (and oversupply) of dentists (Ontario Council of Health, 1981).

Part of governments' symbolic response in this area was typically Canadian: to "study" the situation. Once it became clear that physician numbers were outstripping apparent needs, as well as governments' willingness to pay, a series of physician manpower forecasting exercises was initiated (Aziz, 1974; Canada, 1975; Ontario Council of Health, 1983; Peat-Marwick, 1982). Unfortunately, all these studies had an effect opposite from what was undoubtedly intended. Without exception the projection methodologies adopted had at least two common shortcomings that assured conclusions of a balance between physician supply and requirements, or even of a shortage of supply relative to requirements (Lomas et al., 1985a, 1985b).[14] The conclusion was built into the assumptions and could be avoided only by arithmetic error.

First, the forecasts of physician requirements were based not on epidemiologic studies of health needs translated (directly or indirectly) into physician service requirements, but rather on acceptance of the physician expenditure or utilization data of the studies' base years as a proxy for "need". This utilization approach to requirements estimation is based on the key assumption that requirements are equivalent to utilization, that what is provided is what is needed (Lomas et al., 1985b). By extrapolating this need proxy into the future, taking account of such factors as population growth and demographic changes, an estimate of future physician requirements could be generated. Hence, all the activities performed by physicians in the base year were assumed to be physician service requirements, regardless of their effectiveness, or the possibility that some portion of them could be delivered equally effectively and less expensively by non-physicians. This assumption also ignores the fact that the incomplete agency relationships between practitioners and patients tend to facilitate the expansion of service provision to meet practitioner as well as patient objectives. If physician oversupply does indeed result in increased utilization (recall the earlier discussion), then basing future physician requirements on current utilization data will merely perpetuate and apparently justify an oversupply of physicians into the future.

Second, the future requirement for physicians was always calculated based on adjustments only for factors that would increase that requirement, e.g., population growth, demographic shifts toward a population mix requiring more *physician* services, proposed reduced hours of work for physicians, more female physicians in the total stock (most of whom, it was assumed, would work shorter hours and fewer years than males), new technology that would increase requirements for specialists, and so on. None of the studies introduced into the extrapolation of future requirements any requirements-reducing factors such as changes to the relative roles of different types of health manpower, or potential changes to the financial or structural incentives within the health care system. The existing roles of health manpower and the existing financing and delivery modes were "frozen" into the future, assuming a continuance of physician domination of health services. The assumptions underlying the projections assured findings of future shortages at the current medical school output and immigration rates.

Not surprisingly, with a growing and aging population (and primarily a series of physician panels making requirement decisions), the studies recommended what Bloom and Peterson (1979) have called physician manpower expansionism. Far from signalling to physicians that they were in oversupply, these inappropriate methodologies provided significant ammunition for the profession and for medical schools who wished to resist attempts to reduce domestic training of physicians.

By the end of the 1970s it was becoming clear to governments that their indirect control policies and attempted "symbolic" messages were not working. In fact, these policies of the second phase were doing more harm than good by squeezing non-physician manpower through hospital budgets and providing "planning studies" encouraging those who wished to continue increasing physician supply. Physician supply policies were also retarding the development of alternative manpower categories, not only by meeting in the present, but also by planning and producing the output to meet in the future, the health services requirements that nurse practitioners or midwives could just as easily provide. This realization, coupled with public sector fiscal restraint that had been growing tighter throughout the latter half of the 1970s, moved manpower policy into its third phase of more direct controls on physician supply.

The precipitating factor for this policy reappraisal was the completion in 1980 of a second review of Canada's health care system by Justice Emmett Hall (Hall, 1980), in which he warned of an impending or actual physician oversupply. Some provinces moved to control output with fairly immediate and direct responses. Both Manitoba and Quebec cut first-year medical school enrolment by 10 percent in the early 1980s. The federal-provincial Advisory Committee on Health Manpower (Canada, 1984) included among its recommendations a policy of enrolment cuts of 20 percent starting in 1985, as well as recommendations to reduce immigration even further, reduce the training opportunities for specialists and encourage foreign visa trainees to return to their countries of origin. These national recommendations have not yet been approved by individual provinces. They did, however, receive significant publicity as (arguably) the most widely read Report never to have been released publicly by Health and Welfare Canada.

Some provinces have started their control policies at the postgraduate enrolment end of the production spectrum. Hence Ontario has been trying to reduce, or at least to reallocate, the slots available for specialty training, presumably in the belief that specialists command and demand more health care resources than general practitioners.[15] While as a supply control policy this appears to be entering the production process from the wrong end, it has had the positive side effect of encouraging the teaching hospitals, with some help from the Ministry, to develop and utilize expanded duty nurses in roles previously filled by specialty residents (e.g., in intensive care units), and to expand the role of some technicians (e.g., respiratory technologists).

In the provinces that have historically failed to impose any control on their physician supply, the response has had to be particularly drastic. British Columbia, and to a lesser extent Alberta, have been trying to put limits not on the production process, but on the actual stock of practising physicians. The numbers of certain specialties allowed to bill the provincial plan in specified areas were restricted in a direct attempt to bring some semblance of control to one of the two largest open-ended fiscal responsibilities of the provinces (the other being welfare payments). Clearly, policies with such potential for confrontation are undesirable but are perhaps necessary given the total failure to address the issue earlier with more fundamental solutions. Done on this province-specific basis, they are also clearly short-run solutions that do nothing to stem the flow of physicians into the total Canadian stock and even less to encourage friendly relations with neighbouring provinces that have no such billing restrictions.

Most recently, however, the B.C. initiative has run up against an even more significant barrier. The provincial Supreme Court (1985) has expressed the view, in the case of a petition by an affected physician, that the policy of restricting billing numbers "does preclude the Petitioner from practicing her profession" (p. 23) and is therefore contrary to the Canadian Charter of Rights and Freedoms. (The actual *judgement* was that the B.C. government did not have adequate legislative authority for its actions.) If this view survives both appeal and changes to B.C. legislation, manpower policy initiatives in this area will have been effectively precluded. Governments will have been placed in the curious position of being *required* to provide access to provincial health insurance plans for all licensed physicians. Insofar as physicians are able to generate demand for their own services, this is tantamount to providing them with the unique right of a guaranteed income upon graduation! While this guarantee may uphold the rights of individual professionals, it would do so at the expense of the rest of the community. Such a judgement would clearly increase the difficulty of injecting a role for the collective interest of society/government and as such should be a cause for serious concern among health policy makers.

The specific difficulty encountered by B.C. may also be taken to illustrate the problem of trying to address the issue of health manpower numbers and distribution *after* the horses have bolted. By failing to adopt appropriate policies at the start of national health insurance, provinces have been forced to try these questionable "emergency measures" that so far have met with judicial rebuff and are of little value as long-run solutions to their self-created problems.

By the 1980s most provinces had also introduced some policy initiatives to address the question of geographic distribution, thus counteracting any further attempt to justify supply increases under the misguided "over-flowing pot" theory of getting physicians into unattractive locations (Williams et al., 1983). The use of "carrots" in the form of grants or enhanced fee schedules has been most commonly used, but one province, Quebec, has coupled this with "sticks" by paying only a percentage of the fee schedule to new physicians locating in urban areas declared as adequately supplied or oversupplied. Formal evaluations of these programs are yet to be performed, but informal observations and the Quebec government's own reports indicate that they have not been an overwhelming success.

A sense of urgency can be detected in both the federal government's and the provinces' most recent health manpower policies. The build-up in production capacity for physicians in the 1960s and early 1970s, and the policy fixation on physician numbers but inaction on the problem during the 1970s, has resulted in a distorted array of health manpower that is even more dominated by physicians today than at Medicare's outset. While the fact of health insurance gave government reason to be concerned about physician supply, the climate of its introduction was interpreted to mean that government could not employ the tools necessary to exercise control (unless, of course, it was simply to increase the supply). Consequently, the non-physician personnel have been squeezed in the name of physician expenditure control, the oversupply of physicians has reduced the degrees of freedom for introducing new and more appropriate health care personnel, planning methodologies that merely accentuated the problem have been employed, and governments are now desperately scrambling with *post hoc* policies to disengage from an ever firmer entrenchment of a sub-optimal division of labour in the health care system.

System Financing and Structural Policy:
A Publicly Financed Private System

Just as manpower planning and production policies have affected who has been employed to perform what tasks, so too financial incentive and delivery structure policies have influenced manpower roles and opportunities. Even if consideration of the collective public interest had been successfully integrated within a reformed structure of professional governance, and even if the various health manpower personnel had been produced in the right numbers and proportions, without appropriate remuneration mechanisms and service delivery organizations we would be unlikely to see health manpower arrayed in a cost-effective fashion.

It is not our intention here to review all policy development in the financing and organization of the system; this has been done by Hastings and Vayda (this volume). Rather, we wish to highlight the consequences of these policies for the development of an optimal manpower configuration.

The two primary policy areas have been practice and practitioner remuneration, and the structure of delivery organizations. The former is of concern because of its potential as a (dis)incentive to employ the most efficient combination of personnel; the latter because of its potential to create an environment that enables (even encourages) the most efficient use of personnel. We would note, however, that the two areas are by no means independent; alternative practitioner remuneration methods are frequently available only to those working in alternative delivery structures.

National health insurance was, of course, based on a specific remuneration mechanism and on the delivery structures then in place. By providing cost-sharing only for physicians' (and a limited number of other) services, and hospital care, the federal government endorsed fee-for-service remuneration for care delivered by physicians in their private offices or in hospitals.[16] At the least, the *perception* was therefore created that physicians would both deliver services and, by being "gatekeepers", control those who would complement their services in hospitals and in their private offices. However, the legislation did more than merely create this perception. Since almost no provision was made for remuneration of non-physicians outside the hospital, ambulatory care (if it was to be insured care) *had* to be obtained from physicians.[17] In entrenching fee-for-service physician remuneration, universal medical insurance created a disincentive to the delegation of responsibility to individuals requiring less extensive training.

The repercussions of this approach to physician remuneration were brought to governments' attention on a number of occasions by studies and commissions. For example, the Hastings Report (Hastings, 1972) stated: "There are difficulties in reconciling the planning and administrative interests of the system and the team approach...with the present fee-for-service payment system" (p. 26). Yet no substantive national policy initiatives have attempted to move us away from fee-for-service payment, and among the provinces only Ontario has provided the *option* of "payment per patient" (capitation) — an option taken up by less than 0.2 percent of the province's general practitioners (Lomas and Cushman, 1984)![18] The first glimmerings of initiatives to provide for some form of government remuneration of non-physician personnel outside the hospital can be seen in the recently passed Canada Health Act, in which the definition "health care practitioners" has replaced "medical practitioners and dentists" as individuals entitled to remuneration under the Act, but only at the discretion of the individual provinces. As yet there is no evidence that any province is acting on this extension.

One significant reason for this failure to act (either in response to the Canada Health Act or prior to it) has been the unwillingness of the provinces to permit expansion of fee-for-service payment to additional categories of health manpower beyond the initial primary professions. Given the adverse consequences of this form of remuneration, this has been a wise (and successfully executed) policy. However, it has also precluded the use of these personnel in community-based care because of the parallel absence of delivery organizations in the community that would provide remuneration by alternative means. A private practitioner paid fee-for-service who hires substitute personnel will reduce the practice (practitioner) net income unless the practitioner concurrently expands the scope of the practice. In a situation of physician oversupply, this may well involve demand generation, an activity that in itself may be a source of disutility. This conflict of interest inherent in fee-for-service remuneration of private practice discourages deployment of substitute personnel (Evans, 1984).

Governments' initial (and largely continuing) perceptions of their role in health insurance as public "paymasters" who are funding a private health care delivery system has also had significant effects on their willingness to impose or even encourage the development of delivery organizations that could serve as alternatives to the physician's private practice. As pointed out in the paper by Contandriopoulos et al., achievement of the efficiency potential of task delegation is dependent on the existence of work settings that enable this delegation to occur. For example, a single nurse practitioner is unable to complement (on a full-time basis) the workload of a single physician; optimal full-time work for an NP requires a base of more than one physician (Cassels Record, 1981). While group practice by physicians has always been relatively strong in western Canada, the eastern provinces have not shown the same enthusiasm. Thus, according to Wolfson et al. (1978), only 19.6 percent of Ontario physicians were members of income- and expense-sharing groups in 1976.[19]

The most commonly suggested alternative structure has been the community health centre (Hastings, 1972). The Hastings Report, commissioned by the Conference of Federal-Provincial Deputy Ministers, investigated this alternative in detail soon after universal medical insurance had been introduced. The value of such centres in promoting the optimal use of health manpower was explicitly recognized when the report stated:

> In organized and supervised settings, a team of various types of personnel, each member of which carries out specific functions, definitely increases . . . efficiency and productivity . . . compared to situations of solo and largely unsupported forms of care. It is also definitely possible to substitute less highly trained professional and technological personnel for more skilled personnel in organized and supervised settings . . . without any danger to public safety or diminution in quality of health care. (p. 16)

Despite the strong recommendations of this Report in favour of such community health centres, they have not (again, with the exception of Quebec) been introduced in anything more than token numbers and even then have received little support from government, either directly by bringing about favourable conditions for their development, or indirectly by assisting them to defend themselves from the barrage of adverse reactions from professional medical associations (Vayda, 1977; Lomas, 1985).

The only other alternative delivery structure that has emerged is the Health Service Organization (HSO) in Ontario. These are funded by capitation payments and are similar (but not identical) to Health Maintenance Organizations in the U.S. While these facilities have received guarded endorsement from government (Grossman, 1982), they are still merely an option and as such provide little incentive for physicians already suspicious of growing "government control" to become involved.

That these alternative delivery structures do indeed improve work allocation, or at least reduce dependence on physician service delivery, is shown by a recent investigation of their use of general practitioners compared with the predominantly solo fee-for-service system. Based on age-sex adjusted utilization data for 1980, the general practitioner to population ratio in Ontario's fee-for-service system was shown to be more than 20 percent higher than in the province's seventeen HSOs (Lomas and Cushman, 1984). Much of this reduction in physician requirement in HSOs is due to their widespread use of nurse practitioners — personnel that are little utilized by fee-for-service solo physicians.

The failure of the provinces to adopt more aggressive policies to encourage these alternative delivery structures has occurred despite the increased freedom to do so provided by the federal government's move from cost-shared fiscal transfers to block funding in 1976/77. Block funding (in theory) freed the provinces from the restrictions of receiving federal funds only for approved expenditures on hospitals and physicians. The reformed fiscal transfer mechanism has, however, had no noticeable effects on the provinces' willingness to introduce either new remuneration mechanisms for practitioners or alternative delivery structures. Policies in the areas of financing and delivery structure continue to be dominated not by a desire to achieve optimal task allocation, but by a philosophy of capping expenditures on a publicly funded but privately organized system.

Summary

The preceding discussion has served to emphasize two points. First, more efficient manpower use under national health insurance requires that attention be paid to each of the three policy areas described above: professional governance, manpower supply and financing, and delivery organization. Second, governments in Canada have failed to take up the efficiency challenge, and have avoided making the necessary policy decisions required in even one of the policy areas.

In the area of professional governance there has been no significant reform of a system that emerged in an era in which the collective public interest had a minimal role in health care delivery. The granting of self-regulatory privileges has made it difficult for government to introduce the collective public interest alongside a governance structure that still operates in the interests of the primary professions. Protection of those professions and of, at best, only individual patients (quality without resource constraints) are the central tenets of the current mix of regulation and (privately formulated) public policy.

Health manpower policies have been dominated by concerns over physician supply: first the need to increase this supply, then indirectly to control expenditures on services generated by the growing supply, and finally to slow its growth directly. This focus has been at the expense of appropriate policies for other health manpower. Furthermore, the indirect physician supply control measures and the planning methodologies supported (or tolerated) by governments have had the unwanted side effect of further reducing potential roles for other types of health manpower in the system.

Finally, the unwillingness of governments to initiate and support alternative reimbursement or delivery methods has meant the continuance of financial and organizational disincentives to efficient task allocation.

In the next section we try to sketch out the broad parameters of the policy initiatives that are required to achieve a more rational manpower policy under national health insurance.

Toward Optimality: Round Pegs for Round Holes

Optimality in task allocation within the health care system is at least partly dependent on one's viewpoint. Here we take the technical viewpoint of what Alford calls the "corporate rationalizers" whose objectives are to manage the health care system efficiently.[20] There are three aspects to this viewpoint: educational, population need and economic.

From the educational perspective, no category of health manpower would be performing tasks that either severely under-utilize the skills obtained during education or demand unsupervised exercise of skills beyond that education. As we have seen, the current structure of professional governance has left us some distance from that ideal (it has also ensured that the "professional monopolist's" views of optimality have dominated allocation decisions). Second, from the perspective of the population's health needs, the array of skills available from health manpower would be appropriately matched to the nature of the health problems existing in the population. Unfortunately, through manpower planning and supply policies, a focus on categories of health manpower with curative skills has been maintained and strengthened, whereas our health problems are becoming progressively dominated by the chronic diseases that require health maintenance and palliative care skills (Fries and Crapo, 1981; Fuchs, 1984). This may be attributable in part to the absence of any epidemiologically based manpower studies in Canada. Finally, from the economic perspective, this optimal array of manpower would be placed in a system that took full advantage of our current knowledge about the effect of remunerative and structural incentives on cost-effective practice. Our complement of health manpower would be deployed so as to ensure both technical and allocative efficiency. This again has clearly not been the case.

We have argued above that any movement from where we now find ourselves, toward the technically efficient provision of health care, requires the coordinated use of three levers: regulation, manpower planning and policy, and system structure and finance. To date, these levers have been used largely to convert the interests, tastes and preferences of the current primary professions into the policies of health manpower development and deployment. Given governments' unwillingness to impose alternative policies, these have become, by default, government policies. As Evans (1984) has noted, "It is simply impossible to have no policy, though fragmented, inconsistent, ill-considered and excessively costly policy is all too possible" (p. 302).

The unwillingness of government to be more aggressively involved in formulating health care policy reflects a failure to grasp the full implications of publicly funded health care services. The nature of health care as a product, the informational asymmetry between patient and provider, and our collective interest in the health of others, have resulted in Canadians having chosen public funding of medical and hospital care for all (Evans, 1984). That method of financing carries with it a public trust and responsibility for the collective public interest. Government's failure to impose regulatory, educational and structural policy in the public rather than the professional interest represents more than policy oversight. It reflects an abrogation of that responsibility. The absence of such active policy has led us into a wilderness of inappropriately allocated and organized roles for health manpower personnel.

Imposition of active policy need not necessarily mean direct regulation of specific roles and activities (although this may sometimes be required and desirable). It may also mean imposition of structures, planning methods or remuneration schemes that will *facilitate* performance of appropriate roles and activities. In the three areas of manpower policy outlined above, a judicious mix of these two forms of policy will be required. What we wish to imply here by the use of the term "imposition" is active government policy, as opposed to passive acceptance of policies generated by the vested interests of the health care system that are neither designed nor executed with the collective public interest in mind.

The task is clearly greater now than it would have been fifteen or twenty years ago. The present legacy of uncoordinated or absent policy, and the primary-profession-rich mix of personnel, present a more daunting prospect. We cannot start from scratch and simply plan for the production and distribution of the appropriate number and mix of health care personnel. Rather, we must approach that goal with reduced degrees of freedom as a consequence of the existing number and mix of health care personnel. As we do not yet find acceptable the concept of planned, policy-induced unemployment for physicians or dentists, the way we do for construction workers, auto workers or coal miners, we do indeed have significantly reduced degrees of freedom. Future policy must therefore address the barriers to innovation presented by current professional governance, in order to prevent further restriction of those degrees of freedom by the primary professions. It must also rely on planning methods and forecasts that build in a potential role for all health manpower, to enable an orderly change in the current ratios of manpower, toward a relatively richer mix of substitute professionals. Finally, policy will have to be directed to remuneration and organizational issues that will improve the use of current numbers and mix of manpower and facilitate deployment of changing numbers and mix in the future.

We can be guided in this task by the evidence we currently have, and the evidence that will be produced in the future, on overlapping roles and alternative structures. We are aware of the untoward effects of current professional governance and of the success or failure of some of the attempts at reform (Slayton and Trebilcock, 1978; Muzondo and Pazderka, 1979; Professional Organizations Committee, 1982; Hazelkorn and Christoffel, 1984; Contandriopoulos *et al.*, this volume; Dussault, this volume). Much has been published about the various aspects of introducing, or using more extensively, personnel such as physician assistants (Reinhardt, 1975), nurse practitioners (Spitzer, 1978; Cassels Record, 1981), midwives (Slome *et al.*, 1976), pharmacy assistants (McGhan *et al.*, 1983), dental nurses or their equivalents (Saskatchewan, 1976; Chapko *et al.*, 1985), denture therapists (Dickens, 1981), emergency paramedics (Vertese *et al.*, 1983), and so on; this could all be used to guide our manpower planning and production policies. Evidence that remuneration mechanisms and organizational settings affect manpower deployment comes from studies of the capitation-funded U.S. Health Maintenance Organizations (Luft, 1981), Ontario's Health Service Organizations (Hastings *et al.*, 1973; Lomas and Cushman, 1984) and an extensive general literature on practice structure and organization (e.g., Reinhardt, 1975) and on remuneration systems for practitioners (e.g., Hornbrook, 1983).

We already have sufficient evidence to guide the development of active manpower policy. The frequency and intensity with which supply control policies are now being urged (e.g., Canada, 1984) and the increasingly stark reality of fiscal restraint in the health sector (Bird, 1981) may well be sufficient catalysts for such active policy actually to emerge in the near future. As encouraging policy signals begin to appear, we are confident that a more concentrated research effort will provide further guidance.

Reform in professional governance would involve updating the legislation and regulations to reflect changes that have occurred in the health services environment since the formulation of the governance structure. More specifically, it would remove the barriers to innovation, both in the areas of delegation and supervision of acts from primary professions to substitutes, and in the implicit embargo on various forms of remuneration and various types of practice setting competitive with private, fee-for-service practice.

The enforcement of implicit embargoes is made possible by the failure to remove control over issues of importance to the collective public interest from the self-administered codes of professional groups. Professional codes come to be used as a trade-off game between the three interest elements. Measures to protect the professions' own interests are sold as the protection of the interests of individual patients in order to counteract the collective public interest. Thus when the Minister of Health in Ontario requested that the College of Physicians and Surgeons pass a regulation requiring prior notification of a physician's intention to extra-bill above the Medicare schedule, the request was refused. This regulation allegedly would have interfered with "the independence of doctors and their methods of dealing with their patients" (*Globe and Mail*, 1983). The regulation was in fact intended to improve the information with which consumers choose practitioners — a contribution to the collective public interest as well as to individual rights.[21] The real issue here is why the College should have any say at all over this aspect of practice activity. It has nothing to do with maintenance of the technical content of the professional discipline, for which restricted entry by way of educational qualifications and licensure was introduced. More troublesome still is the fact that this particular example of prior notification is even required under ordinary contract law (*Globe and Mail*, 1982).

Self-regulatory control should be restricted to those aspects of professional practice that bear directly on the competence of the practitioner. All else, including remuneration policies and allowable practice organizations, should be under the direct control of government or alternative third party representatives of the collective public interest. This change would restrict the self-regulatory powers of the primary professions to that area in which they should originally have been targeted, i.e., intra-professional matters.

This change alone, however, will not remove the control of the primary professions over practitioners who can competently and safely substitute for them in their fields of exclusive practice. Because the practice rights of the primary professions are *exclusive*, they have been enabled to consider these potential substitute personnel as an intra-professional matter; they choose how, whether, when and to whom delegation of which aspects of "their" practice field should occur. Thus the federal report on community health centres was moved to recommend as early as 1972 that "professional statutes should be amended, where necessary, to ensure that no profession can, directly or indirectly, regulate the members of another profession or occupation" (p. 40). As described in the following papers by Contandriopoulos et al. and Dussault, this goal of improved task delegation was one of the two objectives of the establishment of the Office of Professions of Quebec in 1973. The experience recounted there suggests that merely setting up a framework to encourage voluntary delegation by the primary professions does not work. What become "delegated" are either acts already being performed by the potential substitute personnel, or acts that are not even part of the primary professions' exclusive fields!

The conclusion therefore seems unavoidable that the collective public interest requires significant incursions into the primary professions' self-regulating privileges over an exclusive field of practice. Not only might Quebec soon resort to the as yet unused portions of the 1973 legislation that entitle it to impose delegation regulations on the professions, but similar provisions may also be developed in other provinces.[22]

But if there is one major theme running throughout this paper, it is that each of the three policy avenues is necessary *but not sufficient* for an efficiency-improving use of resources in the delivery of health care. While changes to regulations make more useful the planning for production of different types of health manpower, neither will work in isolation. Similarly, an isolated community health centre policy initiative may simply result in many empty community health centres scattered around a province.

With the necessary regulatory changes in place, manpower requirements estimation may proceed in the knowledge that the recommended mixes of personnel are not precluded by statute. Similarly, policies designed to change remuneration mechanisms or to encourage community health centres where "teams" of practitioners would be available are far more likely to succeed when codes of self-administered professional regulations cannot be used by their competitors as roadblocks to their development, and when the results of requirements forecasts have been translated into education policy.

However, we will be significantly restricted in these attempts if the planning methods we use to calculate our future manpower requirements continue to focus on isolated categories of personnel (usually physicians) and to accept the current delivery arrangements as unchanging into the future. We must adopt an approach to health care resources planning that recognizes not only the division of tasks between personnel in new ways, but new trade-offs between personnel and technology — both "embodied" technology in the form of equipment and "disembodied" technology in the form of remuneration schemes or practice organization. The primary stimulus for this type of planning would be the explicit recognition that we operate under resource constraints in the health care system, and that we could be doing much better than we are, either in improving community health status or in freeing up resources for other non-health care uses.

The steps in such a planning approach to establish health care *resource requirements* have been detailed elsewhere (Lomas et al., 1985b). Here we provide only a short summary.

First, the health needs of a population would require identification, or estimation, and enumeration. Then, all the *effective* health care *services* that can contribute to maintaining or improving the population's health should be established (McNutt, 1981). This epidemiologic approach to service requirements would define need for health care services on the basis of current evidence on the effectiveness of current technologies in meeting population health status deficits. Thus it would take as its base the current and projected health of the population, not, as has been the common case, current and projected services as provided by current configurations of health care personnel and organizations.

Second, this health care services requirement may be provided by any number of combinations of resources (personnel, supplies, space and equipment), of which the primary professions will be only one category. Although certain services may require the specialized training of a particular class of professionals (supplemented by complementary facilities and equipment), and may admit no substitutes, most do not. Other personnel may be equally effective in providing significant segments of service requirements. And although some portion of that servicing may require some degree of supervision by the more highly trained levels of personnel, there will also be a segment of services that each class of personnel will be able to deliver unsupervised. Most such services are presently defined and viewed by the rigidity of the present structure of professional governance as requiring primary professionals. Thus the second stage will amount to matching service requirements with personnel skills and training to establish the required mix of health care personnel.

The third stage then takes us into the third of our policy avenues: remuneration and organization. It is the aim of this third stage to ascertain the combination of financing and organization most likely to facilitate the deployment of the most effective and efficient mix of personnel and other resources established in the previous stage. Leaving the current system of fee-for-service payments to private practices as the dominant combination of financing and organization is unlikely to result in the desired configurations, even in the presence of changed regulatory legislation and with the requisite mix of trained personnel available. Our present knowledge on how various remuneration and organizational schemes affect health manpower requirements can be a significant input into this process. We will return to that evidence below.

Turning these optimal future manpower requirements into actual current production policies brings one up hard against the constraints of the current supply and mix of health care manpower. There is little value in producing manpower to perform tasks already being performed by others, even if these others are not the optimal category for the services. Now and for some time into the future we will encounter the inhibitory effects of a "slack" supply of the primary professions on innovations of new manpower roles (Ginzberg, 1983). If unemployment among primary professions is socially unacceptable (as it appears to be) then the only alternative is to match progressive reductions in the supply of these primary professions by corresponding increases in supply of substitute categories directed toward the mix and numbers of health manpower estimated in stage two. Such "phasing" calculations have already been performed for some categories of medical (e.g., Lomas and Stoddart, 1985) and dental (e.g., Kilpatrick et al., 1972) manpower. Thus manpower supply and education come to be used as active policy levers for achieving optimal resource use, rather than as passive tools that maintain current mixes of personnel. The recent actions and recommendations to restrict production of the primary professions in Canada (e.g., Canada, 1984) are clearly the first steps in moving toward the necessary taut supply of those professions.

Thus far arguments have been put forward to ensure that an appropriate pool of manpower will be available and that the direct barriers to its use from current professional governance would be removed. The latter would have to rely largely on imposition (or removal) of specific regulatory measures, the former merely on the imposition of general planning constraints and various production quotas that can be reinforced through appropriate funding incentives to the affected educational institutions (Bovey, 1984).[23] To achieve optimal use of manpower in the actual delivery of services will require the imposition of similar general incentives by way of remuneration and practice organization policies — injecting an efficiency imperative into delivery arrangements.

On one level, the incentives must be for groupings of personnel who serve large enough populations of patients to make viable broad teams of health personnel. While the hospital already provides this potential environment for inpatient care, there is no widespread equivalent for ambulatory care. On another level, the manner in which these groups are funded and the remuneration schemes adopted for their practitioners must encourage adoption of optimal manpower arrays.

There is a voluminous and fast-growing literature on the potential and pitfalls of alternative payment mechanisms, either in isolation or in concert with organizational contributions.[24] The main thrust of the present paper is clearly not to break new ground in that area. But we have emphasized its importance, as the third in an inseparable triad, and it seems useful to close, therefore, with a brief look at the directions in which that literature appears to be moving.

Grouping of practitioners in ambulatory care settings has been increasing only gradually over the years, and this trend will presumably continue into the future (Roemer, 1981; Hastings and Vayda, this volume). However, barriers and disincentives to more rapid development of multi-disciplinary groups exist at the attitudinal level for physicians (Boan, 1966; Wolfson et al., 1978; Taylor et al., 1984) and dentists (*Toronto Star*, 1981) and at the level of current government policy (Vayda, 1977; Lomas, 1985). The absence of any significant number of alternative funding mechanisms for these groups was described earlier in this paper; this absence has resulted in few advantages being presented to encourage more use of group practices in any form.[25]

Capitation funding for incorporated group practices or community health centres would at least encourage the use of a broader array of health care personnel. It is not clear, however, whether in isolation this would be a sufficient incentive to increase significantly the overall efficiency of our use of health manpower. Such an isolated policy change would not be likely to induce physicians (or other primary professionals) to drop fee-for-service private practice. Some in Canada argue that this can only be achieved when a competitive element is introduced into the system, such that the advantages achieved by some groups in using resources efficiently can be shared with consumers in the form of lower costs or enhanced service packages (Stoddart, 1985; Stoddart and Seldon, 1984; Evans, 1980). In this scenario the structure of a competing health care services market would be imposed on the system to introduce the efficiency imperative that is currently lacking. The key characteristic of this competitive scenario is that the information asymmetry between patient and practitioner that prevents most patients from choosing appropriate treatment regimens would not affect their choice of alternative service benefit packages. In other words, while one may not wish patients to be responsible for choosing specific courses of treatment, there is no reason why they should not be able to choose between competing packages of benefits (Barer et al., 1979) which would presumably be "priced" to reflect the resource costs of providing those benefits. As Enthoven (1978) has noted in favour of the competitive approach:

> The government cannot reorganize the health care economy by direct action. People would resist such changes involuntarily imposed. And nobody can bring about such a change quickly. But the government can change the underlying economic incentives so that consumers and providers of care can benefit from forming and joining organized systems that use resources wisely. The delivery system would then be forced to reorganize itself in response to consumers who are seeking out and choosing what is in their own best interest. (p. 711)

Such schemes are not without their problems, particularly in the current Canadian environment of free choice of provider and universal public funding, but there is no reason to believe that those problems are insurmountable (Stoddart and Seldon, 1984).

Conclusion

We have proposed changes in professional governance and alterations in manpower supply policies which, if coupled with a more competitive system of health care service delivery, could well lead to a more efficient and effective number and mix of health care personnel in Canada. This outcome obviously cannot be guaranteed. But our description of the current array of health manpower and our analysis of the history of manpower policy in Canada lead us to believe that what we have suggested in this last section certainly looks more promising than a continuation of the current approach. Although there may be short-term advantages for governments in avoiding the inevitable opposition of the primary professions to the adoption of active manpower policies, these gains will be significantly outweighed by the political and pecuniary losses that will accrue in the future if the situation is left unchanged.

Data Appendix

Population figures used to calculate the practitioner to population ratios in all tables were obtained from the following sources:

1968-69: Canada Health Manpower Inventory (CHMI), 1973, Department of National Health and Welfare.
1970-75: Statistics Canada, Quarterly Population Estimates, cat. no. 91-001, 1982.
1976-83: Statistics Canada, Quarterly Population Estimates, cat. no. 91-001, Vol. XII(2), September 1984.
1970-79 estimates are inter-censal; 1980 is final inter-censal
estimate; 1981 is post-censal estimate; 1982 is updated post-censal
estimate; 1983 is preliminary post-censal estimate.

Table 1 physician data are for active physicians including interns and residents, and are derived from information provided by L. Rehmer, Health Information Division, Information Systems Directorate, Policy Planning and Information Branch, Department of National Health and Welfare. The data are based on computer tapes purchased from Sales/Marketing Systems, Scarborough, Ontario, for general practitioners and specialists and on provincial sources for interns and residents.

Dentist data are from CHMI (1983) for 1972 to 1982, CHMI (1980) for 1969 to 1971, CHMI (1972) for 1968. The sources for these were the Bureau of Dental Statistics, Canadian Dental Association and provincial dental licensing authorities.

Pharmacist data are from CHMI (1983) for 1972 to 1982, CHMI (1979) for 1968 to 1971. The sources were the Canadian Pharmaceutical Association, Ordre des pharmaciens du Québec and the governments of the Yukon Territory and the Northwest Territories.

Optometrist data are from CHMI (1983) for 1972 to 1982, CHMI (1979) for 1968 to 1971. The sources were the Canadian Association of Optometrists and the governments of the Yukon Territory and the Northwest Territories.

Table 2 data on all three physician components are from CHMI (1983) for 1972 to 1982 and CHMI (1979) for 1968 to 1971; intern and resident data for 1983 are from L. Rehmer (see Table 1 above). The sources for general practitioners (which includes "family physicians") and specialists were the computer tapes of Sales/Marketing Systems, Scarborough, Ontario. The sources for interns and residents were provincial governments.

Table 3 data for nurses are for full-time and part-time employed in all forms of nursing including patient care, teaching, research and administration where professional training in nursing is required. The sources were CHMI (1983) for 1972 to 1982, CHMI (1979) for 1968 to 1971. From 1979 to 1982, data editing was improved and the data include only nurses registered in a specific province *and* employed in that province.

Nursing assistant data are for full-time and part-time qualified nursing assistants employed in public general and allied special hospitals, in tuberculosis sanatoria (1968 to 1976 only) and in mental institutions. There are three sources: CHMI (1978) for 1968 to 1971 and CHMI (1983) and Statistics Canada, *Hospital Annual Statistics*, for 1972 to 1981. The latter are annual issues, cat. no. 83-232 from 1976 to 1981-1982, and annual issues in three volumes from 1972 to 1975, of which Vol. I, cat. no. 83-227 contains personnel data. The Statistics Canada series is used from 1972 to 1981. In order to make these data comparable with the CHMI data for 1968 to 1971, however, they were adjusted by the average difference between the CHMI and the Statistics Canada series during the period of overlap, 1972 to 1980. This was an upward adjustment of 8.5 percent.

Physiotherapist data are from CHMI (1983) for 1972 to 1982 and from CHMI (1979) for 1968 to 1971. The data exclude inactive, temporary, overseas, honourary life and student members of the Canadian Physiotherapy Association.

Table 4 data on laboratory technologists are for active and certified individuals and are from CHMI (1983) for 1972 to 1982, CHMI (1979) for 1968 to 1971. The source is the Canadian Society of Laboratory Technologists.

Respiratory Technologists are registered individuals and the data are from CHMI (1983) for 1972 to 1982, CHMI (1979) for 1968 to 1971. The source is the Canadian Society of Respiratory Technologists.

Radiation Technicians are registered individuals and the data are from CHMI (1983) for 1972 to 1982, CHMI (1979) for 1968 to 1971. The sources are the Canadian Society of Radiological Technicians (1968 to 1973), Canadian Association of Medical Radiation Technologists and Ordre des techniciens en Radiologie du Québec (1974 to 1982).

Table 5 data sources may be found in other tables for: nurses, nursing assistants, physiotherapists (Table 3); laboratory technologists, respiratory technologists, radiation technicians (Table 4); all physicians (Table 1); specialists (Table 2).

Internists data include physicians in internal medicine, medical science, internal medicine and tuberculosis, tuberculosis, internal medicine and cardiology (1968 to 1975); or physicians in internal medicine and sub-specialties (1976 to 1982). Data are from: CHMI (1983) for 1982, CHMI (1982) for 1981, CHMI (1981) for 1980, and so on, until 1968 to 1971, which are all from CHMI (1972). The source is Sales/Marketing Systems, Scarborough, Ontario, and classification is according to the most recently obtained specialty.

Radiologists data include diagnostic and therapeutic radiologists and are from: CHMI (1983) for 1982, CHMI (1982) for 1981, CHMI (1981) for 1980, and so on, until 1971, which are from CHMI (1973) and 1968 to 1970, which are from CHMI (1972). The source is Sales/Marketing Systems, Scarborough, Ontario, and classification is according to the most recently obtained specialty.

Table 6 data for dental school graduates are from CHMI (1983) for 1972 to 1982, CHMI (1979) for 1968 to 1971. The sources are the Bureau of Dental Statistics, Canadian Dental Association (1968 to 1976); Education, Science and Culture Division (now Education, Culture and Tourism), Statistics Canada (1977 to 1982).

Graduates of programs for dental assistants are from CHMI (1983) for 1972 to 1982, CHMI (1979) for 1968 to 1971. The sources are various including individual surveys (1968 to 1972), Health and Welfare Canada (1973-1974), University of British Columbia (1974-1975), provincial ministries and individual colleges (1975 to 1982). For details see CHMI (1979 and 1983).

Graduates of schools of dental hygiene are from CHMI (1983) for 1972 to 1982, CHMI (1979) for 1968 to 1971. The sources are the Bureau of Dental Statistics, Canadian Dental Association (1972 to 1976); Education, Science and Culture (now Education, Culture and Tourism), Statistics Canada (1977 to 1982); Ministry of Colleges and Universities, Toronto, and individual colleges and universities (1978 to 1981); Department of Education, Government of Quebec (1975 to 1982).

Table 7 presents only data already recorded in Table 6.

Table 8 data on nurse practitioners are for active members of the Nurse Practitioners' Association of Ontario who are working full-time or part-time (not necessarily functioning fully as nurse practitioners) or are unemployed. The data were obtained from Ms. T. Tumber from NPAO membership reports for 1975 to 1983.

Dental therapist data are for active and licensed individuals who have graduated from a school of dental therapy and are not in private office practice (these latter numbers are estimated to be: 1976-0, 1977-0, 1978-6, 1979-8, 1980-7, 1981-8, 1982-10, 1983-8, 1984-5). The sources are: A. Uti, Registrar of the National School of Dental Therapy, Regina, Saskatchewan, for graduates licensed with the Northwest Territories Licensing Board; D. Nelson, Saskatchewan Dental Therapist Association for those licensed in Saskatchewan; V. Malazdrewich, Dental Nurses Association and Dental Health Workers Board, Brandon, Manitoba, for Manitoba licencees.

Table 9 data on graduates of Canadian medical schools and immigration of individuals who give medicine as their intended occupation were obtained from Association of Canadian Medical Colleges Forum, April/May (1981) for 1961 to 1980, CHMI (1983) for 1981-1982. The source for immigration data is the Department of Employment and Immigration.

Table 10 data are from J. Dobson, Program Development Directorate, Policy and Program Development Branch, Department of Employment and Immigration, Ottawa.

We gratefully acknowledge the assistance provided to us by those named in the foregoing sources.

Notes

1. This should not be confused with *allocative efficiency*, which refers to social decisions about, for example, health care vs. highways or bridges. These are two quite separate issues, one dealing with the allocation of resources among competing uses, the other with different mixes of resources used for the same purpose.

2. We also use medical services almost exclusively as our illustrative model. This is not because the other primary professions are any less important (or problematic), but rather because the medical profession makes such a good example. The problems are, however, quite general.

3. These lines of authority were also reinforced, particularly in the case of physicians and nurses, by the predominance of males and females in the primary and subordinate professions respectively.

4. Of course, focusing on the "input" variable of educational qualifications begs a series of important questions concerning the effectiveness of professional services. It is not enough, in supporting the contention that professionalization protects the interests of individual client/patients, to ensure that particular professionals are able to perform particular services competently. One must also demonstrate that the services themselves are effective, *and*

that professional training and entry qualifications are required to perform them competently.

On the first point, competence, questions are increasingly raised as to the effectiveness of "one-shot" training and qualification, at the beginning of a career, in ensuring the continuing competence of professionals. When a large part of the knowledge of a discipline can become obsolete in ten or twenty years, the maintenance of competence depends on continuing professional education, *and requalification*. At present the former is voluntary, the latter non-existent.

Secondly, the effectiveness of a large proportion of professional services, in medicine in particular, is at best undemonstrated and at worst highly questionable. Nothing in the professional "quality-control" process of restricted entry protects the public against ineffective or harmful services. The growing interest in clinical epidemiology, the systematic and scientific evaluation of the effectiveness of interventions, represents a process of refining the service offering, but no regulatory "transmission belt" exists to translate the findings of this work into professional practice.

Yet the efficacy and continuing competence questions, while threatening to particular professionals, fit comfortably within the ideology and *raison d'être* of professionalism as a system of social control. These questions suggest a tightening of the self-regulatory process, e.g., by mandatory relicensure and more aggressive practice monitoring, the better to "protect the public". The problem is whether professional organizations as *political* bodies are able seriously to undertake activities that may inconvenience or threaten significant numbers of their members.

The consistency of such actions with the overall ideology of professionalism, however, is clear.

But the third question, must one be a professional to perform competently?, strikes at the heart of professionalism. The discovery that volunteers are just as effective as fully trained speech pathologists in aiding language recovery in stroke patients (David *et al.*, 1984) indicates not that individual practitioners are incompetent or that individual services are ineffective, but that in this context at least the profession is irrelevant and serves no useful public purpose. There is then no valid argument, other than professional self-interest, for regulating who may provide such services. Experience, attitude and native ability may affect performance, as in any other activity. But the special educational process, which serves to maintain and transmit a profession's ideology as well as its alleged competence, then becomes a private activity with no social significance.

5. Homeopaths still had representation on the Council of the College of Physicians and Surgeons in Ontario in 1932 when there were only twenty homeopaths practising in Ontario.

6. This subordination was initially achieved by including the activities of the complementary personnel within the primary profession's direct control. Later, when these personnel pressed for their own regulatory structures, subordination was achieved by representation or indirect control by the primary profession over the subordinate. For instance, when dental technicians became a registered profession, their regulations "were to be subject to the approval of not only the Lieutenant Governor in Council, but also the Royal College of Dental Surgeons" (Macnab, 1970, p. 81). Similarly nurses, who obtained their own statutory rights in the 1920s and 1930s, had physician representatives on their Councils and were unable to engage in the practice of medicine except by formal delegation of acts from the Colleges of Physicians and Surgeons.

7. Most of the "excluded" categories came to be recognized later with more restricted fields of practice and only limited powers of self-regulation. In Ontario this was achieved by the Drugless Practitioners Act, first passed in 1925, regulating chiropractors, osteopaths, chiropodists, masseurs and drugless therapists. Physiotherapists were added in 1944.

8. For example, it is common practice for endodontists to complete a root canal by placing a temporary filling, forcing the patient to return to the referring general dentist for removal of the temporary filling and replacement with a permanent filling. When one takes patient time and discomfort as well as duplication of effort into account, it is unlikely that this would be the cost-effective course of treatment. However, it reflects tacit inter-specialty agreements designed to ward off raiding of general dentistry by specialists. "Turf overlap" has also been extremely common in medicine, as general practice by definition overlaps to some extent with each of a growing number of specialties, and particularly with paediatrics, obstetrics and gynecology and internal medicine.

9. We do not mean to imply that the committee is necessarily ineffective because of conflict of interest. But its placement is such as to make that conflict virtually certain, and to give the maximum weight to professional, as opposed to public, interests in the monitoring of professionals' behaviour. Ministry of Health representation on the committee is presumably intended to minimize that potential as a check on the professional interest.

10. To our knowledge the Minister of Health of Ontario has refused to pass a regulation on only one occasion: When the College of Dental Surgeons attempted to make practice under prepayment schemes professional misconduct (*Toronto Star*, 1981). On one occasion a regulation has been imposed: When the College of Physicians and Surgeons refused to pass a regulation making it professional misconduct not to give prior notification of an "extra-bill" to a patient (*Globe and Mail*, 1983).

11. While immigration levels dropped sharply from 1973 to 1978, there was also, as Table 9 shows, a marked increase in immigration from 1978 to 1982. This increase was investigated further by contacting the Department of Immigration directly to separate the immigration categories of "selected immigrant physicians" from "refugee and dependent immigrants with physician as their stated occupation". Clearly it is only members of the former group that are open to health policy leverage. Furthermore, members of the latter group will not necessarily all go into practice as physicians either immediately or in the future because they must first meet provincial licensing requirements. These data, presented below as Table 10, indicate that "selected immigrant physicians" have not been increasing in numbers in recent years:

TABLE 10

THE COMPONENTS OF PHYSICIAN IMMIGRATION
CANADA, 1977-1983[a]

YEAR	SELECTED PHYSICIANS	REFUGEES AND DEPENDENTS	TOTAL[b]
1977	158	149	307
1978	127	134	261
1979	113	187	300
1980	133	247	380
1981	160	222	382
1982	148	314	462
1983	113	239	352

a. See data appendix above for source.
b. Some small discrepancies from the totals in Table 9, are due to the use of a different data source with a slightly different reporting period in 1977-79.

12. The difference is somewhat exaggerated by the exclusion of interns and residents from the 1957 to 1967 series but their inclusion in the 1968 to 1975 series. The trends, however, are quite obvious. The excess of growth in physician stock over that of the population has also occurred because the estimates of population growth by the Hall Commission were far too high (by 1981 those estimates had us 20 percent above the actual population figure), leading to higher than necessary requirement figures for physicians.

13. See also Table 9 in the Barer and Evans paper earlier in this volume.

14. Only the most recent in this series of forecasting efforts (Canada, 1984) even with some of the same methodologic shortcomings, sounds the warning of an impending glut of physicians.

15. Since 1974 Ontario has had a "guideline" policy that the practising physician stock should be divided in the ratio of 55 percent general practitioners to 45 percent specialists, based on the numbers in the registry of the College of Physicians and Surgeons of Ontario.

16. Some provinces, in their own legislation, did provide for alternatives. For instance, in Ontario the Ontario Health Services Insurance Act, 1969, stated: "The Minister may enter into arrangements for the payment of remuneration to physicians or practitioners rendering insured health services to insured persons on a basis other than fee-for-service" (section 20). These, however, were clearly meant as exceptions to a rule.

17. A handful of other practitioners have been granted billing privileges under provincial plans (private physiotherapists in existence before Medicare, chiropractors for a limited portion of their fee, etc.), but the major portion of expenditures was (and is) on physicians' services. Using Ontario as the example again, more than 90 percent of all payments from the provincial plan have consistently gone to physicians (Ontario, 1983).

18. By providing global or line-by-line budgets to some primary care facilities, British Columbia, Saskatchewan, Manitoba, Ontario, Quebec and Nova Scotia have also permitted salaried remuneration of physicians. However, some of these facilities have continued with fee-for-service payment mechanisms and, in any case, outside Quebec the number of such facilities in any province can be counted on the fingers of one hand!

19. More recent data from Taylor *et al.* (1984) indicate that the situation has changed little in the intervening six years, although differences in the definition of group practice make direct comparisons difficult.

20. Alford (1975) refers to "professional monopolists", "equal health advocates" and "corporate rationalizers" as the three interest groups in the health system. He points out that professional monopolists have historically been the dominant force; that the equal health advocates have been and still are a repressed interest (largely because they have no clear lobbying power and focus); and that the corporate rationalizers are in the ascendency, largely by reason of necessity as (in the United States) health care costs cause increasing concern.

21. For further details of the incident see *Globe and Mail*, June 1983, "Ailing Credibility of Doctors". In this instance the self-serving nature of the profession's response was too blatant to ignore and the Minister of Health, for the first time in 102 years of medical self-regulation, imposed the regulation on the College. This prerogative had remained dormant since its introduction in 1975, and has now returned to that state.

22. Ontario is currently engaged in a major, two-year Health Professions Legislation Review started in the Fall of 1983. While it is always possible that this will

confront the issue of how to introduce the collective public interest into professional regulation, misguided focus on consensus-building among the professional and occupational groups alone is unlikely to yield such worthwhile results.

23. While the mix of programs offered by post-secondary educational institutions should be determined by those institutions, they seem unduly ponderous in shifting the size of programs to reflect changing public priorities and "market" conditions. They are, however, quite sensitive to the private interests of the primary professions.

24. In fact, the topics can never be entirely independent, since some forms of remuneration (e.g., fee-for-service, capitation) reflect remuneration to *practices*, while others (e.g., salary) can only be paid to *practitioners*.

25. The observation of Luft (1981) that Health Maintenance Organizations in the U.S. have been able to thrive mostly in areas of physician oversupply may be of some concern. If the thrust of revised manpower planning and supply policies should be to create a "taut" supply of the primary professions to enable improved delegation to occur, this might have the unwanted side effect of simultaneously discouraging the primary professions from starting or joining innovative group practice structures. See also Contandriopoulos (1976). Of course, if the financial incentives available through group practices are attractive enough, they may well overcome this possible problem.

References

Alford, R.R. *Health Care Politics: Ideological and Interest Group Barriers to Reform*. Chicago: University of Chicago Press, 1975.

Aziz, J. *Physician Manpower Requirements*. Ottawa: Department of National Health and Welfare, 1974.

Barer, M.L., R.G. Evans and G.L. Stoddart. *Controlling Health Care Costs by Direct Charges to Patients: Snare or Delusion?* Toronto: Ontario Economic Council, 1979.

Begun, J.W. *Professionalism and the Public Interest: Price and Quality in Optometry*. Cambridge, Mass.: MIT Press, 1981.

Bird, R.M. *Commentaries on the Hall Report*. Toronto: Ontario Economic Council, 1981.

Bloom, B.S. and D.L. Peterson. "Physician Manpower Expansionism: A Policy Review", *Annals of Internal Medicine*, 90, 1979, pp. 249-256.

Boan, J.A. *Group Practice*. Ottawa: Queen's Printer, 1966.

Bovey, E.C. *Ontario Universities: Options and Futures.* The Commission on the Future Development of the Universities of Ontario. Toronto: Ontario Ministry of Education, 1984.

British Columbia Supreme Court. Reasons for Judgement of the Honourable the Chief Justice in the Case of Raziya Mia (Petitioner) and the Medical Services Commission of British Columbia (Respondent), March 21, 1985. Vancouver Registry No. A843209.

Canada. *Physician Manpower in Canada. A Report of the Federal-Provincial Advisory Committee on Health Manpower.* Ottawa, 1984.

Canada. *Report on the Requirements Committee on Physician Manpower to the National Committee on Physician Manpower.* Ottawa: Department of National Health and Welfare, 1975.

Carlson, R.J. "Health Manpower Licensing and Emerging Institutional Responsibility for the Quality of Care". In Havighurst, C.C., ed., *Health Care.* New York: Oceana Publications, 1972.

Cassels Record, J. *Staffing Primary Care in 1990: Physician Replacement and Cost Savings*, Vol. VI. Springer series on health care and society. New York: Springer, 1981.

Chapko, M.K., P. Milgrom, M. Bergner et al. "Delegation of Expanded Functions to Dental Assistants and Hygienists", *American Journal of Public Health*, 75, 1985, pp. 61-65.

Checkoway, B. "The Empire Strikes Back: More Lessons for Health Care Consumers", *Journal of Health Politics, Policy and Law*, 7, 1982, pp. 111-124.

College of Physicians and Surgeons of Ontario. Interim Report. Toronto: February 1983.

College of Physicians and Surgeons of Ontario. Letter from the Office of the President to members, August 12, 1982.

Contandriopoulos, A.-P. "Changer l'organization du système de santé; plutôt que limiter le nombre de médecins", *Canadian Public Policy*, 2, 1976, pp. 161-168.

David, R., P. Enderby and D. Bainton. "Treatment of Acquired Aphasia: Speech Therapists and Volunteers Compared", *Journal of Neurology, Neurosurgery and Psychiatry*, 45, 1982, pp. 957-961.

Denton, F.T., A. Gafni, B.G. Spencer and G.L. Stoddart. "Potential Savings From the Adoption of Nurse Practitioner Technology in the Canadian Health Care System, *Socio-Economic Planning Sciences*, 17, 1983, pp. 199-209.

Detsky, A.S., S.R. Stacey and C. Bombardier. "The Effectiveness of a Regulatory Strategy in Containing Hospital Costs", *New England Journal of Medicine*, 309, 1983, pp. 151-159.

Dickens, B.M. "Report of a Review of Denture Services Related to the Denture Therapists Act, 1974". In *Statement on Denture Therapy*. Toronto: Ontario Council of Health, 1981.

Dubin, C. *Report of the Hospital for Sick Children Review Committee*. Toronto: Queen's Printer, 1983.

Dussault, R. "The Office des Professions du Québec in the Context of the Development of Professionalism". In Slayton, P. and M. Trebilcock, eds., *The Professions and Public Policy*. Toronto: University of Toronto Press, 1978.

Egdahl, R.N. "Health Care Management at the Community Level: Doctors, Hospitals and Industry", *Health Affairs*, 2, 1983, pp. 115-126.

Enthoven, A. "Consumer-Choice Health Plan", *New England Journal of Medicine*, 298, 1978, pp. 709-712.

Evans, R.G. "Beyond the Medical Marketplace: Expenditure, Utilization and Pricing of Insured Health Care in Canada". In Andreopoulos, S., ed., *National Health Insurance: Can We Learn From Canada?* Toronto: John Wiley and Sons, 1975.

Evans, R.G. "Does Canada Have Too Many Doctors? Why Nobody Loves an Immigrant Physician", *Canadian Public Policy*, 2, 1976, pp. 147-160.

Evans, R.G. "Professionals and the Production Function: Can Competition Policy Improve Efficiency in the Licensed Professions?". In Rotenberg, S., ed., *Occupational Licensure and Regulation*. Washington: American Enterprise Institute, 1980.

Evans, R.G. *Strained Mercy: The Economics of Canadian Health Care*. Toronto: Butterworths, 1984.

Friedman, L.M. "Freedom of Contract and Occupational Licensing, 1890-1910: A Legal and Social Study", *California Law Review*, 53, 1965, pp. 487-534.

Fries, J.F. and L.M. Crapo. *Vitality and Aging: Implications of the Rectangular Curve*. San Francisco: W.H. Freeman and Co., 1981.

Fuchs, V.R. "'Though much is taken:' Reflections on Aging, Health and Medical Care", *Milbank Memorial Fund Quarterly*, 62, 1984, pp. 143-166.

Ginzberg, E. "How Many Physicians Are Enough?", *Annals of the American Academy of Political and Social Science*, 468, 1983, pp. 205-215.

Globe and Mail. "MD Loses Against Patient in $27 Suit Over Extra Bill". November 3, 1982.

Globe and Mail. "Won't Obey Fee Rule, Group Says". April 22, 1983.

Grossman, L. "Ontario Health Centres. An Idea Whose Time Has Come". Remarks to the Annual Symposium of the Association of Ontario Health Centres, Toronto, October 28, 1982.

Hall, E.M. *Canada's National-Provincial Health Program for the 1980s*. Ottawa: Department of National Health and Welfare, 1980.

Hastings, J.F. *The Community Health Centre in Canada*. Report of the Community Health Centre Project to the Conference of Health Ministers. Ottawa: Information Canada, 1972.

Hastings, J.F., F.D. Mott, A. Barclay and D. Hewitt. "Prepaid Group Practice in Sault Ste. Marie, Ontario: Part 1: Analysis of Utilization Records", *Medical Care*, 11, 1973, pp. 91-103.

Hazelkorn, H.M. and T. Christoffel. "Denturism's Challenge to the Licensure System", *Journal of Public Health Policy*, 5, 1984, pp. 104-117.

Hogan, D.B. "The Effectiveness of Licensing. History, Evidence and Recommendations", *Law and Human Behaviour*, 7, 1983, pp. 117-140.

Hornbrook, M. "Allocative Medicine: Efficiency, Disease Severity and the Payment Mechanism", *Annals of the American Academy of Political and Social Science*, 468, 1983, pp. 12-29.

Hunter, L.A. "Canadian Competition Law and Occupational Regulation". Address to the University of Toronto, Faculty of Law, Law and Economics Workshop, Toronto, December 1, 1982.

Judek, S. *Medical Manpower in Canada*. Ottawa: Queen's Printer, 1964.

Kilpatrick, K.E., R.S. Mackenzie and A.G. Delaney. "Expanded-function Auxiliaries in General Dentistry: A Computer Simulation", *Health Services Research*, 7, 1972, pp. 288-300.

Krever, H. "National Health Insurance and Problems of Quality". In Andreopoulos, S., ed., *National Health Insurance: Can We Learn From Canada?* Toronto: John Wiley and Sons, 1975.

Lincoln, N.B., G.P. Mulley, A.C. Jones *et al.* "Effectiveness of Speech Therapy for Aphasic Stroke Patients: A Randomized Controlled Trial", *Lancet*, June 2, 1984, pp. 1197-1200.

Lomas, J. *First and Foremost in Community Health Centres: The Centre in Sault Ste. Marie and the CHC Alternative*. Toronto: University of Toronto Press, 1985.

Lomas, J., M.L. Barer and G.L. Stoddart. *Physician Manpower Planning: Lessons from the Macdonald Report.* Toronto: Ontario Economic Council, 1985b.

Lomas, J. and R. Cushman. "Potential Effects of a Competitive System of Health Delivery on Canadian Requirements for Physician Manpower". Paper presented at 75th Annual Conference of the Canadian Public Health Association, Calgary, Alberta, June 26, 1984.

Lomas, J. and G.L. Stoddart. "Estimates of the Potential Impact of Nurse Practitioners on Future Requirements for Physicians in Office-Based General Practice", *Canadian Journal of Public Health,* 76, 2, 1985, pp. 119-123.

Lomas, J., G.L. Stoddart and M.L. Barer. "Supply Projection as Planning: A Critical Review of Forecasting Net Physician Requirements in Canada", *Social Science and Medicine,* 20, 1985a, pp. 411-424.

Luft, H. *Health Maintenance Organizations: Dimensions of Performance.* New York: John Wiley and Sons, 1981.

Macnab, E. *A Legal History of Health Professions in Ontario.* A study for the Committee on the Healing Arts. Toronto: Queen's Printer, 1970.

Malazdrewich, V. Dental Nurses Association of Manitoba, Brandon, Manitoba, 1985. Personal communication.

McGhan, W.F., W.E. Smith and D.W. Adams. "A Randomized Trial Comparing Pharmacists and Technicians as Dispensers of Prescriptions for Ambulatory Patients", *Medical Care,* 21, 1983, pp. 445-453.

McNutt, D.R. "GMENAC: Its Manpower Forecasting Framework", *American Journal of Public Health,* 71, 1981, pp. 1116-1124.

Muzondo, T.R. and B. Pazderka. *Professional Licensing and Competition Policy: Effects of Licensing on Earnings and Rates-of-Return Differentials.* Research Monograph Number 5, Bureau of Competition Policy. Ottawa: Consumer and Corporate Affairs Canada, 1979.

Ontario. *Health Disciplines Act.* Toronto: Queen's Printer, 1975.

Ontario. *OHIP Practitioner Care Statistics, 1981-82 (Pre-Audit).* Toronto: Ontario Ministry of Health, 1983.

Ontario. *Report of the Health Planning Task Force.* Toronto: Queen's Printer, 1974.

Ontario Council of Health. *Medical Manpower for Ontario* (Macdonald Report). Toronto: Ontario Council of Health, 1983.

Ontario Council of Health. *Statement on Denture Therapy.* Toronto: Ontario Council of Health, 1981.

Peat-Marwick. *Western Canada Health Manpower Training Study.* Toronto: Peat-Marwick and Partners, 1982.

Professional Organizations Committee. Reports and Studies. Toronto: Ministry of the Attorney General, 1982.

Reinhardt, U.E. *Physician Productivity and the Demand for Health Manpower: An Economic Analysis.* Cambridge, MA: Ballinger, 1975.

Robertson, R.H. *Health Care in Canada: A Commentary.* Background study for the Science Council of Canada. Ottawa: Information Canada, 1973.

Roemer, M. *Ambulatory Health Services in America.* Rockville, MD: Aspen Systems Corporation, 1981.

Saskatchewan. *A Quality Evaluation of Specific Dental Services Provided by the Saskatchewan Dental Plan: Final Report.* Regina: Saskatchewan Ministry of Health, 1976.

Shaw, G.B. *The Doctor's Dilemma.* London: Harmondsworth Press, 1911.

Slayton, P. and M. Trebilcock, eds. *The Professions and Public Policy.* Toronto: University of Toronto Press, 1978.

Slome, C., H. Wetherbee et al. "Effectiveness of Certified Nurse-Midwives", *American Journal of Obstetrics and Gynecology*, 124, 1976, pp. 177-182.

Smith, W.B. "Hospital Liability For Physician Negligence", *Journal of the American Medical Association*, 251, 1984, pp. 447-448.

Somers, A.R. *Hospital Regulation: The Dilemma of Public Policy.* Princeton: Princeton University Industrial Relations Section, 1969.

Spitzer, W.O. "Evidence That Justifies the Introduction of New Health Professionals". In Slayton, P. and M. Trebilcock, eds., *The Professions and Public Policy.* Toronto: University of Toronto Press, 1978.

Spitzer, W.O. "The Nurse Practitioner Revisited: Slow Death of a Good Idea", *New England Journal of Medicine*, 310, 1984, pp. 1049-1051.

Spitzer, W.O., W.A. Russell and B.C. Hackett. "Financial Consequences of Employing a Nurse Practitioner", *Ontario Medical Review*, 40, 1978, pp. 96-99.

Stoddart, G.L. "Rationalizing the Health Care System". In Conklin, D., G. Cook and T. Courchene, eds., *Ottawa and the Provinces: The Distribution of Money and Power.* Toronto: Ontario Economic Council, 1985.

Stoddart, G.L. and J. Seldon. "Publicly Financed Competition in Canadian Health Care Delivery: A Proposed Alternative to Increased Regulation". In Boan, J., ed., *Proceedings of the Second Canadian Conference on Health Economics*, Regina, 1984.

Taylor, M.G. *Health Insurance and Canadian Public Policy*. Montreal: McGill-Queens, 1978.

Taylor, M.G. "The Role of the Medical Profession in the Formulation and Execution of Public Policy", *Canadian Journal of Economics and Political Science*, 25, 1960, pp. 108-127.

Taylor, M.G., H. Stevenson and A. Williams. *Medical Perspectives on Canadian Medicare: Attitudes of Physicians to Policies and Problems of the Medical Care Insurance Program*. Toronto: York University, 1984.

Toronto Star. "Dentists Fight Prepaid Care". January 27, 1981.

Tuohy, C. "Does a Claims Monitoring System Influence High Volume Medical Practitioners? Attitudinal Data From Ontario", *Inquiry*, 19, 1982b, pp. 18-33.

Tuohy, C. "Smoke and Mirrors: Professional Ideology and Symbolism in Health Policy". In Squire, B., ed., *Proceedings of the Conference on Health in the '80s and '90s and its Impact on Health Sciences Education*. Toronto: Council of Ontario Universities, 1982a.

Tuohy, C. and A. Wolfson. "Self-Regulation: Who Qualifies?". In Slayton, P. and M. Trebilcock, eds., *The Professions and Public Policy*. Toronto: University of Toronto Press, 1978.

Uti, A. Registrar, National School of Dental Therapy, Regina, Saskatchewan, 1985. Personal communication.

Vayda, E. "Prepaid Group Practice Under Universal Health Insurance in Canada", *Medical Care*, 15, 1977, pp. 385-391.

Vayda, E. and R.B. Deber. "The Canadian Health Care System: An Overview", *Social Science and Medicine*, 18, 1984, pp. 191-197.

Vertese, L., L. Wilson and N. Glick. "Cardiac Arrest: Comparison of Paramedic and Conventional Ambulance Services", *Canadian Medical Association Journal*, 128, 1983, pp. 809-813.

Weller, G.R. and P. Manga. "The Development of Health Policy in Canada". In Atkinson, M. and M. Chandler, eds., *The Politics of Canadian Public Policy*. Toronto: University of Toronto Press, 1983.

Williams, A.P., W.B. Schwartz, J.P. Newhouse and B.W. Bennett. "How Many Miles to the Doctor?", *New England Journal of Medicine*, 309, 1983, pp. 958-963.

Wolfson, A., C. Tuohy and C. Shah. "What Do Doctors Do? A Study of Fee-for-Service Practice in Ontario". University of Toronto, Department of Health Administration, 1978, mimeo.

TOWARD AN IMPROVED WORK ORGANIZATION IN THE HEALTH SERVICES SECTOR: FROM ADMINISTRATIVE RATIONALIZATION TO PROFESSIONAL RATIONALITY

André-Pierre Contandriopoulos
Claudine Laurier
Louise-Hélène Trottier

Introduction

The rationalization of patterns of resource use in the health care system has been the source of numerous discussions. Although the era of major expansion seems to have ended in Quebec as well as in Canada at large, health expenditures still account for a relatively important part of the gross national and provincial products. In 1981 they represented 7.6 percent of the Canadian GNP and 8.5 percent of the Quebec GPP. Nevertheless, since 1975, the rate of increase has been low. Canadian health expenditure (relative to national income) increased 1.60 percent between 1980 and 1981. In Quebec, during the same period, it increased by 0.12 percent (Canada, 1984). Some observers feel that the methods used to stabilize expenditure cannot or should not be sustained in the future. Questions about the "underfunding" of the health care system and the ability of the system to meet the needs of the population will, therefore, continue to be debated. Given the current level of state involvement in funding (approximately 70 percent of total health expenditure in Quebec) and the associated revenue requirements, however, it will be a difficult task indeed to convince provincial Treasurers to increase health care spending. In this environment, the rationalization of health care delivery patterns cannot be avoided.

There are many targets for cost control. One is health manpower and particularly professional manpower. It is an important target because a large part of health care costs are related to manpower. Indeed, salaries and other forms of remuneration represent a considerable proportion of health expenditure.[1] Moreover, health care providers play a central role in determining the utilization of resources.

Examination of health manpower policy raises several questions. Are there changes in the structure and use of manpower that would allow for a more efficient health care system? Would a reorganization of work in the health field be advantageous? Can health personnel be used in such a way as to permit specialized human resources to provide the services for which they were actually trained, leaving the performance of simpler tasks to others? Is such rationalization possible?

These are the sorts of questions addressed in this paper. In the first section, we adopt an administrative rationalization approach that leads us to evaluate the economic benefits of changing health manpower organization. The discussion focuses on proposals for a reorganization within the primary medical service sector. Particular attention is given to proposals for the use of nurse practitioners and physicians' assistants. We then examine why plans that seek to rationalize the structure and use of manpower seem difficult to implement despite a generally positive evaluation. This forces us to use another approach based on professional rationality in the second section of the paper. Based on Quebec's experience with task delegation we discuss what appears to be a fundamental obstacle to such an approach: the defensive reaction of professional groups to any invasion of the field of activity that they control.

The Administrative Rationalization Approach: Toward a Reorganization of Manpower in the Primary Medical Services Sector

Proposals for Rationalizing the Structure and Use of Manpower in Primary Medical Services

Proposals aimed at improving the structure and use of manpower in primary medical services range from general statements to specific suggestions. Some analysts suggest multi-disciplinary interaction or teamwork.[2] These general appeals are meant to activate communication and collaboration among categories of existing personnel, especially among professionals. Others suggest that the physician should call on traditional auxiliary workers (medical secretary, nursing assistant, technician . . .) more often than before. Still others suggest using new categories of personnel, without complete medical training, who can take over functions that traditional auxiliaries are not trained to perform. These are the "new health practitioners" (NHP)[3] or "physician extenders"; they include nurse practitioners, paediatric nurse practitioners and adult nurse practitioners as well as physicians' assistants and MEDEX. Here the manpower structure is altered to include a new category of individuals whose training is different from that of traditional auxiliaries, and who, in theory at least, would fit less easily into a hierarchical model that entrusts all clinical decisions to the physician.

The Castonguay-Nepveu Commission had emphasized the nurse practitioner's potential:

> In Quebec, by virtue of the irrational use of medical staff and the forseeable increase in demand for care with the establishment of a universal health insurance plan, the problem of assistants becomes acute. In our view, the solution lies in the establishment of a class of health professionals capable of carrying out a certain number of tasks now reserved for the medical profession.
>
> The Commission believes university-trained nurses can fulfill this role after appropriate training.
>
> (Commission of Inquiry on Health and Social Welfare, 1970b, p. 69)

In Canada, in the early 1970s, the National Conference on Assistance to the Physician made the recommendation "that there be immediate development of programs conjointly by medical and nursing faculties for the education of nurses to become nurse practitioners" (Spitzer et al., 1975, p. 214).

These suggestions, however, have never been put into practice in Quebec. There have been training programs in Canada[4] but these no longer exist (Spitzer, 1984). Nonetheless, in the United States this innovation in health manpower has gained a certain popularity. In 1980 there were fifty-four training programs in the U.S. for physician assistants (PA) and 208 programs for nurse practitioners (Yankauer and Sullivan, 1982). By the end of the 1970s there were approximately 22,100 new health practitioners practising (Cassels Record et al., 1980) and, according to the Graduate Medical Education National Advisory Committee (GMENAC), more than 41,000 are expected to be practising in 1990, which represents a ratio of one NHP to fourteen physicians (Scheffler et al., 1978).

The above proposals were meant to accomplish several objectives such as improving quality and accessibility and controlling costs (Weston, 1980; Celentano, 1978; Lawrence et al., 1977; Storms and Fox, 1979; Scheffler et al., 1979; Breslau and Novack, 1979; Fottler et al., 1978). The cost control objective is the one that interests us here.

Expected Results of a Reorganization of Manpower in Primary Medical Services

We will start by showing how a change in the structure and use of manpower can further cost control. This will also allow us to identify the different variables that must be taken into account when evaluating the economic impact of such a change.

The Logic Underlying the Proposals

When we suggest task delegation to traditional auxiliaries, new health practitioners or a multi-disciplinary team, we are in effect proposing to change the mix of medical service producers. For any given production team, the savings that result from this change may stem from any combination of three processes. First, a change in the mix of producers that allows a better utilization of each person's skills can help reduce costly delays and confusion in the treatment or prevention of illness. In this case, it is increased output for a given number of work hours that results in savings. The second process is related to the substitution of resources. A new mix of producers can save money if certain tasks formerly performed by the physician are entrusted to cheaper human resources. The output rate remains stable but there is a reduction in input costs. The third process works by altering the nature of the services rendered. Having recourse to a multi-disciplinary team interested in practising medicine in a different, less technological manner, could lead to the use of fewer or more effective services for each care episode. In both cases there are potential gains, either immediate (fewer, less technologically oriented services) or long term (more effective services inducing better health and a gradual lessening of needs).

These three processes could lower the cost of a treatment delivered to a given patient by the production team (Figure 1). In recommending the use of traditional auxiliaries, one hopes for a decrease in the cost of resources that does not significantly affect the output rate or the way services function. The multi-

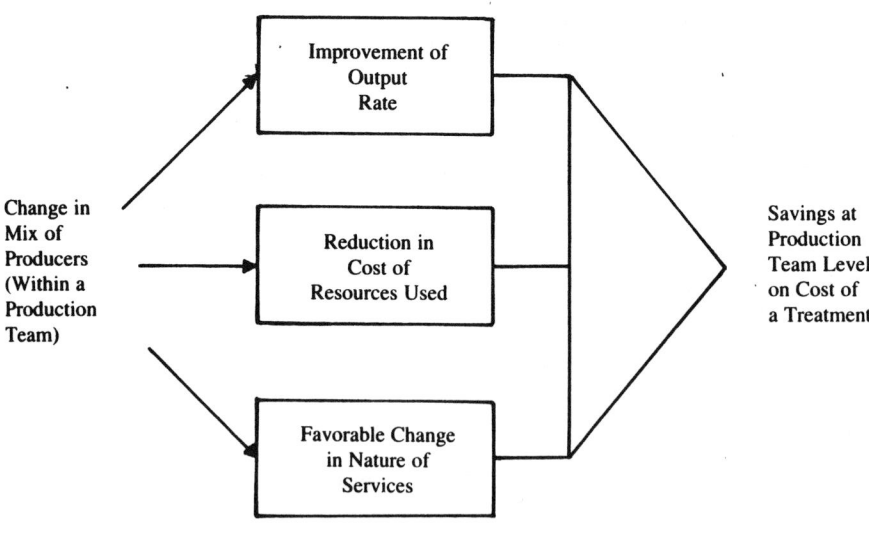

Figure 1

Postulated Logic

disciplinary team, on the other hand, would work by modifying the output rate and maybe even more by altering the nature of services, but it would not necessarily rely on the lesser remuneration of some professionals. Finally, the introduction of new practitioners, as laid out in most of the proposals, can prompt interesting changes through the combined action of the three processes. The reduced cost of resources, however, will probably be the main driving force.

Before drawing any conclusions about cost control in the health care system, we must explore the above logic. First we must ask if the processes advocated will have the desired effects. Then, insofar as they do, we must ask if savings in the cost of a given treatment or case will actually mean a reduction in the global costs of the system, which depend on both unit cost and volume of cases treated. The following section deals with these questions.

Assessment of the Logic

Will the processes described get under way, and if so, to what extent? Will action not produce the opposite effect of that intended? Indeed, although we recognize that by changing the mix of producers we can reduce the cost of resources, increase the output rate and change the nature of services in a positive way, we have to admit that this type of intervention may also produce the opposite effect.

Not only must we be aware of detrimental effects that might show up in places where we expected gains, but we must also worry when they appear in places where we had foreseen no significant change. In evaluating the results of an intervention that expected to benefit from reduced cost of resources, we must check to see if these hopes are being realized. We must also take into account what happens at the output level and at the level of the nature of services.

The overall result depends on the convergence or divergence of the effects obtained by the three processes (or corresponding counter-processes) just described. In turn, the effects of each of these processes will depend on three factors: (1) the nature of the proposed change (multi-disciplinarity), PA, traditional auxiliary . . .), (2) its degree of application (degree of utilization of the new team), and (3) a set of variables particular to the processes concerned. Therefore, the effect on the output rate will depend on the context of the practice (organizational support offered, waiting room, physical and material organization, experience of team members, organization of supervision and consultation . . .). How much is gained or lost in terms of the cost of resources after the introduction of a new team will depend on the level of each member's remuneration and how it evolves. It will also depend on the costs of training these individuals. Finally, the change in services will be influenced by, among other things, the producers' attitudes and abilities and the evolution of technology. Each of these factors must be examined in the assessment.

While activating these various processes may reduce costs at the production team level, hopes can be dashed when, despite a reduction in production costs, there is no reduction in the price paid by the consumer or the third party. Therefore, the possibility that efficiency gains will be captured by providers instead of taxpayers must also be examined.

Finally, the integration of the new team's production to the system's overall production must also be analysed, as must its capacity to modify the global costs to the system. In fact, to this point the assessment involved only one slice of reality. Here, compared with a more traditional organization, reorganization of medical work engenders savings; savings are transferred to the consumer. However, we must explore how this slice, with its positive result, combines with or fits into the overall system (Figure 2). If it simply adds to the existing situation without being able to replace it totally or partially, then the additional investment it implies, minimal as it may be in relation to a competing proposal, can only mean an increase in costs to the system. To bring about a reduction in costs at the system level, a partial, and preferably significant, substitution of the existing reality (in terms of demand, type of clientele and practice context) must take place.

Our reasoning deals only with costs. We are making no judgement on the fit between the need for services and the services used. In fact, a change in the mix of producers could well lead to a better response to needs as well as to an increase in the output rate. If such is the case, then there would not necessarily be a reduction in costs to the system.

The aspects just underlined, which are represented in Figure 2, make it difficult to assess the effects of reorganizing medical work. In the face of this difficulty, we can try to minimize the variability caused by some factors of influence. One way of doing this is to single out a very narrow and specific aspect of reality and to describe the effects obtained in that particular context. Then we arrive at valid but necessarily limited conclusions that do not allow us to assess the effect of the intervention on a larger part of reality. An alternative exists, which reduces the complexity of an overall assessment: certain factors of influence can be excluded from the analysis by postulating in their case a constant or quasi-null effect with the help of the very useful *ceteris paribus* assumption, well known to economists. For example, we will assume that a reorganization of work will not have any significant effects on the nature of the services rendered. Or we will assume that in all settings, the contingencies of practice will have an equivalent effect on the output rate. The overall assessment can also deduce average estimates from a set of effects observed or estimated under different conditions. Even if they do not correspond exactly to the reality of a particular case, these estimates can inform the evaluator as to global tendencies. Finally, one can also obtain an interval that accounts for the range of possible effects. No matter which approach is used and despite efforts made to account for a maximum number of factors, the analysis often remains incomplete and does not

Toward an Improved Work Organization in the Health Services Sector 293

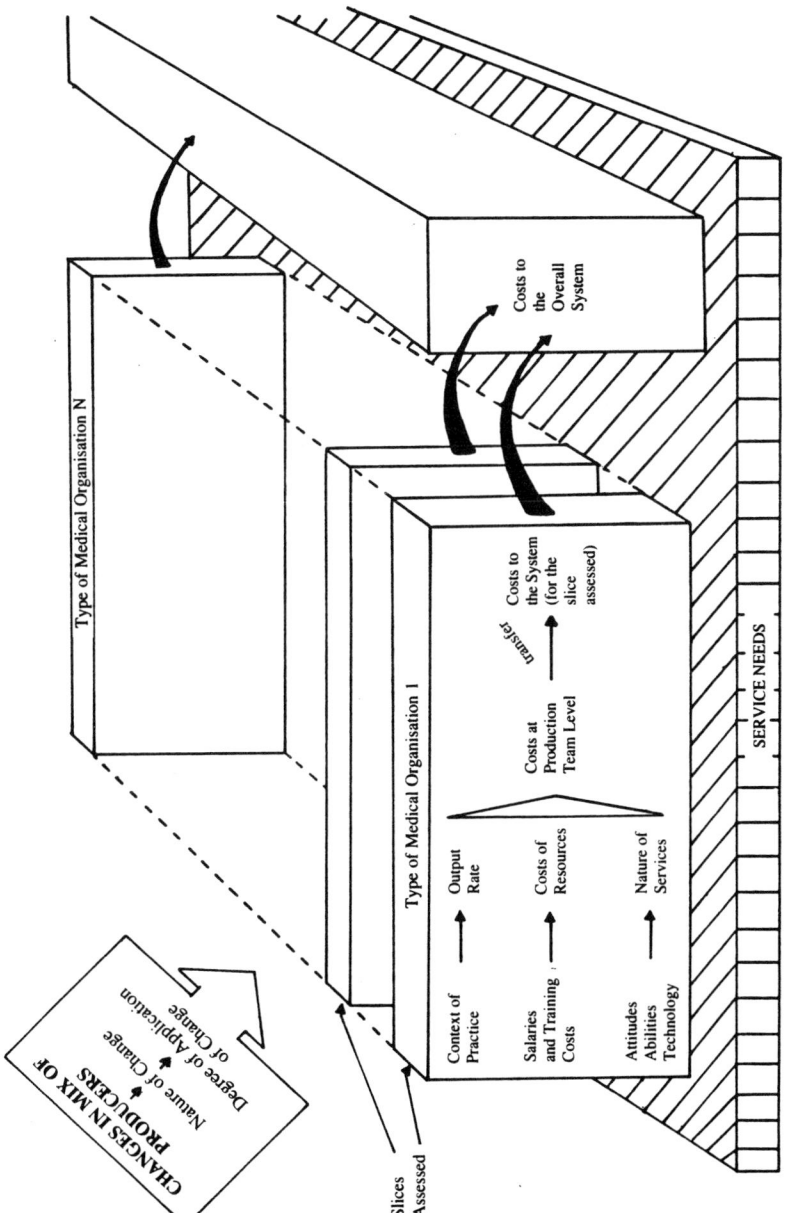

Figure 2
Postulated Logic and System of Care

allow for a precise quantification of overall effects. Only broad tendencies can emerge.

This will be our vantage point for discussing the effects of the reorganization of medical work. We will draw on the enormous amount of literature published on this subject, which we examined in a general way. We will then deal more particularly with the utilization of new health practitioners.

General Tendencies

Effects on Output Rate

In 1977, a group of researchers working with the Kaiser Permanente Health Services Research Center was asked to study the potential of new health practitioners (especially PAs and NPs) in the primary care sector. To assess the output rate of these new resources, they analyzed more than fifteen studies. Of course, they had to deal with data that showed definite variability in the production of individuals and practices since, as we have already underlined, output rate depends on many factors related to practice context. Also, in comparative studies, the question of homogeneity of output complicates the assessment. Indeed, in order to compare the quantities of services produced by different producers or different combinations of producers, we must consider similar services and use comparable production sectors. Moreover, if we want to avoid engaging in the perilous enterprise of comparing only narrowly defined services (e.g., auscultation with auscultation, examination with examination . . .), we must find a global measure of output. In this regard, the Kaiser group uses the concept of office visits (OV). Of course this gives us a general indication of output that, for primary care, has a certain validity, Utilization in this sector is often expressed in terms of numbers of office visits. However, as with all global indicators, the homogeneity in the nature of services can be called into doubt.

Using the office visit concept, the Kaiser team reviewed previous experiences to get information on the length of visits produced by physicians, PAs and NPs, and on the number of visits per day, per week and per year. The increase in number of visits following the addition of an NHP to a given practice and the (physician/NHP) substitution ratio were also explored. The researchers concluded:

> There is substantial evidence that PAs and even NPs can achieve the physician's output rate *given the same context and content*[5] of care within the delegable services . . . . It seems reasonable to assume that, given the same case mix, the same delivery context, and the same product there would be little to choose between the productivity of MDs and NHPs or between that of PAs and NPs . . . . Even if the basic productivity of the NHP, per hour or per day were the same as the physician's, the addition of an NHP to a physician practice would not result in a doubling of the OV output . . . . [In] small practices . . . there is strong evidence that the average increment in

total OVs would be in the range of 40 to 50%. The larger practices may achieve higher marginal products from the employment of an NHP . . . . Most substitution ratios of MDs to NHPs, as calculated in the literature, range from about .50 to .75 (Cassels Record et al., 1981, pp. 51-52).

We should try to explain why the total output of a practice does not double with the addition of an NHP to a physician. This situation is not surprising of course: it is the direct result of a form of task sharing that does not correspond to perfect substitution. If certain tasks (or certain visits) can be taken on by new personnel, others, more complex and probably requiring more time, must be performed by the physician. Also, physicians must spend time supervising and consulting with the NHP. Physicians practising alone or in small groups cannot fully benefit from the introduction of an assistant. In fact, in cases in which demand is sufficient, physician availability for supervision or the capacity of physicians to treat complex cases referred to them by assistants imposes a limit on the contribution they can accept from NHPs. Once translated into hours, this maximal contribution does not necessarily add up to a full-time job for an assistant, and the possibility of offering part-time work is limited. The assistant who joins a solo practice runs the risk of being underemployed. The risk is small in a large practice in which adjustments are more easily made and a supplementary contribution can be absorbed by a slight increase in the working hours of each physician in the group.

If the demand for the type of services provided by assistants is limited, a small practice may not be able to keep the assistant busy, whereas there would be no such problem in a large practice. Such a case might arise if a non-physician must provide specialized services. This situation underlines how important the exact nature of the proposed reorganization is for an assessment of its effects. Hence, most proposals concerning NHPs imply a certain independence (limited by consultation and supervision) between the workloads of the extender and of the physician, a relative independence which is less important where traditional auxiliaries are concerned.[6]

A real increase in a team's output rate requires that the NHP substituting for a physician increases the volume of services already provided by the team by an amount greater than the increase in total work hours resulting from his having been hired. Now the results reported above (substitution rate lower than 1.00, increase of 25 percent when number of auxiliaries are doubled) are not likely to be compatible with such an effect. On the contrary, we observed the opposite effect. Nevertheless, since auxiliaries and NHPs are less costly resources than physicians, it is important to see if the decreased "productivity" (volume of output per worker) of the team is justified when considering cost savings.

Effects on Costs of the Team

Here the situation is clear: the benefits at the cost level will derive mainly from the differences in training and employment costs between assistants and physicians. It may appear easy to compare training costs, but things become complicated if we consider that assistants and physicians are resources that cannot be completely substituted. It may not be appropriate to treat the difference in training costs between an assistant and a physician as a difference that can be recovered by the system, even if we only consider tasks in which an assistant can replace a physician. A physician's training, which is longer and most costly, allows him, among other things, to supervise assistants. Thus, the cost of a service by a PA or an NP is related to the training expense of this type of personnel and also to the training expense of the physician supervising him or her. Despite this phenomenon, it would be surprising if the total training costs of a physician/NHP team that is able to provide a given volume of services were higher than those of a physicians' team providing the same volume of services. This is also the case, only more so, with traditional auxiliaries.

When assessing the difference in employment costs between assistants and physicians, one must also consider supervision costs. However, the difference in remuneration between physicians and assistants is expected to be so great[7] that it is still efficient, even considering a conservative substitution ratio of 0.50, to use assistants. The potential savings will of course depend on how this remuneration evolves. Using a mathematical model, Schneider and Foley (1977) estimated that the economic benefits resulting from the use of physician extenders declined rapidly when the ratio between extenders' salaries and physicians' salaries reached a certain threshold (0.52 in their case). Contrary to studies undertaken elsewhere (Reinhardt, 1975; Hadley, 1974), Contandriopoulos (1976) noted that in Quebec the growth in output rate resulting from the use of traditional auxiliary personnel was not always justified by the salaries the physicians gave them. His results emphasize the importance of salary level in a given time and place. However, it should be possible, despite this discordant note, and taking into account what has been said about output rate and resource costs, to restrain the unit costs of health care by modifying the utilization of manpower. Lawrence observes that "in sum the limited number of studies available suggest that NHP are generally cost effective in the settings examined" (Lawrence, 1981, p. 7).

Individual variations, remuneration level and training costs must be considered, but for the time being the proposal remains an interesting one. However, one must ask if the effects on the nature of services might modify this rather positive assessment.

Effects on the Nature of Services

Debate about the nature of services inevitably leads to the question of quality. This is an important question, since quality is always presented as a sacred objective easily threatened by any change to the system, however slight. In fact the banner of quality is always raised either to promote or to condemn a proposed change. If necessary, a repertoire of anecdotes will surface, among which, inevitably, is the case of Mr. X whose lot would have been infinitely better or worse if the situation favoured by some had prevailed.

Quality should not be taken for granted when services generally provided by physicians are offered by another category of personnel. The claim of equivalent quality should be verified. Of course this process, like the process of assessment of productivity and costs, is full of pitfalls. The concept of quality is so complex that it is difficult to do it complete justice. Between the technical aspects of services and their interpersonal components, between the need for continuity and the need for individual quality, between "absolutist" and "individual" definitions (to use terms suggested by Donabedian, 1980), there is always the risk of favouring one concept of quality over another. Moreover, perhaps the sacred character of the quality objective should be questioned. One must realize that at a given point in time there is an optimal quality level that a society can financially allow itself to reach and an ideal level that it is unreasonable to aim for (Vuori, 1980). These factors having been put forward, what do we find in the literature on the subject of the quality of services provided by different types of personnel?

There are numerous studies on the subject. Two authors, Sox (1979) and Lawrence (1978), have summarized them.[8] A similarity in performance was observed for process measures as well as for outcome measures. Lawrence confirms Sox's review, noting that "in sum the available literature on NP- and PA-provided quality suggests that those practitioners do not adversely affect care process or outcomes . . ." (Lawrence, 1978, p. 10).

One of the studies mentioned by Sox and Lawrence, a study conducted by a group of researchers in the early 1970s (Spitzer et al., 1974; Sackett, et al. 1974), is especially familiar to Canadians. It has the merit of having dealt with a reasonable number of patients (296 in the nurse practitioners' group) and care episodes, of having randomized the families investigated, and of having measured several aspects of quality. The authors conclude that a nurse practitioner can provide primary care as effectively and safely as a physician.

Let us note that the studies examined by Sox and Lawrence seem to agree with recent studies (Goldberg et al., 1981). To that effect Spitzer mentions that "in studies published since 1978 there has been no change in the general thrust toward verdicts of adequate quality of care" (Spitzer, 1984, p. 1049). As for a certain degree of moderation or wisdom that NHPs might eventually demonstrate in their use of resources, and that could prove efficient at the cost level, the Kaiser group notes that "for each of the two primary groups of NHPs — PAs (including MEDEX) and NPs — there are research findings that show both greater use of laboratory and X-ray procedures and a smaller or similar use, as compared with physicians" (Cassels Record et al., 1981, p. 58).

These studies were obviously conducted in special circumstances: the settings were generally receptive to the use of medical assistants, and these assistants, fresh out of training programs and eager to prove their skills, devoted all their energies to their work. One must therefore remain cautious about generalizing results obtained in different settings, with different individuals and at different periods. Moreover, it is always possible to put the blame on the necessarily limited number of patients studied, by referring to a few cases that, though rare, could be seriously affected by a reorganization of medical work. Be that as it may, everything points to the fact that, if caution and intelligence are used in the delegation of tasks, an important number of medical activities could be delegated to non-physicians without threatening the quality of care provided. Rather, if this delegation leads to savings, one can consider reinvesting resources in other fields such as research, the delivery of more specialized or preventive services, or the promotion of better accessibility, all of which could lead to a general improvement in the state of public health.

Effects on Costs to the Health Care System

As we have seen, the savings achieved at the production team level will only benefit the system if they are transferred to it. This can only occur if the payment procedure allows it. Savings will only be transferred to the system (and eventually to the taxpayer) if the payment procedure is consistent. In fact, if the visits provided by an NHP employed by a physician or a practice are reimbursed at the same rate as that demanded by a physician, the employer benefits and is thus encouraged to take on assistants. This equal reimbursement-for-equal-services scheme was proposed in the U.S. (see Scheffler *et al.*, 1978). But unless the employer is the state or a consumer collective, the savings achieved will not lower the costs to the system (in the short term).

In a system of universal insurance in which a practice cannot compete by lowering its prices, savings can only come from a negotiated adjustment of rates for services that can be delivered by assistants (gradual reduction, increase freezes, differentiated rates depending on the type of producer . . .).

Finally, as the previously described framework of analysis had foreseen, one must be wary of the ability of change proposals to modify the overall reality, and of possible attempts on the part of the new team to take the place of an important slice of this reality. This substitution will only materialize if an NHP is trained and then employed in a case in which a physician would formerly have been used. It will only be significant insofar as services (or visits) traditionally delivered by a physician are entrusted to assistants. The substitution ratio and the increase in the volume of services previously described are proof that the situation is encouraging in this respect. Among other things, these data show the conception certain organizations have, in some circumstances and at a given time, of the contribution that the NHP can make. Theoretically, this contribution could be more important. The Kaiser group assessed how many visits assistants could provide without threatening quality. A panel of professionals developed beforehand a set of criteria defining the problems that should be dealt with by a physician only (cases in which there was either an immediate mortality risk, a high probability of wrongly diagnosing an important problem, the possibility of rapid and serious deterioration, or in which the treatment was complex). These criteria were then applied in a review of adult patient-records in the Kaiser-Permanente Health Plan. According to this analysis, 83 percent of the visits were judged appropriate for delegation to an NHP, provided there was general supervision in most cases and consultation in some cases. When conducting a comparable analysis of data provided by the National Ambulatory Medical Care Survey, the researchers noted a "delegability" of 78 percent (Cassels Record et al., 1981). For their part, Rabin and Spector (1980) asked three panels, each composed of six physicians who were aware of the potential of NHPs, to assess the contribution that this type of personnel could have made to a set of primary care visits provided by physicians belonging to the committee. The panels concluded that 8 percent of the visits could not have been confided to assistants, either totally or in part. More than 48 percent could have been totally delegated. For the remaining 43 percent, the NHP could have shouldered part of the responsibility but the physician's skills would have been needed also.

Despite persisting doubts, the case for a reorganization of manpower, especially when it assumes the utilization of NHPs, has gained enough positive points to deserve serious consideration. The new health practitioners constitute a type of personnel that is interesting by virtue of its potential capacity to relieve the physician of a considerable portion of his activities at a justifiable cost while maintaining an adequate output rate and quality of services. Denton et al., (1983) recently estimated that for the whole of Canada in 1980, the savings related to the use of nurse practitioners could have represented (very conservatively) 10 percent to 15 percent of expenditure for medical services.

It is therefore justified to think of using NHPs in the health care system. Why then do these proposals not seem to be materializing on a broad basis? Or, put another way, why are they encountering important or permanent difficulties?

The Pitfalls of Such Proposals

Obviously, the idea of using NHPs has not convinced everyone. In the U.S., for example, various studies have attempted to see if physicians were ready to hire an NHP. Fottler (1979) summarizes five studies of this type. In most of the studies, fewer than 50 percent of the physicians were inclined to use an NHP.[9]

Of course, physicians' interest is related to a given legal and economic context. For physicians as well as for health services organizations, the delegation of additional medical work requires a suitable context. Thus, structural obstacles that impede the reorganization proposed here must be faced. These obstacles have to do with the legal status, reimbursement and training of the personnel required by such proposals. Bates (1975) writes, appropriately, that "it does not make sense to train such nurse practitioners with both government and private funds, only to have state agencies or professional boards declare their practice illegal".

In order to benefit from task delegation, one must legally allow those to whom one wishes to delegate medical work to perform the tasks. This would not only confirm the assistant in the role he or she may claim and the tasks he or she may perform, but it would also free the physician from the obligation to shoulder total responsibility for delegated interventions. In cases in which the physician might become the employer of these assistants, this limitation on legal responsibility is important. A study has revealed that one of the reasons put forth by a sample of physicians for not hiring a nurse practitioner turned on this point; for almost 18 percent of the respondents the legal responsibility they would have to shoulder partly explained their reluctance to employ an NP (Fottler et al., 1978; Fottler, 1979). What is true for legal changes is also true for changes in reimbursement policies: "It does not make sense to train nurse practitioners skilled in ambulatory care and interested in the care of the poor and the aged and then provide no reimbursement mechanisms through Medicaid and Medicare so that they can be paid for their services" (Bates, 1975, p. 704).

Finally, a last structural condition for initiating a reorganization of medical work is the adequate training of the personnel that are going to take over the delegated tasks. Obviously, if well-trained NHPs are not available, they will not be used.

All things considered, however, the structural adjustments do not constitute insurmountable problems *per se*. Laws and reimbursement can be changed; training can be improved. In short, ways can be found to make adjustments to the system, so long as the desire to do so exists. But does the desire exist? Or are there forces militating in favour of the *status quo*, and is this not where the greatest difficulties lie? Is there a resistance to change on the part of consumers and/or on the part of producers?

The resistance of consumers, if it exists, may not be as important as one might think. As reported by Sox (1979), Lawrence (1979) and Spitzer (1984), the experiments undertaken to date have shown that patients are highly satisfied with the services provided by an NHP. Consumers have expressed some reservations (Storms, Fox, Breslau and Novack, 1979): they have considerable trust in their physicians and they recognize his or her involvement in numerous tasks as necessary. But they are nonetheless ready to accept NHPs' contribution as long as the latter are adequately supervised.

However, the attitude of the providers in this matter presents more of an obstacle than the attitude of the consumers. Even if legal status, training and reimbursement policies facilitate a change in the structure and use of manpower, providers may still have a sceptical attitude toward the economic advantages of such a change. Despite the results mentioned above and some success stories, the majority of physicians and health service organizations may think that the economic potential of their work will not materialize for them. If the suggested reorganization does not have other highly valued consequences (improved accessibility, improved quality), it will find very few supporters.

This sceptical attitude may be prompted by the fact that providers and planners do not perceive the task distribution implied in the proposals in the same way. In this respect it is interesting to look at attitude studies that attempt to determine how physicians define the NHP role and which tasks they are ready to assign to them. Fottler again summarizes some of these studies:

> [Studies] show that while the majority of physicians agree that many more tasks could be delegated, they prefer that physician extenders carry out specific tasks involving the limited management of defined patient services rather than total independent management of patients. It is also compatible with the concept that while the other occupations should be involved with patient "care" only physicians should be directly involved with patient "cure". Physicians appear to view extenders as technicians but not as colleagues capable of working more or less independently.[10] (Fottler, 1979, p. 544)

Thus it seems that, while not completely opposed to the concept of NHPs or task delegation, physicians as individuals have a limited role in mind for assistants. This does not correspond to the scenario planners devised for purposes of rationalization. Moreover, the positions adopted by the whole of the medical profession are in line with those reported by the respondents in attitude studies.

At this group level, the determination on the part of physicians to moderate and control their use of NHPs is clear. In the U.S., for example, medical organizations insisted on a subordinate position for NHPs. In 1978, an inquiry commission set up by the American Academy of Family Practitioners stipulated that:

> Because of the present physician shortage and maldistribution and the goal of the AAFP to provide excellence in health care to all people of America, the adequately trained assistant to the physician is welcome in some situations as a means of assisting in overcoming the current defects in health care delivery. The AAFP believes that the training programs preparing all types of assistants to the physician should be constantly monitored to assure the quality of training provided and that the number of graduates produced is limited to meet demonstrated needs. (Cassels Record *et al.*, 1981, p. 140)

In June 1972, the House of Delegates of the American Medical Association recommended that physicians' associations exercise a control over the PAs by approving the following, on an individual basis: the PA, the physician supervising him or her and the description of tasks to be performed by the PA (Greenwood *et al.*, 1980).

For their part, Yankauer and Sullivan write:

> In 1970 . . . the American Medical Association acting on its own initiative and without consulting the nursing profession issued a statement to the effect that, as a stopgap measure, the physician shortage could be alleviated by training thousands of nurses to practice as "physician's assistants" . . . . [The statement's] wording and later interpretation clearly placed the nurse in the position of a girl Friday who functioned only at the doctor's beck and call. (Yankauer and Sullivan, 1982, p. 257)

The *status quo* was given clear support in certain cases.[11] The reactions of the American medical profession show a resistance to the type of reorganization planned in the perspective of administrative rationalization. This resistance may explain why the proposals were not implemented in some cases. It might also explain why, in other cases, proposals were modified to such an extent that their essence was lost. However, by closely examining the Quebec experience we will be able to analyze how, and according to what rationale, professional groups can thwart plans to rationalize health care work.

The Professional Rationality Approach: Analysis of the Failure to Reorganize Professional Work — The Case of Quebec

There have never been nurse practitioners or physician assistants in Quebec and little has been done to introduce this new type of assistant into the health sector. Instead, the Quebec government has devoted its energies to rationalizing the tasks and functions of health professions already in existence.

Quebec's determination to do so led to reforming the Professional Code and instituting a formal procedure for the delegation of tasks. This determination to change is in keeping with the reform movement in the health care sector, which is characterized by the dominant presence of the state and the systematic recourse to legislative apparatus in order to standardize the organization of the health care system throughout the province, which, in turn, has left little room for pilot experiments and spontaneous initiatives. This situation has hardly been favourable to the development of new categories of assistants.

State intervention in the health sector is not peculiar to Quebec, but it is clearly stronger here than in other Canadian provinces or in the U.S. Recourse to legislation obviously gives the Québécois experience a particular character, but it also means that the reactions of professionals to the reorganization and decompartmentalization of their tasks are stronger in Quebec than elsewhere. These reactions have manifested themselves not quietly but publicly ever since the mid-1960s. In this sense, the Québécois experience is most revealing of what is happening, though in less spectacular fashion, elsewhere in Canada and the U.S.

Furthermore, Québécois experience shows how the leading professions have means of impeding any attempt to infringe on their field of practice. It also shows the limited hold our political and legislative structures have on the organization of professional work. For example, the main objective in reforming the Professional Code was to dissociate the function of protecting the public from that of defending interests of the members of the profession. However, the professional orders in Quebec continue, to this day, to be highly corporatist. Here is another example. The delegation of tasks by physicians to other categories of professionals has only made official a *de facto* situation. Despite the reform of professional corporations (known as Colleges outside Quebec), the division of tasks and functions among health professionals has not changed in any fundamental way.

It is this failure to achieve change that we will attempt to analyze. First, we will see how the professions and professionalism are defined by social scientists. This will allow us to understand better the principles of work organization in the health sector. Then we will describe the basic parameters of the Professional Code Reform and the effects of state intervention on the organization of professional corporations. Finally, in order to pinpoint the means certain professions have of keeping their fields of practice intact, and in order to understand the state's partial failure to intervene in the division of professional labour, we will examine professional reaction to the task delegation policy imposed by the government.

Professions and Professionalism

It is not easy to define a profession or professionalism. Not only do these concepts correspond to very different realities from one society to another (Haug, 1975), but they also refer to occupations with characteristics and statuses that virtually cannot be compared.

At first, social scientists thought the professions were a particular type of occupation. From this vantage point, sociologists have tried to define the professions by establishing their specific attributes and their common characteristics in order to distinguish them from other categories of work.[12] Lists of attributes were drawn up specifying what seemed to be the general parameters of the professions: the nature of the activity engaged in and its altruistic character (Elliot, 1972); the specialized knowledge and time necessary for training (Barber, 1965; Moore, 1970); the personal nature of the professional-client relationship (Reeder, 1972). This approach did not prove very fruitful because it was unable to come up with any definition of the professions (Bohnen, 1977; Johnson, 1977).

Today we no longer seek the characteristics the professions have in common in the nature of their activity but rather in the type of social controls to which their members are subjected and in the characteristics of their clientele, that is, the people who generate the demand for their services. Therefore, the different types of professions are divided into two broad categories: the liberal professions such as medicine and law, and the auxiliary professions, defined by some authors as technical professions (Strauss, 1967; Freidson, 1970; Wolinsky, 1980) or organizational professions (Sarfatti-Larson, 1977). The auxiliary professions must further be subdivided into the intermediate professions, of which nurses are a perfect example, and the sub-auxiliary professions, such as that of the nursing assistants.

This approach views professionalism as a particular type of occupational control that amounts to peer control (Johnson, 1977).[13] In the case of the liberal professions, this internal control is the main, if not the only, control regulating the quality of the activity. Moreover, a vast and heterogeneous clientele stimulates demand for services on a direct basis, which gives producers an important margin for manoeuvring when it comes to defining a client's needs and the manner in which they are to be met (Johnson, 1977).

In the case of the auxiliary professions, peer control is limited by various external controls.[14] One of these takes the form of the salaried employee status held by the members of these professions who work for big firms or institutions. Hence, their practice is controlled externally both by hierarchical structures and by the bureaucratic constraints that govern the work organization of salaried workers (Mauksch, 1967; Freidson, 1970; Reverby, 1975, 1979). Moreover, these occupations are limited by a second external control flowing from the very nature of those who directly stimulate demand for their services. Johnson (1977) defines this type of control as "oligarchic and corporate patronage". Other authors who have looked more closely at work organization in the health sector maintain that this control is a result of the position of dependency in which the medical profession holds the auxiliary professions (Friedson, 1970; B. and J. Ehrenreich, 1975; Wolinsky, 1980). The control exercised by the members of the medical profession over access to services, referral to other professionals, and diagnosis and treatment protocols, makes this profession the first consumer of auxiliary services. As a consumer of auxiliary services, the medical profession is an organized and homogeneous group that controls the practice of the auxiliary by determining the needs of the client (diagnosis) and the manner in which these are to be met (care and treatment protocol).

There is another type of control being exercised in the health sector today, one that limits the leading as well as the auxiliary professions. Johnson (1977) speaks of mediative control in which the producer-consumer relationship is mediated by a third party in order to rationalize production and regulate the market. In Quebec the growing amount of state intervention in the health services sector immediately brings to mind this mediative control, but as Johnson indicates, this control may also be exercised by private firms such as insurance companies.

According to social scientists, since the turn of the century there has been a gradual but real increase in the external controls placed on the professions. Although the leading professions do not seem to be as affected by these controls, there is an increasing tendency to put their members on regular salary. Also, third parties are trying to control their practice in order to rationalize production and regulate the market. Though the controls exercised over the leading professions are increasingly more effective, their clientele continues to be vast and heterogeneous, peer control is still extremely important and their therapeutic freedom is held onto tightly. Such is not the case for the auxiliary professions. Peer control, which is limited by hierarchical, oligarchic and mediative controls, is more an artifact than a reality (Sarfatti-Larson, 1977). In this paper, professionalism is therefore understood as a particular type of occupational control that corresponds to peer control. From this point of view, professional occupations are those in which a member's practice is mainly or partly controlled by his or her colleagues.

The General Parameters of the Professional Code Reform

Since 1973, the Professional Code of Quebec has governed professional corporations, of which twenty-one are exclusive professions and seventeen have reserved titles. Exclusive professions have two monopolies: one over title and another over field of practice. The reserved title confers only one monopoly, the title. Excluding social workers and psychologists,[15] twenty of these professional corporations work in the health sector: twelve have an exclusive right to practice,[16] and eight a reserved title.[17] The Professional Code Reform has granted new prerogatives to some of the already existing professional corportions (nurses, for example, obtained a definition of their field of practice).[18] As well, nine new professional corporations were constituted, all operating in the health sector.[19]

State adoption of the Code also served to remind the professional corporations that their principal social function is to protect the public. In fact, the legislation narrows down the role of the professional corporations to this function, and leaves the task of defending the socio-economic interests of its members to unions or similar associations.[20] The government took a series of measures to ensure that professional corporations would meet their responsibilities. It asked that representatives be appointed to the Bureau of Professional Corporations, obliged the latter to set up a professional inspection committee and a committee on discipline, and created the Office des Professions du Québec. The Office is a para-governmental agency, the function of which is to see that each corporation ensures the protection of the public. More generally, it is also supposed to see that each corporation conforms to the Professional Code and to its constituent laws.

The reorganization of professional corporations did not stop here. The state also granted itself the means of intervening more directly in the professional division of labour. A device was introduced in the Professional Code Reform by which certain exclusive professions[21] were required "to determine from among the tasks reserved to its members the tasks which may, without danger to the public, be delegated to classes of persons other than its members" (Dussault and Potvin, 1983, p. 3). Only the nurses' regulation stipulates that nurses' tasks are to be delegated to nursing assistants. The other professional regulations do not mention who these other classes of persons are to whom tasks can or must be delegated.

The Office des Professions has in this respect three responsibilities. First, it must see to it that professional corporations required to delegate tasks reserved to their members do in fact perform the delegation. Second, the Office must be consulted before the adoption of such a regulation. Third, in cases in which professional corporations do not put this task delegation into effect, the Office can supersede the corporations and impose the regulation.

Although the exclusive right to practice is maintained in the Professional Code, the government recognizes that this monopoly must no longer hinder the development of fields of practice. The aim of task delegation is therefore to favour flexibility in the professional fields by introducing a less rigid division of tasks among professionals. Its objective is also to legalize the informal task delegation that occurs in health institutions.

In short, with the reorganization of professional corporations in Quebec, the government acknowledged new professional corporations, incorporated others and made known to all the professional corporations that their main, if not their only, function is to protect the public. It created the Office des Professions to ensure that the corporations meet their social responsibilities. And, while maintaining the privilege of exclusivity, it gave itself the means of intervening more directly in the process of the division of tasks among professionals through task delegation regulations, so as to decompartmentalize the fields of professional activity and stimulate professional collaboration.

State Intervention and Professional Corporations

Through the creation of the Office des Professions, the legislature acknowledges that "in matters of professional services, as in other fields of social or economic activity . . . the producers cannot assume alone and without external controls the defense of consumers or of the general public"[22] (Office des Professions du Québec, 1976, p. 9). In fact, the state thus admits that the traditional forces regulating the professional services market are no longer effective and that it must intervene more directly in order to protect the public.[23]

The formal task delegation procedure is the means used by the state to decompartmentalize fields of activity. By introducing task delegation and subjecting this procedure to the supervision of the Office des Professions, the state acknowledges here also that changes have occurred in professional work organization.

It recognizes that the compartmentalization of fields of activity, along with the increase in numbers of different occupations, has had negative effects on professional work organization and that it must now intervene more directly in order to rationalize the division of labour.

From a logical point of view, this task delegation mechanism imposed by the state is as incompatible with professionalism as are external controls. The monopoly on title and field of practice conferred on members of a professional corporation by the exclusive right to practice is aimed precisely at closing down a field of practice, thereby allowing the elimination of incompetent persons likely to cause serious prejudice to the public. Now, closing down a field of practice in order to protect the public (which has the direct, intended result of eliminating competition among producers of the same service) is the very *raison d'être* of professionalism. Consequently, the decompartmentalization of fields of practice, regardless of the form it takes, is a rather serious attack on this type of occupational organization.

The advent of task delegation does not mean that the Quebec government is trying to re-introduce competition among producers of the same service. On the one hand and in keeping with the spirit of the Professional Code, the compartmentalization of fields remains a necessary means of insuring the protection of the public in cases in which the professional enjoys a wide autonomy of practice (Gaudreau, 1983); that is, in which the relationship with the client is of a strictly personal nature involving no witness to the quality of services rendered.[24] On the other hand, by asking exclusive professional corporations to determine the tasks that can be delegated, the state is restoring their traditional power of delegation; that is, the power to define the scope of practice of the auxiliary professions.

In conclusion, even though the state is not trying to destroy professional organizations, it would seem, since it is maintaining the privilege of exclusivity and the delegating power of the leading professions, that it has to attack the very foundations of professionalism if it wants to offset the negative effects of this kind of occupational control on work organization in the health sector.

The increase in type of occupations and their specialties, largely dependent on the development of knowledge and technology, has taken a particular form in the health sector since World War II. The closing of certain fields of practice at the turn of the century and the absence of competition among producers of the same service have resulted not only in the expansion of occupations, but also in a narrow and rigid division of labour among related specialties. Another result has been the organization of health occupations into an increasingly complex hierarchy.

Denounced by the Castonguay-Nepveu Commission (Commission of Inquiry on Health and Social Welfare, 1970) as costly and unproductive, the complex hierarchical organization of health occupations and the rigid compartmentalization of professional fields are the negative results of the very professionalism the state wanted to offset by instituting task delegation. The state wanted to render the division of labour in the health sector more flexible in order to encourage the efficient and rational use of manpower and to promote team and multi-disciplinary work. In short, it wanted to re-establish a basis for agreement among professionals in order to reactivate a harmonious collaboration among them. This collaboration existed before the 1960s,[25] but the anarchical development of occupations with narrow and rigid boundaries, subjected to exclusive professions, involved the various categories of producers in an almost permanent process of negotiation concerning the limits of their fields of practice (Freidson, 1976). With each occupation tied to its own bargaining power, to economic alliances among professional groups, and to actual agreements with the medical profession, these negotiations gradually became a vivid and almost constant source of conflict.

The controls that the Quebec government is trying to exercise over professional corporations and the division of labour in the health sector stem from the particular development of this sector over the past thirty years. With these controls, aimed at offsetting the negative effects professionalism has had on the division of labour in this sector, the government is imposing itself as an active agent in the organization of professions and their services. The professionals' reaction has been tantamount to the destabilization that can come about when a new actor is introduced into the economic sector. There can be two reactions: the fear of losing professional privileges or the hope of gaining greater social recognition.

Professional Reaction to Task Delegation[26]

The formal task delegation process began in 1974, but it was only in May 1980 that these regulations were adopted in the case of medical and nursing tasks. Slowness to adopt these regulations cannot be attributed to the newness of the task delegation phenomenon in the health sector, nor to opposition expressed by the professionals to the formal delegation imposed by the Professional Code.

As we have just seen, task delegation among health professionals is far from a new phenomenon. The leading professions have easily delegated tasks to auxiliary professions as the need was felt, and also as a result of scientific discoveries, technological developments and the ever more specialized training of auxiliary professionals. This delegation, however, was informal. It took into consideration the experience that these professionals had of working together, the savings it allowed in terms of time and money and the particular characteristics of each field of practice (general, specialized or university hospitals, private offices, etc.). Over the years, however, this informal delegation has led to legal problems that the professions hoped to mitigate with the formal delegation of tasks. Dussault and Potvin (1983) note that in the medical sector, at least, physicians, nurses and nursing assistants welcomed from the very beginning this formal procedure of task delegation. Physicians saw it as a way of clarifying the limits of their legal responsibility in situations in which medical tasks were performed by persons other than physicians; nurses and nursing assistants saw in it the possibility of legalizing routine medical tasks performed by members of both their groups.

Neither lack of familiarity with the procedure itself nor professional opposition to formal delegation can be blamed for the slow adoption of delegation regulations. The only explanation seems to be the professionals' fear of defining too narrowly the boundaries of their own fields of practice. Negotiations among professionals stumbled over this problem, which is why different strategies to maintain their professional fields intact were more or less consciously set up by the parties involved.

The Strategies

In order to maintain and expand their fields of practice, the delegating professions have adopted very similar strategies. Even though these professions are legally bound to delegate only tasks that are exclusive to them, they began by delegating tasks that were not. For example, the first regulation proposal presented by physicians in March 1976 mentioned several tasks as likely ones to delegate to nurses or nursing assistants, which in fact already belonged to nursing. The same phenomenon occurred in the case of physiotherapists and rehabilitation technicians: at first, physicians tried to delegate to them tasks such as whirlpools or massages that did not belong to physicians exclusively (Corporation Professionelle des Physiothérapeutes du Québec, 1984). In May 1976, the nurses presented their first regulation proposal regarding nursing assistants. They adopted the physicians' strategy of trying to delegate to nursing assistants tasks that already belonged to this profession.

Of course these regulation proposals were turned down by the Office des Professions. However, this strategy was meant to enable the delegating professions to protect their fields of practice by expanding them. In other words, by delegating tasks that already belonged to other professions, the delegating professions were asserting that these tasks formed an integral part of their own fields of practice.

The other strategy adopted by physicians (the dentists followed suit) consisted in supporting sub-professionals, such as nursing assistants and rehabilitation technicians (the dentists supported the dental assistants), against the intermediate professionals, such as nurses and physiotherapists (dental hygienists in the case of dentists).[27] This strategy had a double objective: one professional, the other economic.

The professional objective was to remind the intermediate professionals that they are subordinate to the leading professions. In other words, the intermediate professions cannot hope to widen the scope of their fields of practice nor to increase their autonomy if they manifest too explicitly their desire for independence and if they do not remain in a position of respect and submission to the leading professions. The support given to sub-professionals is a traditional strategy on the part of the delegating professions to maintain control over the whole of the activities of their sector. By delegating tasks to these professions and by guaranteeing them a certain autonomy with relation to the intermediate professionals, the leading professions are establishing narrow boundaries between the auxiliary professions in their sector as well as maintaining the professional hierarchy and the subordination of the auxiliary professions.

In economic terms, it was necessary for physicians in private practice to be able to continue working with nursing assistants, whose services are less costly than those of nurses. In this delegation process, it was imperative that physicians support the sub-auxiliary professions if they wanted these to remain in existence and to maintain a certain autonomy of practice. Without this autonomy there was no longer any interest, not even an economic one, in working with members of these professions.

The task delegation regulations adopted were an outcome of this strategy. The support given to nursing assistants by the medical profession and the Office des Professions forced the nurses to grant nursing assistants more tasks than they would have liked, but it allowed physicians to keep their field of practice intact and to maintain their dominant position.

Medical and Nursing Task Regulations

The medical and nursing regulations adopted in 1980 are negotiated agreements between the different parties. Despite the diametrically opposed interests involved and the deep rifts that occurred throughout the negotiations, the professions involved seem to have succeeded in meeting the new demands imposed by the formal task delegation procedure without losing or gaining too much autonomy.

By supporting the nursing assistants, physicians succeeded in maintaining the traditional hierarchy and order in this sector. Supported by the Office des Professions and by the medical profession, nursing assistants maintained and perhaps even increased their autonomy of practice. The nurses, who wanted to become "the required intermediary between physicians and assistants"[28] (Dussault and Potvin, 1983, p. 37), did not succeed. Instead they ended up delegating to the assistants more tasks than they had intended.

In 1980, nurses seemed to be the losers by the medical and nursing tasks regulations, but four years later they admit, along with the physicians and the nursing assistants, that these regulations actually changed nothing in their practice and in the task distribution of the parties concerned (Dussault and Potvin, 1983). Moreover, they were able to get around them thanks to the definition of their field of practice conferred by the government in 1973. After a period of formally conforming to the medical task regulations, they now interpret them liberally. Today they use this definition to perform tasks that local practice conditions allow them to usurp without becoming illegal.[29]

A liberal interpretation of these regulations is facilitated by the difficulties encountered by institutions in applying them. It is estimated that only one quarter of the institutions concerned have applied delegation regulations. Physicians, who would have preferred to set up a delegation guide rather than having to delegate by list of tasks, expected such difficulties. According to them, provincial delegation by list of tasks is too rigid and leaves no room for the distinctive features of institutions and the specific features of the different types of practices. In the physicians' opinion, provincial regulations should serve solely to establish certain markers for the local delegation.

Lately, nurses seem to prefer less formal negotiations. Faced with delegating tasks to nursing assistants, they are now questioning the pertinence of setting up a provincial delegation by list of tasks. It is becoming increasingly obvious to nurses that provincial delegation should be no more than a "guide, a set of practice norms or regulating principles"[30] (Larose, 1983, p. 23).

According to physicians and nurses, provincial delegation policy is trying to standardize a situation that cannot be standardized because of the many differences between practice locations and because the division of tasks among professionals is not, nor can be, everywhere the same. In fact, what these two professional groups are advocating with the delegation guide is a return to informal negotiations between professionals and, by the same token, a reduction of the government's role in the division of tasks among professionals. So the game is not over yet. The difficulties encountered in applying these regulations locally may lead the Office des Professions and the government to consider the delegation guide as an acceptable solution.

Discussion

In the light of the events we have just examined, it is obvious that the Professional Code Reform and the delegation policy allowed the auxiliary professions in the medical and nursing sectors to increase formally the autonomy of practice they enjoyed. It is also obvious that the medical profession succeeded in maintaining intact its field of practice. It also succeeded in maintaining the dominant position it holds over the other professions in this sector.[31]

This formal increase in autonomy of practice of the auxiliary professions did not increase their real autonomy. We can only note that since the professions in this sector agree that task delegation regulations have changed nothing in task distribution, these regulations have actually only confirmed a *de facto* situation. Nonetheless, by legally recognizing nursing assistants as a profession for the first time and by defining nurses' field of practice, the Professional Code has formally increased the means available to these occupations to defend their fields of practice and to reduce their vulnerability in the context of task delegation.

The medical and nursing professions were able to arrive at regulations mainly because the physicians' and the nurses' fields of practice were not really challenged in this first formal delegation negotiation. Another reason is that the state's economic interests and the physicians' professional interests called for a common strategy: supporting the nursing assistants with regard to task delegation from the nurses. For the government as for physicians in private practice, the use of nursing assistants has certain economic advantages as long as the latter enjoy a measure of autonomy — that is, as long as their practice does not require that they be too narrowly supervised by nurses. Moreover, the entire medical profession stands to gain from supporting nursing assistants; such support reduces the control nurses have over the particular field of treating the sick and maintains their subordinate position. This common strategy, backed by interests particular to the state and the medical profession, served to prevent the development of conflicts between the Office des Professions and the physicians. It also facilitated negotiated agreements in the medical and nursing sectors.

Despite its being a negotiated agreement, formal task delegation did not succeed in making the fields of activity more flexible. All the professionals agree on this point. For them, the provincial delegation policy has made the fields of practice more rigid, not leaving enough room for agreements and local planning. The difficulties involved in putting these regulations into effect in institutions seem to support the professionals' claim. However, we must not lose sight of the fact that their determination to return to an informal negotiation of their fields of practice is actually aimed at reducing the state's control over the division of labour among professionals and at giving professionals back their traditional manoeuvring margin. Strengthened by the professional privileges they obtained in 1973, nurses and nursing assistants feel they are now able to return to informal negotiations of the limits of their fields of practice. Hence, by increasing the professional privileges of the auxiliary professions, state intervention only served to re-establish the traditional collaboration among the professionals in this health sector. At the same time, increasing these professional privileges has led to the further compartmentalization of the fields of activity and increased the professional means, available to these occupations, of fighting back attempts to usurp their fields of practice.

While upholding professionalism, the Professional Code Reform and the task delegation procedure afforded the state a means of reducing the negative effects of this mode of occupational organization. The state could not offset the negative effects of professionalism without touching the physicians' field of practice or further compartmentalizing nursing. Actually, state intervention only consolidated the professional structure of the medical and nursing sectors. By so doing, it did not succeed in softening the boundaries of the fields of practice, nor did it succeed in distributing tasks differently among related specialties. At the most, it made possible a more harmonious collaboration among the parties concerned. But for how long? When the fields of practice are narrow and compartmentalized, such collaboration is temporary and a crisis is always latent.

In summary, the Québécois experience shows that if the government wants to intervene in order to rationalize the organization of professional work, it must come to terms with the interests and reactions of the leading professions. This constraint limits its capacity to intervene. It also forces government to follow the logic of professionalism (the closing down of fields of activity to protect the public) and its division of labour (upholding the professional hierarchy by establishing narrow boundaries between auxiliary professions). Even when the state uses legal and coercive means, as in Quebec, its impact on the professional sector is limited — unless, that is, the leading professions have something to gain by it. If the state cannot prevent the leading professions from obstructing the rationalization of their tasks, how can new participants in the health sector (such as the new health practitioners who also encroach on physicians' field of practice) hope to gain recognition if they have no professional prerogatives? The organization of health work is based on professionalism in the name of public protection. Any new participant in the professional sector must come to terms with this basic fact, if this mode of work organization is to continue.

Conclusion

There are two ways of perceiving the reality of the health care system. One uses administrative, and the other professional, rationality. Consequently, the question can be approached in two directions. On the one hand, administrative rationality calls for an analysis of work performed in the health care system. This analysis shows that it would be feasible in terms of service quality, and desirable in cost terms, to replace physicians with other professionals for certain activities. Indeed the training of these other professionals is more directly oriented toward the activities concerned, whereas physicians represent qualified, specialized and costly manpower.

On the other hand, professional rationality entails an acknowledgement of professionalism. Professionalism is based on the need to protect the population, which is not always capable of appreciating its need for services, by ensuring good quality services.

Professionalism built on this need by delegating to the professions the responsibility for control over their own activities. This control led to a monopoly on title and field of activity. However, establishing control over a field of activity in order to protect the public can only limit the possibility of establishing a better work organization in the field.

In the first four sections of this paper, we used a general model and the available literature to explore the possible effects of reorganizing the health services sector. This analysis showed that it is theoretically possible to reduce service costs without reducing their quality. This can be done by making more extensive use of already existing, non-physician professionals and traditional aides, or by introducing new health practitioners (NHP).

Then, we looked at the reasons that could explain why NHPs have not found a place in Canada, despite encouraging results, and why the use of existing personnel, through task delegation among other things, remained limited. We did this by studying the case of medical and nursing task delegation in Quebec. That province's experience seemed particularly interesting to us because, with the setting up of a public health insurance plan, the organization of the professions was modified in order to induce professionals to take more seriously their mandate to protect the public. This modification took the form of a centralized code that defines the functions of each professional corporation.

We noted that, despite a legal context whose aim is to achieve a better organization of professional activity by defining the tasks that can be delegated from one profession to another, and after a long series of confrontations, the *status quo* prevails.

As this paper's analysis shows, there is not much likelihood of seeing the establishment of a better work organization in the health services sector if this organization is not acceptable to the leading professions. In places such as Canada where there are strong leading professions, especially physicians, and where the number of their members is increasing more rapidly than the population, there is no chance, under the present circumstances, that a new profession will see the light or even that other professions can expand their fields of practice.

Acknowledgements

The authors wish to thank the following persons for their comments on a preliminary version of this text: A. Archambault (Faculty of Pharmacy, University of Montreal), F. Champagne (G.R.I.S., University of Montreal), P. Bergeron (Quebec Ministry of Social Affairs), M.-A. Fournier (G.R.I.S., University of Montreal), B. Maheux (G.R.I.S., University of Montreal), A. Lemay (G.R.I.S., University of Montreal), R. Pineault (G.R.I.S., University of Montreal), J. Rochon (Faculty of Medicine, Laval University) and G. Rivard (Faculty of Medicine, Laval University).

The assistance of Yolaine Mottet and the secretarial staff of GRIS is also gratefully acknowledged, as is the translation work of M.P. Smargiasso and L. Valois.

Notes

1. In Quebec, physicians' gross remuneration represented 18.8 percent of public health expenditure in 1982-1983 (Quebec Health Insurance Board, 1983). For the same period, salaries and fringe benefits of non-physician personnel

constituted approximately 75 percent of the operating expenses of general hospitals (Ministry of Social Affairs, 1984).

2. In Quebec, the Commission of Inquiry on Health and Social Welfare (the Castonguay-Nepveu Commission) greatly contributed to popularizing this line of thought. The Commission's final report states that "in all sectors of human activity and even in research, the need for multidisciplinary teams under flexible and well-defined leadership is being felt and the formula generally gives excellent results. The health system should encourage, by all the means available, establishment of multidisciplinary teams" (Commission of Inquiry on Health and Social Welfare, 1970a, p. 30).

3. The NHP is not a homogeneous group. It includes two broad categories of practitioners: the nurse practitioners (NP) and the physician assistants (PA). These categories are also relatively heterogeneous, grouping together Primex, MEDEX, paediatric NPs, family practice NPs, etc. Yankauer and Sullivan (1982) discuss the differences and similarities between NPs and PAs. The skills that the NP and PA programs develop seem to be similar except that in the case of NPs more emphasis is put on patient education. But their respective roles are the same for the most part: both perform medical tasks that do not necessarily require full medical training, particularly tasks in the field of primary health care.

4. McMaster University offered a program for nurse practitioners (Spitzer and Kergin, 1973), and Newfoundland's Memorial University offered a training program for family practice nurses (Chambers et al., 1977).

5. Italics added.

6. Reinhardt and Smith (1974) reported that if the physicians they had studied doubled the number of (traditional) auxiliary employees, they could increase the hourly output of their practices by 20 percent to 25 percent. Hadley (1974) refers to studies by Kehrer and Zaretsky (1972) and by Kimbell and Lorant (1972). Both studies produced results consistent with those of Reinhardt and Smith (1974). In Quebec, if the physician doubled the number of auxiliary employees, he would increase his hourly output by 25 percent to 40 percent, depending on the specialty (Contandriopoulos, 1976).

7. For example, the Kaiser group sets the NHP remuneration/physicians' remuneration ratio at 0.38 (Cassels Record, 1980). In Canada, Denton et al. (1983), when estimating potential gains resulting from the introduction of nurse practitioners, set this ratio at 2/7 (0.29).

8. Sox listed more than forty articles and analyzed more closely those (about twenty) that compared the physicians' performance with that of non-physicians in the delivery of comparable tasks. In eight of the studies, comparability was established by a random selection of patients treated. On the whole, the quality of care provided by the NHPs was equal to that provided by physicians.

These conclusions are repeated in three studies that assessed the response produced by a nurse practitioner and by a physician when the same case was presented to them, and in nine studies that used a non-randomized design.

9. Studies by Borland *et al.* (1972), and Parker and Delahunt (1972) reported on the attitude of physicians in Pennsylvania and Texas respectively. They obtained rates of 70 percent and 47 percent, respectively, on respondents ready to employ PAs. Lawrence *et al.* (1977), and Fottler himself, noted that 33 percent and 29 percent of their respondents, respectively, were ready to employ a nurse practitioner. To Fottler's summary we can add the Burkett *et al.* study (1978) in which 36 percent of the respondents were interested in using a nurse practitioner. These proportions may well be overestimated. The hypothesis that there was a selection of respondents, retaining only those favourable to NHPs, is a plausible one, given the low rate of responses obtained. For example, the non-response rates in the Lawrence, Fottler and Burkett studies are, respectively, 62 percent (Lawrence *et al.*, 1977), 63 percent (Fottler, 1979) and 40 percent (Burkett *et al.*, 1978), and the biased response hypothesis was verified by Fottler *et al.* (1978). Moreover, one must bear in mind that while attitudes may be conciliatory, considerably less enthusiasm may be expressed in actual behaviour.

10. Making similar comments are Burkett *et al.* (1978) and Breslau and Novack (1979).

11. According to Mauksch, "a number of State Medical Societies, as for instance in Texas in 1977, openly opposed revisions of nurse practice acts which would update nursing practice. In Tennessee, the Medical Society did not support the Nurse Association's endeavour to legalize the practice of physician-supervised prescription writing by nurse practitioners of protocol listed drugs. In New Jersey, the Medical Board of Examiners charged two nurse practitioners with practicing medicine . . ." (Mauksch, 1978, p. 1075).

12. This approach, which is generally known as trait analysis, dominated the scientific field of the sociology of the professions from the 1930s to the end of the 1960s. It was first acknowledged by Carr-Saunders and Wilson (1933).

13. This type of occupational control is the product of a period in which the development of knowledge and socio-economic changes went hand in hand with aristocratic values that were still popular (Elliot, 1972). The liberal professions succeeded in imposing the superiority of their services, eliminating competition and gaining exclusive rights over a vast field of practice (Sarfatti-Larson, 1977). They did this by embroidering on the gentleman's ethic, by claiming the right to high social status and control of their activities, and by invoking their know-how and specialized knowledge (Bohnen, 1977) in order to adapt themselves to the industrial era. Professions created in the twentieth century were not able to eliminate competition so easily, much less acquire exclusive rights over a vast field of practice.

14. For Sarfatti-Larson (1977), the external controls imposed on the auxiliary professions are an indication of the separation that occurs in professionalism between market control and the struggle for professional status. This brings the author to conclude that professionalism today is no more than an ideology.

15. These two professional corporations hold a reserved title only.

16. The professional corporations with an exclusive right to practise in the health sector are: hearing-aid acousticians, chiropractors, dentists, dental technicians, nurses, physicians, veterinary surgeons, dispensing opticians, optometrists, pharmacists, podiatrists and radiology technicians.

17. The professional corporations with a reserved title in the health sector are: dietitians, occupational therapists, dental hygienists, nursing assistants, speech therapists and audiologists, physiotherapists, dental technicians and medical technologists.

18. Although the nursing profession in Quebec has been an exclusive profession since 1946, the 1973 reorganization consolidated this monopoly by officially defining its field of practice. Before the reorganization, a list of prohibited tasks limited their practice, forbidding them "to give medical consultations, to prescribe medication or to practise medicine". Even so, their field of practice was not defined (Trottier, 1982).

19. Four of these new professional corporations have obtained exclusive rights to practice. These are: hearing-aid acousticians, chiropractors, dental technicians and podiatrists. The remaining five were granted a reserved title. These are: occupational therapists, dental hygienists, nursing assistants, physiotherapists and medical technologists.

20. In Quebec, this separation seemed to come easily. Indeed, following the establishment of hospitalization insurance (1961) and medical insurance (1970), and given the particular modes of administration of health services that these developments led to, members of professional corporations rapidly formed unions or similar organizations in order to defend their socio-economic interests better. State intervention gave a particular structure to the organization and administration of health services. Hospitals, for example, are autonomous public corporations financed almost exclusively by a global budget provided by the state. But salaries and the general work conditions of hospital employees are negotiated provincially between the government and the unions. In a reluctant effort to adjust, members of the professions joined these unions during the 1960s and early 1970s. This movement affected physicians and pharmacists as well as members of the auxiliary professions. In 1963, general practitioners grouped together to form the Fédération des médecins omnipraticiens du Québec (FMOQ) and in 1965, specialists formed the Fédération des médecins spécialistes du Québec (FMSQ). They hoped that these federations would be better able to defend their socio-economic

interests than the Collège des médecins (Contandriopoulos and Fournier, 1983). It was also at the beginning of the 1960s that the members of organizational professions working in hospitals, such as nurses, began to improve their work and salary conditions.

21. In all, there are seven professional corporations that, by virtue of their constituent laws, are required to determine through regulations the tasks that may be performed by classes of persons other than their members. These are: chemists, dentists, nurses, physicians, optometrists, pharmacists and podiatrists.

22. Authors' translation of: "qu'en matière de services professionels comme dans d'autres domaines de l'activité économique ou social . . . les producteurs ne peuvent assumer seuls et sans contrôle externe la défense des intérêts des consommateurs ou du public en général".

23. The creation of the Office des Professions follows a line of thinking similar to the one that led the government to adopt anti-trust laws. With these laws, the state recognized that market forces were no longer effective to maintain competition in the presence of monopolies, and that it had to intervene more directly in order to protect consumers.

24. In accordance with this line of thinking, hearing-aid acousticians, chiropractors, dental technicians and podiatrists (recognized and incorporated for the first time in 1973) were given exclusive right to practice.

25. The organization of health services and the administration of medical care, based for more than a century on the principle of human charity, are no longer inspired by this altruism. Today we are dealing with a complex work organization in which many specialized workers defend their economic interests as aggressively as workers in the goods sector, and in which the difficulties of professional collaboration often become more important than the ultimate end of these services, which is the treatment and care of the sick. Submission to the medical profession and respect for the judgement of its members were once determining factors in professional relationships in the health sector. They have now been replaced by the determination of the auxiliary professions to obtain recognition of their fields of practice. We have gone from submission and respect to claims and negotiated collaboration, a collaboration that could require renegotiation at any time.

26. This section is based on Dussault and Potvin (1983).

27. It was very difficult for nurses to use the same strategy, because the regulation specifies that they must delegate tasks to nursing assistants.

28. Authors' translation of: "l'intermédiaire obligé entre les médecins et les auxiliaires".

29. When the medical tasks regulations were adopted, the Order of Nurses recommended to its members that they perform only those tasks formally mentioned in the regulations. Today, the Order encourages its members to accept a liberal interpretation of the regulations. As long as the tasks conform to their field of practice, i.e., are legal, there is no reason, according to the Order, why they cannot be performed.

30. Authors' translation of: "un guide, un ensemble de normes de prâtique ou de principés directeurs".

31. The same cannot be said for dentists. The task delegation regulations seem to have reduced the influence they enjoyed over the auxiliary professions in their sector, and they are now faced with higher competition for their services. The professions concerned were unable to reach an agreement with regard to the delegation of dental tasks and the regulation adopted in May 1982 was passed by decree following a proposal submitted by the Office des Professions. This decree allowed dental hygienists to increase their real autonomy of practice while dentists saw their field of practice reduced. However, the matter is not completely settled yet in this sector. The Order of Dentists and the Dental Surgeons Association are contesting this by-law. The Order has also instituted a petition for a declaratory judgement to be rendered on the right of the Office des Professions to make substantial amendments to a regulation proposal drafted by a professional corporation (on this subject, see Dussault and Potvin, 1983).

References

Barber, B. "Some Problems in the Sociology of Professions". In K.S. Lynn, ed., *The Professions in America*. Edited by Kenneth S. Lynn. Boston: Houghton Mifflin, 1965, pp. 15-35.

Bates, B. "Physician and Nurse Practitioner: Conflict and Reward", *Annals of Internal Medicine*, 82, 5, May 1975, pp. 702-706.

Bohnen, L. "The Sociology of the Professions in Canada". In *Four Aspects of Professionalism*. Ottawa: Consumer Research Council Canada, 1977, pp. 1-36.

Borland, B.L., F.E. Williams and D. Taylor. "A Summary of Attitudes of Physicians on Proper Use of Physicians' Assistants", *Health Service Reports*, 87, 1972, p. 467.

Breslau, N. and A.H. Novack. "Public Attitudes Toward Some Changes in the Division of Labor in Medicine", *Medical Care*, 17, 8, August 1979, pp. 859-867.

Breslau, N., G. Wolf and A.H. Novack. "Correlates of Physicians' Task Delegation in Primary Care", *Journal of Health and Social Behavior*, 19, 12, December 1978, pp. 374-384.

Burkett, G.L., M. Parken-Harris, J.C. Kuhn and G.H. Escovitz. "A Comparative Study of Physicians' and Nurses' Conceptions of the Role of the Nurse Practitioner", *American Journal of Public Health*, 68, 11, November 1978, pp. 1090-1095.

Canada. Health and Welfare Canada. *National Health Expenditures in Canada, 1970-1982*. Ottawa: Policy, Planning and Information Branch, Information Dissemination Unit, 1984.

Carr-Saunders, A.M. and P.A. Wilson. *The Professions*. Oxford: Clarendon Press, 1933.

Cassels Record, J. and M.R. Greenlick. "New Health Professionals and the Physician Role: An Hypothesis from Kaiser Experience", *Public Health Reports*, 90, 3, May-June 1975, pp. 241-246.

Cassels Record, J., M. McCally, R.H. Blomquist, B.D. Berger and M.A. McCabe. *Staffing Primary Care in 1990: Physician Replacement and Cost Savings*. New York: Springer, 1981.

Cassels Record, J., M. McCally, S.O. Schweitzer, R.M. Blomquist and B.D. Berger. "New Health Professions After a Decade and a Half: Delegation, Productivity and Costs in Primary Care", *Journal of Health Politics, Policy and Law*, 5, 3, Fall 1980, pp. 470-495.

Celentano, D.D. "New Health Professional Practice Patterns", *Medical Care*, 16, 10, October 1978, pp. 837-849.

Chambers, L.W., P. Bruce-Lockhart, D.P. Black, E. Sampson and M. Burke. "A Controlled Trial of the Impact of the Family Practice Nurse on Volume, Quality and Cost of Rural Health Services", *Medical Care*, 15, 12, December 1977, pp. 971-981.

Commission of Inquiry on Health and Social Welfare. *Report of the Commission of Inquiry on Health and Social Welfare, Part Two*. Government of Quebec, Quebec, 1970.
a) Volume IV, tome II, Second Title: The Health Plan, p. 30.
b) Volume IV, tome IV, Third Title: Resources, p. 69.

Contandriopoulos, A.P. *Un modèle de prévision de la main-d'oeuvre médicale*. Rapport final, programme national de recherche et développement en matière de santé, (605-21-48), Université de Montréal, Montréal, 1976, p. 261.

Contandriopoulos, A.P. and M.A. Fournier. *Compensation of Physicians in Quebec, Canada*. Groupe de recherche interdisciplinaire en santé, Université de Montréal, Montréal, 1983.

Contandriopoulos, A.P. and M.A. Fournier. *Les services médicaux au Québec.* Groupe de recherche interdisciplinaire en santé, Université de Montréal, Montréal, 1983.

Corporation Professionnelle des Physiothérapeutes du Québec. *Mémoire de la Corporation professionnelle des physiothérapeutes du Québec présenté a l'Office des professions du Québec concernant le projet de délégation d'actes médicaux aux techniciens en réadaptation physique par les médecins.* Montréal, 1984.

Denton, F.T., A. Gafni, B.G. Spencer and G.L. Stoddart. "Potential Savings from the Adoption of Nurse-Practitioner Technology in the Canadian Health Care System", *Socio-Economic Planning Sciences*, 17, 4, 1983, pp. 199-209.

Donabedian, A. *Explorations in Quality Assessment and Monitoring: Volume I The Definition of Quality and Approaches to its Assessment.* Ann Arbor: Health Administration Press, 1980.

Dussault, G. and L. Potvin. *L'Etat et la divison du travail sanitaire: la politique de délégation des actes médicaux, infirmiers et dentaires au Québec.* Département des relations industrielles, Faculté des sciences sociales, Université Laval, Québec, 1983.

Ehrenreich, B. and J. Ehrenreich. "Hospital Workers: Class Conflicts in the Making", *International Journal of Health Services*, 5, 1, 1975, pp. 43-51.

Elliot, P. *The Sociology of the Professions*, London: MacMillan, 1972.

Evans, R.G. "Does Canada have too many doctors? — Why nobody loves an immigrant physician", *Canadian Public Policy*, 2, 2, Spring 1976.

Evans, R.G. and M.F. Williamson. *Extending Canadian Health Insurance: Options for Pharmacare and Denticare.* Toronto: University of Toronto Press, 1978, esp. Ch. 6.

Fottler, M.D. "Physician Attitudes Toward Physician Extenders: A Comparison of Nurse Practitioners and Physician Assistants", *Medical Care*, 17, 5, May 1979, pp. 536-549.

Fottler, M.D., G. Gibson and D.M. Pinchoff. "Physician Attitudes Toward Nurse Practitioners", *Journal of Health and Social Behaviour*, 19, 9, September 1978, pp. 303-311.

Freidson, E. "The Division of Labour as Social Interaction", *Social Problems*, 23, 3, 1976, pp. 304-313.

Freidson, E. *Profession of Medicine. A Study of the Sociology of Applied Knowledge.* New York: Harper and Row, 1970.

Gaudreau, R. "L'exercice illégal des professions et l'usurpation de titres réservés", *Revue générale de droit*, 14, 1983, pp. 45-92.

Goldberg, G.A., D.M. Jolly, S. Hosek and D.S.C. Chu. "Physician's Extenders' Performance in Air Force Clinics", *Medical Care*, 19, 9, September 1981, pp. 951-965.

Greenwood, J.G., R.F. Hill, T.R. Godkins and W.D. Stanhope. "Physician Assistants: Job Descriptions and Practice", *Inquiry*, 17, Summer 1980, pp. 137-144.

Hadley, J. "Research on Health Manpower Productivity: A General Overview". In Rafferty, J., ed., *Health Manpower and Productivity*. Lexington: D.C. Heath, 1974, pp. 143-204.

Haug, M. "The Professionalization of Everyone?", *Sociological Focus*, 8, 3, 1975, pp. 177-213.

Johnson, T.J. *Professions and Power*, 2nd ed. London: MacMillan, 1977.

Kehrer, B.H. and H.W. Zaretsky. "A Preliminary Analysis of Allied Health Personnel in Primary Medical Practice". Working Paper, Center for Health Services Research and Development, AMA, Chicago, 1972.

Kimbell, L.J. and J.H. Lorant. "Production Functions for Physicians' Services". Working Paper submitted by Human Resources Research Center to Economic Analysis Branch, NCHSRD, HSMHA, DHEW, under Contract No. HSM 110-70-354, December 1972.

Larose, O. "Règlement d'autorisation des actes infirmiers et des actes médicaux", *Nursing Québec*, 3, 2, Janvier-Février 1983, pp. 22-23.

Lawrence, D. "Physician Assistants & Nurse Practitioners: Their Impact on Health Care, Access, Costs and Quality", *Health & Medical Services Review*, 15, 4, April 1977, pp. 298-310.

Lawrence, R.S., G.H. DeFriese, S.M. Putnam, C.G. Pickard, A.B. Cyr and S.W. Whiteside. "Physician Receptivity to Nurse Practitioners: A Study of Correlates of the Delegation of Clinical Responsibility", *Medical Care*, 15, 4, April 1977, pp. 298-310.

Mauksch, H.O. "The Organizational Context of Nursing Practice". In F. Davis, ed., *The Nursing Profession: Five Sociological Essays*, 2nd ed. New York: John Wiley, 1967, pp. 107-137.

Mauksch, T. "The Nurse Practitioner Movement — Where Does It Go From Here?", *American Journal of Public Health*, 68, 11, November 1978, pp. 1074-1075.

Ministry of Social Affairs, Service de l'évaluation des programmes de santé, Série Etudes et Analyses. "Comparaison Québec-Ontario Evolution des Dépenses de Santé pour les soins en établissements, 1978-1979 à 1982-1983", juillet 1984.

Moore, W.E. *The Professions: Roles and Rules.* New York: Russell Sage, 1970.

Office des Professions du Québec. *L'évolution du professionalisme au Québec.* Québec: 1976.

Parker, A.J. and J.C. Delahunt. "Tasks for the Physician's Assistant: Reactions of Urban Physicians", *Dallas Medical Journal,* 49, 1972, p. 281.

Quebec Health Insurance Board. "Statistiques Annuelles 1983". Quebec: 1983.

Rabin, D.L. and K.K. Spector. "Delegation Potential of Primary Care Visits by Physicians' Assistants, Medex and Primex", *Medical Care,* 18, 11, November 1980, pp. 1115-1126.

Reeder, L.G. "The Patient Client as a Consumer: Some Observations on the Changing Professional-Client Relationship", *Journal of Health and Social Behavior,* 13, 4, 1972, pp. 406-411.

Reinhardt, U.E. *Physician Productivity and the Demand for Health Manpower.* Cambridge: Ballinger, 1975.

Reinhardt, U.E. and K.R. Smith. "Manpower Substitution in Ambulatory Care". In Rafferty J., ed., *Health Manpower and Productivity.* Lexington: D.C. Heath, 1974, pp. 3-38.

Reverby, S. "The Emergence of Hospital Nursing", *Health/PAC Bulletin,* No. 66, 1975, pp. 7-16.

Reverby, S. "The Search for the Hospital Yardstick: Nursing and the Rationalization of Hospital Work". In S. Reverby and D. Rosner, eds., *Health Care in America: Essays in Social History.* Philadelphia: Temple University Press, 1979, pp. 206-225.

Sackett, D.L., W.O. Spitzer, M. Gent and R.S. Roberts. "The Burlington Randomized Trial of the Nurse Practitioner: Health Outcomes of Patients", *Annals of Internal Medicine,* 80, 2, February 1974, pp. 137-142.

Sarfatti-Larson, M. *The Rise of Professionalism. A Sociological Analysis.* Berkeley: University of California Press, 1977.

Scheffler, R.M., J.D. Weilsfeld, G. Ruby and E.H. Estes. "A Manpower Policy for Primary Health Care", *New England Journal of Medicine,* 298, 19, May 11, 1978, pp. 1058-1062.

Scheffler, R.M., S.G. Yoder, N. Weilfeld and Ruby, G. "Physicians and New Health Practitioners: Issues for the 1980s", *Inquiry,* 16, 3, September 1979, pp. 195-229.

Schneider, D.P. and W.J. Foley. "A Systems Analysis of the Impact of Physician Extenders on Medical Cost and Manpower Requirements", *Medical Care,* 15, 4, April 1977, pp. 277-297.

Sox, H.C. "Quality of Patient Care by Nurse Practitioners and Physician's Assistants: A Ten Year Perspective", *Annals of Internal Medicine*, 91, 3, September 1979, pp. 459-468.

Spitzer, W.O. "The Nurse Practitioner Revisited: Slow Death of a Good Idea", *New England Journal of Medicine*, 310, 16, April 19, 1984, pp. 1049-1051.

Spitzer, W.O., J.R. Gilbert and D.J. Kergin. "The Nurse Practitioner in North America: From Concept to Reality", *International Journal of Dermatology*, 14, 3, April 1975, pp. 214-219.

Spitzer, W.O. and D.J. Kergin. "Nurse Practitioners in Primary Care I. The McMaster University Educational Program", *Canadian Medical Association Journal*, 108, April 21, 1973, pp. 991-995.

Spitzer, W.O., R.S. Roberts and T. Delmore. "Nurse Practitioners in Primary Care VI. Assessment of their Deployment with the Utilization and Financial Index", *Canadian Medical Association Journal*, 114, June 19, 1976, pp. 1103-1108.

Spitzer, W.O., D.L. Sackett, J.D. Sibley, R.S. Roberts, M. Gent, D.J. Kergin, B.G. Hackett and A. Olynich. "The Burlington Randomized Trial of the Nurse Practitioner", *New England Journal of Medicine*, 290, 5, January 31, 1974, pp. 251-256.

Storms, D.M. and J.G. Fox. "The Public's View of Physician's Assistant and Nurse Practitioner: A Survey of Baltimore Urban Residents", *Medical Care*, 17, 5, May 1979, pp. 526-535.

Strauss, A. "The Structure and Ideology of American Nursing: An Interpretation". In F. Davis, ed., *The Nursing Profession: Five Sociological Essays*, 2nd ed. New York: John Wiley, 1967, pp. 60-108.

Trottier, L.-H. *Evolution de la profession infirmière au Québec de 1920 à 1980*. Mémoire de maîtrise, Département de sociologie, Université de Montréal, Montréal, 1982.

Vuori, H. "Optimal and Logical Quality: Two Neglected Aspects of the Quality of Health Services", *Medical Care*, 18, 10, October 1980, pp. 975-985.

Weston, J.L. "Distribution of Nurse Practitioners and Physician Assistants: Implications of Legal Constraints and Reimbursement", *Public Health Reports*, 95, 3, May-June 1980, pp. 253-258.

Wolinsky, F.D. *The Sociology of Health. Principles, Professions and Issues*. Boston, Little, Brown, 1980.

Yankauer, A. and J. Sullivan. "The New Health Professionals: Three Examples", *Annual Review of Public Health*, 3, 1982, pp. 249-276.

COMMENTARY

René Dussault

When addressing the issue of health manpower, I cannot help thinking that we are in the same position as nineteenth-century fishermen who had to answer this very basic question: "How do you weigh a whale?" And I am afraid we are in no better position today than was the wittiest of them, whose answer simply was, "You bring it to the whale weigh station". Of course, while we are aware that there are many power stations around, we know that there is no such thing as a manpower station where our multi-faceted health care beast could be brought and trimmed so as to meet future health care needs efficiently.

I will concentrate my comments on the regulatory aspects of a manpower policy, and specifically on the part of the paper by Contandriopoulos *et al.* that deals with the failure until now in Quebec to reorganize professional work through professional regulations.

It is true that when we attempted an overall reform of the professions in 1973, in particular through the enactment of the Professional Code, better known as Bill 250, we tried to "give life" to two birds with one stone!

First we clearly established the protection of the public as the main reason for the legal recognition of professions and as the main goal to be pursued by the various self-governing bodies. Second, we tried to use professional regulations to rationalize professional work. While we have succeeded reasonably well on the first count, to date we have failed on the second.

In this respect, I should note that the reform was mainly triggered by the problems encountered in the health sector, although it encompassed all the professions. This explains why twenty out of the thirty-eight groups recognized as "professions" in the Professional Code are directly involved in the health sector. In fact, nine of the twenty received their first legal recognition in the Professional Code. Some of these "new professions" were given an exclusive right to practise: chiropractors, denturologists, podiatrists, hearing aid acousticians. Others were given a reserved title only: physiotherapists, occupational therapists, nursing assistants, dental hygienists, medical technologists.

Although the recognition of these nine new health professions was justifiably based on the principle of protection of the public and in some instances brought a beneficial truce to inter-professional conflicts, it did not reduce the complexity of the regulation of health manpower. It did, however, end two long battles in particular: one between the medical profession and the chiropractors, and the other between dentists and dental technicians, now called denturologists because of their expanded functions. Furthermore, in these cases the official recognition of the two emerging professions cut into the powers of the two major traditional ones.

Our attempt to rationalize professional work through professional regulations met with less success when we tried to implement four other principles.

The first was that no professional group should be under the control of another, at least in terms of professional status. We therefore had to recognize distinct professions for the dental hygienists, podiatrists and hearing aid acousticians, who otherwise might have been placed under the control of parent professions (medical doctors and dentists).

The second principle was that autonomy in terms of professional status should not always mean total autonomy in terms of professional practice. We therefore retained, by law, functional links between the members of different professions in their day-to-day practice. The prescription mechanism caused no great problem because of the tradition behind it (medical doctor vs. dispensing opticians or pharmacists; dentist vs. dental technicians). It was a different matter altogether, however, to allow the public direct access to two different and autonomous professions, but to require patients to obtain a certificate from a member of one profession in order to consult a member of another.

It did not work! For example, one law specified that "no denturologist may perform the taking of impressions and occlusions, the trying, fitting, adjusting, replacement or sale of removable dental prostheses to replace natural dentition, unless he is shown a dental health certificate issued by a dentist during the preceding year". This has remained a dead provision, however, and has proved unenforceable. This failure seems certain to be repeated in Quebec where a draft regulation concerning the practice of acupuncture by non-medical personnel requires the same kind of certificate, provided in this case by physicians.

The third principle was that for each profession recognized by law, an introduction should be given in the law as to which professional activities a member might engage in. Therefore, where the law previously provided a general definition of the scope or field of practice only for those professions with an exclusive right to practise, the Professional Code also provided such a definition for the seventeen professions with only a reserve of title. In these cases, of course, there was no closed field of practice and the definition was explanatory only.

We viewed this approach as an improvement over the old one in which, for example, a nursing assistant was defined in a circular way to be a member of the self-governing body of nursing assistants. Now the Professional Code states that a nursing assistant may, in addition to the specific activities he or she is allowed to engage in by law, "provide the nursing care required for the treatment of the sick".

The approach has its drawbacks, however, and has forced us to put into the Nurses Act a definition of their exclusive field of practice that is distinct from that of both the medical profession and the nursing assistants. Although this was a "first" in North America, it made it more difficult to implement the fourth principle, which dealt with the application of the mechanism for the delegation of professional tasks or acts.

The fourth principle, specifically, was that the major health professions were required by law to authorize, through regulations, certain classes of people other than their members to execute certain tasks traditionally reserved for the major professions. The objectives were to give some flexibility to the exclusive fields of practice and to legalize *de facto* situations. Provision was made for the Quebec Professions Board, a general supervisory body with responsibility for monitoring the whole reform, to step in and enact the regulation in cases in which the major professions failed to act.

As originally conceived, this mechanism for the delegation of acts was intended to allow physicians or dentists, for example, to delegate acts that were clearly within their field of practice as defined by the Medical Act or the Dental Act. The immediate goal was to legalize *de facto* situations (e.g., intravenous injections by nurses). The ultimate goal was to allow, under certain conditions, nurses to become nurse practitioners and dental hygienists to become dental nurses.

Ten years later, we must acknowledge that we have failed on both counts. The Professions Board did not dare use its sweeping powers, nor was it pushed to do so by the Social Affairs Minister, who had to negotiate schedules of fees with the representative bodies of these two professions. Furthermore we have witnessed a definite shift, if not a complete deviation, from the original goal, since the beginning of the application of this regulatory mechanism.

Led by the physicians, groups responsible for the adoption of a regulation for the delegation of acts have all profited from the opportunity by attempting to define their respective fields of practice in a more precise, detailed and exhaustive fashion. Indeed, instead of limiting themselves to important acts requiring substantive medical or nursing skills, physicians and nurses, for example, concentrated on delegating acts that were not within their exclusive fields of practice even prior to the passage of the code. The latest example of this is the proposal by physicians to "delegate" to rehabilitation technicians acts that those technicians may currently perform.

A return to the spirit and letter of the Professional Code concerning the delegation of acts would require that physicians be allowed to delegate only those acts already clearly within their field of practice as described in the Medical Act. Where there is doubt concerning the purely medical and exclusive nature of an act, it is better to disallow delegation of that act. To do otherwise would allow physicians to resolve litigious cases in their favour and to extend without justification the scope of their exclusive field through the adoption of regulations for the delegation of acts. Indeed, that an act must be delegated in order to allow another group to execute it presupposes that it belongs clearly to the exclusive field of practice of the delegating group. The adoption of such a restrictive criterion in the application of this regulatory mechanism would have two advantages. It would realign the mechanism with its original purpose — a greater flexibility in exclusive fields of practice — while avoiding the extension of the boundaries of exclusive practice.

It should be noted that a recent application of this fourth principle has resulted in the recognition of respiratory technicians as a profession with reserved title under the Professional Code.

In conclusion, the Quebec experience demonstrates the difficulties associated with a regulatory approach to the rationalization of professional work. The strength of the major professions often makes regulatory action more harmful than useful. The alternative approach involving the negotiation of collective agreements with professional associations or syndicates seeking to protect their "rights", however, may not be any less difficult.

COMMENTARY

Pierre Bergeron

The benefits expected from the introduction of physician assistants or nurse practitioners and their impact on the nature, accessibility and costs of primary health care services have been outlined and discussed in detail by Contandriopoulos *et al.* It could be, however, that the introduction of less intensively (and expensively) trained personnel is a good idea that has some drawbacks.[1]

First, it would create a new group of health professionals. The existence of numerous professional groups and specializations in the health care field already causes problems in the allocation of tasks and the assignment of responsibilities. It also generates inter-group rivalries. The addition of yet another professional group will not improve this situation.

Moreover, we must remember that productivity gains are greater in large group practice settings. Solo practice settings offer little or no opportunity for such gains. Because group practice is mostly an urban phenomenon, the effective use of nurse practitioners by physicians is unlikely to reduce the accessibility gap between urban and rural regions.

In order for productivity gains to improve accessibility in peripheral areas, therefore, it would be necessary to integrate new, formally autonomous professionals into organizational settings, such as Quebec's community services centres (CLSCs). For the present, such arrangements exist only in very isolated areas, far away from significant population centres. We must bear in mind that any broadening of this approach would be deemed by many as the creation of "two-class" medicine: physicians in urban and semi-urban areas and nurses elsewhere.

All this strikes me as rather futile, however, since the prospect of introducing nurse practitioners into the Canadian health care system is as good as dead. The sad fact is that as soon as we move away from the rational consideration of the benefits resulting from their introduction and recognize the current distribution of power in the health care system, we must realize, as Spitzer has recently concluded,[2] that there is no room for nurse practitioners. Currently there is an oversupply of physicians. Decelerating growth in the stock of physicians and then reducing that stock for the purpose of introducing a substitute professional seems unrealistic. In this context, the "good idea" of introducing nurse practitioners into the Canadian health system was almost certainly doomed to fail.

It is a significant failure. There are, of course, other ways to improve the quality and accessibility of primary health care services, and other ways to save money. But the failure of the nurse practitioner movement means that a large part of primary health care will continue to be dispensed by over-paid and over-trained professionals.

This not only restricts the efficiency of our health system but may also lead some physicians to restrict themselves to routine practices, thereby diminishing their ability to perform more difficult medical interventions.

The causes of the failure to bring these practitioners onstream are of the utmost importance. In my opinion, this failure is the result of the distribution of power in the health care system. If those holding power are in fact systematically resisting a more efficient use of manpower, then our ability to achieve broader system goals relating to quality and access as well as efficiency is called into question.

The power of professional groups is manifest in such things as the reimbursement for their services by health insurance boards, legal standing and prerogatives, authority to prescribe drugs, access to hospital and other institutional resources, immunity from competition and the consequences of surplus labour, level of income, political clout and, finally, their ability to exclude consumers from debates concerning their members. As a rule, most attributes of this power are associated with the state of knowledge and the social, economic and political context. However, some have been enshrined into laws or have been implied by past political decisions on the intervention of the state in matters of health. These laws and decisions bear the stamp of the state of knowledge and of the political context of the time at which they were voted in or taken. They also restrict the ability of the system to adapt to current and future values and constraints.

The introduction of public health insurance in Quebec is a good illustration of this phenomenon. In the late 1960s, two characteristics of the social and political context were to the advantage of the medical profession. Because accessibility was the primary aim of the implementation of a public, universal health insurance scheme, it was imperative that physicians be attracted into the system. The significance of this was reinforced by the expectation that the lifting of financial barriers would increase the demand for care in a context of sustained population growth. Moreover, reform was not limited only to the health care system but was aimed at the whole domain of social affairs. It would have been politically unwise to provoke resistance to reform. Thus, the basic features and privileges of the then current health care system were maintained. Public health insurance simply changed the source of the third party payment of physicians.

The whole insurance scheme, and the type of relationship with professional groups that it presupposed, was based on the premise that the first interest of physicians was to deliver care of the best possible quality to the public. Because quality control was the exclusive domain of the medical societies, the integration and control of physicians in hospitals were thought to be a matter of gentlemanly cooperation. The provision of medical services was seen as something independent of hospital management. The impact of medical practice on hospital resource use was unknown, or ignored. This view was both illustrated and reinforced by the existence of two distinct federal programs for hospital and medical insurance.

Reflecting the state of knowledge at the time and prompted by optimistic budgetary forecasts, the insurance scheme was an open-ended one, responsive mostly to shifts in demand. It assumed that needs, and services directed toward those needs, were objective and measurable entities. Demand was viewed as a function of need and was assumed to determine the level of services provided. And it was expected that when needs had been met, demand and utilization would level off.

These assumptions have been contradicted by experience which has shown the definition of health and health needs to be rather elastic. The demand for health services has also been found to vary from society to society according to socio-economic values. Similarly, the level of services required to meet that demand can vary greatly depending on the availability of resources. In the current economic context, the limits to our ability to pay conflict with the inner logic of an open-ended system. The Quebec system has not been characterized by ever-increasing expenditures but this is only because various expenditure control mechanisms have been introduced: stringent controls on hospital budgets, salary restrictions for nurses and other hospital workers and a cap on fee-for-service remuneration of physicians.

Even though many of these short-term adjustments have helped to meet current budgetary constraints, cost control remains basically a matter of cost capping. The true solution lies somewhere else. We must move from a relatively open-ended system to a system that maintains an equilibrium. We must solve the needs/resources equation. Yet many features of our health system are a legacy of the late 1960s and work against the achievement of that equilibrium. For example, in the 1970s Quebec's population grew very slowly while the number of new physicians increased to the point of surplus, and this happened without producing either physician unemployment or a better geographical distribution of physicians. Further, it is generally agreed that the behaviour of physicians is quite sensitive to the economic incentives of a fee-for-service mode of remuneration, and that physicians may provide services for motives beyond that of clinical benefit to their patients.

A better understanding of health risk factors associated with certain lifestyles and with the physical and social environments of individuals has underscored the limited capability of curative medicine to improve the health status of the population. But this does not accord with a system organized around individual curative services. The technological explosion, mostly in diagnostic machines and techniques, has increased the dependence of physicians on the technical resources of hospitals, while the organization of medical practice leaves physician behaviour relatively unaffected by the costs involved.

To achieve a more stable balance, our health system must encourage and make visible several necessary trade-offs: between the citizen's ability to pay and the level of public health expenditures; between health expenditures and expenditures for education or transportation (for example); between medical and hospital services and less intensive services; between wages/salaries and capital expenditures; between professional autonomy and the need to manage groups of professionals in institutional settings; between the individual aims of various establishments and regional complementarity; and between individual and collective interests. A balanced system must link a given pool of resources with the needs and choices of the population to be served and must do so in an equitable and efficient manner.

These are not new ideas. They have been around for years. But our progression toward a balanced system requires adjustments to today's incentives, constraints, limits and powers.

In the case of medical manpower, the "rules" of the system are such that the number of physicians *per capita* continues to increase, even though we have more physicians than needed according to generally accepted norms. These same rules ensure that surplus physicians will not pay a price through personal unemployment, but that society will pay, through additional health expenditures. Moreover, increases in the physician-to-population ratio will stimulate a spillover of physicians' activities into areas peripheral to traditional medical practice. We can already see some spillover in the field of community health. We may see more in the management of health services and nursing activities. At the same time, because health spending will be bounded by society's capacity to pay, the proportion of total health expenditure allocated to the remuneration of physicians will rise, unless their average *per capita* remuneration is sharply reduced.

Could this scenario be changed? Governments could intervene through rules and regulations. For instance, we might place a ceiling on the number of physicians who, for given regions, could be reimbursed by the health insurance board. We would then have to set rules defining who would and who would not be reimbursed, establish procedures to select those who would replace departing or deceased physicians and advocate guidelines governing the buying and selling of what would amount to rights of participation in the health insurance plan. Non-participating physicians could move to another province or country. They could work in another field of activity or be unemployed. More important, they might also push for the development of a privately insured, parallel system of care. The British Columbia government has moved in the direction of restricting billing numbers. It will be very interesting to see the final results of this move.

Because Quebec produces many more physicians than it needs, it seems necessary there to limit the number of students in medical schools. But how many students should be trained? Less than are currently trained, but how many less? And should forecasts of "needed" medical manpower be based on projections reflecting current use of medical services and current medical practice, or should they assume future changes in the organization of health services?

In any case, it seems that nobody is pressuring the government to limit the number of new physicians. Consumers dislike waiting time and waiting in lines; they want easy and immediate access. The medical profession often stresses that shortages of physicians exist in certain specialties. It seldom acknowledges manpower surpluses so long as the average income of physicians is not threatened. Universities decide on the number of medical student admissions according to the number of places they have in their medical schools and will not risk being accused of elitism by further reducing the number of admissions. Finally, the political benefits of acting to restrict admissions will be slow to surface, and are unlikely to be obvious by the end of a four- or five-year electoral mandate. All the actors, therefore, have a convergent interest in favour of inaction. It seems that only catastrophes can shake such a situation. Therefore, it seems important that we make good use of the opportunity provided by budgetary constraints and that we do not wait for a real catastrophe.

Structural sources of balance must be introduced. In my view, allowing for greater consumer voice is a promising avenue. We should be able to reach a point at which public sentiment, because it has grown conscious of the consequence of surplus medical manpower, would force government to restrict the training of new physicians and put a ceiling on the number of physicians who could be reimbursed by the health insurance board.

Such involvement of the population is far beyond the often symbolic participation of lay people on the boards of hospitals, social services agencies and other organizations providing health care. Rather, it is the same kind of involvement sought by those who support the provision of an opportunity for thousands of individual decisions within a framework similar to the Health Maintenance Organizations in the U.S. and by those who favour regionalization with political and budgetary decentralization. Further, this involvement could be stimulated by pressure groups not unlike consumers' rights movements. But this involvement does not in any way mean a return to the free market, the deficiencies of which are well known.

Finally, over the short term, it would be interesting to identify and isolate health expenditures from total public expenditures and to set up a distinct financing mechanism for them. This would make trade-offs more visible, and it would be easier to show the impact of growth in medical manpower. It might even become possible to go beyond conventional bargaining with health professionals, and to place debates over their incomes within the framework of available resources.

The challenge of the coming years will be to ensure that the population acquires an effective right to choose the type and quantity of health services it is willing to pay for, instead of having those decisions resolved by confrontations between the profession and the state. The challenge will be to initiate and support a new dynamic in which the population will be involved, and with sufficient flexibility for the development of new policies promoting effective and efficient health care delivery.

Notes

1. The views presented in this paper are those of the author and not necessarily those of the Department of Social Affairs, Quebec.
2. Spitzer, W.O. "The Nurse Practitioner Revisited: Slow Death of a Good Idea", *New England Journal of Medicine*, 310, 1984, pp. 1049-1051.

V

ORGANIZATION OF DELIVERY

HEALTH SERVICES ORGANIZATION AND DELIVERY: PROMISE AND REALITY

John E.F. Hastings
Eugene Vayda

Introduction

The year 1970 opened with a sense of optimism and promise for the Canadian health care system, although concerns about future cost projections were emerging. Canadians could look back with pride on what had been accomplished in health care services and financing since the end of World War II (Taylor, 1978; Taylor, 1984; LeClair, 1975; Gelber, 1959; Hastings, 1971; Vayda, Evans and Mindell, 1979; Vayda and Deber, 1984). Beginning in 1948, the National Health Grants Program (conditional grants-in-aid to the provinces) had provided a stimulus to the provinces for a wide range of services, such as health planning, public health, hospital construction, laboratory and radiological services, cancer diagnosis and therapy, and the training of public health physicians and nurses. In 1957, the federal Hospital Insurance and Diagnostic Services Act (again using the conditional grant-in-aid approach) opened the way to universal coverage through provincially administered programs for standard ward inpatient hospitalization, emergency services and specified diagnostic services. The Royal Commission on Health Services in its 1964 Report (Canada, *Royal Commission on Health Services*, 1964 and 1965) recommended federal support to the provinces, on a similar basis, for the insurance of physician services and the inclusion, on a phased basis, of a range of other services. The federal Medical Care Act of 1966 came into effect on July 1, 1968, and by early 1971 all provinces had programs in effect.

The Royal Commission also predicted a shortage of physicians and other health professionals and recommended increases in the number of graduates from existing professional schools and the development of new schools. In 1966, the federal Health Resources Fund was established (also on a cost-shared basis) from which the federal government would contribute to approved projects for planning, constructing, and renovating teaching and research facilities for health services personnel.

The Canada Assistance Plan of 1965, which was aimed at consolidating federal contributions to the provinces for public assistance recipients, included financial assistance for any health services a province might decide to provide for beneficiaries beyond benefits already covered under universal programs.

Thus, by 1970, a number of major programs were in place across the country. As a result of the federal-provincial agreements, there was a high degree of comparability in benefit coverage across provinces. Through immigration, large numbers of medical, nursing and other personnel were entering Canada. There was also a marked increase in health personnel graduating from Canadian education and training programs. The acute hospital system had begun to grow earlier. Population growth continued through immigration and natural increase, although the natural increase had slowed dramatically in the mid-1960s and was still slowing. The economy was buoyant. Science and technology offered hope of a more healthful future. The preceding years had also seen the development of a universal pension program, the extension of social assistance benefits, public funding for low cost housing and a broadening of opportunities for young people, in particular through expansion of the post-secondary education system.

An air of optimism pervaded society and it seemed only a matter of time until all health services would be insured or provided as part of comprehensive health and social benefits systems. Canadians faced a more equitable future in which the experiences of deprivation in the dustbowl and depression years of the 1930s would no longer be possible. The atmosphere was captured by the recommendation of the Royal Commission Report "that as a nation we now take the necessary legislative, organizational and financial decisions to make all the fruits of the health sciences available to all our residents without hindrance of any kind . . . . There can be no greater challenge to a free society of free men" (Canada, *Royal Commission on Health Services*, 1964).

But data on trends in costs and expenditures, especially under hospital insurance, had by the end of the 1960s awakened concerns about health care utilization, rising costs and escalating expenditures. In the first half of the 1970s a series of studies and reports made recommendations for immediate cost and expenditure containment. They also recommended more sweeping changes in the ways in which health services were provided in order to improve efficiency and effectiveness in the long term. The studies took place in a context of almost continuous federal-provincial discussions about revision of the federal-provincial cost-sharing arrangements, in particular for the hospital insurance and medical care programs (Van Loon, 1978).

Without increased financial and planning flexibility that would allow them to rationalize services, develop a broader spectrum of services and build in incentives for less costly alternatives to acute hospital care and physicians' services, the provinces saw themselves facing enormous health delivery system and funding problems in the near future. These health care sector concerns coincided in the large provinces of Ontario and Quebec with a growing sense of provincial identity and power. In Quebec, there was the added impetus of the socio-political transformation being brought about in almost every sector of life through the "Quiet Revolution", now no longer quiet as separatist sentiment coalesced into a potent political force. The demand for greater provincial power over constitutionally assigned responsibilities, including health care, and for greater taxing access was not limited to the two central provinces. The emerging new centres of economic and political power, in Alberta and British Columbia, were also pushing for more independence. Even the poorer provinces recognized the need for greater flexibility in shaping their systems. Yet the cost-sharing programs with the steering effect of "50 cent dollars" for acute hospital care and physicians' care made a shift in emphasis difficult. On the other hand, the provinces were also concerned about any change that might reduce the earmarked federal contributions for their programs and remove the equalization component for the poorer provinces in the cost-sharing formula. In short, all the provinces, to a greater or lesser extent, wanted to assume greater responsibility and to free themselves from the high degree of federal control implied by the conditional grant-in-aid approach, but without reduced federal financial contributions.

The federal government recognized the provincial concerns and, moreover, was itself anxious about rising financial demands under the cost-sharing arrangements over which it had little control because of the open-ended reimbursement formula. However, the federal government wanted to retain its financial leverage in order to maintain the nation-wide characteristics of comprehensiveness, universality, public administration and portability in the provincial systems. In the early 1970s the time seemed ripe for change.

In May 1971, the federal government proposed replacement of the shared-cost approach to financing on a post-audit basis with a *per capita* federal grant to the provinces that would be modified annually according to an escalation formula based on changes in the GNP and independent of changes in actual expenditure. So long as agreed national standards were maintained, the federal funds could be used by a province as it saw fit. An equalization component would be included to continue proportionately greater help to the poorer provinces. Significantly, the proposal also included a $30 *per capita* "thrust fund" on a one-time only basis for the provinces to use in re-organizing their health care systems (Van Loon, 1978). Although discussions continued between the federal government and the provinces, no agreement was reached until 1977 when the Established Programs Financing Act (EPF) came into effect (Canada, *Federal-Provincial Fiscal Arrangements* . . ., 1977).

Studies and Reports: Years of Ferment and Promise

Federal Studies

Commissions and studies were undertaken at the federal level and in almost all provinces in the first half of the decade. Arising from proposals in the federal Task Force Reports on the Cost of Health Services (Canada, *Task Force Reports* . . ., 1969), two federally funded studies were established. In 1971 the Nurse Practitioner Study (Canada, *Report of the Committee on Nurse Practitioners*, 1972) recommended support for the development of programs of training for nurse practitioners. Two types were foreseen: those who would serve as physician extenders generally and those who would work as physician alternatives in the North and in rural areas where it was difficult to attract full-time doctors. The 1974 Report of the Burlington, Ontario Nurse Practitioner Trial (Spitzer *et al*, 1974; Spitzer, Russell, and Hackett, 1973) confirmed both public acceptance and the utility of nurse practitioners as members of group practice teams, while identifying the need for payment mechanisms that did not reduce the incomes of the physicians in the groups. Otherwise there would be a disincentive to employ nurse practitioners. A number of education and training programs in university faculties of nursing were established, but now only one program, exclusively for the North and remote areas, remains.

Although the concept has been shown to be theoretically and practically applicable, it has foundered on a combination of factors. They include: the opposition of organized medicine to extensive use of nurse practitioners in the light of growing physician numbers; the reluctance of governments to finance personnel who could generate additional services and costs and be largely financial "add-ons"; and even some lack of unanimity among the nursing profession itself about this new group of colleagues (Spitzer, 1984; Lomas and Stoddart, 1982).

The other federally initiated study was the Community Health Centre Project (Canada, *The Community Health Centre in Canada*, 1973), which grew out of concerns at both levels of government over accelerating health care expenditures. There was a growing belief that substantial shifts could be made from acute hospital inpatient care and physicians' care to less costly alternatives, including community health centres. The belief drew on published experience from group practice pre-payment programs, Health Maintenance Organizations (HMOs) and Office of Economic Opportunity health centres in the U.S. But there was also Canadian experience with the Saskatchewan Community Clinics, and the Ontario programs at Sault Ste. Marie (Hastings *et al*, 1970a, 1970b, 1973; Mott, Hastings and Barclay, 1973), and at St. Catharines, founded in the mid-1960s under union sponsorship and based on the group practice pre-payment model. The various reports indicated that these types of programs could achieve reductions of from 15 to 50 percent in inpatient acute hospital admissions (Enthoven, 1980; Luft, 1981) by an emphasis on ambulatory diagnosis and care provided by a team that was composed of a full range of health professionals, not only physicians. These programs with their different patterns of practice and staffing were seen as responding to more than costs. Many emphasized prevention, health promotion, social counselling needs and a broader "people-centred" approach that involved the community served in both policy and management of the program.

The Community Health Centre Project Report made three principal recommendations:

1. The development by the provinces in mutual agreement with public and professional groups of a significant number of community health centres, as described in this Report, as non-profit corporate bodies in a fully integrated health services system.

2. The immediate and purposeful re-organization and integration of all health services into a health services system to ensure basic health services standards for all Canadians and to assure a more economic and effective use of all health care resources.

3. The immediate initiation by provincial governments of dialogue with the health professions and new and existing health services bodies to plan, budget, implement, coordinate and evaluate this system; the facilitation and support of these activities by the federal government through consultation services, funding and country-wide evaluation.

(Canada, *The Community Health Centre in Canada*, 1973)

The climate seemed favourable for implementation since approval in principle was given by the three major federal parties and the three large national professional associations (Canadian Medical Association, Canadian Nurses' Association and Canadian Hospital Association) at an August 1972 joint meeting. The availability of the $30 *per capita* "thrust fund" for innovation in the system as a part of the federal proposals to the provinces for renegotiation of the cost-sharing agreements provided potential capital and development seed money. The need for regionalization of services, coordinating mechanisms, a broader socio-medical care model and greater community participation was widely recognized across Canada. At about the same time a number of provincial commissions, to be outlined shortly, were making similar proposals for reorganization.

The honeymoon was brief (Hastings, 1978). The Canadian Medical Association backed off from its initial support because of the strong negative reaction from provincial medical associations. The latter objected to proposals for alternatives to fee-for-service payment of physicians, system changes aimed at greater planning and co-ordination on a regional basis, enhanced community participation in decision-making, and a greater use of other health and social service professionals. Provincial hospital associations were also lukewarm because of the implication of shifting some of the emphasis from hospitals to the new centres. Hospitals were also anxious about the proposed regional and community systems with public boards as planning, coordinating and, in time, operational agencies and the suggestion of a global budget to encompass all services in a region or community as a means for encouraging variety in delivery modes and trade-offs among services. Subsequently, failure to negotiate cost-sharing agreement changes based on the federal proposals and mounting concerns about a continuing rise in hospital costs led to the dropping of the federal "thrust fund" proposal. Revenue for start-up and capital costs from the federal government was no longer available to the provinces. Equally important was the reluctance to implement a "lock-in" principle for populations served by the centres and to develop incentive mechanisms for "trade-offs" between the various service elements in a region or community, especially between primary care settings and hospitals. Such "trade-offs" are essential to effective planning and to the realization of cost savings on a system-wide basis. As well, some saw community health centres as a form of "socialized medicine" and rejected them on ideological grounds. Thus despite widespread consumer, media, and non-medical and non-dental professional support, relatively few centres have been established outside Quebec. Even in Quebec they provide personal health care only to a relatively small portion of the population. (See the section below on the Organization of Medical Practice and Personal Health Care Services.)

Provincial Studies

A number of provincial studies were also carried out during the early 1970s. The White Paper on Health Policy in Manitoba (Manitoba, *White Paper . . .*, 1972), Health Security for British Columbians (Foulkes, 1973), Health Care in Nova Scotia, "A New Direction for the Seventies" (Nova Scotia, *Health Care . . .*, 1972) and the Report of the Health Planning Task Force in Ontario (Ontario, *Report . . .*, 1974) all recommended extensive restructuring of the health care system in their respective provinces. All discussed the problems in their current systems and recommended a closer integration of health services. The precise recommendations included a varying mix of proposals:

— decentralization of some of the responsibility for services planning and provision to regional and community boards;
— the development of health teams based in ambulatory care centres (variously called community health centres, primary care centres and human resource centres);
— hospitals to be part of a referral system fully integrated with other forms of care;
— greater emphasis on home care and other community-based care;
— the extension of provincial programs to cover personal care benefits not currently included;
— greater government involvement in health manpower planning;
— increased provincial oversight of the health professions;

— the development of an integrated network of laboratory and related diagnostic services;
— improved information, records and referral systems.

Quebec: Study and Restructuring

The most comprehensive study was carried out by the Commission of Inquiry on Health and Social Services in Quebec (Castonguay-Nepveu) which in its 1970-1971 reports recommended a fundamental restructuring of health and social services (Quebec, *Report* . . ., 1970-71). With the subsequent election of Castonguay and his appointment as Minister of Social Affairs, enabling legislation was passed (Quebec, *Law on Health and Social Services*, 1971). As Gosselin has written:

> We were hoping to gradually abandon the traditional closed (medical) model and adopt a more open social model; therefore we chose to focus our efforts on preventive programs as well as on curative programs. And all this would ostensibly be accomplished through intensive involvement of the local people including the communities, health care managers and professionals, citizen groups, associations, and so on. Health would be delivered through a variety of establishments, each one with a specified role and tightly linked to one another, both horizontally and hierarchically. (Gosselin, 1984, p. 8)

With the Ministry of Social Affairs (MSA) at the top of the pyramidal administrative structure, where ultimate and overall responsibility for the system rests, the province is divided into twelve regions, each with a regional Health and Social Service Council (CRSSS). Initially advisory, promotional and facilitating in function, the councils have as their present mandate the provision of region-wide communications, planning (both long-range and programmatic), and consultation. Also included are responsibility for approving renovations and expansion of facilities, and operational budgets. Other functions include establishing links, shared programs and coordinating mechanisms, developing specified services, ensuring cost control and efficiency, and evaluating institutions and programs.

Hospitals and social services are now under public operation. Preventive and public health services have been integrated, in large measure, with the curative system (Casonguay, 1975; Brunet, 1981; Trent, 1984). As in other provinces, the funding of hospitalization and physicians' services for the population is through a government plan.

Regions are divided into sub-regions, each with a Department of Community Health (DSC) located in an acute care hospital (Pineault, 1984). The responsibility of the DSCs is to provide a range of planning services, including studies of health needs, program planning and development, co-ordination among establishments, and program evaluation. As well they carry out epidemiologic studies and

344   John E.F. Hastings & Eugene Vayda

Chart
Quebec's Health System

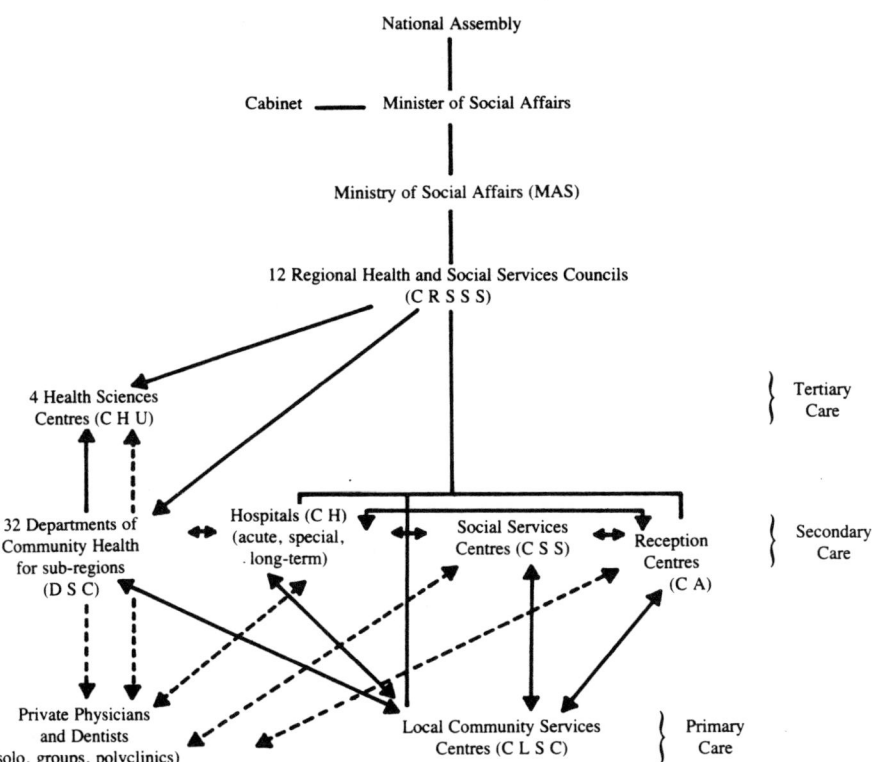

NOTES: Solid lines represent the interrelations among the public components of the system. The broken lines represent the interrelations between the majority of doctors and dentists, who are in forms of private practice, and the components of the public system. It should be noted that they receive payment through the public plan, although they function as independent practitioners.

ensure the availability of occupational health services. Currently most also provide personal preventive services for populations not yet served by new primary level entities, known as Local Community Service Centres (CLSC). The CLSCs provide primary level health and social services, preventive, diagnostic and treatment, and act as the point of referral to the specialized health and social services at the secondary care level of the network.

At the secondary level are the Community Hospitals (CHs) which provide special investigative services and some tertiary level services in addition to secondary care. For tertiary referral care, professional education, specialized planning, consultation and research purposes, the health services are related to the four Health Science Centres (CHUs) in the province. Also at the secondary care level, there are Reception Centres (CAs) which include social service, institutional, and residential facilities and programs, and the Social Service Centres (CSSs) which provide non-institutional social services other than those provided by the CLSCs.

Most physicians are still in private practice, either solo or in groups. In response to the CLSCs, physicians developed polyclinics and group practices, usually made up of general practitioners but sometimes with a mix of general practitioners and specialists. This development has now largely stabilized. The predominant method of payment for doctors continues to be fee-for-service but in the CLSCs is a combination of salary and sessional payments. The present government has indicated its intention to shift to a salaried basis for most physicians in the next few years.

Accomplishments

In the provinces other than Quebec, the accomplishments remain well short of the visions of the various reports. Yet there have been some accomplishments. Regionalization and decentralization of delivery of selected services are accepted concepts in the planning and delivery system, although the precise meaning and extent of implementation are variable from province to province. No province has relinquished financial control and transferred unfettered executive powers to the region or community. In Newfoundland and Labrador, Regional Boards operate hospitals and government clinics under a global budget and it is now proposed to include nursing homes (Newfoundland and Labrador, *Royal Commission on Hospital and Nursing Home Costs*, 1984). New regional planning and advisory bodies appointed by the Minister and known as District Health Councils (DHCs) were introduced in Ontario beginning in 1974 and now cover almost the entire province (Dixon and Kirkland, 1972; Ontario, *Final Report of the Steering Committee for the Developmental Assessment of District Health Councils in Ontario*, 1983). Some other provinces have developed or are considering similar concepts.

The range of services and benefits provided under health insurance has broadened in all provinces, although the extent of benefits varies. The mix now includes full or partial drug benefits (usually for selected categories, such as the aged and the indigent), dental benefits (for example, for children) and home care for the chronically ill. Increasingly, chronic care, nursing home facilities and residential facilities for various groups (for example, the aged and the mentally and physically handicapped) are being fully or partly funded publicly. Nursing home and residential care, and some aspects of home care, are provided in large measure by the private sector, both non-profit and for-profit.

There has been some shift from an institutional focus to ambulatory and community care, in part because of government constraint on hospital budgets and because of a growing sense that institutional care is not optimal care in many instances. But the shift has been limited to date, and the institutional focus of the system remains strong.

Health and social services have been integrated provincially and regionally in Quebec, as noted earlier. Other provinces, such as Manitoba and some years ago New Brunswick, tried forms of political and administrative integration at both levels but later reverted to separate ministries. Recently, however, New Brunswick announced its intention to move again to an integrated health and social service system (Robertson, 1984). Some provinces — Ontario for example — have established social policy secretariats or ministries to facilitate planning and co-ordination among human service ministries, such as health, welfare and education. The best way to promote closer working relationships provincially and regionally still remains elusive.

In most provinces there are a variety of local co-ordinating mechanisms being tried on a voluntary basis among services. For example, in the Halifax region, the Cobequid Multi-Service Centre and system (Stewart, 1982) brings together a range of social and health agencies in a co-operative network. The publicly encouraged CLSCs, and centres in Quebec, Manitoba and British Columbia (Talbot, 1978) incorporate a variety of human services. But even in Quebec the centres cover only a relatively small proportion of the population. In New Brunswick, a single organization has recently been proposed for a broad range of health and social services in specified zones and areas. Over a three-to-five year period local community service management boards would replace the initially proposed advisory boards (Robertson, 1984).

Arising from the Castonguay Report, a provincial board supervising more than forty health and other professions has been established in Quebec. In Ontario, the 1970 Report of the Committee on the Healing Arts (Ontario, *Report . . .*, 1970) led to the addition of public representatives to the governing bodies of the major health professions and to the establishment of an overriding provincial Health Disciplines Board made up entirely of non-professional members of the public.

Other provinces have increased public representation, supervision and accountability for the major health professions.

Most of the federal and provincial reports recommended increased community and consumer participation in policy formulation and decision-making within the system. However, there have been relatively slow changes in the middle and upper class and professional predominance in the membership on provincial and regional advisory bodies, such as the Ontario Council of Health and DHCs, and on local hospital, public health and voluntary agency boards. Even in Quebec, where the new structure mandates the election and naming of some consumers to the various governing bodies, several commentators have noted the relatively weak position of consumer members when compared with health professionals and bureaucrats (Bégin, Bheres and Wallot, 1978; Godbout, 1981; Hastings, 1984). Indeed, one of the phenomena of the decade has been the steady growth in professional qualifications, responsibilities and power of health administrators and bureaucrats (Hastings, *et al.* 1981). Their power is likely to increase as more sophisticated management and information systems are introduced. In contrast to the gradual change in consumer participation on decision-making bodies, consumer-based self-help and advocacy groups and voluntary organizations focused on the needs of patients with particular diseases have increased dramatically in numbers during the past decade.

No account of the 1970s and early 1980s would be complete without reference to the increased interest in health maintenance and promotion, disease prevention and fitness. The major impetus was *A New Perspective on the Health of Canadians* (Lalonde, 1974). This Report formulated the Health Field concept consisting of four broad elements: human biology, environment, lifestyle and health care organization. It gave focus and impetus to the already developing public interest in lifestyle and fitness. There has been interest also among professionals and governments in the identification of risk factors and high risk groups, preventive interventions, health promotion and regulatory strategies. Canada has also been affected by world-wide concerns about the dangers to life and the environment from pollution by human and industrial waste, acid rain and the threat of thermo-nuclear disaster. There is a new recognition of the intimate relation between health in its fullest sense and socio-economic and political policies and actions in society, although there is ambivalence about tackling the socio-economic adjustments that a solution of some of the problems will require. The potential for improved health status embodied by the Lalonde Report is still unrealized. Comprehensive long-term goals and programs in prevention and health promotion are not yet firmly established as major priorities provincially or federally.

Organization of Medical Practice and Personal Health Care Services

Overview

Medical and personal health care services are largely fragmented and uncoordinated. Canada offers few examples where a full range of integrated health services is provided for defined population groups. Ambulatory and hospital services are frequently the responsibility of different physicians; services in emergency departments are provided by yet other physicians who may be hospital employees, individual practitioners or members of organized groups. Occupational health and public health are separate from each other and from personal health care, except to some extent in Quebec where the DSC has overall responsibility to see that occupational health services are available and may itself provide these for industries without their own services (Pineault, 1984). Specialization, a natural result of increasing technology, has also contributed to the fragmentation of patient care. Fragmentation has persisted despite repeated exhortations for coordination.

Although recent data are scanty, it seems clear that the predominant pattern of medical practice in Canada is still solo practice. A recent survey of physician attitudes in five provinces found that, on average, 50 percent of doctors were in solo practice, ranging from 43 percent in Quebec to 57 percent in Ontario (Taylor, Stevenson and Williams, 1984), although there is some evidence that younger physicians are moving to group practice. In solo practice each physician has an independent practice and office, although many solo practitioners work in medical arts buildings. Some solo physicians are located in ambulatory care units in or adjacent to hospitals. Most have admitting privileges at one or more hospitals and have established referral patterns based on their hospital appointments and/or their office locations. To provide round-the-clock coverage, some have arranged sharing of night, weekend and vacation coverage with other colleagues. As a result, solo practice describes business and billing arrangements, not necessarily the way in which patient care is provided. Despite the obvious interdependence of practitioners, more formal organizations have been slow to develop.

Physicians may share office space and office personnel. Such sharing may be informal or it may be formalized by partnerships or other contractual arrangements. Some physicians employ other physicians. With the post-World War II growth of medical faculties and the concomitant increase in the numbers of "full-time" clinicians, hospital and university-based groups have been developed, but their financial and contractual arrangements are extremely varied. Many teaching hospitals and some community hospitals have outpatient clinics. Before universal insurance these clinics primarily served indigent populations; now they can and do serve more representative population groups.

Some family practice training programs have incorporated hospital-based groups of family physicians as training sites. Although their primary mission is education, patient care has been a key part of their work.

More formal organizations include group practice, the Quebec polyclinics, team practice and community health centre practice. Group practice is usually defined as three or more physicians working together with shared records and an agreed on mechanism for income distribution. Groups may consist of single specialties such as anaesthesia or radiology, or multiple specialties with or without general or family practitioners. Groups employ nurses and other health professionals. Team practice implies the inclusion of other non-physician health professionals as colleagues, a status that is hard to reconcile with an employer-employee relationship. Ideally, team practices operate in health centres; a community health centre implies a health care team that serves a defined population group.

The 1972 Report of the Community Health Centre Project to the federal Health Minister defined a community health centre as

> a facility or intimately linked group of facilities, enabling individuals and families to obtain initial and continuing health care of high quality. Such care must be provided in an acceptable manner through a team of health professional and other personnel working in an accessible and well-managed setting. The community health centre must form part of a responsive and accountable health care system. In turn the health services must be closely and effectively co-ordinated with the social and related services to help individuals, families, and communities deal with the many sided problems of living. (Canada, *The Community Health Centre in Canada*, 1973)

Ontario in 1982 added global funding in lieu of fee-for-service payment to its community health centre definition, following the example set by Saskatchewan in 1972. Physicians in Ontario were also offered the opportunity to organize themselves into Health Service Organizations (HSOs) and receive their payment on a capitation basis (Grossman, 1982).

A recent Ontario review of organized health services focused mainly on primary care (Ontario, *Report of the Task Force to Review Primary Care*, 1982). Primary care is important because it is the point of entry, the coordinating apparatus and the gatekeeper. The review, while dealing with primary care, also indicated the need for integrating primary and secondary care; but rather than suggesting more formal structures for integration of levels of care it stated, "When patients are referred to services outside the centre, it is important that the Health Centre be informed and aware of the services provided by the referral group". "Informed and aware" does not assure or imply integration. The Report does speak of the primary care sector within the context of the entire health care system, but no suggestions for integration are made. Any plan that includes only primary care is inadequate because coordination with secondary and tertiary care and other health related services is not an integral part of the system.

The development of organized health care practice in Canada has not been extensive. Group medical practice has been established, primarily, in the past six decades. Initially there was considerable physician opposition to group practice but a survey by the Canadian Medical Association indicated that physician acceptance of group practice was increasing.

Despite some increase in group practice (it now includes in one arrangement or another just under one-half of Canada's practitioners), there has been little growth of multi-specialty group and team practice serving defined and clearly identified population groups. Of the community health clinics that grew out of the 1962 Saskatchewan doctors' strike, only three large ones and a few smaller ones have survived into the 1980s. At least one, in Regina, has had considerable unrest with board and physician turnover (Barer, 1981). Until 1972 the Saskatchewan community health clinics were paid on a fee-for-service basis and medically generated fees were used to pay both physicians and other health centre workers. In 1972 the community health clinics were finally offered global funding instead of fee-for-service.

In Ontario there were two programs that attempted to organize comprehensive health care services for defined population groups on the pre-paid group practice (PPGP) model. The first, in Sault Ste. Marie, began in 1963 amid hope and intense medical opposition. The physicians staffing this program had to be imported from outside the community; it was many years before there was even marginal acceptance of the group practice physicians by the rest of the Sault Ste. Marie doctors (Lomas, 1984). Although this program, after Medicare was introduced, was forced to adopt modifications that have essentially removed it from the PPGP model, it continues as a successful program in which a multi-specialty team of physicians and other health professionals serves a defined and voluntarily enrolled group of residents, now numbering almost one-half of the Sault Ste. Marie population. The program is the responsibility of a community-based board of trustees.

Another PPGP type of program, in St. Catharines, was not so fortunate. It began in 1968, two months before universal medical care insurance was implemented in Ontario. Like the Sault program it was union sponsored (steel workers in the Sault, auto workers in St. Catharines). Physicians were imported into St. Catharines and they, too, encountered professional opposition. Constraints on the St. Catharines program, largely engendered by professional animosity coupled with an inability to enrol a sufficiently large and stable membership, ultimately resulted in the demise of the program in 1979.

Experience of Health Maintenance Organizations and Pre-paid Group Practice in the U.S.

The organization of health care services is essential to improve their coordination and accessibility and to reduce costs or increase insured benefits. The highest degree of organization of medical and health care services on this continent is found in pre-paid group practice in the U.S. While this is included under the Health Maintenance Organization (HMO) rubric, it is quite different from the other HMO category, Independent Practice Associations (IPAs). IPAs are loose organizations (occasionally sponsored by medical societies) that contract with physicians to deliver services from their private offices. PPGP, on the other hand, implies a much tighter organization.

In PPGP, physicians are organized into multi-specialty group practices to provide or arrange a full range of insured services for defined and enrolled populations. Medical groups, such as those associated with the Kaiser-Permanente organization, include virtually all the medical specialties. Smaller and newer programs contract for more highly specialized services but include primary care practitioners and commonly used specialists on a full-time basis. The PPGP medical groups may be independent partnerships or professional organizations that contract with the pre-paid program (group model) or the programs may employ the physicians (staff model). Associated with the PPGP groups are many different types of health professionals, such as nurses, technologists of various kinds, social workers and psychologists. Because payment to the medical group is by salary or capitation, there are incentives to utilize non-physician health professionals to the fullest extent since they are generally less costly than physicians. While PPGP is not exactly the type of team practice envisioned in the Community Health Centre Report, pre-paid programs in the U.S. do use many different non-physician health professionals and the groups operate on a collegial basis. Many programs have community control or at least community input.

PPGP physicians practise together in facilities of varying size. In programs that own hospitals, some ambulatory facilities are located there. When hospitals are not owned, PPGP programs attempt to arrange contracts with limited numbers of hospitals or to arrange hospital privileges for all their physicians in a few hospitals (Yedidia, 1969). For physicians, the advantages of PPGP practice include assured night and vacation coverage, reasonable work schedules, access to consultants, a full practice and a guaranteed income from the first day of practice. Over the years perceived constraints on physician autonomy have come to be outweighed by the advantages of group practice; at the same time, the supply of physicians continues to grow rapidly. In the present U.S. market, recruitment of physicians to PPGP is no longer a problem.

The patients served by these programs are all enrolled members. They pay or have paid on their behalf a monthly premium that entitles them to a full range of primary, secondary and tertiary health care services in health centres, hospitals or their homes. There are no fees for individual services. Enrollees agree (except in emergency situations) to use only the services provided by the program during the period of their enrolment, which is usually one year and may then be renewed or cancelled. Services used outside the program, except for emergency services, are not insured; they must be paid for by the enrollee.

Another key element of PPGP is its organizational structure. In consumer-sponsored PPGP, the board of trustees is elected by the enrolled membership. Programs that are not consumer-sponsored have community representation on their boards. The board and its administrative infrastructure enrols members, owns or contracts with hospitals, employs or contracts with groups of physicians, and has general managerial and fiscal responsibility for the program. PPGP programs in the U.S. operate under enabling state legislation.

With this model, PPGP programs have achieved coordination and integration of health care services with costs substantially less than comparable fee-for-service practice (Luft, 1981; Somers, 1981; McColl, 1966). However, savings are usually not realized in the early years of a program because of the start-up costs involved and because of the time needed to develop efficient operation. Savings have been achieved mainly by reductions in hospitalization, largely through reductions in numbers of admissions of from 20 percent to 50 percent coupled with small reductions in average lengths of stay (Manning *et al.*, 1984; Barer, 1981; Luft, 1981; Somers, 1981). The reduction in numbers of admissions has been due to lower rates for controversial discretionary operations, such as tonsillectomy and hysterectomy, as well as for some acute conditions, such as pneumonia, and greater use of ambulatory surgery (Manning *et al.*, 1984; Vayda, Mindell and Rutkow, 1982). Admissions solely for diagnostic assessments have been virtually eliminated. The Kaiser-Permanente Health Care Program, which owns and operates its own hospitals, averages 1.5 acute care beds per 1,000 enrollees, while the Canadian average is 4 or more. While quality of care is difficult to measure, it is at least as good in PPGP as in community practice (Luft, 1981; Somers, 1981).

Comparable Canadian Models and Experience

The program in Sault Ste. Marie which began in 1963 was closely modelled on PPGP in the U.S. Voluntary enrolment was permitted in Ontario at that time. Although the program was not formally linked with a hospital, there were only two hospitals in the community, located next to each other. The program succeeded, after considerable difficulty, in obtaining admitting privileges for its physicians at both hospitals. The performance of the Sault program, measured in 1967-1968, mirrored PPGP outcomes in the U.S. Hospital discharge rates for the Sault program were 109.5 per 1,000; for Prudential Insurance Plan subscribers in Sault Ste. Marie the rate was 136.4. The average length of stay was slightly less in the Sault program, 8.95 vs. 9.32 for Prudential (Hastings *et al.*, 1970a, 1970b; Mott, Hastings and Barclay, 1973). With the advent of universal medical care insurance in Ontario in 1968, meaningful enrolment was essentially ended since controls on out-of-plan utilization were eliminated. Sault health plan members could go anywhere for their medical services and the Sault program was financially liable for the costs incurred. Although the program was paid an increased capitation amount prospectively in anticipation of decreased hospital use by its members, hospital use by Sault plan members increased once controls on out-of-plan use were lifted. Nonetheless, hospital use remains below that for the other doctors in the community (Vayda, 1977).

It was the same lack of meaningful enrolment and the resulting inability to control out-of-plan use that forced the St. Catharines program to move from capitation payments to a line-by-line budget in 1971, cost reimbursement in 1973 and program dissolution in 1979. The financial survival of the Sault Ste. Marie program was possible only because the program increased its volume of fee-for-service work for non-plan members. After years of uncertainty, the Sault Ste. Marie program benefited in the early 1980s from improvements in its contract with the Ontario Ministry of Health negotiated in 1979. Instead of being financially liable for all costs incurred by members when they used non-plan services, the plan lost only the capitation payment for those months when subscribers used outside services that they could have obtained at the plan's health centre (capitation negation). The Sault program's capitation payment was also adjusted for the age and sex mix of its population and the capitation payment included extra funding for additional services provided by the program (for example, counselling, optometry, physiotherapy, laboratory). Further, incentive payments for reduced hospital use were included under the ambulatory care incentive plan (ACIP) and hospital use was based on the Algoma district, not the provincial average. These changes, coupled with the Ontario Ministry of Health's decision in 1982 to change Health Service Organizations (HSOs) and Community Health Centres (CHCs) from experimental to established programs (Grossman, 1982), have, for the present, solidified the funding foundation for the Sault program and for most of the eighteen HSOs and ten CHCs in Ontario. However, HSOs and CHCs (including the 40,000 or more members in the Sault program) have enrolled only 2 percent of the Ontario population and account for only 2 percent of Ontario expenditures for physician services.

An analysis in 1982 of health centres, variously defined (Kagis, 1982), reported a total of only 159 in Canada, with 112 CLSCs in Quebec where they have been actively promoted, twenty-eight in Ontario and nineteen in the rest of Canada. Quebec has recently indicated its intention to increase the number of CLSCs to about 150. Although national interest in community health centres remains, nowhere, even in Quebec, has large scale regional establishment of significant numbers of community health centres been carried out. This step was recommended in the Report of the Community Health Centre Project as necessary before real evaluation of their system-wide impact on services, costs and organization could be done. Nor, as yet, have there been specific experiments on tying together hospitals and health centres with a global organization and budget in order to see what incentives and "trade-offs" will facilitate shifts in service and utilization to lower cost alternatives.

Constraints in Canada

The organized delivery of health care services has failed to grow and thrive for a number of reasons. These reasons become apparent when the key features of PPGP are re-examined in the Canadian context.

Provider Factors

Although physician acceptance of group practice is growing, there is considerable evidence of the continued opposition of individual physicians and organized medicine to either salary or capitation forms of payment. As well, there is resistance to an employed status for physicians, although in the U.S. that resistance appears to be decreasing under pressure of increasing numbers and the absence of guaranteed reimbursement. Most physicians (and dentists) are, however, still bitterly opposed to being employed by a community-controlled board of directors. They fear a loss of autonomy and ultimately reduced control of both the practice of medicine and their incomes. The Ontario HSO arrangement which entails, essentially, physician-sponsored group practices paid by capitation instead of fee-for-service, may overcome some physician concerns regarding employed status; HSOs do not mandate consumer involvement or input.

Increasing organization and control are also opposed on ideological grounds by a majority of Canadian physicians. Ideological opposition has been defined as "a tendency to take positions consistent with professional self-interest, avoiding or disregarding information that could undermine or qualify those positions" (Taylor, Stevenson and Williams, 1984). Opposition by physicians and their unwillingness to participate in organized programs that are characterized by community involvement and alternative payment mechanisms may prove to be less of a factor over time because of the increasing numbers of physicians, decreasing population to physician ratios, and the resulting competition for financially viable practice locations. To date, however, Canadian physician incomes have been maintained in spite of increasing numbers. Thus there has been little incentive to change modes of practice and payment. The entry of more women into medicine could overcome some ideological opposition because organized practice is also associated with regular working hours and as such is more compatible with family responsibilities.

Physicians are, of course, not the only providers involved. Team practice requires modification of the authoritarian stance of physicians, and other providers, especially nurses, are demanding equal and indeed independent status in patient care (Canadian Nurses' Association, 1984; House of Commons, *Minutes . . . on Bill C-3*, Feb. 19, 1984). The many studies of team practice in the U.S., particularly in relation to Office of Economic Opportunity (OEO) sponsored neighbourhood health centres, have identified major problems when different health professionals work together (Wise *et al.*, 1974). It is not sufficient to house a varied group of health professionals in a single building or program and expect them to function harmoniously and productively. Considerable time, commitment and work is required. For some health professionals, team practice may prove impossible under any circumstances.

Hospitals are another provider group that must be considered. The model of hospital-based or hospital-affiliated comprehensive health care programs is almost unknown in Canada. All hospitals operate emergency departments. Some family practice teaching clinics are located in hospitals, and most teaching hospitals do operate outpatient or ambulatory care facilities, in a few cases outside the hospital. However, to date most hospitals have not seen ambulatory care as a major responsibility. As well, responsibility for the total health care for a community does not come within current hospital terms of reference. Hospitals may view potential relationships with a provider group and an organized community consumer group as possible threats to their autonomy and mission. The comprehensive program would also have concerns, since its power base within the hospital would be small and this could limit its growth and development. Finally, in spite of budget constraints for hospitals, there has been only a limited incentive to change, because in most provinces (except Quebec) annual deficits have been covered by the provincial government.

Individuals with administrative skills necessary to plan and implement comprehensive health care programs are still relatively scarce in Canada. Because of the paucity of such programs, this kind of management has not been seen as a career option (Hastings *et al.*, 1981). However, the graduate education programs for health administrators now include opportunities for acquiring knowledge of and experience in non-hospital settings.

Government Factors

The major problem requiring intervention by provincial governments is enabling legislation to deal with the problem of active enrolment of members or subscribers. The implications of enrolment for the consumer will be considered in the next section. At the heart of PPGP, and HMOs generally, is an enrolled subscriber group which, once enrolled, must obtain all services from the program. Services obtained outside the program become the financial responsibility of the patient. No provincial government has yet been willing to adopt such an enrolment provision because it might be interpreted as depriving individuals of comprehensive coverage "on equal terms and conditions" and thus could conflict with federal requirements for universality. Ontario is now attempting to deal with the problem of enrolment in a limited way by what is called capitation negation (CN). CN is a fiscal arrangement under which the capitation payment is not paid by the province to a program for any month in which an enrollee obtained services from physicians who were not affiliated with the program. As a result the program is at limited financial risk; the government assumes the greatest risk since it must pay the bills incurred and only withholds the capitation payments. The user of services is not at risk in any way. HSOs could abuse CN by encouraging high users of service and sicker patients to use non-plan providers, thus limiting their own costs while losing only the capitation payment. Enrolment might be possible if it were universal and each resident were registered with an individual provider or a grouping of providers. This is the current arrangement in England and the basis for a plan proposed by Enthoven in the U.S. as "consumer choice", and by Stoddart for Canada. Without meaningful enrolment, program planning is extremely difficult. Without limits on out-of-plan use, planning of facilities and staff is meaningless. The issue of enrolment or definition of population served must be resolved if comprehensive population-based programs are to operate in a cost-effective and economic way.

Enrolment also raises the issues of advertising and marketing. Presently, in Ontario, patients can only "sign up" for the programs in clinic offices, usually at the point of service. In PPGP and HMOs generally, competing programs are offered to groups of consumers who may periodically enrol or disenrol and join other programs. There are no limitations on the description of competing programs to potential enrollees, and enrolment outside medical offices is allowed. In Canada, bans on advertising by provincial Colleges of Physicians and Surgeons make program description a potential ground for professional misconduct charges against associated physicians, and loss of medical licensure. Enabling legislation must allow for program description and enrolment in the community and the workplace as well as the clinic offices.

Health centres and related programs are based on different staffing patterns and uses of personnel. Inhibitory regulations constraining the substitution of lower for higher cost personnel remain in many provinces, although some, such as Quebec, have eliminated certain constraints.

Finally, comprehensive programs cannot begin without planning and without capital and start-up funds. Planning is necessary to identify areas and population groups in which a market and a need for comprehensive services exists. It is essentially market research. Without such planning, programs could be started in locations where there was no need or demand. The facilities in which programs are housed must reflect functional planning, or program goals cannot be achieved. New centres will be needed, or existing structures (such as sections of hospitals) will require remodelling. The Report of the Community Health Centre Project recommended capital and start-up funding, but this failed to materialize because the offer of federal "thrust fund" monies was withdrawn when federal-provincial funding negotiations collapsed. The Fiscal Arrangements and Established Programs Act of 1977, which restructured federal funding for the cost-shared programs, made no provision for funding for health centre programs. Neither has the issue of start-up money for community health centres been addressed in the new Canada Health Act of 1984 (Vayda and Hastings, 1984; House of Commons, *Minutes . . . on Bill C-3*, Feb. 14, 1984). It should be noted that in the U.S. more than $360 million was made available over a ten-year period to stimulate HMO development, of which about $145 million was in grants and the remainder in loans and loan guarantees. Ten percent of that amount in Canada (0.1 percent of annual health care spending for ten years) would assure start-up funds for a health centre program large enough to have an impact on the system. However, in the present climate of cost containment, funds for planning and development for new delivery approaches have been difficult or impossible to obtain. Although provincial budgets for health care have increased in real terms, the new monies have been used to pay for the existing system. Except in Quebec, almost none have been made available for developing new comprehensive programs, even though such programs have the potential for long-term cost savings. Governments and their bureaucracies have been reluctant to appear to be actively promoting changes opposed by major provider interests. One solution could be to develop an agency similar to the federal Central Mortgage and Housing Corporation and the provincial housing authorities, to provide low interest capital and start-up funds for alternative delivery programs.

Consumer Factors

Except in the past decade in Quebec, and to a limited degree in British Columbia, Manitoba, Saskatchewan and Ontario, consumers have not played a significant role in the organization and delivery of their personal health care services (Hastings, 1984). Public education and the generation of public interest would be essential for any widespread growth. For consumers to relinquish their rights to unlimited and unrestricted free choice, inducements and incentives would also be necessary. Major incentives would be the elimination of additional patient charges, comprehensive and co-ordinated care ("one-stop" health care) including a range of supporting professional services such as social work, nutrition, counselling and physiotherapy, and ultimately increased benefits, such as dental care, which could be generated from cost savings resulting from greater efficiency of operations.

Conclusions

Provider attitudes and beliefs, lack of government support, lack of enabling legislation for enrolment and advertising, lack of capital and start-up funding especially for consumer-sponsored programs, and cost constraints associated with an ailing economy — all these have contributed to the lack of growth of comprehensive community-based programs in Canada. Quebec, in this decade, has been the exception, yet even in Quebec the development of the professionally encouraged polyclinics and straitened economic circumstances have limited the growth of CLSCs in recent years. There is, however, an indication that some further CLSCs will be established in the next few years. The situation in Ontario, while more favourable than two years ago, is still unclear. To date, growth of health centres and HSOs has been modest (Frankford, 1984; Goldberg, 1984). Moreover, Ontario government support for new community health centres has been limited largely to those for high risk and under-served populations. They are seen as programs for such groups rather than for the population as a whole. HSOs, on the other hand, are (with the exception of the Sault program) physician sponsored, not community based.

Overall, the constraints and difficulties are formidable but not prohibitive. The rhetoric calls for a pluralistic system with multiple models, but to date, the reality has been that the political, social, economic and legislative structures in Canada have in effect bolstered the prevailing system based on independent fee-for-service practice. In other words, we have public payments for a private system. Coordination and integration, when they have occurred, have been *ad hoc*. The political, economic and social pressures have not yet reached a critical level and there have been relatively weak incentives for the present system to change.

What may emerge is a typically Canadian model that operates in spite of the constraints. Enrolment with capitation negation may prove acceptable as long as reasonable marketing is permitted and enrolment allowed in sites other than clinics or physicians' offices. While there will almost certainly be professional opposition, it appears that considerable numbers of physicians would accept capitation or salaried arrangements and could be recruited to health centres. Certainly any program that integrated primary care with secondary and tertiary care, hospital and ambulatory care, and medical with other human services could prove to be an important advance. Funding, enabling legislation, the removal of existing regulatory constraints on the wider use of alternative personnel and public education would be necessary first steps. Governments would need to assume stimulative rather than responsible stances for new programs. At the same time they would have to be prepared to hold the line on hospital and medical expenditures so as to create a climate in which existing services would be prepared to consider change. Another key ingredient would be consumer control or meaningful consumer input. The resulting programs would then have the possibility of being comprehensive, coordinated, population based and modelled on community health centre principles.

Hospitals and the Institutional Sector

Provincial Approaches to Control Resource Use

The 1970s and the 1980s have seen some change in the hospital and institutional sector. Although it remains the area of greatest cost in health care, accounting for about 54 percent of all expenditures, there has been a record of some success in containing expenditure increases by a combination of "direct administrative limits on budgets and availability of facilities, combined with powerful moral suasion to discourage excessive use of hospitals" (Vayda, Evans and Mindell, 1977). The provinces have also limited the introduction of high technology such as CAT scanners. Global budgeting, coupled with ceilings on permitted increments in operational budgets, has forced acute hospitals to close beds and to develop better procedures for admission, bed use and discharge. They have also been forced to examine their staffing patterns and to introduce a range of other administrative efficiencies including joint support services such as laundry, food services and biomedical engineering (Pynn, 1983; Chang and Prud'homme, 1982). In some cases hospitals have contracted out selected support services to private firms when efficiencies and savings seemed possible.

Regionalization

In addition to tightened provincial control, new regional planning and approval bodies in some provinces, such as DHCs in Ontario and CRSSSs in Quebec), must now approve all proposals for new capital investments, technology and programs. The planning bodies have also studied and promoted the rationalization of existing specialized services in communities with more than one hospital. Basic specialty services, such as obstetrics, paediatrics and psychiatry, and tertiary services, such as renal dialysis and trauma care, have been allocated on a community or regional basis. Since the process is still largely persuasory, the ultimate location of services seems to be related more to political trade-offs among hospitals than to a fully rationalized planning approach. Even so, there have been reductions in service overlap in many communities. Some communities and regions have even been able to move to a fairly effective regional referral system from smaller community hospitals to tertiary care teaching institutions with designated catchment areas. For example, in Hamilton, Ontario, the advent of a new medical school and teaching hospital stimulated the development, through, first, a regional hospital council and, later, the District Health Council, of community-wide purchasing and laboratory programs (Hamilton-Wentworth DHC, 1983), a regional placement and coordination service (Hamilton DHC, 1973; Hamilton-Wentworth DHC, 1982-1983), and specialized service roles for individual hospitals (Hamilton-Wentworth DHC, 1970), resulting in a health services network (Hamilton-Wentworth DHC, *et al.*, 1983). However, in an essentially voluntary context the extent of achievement is variable. For example, it took several years before a major trauma centre in one Toronto hospital began to receive large numbers of referrals from neighbouring hospitals.

In Quebec, the restructured system has led to considerable service rationalization within most regions (Gosselin, 1984). One of the more interesting steps in the Quebec restructuring has been the placing of public health planning and management in new entities called DSCs located in regional hospitals, as described earlier. In Newfoundland and Labrador, Regional Health Boards currently operate hospitals and other government health clinics under a global budget. A recent Royal Commission has proposed including nursing homes under this arrangement (Newfoundland and Labrador, 1984).

Increased Efficiency in Patient Care

Among steps taken to conserve the use of acute care beds have been increased emphasis on outpatient diagnostic work-up and services, earlier ambulation for many types of patients (for example, post-delivery, post-surgery), progressive patient care with patients assuming responsibility for an incremental range of their personal needs, and day surgery units. In some locations day surgery now makes up 25 percent or more of the total surgical workload. The development of day surgery was delayed because of inappropriate financial incentives and because, where day surgery was not combined with bed reductions, overall utilization increased (Shah, 1980).

Extended Care

Lowered bed targets of 3.5 to 5 beds/1,000 population in the provinces have led to a reduction in available acute beds *per capita* from their peak in the 1960s. The reductions have usually been accompanied by increased provincial government support for the development of convalescent and chronic care facilities, usually in separately administered institutions. (Funding for capital development and operational costs related to the non-acute levels of care comes from the provinces, although some provinces also impose some direct *per diem* charges on patients. Such charges are permitted (within limits) by federal legislation, which otherwise seeks to prevent direct billing of patients, when the institution is the place of residence of the person.) The provision of $20 *per capita* for extended care under the EPF agreements has also been a stimulus. In some provinces acute hospital beds have simply been redesignated as long-term care. For example, in Manitoba and Quebec acute hospitals were required to convert 10 percent of acute beds to chronic, extended and geriatric care (Clarkson, Vayda and Maxwell, 1975). Thus the total number of beds, both acute and chronic, did not increase. More recently, and in part stimulated by private sector experiences in both the U.S. and Canada, some acute care hospitals have developed joint administration for different levels of care in different institutions, including acute and convalescent care (for example, St. Joseph's Health Centre, Toronto) and sometimes chronic care and nursing home care as well (for example, plans by Ottawa Civic Hospital). New Brunswick has recently announced its intention to encourage greater coordination among levels of hospital care, other institutional care and community care under consolidated area boards and management teams (Robertson, 1984). Currently the extramural hospital concept, whereby the hospital has extended its services to include home care, is being developed in several communities in New Brunswick. Some programs, such as the Baycrest Centre in Toronto, include a range of care for the aged, including chronic, nursing home, protected residential, and day care and community care coupled with close liaison with an acute care hospital (Ruth and Rudin, 1973; Rudin and Jesion, 1983).

Community Care and Home Care

One of the areas of rapid development in most provinces has been that of province-wide home care (Shapiro, 1979) on a community basis. Such care is usually under public health sponsorship, but is sometimes contracted to voluntary agencies, such as the Red Cross or the Victorian Order of Nurses. As noted above, home care in several New Brunswick communities is sometimes provided by hospitals and former patients. However, as yet province-wide programs do not exist in Prince Edward Island or Nova Scotia. Most programs limit services to post-hospital patients, for maximum time periods; some now accept patients with medical problems directly from the community. Comparatively few home care programs funded by Ministries of Health include people with essentially social needs. Home care in Canada is characterized, from province to province and in various communities within any province, by its diversity in organization, eligibility and services. In some communities services do not yet exist; in others they are minimal and restricted to nursing and some homemaking; and in others they include a wider range of services, such as physiotherapy, dietary assistance, podiatry and shopping services. Overall, the support for and provision of community care services remains well below the level required if these services are to become a significant alternative to the institutional sector and to make possible a shift in the heavy institutional focus of the present system or a reduction in numbers of beds.

Emergency and Ambulatory Care

Urban hospitals in particular have moved to organize their emergency departments, sometimes with physicians who do only emergency work (now recognized as a specialty), and in some instances separating emergencies from non-urgent primary care services. The latter can then be referred to contiguous family practice units or clinics, as at the Winnipeg Health Sciences Centre (Clarkson, Vayda and Maxwell, 1975). A few hospitals have developed special ambulatory care clinics and separate health centres to meet the needs of downtown populations and ethnic groups (for example, Mt. Sinai and St. Michael's Hospitals, Toronto). In a few cases ambulatory care centres are established to preclude or delay the need for full-scale hospital development (for example, St. Joseph's Ambulatory Care Centre being proposed for the east end of Hamilton). None of these represent coordinated and population-based global health programs, such as pre-paid group practice or the centres proposed by the Community Health Centre Project Report. Rather, they are opportunistic responses by individual institutions or local planning bodies.

Hospices and Palliative Care Units

Another development in Canada within the past decade is the establishment of hospices and/or palliative care units for terminal patients. Such units may be free standing or attached to acute care hospitals. This movement grew out of concern for the emotional and social needs of dying patients, which the regular acute hospital services were not designed to meet, and the recognition that many people in today's society cannot be adequately cared for at home by families or are living alone (Mount, 1976; Shephard, 1977; Greenway, 1979; Freedman, 1979). Although hospices and palliative care units are still comparatively few in number, they have drawn increased attention to the particular needs of terminally ill patients.

Technology and Computerization

More than any other sector, hospitals, and particularly acute care hospitals, have experienced the impact of changing technology. This has led to the increased automation of many services, such as food, supplies handling and pharmacy. More recently computerization is being introduced for management information systems and operational purposes (McDermit, Bernstein, and Harmer, 1983; Crewson, 1984; Protti, 1984). Hospitals may in the near future be linked with other hospitals, health centres, and physicians offices, even at considerable distances, via modern communication systems, including satellites (House, 1984). Outside the hospital sector the introduction of computerization has been slower. The hospital of the future undoubtedly will be a highly sophisticated technological system. How to maintain human dimensions and a humane perspective in care will be a major challenge (Wright et al., 1984; Brown, 1984). It also seems probable that, as more sophisticated information systems become available at manageable cost, there will be growing pressures for closer coordination and integration of hospitals and other health and related services into a single network of community and, ultimately, province-wide services. Such changes may occur in spite of the desire of individual practitioners, programs and institutions to remain autonomous.

Quality Control, Accreditation and Performance Assessment

Another emphasis throughout the hospital system has been a growing interest in utilization review, audit and quality assessment. The Canadian Council on Hospital Accreditation (Canadian Council on Hospital Accreditation, 1982; Swanson interview, 1982; Limongelli, 1983), a voluntary accreditation mechanism available initially for larger hospitals, now covers many smaller hospitals and, more recently, mental and long-term care institutions. Although it is voluntary, covering only about 75 percent of institutions, and focuses essentially on structure and process criteria, accreditation is now sought by most hospitals as evidence of their adherence to recognized standards of operation. Governments do not mandate accreditation, but most hospitals see it as advantageous in obtaining support from regional and provincial planning bodies. As part of the process hospitals are required to utilize a variety of professional and administrative audit and peer review mechanisms. Other audit and data systems such as HMRI (Hospital Medical Records Institute), which is required for all Ontario hospitals, regularly provide data to member institutions for internal operational assessment and audit. In other provinces, the U.S.-based PAS (Professional Activity Studies) program is used for these purposes. On the other hand, there has been no mandatory development of review mechanisms comparable to the PSRO in the U.S.

Management Developments

Several other trends related to management and cost control are worth noting. Many larger hospitals are shifting to a corporate model of organization in recognition of budget size and range of services. There is an increasing demand for professionally qualified health administrators. In recent years, a wider range of opportunities for formal education and training, in-service education and continuing education has been developed. (The six university graduate programs have now been joined by a number of full and part-time baccalaureate programs. Most programs have revised their curricula in line with perceived knowledge and skills required for future administrators. The Canadian Hospital Association, in particular, has had major in-service programs for a number of years.) In the early 1970s a Canadian professional association, the Canadian College of Health Service Executives, was established. More recently there has been recognition of the particular needs of health professionals, in particular physicians, who find themselves in management roles in the system. (Examples of programs to assist this group are the new Ontario Ministry of Health-sponsored Executive Development Project at the Department of Health Administration, University of Toronto and the joint program between the Canadian Medical Association and the Canadian College of Health Service Executives.)

Recently, some provinces have encouraged hospitals to develop financially remunerative services, such as shops, parking and catering. The income from these activities can be retained and used for special needs that are not covered by provincially-derived budgets. In Ontario this has been called the BOND (Business-Oriented New Development) Program. Except for a few large urban hospitals, which have acted vigorously to develop a variety of revenue-making schemes (for example, Ottawa Civic with an internal mall of shops) and even to bid on joint management proposals for other hospitals and extended care institutions, the impact has been limited to date.

Experiments with alternative reimbursement mechanisms are under way in a number of provinces. Most of these are variants of the Diagnosis Related Group (DRG) patient classification, sometimes called the Case Mix Management Approach (Zuckerman, 1983; deMora, Legros and McGeorge, 1983). This has focused attention on the content of care given by individual physicians and hospitals for specific patient categories, to make physicians more aware of how their actions affect the use of resources and costs. DRGs have also emphasized the need for more sophisticated computer-based information systems for management. It is too early to assess the extent to which this approach may be applicable to province-wide reimbursement under a universal system. At present, it is not seen by most observers as replacing global budgeting but rather as a means of providing additional information to stimulate greater involvement by doctors and other health professionals in planning and resource allocation.

Conclusions

In summary, the institutional sector has become the most sophisticated and resource conscious sector in the health care system, in large part under the driving force of cost containment. Many hospitals have achieved an increasing degree of internal efficiency and innovation in providing a greater variety of services both intramurally and in the community. More sophisticated management and information systems are making possible a gradual trend to multi-unit and multi-level systems of management in some communities. Private sector firms have been particularly active in this regard in the nursing home and residential institutional care fields. They are clearly interested, if the opportunity presents, in expanding into the acute hospital area. However, planning is still largely dependent on the interest and ability of individual institutions and communities to respond to pressures and opportunities. There is ample room for the more aggressive and entrepreneurially-minded institutions and organizations to diversify and add new services. Although this is in one sense a positive form of competition, it could lead to a distortion of service patterns and an emphasis on the interests of particular hospitals and/or organizations with access to capital and management expertise rather than to a balanced and rationalized meeting of community needs. Strategic planning is still weak and even suspect on both ideological and practical grounds in many government Ministries of Health, regional planning bodies, and among many health professionals and managers in the health care system. And the time frame for planning does not easily fit that of the political system.

Public Health

Uncertainty and Changes

At the beginning of the 1970s, full-time public health services, staffed by a medical health officer (MHO or MOH), public health nurse, sanitarians, and sometimes other personnel, such as public health dentists, nutritionists and health educators, were in place in all provinces. Public health units were usually decentralized extensions of provincial health departments on a district basis, except in Ontario and Alberta where they were administered by locally autonomous boards of health. In larger Canadian cities, boards of health related to city government operated municipal health departments. Success in the first half of the century in the control of infectious diseases, in maternal, child and school health, and in sanitation had created uncertainty about the current and future roles of public health. It was unclear whether a separate public health agency was necessary in the community. In particular, there were concerns about the role of the Medical Health Officer as the head of the local public health program. This period coincided with the retirement of many MHOs, and recruitment of new ones was often difficult. At the same time, nurses were becoming increasingly discontented with medical control, discontent that was particularly apparent in public health where strong nursing programs operated in most health units, sometimes under relatively weak medical leadership. Thus, by 1970, the stage was set for change in both the organization and the functions of public health as a whole, and in the place of the MHO (Schwenger, 1971).

It appeared for a time that many provinces, motivated partly by the shortage of qualified personnel, would move to having professional non-physician managers replace the MHO as directors of district and municipal public health services. Medically qualified public health personnel would then serve as epidemiologists and planners, in some instances at the regional or provincial level. Many water, sewage and pollution control functions were placed in ministries other than health. Experiments with seconding public health nurses to medical groups and even to individual physicians suggested that many personal preventive services could be moved to physicians' offices. In Manitoba, for example, as a result of the 1972 White Paper on Health Policy (Manitoba, *White Paper . . .*, 1972), health and social services were merged provincially and regionally. At the regional level, the executive posts went to non-physicians. The 1974 Report of the Health Planning Task Force in Ontario, influenced by the British community medicine model, emphasized the role of the public health physician as epidemiologist, not administrator (Ontario, *Report . . .*, 1974). Even public health advocates questioned whether, in light of the shortage of new recruits for training, medical health officers should continue as public health unit directors in all jurisdictions (Schwenger, 1971).

Quebec

Quebec, as part of the restructuring of its health system, abolished its public health units and moved them and their former staffs into thirty-two Departments of Community Health (DSCs) located in designated regional hospitals (Pineault, 1984). The physician head of a DSC was responsible for planning and epidemiology in the region. The intent was to move personal public health services into the CLSCs. Although Quebec reorganized its public health delivery system, physicians trained in community medicine directed the DSCs. On the other hand, the directors of the new CLSCs that provide personal health services are not physicians. Some DSC personnel feel that they should be located in closer relationship to the CRSSS, the regional health and social services planning body (Hastings, 1984).

In regional hospitals, DSC staff have limited involvement with clinical colleagues and their planning role may be seen as suspect by other hospitals and programs in the region. Planning functions for regional health services tend to take precedence over public health. Pineault has written that it is too early to assess the overall public health and preventive impact of the new structures, since the process of change is still under way. "The results, while not spectacular, compare favourably with those recorded in other Canadian provinces" (Pineault, 1984).

A Rebirth and a Renewed Mandate

More recently, a number of developments have led to a new emphasis on public health (or as it is often now called, community health) in most provinces. There have been growing concerns about new infectious diseases, such as Acquired Immune Deficiency Syndrome (AIDS), together with a recognition that some old ones, such as infectious hepatitis, are not yet under control. The increasing importance of chronic diseases, coupled with trends to earlier discharge of hospitalized patients and to the deinstitutionalization of mental patients, have combined to create a new emphasis on community and home care. The 1974 Lalonde Report renewed interest in primary prevention, health promotion and community-wide interventions. One problem, as the emphasis on primary prevention and promotion gains momentum, may be the potential for conflict over goals and program support between the new focus and social/nursing support services for the elderly and discharged mental patients, which are currently major functions of public health nurses.

Ontario, for example, has recently replaced its largely permissive public health legislation with a new Act that mandates a range of baseline programs and services in public health units while confirming the executive role of the MHO (Ontario, Health Protection and Promotion Act, 1983). The Quebec changes have been discussed earlier. Outside Ontario and Quebec, most, although not all, of the provinces have moved to strengthen their regional public health units, programs and staffs. More recently, reports such as Toronto's "Public Health in the 80's" have pointed up the local need for programs aimed at modern community needs and staffed by well-qualified personnel (Toronto, *Public Health . . .*, 1978).

The strengthening of education and training programs for public health physicians, public health nurses and others entering public health careers, as well as a trend for physicians now entering the field to go on to the Royal College specialty qualifications, have coincided with the renewed recognition of the significance of public health. In 1978, five candidates successfully completed the speciality examination of the Royal College of Physicians and Surgeons of Canada in Community Medicine; in 1983 there were sixteen successful candidates. The residency training program at the Division of Community Health, University of Toronto, had three residents in 1978 and twenty-eight in 1983, of whom sixteen were funded by the Ontario Ministry of Health. The residency program at Laval had twenty-one residents in 1984, of whom nineteen were provincially funded. A new generation of more fully qualified public health personnel is moving into the field. Although the rate of change varies across the country, the trend seems to be toward an increased role for public health in the next decade (Terris, 1983).

Mental Health

The landmark report *More for the Mind* (Tyhurst et al., 1963) recommended that mental health services in Canada should be based on five principles:

1. *Medical integration*: That psychiatric services be integrated with the physical and personnel resources of the rest of medicine.

2. *Regionalization*: That psychiatric treatment services be established in centres of population on a regional basis and that a wide range of psychiatric services be established in the larger communities.

3. *Decentralization*: That the management and administration of psychiatric services be decentralized.

4. *Continuity of care*: That close cooperation among treatment personnel and coordination of psychiatric services be maintained to ensure that the patient receives appropriate help in his community through all phases of his illness without interruption.

5. *Coordination*: That local psychiatric services in hospitals, clinics and other centres be coordinated to promote maximum effectiveness.

What has happened in the intervening years? Currently there are four main providers of care for the mentally ill:

1. *Psychiatric or mental hospitals run by the provinces.* Although the number of hospitals has been reduced and the number of inpatients cut by more than one-half, these hospitals continue in most parts of Canada to be the main site of care for long-term patients. They are also the main site for referral of more severely ill or more difficult short-term patients from the general hospital psychiatric units in their areas. As well, the majority of court-referred patients are sent to the mental hospitals. Wasylenki notes that in Ontario, for example, the provincial mental hospitals still account for some 50 percent of public expenditure on mental health services (Wasylenki, 1983), although in other provinces, because of a shift in the system of care, the percentage is as low as 35 percent (Manitoba, *Mental Health Services in Manitoba*, 1983). In some provinces their management has been modified from a civil service line structure to community management or advisory boards. There is also a greater emphasis on professionally qualified managers or on the acquisition of management skills by medical directors.

2. *Psychiatric units in community general hospitals.* Such units began more than twenty years ago, but their major growth has occurred in Canada since 1969.

Their numbers have more than doubled, in large part in response to public Medicare plans that paid for psychiatric services in general hospitals but not in provincial mental hospitals where care had been publicly financed for many years. The hospital psychiatric units were initially and primarily intended to provide acute and crisis-oriented care for short-term patients on an inpatient basis, and consultation to the other clinical services in the hospital. Until recently, outpatient and follow-up care was limited.

The concept of the pivotal general hospital psychiatric unit put forward by some advocates, most recently the Heseltine Report in Ontario (Heseltine, 1982), has been implemented in only a few localities in Canada (Richman, 1983). It assumes that the general hospital psychiatric unit staff are qualified to handle the full range of psychiatric diagnoses, and both short and long-term care. The staff would also provide leadership in establishing outpatient and community follow-up programs, and in coordinating a network of community services and programs. Heseltine also envisioned the disappearance, over time, of most traditional mental hospitals. Richman (1983) notes that the model that has most commonly evolved in Canada is a growing referral relationship between regional mental hospitals and the general hospital psychiatric units in their catchment areas. These relations have developed slowly, and a fully planned and coordinated system, let alone a network of comprehensive community services, has been most difficult to achieve.

3. *Private and independently practising professionals in the community (psychiatrists, psychologists, social workers and others).* Psychiatrists provide care to individual patients and are either reimbursed by the provincial medical care plan, or bill the patient directly and the patient in turn is reimbursed. Other independent professionals bill the patients directly; those charges are not normally covered by Medicare. Many psychiatrists, but few other professionals, have admitting privileges to general hospital psychiatric units. The clientele served tend to be short-term and acute care patients, drawn predominantly from middle and upper socio-economic groups.

4. *A wide range of community-based agencies that provide various types of mental health services.* Some are non-profit, such as visiting nurses, but others are for profit. Many derive their income from both public and private sources. There is considerable dependence on volunteers and untrained staff in some of the agencies. The degree of involvement and coordination of the community agencies with psychiatric units and mental hospitals varies but is often tenuous. Some of the self-help oriented groups concerned with social, rehabilitation and residential needs hold therapeutic philosophies opposed to those in the formal psychiatric milieu. Some see their primary role as one of advocacy. Most community-based organizations exist only in larger communities. Small communities and rural areas may have only the services provided through public health units or visiting diagnostic and/or follow-up teams from the regional mental hospital.

Changes and Issues

A major change in the care of the mentally ill or handicapped (and to a lesser extent of the physically handicapped as well) in the past two decades has been deinstitutionalization, an approach by which chronically ill psychiatric patients on psychoactive drug therapy are discharged into the community from the large mental hospitals (Bassuk and Gerson, 1978). The concept arose from a spirit of reform, and revulsion against the large and often primarily custodial mental hospitals, and was made possible by the dramatic advances in psychopharmacology. The new drugs are potent in effect, but they also have potent side effects. Further, their impact depends on patient compliance. Effective follow-up over time and the ability to re-admit as necessary are thus essential. Also needed are a coordinated range of flexible and patient-oriented preventive, social, rehabilitative, residential and occupational services in the community, perhaps coordinated through community mental health centres. Another important influence on the push for deinstitutionalization was the promise of sharply reduced inpatient and custodial costs, not unappealing in a time of growing concern about rising health care costs.

The reality is that there has been insufficient funding, planning and preparation of communities for the new approach. The range of services envisioned was not developed on a coordinated basis. Few community mental health centres were established, and thus they were not able to provide the hoped for coordination and focus. Mental hospitals were dramatically reduced in numbers and size. For some the result was more rapid and effective treatment. But as a recent study in Metropolitan Toronto shows (Wasylenki *et al.*, forthcoming), even with both formal and community service resources far in excess of those available in most other regions, there has been inadequate follow-up, a shortage of appropriate forms of housing, little or no social and recreational services, and few occupational and rehabilitation programs. Communities have been fearful and reluctant to accept into their midst discharged patients, or residential and rehabilitative services such as group homes.

One result has been what is called the "revolving door" phenomenon. Mental hospital admission rates have gone up 25 percent, and some two-thirds of these are re-admissions. Between 35 and 50 percent of discharged patients are re-admitted within a year of discharge. In the Toronto study only 19 percent were employed after two years, 30 percent to 50 percent had no family support, more than one-third were dependent on public assistance and nearly 48 percent had serious financial problems. After one year one-third were living alone and 35 percent were still in boarding or rooming houses. Two-thirds reported serious social and recreational problems (Wasylenki, *et al.*, forthcoming).

In summary, although major changes have occurred in mental health services, implementation of the principles enunciated in *More for the Mind* and other subsequent reports remains unattained.

Services in Remote and Under-Serviced Areas Within the Provinces

Some provinces have programs to subsidize the establishment and maintenance of practices by doctors, dentists and other personnel in areas of the provinces designated as under-serviced. Many areas that formerly had problems attracting doctors and dentists, but that were close to larger centres, are now able to receive services through these programs. The provision of services for more remote and isolated communities has also improved to some degree, but it still remains a serious problem in most provinces, despite the almost 100 percent increase in physician numbers in the past fifteen years. Quebec has introduced a differential fee schedule, with medical graduates settling in designated under-serviced areas receiving 130 percent of the provincial fee schedule and those settling in cities receiving only 70 percent for the first three years of practice. To date, this approach does not appear to have been a sufficient incentive or disincentive to resolve the manpower distribution problem.

Health Services for Indians and Inuit, and in the North

Health services in the larger communities in the Northwest and Yukon Territories are provided on a similar basis to those in the provinces. Public health services are provided on contract by the Medical Services Branch of Health and Welfare Canada. For more remote settlements in the Territories and for the Indian and Inuit peoples living in the Territories and in remote areas of the provinces, personal as well as public health services are provided by Medical Services Branch through a network of hospitals, nursing stations and health centres. Some of the provinces, on behalf of the federal government, provide personal health care to Indians in more populous areas under the provincial plans, while in others Medical Services Branch continues to be the provider. The Medical Services Branch primary care program is based on public health nurses and other personnel working from nursing stations and on indigenous Family Health Aides specially trained to work in small settlements and bands. In some zones, agreement has been reached with medical schools and hospitals to provide permanent, visiting and tertiary back-up services.

The federal services have come into considerable question in recent years both by the native peoples themselves and by other observers (Young, 1984). Some see the federal services as paternalistic and not responding to perceived native priorities. It is argued also that health services are only part of a much wider and more complex problem facing the native people, many of whom have inadequate diets, housing, sanitation, educations, jobs and income. Thus, it is a difficult and confusing time for personnel working in the federal service.

There has been growing government and native recognition that resolution of the issues will require a broad and coordinated approach to the socio-economic and cultural needs of the native peoples. Central to this is solution of the political issues of self-government and creation of an economic base, perhaps through native resource and land rights (Young, 1984; Canada, *Medical Services Annual Review, 1981*). Current federal policy is to encourage the native people to develop their own boards of health. An increasing number of native communities are thus assuming some or full responsibility for employing staff and running their own primary care services.

In summary, federal services are currently in transition. Questions of jurisdiction, accountability, staffing and emphasis will require further clarification as the broader socio-economic and political issues are resolved.

The Private Sector

Although health care in Canada is now largely publicly funded and regulated, it remains a mixed system with significant elements remaining in the private sector.

During the 1970s, there was a shift to more active intervention by the provinces in manpower planning including control of numbers of residency posts and provision of incentives to enter specialties in short supply and to work in designated under-serviced communities. However, most doctors and dentists, some pharmacists and some other personal health services personnel continue to be independent practitioners. Doctors, dentists, nurses, pharmacists and some others function as members of self-governing and largely self-regulating professions. In some provinces publicly appointed boards with non-health professional representation have been established to provide general oversight of legislation and regulations regarding these professions and of the functioning of the professional governing bodies. In most provinces public representation on the boards of the governing bodies has been increased.

The prevailing method of payment for physicians in clinical practice (excluding interns and residents) and for dentists is fee-for-service, although some derive a portion of their income from other forms of payment. Most physician incomes now come either directly or indirectly through provincial medical care insurance plans. Most nurses and other health care personnel are employed on a salaried basis by institutions or programs, although a small proportion of some professions, such as psychologists, social workers and physiotherapists, are in private practice.

Other than federal military hospitals and some facilities in the North, provincial mental hospitals and, in some provinces, certain long-term care institutions, almost all hospitals are owned by voluntary corporations, religious bodies or local governments and are operated by separate boards on a non-profit, public basis. Proprietary general hospitals are rare in Canada. Many convalescent and chronic care hospitals, about 75 percent of nursing homes and some special care facilities remain under non-government auspices, either non-profit or private and for-profit. They must adhere to publicly set standards and derive varying portions of their daily operating charges from public plans.

The licensing, manufacture and distribution of pharmaceuticals remain in the private sector, although government regulations must be followed. Canada is unique among developed countries in having legislation enabling competitive manufacture of patented drugs with a set percentage royalty being paid to the patent-holder, rather than having a period of exclusive patent. The large international firms strongly oppose this, whereas the provinces and other bulk purchasers, as well as consumer groups, support it as a means of holding down drug costs. Public pharmacare programs exist in all provinces; these are usually limited to designated public assistance and low income groups and to those sixty-five years of age and older. Even in provinces with universal drug benefits, such as Manitoba and B.C., there are deductibles and/or co-insurance.

A wide range and number of voluntary health and social agencies remain important in identifying and filling service gaps, in meeting special needs, in the innovation and demonstration of new service approaches, in supporting research, and in supporting public and professional health education. Some charge limited fees for personal services, often on a sliding scale. Government grants have become important sources of funding for many agencies and some, such as visiting nursing groups, may serve as agents of government.

Private insurance was prohibited for services covered under the federal Hospital Insurance and Diagnostic Services Act and Medical Care Act. This prohibition continues with adoption of the Canada Health Act in 1984. As a result, all extra physician charges and hospital user charges must be paid out-of-pocket by the patient. Private insurance is permitted only for non-covered services, such as semi-private accommodation and dental care. More than 90 percent of physician and hospital costs are covered by the universal public programs. Private payments, whether out-of-pocket or privately insured, are limited mainly to nursing homes (40 percent of costs), dental care (90 percent of costs) and drugs and prostheses (75 percent of costs) (Canada, *National Health Expenditures* . . ., 1979).

Recently, in Ontario, two public hospitals have been permitted by the province to enter into contractual arrangements with private hospital management companies (on an individual basis, it appears, rather than as a general policy). One of the two management contracts covers all hospital services and the other covers chronic and extended care beds only. In both instances the private company loaned funds for new construction, thus relieving the province and the communities involved of the responsibility for contributing or raising capital funds. A third hospital has concluded a limited management contract with a private firm. To date the province and the institutions concerned appear to be satisfied with these private-public arrangements (Lacroix, 1984), but the Ontario Hospital Association (Personal Communication, P.L. Wood), consumer groups and the

New Democratic Party (Ontario New Democratic Party, *Health Care Priorities*, 1984) have been sharply critical of both the particular arrangements and the concept. The private sector would like to expand its involvement in institutional management, and perhaps ownership, beyond nursing homes and residential care, where it has a significant role in most provinces to include the acute and chronic hospital field. Those who favour a public and universal approach are concerned with the potential implications for equality of access and services, and for costs, should privatization occur. Recent American experience indicates that privatization in the acute hospital sector appears to be associated with increased rather than decreased costs (Pattison and Katz, 1983). Ontario does not, at this time, seem to be moving as a general policy to greater private involvement in the acute hospital sector. On the other hand, neither does the province seem to be intent on decreasing the role of the private sector in nursing homes, extended care facilities and residential facilities.

The government of Alberta has recently asked a private consulting firm to study the possibility of contracting out the management of its health care insurance program to the private sector. Whether this is a serious intention or a political response to the recent passage of the Canada Health Act remains to be seen.

Consumerism and Self-Help Groups

The Consumer Movement

In line with developments in the western world generally, there has been a widespread growth of consumer groups representing the lower socio-economic groups and the disadvantaged: tenants, welfare recipients, native peoples, women, the aged, single parents, the mentally and physically handicapped. There has also been a dramatic growth of groups concerned about broad social issues, some of which have significant health implications, such as the rights of consumers, energy development, thermonuclear war hazards, the impact of technology in various forms, bioethical issues such as abortion, the impact of urbanization and high rise living on health, and environmental pollution. These groups often cut across socio-economic and political interests and have become important and recognized forces in modern society. They organize meetings, circulate petitions and hold rallies to seek to impress their views on governments, the media and their fellow citizens. Some citizen groups, such as the Canadian Association of Consumers, and some voluntary social policy agencies, such as the Canadian Council on Social Development, regularly monitor and comment on health issues, and present briefs to governments and others. These organizations have achieved added public legitimacy by being invited regularly by government to comment on proposed policy changes. In some cases they may receive some funding support from governments.

Self-Help Networks and Groups

A major component of health care is carried out by people themselves through self-help, family help and social networks (Romeder, 1982). Most simple and minor ailments, such as the common cold, the symptomatology commonly called "flu", headaches, minor cuts and bruises are cared for without formal professional intervention. Health maintenance, questions of diet, exercise and other health related behaviour, as well as minor behavioural/psychological problems within the family, are also commonly dealt with in this manner. Of course, some of these health and illness problems may also be brought to some professional within the formal health care system, usually a family physician, public health nurse or hospital emergency department.

There are also many individuals who for various reasons obtain some health care services outside the formal system. Some people avoid the existing system or feel themselves excluded for social, religious or ethnic reasons. Others feel the prevailing system is unresponsive to their very specific needs or concerns. Thus, for some people, programs catering to women, homosexuals or teenagers have proved to be preferable alternatives to the "mainstream" system. For those who feel excluded as well as those with special problems, self-help groups have been formed. Some, such as Alcoholics Anonymous and the Lost Chord, have been in existence for many years, while others, such as Bereaved Parents, Families of Alcoholics or Families of those with Alzheimer's Disease, have been developed more recently. All groups share a single developmental force: the sense that the dominant system and its practitioners are, for whatever reasons, not fully responsive to their particular problems. Self-help groups usually limit and may even reject professional input; individuals with a common problem band together to help themselves and each other. Although they may lobby from time to time in an attempt to change specific government policies, this is not as a rule their major purpose.

Future Patterns of Organization: Cost-Driven Rationalizations

Underlying most of the reports and proposed changes of the 1970s and early 1980s has been continuing concern about the cost of human services, including health care, and the level of expenditure for these services in relation to the Gross National Product. The recent economic downturn and slow recovery have added to this concern. Will there be sufficient resources to meet the needs of an aging population, growing professional and public expectations, mushrooming scientific-technologic developments, and high service costs. Will there be sufficient resources to allow for real change and innovation? Some groups, including organized medicine, are advocating the reintroduction of some private funding and direct charges to patients. Some of the provinces have undertaken limited re-privatization experiments in the capital funding and management of acute hospitals. But the threat of insufficient resources to pay for acceptable levels of basic services is not regarded as an immediate crisis by most observers, provider groups or consumer groups. Indeed, the level of satisfaction with the system is high. There is, however, unease about the future. Efforts to limit expenditures by budgetary and funding controls and some planning in the acute hospital sector may not be long-term solutions. Further development of the health care system will likely depend not only on continuing prudent constraints on existing services, but even more on incentives for restructuring the system to give greater emphasis to ambulatory care, community-based care, prevention, health promotion and health maintenance. Politically, restructuring is difficult. It affects strong provider interests because some of the resources needed for creating and sustaining changes will have to be transferred from existing health services. Established interests in society, such as industry and agriculture, will also be affected. It remains to be seen whether governments, the public and providers are prepared to take these steps or whether, in spite of the ferment and promise of the early 1970s, we will continue to deal with the issues in a piecemeal fashion until a major crisis erupts. Change needs strong political backing and will.

In the short term, although all signs point to a continuing upward pressure on health care costs, there is little evidence that the provincial governments will alter their current, essentially *ad hoc*, incremental and pragmatic approach to dealing with problems as they emerge (Deber and Vayda, forthcoming). Although planning of individual programs is well accepted, there is little evidence of a will to mandate strategic planning; in part this arises from a suspicion about the concept in Canada. Reluctance also arises because a significant reshaping of the health care system, whatever the promise for greater efficiency in resource use in the long term, will require an initial commitment of additional resources for development, seed money and operational support during the first years of change. At the present time and in the immediate future, economic circumstances in Canada do not offer hope of additional resource inputs to the health care system. The potential for disruption in the system and confrontation with major provider interest groups is considerable. The short-term political "fallout" would also be considerable and the long-term result not assured. Evidence from other countries and from Quebec suggests that in the end compromises result that may sharply reduce the impact of reforms, and that the existing system has an enormous capacity to absorb change without really changing.

For these reasons, we see in the short term a continuation of the gradualist and incremental approaches of the past and present. Of course, when a particularly energetic minister or a committed government comes to power, particular program areas may be developed and important changes implemented. There seems little likelihood in the short term of the introduction of major community-based alternatives to existing prevailing medical practice and institutional modes. Some changes will be developed because of particular local circumstances, but their system-wide impact will be modest.

It also appears likely that for the next three years or so, a major pre-occupation of the federal and provincial governments and of organized medicine will be the administration of the Canada Health Act. How will the different provinces respond to it? Will those who have been most opposed challenge it in the courts? Will ways be found to circumvent some of its requirements. Will the new federal government elected in September 1984 renegotiate and modify the terms? Great pressures undoubtedly will be brought to bear on the new government to do so. The interim period seems likely to be one of posturing, lobbying, negotiations and court challenges to the federal Act and to any related provincial legislation, which will leave little room for significant innovation.

In the longer run, continuing upward cost pressures and the inability to squeeze much more from the existing health care system by current restraint measures may force governments into a more and more direct role in the system's management. This could lead to decisions to experiment seriously with alternative delivery models in sufficient numbers to demonstrate system effects, as was suggested by the Community Health Centre Report, and as shown to be cost effective by HMO experience in the U.S. (Enthoven, 1980; Luft, 1981; Manning *et al.*, 1984). The savings inherent in tying together ambulatory and inpatient care for defined populations and in creating incentives for (and allowing) changes in staff mix, service patterns and utilization are considerable. This change process may be further stimulated by the increasing versatility and sophistication of information and management systems. Such systems could provide mechanisms that facilitate greater coordination and integration among services and programs within communities and regions, without the pressures for more centralized control which such efforts seem so often to imply. Thus a combination of cost pressures and more sophisticated information and management systems may both require and make feasible major system changes, in spite of the inherent resistance of providers, consumers and governments to substantial change.

References

Barer, Morris L. *Community Health Centres and Hospital Costs in Ontario*. Toronto: Ontario Economic Council, 1981.

Bassuk, E.L. and S. Gerson. "Deinstitutionalization and Mental Health Services", *Scientific American*, 238, 2, February 1978.

Begin, Clermont, Harold Bheres and Hubert Wallot. "L'Experience de la Participation dan les Establissements de Santé et des Services Sociaux au Québec: un Bilan", *Can. J. Pub. Health*, 69, 6, Nov./Dec. 1978.

Boan, J.A. *Group Practice*. A study commissioned for the Royal Commission on Health Services. Ottawa: Queen's Printer, 1966.

Brown, Paul. "The Hospital of the Future: Efficient and Humane", *Dimensions in Health Service*, 61, 2, Feb. 1984.

Brunet, Jacques. "An Overview of Developments in the Quebec Health Care System". Presented at Health Sciences Plenary Symposium, Toronto, 1981, mimeo.

Canada. *The Community Health Centre in Canada*, Vols. I-III. Report of the Community Health Centre Project to the Health Minister. Hastings Report. Ottawa: Information Canada, 1973.

Canada. *Federal-Provincial Fiscal Arrangements and Established Programs Financing Act, 1977.*

Canada. *Medical Services Annual Review, 1981*. Ottawa: Health and Welfare Canada, 1983.

Canada. *National Health Expenditures in Canada, 1960-1975*. Ottawa: Health and Welfare Canada, 1979.

Canada. *National Health Expenditures in Canada, 1970-1982*. Ottawa: Health and Welfare Canada, 1984.

Canada. *Report of the Committee on Nurse Practitioners*. Boudreau Report. Ottawa: Department of National Health and Welfare, 1972.

Canada. *Royal Commission on Health Services*, Vols. I-III. Ottawa: Queen's Printer, 1964 and 1965.

Canada. *Task Force Reports on the Cost of Health Services in Canada*. Vols. I-III. Ottawa: Committee on Costs of Health Services, 1969.

Canadian Council on Hospital Accreditation. *Voluntary Hospital Accreditation: What's It All About?* Ottawa: CCHA, 1982.

Canadian Medical Association. *Group Practice in Canada. Report of the Special Committee on Group Practice*. Toronto, 1967.

Canadian Nurses' Association. *Brief to House of Commons Standing Committee on Health, Welfare and Social Affairs in Response to the Proposed Canada Health Act*. Ottawa, 1984 (processed).

Castonguay, Claude. "The Quebec Experience: Effects on Accessibility". Ch. 2 in S. Andreopoulos, ed., *National Health Insurance: Can We Learn from Canada?* Toronto: John Wiley, 1975.

Chang, M. and J. Prud'homme. "Shared Biomedical Engineering: A Cost-benefit Analysis, *Dimensions in Health Service*, 59, 7, July 1982.

Clarkson, C.G., E. Vayda and G. Maxwell. *The Plan for the Redevelopment of the Health Sciences Centre*, Vol. I. Winnipeg: Ministry of Health, 1975.

Crewson, H.A. "Manitoba's Computer Model: A Co-operative Venture", *Dimensions in Health Service*, 61, 2, February 1984.

Deber, R.B. and E. Vayda. "The Environment of Health Policy Implementation: The Ontario, Canada Example". In *Investigative Methods in Public Health*, G. Knox, ed., Vol. III, *Oxford Textbook of Public Health*, W. Holland, ed.-in-chief. Oxford University Press (forthcoming).

deMora, J., G. Legros and K. McGeorge. "Case Mix Management: One Approach Revealed", *Dimensions in Health Service*, 60, 7, July 1983.

Dixon, Maureen and Ann Kirkland. *The Organization of District Health Councils in Ontario*. Toronto: University of Toronto, Department of Health Administration, 1972.

Enthoven, A.C. *Health Plan*. Ontario, California: Addison-Wesley, 1980.

Foulkes, Richard G. *Health Security for British Columbians*. Victoria, B.C.: Health Security Programme Project, 1973.

Frankford, Robert. "Taking an Inside Look at the H.S.O. If These Organizations Succeed They May Have Large Medical Implications", *The Medical Post*, July 10, 1984.

Freedman, Theodore. "Palliative Care. A Process of Change", *Hospital Trustee*, November/December 1979.

Gelber, Sylvia M. "Hospital Insurance in Canada", *I.L.O. Review*, 79, 1959.

Godbout, Jacques. "Is Consumer Control Possible in Health Care Services? — The Quebec Case", *Int. J. Health Services*, 11, 1, 1981.

Goldberg, Ted. "The Canadian National Health Insurance Program: Impact of Policies on HMOS". Presented at 1984 Group Health Institute, Philadelphia, June 11, 1984 (processed).

Gosselin, Roger. "Centralization/Regionalization in Health Care: The Quebec Experience", *H.C.M. Rev.*, Winter 1984, p. 8.

Greenway, Kathryn R. *Hospice Care in Canada: A Review*. Presented at Ontario Psychiatric Association, Toronto, February 1979 (processed).

Grossman, Hon. Larry, Minister of Health, Ontario. "Ontario Health Centres — An Idea Whose Time Has Come". Speech to Association of Ontario Health Centres, Toronto, October 28, 1982 (processed).

Hamilton District Health Council. "Assessment and Placement Services of the Hamilton District Health Council", *Second Annual Report*, 1973.

Hamilton-Wentworth DHC. "Assessment and Placement Services of Hamilton-Wentworth". *Annual Report*, 1982-83.

Hamilton-Wentworth DHC. *The Hamilton Health Services Laboratory Program*, April 1983 (processed).

Hamilton-Wentworth DHC. Faculty of Health Sciences, McMaster University, Mohawk College, Chedoke-McMaster Hospital, Hamilton Civic Hospitals, Hamilton Psychiatric Hospital, St. Joseph's Hospital, and St. Peter's Centre, "The Health Services Network, Hamilton Ontario", September 1983 (processed).

Hamilton-Wentworth DHC. "A Look at the Programmatic Approach to Health Care Delivery in the Hamilton District", July 1970 (processed).

Hastings, J.E.F. "Community Health Centres — What's Happened Since the Hastings Report? — Neither Sweet nor Sour". Presented at 19th Annual Refresher Course: Issues in Community Health. University of Toronto, Division of Community Health, Toronto, March 17, 1978, mimeo.

Hastings, J.E.F. "Federal-Provincial Insurance for Hospital and Physicians' Care in Canada", *Int. J. of Health Services*, 1, 4, 1971.

Hastings, J.E.F. *Patterns of Community Participation in Primary Health Care — Canada*. Part of a nine-country study report. Copenhagen: World Health Organization, Regional Office for Europe, 1984, forthcoming.

Hastings, J.E.F., W.R. Mindell, J.W. Browne and J.M. Barnsley. "Canadian Health Administrator Study", *Can. J. Pub. Health*, 72, suppl. 1, March/April 1981.

Hastings, J.E.F., F.D. Mott, A.T. Barclay and D. Hewitt. "Prepaid Group Practice in Sault Ste. Marie, Ontario, Part I; Analysis of Utilization Records", *Med. Care*, 11, 2, March-April 1973.

Hastings, J.E.F., F.D. Mott, D. Hewitt and A.T. Barclay. "An Interim Report on the Sault Ste. Marie Study: A Comparison of Personal Health Services Utilization". A joint Canada - World Health Organization Project. *Can. J. Pub. Health*, 61, 4, July/August 1970a.

Hastings, J.E.F., F.D. Mott, D. Hewitt and A.T. Barclay. "The Sault Ste. Marie Study: Utilization of Health Services under Different Organizational Patterns for the Delivery of Personal Health Care. An Interim Report on the Utilization of Laboratory and Diagnostic Radiological Services". Presented to Medical Care Section, 98th Annual Meeting, American Public Health Association, Houston, October 26, 1970b, mimeo.

Heseltine, G.F. "Blueprint for Changes: The Next Ten Years". Discussion document. Toronto: Ontario Ministry of Health, 1982.

House, A.M. "Satellite telemedicine system to support offshore health care", *C.A.D.C.J.*, Winter 1984.

House of Commons. *Minutes of Proceedings and Evidence of the Standing Committee on Health, Welfare, and Social Affairs Respecting: Bill C-3 Canada Health Act.* Ottawa: Queen's Printer, Issue no. 4, February 19, 1984.

House of Commons. *Minutes of Proceedings and Evidence of the Standing Committee on Health, Welfare, and Social Affairs Respecting Bill C-3, Canada Health Act.* Ottawa: Queen's Printer, Issue no. 5, February 14, 1984.

Kagis, Maya. "Here's Looking Back at Us!", *Healthlink*, No. 1, Fall 1982. (Newsletter of Association of Ontario Health Centres)

Lacroix, Raymond. "The Hawkesbury Experiment: A Major Step Forward", *Dimensions in Health Service*, 61, 1, January 1984.

Lalonde, Marc, Minister of National Health and Welfare. *A New Perspective on the Health of Canadians, A Working Document.* Ottawa: Government of Canada, 1974.

LeClair, Maurice. "The Canadian Health Care System". Ch. 2 in S. Andreopoulos, ed., *National Health Insurance: Can We Learn from Canada?* Toronto: John Wiley, 1975.

Limongelli, Fulvio. "Accreditation: New Standards Published", *Dimensions in Health Service*, 60, 7, July 1983.

Lomas, Jonathan. *First and Foremost in Community Health Centres: The Centre in Sault Ste. Marie and the CHC Alternative.* Toronto: University of Toronto Press, 1985.

Lomas, Jonathan and Greg L. Stoddart. "Estimates of the Potential Impact of Nurse Practitioners on Future Requirements for General Practitioners". Hamilton: McMaster University, Department of Clinical Epidemiology and Biostatistics, 1982 (processed).

Luft, Harold S. *Health Maintenance Organizations: Dimensions of Performance.* Toronto: John Wiley, 1981.

Manitoba. *Mental Health Services in Manitoba. A Review and Recommendations.* Winnipeg: Mental Health Working Group, 1983.

Manitoba. *White Paper on Health Policy.* Winnipeg: Cabinet Committee on Health, Education and Social Policy, 1972.

Manning, H.G., A. Leibowitz, G.A. Goldberg, W.H. Rogers and J.P. Newhouse. "A Controlled Trial of the Effect of a Prepaid Group Practice on Use of Services", *N. Eng. J. Med*, 310, 23, June 7, 1984.

McColl, W.A. *Group Practice and Prepayment of Medical Care.* Washington, D.C.: Public Affairs Press, 1966.

McDermit, Robert E., M. Bernstein and Elizabeth Harmer. "U.B.C. Hospital: A Computer in Every Corner", *Dimensions in Health Services*, 60, 8, August 1983.

Mott, F.D., J.E.F. Hastings and A.T. Barclay. "Prepaid Group Practice in Sault Ste. Marie, Ontario. Part II: Evidence from the Household Survey", *Med. Care*, May-June 3, 1973.

Mount, Balfour M. "The Problem of Caring for the Dying in a General Hospital: The Palliative Care Unit as a Possible Solution", *Can. Med Assoc. J.*, 115, July 17, 1976.

Newfoundland and Labrador. *Royal Commission on Hospital and Nursing Home Costs*. St. John's, 1984.

Nova Scotia. *Health Care in Nova Scotia — A New Direction for the Seventies*. Halifax: Nova Scotia Council of Health, 1972.

Ontario. *Final Report of the Steering Committee for the Development Assessment of District Health Councils in Ontario*. Toronto: Ontario Ministry of Health, 1983.

Ontario. *Health Protection and Promotion Act*. R.S.O., 1983.

Ontario. *Report of the Committee on the Healing Arts*. Toronto: Queen's Printer, Vols. I-III, 1970.

Ontario. *Report of the Health Planning Task Force*. Mustard Report. Toronto: Government of Ontario, 1974.

Ontario. *Report of the Task Force to Review Primary Care* (Chairman, J.F. Mustard). Toronto, 1982 (processed).

Ontario New Democratic Party. *Health Care Priorities*. Toronto, 1984 (processed).

Pattison, R.V. and H.M. Katz. "Investor-Owned and Not-for-Profit Hospitals: A Comparison Based on California Data", *N. Eng. J. Med.* 309, 1983.

Pineault, Reynald. "The Place of Prevention in the Quebec Health System", *Can. J. of Pub. Health*, 75, Jan./Feb. 1984.

Protti, Denis J. "The Dawn of a New Age: Competence in Health Care", *Dimensions in Health Service*, 61, 2, Feb. 1984.

Pynn, David J. "Shared Food Services: An Appetizing Idea", *Dimensions in Health Service*, 60, 6, June 1983.

Quebec. *Law on Health and Social Services*. Quebec: Official Editor, S.P.Q., Ch. 48, 1971, and *Amendment*, S.R.O., Ch. 48, 1981.

Quebec. *Report of the Commission of Enquiry on Health and Social Welfare*. Castonguay-Nepveu Report. Quebec: Official Publisher, 1970-71, Vols. I-VIII.

Richman, A. "Advances in Therapeutics and Diagnosis: Reassessing Problems in Care", *Annals R.C.P. and S. Canada*, 16, 5, 1983.

Robertson, Hon. Brenda. "Remarks by The Honourable Brenda Robertson, Minister, Social Program Reform", *Budget Estimates*. Fredericton, June 8, 1984 (processed).

Romeder, Jean-Marie. *Self-Help Groups in Canada*. Ottawa: Program Information Unit, Health and Welfare Canada, 1982.

Rudin, S.E. and M. Jesion. "Baycrest: It Tries Hard to Keep Patients Out", *Dimensions in Health Service*, 60, 7, July 1983.

Ruth, S. and E.S. Rudin. "The Baycrest Experience: Make Your Beds go Further", *Can. Hospital*, May 1973.

Schwenger, C.W. "Future Education of Physicians in Public Health". Editorial in *Can. J. Pub. Health*, 62, 1, Jan./Feb. 1971.

Shah, C.P. "Day-Care Surgery in Canada: Evolution, Policy, and Experience of Provinces", *Can. Anaesth. Soc. J.*, 27, 1980.

Shapiro, Evelyn. *Home Care: A Comprehensive Overview*. Ottawa: Health and Welfare Canada, Policy Planning and Information Branch, Sept. 1979 (unpublished; processed).

Shephard, David A.E. "Principles and Practice of Palliative Care". Report of an international seminar, Montreal, Nov. 3-5, 1976. In *Can. Med. Assoc. J.*, 116, March 5, 1977.

Somers, A.R. *The Kaiser-Permanente Medical Care Program: A Symposium*. New York: The Commonwealth Fund, 1981.

Spitzer, W.O. "The Nurse Practitioner Revisited: Slow Death of a Good Idea". Editorial in *N. Eng. J. Med.*, 310, April 19, 1984.

Spitzer, W.0., W.A. Russel and B.C. Hackett. "Financial Consequences of Employing a Nurse Practitioner", *Ont. Med. Rev.*, 40, 1973.

Spitzer, W.O., D.L. Sackett, J.C. Sibley, R.S. Roberts, M. Gent, D.J. Kergin, B.C. Hackett, A. Olynick *et al.* "The Burlington Randomized Trial of the Nurse Practitioner", *N. Eng. J. Med.*, 290, 1974.

Stewart, M. "Nova Scotia's Multiservice Health System," *Dimensions in Health Service*, 59, 5, May 1982.

Stoddart, Greg L. *Appendix A* in Ontario, *Report of the Task Force to Review Primary Care*. Toronto, 1982 (processed).

Stoddart, Greg L. "Rationalizing the Health Care System". Paper prepared for Ontario Economic Council. *Conference on Ottawa and the Provinces: The Distribution of Money and Power*, May 1984, forthcoming.

Swanson, A. Interview in *Dimensions in Health Service*, 59, 24, July 1982.

Talbot, John. "Community Human Resources and Health Centres in British Columbia". Presented at "19th Annual Refresher Course: Issues in Community Health", University of Toronto, May 17, 1978, mimeo.

Taylor, M.G. "The Canadian Health Care System, 1974-1984". Paper presented for *Health Policy Conference on the Canadian Health Care System*. The Banff Centre School of Management, Banff, Alberta, August 1984. (Ch. 1. Medicare at Maturity 1987)

Taylor, M.G. *Health Insurance and Canadian Public Policy: The Seven Decisions That Created the Canadian Health Insurance System*. Montreal: McGill-Queen's University Press, 1978.

Taylor, M.G., H.M. Stevenson and A.P. Williams. "Medical Perspectives on Canadian Medicare: Attitudes of Canadian Physicians to Policies and Problems of the Medical Care Insurance Program". Toronto: York University, 1984. (Special computer run on numbers of physicians in group and solo practice.)

Terris, M. "The Complex Tasks of the Second Epidemiologic Revolution". The Joseph W. Mountain Lecture. *J. of Pub. Health Policy*, 4, 1, March 1983.

Toronto, Local Board of Health. *Public Health in the 1980s*. Report of the Health Planning Steering Committee, Toronto, May 1978.

Trent, Bill. "Quebec's Struggle for Community-based Medicine", *Can. Med. Assoc. J.*, 130, May 1, 1984.

Tyhurst, J.S. et al. *More for the Mind: A Study of Psychiatric Services in Canada*. Toronto: The Canadian Mental Health Association, 1963.

Van Loon, R.K. "From Shared Cost to Block Funding and Beyond: The Politics of Health Insurance in Canada", *J. Health Politics, Policy and Law*, 2, 1978.

Vayda, Eugene. "Prepaid Group Practice under Universal Health Insurance in Canada," *Med. Care*, 15, 5, 1977.

Vayda, Eugene and Raisa B. Deber. "The Canadian Health Care System: An Overview", *Soc. Sci. Med.*, 18, 3, 1984.

Vayda, Eugene, Robert G. Evans and William R. Mindell. "Universal Health Insurance in Canada: History, Problems, Trends", *J. Comm. Health*, 4, 3, 1979.

Vayda, Eugene and J.E.F. Hastings. "Brief to House of Commons Standing Committee on Health, Welfare and Social Affairs in Response to the Proposed Canada Health Act". Toronto: 1984 (processed).

Vayda, Eugene, William R. Mindell and Ira M. Rutkow. "A Decade of Surgery in Canada, England and Wales, and the United States", *Arch. Surgery*, 117, June 1982.

Wasylenki, D. Lecture in course CHL 3001, "Canada's Health Care System", Graduate Department of Community Health, University of Toronto, November 1983.

Wasylenki, D., P. Georing, W. Lancee, L. Fischer and S.J.J. Freeman. "Psychiatric Aftercare in a Metropolitan Setting", *Hospital and Community Psychiatry*, forthcoming.

Wise, Harold, R. Beckhard, I. Rubin and A. Kyte, eds. *Making Health Teams Work*. Cambridge, Mass.: Ballinger, 1974.

Wood, P.L. Ontario Health Association. Personal communication to Eugene Vayda, October 18, 1983 and January 24, 1984.

Wright, P.A., D. Le Touze, R. Shillington and C. Thompson. "Hospital of the Future: A Project Updated", *Dimensions in Health Service*, 61, 2, February 1984.

Yedidia, A. *Planning and Implementation of the Community Health Foundation of Cleveland*. Arlington, VA: U.S. Department of Health, Education and Welfare, 1969.

Young, T. Kue. "Indian Health Service in Perspective: A Socio-historical Perspective", *Soc Sci. Med.*, 18, 3, 1984.

Zuckerman, Alan M. "Diagnosis Related Groups: Applications for Canada", *Health Managment Forum*, 4, 4, Winter 1983.

COMMENTARY

Jacques Brunet

Introduction

Drs. Hastings and Vayda's paper is an excellent overview of the evolution of health service organization and delivery in Canada during the past decade. They review the studies and reports published by the federal and provincial governments, the organization of medical practice, public health and mental health, the institutional sector and the private sector; they also consider the future of the health system. My comments will consider the main changes necessary in health service organization fifteen years after Medicare, and I will refer often to the Quebec experience.

There is general agreement in Canada that the health system is functioning adequately, is well accepted by the public and has succeeded in containing cost. Its main objectives of universality, accessibility and quality to a large extent have been attained.

Canadians in general, and Quebecers in particular, are very proud of their health system. They resist any major changes in the organization and delivery of services, as illustrated by the public backing of the new Canada Health Act (1984), which is intended to eliminate extra-billing and user fees.

The organization of health services in Canada promotes accessibility and universality. This has recently been reinforced by Parliament's approval of the Canada Health Act. It appears that the Act is making changes and innovation in the organization of health services more difficult. The main barrier is legislative, but we should not forget the resistance to change on the part of institutions, professionals and the general public. However, changes and innovation are essential in maintaining a dynamic health system. It is from this perspective that I will consider the main organizational changes that appear desirable in the near future.

The health system has contributed to the improvement of the health status of Canadians. Recent data show longer life expectancy, diminution of infant and perinatal mortality, and decreased mortality due to ischemic disease, road accidents, cancer of the cervix and lung cancer in men. The delivery system is only partly responsible for these improvements, but there is some evidence that it plays a role (Conseil des Affaires sociale et de la Famille, 1983).

Definition of Health Goals

The orientation of the health system should rest on defined health goals that are judged to be priorities by governments. This would help the various actors in the delivery system to coordinate their activities toward improving the health status of the population and would also facilitate the evaluation of programs in the health system.

The definition by federal and provincial governments of general goals for improving health status should become a political imperative. In Quebec, the following general goals have been defined by a provincial committee on Health Promotion and submitted to the Minister:

1. The improvement of life expectancy in good health (without serious physical or mental limitation).
2. The reduction of premature mortality, in particular violent death.
3. The reduction of inequalities in health.
4. The reduction of the frequency, gravity and impact of chronic disease.
5. The diminution of the incidence, gravity and impact of mental health problems.

In the near future, we hope that the Minister of Social Affairs will adopt these or other general goals. Thereafter it will be necessary to define more specific goals and programs for health promotion. The choice of such goals is difficult. Their specificity can be related to age group, health problems or the environment. In Quebec, we have decided to group them by age: infants from zero to five years, youth from six to twenty-four, adults from twenty-five to sixty-four, and the aged from sixty-five and on.

It is unfortunate that the health data available impose a rather medical formulation on the problems, even though the causes of morbidity and mortality largely lie outside the health delivery system. Health promotion relies heavily on communicating practical ways of avoiding health risks. As an illustration, let me mention a few specific goals that have been chosen by the committee:

1. To diminish the number of low-weight infants at birth.
2. To reduce violent death in youth, particularly death from motor vehicle and motorcycle accidents and suicide.

3. To improve the diagnosis and treatment of hypertension in order to reduce later complications of the disease.
4. To improve alternative services for the aged that allow them to remain in their community.

The health service organization and delivery system is not familiar with such goal-setting processes. The system requires a profound change in attitude on the part of hospital administrators, professionals and physicians. But we believe that it is a necessary step if the health system is to improve the health status of the population and not just respond to demand.

Let us now examine the organizational and financial changes that appear necessary to improve the health service delivery system.

Organizational Changes

The health service organization and delivery system in Canada is one of the best systems in the world. As mentioned in Drs. Hastings and Vayda's paper,

> Further development of the health system will likely depend not only on continuing prudent constraints on existing services, but even more on incentives for restructuring the system to give greater emphasis to ambulatory care, community-based care, prevention, health promotion and health maintenance.

I agree entirely with their statement and feel that future changes should move in the following directions:

Primary Care or Community-based Care

In the province of Quebec, the first priority remains the completion of the community centres (CLSC). These community-based institutions are necessary to guarantee that health services are related to the needs of the population served. In Quebec the actual number of CLSCs is around 110, and about fifty more are necessary to complete the system of first-line care.

These community centres are responsible for primary health and social services in a defined community. They are seen as an alternative to traditional individual medical care, and the services that they offer are based on community needs. They are responsible for home care services. They also offer support to the young and the aged. This approach implies the development of ambulatory care and alternative services, instead of in-patient services.

Deinstitutionalization

Similarly, every possible effort should be made to promote deinstitutionalization. This applies to care for the aged, but also for the mentally retarded, psychiatric patients, the severely handicapped, etc. The objective is to improve the quality of life, and every effort should be made to maintain these individuals in their community. This would entail increased emphasis on community-based services rather than on making available more hospital or nursing home beds.

Quebec has made great progress in this direction in the past ten years, and most actors in the system accept this orientation. However, the transition remains difficult and more alternative resources are necessary.

Acute Care Hospitals

In hospitals we observe two divergent trends. First, the acute care hospital is increasingly becoming an intensive care unit and the daily cost is increasing rapidly. This trend will continue and become the characteristic of the hospital of the future. To control cost, however, hospitals tend to develop ambulatory activities such as day surgery, day hospitals (mostly for the aged) and outpatient diagnostic facilities.

The second trend in acute care hospitals is the increasing number of long-term care patients in acute care beds. These patients should be relocated in more appropriate institutions or units. Every effort should be made either to return patients back to their community with adequate services or to relocate them to more appropriate institutions. This may mean that some acute care hospitals will become, in part or in whole, long-term care hospitals. In Quebec, for instance, 10 percent of the total beds in each acute care hospital have been identified as long-term beds in specific units for long-term care. This is a difficult but rational decision that should be upheld.

Geriatric Care

Health services for the aged are inadequate in our system. The needs and expectations of the elderly are different from those of adults or children; they tend to be more insecure and more dependent. Changes in their health status are often the result of social needs, and health services are not adapted to such needs. For the primary care system and hospitals to adapt to the special needs of the elderly will require a change in attitude on the part of the professionals, and a change in the organization of the services, including the introduction of geriatric units for some specific acute care patients, re-adaptation units, day hospitals and home care services.

I consider this to be the major challenge for the health system in the next decade. More physicians, nurses, physiotherapists, ergotherapists and other professionals will be required in geriatrics and gerontology. Some resource reallocation or transfer to the aged population appears necessary to improve the quality of services. The health service organization and delivery system should consider the care of the aged as a new challenge and make every effort possible to help the elderly maintain their autonomy and improve their quality of life.

Health Promotion and Maintenance

Health promotion and maintenance is a fundamental goal of the health service organization and delivery system. Health promotion is not meant to replace curative health services, but rather to improve the efficiency and effectiveness of the existing systems.

The public health sector plays an essential role in health promotion and maintenance. New knowledge has drastically modified priorities in the public health field, and there is general agreement that health promotion and maintenance, preventive programs and epidemiology are major responsibilities of the public health sector.

As Drs. Hastings and Vayda mentioned, Quebec has transferred all public health staff and activities to designated regional hospitals and has set a four-year program for residents in community medicine. Planning, health care organization and epidemiology are part of their training.

In Quebec, departments of community health (DSC) are responsible for the public health of a defined territory. Their dynamism and involvement in health promotion and maintenance, epidemiology and program evaluation illustrates the crucial role that they play in the orientation of our health system. This example highlights the need for organizational change in our health service delivery system.

Financial Changes

We have already discussed at this meeting the economic aspect of the health system and its rigid organization. The health system is expensive. Many of us are worried about the level of expenditure in the health field in relation to the Gross National Product. Will it be possible to control the level of expenditure in the next decade? Do we see sufficient improvement in morbidity and mortality to justify our investments? Can we improve the quality and efficiency of our health service system?

Health system costs have remained under control in Canada during the past decade, as Barer and Evans have demonstrated. This has been achieved through severe controls by provincial governments on the size of hospitals, their budgets, the number of acute care beds and new technology.

This policy has been successful in the past, but what about the future? The aging of the population, the increase in demand, the development of new technology and the principle of "accessibility for all" confirmed by the new Canada Health Act are serious sources of concern.

It therefore appears that a number of measures are necessary to maintain our record of cost-control. The more significant of these are: to enforce global budgets for hospitals, to limit the growth of hospital bed capacity, to freeze or reduce the number of acute care beds in each province, to create incentives that encourage less expensive types of care, to limit the growth of the physical stock to 1 percent per year and to limited the increase in remuneration for physicians and hospital employees to less than the increase in the consumer price index.

There is nothing in the experience of the United States that suggests that profound change is needed in our system. All Canadians have free access to health services, yet our share of Gross National Product devoted to health is less than that of the U.S.

Conclusion

The changes in health care organization and delivery that I have suggested are aimed at improving the quality, accessibility and efficiency of the system. Our ultimate goal remains the improvement of health status and of quality of life. It is essential, however, that we consider health services as only one part of health policy. The enrichment of the concepts of health appears to be the fundamental issue. Health should be the result of a process of adaptation between the individual and his environment in which healthy individuals are those able to engage in normal daily activities.

Reference

Conseil des Affaires sociales et de la Famille. *La Santé des Québécois: Des problèmes prioritaires.* Gouvernement du Québec, 1983.

VI

CONFLICT MANAGEMENT

CONFLICT AND ACCOMMODATION IN THE CANADIAN HEALTH CARE SYSTEM

Carolyn Tuohy

Introduction

In global perspective — indeed, even in the context of western industrial nations — the similarities between Canada and the United States are far more striking than their differences. They are both pluralist liberal democracies (as opposed, for example, to the "corporatist" or "quasi-corporatist" democracies of Western Europe and Japan).[1] Their party systems are each dominated by two major parties espousing variants of a liberal democratic ideology. And they are federal states in which both national and sub-national governments are involved in most areas of public policy.

Because of these very similarities, the marginal differences in our political cultures, institutions and public policies can be mutually instructive, whether we consider them as dependent or independent variables. The arena of health care policy provides a particularly interesting case.

As an essentially similar medical technology has evolved in marginally different cultural and institutional contexts, the public policy responses in Canada and the U.S. have differed significantly. Understanding these differences, and their likely future development, requires us to consider the histories of conflict and accommodation among interests in the health care field in the two countries. And those histories have been shaped not only by broad technological, cultural and institutional forces, but also by the strategic behaviour and pragmatic judgements of political and economic actors at particular historical junctures.

The purpose of this paper is to trace in general outline the evolution of these dynamic and complex processes in Canada and the U.S. It begins by sketching the broad cultural and institutional similarities and differences in the political systems of the two countries, as relevant to an understanding of health care policy. It then traces a brief history of the conflicts and accommodations that have led to the current *status quo*. Finally, it attempts to suggest the lines of future development.

Political Culture

Collective Ideologies: Canada vs. the U.S.

Perhaps the most frequently noted broad difference between the political economies of Canada and the U.S. is Canada's greater "collectivism". Broad indicators of this phenomenon, though crude, are generally consistent. In 1982, total government expenditure in Canada as a share of Gross National Product (GNP) was 40 percent; in the U.S. the comparable figure was 35 percent.[2] Differences in "welfare state spending" are in the same direction, though less marked. In 1979 government spending on health, education, social security, welfare, and housing and community amenities represented 21 percent of GNP in Canada and 18 percent in the U.S.[3]

These differences, however, need to be seen in historical and comparative perspective. Government spending as a proportion of GNP in the two countries was roughly similar from the 1930s through the 1960s (with the exception of the World War II period in which U.S. government spending was vastly greater); only in the 1970s did the Canadian proportion rise to three to seven points above the U.S. figure. Furthermore Canada and the U.S. are in the mid-range among OECD countries: Japanese and Australian government spending represented about 31 percent of GNP in 1981, while in the Netherlands the share stood at 59 percent.[4]

Crude measures of economic inequality in the two countries, which reflect the impact of redistribution policies, among other factors, are markedly similar. In the mid-1970s the share of national income (after tax) received by the poorest population decile was 1.5 percent in both Canada and the U.S., as opposed to 2.5 percent in West Germany, 2.4 percent in the United Kingdom and 2.9 percent in Sweden.[5] As for regional economic inequality, the two countries are again very similar: the "Gini" index of inequality in *per capita* income among provinces/states was identical in the mid-1970s and indicated a degree of inter-regional inequality greater than that which existed in Germany, Australia or the U.K., similar to that in France and less than that in Italy.[6]

Nonetheless, there are dimensions of "collectivism" in Canadian political culture that have been particularly significant in the evolution of health care policy and that need to be examined at some length. A classic elucidation of the roots and character of collectivist strains in Canadian political culture is presented by Horowitz.[7] He extends and modifies the approach developed by Hartz and applied to Canada by McRae,[8] an approach which posits that the societies founded by European colonists (e.g., the U.S., English Canada, French Canada, Latin America, Australia) can be understood as "fragments" thrown off from the mother country which took root and developed independently in the new frontier. As Horowitz describes this approach:

> The key to the understanding of ideological development in a new society is its "point of departure" from Europe: the ideologies borne by the founders of the new society are not representative of the historic ideological spectrum of the mother country. The settlers represent only a fragment of that spectrum. The complete ideological spectrum ranges — in chronological order and from right to left — from feudal or tory through liberal whig to liberal democrat to socialist. French Canada and Latin America are "feudal fragments". They were founded by bearers of the feudal or tory values of the organic, corporate, hierarchical community; their departure from Europe is before the liberal revolution. The United States, English Canada and Dutch South Africa are "bourgeois" fragments, founded by bearers of liberal individualism who have left the tory end of the spectrum behind them. Australia is the one "radical fragment" founded by bearers of the working class ideologies of mid-nineteenth century Britain.[9]

Most significantly, this fragmentation process in a sense arrests ideological development:

> The full ideological spectrum of Europe develops only out of the continued confrontation and interaction of its four elements; they are related to each other, not only as enemies, but as parents and children . . . . In escaping the past, the fragment escapes the future, for "the very seeds of the later ideas are contained in the parts of the old world which have been left behind".[10]

The tension (or lack thereof) between collectivist and individualist strains in different political cultures can be understood in these terms. Both toryism and socialism view society as a community, an organic entity in which all parts function for the good of the whole. Toryism justifies an inequality of condition in the interests of the collective good: the positions of various "estates" are grounded in a comprehensive framework of social values prescribing their functional responsibilities, their social obligations and, to a large extent, the just rewards attached to the fulfilment of these responsibilities and obligations. The bourgeois reaction to this inequality of condition is to attack ascribed privilege and to emphasize equality of individual opportunity, first in the ownership of property, then in access to the franchise and the largesse of the state. Socialism, in turn, extends this egalitarianism to embrace equality of condition, emphasizing common (at first, class and then community) interests over individual interests. In a culture with no vestigial memory of the organic corporate concepts of toryism, such an appeal has less resonance.

Hartz and McRae, and later Horowitz, have applied this approach in discussing the differences between Canadian and U.S. political culture. Both English Canada and the U.S. are bourgeois "fragments" thrown off from England, and hence both cultures are dominated by liberal individualism. Through a war of independence, moreover, the American republic renounced any vestigial toryism and founded a society explicitly dedicated to principles of Lockean liberalism. "Loyalists" in English Canada, on the other hand, while basically bourgeois liberals, retained and defiantly preserved what Hartz has called a tory "streak" or "touch". French Canada, moreover, dominated by the hierarchical Roman Catholic Church, preserved its "feudal fragment" faithfully into the mid-twentieth century.

Horowitz develops the Hartzian insight regarding Canada's tory touch to explain two Canadian phenomena which contrast with the U.S.: the greater vigour and electoral success of an indigenous socialist movement, and the presence of "red toryism". The social democratic New Democratic Party has formed the government in three provinces at various times, and is an established third party elsewhere in the country, at the federal level as well. (Horowitz did not address the then-nascent development of a socialist strain within the Quebec separatist movement, although it is consistent with his argument.) In Horowitz's view, a socialist party was able to establish itself in Canada because its ideas were not alien. Socialist ideas "'fit' with a political culture which already contained some non-liberal components".[11] Furthermore, those ideas were borne by British immigrants who were not considered "foreigners". In the U.S., in contrast, there were no tory echoes with which socialist ideas of community could resonate, and socialism was carried by immigrants from political cultures foreign to the dominant ethnic groups. In Horowitz's terms, "in Canada, socialism is British, non-Marxist and worldly; in the United States it is German, Marxist and other worldly".[12]

"Red toryism" is Horowitz's term for a variety of admixtures of tory conservative and socialist elements, a term that has since entered the political lexicon in Canada. It refers to the willingness of some conservatives to support programs (such as Medicare) tending toward a greater equality of condition, or (less commonly) the willingness of social democrats to preserve traditional institutions (such as the monarchy) that express community values, even though those institutions may contribute to the perpetuation of an inequality of condition. It is an ideology that emphasizes the social responsibilities and obligations of those who hold privileged positions in society, as part of the justification of those privileges. It also encourages a collaboration between the leadership of corporate groups and the state in the pursuit of redistributive policies.

Canadian collectivism, then, can take the form of democratic socialism or of red toryism. But there is also a dimension of collectivism in mainstream bourgeois liberalism in both Canada and the U.S. Both English Canadian and U.S. bourgeois fragments were initially thrown off from England during a period of mercantilism. Much early settlement in New England and in "the lands draining into Hudson's Bay" was accomplished by private companies which, under charter from the Crown, were given jurisdiction over defined (and, in the case of the Hudson's Bay Company, vast) geographic areas. These private corporations, while legally subordinate to the state and used to further public policy goals, nonetheless enjoyed great *de facto* authority and enormous grants of public resources.

This pattern of using private corporations as vehicles of public policy, aided by massive infusions of public capital, has persisted in the U.S. and Canada, although the instruments used have differed somewhat. Canada, by and large, has been more willing to undertake direct public subsidy, often leading to outright public ownership; the U.S. has favoured regulatory action and contracting relationships. In the nineteenth century, Canadian policies were directed toward developing the infrastructure of a sparsely settled ribbon of land in defiance of "natural" continental economic flows. Grants of public land and capital for railway construction, timber and mineral rights for resource extraction, and direct governmental construction of some railways and canals accustomed the Canadian business elite to the view that the state had not only a legitimate role but an obligation to intervene where private capital dared not go.[13] This view led, in the twentieth century, to a greater willingness to accept public ownership as a policy instrument, although in each arena there have been extenuating circumstances: the need to rescue private corporations that had overbuilt as a result of lavish public aid (railways); the desire for self-sufficiency vis-à-vis the U.S. (hydroelectric and nuclear power); the economic problems of serving thinly spread rural populations (telephone);[14] and, more recently, the behaviour of international competitors (aircraft).

The Legitimation of Private Concentrations of Power

One important result of these ideological factors in Canada and the U.S. has been that concentrations of private power have been legitimated in both countries. But the nature of the legitimation has differed in ways significant to the understanding of health policy. The dominant liberal democratic ethic of both countries is pluralistic. It legitimates concentrations of power only to the extent that they are *countervailing*, that they compete with, check and balance each other. As one interpreter of this pluralistic ethic has stated, the freedom of the individual "resides only in the interstices between organizations".[15] One of the major effects of this ideology has been to legitimate the power of private organizations as a check against the power of the state. Indeed, it is one of the ironies (some would say contradictions) of liberal democracy that an ideology so distrustful of concentrations of power, especially the power of the state, should legitimate oligarchies in the private sector.[16]

In Canada, the tory strain provides another source of legitimacy for corporate power, based not on a concept of individual liberty but on one of functional sovereignty. In this view, sovereignty is shared by the government and a variety of functional groups, on the model of medieval guilds and universities. Each group is seen as sovereign in its own functional sphere and bound to the others by virtue of its functioning within the organic whole of society. The ideology is a deferential one in which authority is vested in elites that govern their own spheres and collaborate with each other in the definition and pursuit of over-arching social goals. (In modern "red" toryism, these goals are more redistributive than the "pure" version would countenance.) Corporate bodies, then, have an intrinsic legitimacy as functional parts of the social organism, and not merely an instrumental legitimacy as promoters of the prior value of individualism. And this legitimacy depends on a recognition of the social obligations attendant on their functional responsibilities.

Only socialism, among the ideologies discussed, presents a fundamental challenge to concentrations of private power. In its democratic socialist variant, it legitimates a considerable concentration of power in the state, so long as the institutions of the state are open to influence by those who would pursue socialist policies.

Summary

In short, the ideological spectrum is somewhat more fully developed in Canada than in the U.S. In the latter country, the spectrum is occupied almost entirely by liberal pluralism, ranging from a thoroughgoing defence of individualism (as has often been noted, what American "conservatives" have to preserve is eighteenth- and nineteenth-century liberalism) through "interest group" liberalism (emphasizing the countervailing power of groups representing a variety of interests) to "neo-mercantile" and "welfare state" liberalism (emphasizing to varying degrees both the necessity for co-operation between private groups and the state, to minimize destructive competition, and the responsibility of the state to provide a "safety net" for victims of the competitive market). In Canada, this spectrum is extended to include non-liberal, less individualistic and more "collectivist" components — toryism on the right and socialism on the left. The coexistence of these elements has produced distinctive hybrids: "tory-touched" liberals less distrustful of concentrated power than their U.S. counterparts; "red tories" supportive of redistributive policies implemented through public and private hierarchies; and democratic socialists willing to pursue collectivist goals through the institutions of the liberal state.

These different legitimations of state and corporate power, and challenges to them, have important implications for the evolution of health care policy in

Canada and the U.S. Before proceeding to that discussion, however, it is necessary to trace out some of the central institutional features of the two political systems.

Governmental Institutions

The discussion so far suggests that the legitimate scope of the state is somewhat broader in Canada than in the U.S. In both countries, however, the power of the state is *divided*, and here again the similarities and differences between them have important implications for their capacity for governmental action.

The pluralist, liberal democratic distrust of concentrated power is revealed in the design of U.S. institutions. Monopolies of legislative, executive and judicial power are avoided and authority is divided so that institutions check and balance each other. The involvement of different institutions of government with different power bases in each of the legislative, executive and judicial processes provides numerous "veto points". Canada, in contrast, operates under a tradition of parliamentary supremacy in which the constraints on the authority of Parliament are largely conventional rather than formal. Only in 1982 did Canada adopt as part of its Constitution a Charter of Rights and Freedoms guaranteeing a variety of individual rights against legislative encroachment. Even here, however, federal or provincial legislatures may explicitly over-ride some of the provisions of the Charter.

The formal constraints on Canadian governments derive largely from the relations, not among *branches* of government, but among *levels* (or orders) of government within the federal system. A comparison of Canadian and American federalism may illumine the nature of these constraints.

Like other dimensions of political culture, concepts of federalism in both countries are varied and in some tension with each other. The Canadian Constitution allows for a wide range of interpretation in the distribution of powers to federal and provincial governments.[17] The provincial governments are granted substantial powers by enumeration, including responsibility for "hospitals, asylums, charities and eleemosynary institutions". The federal government, however, in addition to its enumerated powers, has authority to make laws for the "peace, order and good government" of Canada in all matters not exclusively assigned to the provinces. The federal government also has unlimited taxing authority, whereas the provinces are limited to "direct" taxation.[18]

Black has identified five competing concepts of federalism that have characterized Canadians' interpretation of their federal system over time. Two of these — "coordinate" and "administrative" federalism — continue to be relevant.[19] "Coordinate" federalism refers to a concept that:

> accepts the idea that sovereign authority exists within a state, and that it can be divided between, and exercised by, national and re-

gional governments. A fundamental premise holds that these governments are of the same order, equal in rank with each other, and similar in legal status within their constitutionally-determined orbits.[20]

As Black notes, this essentially legalistic concept of federalism "underpins the constitutional status quo [and] is the most conspicuous concept of federalism in Canada".[21] Moreover, it has had a reciprocally strengthening relationship with what Cameron and Dupré have called "the provincialization of regionalism and dualism"[22] — the tendency for regional and Québécois interests to promote their provincial governments as the sovereign authority in matters unique to regions and the French Canadian culture respectively, and the natural tendency for provincial governments to encourage such a view.

This view of Canadian federalism exists in tension with a more pragmatic concept of "administrative federalism". As Black states, "administrative federalism is not a complete theory of federal government; it says only that problems arising from the federal distribution of authority should be approached pragmatically and settled by cooperative action between governments".[23] In Canada, these "problems arising from the federal distribution of powers" largely concern regional economic disparities, the imbalance between the relatively limited taxing powers and the extensive functional responsibilities of the provincial governments, and the emergence of issues (such as the regulation of telecommunications and broadcasting) unforeseen at the time of Confederation in the mid-1800s. Dealing with such problems has required the negotiation of innumerable agreements regarding such matters as conditional and unconditional grants, equalization payments, shared-cost programs and jointly-administered programs. These agreements are struck through a network of inter-governmental committees and conferences culminating in periodic First Ministers' Conferences, and there is considerable disagreement among both participants in and observers of this process over whether it constitutes federal-provincial "diplomacy" among relatively sovereign units or bargaining within an administrative system.[24] The ability of provinces to "opt out" of shared-cost programs, and the movement in the late 1970s from shared-cost funding of "established programs" (hospital and medical insurance and post-secondary education) to block grants and transfers of tax points from federal to provincial levels,[25] have generally been seen as a strengthening of "coordinate" as opposed to "administrative" federalism. The tightening of the federal strings on these transfers by the recent Canada Health Act (to be discussed below) and the rattling of provincial sabres regarding court challenges to the Act are nonetheless evidence that the concept of the conditional grant, with its limitations on provincial autonomy even within constitutionally defined spheres of provincial authority, retains both its vitality and its contentiousness.

In the U.S., "administrative" concepts of federalism clearly dominate all others and have done so for at least a century. The U.S. Constitution establishes broad areas of concurrent jurisdiction for national and state governments with regard to taxing, spending and regulatory powers. Within these broad areas, the actual distribution of authority has been determined through pragmatic negotiation characterized less by concepts of "sovereignty" than by arguments regarding fiscal capacity and political preference. In Grodzin's classic phrase, U.S. federalism resembles less a "layer cake" of divided sovereignty than a "marble cake" of shared responsibility.[26] In this sharing, the federal government is considerably more involved in the details of program delivery at the state level than is the case in Canada. U.S. grants-in-aid carry with them notoriously specific regulations.

Again, however, the differences between the two countries are not clearcut. The U.S. is not without a concept of "coordinate" federalism — a "dual" federalism, as Daniel Elazar, the dean of American federal scholars has put it. In Elazar's terms:

> In handling specific programs, within [the] large area of concurrent powers, the federal and state governments can either divide the responsibility among their separate jurisdictions, each responsible only for its own share of the divided responsibility ("dual federalism"), or divide the work of government cooperatively and share responsibility in each program, with all units directed toward common goals that extend along the entire chain of concurrent powers ("cooperative federalism") and generally overflow into the ostensibly "exclusive" preserves. Though precedent favors the latter approach, the decision must be made anew through the political process in each case.[27]

The greater constraint on governmental action in Canada than in the U.S. imposed by a coordinate concept of federalism can be seen most clearly in the different histories of the adoption of social security measures in the two countries.[28] The U.S. national government adopted a comprehensive social security program in 1935, providing for federally sponsored Old Age, Survivors' and Disability Insurance, inducing the states to enact unemployment insurance programs by providing for federal action should they default, and providing for federal grants-in-aid for state public assistance programs. In Canada, unemployment insurance legislation enacted by the national government in 1935 was struck down by the courts as *ultra vires*. Only after a constitutional amendment in 1941 was it possible for the national government to undertake an unemployment insurance program. A constitutional amendment was also required to allow the national government to assume responsibility for old age pensions in 1952; prior to that time they were a provincial responsibility, aided by federal conditional grants. General public welfare and "categorical" income support programs developed within each province, cost-shared in various ways by the national government, until these programs were absorbed in 1966 into the comprehensive Canada Assistance Plan, which continues as the major federal-provincial shared-cost program today.

One further contrast between Canadian and U.S. federalism needs to be noted. The Canadian national government, and several provincial governments, have been marked by long periods of dominance by a single party: the Liberals in Ottawa, the Conservatives in Ontario, Social Credit and then the Conservatives in Alberta and Social Credit (with one NDP interlude) in British Columbia. The result has been that partisan conflict has tended to occur along the federal-provincial interface as much as, if not more than, within national or provincial governments. The federal-provincial arena, in other words, has become a major locus of partisan as well as regional and jurisdictional conflict. Furthermore, these provincial footholds, together with considerable provincial autonomy, have allowed parties to experiment with programs that were out of step with prevailing policy directions at the national level. This factor, discussed below, has been particularly significant in the health care field.

Canada's federal system presents greater obstacles to comprehensive national programs of health and welfare than does that of the U.S.; however, it also provides stronger sub-national footholds for parties whose policy preferences differ from the priorities expressed at the national level. Within each level of government, moreover, Canada's parliamentary system provides fewer opportunities for the exercise of vetoes than does the American separation-of-powers system. These institutional differences have had significant effects on the histories of conflict and accommodation in the health care systems of the two countries.

Conflict and Accommodation in Canadian Health Care Politics

As is familiar to students of both systems, the organization of health care delivery in Canada and the U.S. has been (or was until the mid- to late 1970s) very similar. Medical services have been provided by physicians in private fee-for-service practice; hospital services have been provided in non-profit institutions owned by voluntary societies, religious orders, municipalities and universities; extended care facilities have been owned by such non-profit groups or by private independent for-profit operators. In general, physicians have not been employed directly by acute care hospitals or extended care facilities. In the former they have been organized as independent medical staffs with individual admitting and treatment privileges. In the latter their involvement has depended on arrangements between individual physicians and their patients or institutional management.

In Canada, these patterns remain basically unchanged, with the exception of extended care. In the U.S., they are being significantly modified with the rise of multi-institutional chains, both for-profit and not-for-profit, and large group practices and Health Maintenance Organizations employing physicians through a variety of remuneration mechanisms.

To a considerable extent, these growing differences in the *organization* of health care delivery can be attributed to the sharp differences in the way health care is *funded* in the two countries. As has been noted by numerous observers of the Canadian health care system, Canada's adoption of comprehensive government-sponsored insurance for hospital services in 1957 and for medical services in 1966 effectively "locked in" existing patterns of delivery by underwriting their costs. The scheme initially reduced whatever incentive providers and consumers had to consider marginal costs at the point of service. Thenceforth, governmental efforts to contain total costs have tended to focus on attempting to hold down rate increases in negotiations with providers, and on restricting the supply of physicians and of hospital beds, equipment and manpower.

Attempts to regulate rates and to limit capital investment in facilities and equipment have, of course, been pursued by U.S. governments as well. But in the U.S. a general reliance on regulation rather than direct public expenditure has limited governmental leverage on costs. In the absence of a central third party payer, it is more difficult to hold the line on medical and hospital rate increases, and it is virtually impossible to negotiate global hospital budgets. One of the major levers for the containment of total costs in Canada has been the negotiation of annual global budgets between individual hospitals and the respective provincial government agencies. The formulae vary across provinces and are continually undergoing revision, but all are based on estimated patient load and approved service patterns, with their associated requirements for staff and supplies. As Evans has noted,[29] what is most significant about these funding formulae, in contrast to the U.S., is that they are not based on units of service (hence they provide fewer incentives for increasing the volume of procedures), and that they separate operating from capital expenses. (Annual global budgets reimburse only operating expenses; capital funds must be sought through a separate process involving municipal as well as provincial governments and, to a lesser extent, private philanthropy.) In the U.S., service unit reimbursement at rates calculated to include both operating and capital costs, together with the lack of a central funding source, have not only made for decreased governmental leverage over costs, but have also had the significant political and economic effect of encouraging the rise of large for-profit hospital chains. Indeed, this phenomenon has been attributed to the strategic behaviour of the chains in maximizing reimbursement and access to capital markets under the hospital funding policies that prevailed in the 1970s.[30] Although these policies are now undergoing some change, they still reimburse both capital and operating expense simultaneously, and suffer from a lack of the bargaining leverage provided by "sole-source" funding.

The other major difference between Canadian and U.S. health care delivery systems — the existence of large pre-paid Health Maintenance Organizations (HMOs) in the U.S., and increasingly their integration into large national networks — can also be attributed in part to differences in funding mechanisms. By adopting a national health insurance scheme, Canada removed much of the economic impetus for the development of pre-paid groups. Canadians effectively pay their health care bills through the public treasury. In the U.S., HMOs may be said to have developed, both politically and economically, in default of national health insurance. Again, the U.S. has favoured regulatory over direct expenditure instruments in attempting to foster the development of HMOs, although the politics of the regulatory process have arguably constrained rather than promoted their growth.[31]

These differences in public policies toward health care cannot simply be attributed to a greater Canadian "collectivism", although collectivist dimensions of Canadian political culture have played a role. Nor can they be attributed to a greater flexibility in Canadian governmental institutions. Although Canada's parliamentary systems provide fewer "veto points" than the U.S. system of checks and balances, its federal structures erect greater obstacles to national action than is the case in the U.S. Rather, as stated at the outset of this paper, the evolution of these public policies must be seen as resulting from complex processes of ideological, partisan, interest group and inter-governmental conflict and accommodation, mediated through a series of pragmatic judgements. These histories can now be traced out in more detail.

The Coming of Medicare

This historical ground has been well covered by Taylor (above) and needs only brief reference here to relate his account to the lines of our argument.[32] Taylor's comprehensive history of the decision-making processes leading to the emergence of the Canadian health insurance system demonstrates the importance of the interplay between the configuration of interests in the health field and the political complexion of Canadian federalism at particular points in time. In 1945-1946 there existed among medical, hospital and insurance interests a remarkable consensus favourable to the establishment of a comprehensive health insurance program in the public sector. This consensus was arguably attributable to a sort of "red toryism" among these groups, without parallel in the U.S. Viewing national health insurance as "necessary, and . . . probably inevitable",[33] these groups supported such a plan in principle and sought to maximize their influence in its development and implementation. Nonetheless, the federal government's proposal for a national health insurance plan cost-shared between federal and provincial governments sank to defeat under the weight of the larger package of inter-governmental financial arrangements to which it was bound.

The resulting delay gave private health insurance plans time to develop and expand. These plans demonstrated to the medical, hospital and insurance communities the viability of alternatives to government-sponsored health insurance. They also blunted some of the general public pressure for government health insurance by providing coverage for the actuarially "insurable". As a result, the strategic consensus in favour of a comprehensive public-sector plan began to unravel, to be replaced by a preference among medical, hospital and insurance industry spokesmen for government indemnification or partial subsidization of the "uninsurable" and the medically indigent, as a supplement to the private sector plans.

While the support for comprehensive health insurance was unravelling among strategic interests in the health field, however, a more favourable climate of federal-provincial relations was slowly developing. The provinces' post-war suspicion that the federal government would consolidate its wartime centralization of power had abated somewhat. Moreover, the "demonstration effect" of provincial hospital insurance plans in Saskatchewan and British Columbia, adopted unilaterally by those provinces in 1947 and 1948 after the collapse of the federal-provincial negotiations, added further impetus to provincial action. Accordingly, in 1957 the climate of federal-provincial relations again dominated the politics of the health care field. This time the result was that a national hospital insurance program, cost-shared between the federal and provincial governments, was adopted in the face of the opposition of providers of both hospital care and insurance.

It is with respect to the introduction of *medical* care insurance, however, that the influence of the general features of Canadian political culture and institutions discussed in the earlier sections of this paper are most apparent. It was a social democratic party, in a foothold provided by the provincial government of Saskatchewan, that in 1962 exercised the political will necessary to adopt a comprehensive public sector medical care insurance program in the face of intense medical opposition culminating in a physicians' strike. The consequences of this pivotal episode were several. First, medical incomes increased dramatically in the first few years of the program,[34] reducing the likelihood of militant medical opposition to the adoption of a similar program nation-wide. Second, the physician's option to bill his patients directly, at rates above the fee covered by the public plan and without jeopardizing his patients' right to reimbursement from the public plan, was part of the strike-settling agreement. It was henceforth viewed by the medical profession as a hard-won right. (Indeed, the only other major physicians' strike surrounding the introduction of Canadian medicare — in Quebec — focused to a considerable extent on this "extra-billing" or "opting out" issue.) Finally, the fact that physicians brought from England on contract by the Saskatchewan government to provide services during the strike remained to staff the then nascent community clinics in the province exacerbated the politicization of the community clinic movement in the province, and the opposition to it, in its formative stages.

The catharsis and the demonstration effect of the Saskatchewan program eased the introduction of national medical insurance in 1968. But the adoption of the program was not without conflict. Medical and insurance interests continued to favour government supplementation of private sector programs. It is significant, however, that the conflict was again channelled along federal-provincial fault lines, not along partisan lines within the national or provincial governments. The Medical Care Act was passed in 1966 under a minority government, with only two dissenting votes in Parliament. But the provincial level was the *locus* of considerable opposition. Ontario, for example, protested that its entry into the program was practically coerced by the federal imposition of a supplementary tax introduced to pay for it. Taylor quotes then Premier of Ontario John Robarts:

> Medicare is a glowing example of a Machiavellian scheme that is in my humble opinion one of the greatest political frauds that has been perpetrated on the people of this country. The position is this: you are taxing our people to the tune of $225 million a year to pay for a plan for which we get nothing because it has a low priority in our plans for Ontario.[35]

Indeed, in the mid- to late 1960s the government of Ontario and organized medicine in the province appeared to be virtually of one mind on the issue of health insurance. The Ontario Medical Services Insurance Plan (OMSIP), established in 1966, provided for a governmentally sponsored plan, with open enrolment and subsidized premiums on a sliding scale related to income, existing alongside commercial and physician-sponsored plans. This program was fully endorsed by the Ontario Medical Association. Indeed, the OMA Board of Directors announced in 1965 that "the principles embodied in the [draft OMSIP] legislation were supported by [OMA] Council and thus represent the present policy of this association".[36] This rapport was doomed with the advent of Medicare.

The Regulation of the Health Disciplines

The adoption of government-sponsored health insurance established provincial governments as major cost-bearers in the health care system. It also lent some urgency to emerging concerns about the adequacy of existing mechanisms for regulating the supply and conduct of health care practitioners. Both Ontario and Quebec established commissions of inquiry in the late 1960s to review the structures and processes of professional regulation in the health field.[37] These reviews deserve some comment and need to be seen in historical perspective.

Traditionally, Canadian governments have delegated the task of occupational regulation in the health field to professional "self-regulatory" bodies. Indeed, in matters of professional regulation generally, Canada and the U.S. have taken similar approaches in granting broad discretionary authority to professional groups. Academic observers on both sides of the border have drawn attention to the "neo-feudal" structures of professional regulation, analogizing the power, if not the formal structure, of modern professional self-regulatory bodies to that of the medieval guilds.[38] This characterization is doubtless overdrawn, but it does reflect the ambiguous public-private status of these state-sanctioned but professionally elected licensing and certifying bodies. The history of Canadian professional regulation is closer to this model than is the U.S. experience. In the health field, for example, Canada did not experience the degree of factionalism and fragmentation of licensing bodies and medical schools that characterized the

U.S. in the nineteenth century. Kett attributes this difference largely to differences in political culture:

> Canadian nationalism then as now contained a dose of Anti-Americanism . . . . There were widespread and not unjustified fears that lax enforcement of licensing laws would invite a descent on Canada by battalions of American quacks armed with republicanism as well as charlatanism. Regulation . . . meant not only safeguards for health but guarantees of stability. Here the reverse was true in the United States. Amidst the democratic agitation of the 1830's, attempts by the profession to secure enforcement of licensing laws had the rubric of monopoly and were given the kiss of death . . . . Medical institutions in America seemed out of step with triumphant egalitarianism; in Canada they appeared to be guarantors of triumphant paternalism.[39]

Furthermore, there is within the "tory-touched" Canadian context a view of professional self-regulatory bodies as having a functional sovereignty that is recognized, but not delegated, by the state. Evidence of a thoroughgoing and explicitly tory view of professional power can be drawn from the legal profession, a central elite group outside the health field. Defending its traditional privileges before a ministerial committee of inquiry in Ontario in 1979, the Law Society of Upper Canada (the licensing body for Ontario lawyers) argued that:

> There is not the slightest doubt that the legal profession is subject to regulation by the Legislature, but to suggest that in some way it was or is the creature of the Legislature is contrary to the fact. It is not the case that the state has delegated certain functions to the Law Society; rather, the state recognized and tolerated the origin and growth of the Law Society within the framework of the state.
>
> The legal profession, as did the other two ancient professions of theology and medicine, evolved over a long period and developed not only the structure of its governing organization but the services it provides. The profession has evolved within the framework of the state but the state did not create the profession.[40]

Without arguing that such is the prevailing view of the corporate power of professional groups in Canada,[41] it is nonetheless important to draw attention to this dimension of the cultural context of professional regulation. The influence of this view can be seen in the deference paid by the Royal Commission on Health Services (the body that in 1964 recommended the introduction of a national Medicare program) to the concept of "free and self-governing professions", upon whose services the program was to be based.[42]

In any event, professional self-regulatory bodies in Canada have traditionally enjoyed a *de facto* if not a *de jure* sovereignty in matters of admission to and discipline within given fields of practice. Until the mid-1970s, rules of entry and of conduct were typically set by bodies entirely composed of members of the profession, without the necessity of government approval. While disciplinary decisions could be appealed to the court by the disciplined member, there was no possibility of appeal of the professional bodies' decisions by non-members (such as complaining clients or refused applicants).

By the late 1960s, however, this degree of professional autonomy was a matter of increasing public concern. First, there was concern about the perceived ability of professional bodies to restrict entry, particularly at a time when governmental subsidization of the consumption of professional services through programs such as Medicare and, to a lesser extent, legal aid, promised to increase the demand for those services. Second, the complaints procedures of professional bodies, involving as they do the judgements of members of the profession about the behaviour of another member, were viewed with growing suspicion in the dawning light of the consumer movement. Third, professionally imposed barriers to an efficient allocation of functions among various types of manpower were also a concern, albeit of somewhat lesser magnitude.

These concerns, as noted, led to the establishment of commissions of inquiry in Ontario and Quebec in the late 1960s, and are reflected in the recommendations of those commissions and the subsequent legislative changes. The structures and processes of professional bodies (of the five "senior" health professions of medicine, dentistry, nursing, pharmacy and optometry in Ontario; a broader range in Quebec) were modified to provide for lay representation on professional governing councils, Cabinet approval of professional regulations, the possibility of unilateral governmental regulatory action in default of action by the professional body, and mechanisms of appeal by non-members from the decisions of professional bodies.[43] As for the re-assignment of professional functions, the Ontario legislation contained a permissive clause, and the Quebec legislation a mandatory clause, providing for various professions to designate by regulation the functions within their respective scopes of practice that might be performed by persons other than their members.

These reforms, as will be argued below, were largely symbolic in effect. They emphasized the social obligations of corporate professional bodies, and their ultimate subordination to the state, while leaving largely intact their *de facto* functional sovereignty. As such, they were acceptable to red tories as well as to pluralist liberals, but they presaged future challenges to professional power.

In the Wake of Medicare and Professional "Reform"

The developments of the 1960s and early 1970s brought changes in both the nature and the locus of conflict in the health policy arena. Three dimensions of change are of particular note: ideological developments within the medical profession, the increasing politicization of non-medical health care providers and the increasing role of provincial governments.

Medical Ideology

We know little about the distribution of medical attitudes on issues of health care policy before the late 1960s in either Canada or the U.S. Studies of medical opinion and ideology that have been undertaken focus on the policy statements of organized medical groups.[44] Nonetheless, it is possible to identify various dimensions of medical opinion and to speculate about trends in their development over time.

Medical ideologies (that is, belief systems regarding the appropriate sources and distribution of authority in society) are shaped by the technological role of physicians and by characteristics of the broader political culture.[45] In particular, the tension between emphases on the individual autonomy of the practitioner and the corporate responsibility of the professional group can be seen in this light. It is fed by the more general tension, in Canadian political culture, between the individualistic emphasis of liberal democracy and the tory sense of an organic society of corporate groups. But it is also rooted in the medical role of applying specialized knowledge of complex biological and psychological systems to individual cases.[46]

At the core of medical ideology is a focus on the quality of care rendered (according to professional norms) in individual cases, and a resultant emphasis on the development of the technological base, on the clinical discretion of the individual professional and on the collegial or "peer review" authority of the profession as a whole over its members. Over time these concepts have become embodied in certain organizational and institutional arrangements such as private fee-for-service practice and separately constituted structures of medical authority in hospitals. The ideology has embraced these arrangements as well, defending the entrepreneurial as well as the clinical discretion of autonomous fee-for-service practitioners.

The tensions inherent in this ideology are being exacerbated by technological changes that have been similar across jurisdictions. As health care technology has become ever more complex and specialized, it has opened up new frontiers for the exercise of clinical judgement and has made routine the functions that once required discretionary judgement. It has given rise to new and sophisticated equipment, new functions and new types of personnel. Hence, on the supply side, it has created the conditions and the incentive for larger scales of organization to integrate these specialized functions and to capture economies of scale, and for mechanisms for the remuneration of teams of health care providers. On the demand side, it has fuelled the demand for financing arrangements that spread the risk to individuals of increasingly costly episodes of care. By necessitating encounters with a variety of personnel and hardware, it has also tended to weaken the sense of trust that derives from an ongoing provider-patient relationship.

Medical ideologies are responding to these changes, in both Canada and the U.S. I shall discuss the U.S. developments in a later section of this paper; here let me keep the focus on Canada, and particularly on some of my own findings regarding medical opinion in Ontario.

In each of two surveys of the attitudes of private medical practitioners in Ontario in the 1970s,[47] I found essentially two versions of the basic professional ideology described above, each version emphasizing somewhat different elements. The majority version tended to emphasize discretion over what might be termed the "derivative" elements of the doctor-patient relationship as embodied in the traditional institutions of private fee-for-service practice. These institutions allow the individual physician to have discretion not only over the choice of treatment in individual cases (clinical discretion), but also over the resources that he invests in his practice, the size of his patient load, the location of his practice, his hours of work and the number and type of his employees (entrepreneurial discretion). Within (and in some tension with) this entrepreneurial majority are locally-based groups of physicians who seek to preserve, for the local group if not the individual physician, discretion over fees in individual cases. In opposing a fixed fee schedule, these physicians defend their ability to function as discriminating monopolists who vary their fees according to the patient's ability to pay. These local groups can maintain such price structures only so long as they do, in fact, function as monopolies — so long as individual physicians do not enter into price competition with each other. Ideological consensus provides one constraint on such competition. Much of the population of physicians who have "opted out" of the Ontario Health Insurance Plan (OHIP) in order to bill their patients directly at discretionary rates is made up of such locally-based groups, bound together by economic strategy, ideology or some admixture of the two.[48]

Less visible, but more strategically located, is a minority whose opinions differ from the entrepreneurial majority in several important respects. These are physicians, usually associated with medical schools, whose central concern is the physician's clinical discretion subject to professionally determined standards, not the defence of the traditional institutions of fee-for-service private practice. I described this ideological variant in a 1976 article:

> [These physicians] share a judgement that both the technological and the political context of modern medicine require that the physician accommodate himself to his peers and to other groups in society in new organizational contexts and power relationships. They accept the view that public bodies have a legitimate voice in the determination of the rate of medical remuneration. They are willing, at the very least, to see medical fees negotiated with a public agency, and further to experiment with mechanisms of remuneration — salary, pooled income and income ceiling arrangements — which limit the economic discretion of individual physicians . . . . They are further willing to experiment with new forms of organization which allow

for considerable non-medical influence in such matters as location and scheduling of health service facilities, and to some extent in establishing the appropriate mix of personnel within these facilities. What they are concerned to protect, however, is professional control over the content and standards of medical practice, in order to ensure that the individual physician retains the ability to exercise his skills according to his own clinical judgement and the standards of his profession.[49]

This is a sort of "red tory" professionalism: a recognition of the social responsibility of the professional group to limit the economic discretion of its members, while maintaining the corporate power necessary to discharge its social obligation to control the quality of service.

It is also noteworthy that the study found younger physicians to be more supportive of organizational change and/or state activity than their older peers. This support appears to derive from a variety of ideological perspectives: red toryism, welfare-state liberalism, democratic socialism and even a sort of "new entrepreneurialism" that sees in large scales of practice and government funding the opportunity for entrepreneurial activity.

Finally, there is a dimension of medical opinion, not revealed to a significant extent in surveys but apparent in political organization and policy pronouncements, that is more socialist in inspiration. Centred on organizations such as the Medical Reform Group, and acting in coalition with labour and other groups on the left, this small minority of physicians denounces private concentrations of power, including medical power, and advocates reform based on the public provision of medical services through community-sponsored centres.

The Politicization of Non-Medical Health Care Providers

During the period in which Canadian medicare was being formulated, such political activity as was undertaken by non-medical health practitioners was largely directed toward ensuring that their services were covered under the plan. Chiropractors and optometrists engaged in successful lobbying efforts to this end. The 1970s witnessed a considerable escalation in political activity on the part of non-medical health care practitioners, spurred largely by the perception of political opportunities in the occasion of the "reform" of professional legislation.

The results of these activities have been mixed. In Quebec, several non-medical groups have succeeded in achieving or consolidating self-regulatory status without significantly expanding their legal scopes of practice. In Ontario, several groups (such as physiotherapists and dental hygienists) have unsuccessfully attempted to negotiate, with the "senior" professions of medicine and dentistry respectively, regulatory changes expanding their scopes of practice and/or loosening supervision requirements.[50] Denture therapists have been somewhat more successful in directly challenging the senior dental profession through intensive legislative lobbying.

Although many of these groups make efficiency arguments for an expansion in their scopes of practice, the nursing profession is particularly notable in this respect. Organized nursing has recently (and especially in the context of the debate surrounding the adoption of the Canada Health Act at the federal level) emerged as a significant advocate of broad-ranging organizational reform in health care delivery.

The Role of Provincial Governments

The adoption of Medicare made provincial governments major cost-bearers in the Canadian health care system. Since the 1977 changes in federal-provincial cost-sharing arrangements, they have been 100 percent at risk for cost increases in health care.[51] As I have argued elsewhere,[52] Canadian provincial governments have three basic types of leverage on the control of these costs (not including the transfer of costs to the private sector — an option to which I shall return below). They may attempt to hold down rate increases in negotiations with providers; they may restrict the supply of manpower, facilities and services; and they may seek to improve the efficiency of the system through organizational change.

Ideological and institutional constraints on the pursuit of these options, however, have meant that, with a few notable exceptions, their effect has been largely symbolic. This is not to suggest that these policies have been insignificant, but rather that their significance cannot be read literally. In the first place, symbolic policies can be seen as signals within the context of an elaborate political game — in Edelman's terms, to recognize that policies have symbolic dimensions is to understand them not as fiats but as "virtuous generalization(s) around which a game is played".[53] Furthermore, some policies have a sort of "summary" significance; they come to be invested with a significance disproportionate to their tangible effect because they draw on broader areas of concern. In that sense symbolic policies and issues have the potential to drain energy and divert attention from broader concerns and conflicts.

Let us consider the first option cited — the attempt to hold down, through negotiation or unilateral action, the unit prices of physicians' services. Battles over the medical fee schedule that forms the basis of payments under government health insurance are highly visible and dramatic. They also serve the purposes of both government and the profession. They galvanize the entrepreneurial majority of the profession into a display of defiance; they symbolize to the public at large that professional power is being held in check by a government concerned about costs; and they offer a catharsis for the mutual suspicions of physicians, bureaucrats and politicians without fundamentally challenging existing power relationships or familiar ground rules. Behind this spectacle, the earned income of full-time physicians bears almost the same relationship to the average industrial wage that it did immediately after the introduction of Medicare, when medical relative incomes reached their historic peak.[54]

This periodic sound and fury performs a symbolic function, not only for the entrepreneurial majority but also for that subset composed of "opted out" physicians. The battle over fees provides a symbolic justification for the existence of the right to opt out of the government plan. It provides evidence of physician dissatisfaction with the level of their remuneration and with the alleged rigidity of government negotiators and hence legitimates the existence of a "safety valve" for disgruntled physicians.

There is also some symbolic merit in the process for the strategic minority of physicians who are not wedded to the fee-for-service principle. The spectacle of the major institutional protagonists on the demand and the supply sides of the system holding each other in check may serve to divert attention from policy options that might be more threatening to the clinical discretion of physicians.

In the hospital sector, public policies have had more substantive effects. Here wage and unit price increases outpaced general inflation through most of the 1970s. But overall costs in the hospital sector did not increase accordingly, reflecting the fact that the level of hospital facilities — manpower, beds, supplies and equipment — available *per capita* actually declined slightly toward the end of the 1970s.[55] Detsky *et al.* have shown that hospital inputs per patient-day remained virtually constant in Ontario from 1972 to 1981 as a result of restrictions on the number of beds and man-hours that were approved by the province as the basis for negotiating hospital global budgets.[56] Because the number of physicians *per capita* is increasing, these policies represent a significant reduction in the hospital facilities available per physician — an effect that extends beyond symbolism and beyond a challenge to medical entrepreneurialism. Although physicians continue to exercise discretion over the use of a leaner hospital system, the direction of policy in this sector increasingly threatens to constrain clinical as well as economic discretion.

Hospital facilities are not the only factors in the health care system that have been subject to governmental restrictions on supply. Limits on the immigration of physicians were introduced, through federal-provincial collaboration, in 1975. Positive net migration of physicians in Canada had peaked at 1,111 in 1969. By 1976 it had declined to 38, and since 1977 Canada has experienced a negative net migration. Nonetheless, the supply of physicians *per capita* in Canada continues to increase. In 1971 the physician-to-population ratio was 1:791; by 1981 it was 1:636.[57] Some provinces are experimenting with reductions in medical school places. Manitoba reduced its first year enrolment by 10 percent in the early 1980s and Ontario is pursuing a policy of limited (2 percent to 5 percent) reductions in selected post-graduate training posts. B.C. and Quebec, on the other hand, are experimenting with restrictions on billing numbers, placing limitations on the number of physicians in given regions who will be eligible for full reimbursement under governmental health insurance plans, and prorating or denying payments to physicians who locate in regions whose quotas have been filled.

Several provinces, moreover, have attempted to develop mechanisms for limiting the volume of service provided by individual physicians. Quebec, for example, prorates fee-for-service payments to individual general practitioners beyond a negotiated target income and links specialist fee increases to utilization trends in order to establish a year-to-year rolling global limit on payments to specialists. Several provinces, including Ontario, B.C. and Quebec, have developed mechanisms for monitoring service volumes and reducing payments to practitioners who exceed "acceptable" limits.[58]

These attempts to restrict supply have not touched central issues of the organization and utilization of health care personnel — the third instrument of cost control discussed above. The effects of changes in the structures and processes of professional regulation have largely been to emphasize the social responsibilities of corporate professional bodies and to signal a closer public scrutiny of their operations. To date, the changes have had virtually no effect on the allocation of functions among health care personnel, although they have in some cases constrained the entrepreneurial discretion of individual professionals or the economic monopoly power of professional groups.

The Quebec Office des Professions, in the course of an extensive review and coordination of the regulations of professional bodies to ensure their conformity with the umbrella statute, the Professional Code, has enforced on several professions regulatory changes removing barriers to inter- and intra-professional competition within existing scopes of practice. Attempts to rationalize the allocation of functions through regulations under "delegation" clauses, however, have been frustrated by the strategic behaviour of professional groups attempting to "delegate" (and hence to claim jurisdiction over) functions already arguably within the scope of practice of the delegatee group. Those regulations that have been passed under delegation clauses have had little or no effect in practice.[59] In Ontario, no regulations have been passed under "delegation" clauses; nor is this likely pending the completion of a current review of the legislation governing all health disciplines in the province. Governmental authority to over-ride professional regulatory bodies under the Health Disciplines Act has been used twice: once in refusing to approve a regulation passed by the Royal College of Dental Surgeons that effectively would have defined participation in pre-paid practice as "professional misconduct" for dentists; and once to pass a regulation, after the College of Physicians and Surgeons had refused to do so, defining as professional misconduct the failure to inform a patient that professional charges would exceed the amount covered by the government plan. Both of these governmental actions challenge only the entrepreneurial discretion, not the functional authority, of the professions.

Experimentation with forms of health care delivery alternative to private fee-for-service practice, such as clinics funded on a capitation or global budget basis under contract with the government insurance plan, is advanced farther in some provinces (notably Saskatchewan and Quebec) than in others, but such models remain peripheral to the mainstream health care delivery system. In Ontario, Health Service Organizations (HSOs), on the model of American HMOs, have been treated as perennial pilot projects whose development has been hampered by lack of systematic evaluation and by constraints in existing funding mechanisms. As Stoddart has noted, "Funds for innovation or experimentation with potentially cost-effective alternative financing and delivery arrangements are severely limited due to the sheer size of financial commitments to existing programs".[60] Again, Ontario's policy toward HSOs appears to have more symbolic than tangible effects. It signals governmental willingness to consider alternative delivery modes, without providing the concrete support necessary to build on these experimental footings.

There is, of course, yet another option potentially open to governments concerned about the magnitude of health costs in their budgets: the option not to control but to shift costs to the private sector through charges to patients, either uniform across providers or imposed at the provider's discretion.[61] This option has stirred much recent debate in Canada, and enjoys broad support within the medical profession. The entrepreneurial majority view it as a way of preserving "private" practice, while the strategic "red tory" minority view it as a way of increasing the total funds available to the health sector and hence of obviating the supply restriction, which they see as increasingly threatening the technological base and their own clinical discretion.

(Significantly, the hospital community has been less enthusiastic about user charges. Alberta hospitals have not taken up an option granted to them by the province in January 1984 to impose *per diem* charges on patients up to specified maximums, and the Catholic Health Association of Canada, representing Catholic hospitals, has taken a policy position opposing user fees and extra-billing. Hospitals have generally been more concerned with pragmatic negotiations over the bases on which hospital global budgets will be calculated, and about the loosening of the restrictions on supply that have characterized these budgets.)

Again, the arena of conflict over cost-shifting has been inter-governmental. The Canada Health Act, passed in April 1984 with the unanimous support of all parties at the federal level but in the face of provincial opposition, would appear to close the door on the pursuit of this option, by reducing federal cash transfers to each province by an amount equal to the dollar amount of charges to patients for insured services above governmental insurance coverage — a "dollar for dollar" penalty for direct patient charges.

The economic implications of extra-billing and user charges in Canada are not negligible. Although physician charges to patients above government benefits constitute a small proportion of total physician billings, extra-billing tends to occur on a geographically "clustered" basis, with all or most members of a given specialty in a given locality engaging in the practice. Hence financial barriers to particular medical services in certain localities may be substantial.[62] User charges for acute care hospital services are not wide-spread, although British Columbia, Alberta and New Brunswick levy small hospital *per diem* or admission charges. The potential efficiency and equity effects of a broader implementation of such charges has been the subject of considerable debate but little empirical analysis.[63]

The salience of the extra-billing and user charge issue in Canada, however, derives more from its symbolic than from its economic significance. It allows the debate to be contained within the nexus of relationships among the established providers of health care and the federal and provincial governments, without threatening those relationships in ways that changes in the "industrial organization" of health care might do. Nonetheless it draws on (and provides a limited focus for) the broader issue of the role of the private sector and/or market forces in the delivery of health care in Canada. In this light, the provisions of the Canada Health Act may be seen less as outright sanctions against direct patient charges than as "virtuous generalizations" around which will be played the game of developing regulations and federal-provincial agreements defining compliance.

Comparisons With the U.S. Experience

The Absence of Comprehensive Health Insurance
and the Coming of the Corporation

A full treatment of patterns of conflict and accommodation in the U.S. health policy arena is well beyond the scope of this paper, but a few dimensions of comparison and contrast with Canada can be noted here. At one level, conflicts over national health insurance in the U.S. have been conducted, to a much greater extent than in Canada, along broad ideological and partisan lines.[64] The extent to which the state may legitimately intervene in this arena, and the instruments that it may legitimately use, are continually at issue.

At another level, the multiple institutional clearance points of the U.S. system — the relatively independent legislative, executive and bureaucratic organs of government at both federal and state levels, and the judiciary — have provided affected interests with numerous footholds from which to block, or wrest substantial modifications in, the various proposals that proceed through the system. (The generous hospital cost-reimbursement formulae originally developed under Medicare, achieved through a whip-sawing of Congressional committees and administrative agencies, are examples of such concessions, granted to ensure hospital cooperation and a "proper take-off" for Medicare.[65] And this "pot-sweetening" pattern is being repeated in current experiments with Diagnostic Related Group reimbursement.)[66] Furthermore, these footholds allow various interests to plead special cases for governmental coverage of specific groups, even in the face of ideological opposition to more general governmental intervention.[67]

As a result, instead of comprehensive national health insurance, the U.S. has an array of programs. Eligibility for these programs is determined by age, income or other categorical definitions of need. Their administration is divided between the private and the public sector and among levels of government. None of the numerous proposals for national health insurance have cleared the ideological, partisan and institutional hurdles of the political system. The most recent "propitious moment" was lost in 1974, overtaken by the events of Watergate.[68] Furthermore, both federal and state governments have increasingly turned to regulatory as opposed to expenditure instruments. Providing examples of this trend were the requirement that employers offer an HMO option to their employees, the certification of eligible HMOs and the regulation of the expansion of hospital facilities by requiring certificates of need from state planning agencies. Together with the conditions placed on Medicare and Medicaid reimbursement, these regulations constitute a potentially substantial set of constraints on private sector decision-making. Moreover, lacking the control that might be afforded by sole-source comprehensive funding, governments have elaborated these requirements into a complex network of provisions, including both concessions to encourage compliance (pot-sweetening) and restrictions to prevent evasion (loop-hole closing).

The absence of comprehensive health insurance, and the presence of incentives embedded in the complex structures of regulation and conditions on public funding, have shaped the configuration of interests that now occupy the U.S. health policy arena. Most notably, they have led to the emergence of large corporate enterprises on both supply and demand sides of the economic and political systems.

On the supply side, as noted earlier and as chronicled by Starr, large multi-institutional chains, both for-profit and not-for-profit, are increasingly significant political and economic actors. The for-profits are considerably more concentrated. The top three firms (Hospital Corporation of America, Humana and American Medical International) operate nearly three-quarters of the beds in the for-profit sector, while the top three non-profits (Kaiser Foundation, Sisters of Mercy, Sisters of Charity) operate less than 10 percent of the non-profit beds.[69]

Starr identifies five dimensions of what he calls the "increasing integration of control" in the health care industry:

1. *Change in type of ownership and control*: the shift from non-profit and governmental organizations to for-profit companies in health care.

2. *Horizontal integration*: the decline of freestanding institutions and the rise of multi-institutional systems, and the consequent shift in the locus of control from community boards to regional and national health care corporations.

3. *Diversification and corporate re-structuring*: the shift from single-unit organizations operating in one market to "polycorporate" and conglomerate enterprises, often organized under holding companies, sometimes with both non-profit and for-profit subsidiaries involved in a variety of different health care markets.

4. *Vertical integration*: the shift from single-level-of-care organizations, such as acute care hospitals, to organizations that embrace the various phases and levels of care, such as H.M.O.s.

5. *Industry concentration*: the increasing concentration of ownership and control of health services in regional markets and the nation as a whole.[70]

On the demand side, large scale corporate enterprises are increasingly significant as well. The escalating costs of health insurance or service plans provided as employee benefits are becoming a matter of increasing concern to employers. Employer coalitions or "business councils" concerned with health care issues have been established at national, state and local levels. Individual corporations as purchasers of health coverage for their employees are exploring a variety of relationships within health care insurers and providers, and are experimenting with incentives to their employees to reduce the costs of their consumption of health care services.[71] Chrysler corporation, for example, has asserted that nearly $600 of the price of every 1984 Chrysler car and truck is attributable to medical costs (including employee health benefits provided by Chrysler and its suppliers, and Medicare payroll taxes).[72] The Chrysler example is interesting, although it is atypical (its health insurance premium payments per active employee are considerably higher than average), because it has sought to publicize its case to highlight the problem. Not coincidentally, its board of directors included (until very recently) three major actors in the U.S. health policy arena: Chairman Lee Iaccoca (former president of Ford Motor Co.) and Douglas Fraser (former president of the United Auto Workers), who together negotiated health benefits at Ford that set the standard for many other collective agreements, and Joseph Califano, Secretary of Health, Education and Welfare in the Carter Administration. Chrysler is experimenting with systems of prospective review within its own insurance plan and will attempt to institute co-payments or deductibles — partly, it maintains, to increase the attractiveness to employees of its HMO option. The attempts, however, are likely to meet with stiff labour opposition. Ironically, business interests appear to be adopting positions more favourable to organizational innovation in health care delivery, while the traditional advocates of reform in the health care system — the labour unions — are concerned with maintaining existing benefits in compensation plans.[73]

Indeed, American "neo-liberals" such as Reich point out the extent to which health and social services are increasingly delivered and funded through such corporate networks:

> The federal government already is undertaking massive social service programs administered through American firms. In 1982, for example, the government provided workers with $16.6 billion worth of health insurance (representing the tax-free part of more than $55 billion in medical coverage provided by firms). Direct federal outlays for Medicare and Medicaid were around $80 billion. So the total federal [government] cost of health care in 1982 was approximately $97 billion — one-fifth of which went to American workers through their firms . . . . We should not underestimate the magnitude of the changes that will be entailed in completing this transformation of the American work community, extending its benefits to those who are now excluded and rendering it more democratic.[74]

In his advocacy of the use of private corporations as instruments of social and economic dimensions of public policy (as well as his emphasis elsewhere in his argument on the need for collaboration between private and public sector actors to improve productivity and protect and expand international markets for American goods and services), Reich might better be termed a "neo-mercantilist". As he in part recognizes,[75] he and the school of thought which he represents are true to that important dimension of American political and economic culture; and the approach is likely to have significant influence on thinking about health policy in the U.S. in the next decade.

Medical Ideology

These political, economic and organizational developments, together with an increasing supply of physicians (in the U.S. as in Canada), are related to ideological developments within the U.S. medical profession. Medical ideology, at least as represented by the pronouncements of organized medicine, has traditionally drawn on the cultural strength of pluralist liberal democratic concepts to justify its concentrated power. The policy positions and political activities of organized medicine, particularly the American Medical Association, have used the language of free enterprise and freedom of choice, and alliances with business interests, to make the case opposing state intervention in the health care arena and to defend as much entrepreneurial discretion for individual physicians as is consistent with the maintenance of local price-discriminating monopolies.[76] Although these strains have been significant in the policy positions of Canadian organized medicine as well, they have been tempered in the Canadian context by a red toryism emphasizing the social obligations of medicine and rendering the organized profession, like other elite groups, somewhat more prepared to collaborate with the state in the formulation and implementation of redistributive policies.

Studies in the late 1960s and the 1970s, however, suggest the development of dimensions or clusters of opinion within U.S. medicine open to a broader sharing of authority and to organizational change. As in Canada, these attitudes are more likely to be found among physicians associated with medical schools, and among younger physicians.[77] Indeed, there is a broad similarity among recent studies of medical opinion in the U.S. and Canada, whether based on surveys or on official pronouncements, although it is difficult to estimate the comparative size and political significance of the clusters that they reveal. Taken together, U.S. studies suggest the existence of a "traditional" or "monopolistic" cluster (defensive of traditional patterns of medical authority), a "liberal" or "corporate rationalist" cluster (supportive of organizational innovation, state action and a broader sharing of medical authority, subject to a variety of provisos), and a "radical" cluster (too small to be identified in surveys but apparent in case studies or reviews of policy statements, and supportive of public, community-based control of health care delivery).[78]

These clusters bear comparison with those identified in the Ontario profession, as discussed above. The "traditionalist" cluster would appear to be similar to our entrepreneurial majority, although U.S. researchers have not investigated the tension implicit in its defence of the individual and the collective interests of medical practitioners. The "liberal" cluster is similar to Ontario's red tories, although the former lack as firmly rooted a rationale for preserving the collegial authority of the profession. Finally, the "radical" or "community" cluster is distinguished in both countries by its small size, although it may be somewhat more legitimate in Canada through its connection with NDP policy.

The "coming of the corporation"[79] in the U.S. presents a challenge to each of these clusters of opinion. To the "traditionalists" it preserves the possibility of medical entrepreneurialism, but it extends the potential scope of participation in the management and ownership of health care delivery firms to include non-medical administrators, investors and possibly other health care workers. (It has been argued that the major challenge to the traditional power base of the medical profession comes not from government intervention but from the rising importance of administrative skills in the management of an increasingly complex medical technology, and from the large capital investment necessary to acquire the equipment and facilities that it demands.)[80]

"Liberals" accept the need to share power more broadly with administrators, other health care workers and public or private sector providers of capital. Their challenge will be to defend the scope of their clinical discretion within these corporate forms (as they have done through the organization of medical staffs within Kaiser). To the "radicals", these large corporate enterprises represent a further elaboration of the "medical-industrial complex",[81] which is no more (and perhaps less) open to consumer and worker involvement in decision-making than were earlier forms of delivery.

Inter-Professional Relations

As noted earlier, patterns of professional regulation are essentially similar in both the U.S. and Canada. But the emergence of larger-scale corporations and the greater flexibility of billing procedures in the U.S. provide an institutional framework potentially more supportive of a re-allocation of functions among health care personnel. Large-scale practice provides a context in which non-medical personnel can be nominally supervised by medical personnel, and flexible billing allows physicians, as employers or employees, to capture some of the rents for this supervision. A further set of obstacles to the optimal utilization of auxiliaries — those that arise from the "labour-managed" aspects of professional practice — are avoided in those firms that are owned and/or managed by other than their professional employees.

The effect of these organizational forms on the utilization of health manpower may extend beyond their own structures, through a "demonstration effect" legitimating such breaks with traditional patterns,[82] and strengthening the case for regulatory change where required to facilitate their evolution.[83]

Future Developments

We should not be sanguine about the effects of these developments in the U.S. on either allocative or technical efficiency in the health care field. The emergence of multi-institutional, investor-owned chains is a response to their potential to generate high returns to investors by maximizing reimbursement and by gaining favourable access to capital markets.[84] Studies of differences in patterns of service between for-profit and non-profit institutions, and between chains and independents, show varying results; but at best they suggest no cost savings in the for-profit sector and at worst they suggest higher mark-ups on and utilization of ancillary services.[85] As Pattison and Katz have noted, however, strategies of revenue maximization depend on existing reimbursement mechanisms, and continued success will depend on the ability of these corporations to influence and to adapt to changes in reimbursement policies.[86]

Similarly, the economic implications of corporate re-structuring depend on the relative political and economic success of what Starr calls "vertical" (HMO) as opposed to "horizontal" (multi-institutional chains) integration. The former, as has been extensively documented, has the potential to yield significant improvements in the cost-effectiveness of medical care, largely by reducing hospitalization.

Starr rightly notes that "competition among types of corporate medical care is extraordinarily sensitive to the vagaries of politics".[87] These politics are likely to result, in the foreseeable future, in piecemeal changes at both federal and state levels. Comprehensive change is stymied by the existence of numerous veto points in the system and by "the conservative assimilation of reform".[88] Such changes as have occurred at the federal level, notably the Tax Equity and Fiscal Responsibility Act of 1982, have been concerned largely with shifting costs to employers and patients, with moving from a service unit basis to an episode basis for the negotiation of hospital cost reimbursement under Medicare, and, under the Budget Reconciliation Act of 1981, with providing for waivers of federal conditions on cost-sharing to allow states to experiment with cost-containing innovations in their Medicaid programs.

Such state-level experimentation is now well under way. California has recently established a system of state contracting with selected corporate providers to treat MediCal inpatients at an all-inclusive *per diem* rate.[89] Arizona, the only state without a Medicaid program, is to receive a fixed annual grant from the federal government to contract with providers such as HMOs to provide comprehensive care to indigents on a pre-paid capitation basis.[90] But innovations are likely to remain piecemeal and *ad hoc* (as Meyer has noted, "Today Congress probably would not even be willing to pass a law ratifying the changes that have already taken place, let alone one which would advance the process"),[91] and their efficiency implications are by no means consistently positive.

Canada: Future Developments

The agenda of the health care policy debate in Canada is likely increasingly to include issues of alternative modes of delivery, including the issue of the appropriate role of private for-profit corporations. That role may be allowed to increase by design, notably in the provision of institutional care. Examples include the expanding role of private corporations such as Extendicare in the ownership and management of nursing homes, and the as yet experimental contracts for the private management of public general hospitals, such as that between the Ontario government and AMI (Canada) Ltd., a subsidiary of American Medical International, for the management of the Hawkesbury General Hospital. On the other hand, private sector expansion may occur as a by-product of policies that restrict supply in the public sector. It is likely, for example, that policies such as the restriction of billing numbers will generate strong pressures to allow private insurance coverage for the services of physicians practising privately outside the system. Moreover, the pressure of the U.S. example is likely to impinge on the Canadian debate, as the implications of U.S. models in terms of efficiency, technological progress and equity are disputed by Canadian interests.

One notable example of the recent evolution of this debate in Canada is a brief presented by the Ontario Medical Association to the Ontario Minister of Health urging the adoption of an "incentive-based" approach to the organization of health care delivery. Their recommendations deserve to be quoted at some length:

> The major flaw in the system is its open-ended nature, which makes it almost impossible for either providers or consumers to be efficient in the use of resources . . . . The incentive-based approach to this

problem incorporates financial rewards to both providers and consumers of health care. The rewards are based on making discretionary choices which result in a more efficient use of the system. Consumers, for instance, would be free to choose among competing delivery models . . . . Some, of course, will instantly say that this is a return to marketplace competition. To some degree it is, but we recognize fully the problems inherent within this approach and are more than willing to address them. The most visible of these problems is the requirement for direct consumer cost.[92]

The OMA addresses this problem of direct consumer cost by proposing that the poor be "guaranteed access to first-rate medical services", that providers be free to choose among methods of remuneration and practice organization, that consumers be free to choose among competing groups of providers, and that implementation be gradual and carefully evaluated.[93]

This OMA position is remarkable for a number of reasons. To some extent it represents a Canadian version of "the conservative assimilation of reform". This conservative aspect is particularly apparent in the fact that, in presenting this position in his farewell address, the OMA president went on to dismiss, through a sort of "guilt by association" tactic, organized nursing's attempts to raise broad issues of organizational reform. He noted that proponents of a preventive emphasis in the health care system "come in many guises: nurses, chiropractors, naturopaths, nutritionists, fitness specialists, even herbologists, aura balancers, finger-pressure massagers and brain clearers",[94] and suggested that these groups were really seeking "unrestricted access" to health care funding, which, if granted, would simply make them an "add-on expenditure" and not a substitute for physicians. Furthermore, the position regarding "freedom of choice" for providers and consumers is consistent with a line of OMA argument reaching back to pre-Medicare days.

Nonetheless, the emphasis on efficiency and the recognition of the problem of "open-endedness" is relatively new, and represents an openness to significant organizational change. This position draws on a variety of ideological strains within the OMA membership, including not only the red tories who have supported organizational innovation for some time, but also what might be called the "new entrepreneurs": physicians who see the possibility, and indeed the necessity, of re-interpreting entrepreneurial discretion and re-focusing entrepreneurial energy in new forms of practice. To a considerable extent, this OMA position marks a generational change in the association's leadership.

Also on the agenda in Canada, although less likely to be championed by any of the major protagonists, is the issue of the potential role of market forces *within* the public sector. Policies along these lines may be developed and promoted by "policy entrepreneurs" in academe and government. Stoddart, for example, has argued persuasively for the efficiency potential of competing delivery modalities within a publicly financed system.[95]

Organizational innovation, either private or public, may, however, be somewhat constrained by the provisions of the Canada Health Act. Its requirement that provinces, in order to qualify for full federal contributions, must provide insured health services on "uniform terms and conditions" may, as Stoddart has noted, inhibit experimentation with competing delivery modalities within the public system.[96] Furthermore, its strictures against extra-billing, interpreted literally, would deprive private sector entrepreneurs of one discretionary instrument of revenue maximization: price (although the Act is neutral with respect to the instruments of volume and mix of service).

Provincial responses to the federal legislation have not yet been fully formulated. Its provisions have been seen as an affront to provincial sovereignty even by those provinces that support its basic public policy direction.[97] Despite some sabre-rattling regarding court challenges, however, it is likely that federal-provincial conflict will now shift to the regulatory arena, and to negotiations over the terms of compliance with the Act. (Given the bipartisan and broad public support for the legislation, it is unlikely that the statute itself will be changed.) Although the atmosphere of federal-provincial relations may well become warmer with a change in government at the federal level, it is likely that Canadian health care policy in the foreseeable future will continue to be marked by federal-provincial conflict, particularly given the constraints imposed by the Canada Health Act. A number of factors increase the likelihood of such conflict: the continuing vitality of a concept of provincial sovereignty in matters under provincial jurisdiction; the increasing pressure on provincial governments, as cost-bearers at the margin, to control costs without reducing service to politically unacceptable levels; and the ensconcement of governing parties with market-oriented ideologies in several provinces (not only social democrats gain provincial footholds in Canada).

Summary and Conclusions

This comparison of the past and possible future evolution of health care politics in Canada and the U.S. has revealed several ironies. The Canadian medical profession, motivated in part by the red tories in its ranks and in part by the sense of inevitability after the contest of wills in Saskatchewan, ceded in the 1960s and 1970s much more of its discretion over the financial dimensions of medical care than its U.S. counterpart was prepared to grant. Yet it may find itself in the 1980s and 1990s better positioned to defend the core of its power: control over the exercise of clinical judgement. The ideology that has shaped the accommodation between the state and the profession in Canada emphasizes functional sovereignty. Accommodations in the U.S. have been shaped by an ideology emphasizing competition and countervailing power and provide a weaker base from which to oppose competition from non-medical groups. Even more significantly, the adoption of sole-source government financing for medical and hospital services in Canada foreclosed by fiat private insurance firms from much of the health care field. Also, through the design of reimbursement mechanisms, it provided few opportunities or incentives for organizational innovation. Hence the coming of the corporation, which presents a major threat to medical sovereignty in the U.S. (by increasing the likelihood of the involvement of nonmedical actors and their objectives at both the managerial and the clinical levels of health care firms) has been retarded if not forestalled in Canada. And in that period of delay, ongoing ideological development in the medical profession itself may allow it to collaborate with government in the development of delivery models less threatening to medical functional sovereignty.

Another irony, given the historical tendency in the U.S. for the federal government to attach far more detailed conditions to transfer payments to the states than is the case in Canada, is the possibility that Canadian provinces may be more constrained in organizational innovation under the blanket restrictions of the Canada Health Act than are U.S. states under waivers of detailed federal conditions.

When all this is said, however, we return to our observation at the outset of this paper, regarding the basic similarities between Canada and the U.S. And indeed, it is likely that the public policy gap between the two countries will narrow somewhat in the future. In Canada, conflict and accommodation will occur over private encroachments on an essentially publicly-funded system; in the U.S. the issue will be the extent of public intervention in the private sector. Many of the efficiency and distributive issues will be similar, and our experience mutually instructive.

The arenas and the protagonists will, however, continue to be somewhat different. In the U.S., corporate bodies with concentrated power, including the medical profession, health care corporations, corporate purchasers of medical services, unions and universities, will continue to contend in both public and private arenas. In Canada, large corporations on the supply and demand sides will continue at least for a time to be interested by-standers, and conflict is likely to be more contained — channelled and accommodated within the relationships linking established health care providers and federal and provincial governments.

Notes

1. The terms are from H. Wilensky, "Political Legitimacy and Consensus: Missing Variables in the Assessment of Social Policy", in S. Spiro and E. Yuchtman-Yarr, eds., *Evaluating the Welfare State: Social and Political Perspectives*. New York: Academic Press, 1983.

    Corporatist democracies institutionalize collaboration among business, government and labour in the formulation and implementation of public policies; quasi-corporatist democracies lack the full-scale participation of labour.

2. Andrew Sharpe, "A Quantitative Analysis of the Development of the Welfare State in Canada". A paper presented to the annual meeting of the Canadian Political Science Association, University of Guelph, Guelph, Ontario, June 10, 1984, p. 18.

3. *Ibid.*

4. *Ibid.*, p. 24.

5. Robert Reich, *The Next American Frontier.* New York: Time Books, 1983, pp. 283-284. As another benchmark, however, the figure for France was 1.4 percent.

6. Michael Jenkin, *The Challenge of Diversity: Industrial Policy in the Canadian Federation.* Ottawa: Science Council of Canada, 1983, p. 30.

7. Gad Horowitz, "Conservatism, Liberalism and Socialism in Canada: An Interpretation", *Canadian Journal of Economics and Political Science*, 42, 2, May 1966; reprinted in Orest Kruhlak *et al.*, eds., *The Canadian Political Process.* Toronto: Holt, Rinehart and Winston, 1970, pp. 47-74.

8. Louis Hartz, *The Liberal Tradition in America.* Toronto: Longmans, 1955; Kenneth McRae, "The Structure of Canadian History", in Louis Hartz, ed., *The Founding of New Societies.* Toronto: Longmans, 1964.

9. Horowitz, *op.cit.*, footnote 7, pp. 47-48.

10. *Ibid.*, p. 48. The quotation is from Hartz, *The Founding of New Societies*, p. 25.

11. Horowitz, *op.cit.*, footnote 7, p. 61.

12. *Ibid.*

13. See Kenneth McNaught, *A History of Canada.* Penguin, 1970, esp. pp. 173-75, 222.

14. Alexander Brady, "The State and Economic Life in Canada", in Kenneth Rea and J.T. McLeod, eds., *Business and Government in Canada*, 2nd ed. Toronto: Methuen, 1976.

15. Corinne Lathrop Gilb, *Hidden Hierarchies: The Professions and Government.* New York: Harper and Row, 1966, p. 19.

16. This theme has been developed by, among others, Henry Kariel, *The Decline of American Pluralism.* Stanford: Stanford University Press, 1961; Grant McConnell, *Private Power and American Democracy.* New York: Alfred Knopf, 1966; and Theodore Lowi, *The End of Liberalism.* New York: Norton, 1969.

17. David Cameron and J. Stefan Dupré, "The Financial Framework of Income Distribution and Social Services", in Stanley M. Beck and Ivan Bernier,

eds., *Canada and the New Constitution: The Unfinished Agenda*, Vol. I. Montreal: Institute for Research on Public Policy, 1983, pp. 333-399.

18. The distinction between direct and indirect taxation is, however, not clear, and has been the subject of considerable constitutional litigation. See Edwin R. Black, *Divided Loyalties: Canadian Concepts of Federalism*. Montreal: McGill-Queen's University Press, 1975, p. 127.

19. Black, *op. cit.*, footnote 18. The other three concepts are "centralist", "compact" and "dualist". Black's book was written before the 1976 election of the Parti Québécois in Quebec attested to the re-invigoration of a "dualist" concept of federalism, although the "sovereignty-association" model proposed by the Parti Québécois itself strains at the bounds of what can be considered a federal system at all.

20. *Ibid.*, pp. 113-114.

21. *Ibid.*, p. 144.

22. Cameron and Dupré, *op. cit.*, footnote 17.

23. Black, *op. cit.*, footnote 18, p. 106. See also Donald Smiley, *Canada in Question: Federalism in the Eighties*. Toronto: McGraw-Hill Ryerson, 1981.

24. Richard Simeon, *Federal-Provincial Diplomacy: The Making of Recent Policy in Canada*. Toronto: University of Toronto Press, 1972; Richard Shultz, *Federalism, Bureaucracy and Public Policy: The Politics of Highway Transport Regulation*. Montreal: McGill-Queens University Press, 1980.

25. The complex federal-provincial financial arrangements under the major jointly funded programs reflect, among other things, provincial jurisdictional jealousies. Most notable are the "opting out" provisions, exercised in one form or another by Quebec since the 1960s under the Canada Assistance Plan and the "Established Programs". Under the most recent version of Established Programs Financing, federal contributions to the provinces are in the form partly of conditional cash transfers and partly of unconditional transfers of "tax points". Quebec receives, in lieu of part of the federal cash transfer, an additional 8.5 personal income tax points above the 13.5 granted to the other provinces. Adjustments are made, however, to ensure that the value of transfers to Quebec is identical to what it would be under the formulae applying to other provinces. In these somewhat fictional terms, federal cash transfers to Quebec constitute about one-third of total federal contributions to that province under EPF, as compared with a proportion of about one-half in the case of other provinces.

26. Morton Grodzins, "The Federal System", in the American Assembly, *Goals for Americans*. Englewood Cliffs: Prentice-Hall, 1960, p. 265.

27. Daniel Elazar, *The American Partnership*. Chicago: University of Chicago Press, 1962. Elazar has persuasively shown that, even in the nineteenth century, the rhetoric of states' rights, before and after the Civil War, tended to obscure the reality of inter-governmental collaboration and shared responsibilities.

28. For a development of this argument, see Keith Banting, *The Welfare State and Canadian Federalism*. Montreal: McGill-Queen's University Press, 1982.

29. R.G. Evans, "The Welfare Economics of Public Health Insurance: Theory and Canadian Practice", in L. Soderstrom, ed., *Social Insurance*. Amsterdam: North-Holland, 1983, p. 72.

30. Robert V. Pattison and Hallie M. Katz, "Investor-Owned and Not-for-Profit Hospitals: A Comparison Based on California Data", *New England Journal of Medicine*, 309, 6, pp. 347-353; Paul Starr, *The Social Transformation of American Medicine*. New York: Basic Books, 1982, pp. 428-449.

31. Starr, *op. cit.*, footnote 30, p. 401.

32. Malcolm Taylor, *Health Insurance and Canadian Public Policy: The Seven Decisions that Created the Canadian Health Insurance System*. Montreal: McGill-Queen's University Press, 1979.

33. *Ibid.*, p. 23.

34. R.G. Evans and A.D. Wolfson, "Moving the Target to Hit the Bullet; Generation of Utilization by Physicians in Canada". A paper prepared for the National Bureau of Economic Research Conference on the Economics of Physician and Patient Behaviour, Stanford University, Stanford, California, January 27-28, 1978.

35. Taylor, *op. cit.*, footnote 32, p. 375.

36. Ontario Medical Association, "Transactions of Council", *Ontario Medical Review*, March 1965, p. 207.

37. Government of Ontario, Committee on the Healing Arts, *Report*, Vols. I-III. Toronto: Queen's Printer, 1970; Government of Quebec, Commission of Inquiry on Health and Social Welfare, *Report*, Vol. VII, Tome I, *The Professions and Society*. Quebec: Quebec Official Publisher, 1971.

38. See, for example, Gilb, *op. cit.*, footnote 15.

39. Joseph F. Kett, "American and Canadian Medical Institutions, 1800-1870", *Journal of the History of Medicine and Allied Sciences*, 22, 4, 1967; reprinted in S.E.D. Shortt, ed., *Medicine in Canadian Society: Historical Perspectives*. Montreal: McGill-Queen's University Press, 1981, p. 195.

40. Law Society of Upper Canada, *Brief* to the Professional Organizations Committee, MInistry of the Attorney General, Toronto, April 1979, pp. 4-5.

41. Indeed, this interpretation was disputed by the ministerial committee of inquiry to whom it was addressed. The Canadian Bar Association, Ontario Branch, which had advanced a similar argument, subsequently modified it to recognize the existing requirement (since 1970) that regulations of the Law Society be approved by the Lieutenant-Governor-in-Council. Canadian Bar Association, *Brief* to the Professional Organizations Committee, Ministry of the Attorney General, Toronto, May 1979, p. 48; and Supplement, June 1979, p. 1.

42. Government of Canada, Royal Commission on the Delivery of Health Services, *Report*, Vol. I. Ottawa: Queen's Printer, 1964, p. 11.

43. These two pieces of legislation are reviewed in Carolyn J. Tuohy, "Private Government, Property and Professionalism", *Canadian Journal of Political Science*, 9, 4, December 1976, pp. 668-681.

44. See, for example, Oliver Garceau, *The Political Life of the American Medical Association*. Cambridge: Harvard University Press, 1941; D.L. Hyde and R. Wolff, "The American Medical Association: Power, Purpose and Politics in Organized Medicine", *Yale Law Journal*, 63, 1954, pp. 900-1000; Bernard Blishen, *Doctors and Doctrines*. Toronto: University of Toronto Press, 1969.

45. The literature on ideology is vast and not entirely conceptually consistent. Common to all approaches is a treatment of ideology as systematic (i.e., as comprising an inter-related set of beliefs and opinions), as identifying sources of authority (both in the sense of legitimate power and of "truth"), and as having an affective as well as a cognitive component. Some approaches, however, treat ideological formation as related to psychological development; others emphasize its function in the defence of interests (particularly those interests arising from technological roles) or in rationalizing contradictions entailed in certain roles. For a comprehensive review of the psychological approaches, see Jeanne M. Knutson, *The Human Basis of the Polity*. Chicago: Aldine-Atherton, 1972; for a classic exposition of the "legitimation of interest" approach, see Karl Mannheim, *Ideology and Utopia*. New York: Harcourt, Brace and World, 1939; and for a seminal "role strain" work, see S.M. Lipset, *Political Man*. New York: Anchor, 1964. Usage in this paper draws most heavily on the concept of legitimation of interests arising from technological roles.

46. The discussion in this section draws heavily on my earlier paper, "Smoke and Mirrors: Professional Ideology and Symbolism in Health Care Policy", *Proceedings of the Conference on Health in the 80s and 90s*. Montebello,

Quebec, March 14-17, 1982. Toronto: Council of Ontario Universities, pp. 185-203.

47. Carolyn J. Tuohy, *The Political Attitudes of Ontario Physicians: A Skill Group Perspective*, PhD dissertation, Yale University, 1974; Alan D. Wolfson, Carolyn J. Tuohy and Chandrakant P. Shah, *What Do Doctors Do? A Study of Fee-for-Service Practice in Ontario*. Toronto: Physicians' Services Incorporated Foundation, 1978, esp. Appendix C.

48. Alan D. Wolfson and Carolyn J. Tuohy, *Opting Out of Medicare: Private Medical Markets in Ontario*. Toronto: University of Toronto Press, 1980.

49. Carolyn J. Tuohy, "Medical Politics After Medicare: The Ontario Case", *Canadian Public Policy*, 2, 2, Spring 1976, pp. 203-204.

50. See, for example, Joan Boase, "Regulation and the Paramedical Professions: An Interest Group Study", *Canadian Public Administration*, 25, 3, Fall 1982, pp. 332-353.

51. As Soderstrom and Kapsalis have demonstrated, even before 1977 the marginal cost of health care was considerably higher for the provinces than for the federal government. Lee Soderstrom, "Federal-Provincial Cost-Sharing: Can Ottawa Influence Provincial Health Policies Using Financial Carrots?", in J.A. Boan, ed., *Proceedings of the Second Canadian Conference on Health Economics*, Regina, Saskatchewan, September 9-11, 1983. Regina: University of Regina, 1984, pp. 375-426; C. Kapsalis, "Block Funding and Provincial Spending on Social Programs", Discussion Paper no. 210. Ottawa: Economic Council of Canada, 1982.

52. Tuohy, "Medical Politics . . ." and "Smoke and Mirrors . . .", *op. cit.*, footnotes 49 and 46.

53. Murray Edelman, *The Symbolic Uses of Politics*. Urbana: University of Illinois Press, 1964, p. 47.

54. The average income of full-time physicians in Ontario now stands at more than five times the average industrial wage. This compares with a ratio of 4.3 in 1961, 5.7 in 1971 and 4.1 in 1979. The latter figures are from Paul C. Weiler, *Report of the Chairman, Joint Committee on Physicians' Compensation for Professional Services*, March 8, 1982, p. 30. Current estimates are based on Ontario Ministry of Health updating of Weiler's calculations of the earnings of full-time Ontario physicians, and Statistics Canada, *Monthly Labour Statistics*, regarding the average industrial wage.

55. Richard Bird, "The Public Finance of Health Care: Reflections on the Hall Report", in *Commentaries on the Hall Report*, Ontario Economic Council Discussion Paper. Toronto: Ontario Economic Council, 1981.

56. A.S. Detsky, S.R. Stacey and C. Bombardier, "The Effectiveness of a Regulatory Strategy in Containing Hospital Costs", *New England Journal of Medicine*, 309, 3, pp. 151-159.

57. Darrel Weinkauf, "M.D.: Population Ratios and Manpower Planning", *Ontario Medical Review*, October 1982, pp. 666-669.

58. Ontario's experience with its Medical Review Committee, located within the College of Physicians and Surgeons and charged with reviewing and, when deemed necessary, investigating "aberrant accounts" referred to it by the government insurance agency, is particularly interesting for the light it sheds on one aspect of the accommodation between the profession and the Ontario government. See Carolyn J. Tuohy, "Medical Politics . . .", *op. cit.*, footnote 49, and "Does a Claims Monitoring System Influence High-Volume Medical Practitioners? Attitudinal Data from Ontario", *Inquiry*, 19, Spring 1982, pp. 18-33.

59. André-Pierre Contandriopoulos, Claudine Laurier and Louise-Hélène Trottier, "Towards an Improved Work Organization in the Health Services Sector: From Administrative Rationalization to Professional Rationality", this volume.

60. Greg Stoddart, "Rationalizing the Health Care System", in T.J. Courchene, D.W. Conklin and G.C.A. Cook, eds., *Ottawa and the Provinces: The Distribution of Money and Power*, Vol. II. Toronto: Ontario Economic Council, 1985, p. 6.

61. For a review of these options, see M.L. Barer, R.G. Evans and G.L. Stoddart, *Controlling Health Care Costs by Direct Charges to Patients: Snare or Delusion?* Ontario Economic Council Occasional Paper #10, Toronto, 1979.

62. Alan D. Wolfson and Carolyn J. Tuohy, *op. cit.*, footnote 47.

63. Barer *et al.*, *op. cit.*, footnote 61, pp. 56-60.

64. See, for example Theodore R. Marmor, *The Politics of Medicare*. Chicago: Aldine, 1973, esp. pp. 108-109.

65. Starr, *op. cit.*, footnote 30, p. 376.

66. R.R. Henderson and J.J. May, "The Business Community Looks at DRG-Based Hospital Reimbursement", *Health Affairs*, Spring 1983.

67. A striking case is the extension of Medicare to patients with end-stage renal disease. See Daniel Greenberg, "Renal Politics", *New England Journal of Medicine*, 298, June 22, 1978, pp. 1427-1428; and Starr, *op. cit.*, footnote 30, pp. 442-443.

68. Starr, *op. cit.*, footnote 30, p. 405.

69. *Ibid.*, p. 432.

70. *Ibid.*, p. 429.

71. See, for example, Jack Meyer, "Federalism Strikes Back in Health Policy", *Regulation*, November/December 1982, p. 17.

72. David E. Rosenbaum, "Chrysler, Hit Hard by Costs, Studies Health Care System", *New York Times*, March 5, 1984, pp. 28-29.

73. *Ibid.*

74. Reich, *op. cit.*, footnote 5, pp. 250, 254.

75. Reich does not use the term, nor does he deal with the role corporations, subsidized in various ways by the state, played in colonization and later in the opening of the West. But he does present his prescriptions as an extension of the strategic coordination among large-scale enterprises and state activity which characterized the "era of management" in the U.S. (1920-1970) as a reaction against the "decentralized, piecemeal, idiosyncratic and unreliable" forms of political and economic organization that marked American industrial activity in the nineteenth century. *Op. cit.*, footnote 5, pp. 24, 83-105.

76. The classic treatment is Reuben Kessel, "Price Discrimination in Medicine", *Journal of Law and Economics*, October 1958, pp. 20-53. See also Garceau, *op. cit.*, footnote 44; Hyde and Wolff, *op. cit.*, footnote 44; Marmor, *op. cit.*, footnote 64.

77. See, for example, Lee Goldman, "Doctors' Attitudes Toward National Health Insurance", *Medical Care*, 12, 5, May 1974, pp. 413-423; Lee Goldman, "Factors Related to Physicians' Medical and Political Attitudes: A Documentation of Intraprofessional Variations", *Journal of Health and Social Behaviour*, 15, 3, September 1974; J. Colombotos, "Physicians and Medicare: A Before-After Study of the Effects of Legislation on Attitudes", *American Sociological Review*, 34, 1969, pp. 318-334; J. Colombotos, "Physicians' Response to Change in Health Care: Some Projections", *Inquiry*, 8, 1, March 1971, pp. 20-26; J. Colombotos, "Physicians View National Health Insurance", *Medical Care*, 13, 5, May 1975, pp. 369-396; David Mechanic, "Factors Affecting Receptivity to Innovations in Health Care Delivery Among Primary Care Physicians", in Mechanic, ed., *Politics, Medicine and Social Science*. New York: Wiley, 1974.

78. In addition to the sources in the previous footnote, see Robert Alford, *Health Care Politics*. Chicago: University of Chicago Press, 1975; and Charlene Harrington, "Medical Ideologies in Conflict", *Medical Care*, 13, 11, November 1975, pp. 905-914.

79. The phrase is from Starr, *op. cit.*, footnote 30, pp. 420 ff.

80. *Ibid.* See also Victor Fuchs, "The Battle for the Control of Health Care", *Health Affairs*, 1, 3, Summer 1983, pp. 5-13; and Tuohy, *Political Attitudes*,

op. cit., footnote 47.

81. A.S. Relman, "The New Medical-Industrial Complex", *New England Journal of Medicine*, 303, 1980, pp. 963-970.

82. M.D. Fottler, G. Gibson and D.M. Pinchoff, "Physician Attitudes Toward the Nurse Practitioner", *Journal of Health and Social Behavior*, 19, 3, September 1978, pp. 303-311, esp. p. 310.

83. J.L. Weston, "Distribution of Nurse Practitioners and Physician's Assistants: Implications of Legal Constraints and Reimbursement", *Public Health Reports*, 1980, pp. 253-258.

84. Pattison and Katz, *op. cit.*, footnote 30; Lawrence Lewin, R.A. Derzon and R. Margulies, "Investor-Owned and Non-Profits Differ in Economic Performance", *Hospitals*, July 1, 1981, pp. 52-58.

85. See sources in preceding footnote for evidence of differences. For a finding of no systematic differences, see Frank A. Sloan and Robert A. Vracu, "Investor-Owned and Not-for-Profit Hospitals: Addressing Some Issues", *Health Affairs*, 2, 1, Spring 1983.

86. Pattison and Katz, *op. cit.*, footnote 30.

87. Starr, *op. cit.*, footnote 30, p. 442.

88. *Ibid.*, pp. 393-405.

89. Pattison and Katz, *op. cit.*, footnote 30, p. 353.

90. Jack A. Meyer, *op.cit.*, footnote 71, p. 17; Jon B. Christianson, D.G. Hillman and K.R. Smith, "The Arizona Experiment", *Health Affairs*, 2, 3, Fall, 1983, pp. 88-103.

91. Meyer, *op.cit.*, footnote 71, p. 18.

92. W. Murray McAdam, "Incentives Recommended for Health Care System", *Ontario Medical Review*, September 1983, p. 342.

93. *Ibid.*

94. *Ibid.*, p. 343.

95. Greg L. Stoddart, "Publicly Financed Competition in Canadian Health Care Delivery: A Viable Alternative to Increased Regulation?", in *Proceedings of the Conference on Health in the 80s and 90s*, Montebello, Quebec, March 14-17, 1982. Toronto: Council of Ontario Universities, pp. 173-184.

96. Stoddart, "Rationalizing . . .", *op.cit.*, footnote 60.

97. A joint statement issued by a meeting of all provincial health ministers in October 1982 set the tone for provincial reaction throughout the development of federal legislation. It announced the conviction that health care

delivery "remain within the provincial jurisdiction", and declared that the proposed federal legislation presented "a grave threat to the ability of the provinces to meet our constitutional responsibilities to deliver health services to the Canadian people". Ian Mulgrew, "Health Ministers Fear Ottawa Power Grab", *The Globe and Mail*, Toronto, October 2, 1982.

COMMENTARY

K.J. Fyke

Introduction

I would like to respond to Professor Tuohy's paper by pointing to some key factors within the health system that have had a substantial effect on the organization and delivery of health services.[1] I believe Professor Tuohy has provided a valuable sketch of the social, political and technological context in which health policy has developed in Canada and the United States. She has also offered an insightful description of what she calls the "complex processes of ideological, partisan, interest group and intergovernmental conflict and accommodation, mediated through a series of pragmatic judgements". This analytical framework leads Professor Tuohy to conclude that, in Canada, the development of comprehensive hospital and medical care insurance and, more recently, the reinforcement of this comprehensive insurance scheme by the Canada Health Act has to a great extent locked Canada into a set pattern with respect to the organization and delivery of health services. A key element of this organizational structure, according to Professor Tuohy, is the powerful position of key health professions, specifically the medical profession.

Professor Tuohy explains how the development of comprehensive medical insurance in Canada, on the one hand, has caused the medical profession to cede "much . . . of its discretion over the financial dimensions of medical care", but, on the other hand, has enabled it to defend "the core of its power: control over the exercise of clinical judgement". Physicians' control over the exercise of clinical judgement entails substantial control over their scope of practice and consequently the scope of practice of other professions. This control, in turn, means that attempts by provincial governments to reorganize the health system to achieve a more efficient allocation of functions to less expensive professions has been stymied.

In general, I find myself in agreement with Professor Tuohy's argument. It seems clear that comprehensive medical and hospital insurance has become a motherhood issue in Canada — or, at least, in most provinces of Canada. The provisions of the federal-provincial financial arrangements have definitely made innovation in the control or moderation of the supply of services difficult. Yet there have been innovations, perhaps to a greater extent than Professor Tuohy allows. There are also some forces or developments within the health system that, I believe, will bring further innovation and change.

I base much of the following discussion on my experience in the province of Saskatchewan. As Professor Tuohy points out, this province has had a major "demonstration effect" on the rest of the country with respect to hospital and medical insurance. It may be that there will also be — or has been — a demonstration effect with respect to some of the issues discussed below.

The Expanding Role of Non-Medical Professions

Over the past twenty years or so, the role of the non-medical health professions in the provision of health services has expanded dramatically. This has been especially true in Saskatchewan, where the problem of providing services to a small population spread over a vast territorial area combined with a shortage of medical professionals has demanded innovation.

The provision of psychiatric services in Saskatchewan is a good example. That province, like many other parts of Canada, has suffered from a chronic shortage of psychiatrists. Consequently, it has not been possible to make the services of psychiatrists available at the local level. Instead, Saskatchewan has developed multi-disciplinary teams of health professionals who hold regional and district clinics throughout the province. These teams consist of psychiatrists, psychologists, social workers and community mental health nurses. I am not suggesting that social workers, nurses and psychologists are practising medicine in place of the psychiatrist, but that they are providing a number of very important services, at least some of which psychiatrists themselves might be providing were they available in greater supply. I think that in an important way this constitutes a reallocation of functions from physicians to other traditionally less expensive practitioners.

The argument may be made that the functions carried out by the non-medical psychiatric workers are functions marginal to the medical profession. I think there are two responses to this:

1. From an economic point of view, the fact that non-medical workers are providing services that physicians might be providing (even though they may not, strictly speaking, be medical services) means that governments are providing services at lower cost. I recognize that in the case of psychiatrists/non-

psychiatrists we may be talking of providing services by non-psychiatrists or not providing services at all. In other words, these services could be seen as add-on costs. But I suspect that in the absence of these services we would see demand displaced to some extent to hospitals and to general practice physicians.

2. From the viewpoint of the medical community, we can see the expanding role for non-medical professions as an expansion of the whole territory of health care. This territory has grown so that physicians are only one group among many health care providers. "Patients" no longer deal on a one to one basis only with their doctors (and nurses, in the hospital setting), but also with speech pathologists, audiologists, chiropractors, optometrists, chiropodists, psychologists, public health nurses, physical and occupational therapists, etc. Does this mean simply that the territory has expanded while the physician, as Professor Tuohy suggests, still retains control over his "province"?

In response I would say that, in the first place, being one province among many — even if you are the biggest province — is different from being the only province. One crucial respect in which it is different is that physicians are now only one of many professions after government dollars and, as Professor Tuohy notes, after "corporate" power. But a second and more crucial point is that the cumulative effect of all the new professions may be a reduction in the size or at least a change in the shape of the "province" controlled by physicians. I would like to illustrate this point by looking at the role some other professions are taking in Saskatchewan.

There, patients are now visiting optometrists to care for their eyes, chiropractors to care for their backs, chiropodists to care for their feet, physical therapists to care for muscle and joint problems, etc. It is true that some of these services are on referral from a physician and may be nominally under his direction, but inevitably these professions are taking on a role in the diagnosis, assessment and treatment of health conditions independently of physicians. The reaction of the medical community to the role of chiropractors and, more recently in Saskatchewan to the role of chiropodists and physical therapists, suggests that they see or fear an invasion of their territory. I admit that for each individual non-medical profession the invasion may seem small or negligible, but I wonder if the cumulative effect over time, and future developments, will not add up to a reorganization of the health system of considerable importance.

The Aging Population and its Effect on the Organization of the Health System

Another development of major importance to the health system is the aging of the population. Changes in the age structure of the population are altering the environment of medical practice and may, in the long run, affect the scope of physicians' practice. These developments may be seen most clearly in Saskatchewan, where the aging of the population is more advanced than in much of the rest of Canada.

More than 12 percent of the population of Saskatchewan is over sixty-five, one of the largest proportions of any province in Canada. Moreover, a large and growing segment of this elderly population is over eighty-five, the age at which the demand for health service is particularly high. Meeting the health needs of the growing elderly population has presented a major challenge for Saskatchewan. Not only are more resources needed, but different types of resources and different approaches to health care, as well.

The effect of the aging population on medical practice can, in part, be explained by the chronic nature of disease among the elderly. While the focus of much modern medicine is on treatment and cure, the key issue for the elderly is not cure but maintenance or restoration of functional capacity. Certainly, many members of the medical profession recognize this aspect of the health needs of the elderly and are attempting to re-orient the medical profession to address these needs better. But the special needs of the elderly are also pushing the development of non-medical professions and of new approaches to health care. The provincial government has been active in funding the development of many of these non-medical services.

Approximately 8 percent of the elderly in Saskatchewan are institutionalized — in special care homes, private homes or extended care facilities. This is an area in which physicians in the province have had limited interest or involvement. It may be that demands for better care for persons in residential care, combined with pressure to seek new "customers" because of physician oversupply, will result in an expanded role for physicians in this area. If this does occur, however, it will be in the context of an expanding role for physical therapists, occupational therapists, nurses and aides. The point is that a large and growing part of our population will be receiving much primary care from non-physicians. Once again the non-medical territory is expanding, though in this case the medical territory may not be contracting.

For the elderly in the community, a range of preventive, treatment, rehabilitative and palliative services are developing separately from medical services. It is true that the elderly are an important part of the physician's clientele. In Saskatchewan the elderly, making up 12 percent of the population, use about 24 percent of physician services and 47 percent of hospital services. (However, the last figure is somewhat misleading. In any one year, about 25 percent of the elderly are hospitalized; in other words, 75 percent do *not* make use of inpatient hospital services.) But over and above these physician services there is a wide and growing range of health services that the elderly receive and which do not directly involve physicians. These services may constitute, to some extent, a shift of functions from physicians to non-medical workers. These services include audiological evaluations and fitting of hearing aids by audiologists; provision of foot care by chiropodists; provision of home nursing and other home care services by nurses and other workers; adult day care involving nurses, occupational therapists and physical therapists; diabetic counselling by nurses and dietitians; and psychiatric services by social workers, community mental health nurses and psychologists.

A number of these services are seen by the majority of physicians as important services ancillary to medicine, suggesting therefore that they do not constitute an invasion of their territory. However, some of these services or aspects of them have not been without resistance or concern expressed by the medical community. The home care program has raised some controversy because lay assessors determine program eligibility, a decision some physicians feel should be carried out by or controlled by physicians. The recent introduction of a province-wide chiropody program angered the medical community because it felt it had received inadequate consultation. Periodically, there are rumblings from parts of the medical community about the role of audiologists, and some psychiatrists argue that psychologists should limit themselves only to psychometrics. These complaints suggest that the medical profession perceives some loss or potential loss of territory to other professions.

The future development of services for the elderly may expand this invasion of medical territory by non-medical groups. For the elderly in particular, health problems must be addressed in the context of their whole social/living environment. As a result, a broad, holistic approach to preventing and treating their health problems must be undertaken. The provision of appropriate social activities and opportunities for socialization and the provision of support during crises such as bereavement may be as important to preventing depression among the elderly as the provision of anti-depressant drugs and other medical care. But socialization and crisis support involve a wide variety of non-medical professionals from recreation therapists to physical and occupational therapists and community mental health nurses. Moreover, if these services "work", at least some problems that lead to medical visits may not develop, or develop only much later in life.

Prevention and the Changing Nature of Disease

The previous observation leads me to another area on which I would like to comment: the reorganization of the health system. It is well known that over the past fifty years we have seen a dramatic shift in the major causes of premature death and disability in the developed world — principally from infectious diseases as the major cause of death to what has been called by the World Health Organization, "non-communicable diseases".[2] These non-communicable diseases include heart disease, cancer, accidental deaths and injuries, mental disorders and suicide, and they share common risk factors: smoking, inappropriate diet, physical inactivity, risk-taking behaviours, stress and alcohol abuse. Such behaviours are, at least to some extent, avoidable or alterable; consequently, the associated non-communicable diseases are preventable.

The nature of modern disease is of importance to the organization of the health system because the many non-medical professionals have a key role to play in the prevention of these major diseases of the modern era. Health educators, nutritionists, physical fitness instructors, alcoholism/drug counsellors and specialists in media advertising, behaviour change, accident prevention and road design, and others have roles to play that, in many respects, are more important than those of the physician.

There are two effects or possible effects of this multi-disciplinary approach to prevention. First, if prevention works — and I admit that at times this seems a big if — then physicians will be deprived of some of their "customers". Second, whether prevention works to a greater or lesser extent, the number of non-medical "provinces" in the health field are further expanded. As a consequence, the relative size of the medical territory is further diminished, and to some extent the medical territory itself may be infringed upon.

Conclusion

In conclusion, I think the factors I have outlined above may work, in concert with the forces Professor Tuohy has identified, to bring about a reorientation and perhaps a reorganization of the health system in Canada. How rapidly these changes occur will, as Professor Tuohy suggests, be influenced by the social, political and technological context of the future and by the pragmatic judgements of key actors.

Notes

1. The views in this paper are those of the author and not those of Saskatchewan Health or the Greater Victoria Hospital Society.
2. WHO, "The Steering Group Meeting on Integrated Non-communicable Diseases Prevention and Control Programme". Report of a meeting, Geneva, October 1982.

VII

REFLECTIONS AND SYNTHESIS

AMERICAN PERSPECTIVE: IF THE WAR OF 1812 HAD TURNED OUT DIFFERENTLY, WOULD THERE NOW BE PPOs IN MANITOBA OR GLOBAL BUDGETING IN VERMONT? SOME CONCLUDING OBSERVATIONS

Bruce C. Vladeck

Introduction

The formidable task of summarizing a conference such as this one is often equated with development of some sort of grand synthesis. From the welter of observations, insights, digressions and arguments that inevitably arise in five days of discussion, the summarizer is expected to create order, to pull everything into a coherent design, to fit all the pieces into the puzzle. Such a task is not only far beyond the capacity of this commentator but it would also be inconsistent with the tone and attitude that characterized much of the conference itself. For perhaps the most rewarding — and refreshing — aspect of this conference was the way in which participants appeared to agree tacitly that the world is a complex and often confounding place, that most truths are partial or contingent and most research findings conditional and that valid generalizations are hard to come by and harder still to sustain.

So instead of a grand synthesis, I propose sixteen often unrelated statements that are relatively true and at least partially accurate, gleaned from the conference papers and discussions. The first six are mostly about health care financing and economics; the second six mostly about health services organization; the last four primarily about politics. An important *caveat* applies to all of them: While they reflect, to a greater or lesser extent, consensus among conference participants, they are not meant to be consensus statements, and many of the participants might have disagreed strenuously with many of them. They are more accurately characterized as a collection of the commentator's revealed prejudices.

Financing

1. The first point is the most basic. The Canadian experience appears to confirm what most observers always expected: Universal insurance coverage can improve access to health services. The British experience also appears to confirm this belief. In the U.S. there are now somewhere between twenty-five and thirty million people without health insurance of any kind. Since the data quite clearly demonstrate that the lack of insurance is a primary barrier to access to needed health services,[1] this point cannot be emphasized too strongly. If people cannot get care because they do not have insurance — get them insurance.

Under a system of universal coverage, however, there is at any time at least a theoretical possibility that the system will be underfunded. This may lead to rationing by queuing as opposed to rationing by economic or insurance status. Whether or not such queuing currently exists in Canada, or if it does how serious a problem it is, does not really matter. Under circumstances of universal coverage, queuing is the most likely substitute for differential insurance status as a rationing mechanism, if and when rationing occurs. Again, the British experience seems to be relevant here.

2. Single-source or pooled funding appears to be a necessary, if not sufficient, condition for effective cost containment. It has certainly facilitated cost containment in Canada, while those states in the U.S. with the best record on hospital costs are those that have regulated most, or all, of hospital revenues. The data are striking. In the period 1976 to 1981, hospital expenditures in Canada increased at an average annual rate of 10.3 percent. In the U.S. as a whole, they grew at an average rate of 14.0 percent, but in the six rate-setting states studied by Biles, Schramm and Atkinson, the rate was 11.15 percent.[2]

Single-source or pooled funding is a necessary condition for effective cost containment, but is not sufficient by itself. Here, political will appears to be the critical additional variable, as is suggested by the variation in stringency of cost containment across the Canadian provinces (see Barer and Evans).

3. In the presence of appropriate structural characteristics in public finance and federal fiscal relations, governments are more sensitive and likely to respond to cost pressures than are private payers. Examples of the "appropriate" structural characteristics would include Canada since the enactment of the Established Programs Financing Act in 1977, and American states under Medicaid cost-sharing, in which forty-nine of the fifty states are constitutionally required to balance their budgets each year. Conversely, the American federal government felt only limited pressure to constrain the rate of cost increase in the American Medicare program until the effects of the Reagan tax cuts caused a general federal budgetary crisis. In the absence of such a crisis, the ability of the federal government to continue to operate at a substantial deficit made it very difficult to

create adequate political pressure to reduce Medicare expenditures. This point is closely related to the next observation.

4. Large-scale governmental funding of the health sector renders that sector increasingly sensitive to macroeconomic forces, as has been revealed by the recent American experience with Medicare. The conference discussion of the changing attitude in the Manitoba government in the past several years is relevant here, as is the experience of the British National Health Service. The NHS has grown slowly, by international comparisons, in large part because of Britain's poor economic performance relative to other industrialized nations over the past decade or so. And this is despite the relatively favoured status of the NHS within Britain's highly constrained public sector. In the U.S. system, notwithstanding the Medicare experience, the connection between macroeconomic forces and the health care sector remains somewhat more tenuous. The difference arises from the more partial role of government funding, and the diffusion of funding sources across a large number of consumers and institutions.

5. Real *per capita* growth (age-adjusted) of 1 percent per year, or less, appears to be an attainable long-term target for hospital cost increases. This is not just a technical statement, but indeed a policy statement of very considerable magnitude. In the U.S., it substantially alters the debate over the future of Medicare's Hospital Insurance Trust Fund.[3] The experience of sustained controls at this level is confirmed not only in many Canadian provinces, but also in the American states with the most effective hospital regulation programs. It is also interesting to recognize the British NHS budgetary principle of an annual .5 percent increment for "technology". Even in that very highly constrained environment, prolonged periods without real growth in hospital expenditures are apparently unsustainable politically.

6. We know little about how best to pay physicians. I don't believe that the issue of extra-billing in Canada is purely symbolic; rather, it lies at the core of the general policy problem of physician reimbursement. Similarly, it is at the heart of the contemporary American controversy over Medicare reimbursement to physicians. Canada has clearly done an excellent job of controlling the rate of fee increases. Yet, Canada appears to be entirely lacking in effective controls over the volume of services, and many Canadians are worried by that. Similarly, in the American experience we have shown some ability to constrain fee increases, but very little ability to control volume. Moreover, bureaucratic or regulatory controls on volume, such as utilization review of office-based services or procedures, is extremely difficult to do well. In terms of the ratio of administrative burden to effectiveness in changing practice behaviours, it is also generally not cost-effective.

The example of Quebec, where physician payments have been effectively limited by imposition of aggregate caps, may represent a political anomaly in the North American context. But it does bear a striking resemblance to at least one significant proposal for reforming U.S. Medicare practices.[4] It is also identical in principle to the way in which capitated American Independent Practice Association (IPA) model HMOs pay their member physicians.

The operative dynamic on both sides of the border appears to be the effect of "target income" behaviour by physicians in a period of dramatically increasing physician supply, along with a much slower growth in the supply of patients. But, for reasons to be discussed below, the appropriate policy levers may have nothing to do with either target incomes or supply constraints. Nor is either the Quebec model or greater "competition" among "health plans" likely to get us out of this box. The former has too many political liabilities; the latter confuses Microeconomics I with real behaviour. We have not yet begun to experiment seriously with altered fee-for-service incentives, but that is probably the only really plausible direction we can take.

Organization

7. Physician supply is a very potent force, more susceptible to policy intervention in theory than it may be in practice. This foreigner suspects that part of the reason for the apparent Canadian uneasiness about the future of their system lies in concern about the impact of the growing supply of physicians. Medical education is so heavily subsidized by governments in both countries that it would appear quite vulnerable to public policy levers. Yet, it is hard to be very optimistic about significant reductions, given the existing political pressures to maintain the size of the medical education enterprise.

While the growth in physician supply appears to threaten the financial success of the Canadian system, it may also spur greater innovation and impingement on professional autonomy than has previously been the case. In the U.S., much of the innovation in patterns of physician organization, including the employment of physicians in "corporate" settings, appears to have been precipitated by the fears of imminent surplus on the parts of young physicians entering practice.

Conversely, the difficulty of constraining the future supply of physicians raises questions about the wisdom of promoting expanded practice by other categories of professional personnel. The evidence is overwhelming, for example, that nurse practitioners can effectively substitute for physicians. Whether that produces a net benefit to society in an environment of physician surplus seems very questionable.

8. The increased supply of physicians creates possibilities in the organization of medical practice that did not previously exist. Yet the experience both in Canada and in the more regulatory of the American states suggests that it is much easier to control costs than it is to reform the organization of health care delivery. The political price for practitioner acceptance of revenue control may or may not have

to be a guarantee of professional autonomy, as has been suggested in the Canadian case (see Tuohy). But, it does seem to be easier to impose revenue controls than to close unnecessary hospitals, increase the volume of surgery performed on an ambulatory basis, or get physicians to develop more rational and economical referral practices.

In the U.S., for example, there used to be a lot of rhetoric about "integrating planning and rate-setting" in order to ensure that provider responses to revenue constraints moved the system in the right direction. But even those of us most committed to health planning have increasingly had to recognize that while constraining revenues is the best way to control costs in the politically relevant short-to-medium term, it accomplishes little more than constraining revenues.

Perhaps more basically, the disconnectedness of payment reform and organizational change raises questions about the potential confusion of ends and means. Reductions in inpatient capacity, increases in ambulatory surgery or reduced reliance on procedure-oriented specialists may be desirable in and of themselves, but they have been promoted largely through claims of cost-effectiveness. If costs can be reduced without them, however, then one wonders whether they are worth the effort and struggle involved in real behavioural change. An American suspects that this phenomenon may explain some of the apparent frustrations of his Canadian counterparts; the very effectiveness of Canadian economic controls may blunt the impetus for system reform. On the other hand, one can question the value of reform solely for reform's sake.

9. As something of a qualification to the prior point, both Canadian and American experiences suggest that patterns of professional self-regulation and self-governance can present substantial barriers to organizational change in the health system, until there is enough political pressure or commitment to undertake such changes. The U.S. HMO Act of 1971 and professional regulation in Quebec both indicate that these barriers are formidable until one seeks to take them down. Taking them down involves significant political costs, but is not impossible in the presence of adequate political pressures.

10. Cultural differences between the two countries best explain differences in the origins and nature of general innovations in service delivery and patterns of care. The role of the independent entrepreneur or fast-buck artist is substantially more legitimate culturally in the U.S. than in Canada. Certainly, much of what Canadians view as progressive innovation in the American health care system has come about not from concerted public policy development, but rather from the creativity, drive and economic aspirations of a small number of aggressive entrepreneurs. This pattern of behaviour characterizes much of the American economy, although it is a relatively new arrival on the health care scene. My understanding is that it is generally less characteristic of the Canadian economy, in other sectors as well as in health care.

Moreover, as Brown pointed out, during the conference, the bases of legislative representation in the U.S. encourage "policy entrepreneurs" in U.S. legislatures, in contrast to the more rigid Canadian parliamentary party discipline. When organizational and policy entrepreneurs get together, the forces of innovation are particularly potent.

In the American setting, the prevailing political ideology looks with great scepticism on governmentally initiated innovation, while there is an almost excessive premium put on private sector creativeness and innovation. In the absence of such an ideology in Canada, government remains the only really plausible source of programmatic innovation. When, for whatever political reasons, it does not innovate, innovation does not occur. When it does innovate, however, to paraphrase a famous American rhetorician, "It's a beaut".

11. In both countries, the needs of a growing population of frail, elderly persons for comprehensive long-term care services are enormous. Yet this problem is more often mentioned than systematically attacked. In part this is because the provision and financing of services for this population is a provincial or state rather than federal responsibility. In addition, policy makers at all levels of government in both countries are terrified of its fiscal implications. I do believe that there may be more ferment in this area in the U.S. than in Canada. On the other hand, this observation may arise primarily from ignorance of the Canadian system. Or it may stem from the simple fact that there are some fifty sites for potentially innovative policy development in the American federal system but only ten in the Canadian.

12. I am indebted to Crane for the observation that, amid all their differences, Canada and the U.S. appear to share a perceived atrophy in traditional public health activities. Public health professionals further share the view that service dollars drive public health dollars out of government budgets. Several Canadians suggested that public health agencies suffered because Ministries of Health also administered health insurance. However, in the U.S. the general separation of those two functions has not served public health any better.

The case for expanded activities in prevention and health promotion as a way of improving the public's health may be generally compelling, but no sophisticated observer believes that the connection between health and health care is nearly tight enough to ensure that improved health will reduce health care costs. Instead, it may be that we have reached the point in the development of technologies at which health care offers us more efficacious things on which to spend new money than does public health. But that is a complicated subject, more worthy of discussion in a different setting. For purposes of this conference, it is sufficient to say that, like long-term care services for the aged, public health services are those things everyone agrees *should* be talked about — as soon as they get done with the more exciting discussions of hospital finances and physician behaviour.

Politics

13. Federal systems contain enormous levels of diversity within them, which makes generalization of any sort dangerous. This point may, at first glance, appear trivial, but it has extremely interesting implications for the U.S. The apparently lesser variation in the Canadian system than the American may again just be a function of there being ten, rather than fifty-one or fifty-two, units involved.

The important lesson here for an American is that this diversity persists in Canada even within the structure of a basic national commitment to universal access and universal coverage with substantial federal financing. In other words, those in the U.S. who have promoted national health insurance, or even more partial financing reforms such as those contained in the Kennedy-Gephardt Bill, may have suffered a failure of the imagination in thinking through the roles of states and localities. If Quebec and Alberta can both be accurately characterized as participating in the same national health insurance system, then we may have more room to manoeuvre in the U.S. than we have generally believed.

14. The anti-interventionist, anti-governmental ideologies currently prevalent in much of the American culture often produce policies much more interventionist and regulatory than one might expect. Thus, the resistance to public financing of health care has led to substantially greater invasions of professional autonomy in the delivery of services and in the administration of publicly financed health care programs for the poor and the elderly than would apparently be conceivable in the Canadian setting. Similarly, state regulation of hospital costs is substantially more detailed and invasive than the global budgeting that occurs in most Canadian provinces. In large part, this is precisely because it is not connected to more direct government assumption of financing responsibility. When government lacks the leverage of single-source financing, controlling its own costs takes considerably more policing. Indirect cost controls, be they certificate of need or PROs, are inherently more bureaucratically intrusive than direct cost controls.

15. The experience in both Canada and Britain strongly suggests that while it may be politically very difficult to attain publicly financed health insurance, the programs become enormously popular even among conservatives once that battle has been won. Indeed, that also appears to be the case with Medicare in the U.S.; while introduction of Medicare was ardently resisted by organized medical and professional interests, it is now as popular a program as we have. One would hope this would give American politicians substantially more courage than they have shown in this arena in recent years.

16. There is significantly less political consensus in the U.S. than in Canada on national health policy. As a result, health policy in the U.S. is much more susceptible to changes as a result of election outcomes. American elections are

generally more consequential for health policy than Canadian elections, even when Canadian elections produce changes in the partisan control of government. This is true even though health policy is often not a major issue in the U.S. elections. The last time health policy was a major national campaign issue (in 1964), the majority party's position (in support of Medicare) was supported by an overwhelming consensus of the voters.[5]

Conclusion

My good friend Walter McClure, one of the leading advocates of "market-oriented", "competitive" health care strategies in the U.S., often claims that if his policy prescriptions are not adopted, the U.S. health care system will end up looking like Canada's, as though that were the worst of all possible outcomes. After almost a week of talking and thinking about the Canadian health care system, I am convinced both that that would not be such a terrible outcome, and that the "danger" of the U.S. system's looking like Canada's is much exaggerated. We could do much worse — and probably will.

Notes

1. The Robert Wood Johnson Foundation, *Updated Report on Access to Health Care for the American People*. Special Report, no. 1. Princeton, N.J., 1983.

2. Center for Hospital Finance and Management, Johns Hopkins University, personal communication.

3. Bruce C. Vladeck, "Comment on 'Hospital Reimbursement Under Medicare'", *Milbank Memorial Fund Quarterly*, 62, Spring 1984, pp. 272-273.

4. Peter D. Fox, "Physician Reimbursement Under Medicare: An Overview and a Proposal for Area-wide Physician Incentives", in U.S. House of Representatives, Committee on Ways and Means, Subcommittee on Health, *Proceedings of the Conference on the Future of Medicare*, Committee Print WMCP: 98-23. Washington, DC: Government Printing Office, February 1, 1984, pp. 108-120.

5. Theodore R. Marmor, *The Politics of Medicare*. Chicago: Aldine, 1973.

CANADIAN PERSPECTIVE: LEARNING FROM OUR EXPERIENCE

Richard Van Loon

Introduction

"Crisis" must surely be one of the most overused words of the 1980s. It is used by administrators eager to solve one, to their credit and satisfaction. It is used by special interest groups to justify the pre-eminence of their claims. It is used by politicians eager to grab headlines, by reporters eager for bylines, by academics eager to peddle their influence and by anyone else who is eager to gain attention. It should hardly be surprising, then, that it is often used by everyone in the above cast when talking about our health care system.

Yet it is probably fair to say that an air of crisis did *not* suffuse the discussion among the fifty participants at this health policy conference. Concern, yes. Concern that our systems are not sufficiently flexible and adaptive. Concern that costs may be poised to rise rapidly again. Concern about misdirection of resources, about health status that is far less good than it could be, about oversupply of physicians and services, inappropriate modes of technological diffusion and about an array of other problems generated within a highly complex and important social system. But crisis? No. In general, health status indicators are improving slowly and costs are in line with those of most OECD countries. Even if they are escalating a bit too fast and certainly bear watching, they do not seem to be out of control.

It is at best risky and at worst utterly foolish to try to encapsulate briefly the array of concerns that impinge on our health care system in the mid-1980s. However, one theme that suffuses the earlier papers is that the internal dynamics of North American health care systems will not, by themselves, generate either:

1) much further improvement in the overall health of our populations even if we put in a larger portion of our GNP, or

2) a ceiling on overall system costs at any foreseeable level.

The papers and deliberations of this Canadian Health Policy Conference also suggest that effective cost control may be imposed from outside, by government, if there is a universal public health insurance regime, but that this regime will not by itself guarantee cost control. A healthy dose of that elusive variable, political will, is also essential. There was considerably greater doubt about the potential for cost control in a system such as that in the U.S., characterized as it is by a variety of third party insurers in the public and private sector, even though such a system does appear to lead to a much greater variety of practice modes.

In spite of considerable research and a remarkable amount of rhetoric, there remains considerably more doubt about governments' ability to pick up where the health care system leaves off and further improve the health status of North Americans. Beyond a few relatively well-known principles, there still remains some doubt about what "causes good health" and a great deal of doubt about the efficacy of government in promoting even those factors we can identify.

In addition, the conference papers manifest a considerable concern that a supplier-driven, technology-oriented health care delivery system is not able to deal optimally with the development and diffusion of techniques, whether these are in the realm of technological innovation or modalities of practice. Again it would appear that some form of external intervention is often necessary to ensure better forms of patient care.

In Canada, where the relationships between public authorities and a mix of public and private providers dominate much of the discussion, these concerns boil down to the question of what can governments do with, to and for the mix of organizations that constitutes our health care system. Vladeck (this volume) observes that in the U.S. policy and cultural environment, innovation comes from the individual entrepreneur and in Canada from the public sector. This theme is also introduced in Tuohy's paper (this volume). In essence, that leaves three groups of questions for us to struggle with in this paper:

1. What changes should governments seek to effect in our health care delivery system and in other areas that affect the health of Canadians?

2. What types of public policies can they use to encourage that behaviour?

3. What is the likelihood of their making the effort and of succeeding?

The first of these questions can be addressed by looking at the major issues and concerns bearing on our systems in the mid-1980s. The second can be initially addressed as each issue is raised and later by a look at the policy agenda of Canadian governments as they face health care issues in the 1980s. Any suggestions concerning the third question can only be speculative, but at the conclusion of a combined research effort such as this, one should be allowed some room to speculate.

Major Systems Concerns and Problems

Although they break down into an almost infinite array of sub-issues, the major concerns that overhang the Canadian health care system can be categorized into three broad groupings. These deal with costs and funding, with flexibility and adjustability of the system, and with the broad issue of sickness care vs. the encouragement and maintenance of good health. We will deal with each of them in turn.

After several years of rest on a plateau of about 7.5 percent of Gross National Product (GNP), personal health care costs for Canadians moved upward to 8.4 percent of GNP in 1982, the last year for which data were available. (Barer and Evans (above) provide a comprehensive review and disaggregation of health care costs in Canada from 1971 to 1982. At the time of writing no data were available for 1983, but those figures will be essential to establish the trend line for projections to the 1990s.) The decade of stable proportional expenditures in Canada was unique in the western world and, combined with a relatively high level of health status indicators, was a source of considerable pride to Canadians, particularly those making speeches abroad. The jump in 1982 was therefore a source of some concern, a concern that was only partially alleviated by the information that about two-thirds of the increase was accounted for by the 5 percent drop in real GNP that occurred in 1982. Thus, while we still do not know whether it is time to worry, Canadian health policy followers, devoted no less to preventive worry than to preventive medicine, have decided to rejuvenate the concerns about potentially "spiralling health costs" that have lurked just below and sometimes at the surface through the last decade.

Barer and Evans in their paper in this volume undertake an exhaustive analysis of the issue of health care costs. They find wide inter-provincial variance in the success of cost control mechanisms but with a considerable convergence in overall costs over the past decade. While all components of the health care budget have increased, recent trends demonstrate a tendency for costs for physicians' services to escalate faster than those of the institutional sector. Of course the primary driving force has been the rapid increase in numbers of physicians, and Barer and Evans note that, having little control in the short run over physician supply and spotty success at best in controlling physician income, governments have turned to squeezing the global budgets and acute care bed numbers in the hospital sector. This procedure did, over the past decade, leave some room for relative wage increases in the hospital sector and, the authors note, it left considerable room for servicing increases over much of the past quarter century.

There seems no doubt, on the basis of these data, that it was the move by governments into the health insurance field that permitted the relatively good cost/price performance, for trend lines of increasing costs are bent toward the horizontal at or just after the point in time at which such intervention began. The focus of cost control by provinces tends to shift according to political feasibility.

During periods of national wage controls, wage, salary and fee limitations are the method of choice. Indeed the best cost control has tended to occur at that time. At other times restrictions of supply of hospital facilities have been used. At almost no time has really serious attention been given to limiting physician supply, but as Barer and Evans note, "if limiting incomes becomes more difficult, the control of numbers may begin to be taken more seriously".

Control of bed numbers has, of course, been taken quite seriously with the result that, with increasing numbers of physicians, the bed to physician ratio has fallen rapidly. This in itself may constitute a short-run limitation on physician incomes. It also explains the primary care physicians' perception of an underfunding problem as well as the exacerbated internal political struggles in hospitals over access to beds.

Barer and Evans conclude that there is a possibility that relative cost performance under Medicare might now deteriorate, for early successes were based on the relatively blunt instruments of hospital global budgeting and bed count restrictions in acute care institutions. In the 1980s, in contrast, governments must increasingly confront the situation that a good future cost control performance will not be possible unless physician supply is limited or hospital workers' wages are sharply controlled.

In August 1984 provincial ministers of Health began to approach this possibility through a somewhat circuitous route by raising the possibility of global funding for the whole health care sector including physicians' incomes. Presumably this would leave physicians at least partially free to decide among themselves how to handle their own overall funding limitations, perhaps in part by supporting and even encouraging government efforts to limit physician numbers.

The alternative, and it is potentially highly efficacious, if quite contentious, is to intervene in modes of practice and patterns of physician utilization of services. However, given the finding reported by Tuohy (this volume) that most Canadian physicians hold sacred the right to make clinical decisions essentially unencumbered by regulation or restriction, the potential for much intervention in modes of practice may be quite limited. This ideological problem, combined with the discouraging Canadian experience with HSOs and CHCs detailed by Hastings and Vayda (above) and the failures of interprofessional delegation in Quebec outlined in this volume by Contandriopoulos, Laurier and Trottier and by Dussault (this volume) cannot help but lead to some pessimism about the future of government intervention in modes of practice, whether for purposes of cost control or to improve other aspects of the system.

It may be possible to relate cost control issues to the prevalent concern in western countries that the size of the public sector be limited. This could lead to a hypothesis that increased concern to limit the size of government will automatically lend support to attempts to control health care costs. There are, however, reasons to doubt the applicability of this hypothesis to Canada. Given the great popularity of Medicare among Canadians, it is quite possible that its inclusion in the public sector has been a major reason for the relatively high level of Canadian support for government expenditures. Moreover, the revealed preference of the Canadian people and their governments argues against it. After all, health care programs seem always the last to be cut in budget-cutting exercises.

Few Canadian groups have recently expressed much concern with underfunding. Task forces (such as the Parliamentary Task Force on Federal-Provincial Fiscal Relations) and other groups (such as the Canadian Hospital Association) that have studied funding issues have found no evidence of overall problems, although there are always instances in which the distribution of funds could be better. The major exception is the Canadian Medical Association, which has used the issue to try to head off the Canada Health Act as well as to attempt to maximize dollar flows into the health care system.

Both the papers presented in this volume and the deliberations of the conference suggest that funding for the Canadian health care system is adequate. They also suggest, for a variety of reasons, that the outstanding cost control performance of the past decade will be difficult to repeat. Paramount among these reasons is simply the proposition that the paths of least resistance have generally been followed close to their ends. Future controls will have to impinge more directly on either the incomes of providers (particularly, given their numbers, hospital workers), or the nature of practice, or both. These are areas in which resistance is likely to be high. Whether public support will be strong enough for governments to operate successfully in this area remains to be seen.

While other potential components of a cost spiral are also of concern, they are likely either to remain under control or to be of less immediate concern. Thus Battista, Spasoff and Spitzer (above) determine that the cost impact of advancing technology may be much more readily controlled under a universal public health insurance regime than in a mixed private-public insurance regime such as that in the U.S. The aging population distribution will have major effects after the turn of the century but, while considerable planning is necessary, there is likely to be time for Canada to make the necessary adjustments.

There remains one major concern about the financing of the Canadian system and that is the federal-provincial division of costs and the nature of transfer mechanisms. These issues will be dealt with in the concluding section when we touch on speculations for the future.

Adjustment and Flexibility in Service Delivery

In a very large, very important and very high cost system, subject to never-ending technological innovation, there is a constant search for flexibility and adaptiveness in delivery mechanisms. The flexibility may be sought in the name of increased efficiency (to improve cost control, client satisfaction or the outcome of treatment) or it may be necessitated by the nature and, especially, the large and expensive scale of new technology. It is often accompanied by conflict with institutions and personnel accustomed to established ways of doing business.

Several of the papers in this volume consider potential means to improve efficiency through flexibility. Appropriate changes may be induced by dealing with the loci of procedures and practice, the choice of techniques, the mode of practice, and the use of para-professional and professional groups other than doctors. Changes may also be encouraged through the institutional sector and its relationships with other modes of care, particularly home care. We can deal with each of these in turn.

Locus of Procedures and Choice of Technique

There are two sets of issues involved here. The first deals with the question of *which* procedures can be moved out of institutions or handled on an outpatient basis and which among the array of new technologies ought to be adopted into practice. The second raises the question of *how* providers can be convinced to adopt appropriate techniques. Here our focus is primarily on the second set of issues.

Battista, Spasoff and Spitzer indicate that encouraging the diffusion of new techniques is no simple matter. With some important exceptions, evidence of the utility of new techniques tends to be equivocal and diffusion patterns may therefore be uncertain and almost random. Unless the evidence of need for a change is totally overwhelming, practitioners seem unwilling to take the word of other than their peers, so that forcing diffusion from outside the profession is usually very difficult. Thus, for example, even where there does seem to be very great evidence of the desirability of performing a procedure on an outpatient rather than inpatient basis, exhortation by the hospital administrator may fall on deaf ears unless some local medical opinion leader can be convinced to take up the cause. Under these circumstances somewhat more drastic regulatory measures or outright prohibition of performance of a procedure on an inpatient basis and removal of the necessary support services from inpatient availability may be necessary. But that is a highly conflictual approach and will tend, whenever possible, to be avoided by governments and health administrators.

As Tuohy illustrates, the advent of very high technology may tend to introduce added internal strains to the health field. Very expensive and complex technologies such as CAT scanners or very complex surgical procedures require sophisticated administrative backup and may involve an array of non-practitioner specialists. Unlike older and simpler technologies, they are not "hands-on" for the average physician, even for a specialist. Yet many, and perhaps most, physicians love technology and find it no easier than anyone else to resist the temptation to get the newest and best of whatever is available. The price they must pay is acceptance of the kind of complex administrative paraphernalia that is quite inconsistent with their desire to control the technology themselves, and a tension is thereby introduced into the system.

Modes of Practice and the Use of Non-Physician Professionals

If some tensions are introduced through the advent of technological hardware, more are introduced through potential innovations in practice. As Tuohy's research indicates, physicians tend to hold their right to control the non-monetary terms and conditions of their practice more dearly than any other aspect of their working lives. Thus, attempts to encourage — let alone force — them to consider HSOs and other forms of prepaid group practice or to delegate responsibilities to other health professionals have always met with stiff resistance.

Within solo practice there really is not much at issue. Physicians *may* be able to improve the efficiency of their operations by utilizing lower-level professionals but, as Contandriopoulos *et al.* note, there is very often an insufficient volume of business to support this approach.

The situation is much less clear when we consider more complex forms of group practice. Here the U.S. experience is much more varied than the Canadian, and may be quite instructive for us. In the U.S. the combination of public and private third party insurers, fifty different state regulatory regimes and a more entrepreneurial culture have resulted in a much more extensive use of HMOs and other forms of innovative practice organizations than we see in Canada. It has also resulted in a much wider use of surgicentres and polyclinics and, of course, in the proliferation of private hospitals. However, it is crucial to note that it has *not* resulted in lower health care costs, better health indicators or a more satisfied clientele. Indeed, as Hastings and Vayda suggest in this volume, there is some evidence that private hospitals are more costly to operate than public or not-for-profit centres, without necessarily providing better service. There is also abundant evidence that for a start-up period most pre-paid group formats are more costly than solo practice.

There is a difficult comparative problem here because while U.S. health care costs are higher than Canadian, the suspicion is that they would be higher still without the innovative approach to organization that sometimes characterizes U.S. practice. So, what can we conclude? Can we improve either service or cost performance in the quite different Canadian setting by adopting some innovations from American experience, particularly complex modes of group practice? We suffer here from lack of experimental evidence. Much of our information comes from experience with HSOs in Ontario, the province on which Hastings and Vayda report in most detail, but only one significant HSO remains there. In Quebec, which adopted a highly integrated system in the early 1970s, start-up difficulties are now pretty well worked out of the system and, as Barer and Evans report, cost control experience there is comparatively good. However, we lack solid research on other aspects of the CRSSS-based structure. Anecdotal evaluation has moved from largely negative to rather positive, but increasing concerns are also being expressed about the bureaucratization and rigidity of that structure.

The impact on the division of labour between physicians and others in the health care field appears, however, to be much less than we might have anticipated, given Hastings' original enthusiastic endorsement of the community health centre concept in his landmark 1972 report and given Contandriopoulos, Laurier and Trottier's evaluation of the literature that "everything points to the fact that, by using caution and intelligence in the delegation of tasks, an important number of medical activities could be delegated to non-physicians without threatening the quality of care provided". Thus we must ask ourselves what in the Canadian context has conspired to keep us from achieving the benefits we might have hoped for from innovative forms of practice organization. The papers and the conference proceedings had a number of answers to this question.

In part, the problem may be defined as a conflict between professional rationality and administrative rationalization. As defined by Contandriopoulos *et al.*, professional rationality emphasizes the right of individual professionals — particularly those groups of professionals at the top of the hierarchy — to control all aspects of their practice including any delegation of functions to lower level professionals. Administrative rationalization in this context builds on the assumption that most office visits and many, if not most, clinical procedures do not require a physician and can be more efficiently performed by less extensively trained personnel. Contandriopoulos *et al.* and Dussault have both described the Quebec experience in attempting to force delegation of tasks from higher to lower level professionals and their observations are not optimistic. Professional associations — be they physician, nursing or others — appear to have developed a positive genius at subverting delegation procedures, and Contandriopoulos *et al.* are forced to conclude:

> In summary, the Québécois experience shows that if the government wants to intervene in order to rationalize the organization of professional work, it must come to terms with the interests and reactions of the leading professions . . . . Even when the state uses legal and coercive means, as in Quebec, its impact on the professional sector is limited, unless, that is, the leading professionals have something to gain by it. If the state cannot prevent the leading professions from obstructing the rationalization of their tasks, how can new participants in the health sector . . . hope to gain professional recognition if they have no professional prerogatives?

While it is possible to operate a comprehensive, district based, system such as Quebec's under the Canadian form of health insurance, it is quite difficult to operate HMO or HSO type structures that do not have a total regional monopoly; it can be argued that administrative rationalization must be all or nothing. The problem is that the freedom of access provisions of the Canada Health Act mean, in effect, universal self-referral. Under that situation, anyone enrolled in an HSO can, at no cost, visit a non-participating physician and the provincial plan must cover the bill. The difficulties this has imposed on HSO experiments in Ontario are detailed by Hastings and Vayda. Capitation negation (elimination of the capitation payment to the HSO) for the month in which an outside visit is made may be an acceptable compromise, but that still does not provide incentives to patients to remain inside the HSO for all services, perhaps suggesting that if rationalization by reorganization is to be done in Canada, it can only be done holistically as in Quebec. In a health-system variant of Murphy's Law, if any patients can leak out of the rationalized system, they will.

At least equally important may be the "add-on" effect. Most forms of practice rationalization involve adding other types of professionals or other modes of practice to existing systems in the *hope* that they will substitute for some of the existing mix of practice. If there were a shortage of physicians in the system or if human beings were willing to abandon old ways the moment a new one came along, such a hope might be realized. In the real world, however, doctors, already in surplus, are unwilling to surrender procedures to other professionals, and practitioners accustomed to doing things one way are often reluctant to change to another. The result, of course, is not cost savings but new costs added to old ones.

Once again the contrast with the U.S. is striking and paradoxical. There is a great deal more practice variety in the U.S., motivated by a more competitive environment and nurtured on the one hand by a variety of third party insurers and on the other by a greater tendency to regulatory intervention. There is even anecdotal evidence of declining physician salaries combined with a further move into pre-paid group practices. So much for the contrast; the paradox is that all this innovation has not resulted in lower costs or much indication of better levels of service. Indeed, the situation is generally better in the "non-innovative" Canadian system. Maybe, if it is not broken . . . .

The Institutional Sector and Alternative Health Care

Since the institutional sector accounts for approximately two-thirds of health care costs, it is natural to continue to look there for flexibility and further improvements in efficiency. As Barer and Evans point out, there has already been a fairly powerful incentive to efficiency in this sector through the mechanism of global budgeting; but, as was noted in conference deliberations, this incentive has been considerably weakened in many provinces by the inclination of governments to cover deficits at year end.

If it is the case, as Barer and Evans hypothesize, that the relatively easy changes have been made, then perhaps the next cost-cutting innovations will come from the devolution of services and patients from the large institutions to home care and clinical centres outside the hospital. This view is reinforced by an increasing view that home or community based care is more humane and better for the patient.

It is fortunate that there is such reinforcement because it was generally agreed among conference participants that if we expect devolution of services from large institutions to home care to save money, we will be disappointed. While people may be happier with the new services, there is no evidence that the latter can be more cheaply delivered than institutional services; indeed there is evidence to the contrary. As Hastings and Vayda indicate, however, it may be too soon to reach a final judgement on this score since there is still a great deal of experimentation in this area, experimentation that is characteristic of any developing service area.

There are other major problems related to institutional flexibility. In the mental health field we have been shrinking or closing institutions and discharging patients faster than the community appears able to absorb them. Conference participants estimated that up to 30 percent of beds in acute care institutions may still be occupied by patients who do not need to be there. The institutions themselves are large bureaucratic structures, and while this may lead to managerial sophistication, it also leads to a certain amount of slowness of response. Barer and Evans find that a significant portion of the increase in health costs over the past twenty-five years is accounted for by a much increased level of servicing in acute care institutions. Moreover, the increasingly labour-intensive nature of these institutions may have served to diminish their flexibility.

We should not be blinded, however, to the fact that the overall record of flexibility in the institutional sector is quite good. Nor should we be discouraged from anticipating significant results, at least in terms of patient satisfaction and better outcomes, from devolution of some services and forms of care from institutions to the community and the home.

Summary: Conflict and System Adjustability

Health care systems in the Western World have generally been viewed as supplier-driven and, particularly, physician-driven. Since physicians still (correctly) view the system in this light, they do not readily perceive or accept major restraints on it. They can easily see that health systems are the last to be cut and they know well enough that even in tough times, levels of service continue to improve and their incomes tend to escape major restrictions.

Several problems result from the supplier-driven nature of the system together with a burgeoning supply of physicians. Existing physicians, seeking to achieve their target incomes and to provide their patients with the best possible level of care while availing themselves of the use of the acute care institutional facilities to which they have become accustomed, will continue to drive up utilization. (Barer and Evans (this volume) find considerable reinforcement for the target income hypothesis.) Moreover, there is, for these doctors, little incentive to delegate services to other professionals or to engage in administratively more complex and possibly less remunerative, if perhaps less costly, practice modes.

Institutions themselves will continue to attempt to provide higher levels of service and will tend to comply with global budgetary restraints only if their liability for the deficit is very clear. University medical schools, meanwhile, will continue to churn out graduates at a rate greater than necessary — and may be little discouraged by governments only too well aware that hell hath no fury like parents whose child has been denied entrance to medical school. Under these circumstances it should be clear that either increased system flexibility (in a system where the *status quo* has been very good to the providers and is much beloved by the patients) or further restraint and cost control, will be difficult indeed. It will at best be a conflictual business between physicians, institutions and government, and within the system itself.

Yet lest the crisis mentality begin to overtake this paper, it should be noted that the capacity of Canadian society to moderate conflict is great indeed. Let it also be noted that there are some beneficial effects to conflict, and some useful trade offs that can be made.

It is a significant theme of Tuohy that some degree of conflict may be cathartic. She refers most specifically to fee negotiations and arguments about extra-billing, but her points may be generalizable to other aspects of the system. Fee (and perhaps other budgetary) negotiations allow physicians to state publicly their positions and allow provincial associations to mollify their more radically conservative fringes. They allow governments to assure the public that their interest is being protected, and they allow interested members of the public to take sides and express their views. The sound and fury does not, Tuohy notes, make much difference to the outcome, for unless general wage controls are in effect, physicians' fee and income increases have tended to outstrip those of the rest of the population.

Tuohy also notes that there may well be in North American health care systems an implicit trade-off that, if it does nothing to improve flexibility in the Canadian context, does perhaps attenuate conflict. The trade-off is simply between practitioners' incomes and control over their practices. In Canada practitioners' incomes are somewhat limited by virtue of their having to deal with a single third party insurer in negotiations. In the U.S., without being able directly to control incomes, governments have tended to intervene more actively in physicians' use of procedures. Thus in the U.S., ". . . lacking the control that might be afforded by sole-source comprehensive funding, governments have elaborated these requirements into a complex network of provisions, including both concessions to encourage compliance (pot-sweetening) and restrictions to prevent evasion (loop-hole closing)". The situation may be summarized rather briefly: to achieve physicians' compliance in more regulation of their practice would likely cost us at least some money "up front".

Of course it may be argued that strategic planning is essential if government does hold most of the levers and if it wishes to create changes in the health care system. With the notable exception of Quebec, there is remarkably little evidence of the application of such planning in the health care system. There are a number of reasons for this, many of which will be dealt with below in looking at the politics of health care planning. There are, however, two considerations that may be raised at this point.

First, the techniques of any kind of policy and strategic planning are still rudimentary. This is not something policy analysts need to apologize for; we have been at policy planning for less than fifty years and the techniques of data gathering and manipulation, if not those of human judgement, are still improving. However, in the current state of the art, almost any conclusion can still be challenged.

Second, given the still developing state of the art, the need for a great deal of strategic planning in this sector can be challenged. In the absence of certainty about what should be done, or how to do it, perhaps the best form of strategic planning is global budgeting with clearly defined and firm limits. It may be instructive that results in terms of cost-control and health indicators are not markedly different between Ontario, which applies the global budgeting approach to the institutional portion of its system, and Quebec, which is the only Canadian province to attempt comprehensive rational planning in the health field. But the state of data collection and analysis being what it is, we cannot even be entirely sure about the comparison we have just made. No wonder strategic planning may be described as 20 percent science and 80 percent political will.

Health and Health Care

This health policy conference focused much more than its predecessor a decade earlier on health care delivery and dealt less with the issues of preventive medicine, public health or lifestyle interventions to improve health. This is perhaps surprising in the face of knowledge that more health services are not the primary determinants of further improvements in health status. It is by now conventional wisdom that extra money spent on health care services does not produce much improvement in health status indicators.

At first glance, what may seem surprising, particularly in view of Canada's early leadership role in this area as a result of the widely cited *New Perspective on the Health of Canadians* (Canada, 1974), may not be so surprising on subsequent evaluation. First, while it seems evident that further massive expenditures on health care will not produce great improvements in health, it does not follow that great expenditures on other aspects of health policy will. It is not clear how effective governments can be in changing lifestyles and it is not at all clear that their most successful interventions involve large expenditures. The major government activities in public health over the past century have been perhaps the largest cause of improved health but it is not immediately clear that more major projects in this area remain to be carried out.

Second, there is certainly no consensus as to how deeply governments ought to intervene in the lives of individuals. Thus the legitimacy of some of the potentially more effective government programs (banning smoking in public places, for example) could be questioned. However, it is also worth noting that changes do occur over time in such matters; fifteen years ago seat belt laws and bans on smoking in elevators and stores might have been considered excessive governmental interventions.

Third, and perhaps most important, there are a number of factors that have a very great impact on health but that are not really within the purview of health policy. The correlation between unemployment and ill-health is by now well established. Thus one of the major policy contributions to good health would be policies leading to higher levels of employment. Even if anyone knew what these policies should be, it is clear they are not health policies *per se*. To make matters more difficult, strategic planning may be at least as difficult in the other areas which affect health as it is in health policy, and the knowledge base may be a good deal weaker. After all, we have some idea how to cure many health problems. We have almost no idea how to alleviate poverty and those ideas we do have may be extremely difficult to implement.

The foregoing should not be taken to imply that there was not some consideration in the papers and at the conference of the efficacy of prevention and lifestyle change programs. There was, and it was based on the premise that programs dealing with alcohol and drug abuse, motor vehicle safety and smoking are economically sound investments, as are public health measures such as some screening programs, fluoridation, immunization, and surveillance and regulation of food additives. Therefore, discussions and papers focused on how best to carry out these activities.

There appears to be some disagreement on this score. Two lines of reasoning pertain. Some believed that preventive medicine should be largely dealt with by physicians as part of their practice. Battista, Spasoff and Spitzer do not explicitly support this view, but it may be implicit in their paper. Hastings and Vayda adopt this point of view but only explicitly as related to HSOs. Others believe that there is no case for defining preventive activities as part of clinical practice. This view was perhaps most clearly stated by Pran Manga in a 1984 paper prepared for the federal Ministry of State for Social Development:

> Also ill-advised is the incorporation and clinical integration of prevention and health promotion in medical practice or more generally in the health care organization. On the basis of existing evidence there is justifiable scepticism about "preventive medicine" and a growing concern about the potential "medicalization" of disease prevention and health promotion and the consequent expansion of

the health care organization component of the system (the very thing that the new perspective is supposed to resist). There is simply no good case for including prevention and promotion "services" in an entitlement program such as Medicare in Canada. Indeed, it can be argued that the government should do more in the lifestyles and the social and physical environment areas so as to undercut and resist the growing demands by health care provider interests to expand the range and scope of insured services covered by Medicare. The belief that preventive medical services should be generally encouraged is based on the *prima facie* belief that preventive medicine will not only improve health but will save substantial amounts of health care expenditure. Evidence thus far casts doubt on both of these assumptions. There nevertheless may be a few very specific instances where these assumptions may be valid but they in themselves do not call for any significant change in the current policy. Even in such cases, it would be wise to provide coverage in hospital inpatient, public health unit, outpatient or clinic settings and resist including settings such as physician offices. The danger in the clinical integration of health promotion (e.g., counselling and instruction in nutrition, alcohol use, exercise and other lifestyle issues) is that the resulting expenditure will be very difficult to control quite apart from the efficacy of such "clinical" provision of such health promotion services.

Some would also argue that the preventive health field is a promising place to occupy some part of what is viewed as the superabundance of physicians being produced by our medical schools. Of course that does not mean that the expenditures must be covered as insured health services and delivered as part of standard practice.

Reprise: The Policy Agenda

There are a large number of successes in the Canadian health policy field. Near universal access is provided to very high quality health services, and if the Canada Health Act is properly applied, this access will be essentially unencumbered by financial barriers. The Canadian public is highly satisfied with the system and has supported recent policy initiatives such as the Canada Health Act. Consensus on the desirability of a comprehensive publicly financed insurance mechanism is essentially universal. Service levels and access to services have become better and more equal across provinces. Our cost control record has been excellent by international standards. Our health status indicators are highly respectable. Conflict within the system does exist but it appears to be contained at reasonable levels. Much of this combination of successes can be attributed to the nature of our publicly financed insurance system, but ultimately it rests on a pluralistic political culture that also affords substantial legitimacy to government intervention in vital services.

However, the conference also identified a large number of questions and issues that remain on the policy agenda. These include, in no particular order:

1. Do we extend services further (preventive health, lifestyle intervention, etc.)?
2. Can innovative modes of practice be made to work to increase efficiency and effectiveness under current funding regimes?
3. Is government funding excessive, inadequate or about right? What would be the feasibility and efficacy of a firm funding cap?
4. Is the Canada Health Act a solution or a problem? How can adequate flexibility in delivery mechanisms be assured under its terms?
5. What is the role of the consumer in development of health care policy?
6. How do we handle relationships among professional groups and organizations?
7. What *are* we going to do about physician supply? Is the "Canadian way", i.e., the middle road, the worst possible answer?
8. How do we screen, then disseminate, information about innovative techniques so as to ensure effective and efficient use of facilities and technology?
9. What should be the private sector role in the system?
10. How can professional self-regulation best be made to serve the interests of the public and the funding bodies as well as the interests of the professions?
11. How much conflict is acceptable within the health care system? How can it be managed so as neither to stifle innovation nor to endanger the system?
12. Is *any* mode of extra billing necessary or acceptable? Does the system really need a safety valve?

Many of these issues and questions do not have absolute answers. They are resolved by the rolling compromises that characterize pluralistic political systems. However, all of them do form grist for the mill of strategic planning in the public sector and it is to that topic that this paper turns in conclusion.

Conclusions: Setting the Agenda and Strategic Planning in a Mixed But Predominantly Public Sector Environment

There are a large number of restraints bearing on public sector strategic planning and implementation, only some of which are shared by the private sector. The more important of these include bounded rationality, conflict avoidance, basic reallocation difficulties, federal-provincial relations, and the nature and impact of political cycles. Given the array of impediments to change, a very great advantage accrues to the *status quo*, an advantage that may be maximized when the *status quo* is prized by powerful groups with a very high degree of concentrated self-interest in the outcome. That situation does characterize the health sector, and so it is not difficult to see that any major changes are likely to require a strong degree of public consensus in order to support action.

Bounded Rationality

A simple equation will express one of the most important difficulties faced by planners in any system:

> Time restrictions + attention limitations + information costs = bounded rationality.

In any system major decision-makers are likely to have a very great number of decisions thrust upon them. In the political system that situation is accentuated further. Consider that for major decisions not only must the federal and provincial ministers of Health and their top officials be involved, but so also must the first ministers and the ministers of Finance or treasurers. The issues they deal with are extremely complex and there is a myriad of them constantly pressing for attention. Thus it is extremely difficult even to get items on the agenda, and the timing of their arrival is often unpredictable. For example, there is no evidence that public opinion concerning extra-billing or user fees became stronger during the early 1980s and no clear evidence that the situation, at least with respect to extra billing, was deteriorating. The Canada Health Act appeared on the agenda in 1983 rather than in 1980 largely because the leading federal government actors were earlier preoccupied with other issues such as the National Energy Plan, the economy and the Constitution. The combined limitations of time and attention thus restrict the agenda.

To these restrictions must be added the high cost and frequent unreliability of information. In the health policy area the ability to generate information is very substantial and the need for information is prodigious. Yet the reliability of the information being used is frequently dubious and controversial.

Even when an item does "arrive" on the agenda and even if a reasonable amount of reliable information can be brought to bear upon it, it should be noted that the decision will be made in a very noisy atmosphere and often with less attention being paid to what planners might consider pertinent information than they would like. A Cabinet meeting, for example, is characterized by the coming and going of ministers, the constant interruption of messengers and an array of side-conversations among ministers concerned with everything from electoral politics to unrelated policy issues to the quality of the lunch. Key ministers may be absent because of their busy schedules and others may be out of the room at the crucial moment. The "decision" may be very unclear and it may be reopened later or, to some degree, disregarded. If the second scarcest political commodity is a minister's time, surely the scarcest of all political commodities is a minister's attention.

To some degree these problems may be overcome by delegation of decisions. However, decision makers cannot fully delegate risky decisions, and since all the really major health policy decisions are risky (in political and in policy terms), this is a limited solution.

The result is very often no decision at all or, when a decision is made, incrementalism. Moreover even non-incremental decisions are often made incremental in practice. There is nothing inherently wrong in this but it certainly means that most public sector planning systems are some distance away from comprehensive rationality.

Conflict Avoidance

While some conflict may be cathartic and may provide valuable publicity for governments and politicians eager to prove their worth in a popular cause, a major degree of conflict is almost always viewed as undesirable. Thus one of the major criticisms of the Liberal government of Pierre Trudeau was that it was too confrontational in its approach to provinces and to any groups with which it was in disagreement. In a society that places a high value on consensus, the confrontational approach to government is not particularly popular. This is not to say governments will always avoid conflict. Where public support is overwhelming, as it has tended to be in regard to extra-billing or as it was in supporting the Canadianization aspects of the National Energy Policy, the risk will be taken. But even then, if there has been a recent series of controversial decisions, a government may well hold its fire.

The advantage this conflict avoidance behaviour gives to strong, entrenched interests that are willing to dig in to support their positions is quite significant — provided that they are not seen as the aggressors and that they are able, at least partially, to mask their self-interest. That is why, for example, the Canadian Medical Association phrased its fight against the Canada Health Act primarily in terms of underfunding rather than in terms of the physicians' right to extra-bill.

Reallocation Difficulties

In an environment of expenditure restraint, implementing new programs tends to mean restraining or even cutting old ones. Reallocation, however, is always an extremely painful exercise, for to succeed one must cause real pain to a group enjoying the benefits of an existing program in order to provide potential benefits to another. Thus, for a government, cutting old programs is almost always more painful than putting new ones in place which is pleasurable. Reallocation is difficult enough *within* a sector where there is some overlap between winners and losers. It is extremely difficult between sectors where possible winners and real losers have little if any common ground.

Federal-Provincial Difficulties

While the formal division of powers under the British North America Act clearly placed health care in the sphere of provincial jurisdiction, in fact many major health policy issues are shared between the federal and provincial governments. Thus to be effective, strategic planning must often be a joint federal-provincial effort. Over the past decade this has been a dictum more often honoured in the breach than in the observance, a situation which may have reached its nadir in the early 1980s. (Taylor's paper in this volume treats the impact of federal-provincial relations on health policy at much greater length than is possible here.) Discussions during the conference were characterized by the hope that the next few years, with a new government and with the Canada Health Act already passed, would see a return to somewhat more harmonious relations in the health policy field.

While that does seem likely, it may be important to temper our hopes with some degree of caution. As Taylor points out, there has always been a considerable amount of conflict over health policy. This should hardly be surprising. Partisan conflict aside, the federal and provincial governments are inevitably to some degree competing entities. The very existence of parallel governmental structures in a single territorial unit will ensure that perfect harmony over any field of shared jurisdiction is an elusive goal. This will be particularly true in a field characterized by cross winds of competing interests that will attempt to make their views known through those governmental structures.

The situation may be exacerbated by personalities, as it undoubtedly was during the last Trudeau government, but it cannot in any case escape the impact of an internal contradiction within our federal financial system. In our federal-provincial fiscal mechanisms we try to deal with three concepts that Canadians hold as articles of political faith: accountability, redistribution and provincial autonomy. Funds should be spent in such a way that the government can account to Parliament and the taxpayers for the efficiency and effectiveness of expenditures. There should be sufficient fiscal redistribution to permit a reasonably uniform level of services across the country. And yet programs should be delivered in such a way as to ensure that local requirements are met and that the various pieces of our cultural mosaic are adequately taken into account.

Our search among different forms of inter-governmental transfer mechanisms or program arrangements comprises a search for the best possible combination of these features, yet a moment's reflection will unearth a difficult situation: the further we get toward maximizing any two among accountability, redistribution and provincial autonomy, the further away we get from the third. Thus shared cost programs maximize local autonomy and accountability but they do relatively little for redistribution. (Even partially shared cost programs such as HIDS may have negative redistributional aspects. See Taylor's paper in this volume.) Block funding arrangements, such as Established Programs Financing, based on *per capita* entitlements, maximize provincial autonomy and redistribution but leave the federal government unable to account to Parliament for the final use of the funds shipped to provinces. Federally delivered programs with uniform terms and conditions maximize redistribution and accountability but are antithetical to provincial autonomy. In practice the situation is less black and white than that implies. For example, the National Training Act is federally delivered but with very substantial provincial input. Medicare and HIDS were mixed form programs somewhere between shared-cost funding and block grants. But the general paradox remains: all those desirable features cannot be simultaneously maximized.

In the end, then, Canadian federal-provincial fiscal relations are a movable feast, and an arrangement that looks acceptable today is likely to look much less appealing in five years when the sands of public and elite opinion about the appropriate balance of our federalism shift again. We will never find the perfect program. At the highest fiscal level (equalization and tax-sharing) arrangements are renegotiated every five years and a new Fiscal Arrangements Act results. While a five-year time interval is probably too short for health programs — it would create chronic instability — decennial renegotiations might well be appropriate.

Finally, federal-provincial relations in the health care area are bound to remain uncertain and to constitute a difficulty for strategic planning because there are no "right" answers to either of its two most vexing questions, that of the appropriate share of expenditures for either level of government and that of the appropriate jurisdictional split. Since there is no absolute answer available on either score there is bound to be continuing discussion — read "conflict" — on both.

Political Cycles

Strategic planning dealing with a complex system means having to wait for results. As the Quebec government found in implementing the Castonguay-Nepveu Report, major changes take years to work through a system. Ten years might be about the shortest appropriate planning horizon. But the electoral cycle is much shorter than ten years, and within the electoral cycle, the "window" for strategic planning is shorter still. Even in the most optimistic of political situations, such as that afforded the federal Conservative government elected with its huge majority in 1984, eight years (two mandates) is about the longest time span any politician can anticipate. Moreover, during that eight years there will be several Cabinet shuffles; the chances that the federal Minister of Health and Welfare of 1984 will still hold that portfolio in 1992 are close to zero.

When a government is returned from an election, the planning future does indeed look bright. It is thought that four years, maybe even eight, should provide ample time to deal with such problems as the economy or cost containment in health services. By the second year of the mandate, ministers are comfortable in their portfolios and the plans start to flow in. Naturally they all call for increased expenditures and further analysis shows some proposals are quite contradictory to others. In the third year of the mandate, things are fairly well sorted out — an idea of what can be proceeded with and what cannot is now pretty clearly in the government's mind — and some urgent changes will have been proceeding since year one. But, the economy has not generated 5 percent annual growth and the deficit is still high. Various interests affected by potential policy changes have been making threatening noises. Federal-provincial squabbling has broken out. The bureaucracy is slow to change. And what is worse, the 51 percent popular support at the last election is now down to 42 percent and is falling. Maybe a Cabinet shuffle . . . .

By the fourth year of the mandate the election looms. The polls are not really improving and the Opposition may get a new leader. Some provincial governments are now openly questioning the benefits of having a government of the same partisan stripe in Ottawa. In other provinces the Liberals or NDP, left for dead in 1984, have returned from the grave and are in power. Maybe caution should be the order of the day — no big initiatives until after the election — after all the system is pretty good as it is. Besides, we need money for more directly beneficial programs . . . in swing ridings.

So goes the electoral cycle and its impact on strategic planning. Now add to that, in any area of shared jurisdiction, ten more provincial electoral cycles with different periodicity and we see a very considerably shrunken set of opportunities for applying rational strategic planning.

Then Why Does Anything Ever Happen?

Given the nearly infinite array of impediments to policy change the reader must by now wonder why reform ever occurs in health care policy or anywhere else. In fact, it is worth recalling that big changes often do occur only after protracted delays. As Taylor reminds us, publicly financed health insurance has been on the Liberal policy agenda since 1919. Moreover, what seemed like an overwhelming consensus had formed behind it by the end of World War II, fully thirteen years before even the first component was put in place at the national level. Other large social policy programs — old age security, family allowances, child tax credits and unemployment insurance — also had protracted births, if not quite so protracted as health insurance. Even the Canada Health Act — surely only a medium-sized reform of the system — was brought to Parliament only after at least four years of pulling and hauling within the federal government and in the federal/provincial arena.

Smaller (incremental) changes can, of course, occur at any time. Really large changes, however, which automatically will affect strong entrenched interests, will tend to occur under one, or preferably more, of the following circumstances:

1) an overwhelming public consensus;

2) the combination of a very strong concentrated interest and public apathy;

3) a major, well publicized foul-up or disaster, and preferably more than one;

4) a budgetary feast *or* a budgetary famine;

5) (rarely) when a single very powerful actor forces the issue.

While one, and preferably more, of these circumstances is a necessary condition, it is not sufficient. Added to the pot must usually be the passage of sufficient time for the policy concept to migrate from the realm of the revolutionary or the outrageous to the accepted or even the conventional wisdom. Added as well must be a fortunate concentration of major actors. Old age pensions were begun in 1919 when a (then) left-leaning Prime Minister allowed himself to be forced, in a minority government situation, against the wishes of much of his Cabinet by a tiny socialist group in Parliament. Hospital insurance was forced on a reluctant federal Liberal government by the entreaties of a money-strapped Conservative premier in Ontario. Medical care insurance survived a rough provincial reception and a neutral to somewhat hostile federal Cabinet largely because for once in history Canada had a left-leaning Finance Minister. It is the combination of a supportive public environment and a rare alignment of the political stars that is most likely to produce big changes.

What Should Happen?

This health policy conference, however, was not really about big changes. No one was suggesting dismantling Medicare and no one was suggesting a major expansion either. Of course a cost explosion *could* change all that, but if there was a consensus view it was that moderate cost increases are likely but an explosion is not. Discussion therefore centred on middle level reforms such as HSOs and better forms of professional regulation, on administrative matters such as the use of the proper locus for assorted clinical procedures, the management of surgical queues and, perhaps most controversially, on finding some way to deal with the current or future excess supply of physicians.

For the health policy agenda this suggests a "management" orientation for the near future. We would expect:

1. Not much change in the regulation of practice or the use of physician substitutes.

2. Only incremental action to deal with physician supply unless there is a clearly perceived cost explosion.

3. Severe budgetary restrictions only if there is a period of major relative growth in the health sector and the perception that health care costs are taking a lot of money from other sectors.

4. Some considerable de-escalation of overt conflict between federal and provincial governments but a continuation of some underlying conflict.

5. No large retreat by the federal government over extra-billing or user fees but a "reasonable" interpretation of the regulations.

6. Some "side" payments from the federal government to provinces in support of some of the newly fashionable but expensive areas such as home care for the elderly. An immediate return to any form of cost sharing (by the "conventional" 50/50 formula) is unlikely, since the requirement for federal auditing would likely be unacceptable and since, in any case, the 50/50 formula only applied to insured health services, not all provincial health expenditures. On average, in 1983-1984 federal contributions were still one to two percentage points above the 1975-1976 EPF base year shares, so a return to older forms of cost-sharing would not even be profitable for the provincial governments.

7. Not much privatization in the system. Governments are unlikely to give up one of the few things they are perceived to do well.

8. Lots of strategic planning, by planners; little implementation of large strategic schemes, by governments.

If a deliberate reform agenda were to be selected from among the issues raised at the Health Policy Conference, it would probably be to attempt to force the pace somewhat on the physician supply issue. That is an area in which an effective coalition of governments and existing physicians could possibly be forged, and it is one in which all the diagnostic signs point to trouble ahead unless action is taken now. That, combined with continuing attention to good internal housekeeping and a dose of preventive worry about costs, may be an effective approach while we amuse ourselves with watching developments south of the border where some kind of policy explosion may result from what continues to look, to Canadian eyes, like a fascinating example of policy anarchy.

References

Canada. Department of National Health and Welfare. *A New Perspective on the Health of Canadians*. Ottawa, 1974.

Canada. Department of National Health and Welfare. *The Community Health Centre in Canada*, Vols. 1-3. Ottawa: Queen's Printer, 1972.

Manga, Pran. "Next Steps Towards a New Perspective on the Health of Canadians". Report prepared for the Ministry of State for Social Development. Ottawa, 1984.

HEALTH POLICY CONFERENCE ON CANADA'S NATIONAL HEALTH CARE SYSTEM

List of Contributors
(Title and Address at Time of 1984 Conference)

Dr. Morris Barer
Associate Director
Division of Health Services R&D
University of British Columbia
Vancouver, British Columbia

Dr. Renaldo Battista
Professor, Kellogg Centre
Montreal General Hospital
McGill University
Montreal, Québec

Dr. Pierre Bergeron
Directeur
Evaluation des Programmes
Ministère des Affaires Sociales
Gouvernement du Québec
Ste. Foy, Québec

Dr. Jacques Brunet
Directeur general
Centre hospitalier
 de l'université Laval
Ste. Foy, Québec

Dr. Young Mo Cheung
Director
Research & Strategic Planning
Department of Hospitals and
 Medical Care
Government of Alberta
Edmonton, Alberta

Dr. André-Pierre Contandriopoulos
Professor
Département d'administration
 de la santé
Université de Montréal
Montréal, Québec

Mr. René Dussault
Lecturer
Ecole Nationale d'Administration
 Publique
Université de Québec
Ste. Foy, Québec

Dr. Robert Evans
Professor
Department of Economics
University of British Columbia
Vancouver, British Columbia

Mr. Ken Fyke
President
Greater Victoria Hospital Society
Victoria, British Columbia

Dr. John Hastings
Professor
Faculty of Medicine
University of Toronto
Toronto, Ontario

Ms. Claudine Laurier
Assistant de Recherche
Groupe de Recherche
Interdisciplinaire en Santé
Université de Montréal
Montréal, Québec

Dr. Maureen Law
Associate Deputy Minister
Health and Welfare
Government of Canada
Ottawa, Ontario

Mr. Jonathan Lomas
Assistant Professor
Department of Clinical Epidemiology
and Biostatistics
McMaster University
Hamilton, Ontario

Mr. Ken Moore
Assistant Deputy Minister
Department of Hospitals and
Medical Care
Government of Alberta
Edmonton, Alberta

Dr. Robert Spasoff
Professor
Department of Epidemiology
University of Ottawa
Ottawa, Ontario

Dr. Walter Spitzer
Professor, Kellogg Centre
Montreal General Hospital
McGill University
Montreal, Québec

Dr. Greg Stoddart
Associate Professor
Department of Clinical
Epidemiology and Biostatistics
McMaster University
Hamilton, Ontario

Dr. Malcolm Taylor
Professor
Faculty of Administrative Studies
York University
Downsview, Ontario

Ms. Louise Trottier
Assistante de Recherche
Group de Recherche Interdisciplinaire
en Santé
Université de Montréal
Montréal, Québec

Dr. Carolyn Tuohy
Associate Professor
Department of Political Science
University of Toronto
Toronto, Ontario

Dr. Fernand Turcotte
Directeur
Département de médecine social
Université Laval
Ste. Foy, Québec

Dr. Richard Van Loon
Professor
Faculty of Administration
University of Ottawa
Ottawa, Ontario

Dr. Eugene Vayda
Associate Dean, Community Health
Faculty of Medicine
University of Toronto
Toronto, Ontario

Mr. Bruce Vladeck
President
United Hospital Fund of New York
New York, New York

HEALTH POLICY CONFERENCE ON CANADA'S NATIONAL HEALTH CARE SYSTEM

List of Participants
(Title and Address at Time of 1984 Conference)

Dr. Robert Ball
Senior Scholar
Centre for the Study of Social Policy
Washington, D.C.

Dr. Morris Barer
Associate Director
Division of Health Services R&D
University of British Columbia
Vancouver, British Columbia

Dr. Martin Barkin
President and C.E.O.
Sunnybrook Medical Centre
Toronto, Ontario

Dr. Renaldo Battista
Professor, Kellogg Centre
Montreal General Hospital
McGill University
Montreal, Quebec

Mr. David Beavis
Director General
Health and Welfare Canada
Ottawa, Ontario

Dr. Pierre Bergeron
Directeur
Evaluation des Programmes
Ministère des Affaires Sociales
Gouvernement du Québec
Ste. Foy, Québec

Dr. Gerry Bonham
Medical Officer of Health
Calgary Health Services
Calgary, Alberta

Dr. Larry Brown
Professor, Department of
    Medical Care Organization
University of Michigan
Ann Arbor, Michigan

Dr. Jacques Brunet
Directeur général
Centre hospitalier de
    l'université Laval
Ste. Foy, Québec

List of Participants

Mr. Gary Chatfield
President
Extendicare Ltd.
Toronto, Ontario

Dr. Wilbur Cohen
Syd W. Richardson Professor of
 Public Affairs
LBJ School of Public Affairs
Austin, Texas

Dr. David Conklin
Research Director
Ontario Economic Council
Toronto, Ontario

Dr. André-Pierre Contandriopoulos
Professor
Département d'administration de
 la santé
Université de Montréal
Montréal, Québec

Mr. Ralph Coombs
Executive Director
Foothills Hospital
Calgary, Alberta

Mr. Robert Crane
Vice-President, Government Relations
Kaiser Foundation Health Plan
Oakland, California

Dr. Lynn Curry
Vice-President
Canadian College of Health
 Service Executives
Ottawa, Ontario

Professor John Deeble
Head, Research Unit Health Economics
Australian National University
Canberra, Australia

Mr. René Dussault
Lecturer
Ecole Nationale d'Administration
 Publique
Université de Québec
Ste. Foy, Québec

Dr. Carroll Estes
Chairman of the Department of
Social and Behavioral Sciences
University of California
San Francisco, California

Dr. Lynn Etheredge
Professor
Urban Institute
Washington, D.C.

Dr. Robert Evans
Professor
Department of Economics
University of British Columbia
Vancouver, British Columbia

Mr. Gary Frey
Vice-President
The Banff Centre
Banff, Alberta

Mr. Ken Fyke
President
Greater Victoria Hospital Society
Victoria, British Columbia

Dr. Murray Grant
General Accounting Office
National Institute of Health
Bethesda, Maryland

Dr. John Hastings
Professor
Faculty of Medicine
University of Toronto
Toronto, Ontario

Mr. Donald Junk
Assistant Deputy Minister
Policy Development
Alberta Hospitals and Medical Care
Edmonton, Alberta

Mr. Steve Kenny
Executive Director
Medical Services Plan
Medical Services Commission
Government of British Columbia
Victoria, British Columbia

Dr. Bryan Kirk
Associate Dean
Faculty of Medicine
University of Manitoba
Winnipeg, Manitoba

Dr. Rudolph Klein
Professor
School of Humanities and
 Social Sciences
Bath, England

Ms. Claudine Laurier
Assistant de Recherche
Groupe de Recherche
Interdisciplinaire en Santé
Université de Montréal
Montréal, Québec

Dr. Philip Lee
Professor
Institute for Health Policy Studies
University of California
San Francisco, California

Dr. Fulvio Limongelli
Executive Director
Canadian Council on Hospital
 Accreditation
Ottawa, Ontario

Reverend Everett MacNeil
Executive Director
Catholic Health Association
 of Canada
Ottawa, Ontario

Dr. Ted Marmor
Professor
Centre for Health Studies
Institute for Social Policy Study
Yale University
New Haven, Connecticut

Mr. Jean Claude Martin
President
Canadian Hospital Association
Ottawa, Ontario

Mr. Ken Moore
Assistant Deputy Minister
Department of Hospitals and
 Medical Care
Government of Alberta
Edmonton, Alberta

Dr. James Morone
Professor
Department of Political Science
Brown University
Providence, Rhode Island

Dr. Bernard Nelson
Executive Vice-President
Kaiser Family Foundation
Menlo Park, California

Mr. David Pascoe
Director
Research and Planning Directorate
Department of Health
Government of Manitoba
Winnipeg, Manitoba

Dr. Dot Pringle
Research Director
Victorian Order of Nurses
Toronto, Ontario

Dr. Jean Rochon
Dean
Faculté de médecine
Université Laval
Ste. Foy, Québec

Dr. Harvey Sapolsky
Professor
Department of Political Science
M.I.T.
Cambridge, Massachusetts

Mr. Chuck Shields
Vice-President, Education
Canadian College of Health
   Service Executives
Ottawa, Ontario

Dr. Robert Spasoff
Professor
Department of Epidemiology
University of Ottawa
Ottawa, Ontario

Dr. Greg Stoddart
Associate Professor
Department of Clinical Epidemiology
   and Biostatistics
McMaster University
Hamilton, Ontario

Dr. Malcolm Taylor
Professor
Faculty of Administrative Studies
York University
Downsview, Ontario

Mr. Pat Tidball
Manager
B.C. Pharmacare
Vancouver, British Columbia

Dr. Carolyn Tuohy
Associate Professor
Department of Political Science
University of Toronto
Toronto, Ontario

Dr. Fernand Turcotte
Directeur
Département de médecine
   social
Université Laval
Ste. Foy, Québec

Dr. Richard Van Loon
Professor
Faculty of Administration
University of Ottawa
Ottawa, Ontario

Dr. Eugene Vayda
Associate Dean, Community Health
Faculty of Medicine
University of Toronto
Toronto, Ontario

Mr. Bruce Vladeck
President
United Hospital Fund of New York
New York, New York